THE ROUGH GUIDE TO

Berlin

There are more than one hundred and fifty Rough Guide titles
covering destinations from Amsterdam to Zimbabwe

Forthcoming titles include
Devon & Cornwall • Madeira • Tenerife • Vancouver

Rough Guide Reference Series
Classical Music • Country Music • Drum 'n' bass • English Football
European Football • House • The Internet • Jazz • Music USA • Opera
Reggae • Rock Music • Techno • Unexplained Phenomena • World Music

Rough Guide Phrasebooks
Czech • Dutch • Egyptian Arabic • European Languages • French
German • Greek • Hindi & Urdu • Hungarian • Indonesian • Italian
Japanese • Mandarin Chinese • Mexican Spanish • Polish • Portuguese
Russian • Spanish • Swahili • Thai • Turkish • Vietnamese

Rough Guides on the Internet
www.roughguides.com

Rough Guide Credits

Text Editor:	Andrew Tomičić
Series Editor:	Mark Ellingham
Editorial:	Martin Dunford, Jonathan Buckley, Jo Mead, Kate Berens, Amanda Tomlin, Ann-Marie Shaw, Paul Gray, Helena Smith, Judith Bamber, Orla Duane, Olivia Eccleshall, Ruth Blackmore, Geoff Howard, Claire Saunders, Gavin Thomas, Alexander Mark Rogers, Polly Thomas, Joe Staines, Lisa Nellis, Richard Lim, Duncan Clark, Peter Buckley, Sam Thorne, Lucy Ratcliffe, Clifton Wilkinson, David Glen (UK); Andrew Rosenberg, Mary Beth Maioli, Stephen Timblin (US)
Online:	Kelly Cross, Anja Mutić-Blessing, Jennifer Gold, Audra Epstein (US)
Production:	Susanne Hillen, Andy Hilliard, Link Hall, Helen Ostick, Julia Bovis, Michelle Draycott, Katie Pringle, Robert Evers, Mike Hancock, Robert McKinlay, Zoë Nobes
Cartography:	Melissa Baker, Maxine Repath, Ed Wright, Katie Lloyd-Jones
Picture Research:	Louise Boulton, Sharon Martins
Finance:	John Fisher, Gary Singh, Edward Downey, Mark Hall, Tim Bill
Marketing & Publicity:	Richard Trillo, Niki Smith, David Wearn, Chloë Roberts, Birgit Hartmann (UK); Simon Carloss, David Wechsler (US)
Administration:	Tania Hummel, Demelza Dallow, Julie Sanderson

Acknowledgements

Thanks to Andrew Roth for his excellent update; Andrew in turn would like to thank Susan Hannaford, Natalie Gravenor and Anni Klose. At Rough Guides thanks to Sam Thorne for his help with the editing; Katie Pringle for typesetting; Ed Wright for cartography; David Price for proof-reading; and Narrell Leffman, Kate Davis and Gerrard Kennedy for Basics updates.

The publishers and authors have done their best to ensure the accuracy and currency of all information in The Rough Guide to Berlin; however, they can accept no responsibility for any loss, injury, or inconvenience sustained by any traveller as a result of information or advice contained in the guide.

This sixth edition published January 2001 by Rough Guides Ltd, 62–70 Shorts Gardens, London WC2H 9AH.

Distributed by the Penguin Group:
Penguin Books Ltd, 27 Wrights Lane, London W8 5TZ.
Penguin Putnam, Inc. 375 Hudson Street, New York, NY 10014, USA.
Penguin Books Australia Ltd, 487 Maroondah Highway, PO Box 257, Ringwood, Victoria 3134, Australia.
Penguin Books Canada Ltd, 10 Alcorn Avenue, Toronto, Ontario M4V 1E4, Canada.
Penguin Books (NZ) Ltd, 182–190 Wairau Road, Auckland 10, New Zealand.
Printed in England by Clays Ltd, St Ives PLC
Typography and original design by Jonathan Dear and The Crowd Roars.
Illustrations throughout by Edward Briant.

ISBN 1-85828-682-4

THE ROUGH GUIDE TO

Berlin

Written and researched by
Jack Holland and John Gawthrop

With additional contributions by
Andrew Roth

**ROUGH
GUIDES**

Help us update

We've gone to a lot of trouble to ensure that this sixth edition of *The Rough Guide to Berlin* is accurate and up to date. However, things inevitably change, and if you feel we've got it wrong or left something out, we'd like to know: any suggestions, comments or corrections would be much appreciated. We'll credit all contributions and send a copy of the next edition – or any other Rough Guide if you prefer – for the best correspondence.

Please mark letters "Rough Guide to Berlin" and send to:
Rough Guides, 62–70 Shorts Gardens, London WC2H 9AH or
Rough Guides, 4th Floor, 345 Hudson St, New York, NY 10014.

Email should be sent to:
mail@roughguides.co.uk

Online updates about Rough Guide titles can be found on our Web site at *www.roughguides.com*

The Author(s)

Following jobs as diverse as biscuit-making, beer-barrel rolling and EFL teaching in Greece, **Jack Holland** co-founded the Rough Guides in the mid-1980s. He is co-author of the Rough Guides to New York City, Holland and Amsterdam and lived in Berlin for four years. He currently lives in the Cotswolds and when not in front of the computer spends his time playing with his baby son and persuading his hens to lay the perfect egg. **John Gawthrop** has been a regular visitor to Berlin since 1985, spending much time on the eastern side of the former Wall. He is also co-author of the *Rough Guide to Turkey*.

Readers' letters

We'd like to thank all those readers who wrote in with comments and updates to the previous edition: Hazel Britton; Isabel Cole; Jennifer Curtis; Heather Elton; S. Hendriksen; Martin Isaac; R. Jones; Nick Kay; Reima Kylänen; Charles Lees; Jean Macdonald; Simon Meek; Margaret Mitchell; Ayesha O'Reilly; Su-Lyn Seah; Priti Shah; Mark Tucker; and Clemens Zehnder.

Rough Guides

Travel Guides • Phrasebooks • Music and Reference Guides

We set out to do something different when the first Rough Guide was published in 1982. Mark Ellingham, just out of University, was travelling in Greece. He brought along the popular guides of the day, but found they were all lacking in some way. They were either strong on ruins and museums but went on for pages without mentioning a beach or taverna. Or they were so conscious of the need to save money that they lost sight of Greece's cultural and historical significance. Also, none of the books told him anything about Greece's contemporary life – its politics, its culture, its people, and how they lived.

So with no job in prospect, Mark decided to write his own guidebook, one which aimed to provide practical information that was second to none, detailing the best beaches and the hottest clubs and restaurants, while also giving hard-hitting accounts of every sight, both famous and obscure, and providing up-to-the-minute information on contemporary culture. It was a guide that encouraged independent travellers to find the best of Greece, and was a great success, getting shortlisted for the Thomas Cook travel guide award, and encouraging Mark, along with three friends, to expand the series.

The Rough Guide list grew rapidly and the letters flooded in, indicating a much broader readership than had been anticipated, but one which uniformly appreciated the Rough Guides' mix of practical detail and humour, irreverence and enthusiasm. Things haven't changed. The same four friends who began the series are still the caretakers of the Rough Guide mission today: to provide the most reliable, up-to-date and entertaining information to independent-minded travellers of all ages, on all budgets.

We now publish 150 titles and have offices in London and New York. The travel guides are written and researched by a dedicated team of more than 100 authors, based in Britain, Europe, the USA and Australia. We have also created a unique series of phrasebooks to accompany the travel series, along with the acclaimed series of music guides, and a best-selling pocket guide to the Internet and World Wide Web. We also publish comprehensive travel information on our Web site: *www.roughguides.com*

Contents

Part Four Contexts   319

List of maps

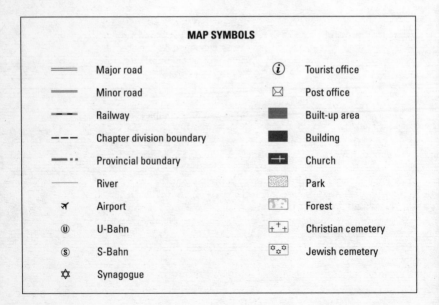

MAP SYMBOLS

═══	Major road	ⓘ	Tourist office
──	Minor road	⊠	Post office
▬▬	Railway	▓	Built-up area
─ ─ ─	Chapter division boundary	▬	Building
▬▬ ▪▪	Provincial boundary	⊞	Church
────	River	▨	Park
✈	Airport	▨	Forest
ⓤ	U-Bahn	+⁺+	Christian cemetery
ⓢ	S-Bahn	✿✿	Jewish cemetery
✡	Synagogue		

Introduction

Das gibts nur einmal
Das kehrt nicht wieder
Das ist zu schön, um wahr zu sein!

It happens only once
It will not come again
It is too beautiful to be true!

Seemingly in a perpetual state of transformation, **Berlin** is an extraordinary city. For over a century, events here have either mirrored or determined what has happened in the rest of Europe, and, more than a decade after the fall of the Berlin Wall, the city is on the move again, working furiously to re-create itself as the capital of Europe's most powerful country and as an international metropolis on a level with London, Paris or New York.

The speed of change has been astounding, with a complete shift in the city's centre of gravity. The area around Zoo Station, the very heart of Berlin when the Wall was in place, has lost much of its lure – there's still plenty of shopping to be had, but the action, both day-time and night-time, is now firmly rooted in the **east**. Scores of trendy bars, restaurants, clubs and galleries have taken over once quiet streets and weekend nights now have a carnival-like atmosphere, the pavements practically impassable. Sleek chrome and glass has replaced crumbling brick throughout the neighbourhoods of Mitte, Prenzlauer Berg and Friedrichshain, yanking them out of a fifty-year slumber, while Potsdamer Platz, nothing but a barren field until a few years ago, is now a bustling entertainment quarter. It's an exciting, infectious scene and, for anyone familiar with the forlorn and unkempt eastern streets of the GDR, a slightly unbelievable one.

The **relocation of government** from Bonn to Berlin has played its part in this renaissance – a titanic undertaking with inevitably profound results, most notably, again, on the eastern side of the city. Not

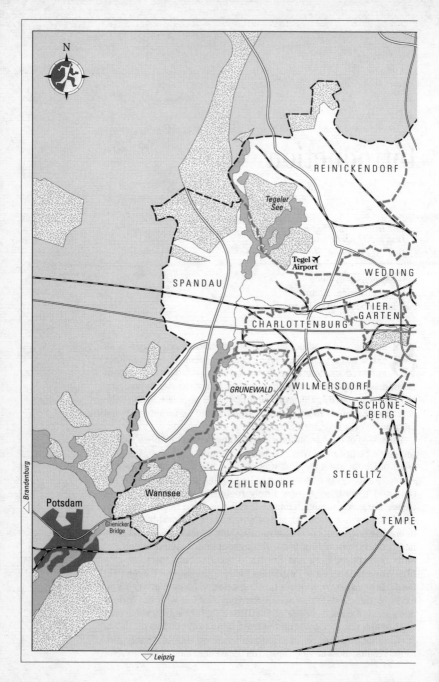

N

REINICKENDORF

Tegeler
See

Tegel ✈
Airport

WEDDING

SPANDAU

TIER-
GARTEN

CHARLOTTENBURG

GRUNEWALD

WILMERSDORF

SCHÖNE-
BERG

Brandenburg

STEGLITZ

ZEHLENDORF

Wannsee

TEMPE

Potsdam

Glienicker
Bridge

▽ *Leipzig*

PANKOW

HOHEN-
SCHÖNHAUSEN

WEISSEN-
SEE

MARZAHN

PRENZLAUER-
BERG

HELLERSDORF

MITTE

FRIEDRICH-
SHAIN

KREUZBERG

LICHTEN-
BERG

✈ Tempelhof
Airport

Friedrichshagen

KÖPENICK

Rahnsdorf

TREPTOW

Grosser
Müggelsee

Grünau

NEUKÖLLN

LHOF

Schmockwitz

Schönefeld
Airport ✈

△ Bad Freienwalde

△ Kostrzyn (Poland)

△ Frankfurt-an-der-Oder & Poland

0   2km

only has the physical demeanour changed, with both new and old buildings housing embassies and ministries to accompany the freshly domed Reichstag, but the influx of politicians and bureaucrats has changed the city's ambience, giving it a sophistication and gravitas that offsets the newly found vitality of the streetlife.

This recent regeneration of the city centre is merely the most visible layer of Berlin's dense and complex past. Heart of the Prussian kingdom, economic and cultural centre of the Weimar Republic, and, in the final days of Nazi Germany, the headquarters of Hitler's Third Reich, Berlin is a weather vane of European history. After the war, the world's two most powerful military systems stood face to face here, sharing the spoils of a city later to be split by that most tangible object of the East–West divide, the Berlin Wall. As the Wall fell in November 1989, Berlin was once again pushed to the forefront of world events, ushering in a period of change as frantic, confused and significant as any the city has experienced. It's this weight of history, the sense of living in a hothouse where all the dilemmas of contemporary Europe are nurtured, that gives Berlin its excitement and troubling fascination.

It was, of course, **World War II** that defined the shape of today's city. A seventh of all the buildings destroyed in Germany were in Berlin, Allied and Soviet bombing razing 92 percent of all the shops, houses and industry here. After the war, Berlin formed the stage for some of the most significant moments in the convoluted drama of the Cold War: the permanent division of the city into communist east and capitalist west, the Blockade of 1948, and, in 1961, the construction of the Berlin Wall. The city became the frontline of the Cold War, and the ideological schizophrenia of East and West is still visible in the city streets. West Berlin made a habit of tearing down its war-damaged buildings and erecting undistinguished modern ones, while East Berlin restored wherever possible, preserving some of the nineteenth-century buildings that had once made the city magnificent. Despite the current feverish construction activity in many parts of eastern Berlin, it's still easy to spot facades scarred by wartime bullets, and common to turn off a main avenue onto a street that appears to have remained unchanged for a century.

Given the range and severity of the events Berlin endured, it's no wonder it emerged far differently from anywhere else in the country. West Berlin's unorthodox character made it a magnet for those seeking alternative lifestyles – hippies and punks, gays and lesbians, artists and musicians all flocked there. Vital to this migration were the huge subsidies pouring in from the West German government to keep that portion of the city alive – with money available for just about everything, Berlin developed a cutting edge **arts** scene and **vibrant nightlife** that continue to this day, long after the grants have dried up. Non-Germans came too, attracted by the city's tolerance. The large numbers of Turks, Greeks and Italians, who originally came as "guest workers" in the 1960s, make Berlin Germany's most cosmopolitan city by far – a fact reflected in the excellent variety of cuisine on offer in the city's **restaurants**.

East Berlin followed this pattern in a more modest way. Much less diverse and considerably less prosperous than its western twin, it was still, as the largest city in East Germany, a draw for nonconformists. No surprise then that it was here, in the late 1980s, that grassroots groups began to call for reform and help set in motion the opening of the Wall on November 9, 1989 – and the eventual collapse of the German Democratic Republic.

What Berlin will be like when the dust from the world's largest building project settles is anyone's guess. Older East Berliners still consider that the West got by far the better deal from unification, and everyone is suffering from an economy greatly weakened by the costs of pulling the two Germanys together. The long-promised financial benefits of a revitalized Berlin will undoubtedly make some residents richer, but will the majority be any better off? The transformation of the city into a vigorous cultural centre, as museums and art collections are shifted and reorganized to integrate facilities in the east and west is encouraging, but how much longer will it take, and how much more will need to be spent? Anxiety and optimism can be found here in equal measure.

Inevitably, the **pace of change** in Berlin, particularly in the eastern part of the city, means that certain sections of this book are going to be out of date even as you read them. New cafés and restaurants open (and close) daily, traffic is rerouted around building sites, and the public transport system is being radically revamped.

One great advantage of unification is that, for the first time since the 1930s, the area **around Berlin** can easily be visited. Potsdam and the magnificent palace of Sanssouci is the obvious day-trip, and it's easy to get into countryside dotted with small towns and villages that preserve a "lost in time" feel.

It's a bracing time to see Berlin. As it seeks to keep its bearings even as its entire foundation has shifted, the city is again making history.

When to go

Lying in the heart of Europe, Berlin's climate is continental: winters are bitingly cold, summers hot. If you're hanging on for decent weather, April is the soonest you should go: any earlier and you'll

Average temperatures												
	Jan	Feb	Mar	April	May	June	July	Aug	Sept	Oct	Nov	Dec
Min °C	-12	-12	-7	-2	2	6	9	8	4	-1	-4	-9
Min °F	10	10	19	28	36	43	48	46	39	30	25	16
Max °C	9	11	17	22	28	30	32	31	28	21	13	10
Max °F	48	52	63	72	82	86	90	88	82	70	55	50

need to don winter clothing, earmuffs and a decent pair of water-proof shoes; this said, the city (especially the eastern part) does have a particular poignancy when it snows. Ideally, the best time to arrive is in May; June and July can be wearingly hot, though the famed Berlin air (*Berliner Luft* – there's a song about it) keeps things bearable. The weather stays good (if unpredictable) right up until October.

Part 1

Basics

Getting there from Britain and Ireland

The most convenient and usually best value way to get to Berlin from the UK is to fly – a journey of around ninety minutes. However, travelling by train through the Channel Tunnel is an easy and quick alternative: the journey time from London to Berlin via Brussels is around twelve hours. Similarly, if travelling by car you can use the Eurotunnel services. There are also ferries to the Hook of Holland and Hamburg from Harwich, which cost significantly less but are often uncomfortable and tiring. There are no direct flights from Ireland to Berlin so your best bet is flying via London.

By plane

Direct **scheduled flights** to Berlin are available **from London** on British Airways, Buzz and Virgin Express. There are three daily BA flights from London Heathrow to Berlin Tegel; Buzz, the low-cost offshoot of KLM, flies between two and three times daily from London Stansted, also to Berlin Tegel; while Virgin Express flies daily from London Heathrow, Gatwick and Stansted to Berlin Schönefeld (for more on Berlin's airports, see *Introducing the city*, p.43). Flying from London to Berlin with the German airline Lufthansa means changing the planes at other

German cities, principally Frankfurt: twice daily from Heathrow, three times daily from Stansted. There are no direct flights to Berlin available from **regional airports**, though BA will arrange a connecting flight from most of them to Heathrow. Additionally, KLM UK flies daily to Berlin Tegel via Amsterdam from almost every British airport (except Gatwick and Luton) and Lufthansa flies from Birmingham and Manchester, again with a transfer in a German city.

Also available, should you want to divide your time between Berlin and other parts of Germany, are the more expensive **open-jaw flights** (fly in to one airport and back from another) and **fly-drive deals**.

The airlines' published return **fare** can cost as much as £300. Special offers apart, the least costly way to fly is normally on a consolidated fare, usually involving booking in advance, a stay over a Saturday night and the risk of being penalized if you change your schedule. Buzz's consolidated direct fare is usually around £120 (inclusive of tax) return, though it can drop as low as £85 (again, inclusive). Consolidated fares with BA, Virgin Express, KLM UK (via Amsterdam) and Lufthansa (via Düsseldorf or Frankfurt) all hover around the £120–130 mark, though this doesn't include **airport tax**, which will add on £20–30 to that figure.

You may find a **cheaper flight** by scanning the travel pages of the Sunday or local evening papers, regional listings magazines, and, in London, *Time Out*. Ceefax is also an extremely good source of discounted flights. There are numerous **discount flight agents and operators** (listed on p.4) offering budget flights – particularly useful to those **under 26** – and specialists like the German Travel Centre in London. In addition, **online** resources such as *www.lastminute.com*, *www.cheapflights.co.uk* and *www.deckchair.com* can offer some of the best discounted fares and last-minute deals available.

By train

Unless you qualify for one of the discounts listed below, there are no savings to be made travelling to Berlin **by train**: in fact, you'll usually pay more than you would going by plane or bus. Students and those under 26 are best served by discounted rail passes.

By far the **fastest** and most popular train route to Berlin begins with **Eurostar** from London

Waterloo to Brussels (2hr 40min), and then onto another train direct to Berlin or via Cologne, a total journey of around twelve hours. Standard return tickets for the complete journey are £159 (with the London–Brussels leg priced at £85, barring special offers, with £75 fares for those under 26); these must be booked a week in advance, require you to spend Saturday night or three nights away, are changeable prior to departure but non-refundable. You can get through ticketing – including the tube journey to Waterloo – from mainline stations in Britain; typical add-on prices are £28 from Edinburgh or Glasgow, £19 from Manchester and £14 from Birmingham.

InterRail, German passes and other offers

If you plan to travel extensively in Europe by train there are better-value options than simply buying a return ticket. The obvious choice is the **InterRail** pass, available from European Rail, RailEurope, any major UK train station or youth/student travel offices; the restrictions are that you must have been resident in a European country for at least six months, and you can't use it for free rail travel within your home country. Since Germany has an extensive train network, the InterRail pass is great value – though more so for under-26s than over-26s – even taking into account the extra supplements you may have to pay on express intercity services. However, there are some private lines, including eastern Germany's narrow-gauge steam train lines, on which passes are not valid. The price of the pass depends on which **zones** you want to travel in; Europe is divided into eight zones, Germany falling into Zone C, along with Austria, Denmark and Switzerland, while neighbouring Belgium, France, Luxembourg and the Netherlands fall into Zone E. Passes are available for one, two, three or all zones: a one-zone pass lasts for 22 days, while all others last a month. A one-zone pass costs £179 (under-26 £129); a two-zone £235 (£169); a three-zone £269 (£195); and an all-zone pass £309 (£219). They can be bought up to two months in advance and in the UK and Ireland all InterRail passes offer discounts on rail travel and cross-Channel ferries en route to the continent.

If you're sixty or over and have a British Rail Senior Card (£18 from any train station), you can get a **Rail Europe Senior Card** for £5, which gives discounts of approximately thirty percent on cross-border train and sea travel in Germany and most of western Europe; both are valid for one year.

Specific **passes for travel in Germany only** can be bought before you go from European Rail, RailEurope or the DER Travel Service (see box on p.7) and other agents – for a full list of national passes contact **German Rail** (see box above), The broadest-ranging pass for travel in Germany is the **EuroDomino**, which offers unlimited travel on the whole train network. Passes are valid for travel for between three and eight days within any one-month period (they do not have to be used on consecutive days). The three-day pass costs £112 (under-26 £86), rising to £165 (£122) for the eight-day pass. Unlike the InterRail pass, the EuroDomino doesn't have any residence requirements – but they're only available for one country at a time.

By bus

Travelling to Berlin by **bus** won't bring any major savings over the cheapest air fares, and the journey will be long and uncomfortable, interrupted every three to four hours by stops at motorway service stations. The one advantage is that you can buy an open return at no extra cost.

Services are run by **Eurolines** (see box opposite) from Victoria Coach Station in London, and are bookable through most travel agents and through any National Express agent. There are two buses daily to Berlin; the journey takes around 24 hours and costs £97 return (£89 for students and under-25s), being only slightly cheaper in winter. It's also worth looking out for special promotions, usually requiring reservation two weeks in advance, which can bring the price down to as little as £79. If you're outside London, Eurolines will book you a National Express coach to London, but with no reductions available on the usual domestic fare. A **Europass** is available for Europe-wide travel for either thirty days (£245/under-26 £195 in high season; £175/139 in low season) or sixty days (£283/227; £219/185) between London and 48 other

---

Train information

European Rail ☎ 020/7387 0444.

Eurostar, 102–104 Victoria St, London SW1E 5JL ☎ 0870/160 6600; *www.eurostar.com*

German Rail (Deutsche Bahn) ☎ 0870/243 5363; *www.bahn.de*

RailEurope (SNCF French Railways), 179 Piccadilly, London W1V 0BA ☎ 0870/584 8848; *www.raileurope.com*

Bus information

Eurolines, 52 Grosvenor Gardens (opposite Victoria Train Station), London SW1W 0AU ☎ 0870/514 3219; *www.eurolines.co.uk*

European cities including Berlin, Hamburg and Frankfurt.

By car: ferries and Eurotunnel

To take your **car** to Berlin you'll need a vehicle registration document and proof of vehicle insurance.

Ferries

The cheapest and most frequent (twice daily, daytime only) Channel crossing for Berlin is the Stena Line **ferry** from **Harwich to the Hook of Holland** (3hr 40min). Five-day returns for a medium-sized car plus driver, travelling over the weekend, are £219 in high season (July and August), and £149 in low season – with extra passengers charged at £22 each; travelling midweek brings the price down to £165 and £119 respectively. Standard midweek returns, which don't have a time limit and include up to four passengers (but you have to leave Tuesday to Thursday and return within the same period, are substantially cheaper at £249 in high season and £189 in low, though frequent special offers can bring prices down to under £100.

From the Hook, the **best route** is Utrecht–Amersfoort–Hengelo–Osnabrück–Hanover–Helmstedt–Marienborn–Berlin: allow about twelve hours to reach Berlin. Both the AA and RAC publish route maps of the areas you'll be passing through, which are free to members.

The route run by **DFDS Seaways** plies **directly** from the UK to Germany. Once there, it's a 285km drive to Berlin, making this the best (though most expensive) route if you want to minimize time actually spent driving. The service runs from **Harwich to Hamburg** all year round – between

three and four times a week – taking nineteen hours. A full berth must be taken, with the cheapest fares (Seapex) booked 21 days in advance avoiding Friday and Saturday; with these fares, taking a standard four-person cabin, each passenger pays £84 per person in low season, rising to £139 in July and August, and car drivers must add on an extra £68, rising to £108 in the high season. Students qualify for a 25-percent reduction on passenger fares.

Eurotunnel

Probably the most convenient way of getting across the Channel is to take the Channel Tunnel train shuttle – **Eurotunnel** (journey time 35–45min). The tunnel entrance is off the M20 at Junction 11A, just outside Folkestone (emerging outside Calais). Services operate around the clock, 365 days a year, with four services per hour at peak periods: because of the frequency of the service, you don't have to buy a ticket in advance; just arrive and wait to board one of the trains – promised loading time is ten minutes.

Tickets are available through Eurotunnel (see box on previous page) or any travel agent. **Fares** vary with the season, time of day and length of stay: it's cheaper to travel between 10am and 6pm and on weekdays, while the highest fares are reserved for weekend departures and July and August. Apart from special offers, standard tickets are fully flexible and refundable and are priced per carload: standard returns are always around £300. However, if you can be more flexible about dates and times, five-day returns offer better value at around £100–150. Look out for the frequent special offers when prices can go as low as £40; booking online will save you an extra £2.

Hitching

Most hitchhikers who start thumbing in the UK will be expected to pay for their ferry passage, and should aim for the Hook of Holland. For all but the absolutely penniless, it's a smarter idea to buy a bus or boat ticket to the port and start hitching from there, following the route outlined above.

If hitching back from or out of Germany, it's worth contacting one of the many Berlin **Mitfahrzentralen** organizations, whose bureaux put drivers and hikers in touch for a small fee and

> **Cross-Channel information**
>
> **DFDS Seaways** Scandinavia House, Parkeston Quay, Harwich, Essex CO12 4QG ☎01255/241234 or nationwide ☎0870/533 3000; *www.dfdsseaways.co.uk*
>
> **Eurotunnel** Customer Service Centre, jct #12 off M20; PO Box 300, Dept 302, Folkestone, Kent CT19 4QD ☎0870/535 3535; *www.eurotunnel.com*
>
> **Stena Line** Charter House, Park St, Ashford, Kent TN24 8EX ☎0870/570 7070; *www.stenaline.co.uk*

a contribution towards petrol. There's a valuable safety factor in this system, since all drivers have to notify the agencies of their addresses and car registration. The usual cost of getting from Berlin to London, for example, is about DM60. *Mitfahrzentralen* can be found at Joachimstaler Strasse 17 (☎1 94 44; daily 9am–8pm); in Zoo Station U-Bahn station, on the platform for line #2, direction Schlesisches Tor (☎1 94 40; daily 8am–9pm); and in Alexanderplatz U-Bahn station at the crossing from line #8 to line #2 (☎24 15 82; Mon–Fri 8am–8pm, Sat 8am–6pm, Sun 10am–6pm). More listings for Mitfahrzentralen can be found in *Tip* and *Zitty* magazines (see pp.46–47).

Inclusive holidays

Since the fall of the Wall, Berlin has featured as a destination for the major **package operators**, and an all-inclusive holiday can prove convenient, if a little pricey, especially for a short break. Prices start from around £200 for a two-night stay, including flights and accommodation in a centrally located hotel. Any high street travel agent will have details of packages; those offered by the DER Travel Service (see box below) are usually reasonable value.

Getting there from Ireland

There are no direct flights from Ireland to Berlin. **From Dublin** Aer Lingus fly to Munich, where you can pick up a connecting flight to Schönefeld, but probably the best option would be to fly to London with Aer Lingus for around IR£80/€101, or with one of the newer, cheaper outfits like Ryanair (IR£49/€62), and then connect up with one of the Berlin-bound flights there (see p.3). Another money-saving option is to fly to London

but book your second flight with one of the London-based discount travel agents (see p.4) before you go. However, to do this you'll need to send proof if you are a student or under 26, and if you live in the Republic you'll need a contact in London to collect the tickets and send them to you.

An alternative to flying from Dublin is to go **from Shannon**: Virgin Express runs a service to Berlin, with a stopover at London Stansted, for IR£200–240 (€250–305) in high season. **From Belfast** most flights to Berlin are with British Airways via London or Birmingham – fares start at £190 (plus tax).

Students and anyone under 26 should contact **Usit NOW**, which generally has the best discount deals on flights and train tickets. **Package holidays** and city breaks are mostly routed via London with an add-on fare for the connection from Ireland.

By car and ferry

Irish Ferries runs services from Rosslare to Roscoff (16hr) and Cherbourg (18hr) on alternate days all year round. Prices vary according to season and size of car, with prices for a small car and two adults starting as low as IR£126/€160 one way (return prices are simply double). Brittany Ferries also operates year round, once a week, crossing from Cork to Roscoff (14hr); prices range from IR£130/€165 one way in low season to IR£234/€297 in high season (return fares are roughly double).

Foot passenger prices vary greatly according to season, with one-way fares from IR£40–80/€51–101 with Irish Ferries, and IR£45–65/€57–82 with Brittany Ferries; returns on both are roughly double the price.

SPECIALIST AND PACKAGE OPERATORS

British Airways Holidays, Astral Towers, Betts Way, London Road, Crawley RH10 2XA ☎01293/723 100; *www.britishairwaysholidays .co.uk*. City breaks starting at £240 (Jan–March) for two nights in a three-star hotel.

DER Travel Service, 18 Conduit St, London W1R 9TD ☎020/7290 1111; *www.dertravel.co.uk*. The national German travel agency, offering a full range of tours, including city breaks in Berlin for £199.

Thomas Cook Holidays ☎01733/418 200; *www.tcholidays.com*. Nationwide holiday company offering competitive packages and flights.

Time Off, 1 Elm Field Park, Bromley, Kent, BR1 1LU ☎0870/584 6363. Flexible city breaks in various price ranges.

Travelscene, 11–15 St Anne's Rd, Harrow, HA1 1LQ (☎020/8427 8800). European city breaks.

AIRLINES IN IRELAND

Aer Lingus Belfast ☎ 0845/973 7747; Cork
☎ 021/327155; Dublin ☎ 01/844 4777 Limerick
☎ 061/474239; *www.aerlingus.ie*
British Airways in the Republic
☎ 1800/626747; in Northern Ireland

☎ 0845/773 3377;
www.british-airways.com
Ryanair ☎ 0870/156 9569 or 01/609 7881;
www.ryanair.com

FERRY COMPANIES

Brittany Ferries ☎ 0870/901 2400;
www.brittanyferries.co.uk

Irish Ferries in the Republic ☎ 1890/313131;
in Northern Ireland ☎ 0800/018 2211;
www.irishferries.com

DISCOUNT AGENTS AND TOUR OPERATORS

Joe Walsh Tours, 8 Lower Baggot St, Dublin
☎ 01/676 7834; 69 O'Connell St, Dublin
☎ 01/872 2555. General budget fares agent.
Student & Group Travel, 71 Dame St, Dublin
☎ 01/677 7834;
www.studentandyouthtravel.com. Student
specialists.
Thomas Cook, 118 Grafton St, Dublin
☎ 01/677 1721; 11 Donegall Place, Belfast
☎ 028/9055 0232; *www.tcholidays.com*.

Package holiday and flight agent, with occa-
sional discount offers.
Travel Shop, 35 Belmont Rd, Belfast
☎ 028/9047 1717. Discount agent.
Usit NOW, O'Connell Bridge, 19–21 Aston
Quay, Dublin ☎ 01/602 1600; 10–11 Market
Parade, Patrick St, Cork ☎ 021/270900;
Fountain Centre, College St, Belfast BT1 6ET
☎ 028/9032 7111; *www.usitnow.com*. Student
and youth specialist for flights and trains.

Getting there from North America

Partly as a result of the presence of US military forces, most German cities are well served by US airlines. There are numerous flights to Berlin from nearly all major North American cities, and fares are among the most inexpensive for transatlantic crossings. The majority of flights land at Tegel airport to the west of the city, with some landing at Schönefeld to the east: for details on how to get to the city centre from either airport, see pp.43–44.

The cheapest and most convenient way to fly from the US or Canada to Berlin is to book a **direct flight** (this means booking a ticket for the entire journey with one airline; it doesn't necessarily mean you will be on a nonstop flight). Searching for special deals to another European city first and then booking a second flight with another airline for the final leg to Berlin will usually take longer and rarely result in significant savings. For Canadians there are no major savings to be made by flying to the US first.

If you're visiting Berlin as part of a wider German or European tour, and flying into one of the other mainland European gateway airports, **trains** are the most economical way to get to Berlin. A Eurail pass is particularly useful, as it can get you from any part of Europe to Berlin. From

England, flying is often just as inexpensive, if not more so, as ground travel.

Shopping for tickets

Barring special offers, the cheapest fare is usually an **Apex** ticket, although this will carry certain restrictions: you will, most likely, have to book – and pay – at least 21 days before departure, spend at least seven days abroad (maximum stay three months), and you tend to get penalized if you change your schedule. There are also winter **Super Apex** tickets, sometimes known as "Eurosavers" – slightly cheaper than an ordinary Apex, but limiting your stay to between 7 and 21 days. Some airlines also issue **Special Apex** tickets to people younger than 24. These will probably cost the same as the lowest Apex fare, but may have an advance purchase requirement of only three days, an "open" return and a maximum stay of a year.

You can normally cut costs further by going through a **discount agent** or **consolidator**, who buys up blocks of tickets from airlines and sells them at a discount. Some agents specialize in **charter flights**, which may be cheaper than any available scheduled flight, but again departure dates are fixed. With all reduced-rate operations, withdrawal penalties are high (check the refund policy).

Especially if you're a **student** or **under 26**, you should contact any of the specialist operators listed below, such as Council Travel, STA, or Travel Cuts in Canada, who may be able to offer substantial discounts on scheduled fares – at the time of writing, low season fares were available for as little as $343 (from New York), $420 (from Chicago) or $502 (from LA).

Regardless of where you buy your ticket, the fare will depend on the **season**. Fares to Berlin are highest from the beginning of June to the end of September; they drop during the "shoulder" seasons (all of October, mid-March to the end of May and December 1–24), and fall to their lowest level for November and from December 25 to mid-March. But don't be surprised to find further

AIRLINES

Air France US: ☎ 1-800/237-2747; Canada: ☎ 1-800/667-2747; *www.airfrance.fr*

American Airlines ☎ 1-800/433-7300; *www.americanair.com*

British Airways US: ☎ 1-800/247-9297; Canada: ☎ 1-800/668-1059; *www.britishairways.com*

Canadian Airlines ☎ 1-800/426-7000; *www.cdnair.ca*

Continental Airlines ☎ 1-800/231-0856; *www.flycontinental.com*

Delta Airlines ☎ 1-800/241-4141; *www.delta-air.com*

Lufthansa US: ☎ 1-800/645-3880; Canada: ☎ 1-800/563-5954; *www.lufthansa-usa.com*

Northwest/KLM US: ☎ 1-800/374-7747; Canada: ☎ 1-800/361-5073; *www.nwa.com*

Sabena ☎ 1-800/955-2000; *www.sabena.com*

Swissair US: ☎ 1-800/221-4750; Canada: ☎ 1-800/267-9477; *www.swissair.com*

United Airlines ☎ 1-800/538-2929; *www.ual.com*

DISCOUNT TRAVEL COMPANIES

Air Brokers International, 150 Post St, Suite 620, San Francisco, CA 94108 ☎ 1-800/883-3273; *www.airbrokers.com*. Consolidator.

Council Travel, 205 E 42nd St, New York, NY 10017 ☎ 212/822-2700 or 1-800/226-8624, branches in many other US cities; *www.counciltravel.com*. Nationwide US organization. Mostly, but not exclusively, specializes in student travel.

Encore Travel Club, 4501 Forbes Blvd, Lanham, MD 20706 ☎ 1-800/444-9800; *www.preferredtraveller.com*. East Coast travel club.

Interworld, 800 Douglass Rd, Miami, FL 33134 ☎ 305/443-4929 or 1-800/468-3796; *www.interworldtravel.com*. Southeastern US consolidator.

Moment's Notice, 7301 New Utrecht Ave, Brooklyn, NY 11204 ☎ 718/234-6295 or 212/486-0500; *www.moments-notice.com*. Discount travel club.

STA Travel, 10 Downing St, New York, NY 10014 ☎ 212/627-3111 or 1-800/777-0112, branches in several other US cities;

www.sta-travel.com. Worldwide specialists in independent travel.

Travac, 989 Sixth Ave, New York NY 10018 ☎ 1-800/872-8800; *www.thetravelsite.com*. Consolidator and charter broker; has another office in Orlando.

Travel Avenue, 10 S Riverside, Suite 1404, Chicago, IL 60606 ☎ 1-800/333-3335; *www.travelavenue.com*. Discount travel agent.

Travel Cuts, 187 College St, Toronto, ON M5T 1P7 ☎ 416/979-2406 or 1-800/667-2887, plus branches all over Canada; *www.travelcuts.com*. Canadian student travel organization.

Travelers Advantage, 3033 S Parker Rd, Suite 1000, Aurora, CO 80014 ☎ 1-800/548-1116; *www.travelersadvantage.com*. Discount travel club.

Unitravel, 11737 Administration Drive, Suite 120, St Louis, MO 63146 ☎ 1-800/325-2222; *www.flightforless.com*. Consolidator.

Worldwide Discount Travel Club, 1674 Meridian Ave, Miami Beach, FL 33139 ☎ 305/534-2082. Discount travel club.

---

variations; Lufthansa, for instance, divides its "high" season into three further "sub-seasons". In addition, the major carriers periodically offer special limited promotional fares – and it is these which generally offer the best value.

Ticket prices quoted below are for midweek travel. Weekend flights cost around $60 extra. All prices are round-trip, exclusive of taxes and subject to availability and change.

Flights from the US

Although there are direct scheduled flights to Berlin from all the major gateway cities (New York, Atlanta, Boston, Washington DC, Miami, Chicago and LA), you'll usually have to stop over in another European city. At the time of writing, Lufthansa has the most competitive fares and the most flights to Berlin.

From the **East Coast**, expect a flying time of approximately nine hours. From New York a regular APEX fare will cost as little as $343 in low season and up to $1050 in high season; from Atlanta $369 (low) or $1240 (high); from Miami $490 (low) or $1250 (high).

From the **Midwest** flight times are roughly ten and a half hours. From Chicago fares are around $420 (low) or $1275 (high).

From the **West Coast** the flying time is approximately thirteen hours. Flying from Los Angeles, the average fares to Berlin are around $665 in low season and $1420 in high season. From San Francisco $750 (low) or $1410 (high). From Seattle $675 (low) or $1420 (high).

Flights from Canada

Canadians have fewer direct flight options than Americans. The widest selections are out of **Toronto** and **Montreal** (10hr), with fares to Berlin from around CDN$850 (low season) to CDN$1270 (high season) on the major carriers, although a **discount travel agent**, such as Travel Cuts, may be able to find you a low season fare from the East Coast for as little as CDN$700. From

Rail contacts

CIT Tours, 15 W 44th St, 10th Floor, New York, NY 10036 ☎1-800/223-7987 or 1450 City Counselers, Quebec, Montreal H3A 2E6 ☎1-800/361-7799; *www.cittours.com*

DER Tours/German Rail, 9501 W Devon Ave, Suite 400, Rosemont, IL 60018 ☎1-888/337-7350; *www.dertravel.com*

Rail Europe, 226 Westchester Ave, White Plains, NY 10604 ☎ 1-800/438-7245; *www.raileurope.com*

ScanTours Inc., 3439 Wade St, Los Angeles, CA 90066-1533 ☎1-800/223-7226; *www.scantours.com*

TOUR OPERATORS IN NORTH AMERICA

Unless stated otherwise, all prices quoted below exclude taxes and are subject to change. Where applicable, round-trip flights are from New York and accommodation is priced per person sharing a double room.

American Express Vacations, 110 East Broward Blvd, Fort Lauderdale, FL 33302 ☎1-800/241-1700; *www.americanexpress.com/travel*. City breaks from $765 (7 nights, land/air all taxes included).

Brendan Tours, 15137 Califa St, Van Nuys, CA 91411 ☎818/786-9696 or 1-800/421-8446; *www.brendantours.com*. Fifteen-day German tour spends two days in Berlin along with Frankfurt, Munich, Dresden etc. (from $2072 land/air).

Caravan Tours, 401 N Michigan Ave, Chicago, IL 60611 ☎312/321 9800 or 1-800/227-2826. Motorcoach tours. "Berlin to Budapest" spends two days in Berlin with stops in Dresden, Vienna and Prague (eleven days from $2995, land only).

DER Travel Services, 9501 West Devon Ave, Rosemont, IL 60018 ☎1-888/337-7350. Customized tours and packages.

Euro Lloyd Tours, 1640 Hempstead Turnpike, East Meadow, NY 11554 ☎516/794-1253 or 1-800/334-2724; *www.eurolloyd.com*. Customized tours and city packages from $699 (three nights land/air).

International Gay Travel Association, 4331 N Federal Hwy, Suite 304, Ft Lauderdale, FL 33308 ☎1-800/448-8550; *www.igtla.org*. Trade group with lists of gay-owned or gay-friendly travel agents, accommodations and other travel businesses.

Maupintour, 1421 Research Park Drive, Suite 3000 Lawrence KS 66049-3858 ☎1-800/255-6162; *www.maupintours.com*. "Berlin to Budapest by Train" – fourteen days from $4715 (land/air).

Trafalgar Tours, 11 E 26th St, New York, NY 10010 ☎1-800/854-0103; *www.trafalgartours.com*. Thirteen-day "Best of Germany" tour (from $1099 – land only).

Travel Bound 599 Broadway, New York, NY 10012 ☎212/334-1350 or 1-800/456-8656. Fully inclusive tour package bookable only through a travel agent.

Vantage Travel 111 Cypress St, Brookline, MA 02146 ☎1-800/322-6677; *www.vantagetravel.com*. Group travel for seniors. River cruises and packages that include Berlin as part of a multi-city itinerary.

Vancouver (12hr) expect to pay from CDN$1100 (low) to CDN$1410 (high).

Train passes

If you're planning to do much **train travel** across Europe, a **Eurail** pass – which allows unlimited free train travel in seventeen European countries, and must be bought before you leave home – might come in useful. The **Eurail Youthpass** (for under-26s) costs US$388/CDN$590 for fifteen consecutive days, US$499/CDN$759 for 21 days, US$623/CDN$947 for one month, US$882/CDN$1341 for two months, and US$1089/CDN$1656 for three months; if you're 26 or over you'll have to buy a **first-class pass**, the corresponding prices for which are US$554/CDN$843, US$718/CDN$1092, US$890/CDN$1353, US$1260/CDN$1916 and US$1558/CDN$2369.

You stand a better chance of getting your money's worth out of a **Eurail Flexipass**, good for a certain number of travel days in a two-month period. This, too, comes in under-26/first-class versions, covering ten days, (US$458/US$654; CDN$697/CDN$995) and fifteen days ($599/$862; CDN$911/CDN$1311).

North Americans are also eligible to purchase more specific passes valid for travel in Germany only, such as the **EuroDomino** pass (see "Getting there from Britain"). These and the wider European passes can be purchased through most travel agents, or try the agents listed in the box below.

Packages and organized tours

Most **package holidays** combine Berlin with other German and European cities, and if you want something based in Berlin alone, you need to choose carefully. A good starting point for further information on packages is the **German National Tourist Office** (see p.17), and of course, your local travel agent.

Getting there from Australia and New Zealand

There are no direct flights to Berlin from Australia or New Zealand; most airlines use Frankfurt as their German gateway. All involve either a transfer or overnight stop en route in the airline's hub city: flying times are around 24 hours via Asia and thirty hours via the US, so the chance to rest up should be taken (if you're not pushed for time, stopovers are also a good way to see places along the way).

Air fares

Regular return **air fares** are seasonally adjusted – **low season** is from mid-January to the end of February and October to November; **high season** is mid-May to August and December to January; the remainder of the year is **shoulder season**.

Tickets purchased direct from the airlines tend to be expensive; travel agents generally offer much better deals, and have the latest information on limited special offers and stopovers. Some of the best **discounts** are offered by

AIRLINES

Air France Australia ☎ 02/9244 2100; New Zealand ☎ 09/308 3352; *www.airfrance.com.au*

Alitalia Australia ☎ 02/9244 2400; New Zealand ☎ 09/302 1452; *www.alitalia.it*

Garuda Australia ☎ 1300/365330; New Zealand ☎ 1800/128510 (toll-free) or ☎ 09/366 1855.

Japan Airlines (JAL) Australia ☎ 02/9272 1111; New Zealand ☎ 09/379 9906; *www.japanair.com*

Lauda Air Australia ☎ 1800/642438 (toll-free) or ☎ 02/9251 6155; *www.laudaair.com*

Lufthansa Australia ☎ 1300/655727 or ☎ 02/9367 3887; New Zealand ☎ 0800/945220 (toll-free) or ☎ 09/303 1529; *www.lufthansa.com*

Olympic Airways Australia ☎ 1800/221663 (toll-free) or ☎ 02/9251 2044; *www.olympic-airways.com*

Qantas Australia ☎ 13/1313; New Zealand ☎ 09/357 8900 or 0800/808767 (toll-free); *www.qantas.com.au*

Royal Brunei Australia only ☎ 07/3221 7757; *www.bruneiair.com*

Singapore Airlines Australia ☎ 13/1011; New Zealand ☎ 09/303 2129 or ☎ 0800/808909 (toll-free); *www.singaporeair.com*

Sri Lankan Airlines Australia ☎ 02/9244 2234; New Zealand ☎ 09/308 3353.

United Airlines Australia ☎ 13/1777; New Zealand ☎ 09/379 3800; *www.ual.com*

DISCOUNT AGENTS

The agents listed below offer competitive discounts on airfares as well as a selection of packaged holidays and tours, and can also arrange car rental and bus and rail passes.

Anywhere Travel, 345 Anzac Parade, Kingsford, Sydney ☎ 02/9663 0411; *anywhere@ozemail.com.au*

Budget Travel, 16 Fort St, Auckland ☎ 09/366 0061 or 0800/808 040, plus branches around the city; *www.budgettravel.co.nz*

Destinations Unlimited, 220 Queen St, Auckland ☎ 09/373 4033.

Flight Centres Australia: 82 Elizabeth St, Sydney ☎ 02/9235 3522, plus branches nationwide – for the nearest branch call ☎ 13/1600. New Zealand: 350 Queen St, Auckland ☎ 09/358 4310 or 0800/354 448, plus branches nationwide; *www.flightcentre.com*

Northern Gateway, 22 Cavenagh St, Darwin ☎ 08/8941 1394; *oztravel@norgate.com.au*

STA Travel Australia: 855 George St, Sydney; 256 Flinders St, Melbourne; other offices in state capitals and major universities – for nearest branch call ☎ 13/1776. New Zealand: 10 High St, Auckland ☎ 09/309 0458; plus branches in major cities and university campuses – for

nearest branch call ☎ 0800/874773; *www.statravel.com*

Student Uni Travel, 92 Pitt St, Sydney ☎ 02/9232 8444; plus branches in Brisbane, Cairns, Darwin, Melbourne and Perth; *sydney@backpackers.net*

Thomas Cook Australia: 175 Pitt St, Sydney ☎ 02/9231 2877; 257 Collins St, Melbourne ☎ 03/9282 0222; plus branches in other state capitals – for the nearest branch call ☎ 13/1771. New Zealand: 191 Queen St, Auckland ☎ 09/379 3920; *www.thomascook.com.au*

Trailfinders, 8 Spring St, Sydney ☎ 02/9247 7666; 91 Elizabeth St, Brisbane ☎ 07/3229 0887; Hides Corner, Shield St, Cairns ☎ 07/4041 1199; *www.travel.com.au*

Usit Beyond, Shortland St/Jean Batten Place, Auckland ☎ 09/379 4224 or 0800/788 336; plus branches in major cities; *www.usitbeyond.co.nz*

agents such as Flight Centres, STA Travel and Trailfinders (see box on above), particularly for students and under-26s; these can help with visas, travel insurance and tours, too. You might also want to have a look on the Internet; *www.travel.com.au* and *www.sydneytravel.com* offer good deals online.

Flights to Europe are generally cheaper via Asia than the US. Fares from eastern Australian cities to major western European cities are common rated, so you pay the same irrespective of destination, with Ansett and Qantas providing a connecting service to the point of departure. From Perth and Darwin these fares are around A$100–300 less via Asia, and A$400 more via the US. Common-rated fares mean you could, alternatively, buy the cheapest possible flight being offered and then either pick up a cheap charter flight or make your way to Germany overland, although this rarely works out as cheaply as buying a discounted air fare all the way.

From Australia

The most competitive rates for flights to Frankfurt via Asia from eastern Australia are with Sri Lankan Air from Sydney, Royal Brunei from Sydney and Brisbane, and Garuda from eastern gateways, all starting at A$1400 in low season, rising to A$2600 in the high season. However, the best deals flying right through to Berlin are offered by JAL from Sydney and Brisbane (with an overnight stopover in either Tokyo or Osaka), and Alitalia and Olympic Airways from Sydney (with a transfer in their respective home ports of Milan and Athens), all for A$1500 low season/A$2600 high season. For a little more Air France, Lauda Air, Singapore Airlines and Qantas can also take you through to Berlin via a transfer in their home cities for A$1800/2600. More expensive still, at A$1900/2800, Lufthansa, in conjunction with a number of airlines (via Bangkok), currently offer the most direct and fastest service to Berlin, with a flying time of around 22 hours.

Via North America, United Airlines teams up with Lufthansa to offer the cheapest deal to Berlin, via a transfer in LA, from A$2199 low season/A$3000 high season.

From New Zealand

Most airlines fly out of Auckland; add between NZ$150 and NZ$300 to the following fares for flights from Christchurch and Wellington respectively. The best deal to Berlin is with JAL (with a transfer or overnight stop in Tokyo or Osaka), for between NZ$1900 low season and NZ$2400 high season, while the cheapest fares to Germany are with Garuda to Frankfurt, via either Jakarta or Denpasar, from NZ$1800/2400. The most direct flights to Berlin are on Lufthansa, which teams up with other carriers to provide a through flight via Bangkok – more expensive at NZ$2300/3000 but faster, while for the same

price Singapore Airlines fly via Singapore and Frankfurt.

Via LA, the best deal to Berlin is with United Airlines-Lufthansa, from NZ$2499/3000.

Round-the-World tickets

Given the high cost of flights from Australasia, and particularly if you're planning to visit Berlin as part of an extended trip, then **Round-the-World tickets**, valid for a year, offer greater flexibility and can be very good value. RTW tickets are put together by an alliance of airlines – such as Star Alliance and Oneworld – and are usually mileage-based with a certain amount of stopovers included; the price rises the further you wish to travel or the more stopovers required. To give you some idea, an RTW ticket, for example, from Sydney/Auckland–Singapore/Bangkok–Rome–Berlin–London–New York–Los Angeles–Honolulu/Papeete–Sydney/Auckland, starts at around A$2399/NZ$2899.

By train

If you intend to explore Germany or extend your trip into Europe, it might be worth buying a **rail pass** before you leave home. The **Eurail Youth Pass** for under-26s is available in fifteen-day, 21-day, one-month, two-month and three-month versions, and varies in price from A$615/NZ$756 for the fifteen-day to A$1730/NZ$2127 for three months. If you're 26 or over you'll have to buy a first-class pass, the corresponding prices for which are A$880/NZ$1082 and A$2475/NZ$3044.

The **Eurail Flexipass** is good for a certain number of travel days in a two-month period and also comes in youth/first-class versions: ten days cost A$725/1040 (NZ$891/1279); and fifteen days, A$950/1370 (NZ$1168/1685.

A scaled-down version of the Flexipass, the **Europass** allows travel in France, Germany, Italy, Spain and Switzerland for (under-26/first-class)

> ### Rail contacts in Australia and New Zealand
> **CIT World Travel** ☎ 02/9267 1255; *www.cittravel.com.au*
> **Rail Plus** Australia ☎ 1300/555003 or 03/9642 8644; New Zealand ☎ 09/303 2484; *www.railplus.com.au*

SPECIALIST AGENTS

There is very little in the way of organized tours to Germany from Australia or New Zealand, and you're better off making arrangements once you're in Europe. However, the agents listed below can help you plan your trip.

Adventure World Australia:73 Walker St, North Sydney ☎ 02/9956 7766 or 1300/363 055, plus branches in Adelaide, Brisbane, Melbourne and Perth; *www.adventureworld.com.au*. New Zealand: 101 Great South Rd, Remuera, Auckland ☎ 09/524 5118; *www.adventureworld.co.nz*. Can arrange car rental, hotel accommodation, tours, train passes; are also agents for Explore's three day "Berlin Experience", which includes accommodation and two half-day city sightseeing tours (from A$389/NZ$460).

European Travel Office (ETO), 122 Rosslyn St, West Melbourne ☎ 03/9329 8844; Suite 410/368 Sussex St, Sydney ☎ 02/9267 7714; 407 Great South Rd, Auckland ☎ 09/525 3074. City stays and cultural tours throughout Germany, offering a wide selection of accommodation, including monasteries.

Insight Holidays, bookings through travel agents only.
First-class city accommodation and bus tours.

Qantas Holidays, 141 Walker St, North Sydney (bookings through travel agents only). Berlin accommodation passes and car rental.

Silke's Travel, 263 Oxford St, Darlinghurst, Sydney ☎ 02/9380 5835. Specially tailored packages for gay and lesbian travellers.

Youth Hostel Associations Australia: 422 Kent St, Sydney ☎ 02/9261 1111, and branches nationwide; *www.yha.com.au*. New Zealand: 173 Gloucester St, Christchurch ☎ 03/379 9970; *www.yha.co.nz*. Organizes budget accommodation and travel throughout Germany for HI members. Adult membership rate A$47/NZ$40.

A$370/550 (NZ$455/676) for five days in two months, on up to A$815/1155 (NZ$1002/1420) for fifteen days in two months; there's also the option of adding adjacent "associate" countries (Austria, Hungary, Benelux, Portugal and Greece). Passes are available through the contacts in the box on opposite, the travel agents listed in the box above or the German National Tourist Office (see p.17).

There's also a **Eurail Saverpass**, **Saver Flexipass** and **Euro Saverpass**. These are first class passes, valid for between two and five people who must be travelling together on all journeys. The cost is slightly less than for the full first-class passes.

Red tape and visas

British and other EU nationals can enter Germany on a valid passport or national identity card. The official time limit for stays in Germany is ninety days, but enforcement of this is fairly lax: it's unlikely, for example, that your passport will be date-stamped on arrival.

US, Canadian, Australian and New Zealand passport holders do not need a visa to enter Germany, and are allowed a stay of ninety days (within any one year). However, you're strongly advised, if you know your stay will be longer than this, to apply for an extension visa from your local German embassy before you go.

> If you are intending to stay on in Berlin and/or find a job, regulations are complex: see "Staying On", p.36.

Visa requirements vary for nationals of other countries; contact your local German embassy or consulate for information. For details of where to find your own embassy or consulate when in Berlin, see *Directory*.

If you want to extend your stay beyond three months, you are expected to **register with the local police** (as is every resident of Germany). First you'll need a *Polizeianmeldungsformular* ("registration form"), available from newsagents

for DM2 (€1). Get a friend, who has already registered and understands the complex German on the form, to help; inaccuracies will cause complications when you go to the police station.

Customs

Within the EU, **EU nationals** travelling across international borders don't have to make a declaration to Customs at their place of entry, and can effectively carry as much in the way of **duty-paid** goods as they want (as long as they're for personal use). However, they can no longer buy **duty-free goods**.

Duty-free restrictions for **non-EU residents** are standard for EU countries at 200 cigarettes (250g of tobacco, or fifty cigars), one litre of spirits and two litres of wine.

German embassies

Australia 119 Empire Circuit, Yarralumla, Canberra 2600 ☎ 02/6270 1911; *www.germanembassy.org.au*

Britain 23 Belgrave Square, London SW1X 8PZ ☎ 020/7824 1300; *www.german-embassy.org.uk*

Canada 1 Waverley St, Ottawa, Ontario K2P 0T8 ☎ 613/232-1101; *www.germanembassy-info.org* Consulates in Montreal, Toronto and Vancouver.

Ireland 31 Trimelston Ave, Booterstown, Blackrock, Co Dublin ☎ 01/269 3011; *germany@indigo.ie.*

New Zealand 90–92 Hobson St, Wellington ☎ 04/736 063.

US 4645 Reservoir Rd NW, Washington, DC 20007-1998 ☎ 202/298-4393; *www.germany-info.org* Consulates in New York, Atlanta, Boston, Houston, Miami, San Francisco, Los Angeles and Chicago

---

Information and maps

There's a wealth of rescources on the Internet too, providing details, often in English, on everything from Berlin's history to its vegetarian restaurants – we've given a selection below.

Before you set off for Berlin, it's worth contacting the German National Tourist Office, which has a lot of useful information on accommodation, what's on in town and the odd glossy brochure.

German National Tourist Offices

Australia Level 2, St Andrews House, Sydney Square, Sydney 2000 ☎ 02/9267 8148.

Britain PO Box 2695 London W1A 3TN ☎ 0990/600 1000 (60p per minute); *german_national_tourist_office @compuserve.com*

Canada postal address only: 175 Bloor St E, Suite 604, North Tower, Toronto, Ontario M4W3R8 ☎ 877/315-6237.

US 122 E 42nd St, New York, NY 10168 New York, NY 10017 ☎ 212/661-7200.

BERLIN ON THE NET

Official site *www.Berlin.de*
The city's official site, with loads of general information, plus the latest events.

Tourist office *www.btm.de*
Web site for the official tourist agency, which includes an accommodation booking service.

Berlin online *www.BerlinOnline.de*
An excellent, all-purpose source for news, business, politics, entertainment, restaurants, listings and the like.

Travel guide *www.gotoberlin.de*
General travel guide geared towards young people.

Train information *www.bahn.de*
The German railway company, with full information on routes, fares and timetables, plus a reservations facility.

Hostels *www.jugendherberge.de*
Listing of HI hostels in Berlin and the surrounding area.

Restaurants *www.berliner-gastronomie.de*
Online restaurant guide with search engine.

State museums *www.smp.spk-berlin.de*
Information on the state museums in the city.

City museums *www.stadtmuseum.de*
City museums online, including the Märkisches Museum and the historic houses in the Nikolaiviertel.

Berlin Wall *www.dailysoft.com/berlinwall*
Illustrated history of, and facts about, the Berlin Wall.

SPSG *www.spsg.de*
Information from the foundation administering the palaces and gardens of Sanssouci and Schloss Charlottenburg.

Die Welt *www.welt.de/english*
English-language articles from *Die Welt* newspaper, packed with Berlin news and culture.

Gay scene *www.sieges-saeule.de*
Berlin's main gay and lesbian city magazine online.

Vegetarian/health food
www.veg.org/veg/Guide/Germany/Berlin.html
Guide to vegetarian restaurants and health food stores in the city.

Once in the city, the **tourist office**, Berlin Tourismus Marketing, can supply a wider selection of bumph than the national offices, including comprehensive listings of the higher-brow cultural events, and help with accommodation (see *Accommodation* p.229). For more information on

---

MAP OUTLETS

AUSTRALIA AND NEW ZEALAND

Mapland, 372 Little Bourke St, Melbourne ☎03/9670 4383; *mapland@lexicon.net*

The Map Shop, 6 Peel St, Adelaide ☎08/8231 2033; *www.mapshop.net.au*

Mapworld, 173 Gloucester St, Christchurch ☎03/374 5399; *www.mapworld.co.nz*

Perth Map Centre, 1/884 Hay St, Perth ☎08/9322 5733; *www.perthmap.com.au*

Specialty Maps, 46 Albert St, Auckland ☎09/307 2217.

Travel Bookshop, Shop 3, 175 Liverpool St, Sydney ☎02/9261 8200.

Worldwide Maps and Guides, 187 George St, Brisbane ☎07/3221 4330; *www.powerup.com.au/~wwmaps*

BRITAIN

Blackwell's Map and Travel Shop, 53 Broad St, Oxford OX1 3BQ ☎01865/792792; *bookshop.blackwell.co.uk*

Heffers Map and Travel, 3rd Floor, in Heffers Stationery Department, 19 Sidney St, Cambridge, CB2 3HL ☎01223/568467; *www.heffers.co.uk*

James Thin Melven's Bookshop, 29 Union St, Inverness, IV1 1QA ☎01463/233500; *www.jthin.co.uk*

The Map Shop, 30a Belvoir St, Leicester, LE1 6QH ☎0116/247 1400.

National Map Centre, 22–24 Caxton St, London SW1H 0QU ☎020/7222 2466; *www.mapsworld.com*

Newcastle Map Centre, 55 Grey St, Newcastle-upon-Tyne, NE1 6EF ☎0191/261 5622; *www.newtraveller.com*

Stanfords, 12–14 Long Acre, London WC2E 9LP ☎020/7836 1321; *sales@stanfords.co.uk*

CANADA

International Travel Maps and Books, 552 Seymour St, Vancouver V6B 3J5 ☎604/687-3320; *www.itmb.com*

Open Air Books and Maps, 25 Toronto St, M5R 2C1 ☎416/363-0719.

Ulysses Travel Bookshop, 4176 St-Denis, Montreal H2W 2M5 ☎514/843-9447; *www.ulyssesguides.com*

US

ADC Map and Travel Center, 1636 I St NW, Washington DC 20006 ☎202/628-2608.

Book Passage, 51 Tamal Vista Blvd, Corte Madera, CA 94925 ☎415/927-0960; *www.bookpassage.com*

The Complete Traveller Bookstore, 199 Madison Ave, New York, NY 10016 ☎212/685-9007; 3207 Fillmore St, San Francisco, CA 94123 ☎415/923-1511; *www.complete.traveller.com*

Elliott Bay Book Company, 101 S Main St, Seattle, WA 98104 ☎206/624-6600; *www.elliottbaybook.com*

Forsyth Travel Library, 226 Westchester Ave, White Plains, NY 10604 ☎1-800/367-7984; *www.forsyth.com*

Map Link Inc., 30 S La Patera Lane, Unit 5, Santa Barbara, CA 93117 ☎805/692-6777; *www.maplink.com*

Phileas Fogg's Books & Maps, #87 Stanford Shopping Center, Palo Alto, CA 94304 ☎1-800/533-FOGG; *www.foggs.com*

Rand McNally, 444 N Michigan Ave, Chicago, IL 60611 ☎312/321-1751; 150 E 52nd St, New York, NY 10022 ☎212/758-7488; 595 Market St, San Francisco, CA 94105 ☎415/777-3131; *www.randmcnally.com*

Travel Books & Language Center, 4437 Wisconsin Ave, Washington, DC 20016 ☎1-800/220-2665.

Traveler'sChoice Bookstore, 2 Wooster St, New York, NY 10013 ☎212/941-1535; *tvlchoice@aol.com*

Note: Rand McNally now has more than twenty stores across the US; call ☎1-800/333-0136 ext 2111 or visit their Web site for the address of your nearest store, or for direct mail maps.

the city's tourist offices, as well as listings maga-zines, see *Introducing the city*, p.46.

Maps

Having a **map** is essential for getting around Berlin; the city is full of little side streets, its long-running boulevards tend to change names every couple of blocks, and Berliners are notorious for giving the wrong directions. By far the most con-venient map of the city is the ingeniously folded *Falk Plan* (DM9.80/€5, DM11.80/€6 for the bet-

ter, enlarged version) which contains an excellent gazetteer and enlarged plans of the city centre. It also includes a map of the U- & S-Bahn system and an index of every street in Berlin and Potsdam. It's available at most bookstores and newsagents.

For public transport, the best option is the *BVG & S-Bahn Berlin Atlas* (DM12/€6.15), which has complete listings and timetables for the U- & S-Bahn system, and bus, tram and ferry routes. It's available at the larger U-Bahn and S-Bahn sta-tions.

Health and insurance

As a member of the European Union, Germany has free reciprocal health agreements with other member states. To take advantage, British and Northern Ireland citizens will need form E111 (stamped), available over the counter from most post offices, which entitles you to free treatment within Germany's public health care system; other EU nationalities need comparable documentation. Without this form you'll have to pay in full for all medical treat-ment, which is expensive – currently DM40 for a visit to the doctor. Non-EU residents will need to insure themselves against all eventualities, including medical costs. No vaccinations are needed for Berlin or Germany.

Regardless, however, of whether or not you're covered by the E111 form, taking out your own **private medical insurance** remains a sensible precaution. It means you'll cover the cost of items not within the EU's scheme, such as dental treat-ment and repatriation on medical grounds, and it will usually also cover your baggage and tickets in case of theft, as long as you get a crime report from the local police. In the case of major expense the more worthwhile policies promise to sort matters out before you pay rather than after, but if you do have to pay upfront, get and keep the receipts.

Health

For minor ailments you'll find a local **doctor** under *Ärtze* in the Yellow Pages – surgeries don't

have standard hours, but generally operate a walk-in clinic for three or four days of the week. Doctors are likely to be able to speak English, but if you want to be certain, your embassy (see *Directory*, p.317) will provide a list of English-speaking ones. For an emergency doctor, call ☎31 00 31; for an emergency dentist, ☎89 00 43 33. In the event of an **emergency**, phone ☎110 for the police, who will call an ambulance for you, or go straight to the casualty unit of one of the major hospitals (there's a list in the *Directory*, p.317).

To get a prescription filled, go to a **pharmacy** (*Apotheke*): pharmacists are well trained and often speak English. Outside normal hours (usu-ally 8.30am–6.30pm), a notice on the door of any *Apotheke* indicates the nearest one open, mean-ing there's a round-the-clock service. Alternatively, call ☎31 00 31 for the same infor-mation. These pharmacies aren't open for brows-ing; you'll be served through a small hatch in the door, so don't be put off by the shops' closed appearance.

Insurance

A typical **travel insurance policy** usually provides cover for the loss of baggage, tickets and – up to a certain limit – cash or cheques, as well as can-cellation or curtailment of your journey. Most of them exclude so-called dangerous sports unless an extra premium is paid. Read the small print and benefits tables of prospective policies carefully; coverage can vary wildly for roughly similar premiums. Many policies can be chopped and changed to exclude coverage you don't need – for example, sickness and accident benefits can often be excluded or included at will. If you do take medical coverage, ascertain whether benefits will be paid as treatment proceeds or only after returning home, and whether there is a 24-hour medical emergency number. When securing baggage cover, make sure that the per-article limit – typically under £500 equivalent – will cover your most valuable possession. If you need to make a claim, you should keep receipts for medicines and medical treatment, and in the event you have anything stolen, you must obtain an official statement from the police (an *Anzeige*). Bank and credit cards often have certain levels of medical or other insurance included and you may automatically get travel insurance if you use a major credit card to pay for your trip.

Even though EU health care privileges exist in Germany, British and Irish citizens would do well to take out an insurance policy before travelling to cover against theft, loss and illness or injury. Travel agents and tour operators are likely to require some sort of insurance when you book a package holiday, though according to UK law they can't make you buy their own (other than a £1 premium for "schedule airline failure"). If you have a good all-risks home insurance policy it *may* cover your possessions against loss or theft even when overseas. Many private medical schemes such as BUPA or PPP also offer coverage plans for abroad, including baggage loss, cancellation or curtailment and cash replacement as well as sickness or accident.

Americans and **Canadians** should also check that they're not already covered. Canadian provincial health plans usually provide partial cover for medical mishaps overseas. Holders of official student/teacher/youth cards are entitled to meagre accident coverage and hospital in-patient benefits. Students will often find that their student health coverage extends during the vacations and for one term beyond the date of last enrollment. Homeowners' or renters' insurance often covers theft or loss of documents, money and valuables while overseas, though conditions and maximum amounts vary from company to company.

Rough Guides Travel Insurance

Rough Guides now offer their own **travel insurance**, customized for our readers by a leading UK broker and backed by a Lloyds underwriter. It's available for anyone, of any nationality, travelling anywhere in the world, and we are convinced that this is the best-value scheme you'll find.

There are two main Rough Guide insurance plans: **Essential**, for effective, no-frills cover, starting at £11.75 for 2 weeks; and **Premier** – more expensive but with more generous and extensive benefits. Each offers European or Worldwide cover, and can be supplemented with a "Hazardous Activities Premium" if you plan to indulge in sports considered dangerous, such as skiing, scuba-diving or trekking. Unlike many policies, the Rough Guides schemes are calculated by the day, so if you're travelling for 27 days rather than a month, that's all you pay for. You can alternatively take out annual **multi-trip insurance**, which covers you for all your travel throughout the year (with a maximum of 60 days for any one trip).

For a **policy quote**, call the Rough Guides Insurance Line on UK freefone ☎ 0800 015 0906, or, if you're calling from outside Britain on ☎ 0044-1243/621 046. Alternatively, you can get a quote or buy a policy online at *www.roughguides.com/insurance*.

Costs, money and banks

Long gone is the time when visitors to the former GDR could wine, dine and entertain themselves for a fraction of the cost of such entertainments in West Berlin. These days the hip new east side, with its upmarket shops and nightspots, has upmarket prices to match. The use of credit cards is steadily increasing for stores but cash is still the currency of choice when it comes to most bars and restaurants.

Assuming you intend to eat and drink in moderately priced places, utilize the public transport system sparingly and not stay in the *Hilton*, the **minimum** you could get by on after you've paid for your room is £17/$25 (or around DM50/€25.50) a day. For this you would get a sandwich (DM5/€2.50), an evening meal (DM20; €10.25), three beers (DM12; €6.15) and one underground ticket (DM4; €2.05), with around DM9 (€4.60) left for museums, entertainments,

etc. A more realistic figure, if you want to see as much of the city as possible (and party at night), would be at least twice that amount.

Accommodation, **transport** and **nightlife** are the most likely to run your budget up. The cheapest hostel dormitory or basic room is around £8/$15 a night; the flat fares of around £1.30/$2 on the bus and U- and S-Bahn network quickly mount up. **Drink** is a little more expensive than most are used to, particularly in the city's more enjoyable nightspots; but the quality – especially of the beer – is significantly higher.

Eating is comparatively cheap, cheerful and varied (food is good value in the shops and in restaurants) for British visitors. North Americans will, however, find prices marginally higher than they are used to. However, many **museums** and other attractions soften their entrance fees for students with ID.

Money

Until December 31, 2001, the currency of Germany is the **Deutschmark**, which comes in notes of DM5 (rarely encountered these days), DM10, DM20, DM50, DM100, DM200, DM500 and DM1000; and coins of DM0.01 (one Pfennig), DM0.02, DM0.05, DM0.10, DM0.50, DM1, DM2 and DM5. The current **exchange rate** is around DM3 to the pound sterling, DM2 to the US dollar. You can bring as much currency as you want into Berlin.

From January 1, 2002 however, the **euro** will take over completely as the legal tender of

---

The euro

Germany is one of eleven European Union countries who have changed over to a single currency, the **euro** (€). The transition period, which began on January 1, 1999, is, however, lengthy: euro notes and coins are not scheduled to be issued until January 1, 2002, with Deutschmarks remaining in place for cash transactions, at a fixed rate of 1.956 Marks to one euro, until they are scrapped entirely on July 1, 2002.

Even before euro cash appears in 2002, you can opt to pay in euros by credit card and you can get travellers' cheques in euros – you should not be charged commission for changing them in any of the eleven countries in the euro zone (also known as "Euroland"), or for changing from any of the old Euroland currencies to any other (French francs to Deutschmarks, for example).

All prices in this book are given in both Deutschmarks and the euro equivalent.

Germany – see the box below. Notes come in denominations of €5, €10, €20, €50, €100, €200, and €500; and coins in €0.01 (one euro-cent), €0.02, €0.05, €0.10, €0.20, €0.50, and €1. Current euro-sterling and euro-dollar exchange rates are €1 to £0.61 and €1 to $0.89.

Travellers' cheques, credit cards and ATMs

Travellers' cheques are the safest way of carrying your money. The usual fee for their purchase is one percent of face value, and they can be cashed in any bank or exchange office and used in the flashier shops. Make sure you keep the purchase agreement and a record of cheque serial numbers safe and separate from the cheques themselves. In the event that cheques are lost or stolen, the issuing company will expect you to report the loss forthwith; consequently, when you buy your travellers' cheques, ensure you have details of the company's emergency contact numbers or the addresses of their local offices. Most companies claim to replace lost or stolen cheques within 24 hours. When you cash your cheques, you'll find that almost all banks make a percentage charge per transaction on top of a basic minimum charge.

Debit and credit cards, once a foreign concept in Berlin, are finally becoming a part of everyday life. Debit cards are commonly accepted, whilst credit cards (at least the major ones such as American Express, Mastercard and Visa) are good in department stores, mid- to upmarket restaurants, an increasing number of shops and petrol stations. Should you want to get **cash** on your plastic, the best way is from any of the various **ATMs** around town. You can withdraw as little as DM50 (€25.50), but they do charge a minimum fee, often around DM4 (€2.05) against two to four percent of the withdrawal. In addition to credit cards, most bank debit cards, part of either the Cirrus or Plus systems, can be used for withdrawing cash, and carry lower fees than credit cards. Various banks will also give an advance against your credit card, subject to a minimum of the equivalent of £60/$100 – stickers in the bank windows indicate which cards they're associated with. American Express card holders can use that company's facilities at Friedrichstr. 172, Mitte (Mon–Fri 9am–6pm, Sat 10am–1pm; ☎2 01 74 00).

An alternative to conventional plastic is **Visa Travel Money** (*www.visa.com*), which comes in

Emergency numbers for lost credit cards	
Access/Mastercard/ Eurocard	☎ 069/7 93 30
American Express	☎ 069/72 00 16
Diner's Club	☎ 069/2 60 30
Visa	☎ 069/79 20 13 33

the form of a disposable debit card pre-paid with dedicated travel funds. Money can be accessed from ATMs worldwide. When your funds are depleted, you simply throw the card away. A 24-hour customer assistance service can be reached from Germany on ☎0800/810 9910.

Banks and exchange

Banking hours are usually Monday to Friday from 9am to 3pm and two days a week to 6pm (usually with a lunch break, the length of which varies depending on the closing time for that day – look at the schedule posted on the door). Branches of the Berliner Bank have the longest hours: the airport branch at Tegel is open daily from 8am to 10pm, and the branch at Kurfürstendamm 24, Charlottenburg, is open Monday to Friday from 9.30am to 6.30pm, and on Saturday from 9.30am to 1.30pm. Deutsche Bank's late opening days are Tuesday and Thursday and their branch at Potsdamer Platz is open till 4pm on Saturdays. It may be worth shopping around several banks (including the savings banks or Sparkasse), as the rates of exchange offered can vary, as can the amount of commission deducted. The latter tends to be a flat rate, meaning that small-scale transactions should be avoided whenever possible. In any case, the several **Wechselstuben** (bureaux de change) around Zoo Station, and particularly the Reisebank in the Alexanderplatz Station, offer better rates, as well as being open outside normal banking hours and weekends.

The most useful and central place for **currency exchange** is the Reisebank exchange office, either at Bahnhof Friedrichstrasse (Mon–Sat 7.30am–8pm, Sun 8am–8pm; ☎20 45 50 96), Zoo Station (Mon–Sat 7.30am–10pm, Sun 8am–10pm; ☎881 71 17) or Ostbahnhof station (Mon–Sat 7.30am–10pm, Sun 8am–4pm; ☎296 43 93); it's open year-round, and will cash travellers' cheques and give cash advances on major credit cards, though subject to a minimum of

DM200 (€102.25). There's a 24-hour ATM that will give cash advances on Visa and American Express cards; and it's also possible to transfer cash to or from any Western Union office here; for more information, call the main office (☎069/2 64 82 01; www.westernunion.com).

Wiring money

The high cost, long wait, and extreme complexity of **wiring money** through a German bank makes it impractical. A much more convenient alternative is a Moneygram, which allows someone to send you money that you can then pick up immediately at a Moneygram agent. There are several in Berlin, including the American Express office noted above (though you must be an American Express cardholder); Thomas Cook, Friedrichstrasse 56; and Euro Change offices in the Europa Center, and at Alexanderplatz S-Bahn Station. The surcharge for a Moneygram runs at about 8–10 percent.

Post, phones and the media

Germany's famed efficiency is apparent in its postal and telephone services: the former is speedy and the latter hassle-free. Both, however, are relatively expensive (although since privatization in 1999 the telephone system has become cheaper).

Post

Central Berlin's most conveniently situated **post offices** (*Postämter*) are at Bahnhof Friedrichstrasse (under the arches at Georgenstrasse 12; daily 8am–10pm) and Budapesterstrasse 42 (Mon–Sat 8am–midnight, Sun 10am–midnight). These are the easiest (and quickest) places to send letters home: mail to the UK usually takes 3–4 days; to North America one to two weeks; and to Australasia over two weeks. There are also separate parcel offices (marked *Pakete*), usually a block or so away.

There's a late-opening post office at Tegel airport (Mon–Fri 7am–9pm, Sat & Sun 8am–8pm) and another office at Strasse der Pariser Commune 8–10, which is open weekdays until 9pm and Saturday until 10pm. Other offices (Mon–Fri 8am–6pm, Sat 8am–1pm) are dotted around town; you can also buy stamps from the small yellow machines next to some postboxes. **Postboxes** themselves are everywhere and unmissable, painted bright yellow. When posting

Berlin postcodes

Each Berlin address has a five-digit post code. In our Listings chapters we've given the district name for each address: this is important since certain street names recur across the city. To find out where each district lies, see our map on pp.x–xi.

However, where you may need to write to a given address, we have included the post code. A complete list of city post codes may be found in the telephone white pages of the inexpensive *BVG & S-Bahn Berlin Atlas*, see "Information and Maps".

a letter, make sure you distinguish between the slots marked for various postal codes. Boxes marked with a red circle indicate collections late in the day and on Sunday.

The two main post offices are also the places to send and collect letters **poste restante**: letters for the Bahnhof Friedrichstrasse branch should be sent to: (Recipient's Name), Postlagernd, Postfiliale Berlin 120, 10612 Berlin; for the Budapesterstrasse branch it's Postlagernd, Postamt Rathausstrasse 5, 10178 Berlin, and collected from the counter marked "Postlagernde Sendungen" (take your passport). **Telegrams** can be sent either by ringing ☎01805/12 12 10, or from any post office. The major post offices also offer **fax services**, and at a cheaper rate than in copy shops and the like.

Telephones

Believe it or not, there are more **telephones** in Berlin than there are people. You can make **international calls** from most phone boxes in the city, which are usually equipped with basic instructions in English. Virtually every pay phone you'll find takes **cards**. These cost DM12 (€6.15) or DM50 (€25.50) and are available from all post offices and some shops. Another option is to use the **direct phone service** facility of the main post offices: a phone booth will be allocated to you from the counter marked *Fremdgespräche*, which

To call Berlin **from the UK** dial ☎00 49 30 followed by the number; **from the US** dial ☎011 49 30 followed by the number; **from Australia** dial ☎0011 49 30 followed by the number; **from New Zealand** dial ☎00 49 30 followed by the number; **from elsewhere in Germany** dial ☎030 followed by the number.

is also where you pay once you've finished. A large number of **phone shops** offering cheap international calling have also sprouted up lately: among others, there's Telecafé at Potsdamerstrasse 164 (Schöneberg); CSB at Gneisenaustrasse 21 (Kreuzberg); and Call Center ACC in Europa Center (Charlottenburg).

Some of the public boxes are marked *International*, with a ringing bell symbol to indicate that you can be called back on that phone. There are international and local phones in Bahnhof Friedrichstrasse and Zoo Station. The cheapest time to call abroad is between 9pm and 8am.

Internet and email

Berlin is a very Internet-conscious city and **online access** is excellent: there are a number of local providers, and Compuserve and AOL (as well as the German T-Online service) have local nodes here. Some of the larger hotels, and many of the

---

PHONING ABROAD FROM BERLIN

Dial ☎00 + IDD country code + area code minus first 0 + subscriber number

IDD CODES

Britain ☎44	USA ☎1	New Zealand ☎64
Ireland ☎353	Canada ☎1	Australia ☎61

TIME

Germany is one hour ahead of GMT, 9 hours ahead of US Pacific Standard Time and 6 hours ahead of Eastern Standard Time. Clocks are turned an hour forward at the end of March and an hour back at the end of September.

USEFUL NUMBERS WITHIN BERLIN

Directory enquiries ☎1 18 33	International directory enquiries ☎1 18 34
Police ☎110	Fire ☎112
English-language directory enquiries ☎11837	Operator wake-up call ☎0 11 41
Ambulance ☎112	

growing number of Internet cafés in the city, also offer ISDN access. **Internet cafés** range from humble affairs in youth clubs to very slick techno palaces; the software is always current, but, of course, in German; costs are about DM5–7 (€2.50–3.60) per half-hour. For a selection of Internet cafés see the *Directory*.

The media

English being the prevalent second language in Berlin, you'll find a good range of newspapers and magazines and – if you're prepared to search – some English-language programmes on the TV and radio.

Newspapers

It's relatively easy to find **British and US newspapers** in Berlin: most of the London-printed editions can be found at lunchtime on the same day and the *International Herald Tribune* is also readily available. *Internationale Presse* (inside Zoo Station; daily 9am–midnight) has a good selection of international newspapers and magazines, as do the Alexanderplatz and Ostbahnhof Stations, and the British Council at Hackescher Markt 1 (see p.46).

Berlin has four **local newspapers**. Two of these are from the presses of the right-wing Springer Verlag: the *Berliner Morgenpost* is a staid, conservative publication and *BZ* is a trashy tabloid. *Berliner Kurier* is another tabloid, less trashy, but more boring. The other main local paper is the *Berliner Zeitung*, originally an East Berlin publication, which covers national and international news as well as local stories.

Of the **national** dailies, the two best-sellers are also from the Springer presses: *Die Welt* (*www.welt.de*), once a right-wing heavyweight, has become somewhat more centrist and now sports a backpage in English, while the tabloid *Bild* is a reactionary, sleazy and sensationalist rag. Recommendable are the Berlin-based *Tagesspiegel*, a good liberal read, and the left-centre *Tageszeitung*, known as *taz* – not so hot on solid news, but with good in-depth articles on politics and ecology, and an extensive Berlin listings section on Friday. It has the added advantage of being a relatively easy read for non-native German speakers. The *Frankfurter Allgemeine*, widely available in the city, is again conservative, appealing to the business community in particular. An English-language version is included as a

supplement in every issue of the *International Herald Tribune*. Hamburg-based *Die Zeit* appears every Thursday and, while left-wing in stance, includes a number of independently written reports on a variety of subjects. A few other papers from the old GDR hang on, like *Neues Deutschland*, once the Party paper.

For details of Berlin's **listings magazines**, see p.46.

If you're in Berlin for the club scene, you might want to check out *Flyer*, a monthly guide to parties and raves, or *030*, which in addition to a party guide has listings of films and other entertainments. Both are free and can be picked up in cafés and bars all over town.

TV channels

Berlin has **five main TV channels**: ARD and ZDF somewhat approximate British channels or a downmarket PBS; VOX and B1 are primarily entertainment channels; ORB is basically a local channel for Berlin and Brandenburg, risen from the ashes of the ex-GDR's two TV stations. All channels seem to exist on a forced diet of US reruns clumsily dubbed into German. With cable TV, available in larger hotels, you'll be able to pick up the locally available **cable channels** (over twenty to choose from, including MTV and BBC World). Of the cable channels, FAB (*Fernsehen aus Berlin* – "TV from Berlin") is a local channel with news footage, celebrity interviews and the infamous "Partnerwahl" dating service.

The number of **foreign films** shown in the original on the above channels has dwindled over the years but it does happen occasionally. If it's listed in the newspaper as *OF* it will be in the original language (usually English or French); *OmU* means that it has German subtitles.

Radio stations

The only English-speaking **radio** stations are the BBC World Service (90.2FM), BBC Radio One (95.8FM) and Star Radio (87.9FM), which daily combines American rock music with the *Voice of America* radio programme. Berlin's radio output is fairly dreadful, with a multitude of stations churning out light music and soft rock, and little else. The best local music station is Fritz Radio (102.6FM), with some decent dance music and rap shows (mainly late at night). For the latest bland pop, try R. S. 2 (94.3FM), and for hits from the last couple of decades try RTL (104.6FM). Also listenable is SFB4 MultiKulti (106.8FM), which has popular music from around the globe, as well as a few different foreign-language news programmes and chat shows. Best of the classical music stations is Klassik Radio (101.3FM). Jazz Radio Berlin (101.9FM) offers jazz and blues.

Opening hours, public holidays and festivals

Large shops in central Berlin are open Monday to Friday from 9 or 10am to 8pm, on Saturday from 9 or 10am to 4pm, while smaller shops or those outside the centre usually close two hours earlier.

British and American visitors will be surprised by the rigidity of Berlin's closing rules: you won't find late-night corner shops or Sunday morning newsagent-grocers here. A few supermarkets and fruit stands, located in main stations such as Bahnhof Zoo, Bahnhof Friedrichstrasse or Alexanderplatz, are **open late** and on Sunday (see *Shopping*) though you pay for the privilege of after-hours shopping; alternatively, you can stock up on basics in any of the Turkish shops of Kreuzberg and Asian shops in Mitte or Prenzlauer Berg on Saturday afternoons. Additionally, lots of bakers open on Sunday from 2 to 4pm.

Many **museums** follow a general pattern of opening 10am–6pm daily except Monday (although there are a few open on Monday too). This, however, cannot be taken as a rule, and to avoid disappointment it's a good idea to double-check opening times before setting off to visit a particular museum. They're open on all the public holidays listed above (even Christmas), but usually close the following day. Remember that almost nothing else opens on public holidays other than cafés, bars and restaurants, so stock up on groceries the day before.

Festivals and events

Berlin's **festivals** are, in the main, cultural affairs, with music, art and the theatre particularly well catered for. Best place to find out what's on and where (and, occasionally, to book tickets) is the **tourist office** in the Europa Center (see p.46): all mainstream events are well publicized in its leaflets and in brochures like *Berlin Programm*.

Other events, apart from the giant techno street party that is the **Love Parade** (in July), tend to be rather staid: one thing to look out for is the Volksfeste, small, local street festivals you often come across by chance from July to September. Most city districts, in the east especially, have their own Volksfeste, which are usually an excuse for open-air music, beer-swilling and Wurst-guzzling. The Feste an der Panke in **Pankow** in September can be fun; the Köpenicker Sommer, held in **Köpenick** in the second half of June, features a re-enactment of the robbery of the Rathaus safe in 1906 by Friedrich Wilhelm Voigt, a cobbler and ex-convict who, disguised as an army officer, conned a detachment of soldiers into accompanying him.

Public holidays

Jan 1; Good Friday; Easter Monday; May 1; Ascension Day; Whitsun; Oct 3 (Reunification Day); 3rd Wed in Nov (Day of Prayer and National Repentance); Dec 24; Dec 25; and Dec 26.

JANUARY

Grüne Woche (*www.gruenewoche.de*). Berlin's annual agricultural show, held in the Messegelände, with food goodies to sample from all over the world.

FEBRUARY

Berlin International Film Festival (*www.berlinale.de*). The third largest film festival in the world, with around twelve days of old and new movies, art house cinema and more mainstream entertainment. Films are usually shown in the original versions with German (and sometimes English) subtitles. The festival is now concentrated around the multiplexes on Potsdamer Platz, though the programme repeats at various cinemas around town; check *Tip*, *Zitty* or the festival's own free daily magazine for listings. Tickets are available from booths in the Potsdamer Platz Arcade or Europa Center, or at participating theatres on the day of the screening. A limited number of season tickets go on sale a week before opening at the Galerie of the Berliner Volksbank, Linkstrasse 10, Potsdamer Platz.

MARCH

Internationale Tourismus Börse (ITB) (*www.messe-berlin.de*). Funkturm Exhibition Halls. Information and goodies from over a hundred countries to encourage tourism and travel.

APRIL

Free Berlin Art Exhibition Early April to early May in the Funkturm Exhibition Halls. Berlin artists show their most recent work. Painting areas for children, too.

MAY

Berlin Drama Festival Various theatres. Large, mainly German-speaking theatre event that has tended towards the experimental in recent years.

German Open Tennis Championship See *Sport* in Listings.

Deutsche Pokalendspiel (German Football Cup Final) From May to June. See *Sport* in Listings.

Und ab die Post From May to June. Exhibition of international experimental art and performance held in the Postfuhramt on Oranienburgerstrasse and organized by the Aktions Galerie (see *The arts*, p.291).

JUNE

Youth Drama Festival Late May to early June. Various venues. Experimentalism rather than professionalism is the name of the game here.

Karneval der Kulturen Early June. Huge parade winding through Kreuzberg with floats featuring music from around the world. A kind of warm-up for the Love Parade.

Fete de la Musique June 21. Bands from all over Europe and beyond come to play in bars, clubs, and other venues around the city.

Christopher Street Day (*www.csd-berlin.de*). Last Sat in June. Parade with lots of floats, music, and costumed dancers celebrating gay pride at the centre of Gay Action Week.

JULY

Love Parade Early July. Huge techno event that takes over much of the city centre and draws determined party people from all over Germany and the rest of Europe.

Classic Open Air Early July. The Gendarmenmarkt makes the perfect setting for this week-long series of very popular outdooor classical concerts.

The Bach Days Second week of July. Celebration of the great Baroque composer and musician in concerts throughout the city.

German-American Festival Truman Plaza (behind Oskar-Helene-Heim U-Bahn). One of the most popular events of the year. Eat junk food and gamble away your marks on lotteries and other carnival games.

German-French Festival Late July to mid-August. Kurt-Schumacher-Damm (near Tegel Airport). Mini-fair with food and music and a reconstruction of a different French town each year.

Heimatklange July to August. Tempodrom at Ostbahnhof. A series of spirited concerts which focus on the music of a different country each year.

continued overleaf

CALENDAR OF EVENTS CONTINUED

AUGUST

Berlin Beta (*www.berlinbeta.de*). A yearly week-long conference on new media which includes a film festival with a much wilder palette than its more established cousin. Non-German films shown in original with English subtitles. Takes place at the Kino Eiszeit and Central cinemas (see *The arts*), plus other venues.

Tanz im August Mid- to late August. Hebbel Theater. A series of dance performances featuring companies and artists from all over the world.

SEPTEMBER

Berlin Festival Weeks Various venues. A wide variety of events and international performers celebrate a different highlight from the history of the arts each year.

ADAC Rennen A chance for motor-racing enthusiasts to hurtle down the Avus, an arrow-straight stretch of autobahn, in their Porsches. Call ☎8 68 62 84 for details.

Art Forum Berlin (*www.art-forum-berlin.de*). A week-long art exposition with an international selection of galleries and dealers representing a broad spectrum of contemporary works. Takes place in Messegelände Berlin at Hammarskjöldplatz-Masurenallee.

Berlin Biennale (*www.berlinbiennale.de*). September to October. A two-month-long biannual international art event centring on the Kunst-Werke (see *The arts*) but spreading out to several other venues around town.

OCTOBER

Berlin Marathon First Sunday of the month. The race begins on Strasse des 17 Juni and ends nearly 50km later, after passing through Dahlem and along the Ku'damm, back at the Kaiser-Wilhelm Memorial Church. To enter, write to SCC Berlin, Berlin Marathon, Waldschuleallee 34, 14055 Berlin (☎3 02 53 70; *www.berlin-marathon.com*): closing date for entries is one month before the marathon.

AAA Exhibition Early October for nine days; Funkturm Exhibition Halls. Motor show organized by the German equivalent of the Automobile Association.

Lesbian Weeks Mehringhof, Gneisenaustr. 2, Kreuzberg ☎6 91 29 71. International forum for discussion, dance, music and celebration of lesbian culture, including a film series at Kino Arsenal.

JazzFest Berlin (*www.berlinerfestspiele.de*). Late October to early November. Jazz of every form and style. Different venues each year; check programme available from the tourist office.

Six-day Non-stop Cycle Race In the Velodrome, Paul-Heyse-Strasse. A Berlin tradition that's been going since the 1920s.

NOVEMBER

Festival of Young Songwriters Five days in early November; ask at tourist office for venue. Forum for young songwriters to discuss and perform their work. Strongly international (and political) in tone.

International Indoor Show-Jumping An annual event that attracts big names from the show-jumping world to the Deutschlandhalle.

Jewish Culture Days Second two weeks in November. Various venues. Concerts, lectures, readings and films that focus each year on Jewish culture in a particular country or place.

DECEMBER

Christmas Street Market Twee Christmas market from the first Sunday in December to December 24 in Breitscheidplatz, between the Europa Center and the Memorial Church.

Rixdorfer Christmas Market Richardplatz, Karl-Marx-Strasse U-Bahn. Pretty Christmas market on one of the oldest surviving squares in Berlin.

Spandau Christmas Market In Spandau's old centre from the end of November and at weekends in the run-up to Christmas.

New Year's Eve Run December 31. Annual run organized by the Berlin Marathon authorities (see contact details above).

Police, crime and personal safety

The Berlin police (Polizei) maintain a low profile; they're not renowned for their friendliness, but they usually treat foreigners with courtesy. They're unlikely to make their presence much felt unless ordered to from on high (which usually happens during demonstrations), in which case the Prussian military mentality goes into automatic pilot, resulting in robotic-type gratuitous violence.

Generally though, the police are very correct, and shouldn't subject you to any unnecessary chicanery – in this country of rule and order it's more likely to be the ordinary citizen who'll spot you jaywalking and tick you off before the police even have a chance to get there.

Petty crime

Although crime in the city has risen rapidly since the fall of the Wall, it still remains quite modest

---

Central Berlin police stations

Headquarters:
Platz der Luftbrücke 6, Tempelhof ☎ 69 95

District stations:
Jägerstr. 48, Mitte ☎ 2 40 55
Bismarckstr. 111, Charlottenburg ☎ 3 30 10
Friesenstr. 16, Kreuzberg ☎ 69 95
Hauptstr. 44, Schöneberg ☎ 7 67 20
Schönhauser Allee 22, Prenzlauer Berg
☎ 5 77 40

---

in comparison with other European cities of the same size. The type you're most likely to encounter is **petty crime**: pickpocketing or bag-snatching in one of the main shopping precincts. Sensible **precautions** against petty crime include: carrying bags slung across your neck and not over your shoulder; not carrying anything in pockets that are easy to dip into; having photocopies of your passport, airline ticket and driving licence, and leaving the originals in your hotel safe; and noting down travellers' cheque and credit card numbers. When you're looking for a hotel room, never leave your bags unattended.

If you do have something **stolen** (or simply lost), you'll need to register the details at the local police station: this is usually straightforward, but inevitably there'll be a great deal of bureaucratic bumph to wade through. Remember to make a note of the crime report number – or better still, ask for a copy of the statement itself – for your insurance company.

The **emergency phone number** for the police is ☎ 110. Occasionally you'll see **emergency posts**: these are about head-high with a button that you press to alert the nearest police station. For an **ambulance** or the **fire brigade**, call ☎ 112.

Personal safety

As far as **personal safety** is concerned, most parts of the city are safe enough, though it's wise to be wary away from the centre, as muggings and casual violence are becoming depressingly frequent. On the whole though, providing you use common sense, you'll be safe walking virtually anywhere alone by day in the city centre. In the suburbs by night, particularly those in the **eastern part of the city**, and on the more far-flung stretches of the public transport system (especially if you're female and/or alone), it's wise to exercise the same caution as you would at home: work out beforehand exactly where you're going so that you don't look lost and vulnerable, don't walk anywhere unlit, always travel with a friend if possible and don't wear or carry anything obviously valuable.

Racial attacks

Since unification, **racial attacks** on guest workers (anyone who comes into Germany to do menial work), Eastern Europeans, naturalized Germans from other countries, and anyone non-White have become an ugly fact of life in Germany. Attacks have been most prevalent in the east, where unemployment and dissatisfaction with the failure of unification to deliver the promised good life have prompted so-called neo-Nazis and skinheads, and a fair number of "normal people", to take out their frustrations on the usual scapegoats. In September 1991, asylum seekers in the town of Hoyerswerda had to be removed en masse following repeated racist attacks on their temporary living quarters; and in Rostock in August 1992 a skinhead mob attacked a hostel full of Eastern European asy-

lum seekers, to the open applause of the locals – and with little opposition from the police. The media, too, play their part. Officially, TV channels and newspapers play down racial attacks or fail to mention them entirely, since this would "incite racial hatred". Critics say that this is officialdom's way of turning a blind eye to the problem – and thereby tacitly condoning it.

In Berlin, racial violence, though fairly rare in central parts of the east, is definitely a risk in outlying areas like **Lichtenberg** or **Marzahn**, which are perceived as neo-Nazi/skinhead strongholds. Such thugs are likely to pick on anyone who stands out – and not only because of their skin colour. Simply being "foreign" or looking unusual is reason enough to be at the rough end of their attentions.

Drugs

Street dealing of hard and soft **drugs** goes on around the back of the Gedächtniskirche and at the junction of Kurfürstenstrasse and Potsdamer

Strasse. Possession of any of the usual substances is illegal, and anyone caught with them will face either prison or deportation: consulates will not be sympathetic towards those on drugs charges.

Travellers with disabilities

You'll find that access and facilities are good in Berlin, although the western part of the city is currently better equipped than the east, where things are slowly being improved. Most of the major museums now have wheelchair access, as do many other public buildings. The offical U- and S-Bahn map indicates which stations are accessible by wheelchair, and Deutsche Bahn operate an advisory service for rail travellers with disabilities (see box below).

The best source of information in Berlin is **Movado**, Langhansstrasse 64, Weissensee (☎4 71 51 45; www.movado.de), an activist group devoted to the issue of access for people with restricted mobility. They have a great wealth of information on wheelchair-accessible hotels and restaurants, city tours for disabled travellers and

local transport services. Their online databank, at www.berlin.de/home/Skript/movado/search, lists over 40,000 buildings in Berlin, including hotels, restaurants and theatres, indicating their degree of accessibility. An alternative is the **Fürst-Donnersmarck-Stiftung**, Dalandweg 19, Steglitz (☎7 69 70 00; www. fdst.de), a foundation providing treatment and services for the disabled. Although they no longer run a hostel for travellers with disabilities, they do have plenty of information about accessibilty. **Berlin Tourismus Marketing** (tourist office) also has details on suitable accommodation.

If you are registered disabled then you're allowed to use Berlin's excellent free **Telebus** service, Esplanade 17, Pankow (Mon–Fri 9am–3pm; ☎41 02 00). After being issued with

CONTACTS FOR TRAVELLERS WITH DISABILITIES

GERMANY

Deutsche Bahn MobilitätsServiceZentrale
☎01805/51 25 12. The German rail company's advisory service for travellers with disabilities.

Deutscher Paritätischer Wohlfahrtsverband, Brandenburgische Str. 80, Wilmersdorf, Berlin ☎86 00 10; *www.paritaet.org/berlin*. Umbrella group of disabled and self-help organizations, useful for finding addresses of more specific groups.

Reiseagentur für Behindertenreisen Carsten Müller, Strasse 6, 116, Hohenschönhausen, Berlin ☎9 24 40 35; *www.behindertenreisen-cm .de*. Travel agent specializing in tours and destinations for disabled travellers.

AUSTRALIA AND NEW ZEALAND

ACROD (Australian Council for Rehabilitation of the Disabled), PO Box 60, Curtin, ACT 2605 ☎02/6282 4333; 24 Cabarita Rd, Cabarita, NSW 2137 ☎02/9743 2699. Provides lists of travel agencies and tour operators for people with disabilities.

Barrier Free Travel, 36 Wheatley St, North Bellingen, NSW 2454 ☎02/6655 1733. Independent consultant – draws up individual itineraries for people with disabilities for a fee.

Disability Information & Resource Centre, 195 Gilles St, Adelaide, SA 5000 ☎08/8223 7522; *www.dircsa.org.au*. Provides details of organizations offering holiday and travel information.

Disabled Persons Assembly, 4/173–175 Victoria St, Wellington ☎04/801 9100; *www.dpa.org.nz*. Resource centre with lists of travel agencies and tour operators for people with disabilities.

BRITAIN

Holiday Care Service, 2nd Floor, Imperial Building, Victoria Rd, Horley, Surrey RH6 7PZ ☎01293/774535, fax 784647, Minicom ☎01293/776943; *www.holidaycare.org.uk*. Free lists of accessible accommodation and information on financial help for holidays.

RADAR (Royal Association for Disability and Rehabilitation), 12 City Forum, 250 City Rd, London EC1V 8AF ☎020/7250 3222, Minicom ☎020/7250 4119; *www.radar.org.uk*. Advice on holidays and travel abroad. They also produce, in conjunction with Holiday Care, a guide called *Getting There* on travel abroad (transport only; £5 inc. p&p).

Tripscope, Brentford Community Resource Centre, Alexandra House, Brentford High St, Brentford, Middlesex TW8 0NE ☎0845/758 5641; *www.justmobility.co.uk/tripscope*. National telephone information service offering free advice on UK and international transport and travel for those with a mobility problem.

NORTH AMERICA

Access First Travel, 239 Commercial St, Malden, MA 02148 ☎1-800/557-2047. Up-to-date information for disabled travellers.

Directions Unlimited, 123 Green Lane, Bedford Hills, NY 10507 ☎1-800/533-5343. Tour operator specializing in custom tours for people with disabilities.

Jewish Rehabilitation Hospital, 3205 Place Alton Goldbloom, Chomedy Laval, PQ H7V 1R2 ☎450/688-9550, ext 226. Guidebooks and travel information.

Mobility International USA, PO Box 10767, Eugene, OR 97440 ☎541/343-1284 (voice & TDD); *www.miusa.com*. Information and referral services, access guides, tours and exchange programmes. Annual membership $25 (includes quarterly newsletter).

Society for the Advancement of Travel for the Handicapped (SATH), 347 Fifth Ave, Suite 610, New York, NY 10016 ☎212/447-7284; *www.sath.org*. Non-profit-making travel industry referral service that passes queries on to its members as appropriate.

Travel Information Service ☎215/456-9600. Telephone only information and referral service for disabled travellers.

Twin Peaks Press, Box 129, Vancouver, WA 98666 ☎360/694-2462 or 1-800/637-2256; *www.pacifier.com/twinpeak*. Publisher of the *Directory of Travel Agencies for the Disabled* ($19.95), listing more than 370 agencies worldwide; *Travel for the Disabled* ($19.95); the *Directory of Accessible Van Rentals* ($9.95) and *Wheelchair Vagabond* ($14.95), loaded with personal tips.

Wheels Up!, PO Box 5197, Plant City, FL 33564-5197 ☎1-888/389-4335; *www.wheelsup.com*. Provides discounted air fare, tour and cruise prices for disabled travellers. Also publishes a free monthly newsletter and has a comprehensive Web site.

a pass and number, you call the service and one of their fifty taxis or seventy buses will pick you up and take you to your destination. For people in wheelchairs, the buses need to be booked at least a day in advance, the taxis a few hours.

A café-bar designed especially, but not exclusively, for disabled people, **Blisse 14** (Blissestr. 14, Wilmersdorf; ☎8 21 20 79; *www.fdst.de*) is a good meeting place with lots of useful information and a wide range of food and non-alcoholic drinks.

Women's Berlin

There are around a hundred women's organizations and permanent venues in Berlin, offering information and advice, courses, performances and partying. They're testimony to a struggle for equal rights which began before the revolution of 1848 and sidestepped a complete ban from 1850 to 1908 on women's right to political assembly.

Not that women can yet afford to rest on their laurels. A short-lived Red-Green senate a few years ago briefly opened the public purse to hitherto voluntary-funded women's organizations but proved, perhaps inevitably, to contain more promises than pfennigs. Similarly, recent improvements in maternity provision – while long overdue and very welcome – were fuelled primarily by a concern for the falling birthrate. They also help underpin a "return to family values" which, given the present unforeseen strain on resources and employment, along with the increased electoral support for right-wing parties, could mean that further improvements to the welfare provision for women are unlikely.

Harassment

Compared to many other European cities, Berlin is basically safe for women to visit. **Sexual harassment**, if committed at all, is generally of the verbal kind. With caution, it's safe to use the U- and S-Bahn and walk around at night: streets are well lit, and dawdling for hours in late-night cafés is standard practice. Obviously you should use common sense, but even the rougher neighbourhoods (say east Kreuzberg or Friedrichshain) feel more dangerous than they actually are: the run-down U-Bahn stations at Kottbusser Tor and Görlitzer Bahnhof (both in largely immigrant districts) or S-Bahn stations Warschauer Strasse and Ostkreuz look alarming when compared to the rest of the system, but wouldn't stand out in most other European cities. Kurfürstenstrasse U-Bahn is in the traditional red-light district, and worth avoiding if you're on your own at night. See also the box on "Racial Attacks", p.30.

The listings below cover a cross-section of women's groups: don't worry if your German is nonexistent – there's always someone who speaks English. For **women-only bars and cafés**, see *Cafés and bars* in Listings.

Health and crisis centres

Feministisches Frauengesundheitszentrum, Bamberger Str. 51, Schöneberg ☎2 13 95 97. (Tues 10am–1pm, Thurs 10am–1pm & 5–7pm). Well-organized feminist health centre for advice, therapy and seminars.

Frauenkrisentelefon, ☎6 15 42 43 (Mon & Thurs 10am–noon, Tues, Wed & Fri 10am–noon & 7–9pm Sat & Sun 5–7pm). Phone-in service offering sympathy and practical advice in a crisis.

LARA, Tempelhofer Ufer 14, Kreuzberg (Mon–Fri 9am–midnight; hotline ☎2 16 88 88). Rape victim crisis centre.

Pro Familia, Ansbacherstr. 11, Schöneberg ☎2 13 90 13; U-Bahn Wittenbergplatz (Mon–Thurs 6–9pm, Sun noon–2pm). Impartial abortion referral clinic, advice on pregnancy and the morning-after pill.

Rape Crisis Line ☎2 51 28 28 (Tues & Thurs 6–9pm, Sun noon–2pm).

Selbstverteidigung für Frauen, Hauptstr. 9, 3rd Gartenhaus, 5th floor, Schöneberg ☎7 81 94 32 (Mon 4–6pm, Thurs 5.30–7pm; also first Wed in month until 7.30pm). Fairly strenuous courses in self-defence.

Wildwasser e.V. Beratungsstelle, Mehringdamm 50, Kreuzberg ☎7 86 50 17; U-Bahn Mehringdamm (Mon–Fri 9.30am–6pm). Advice for sexually abused young women.

Women's centres

EWA, Prenzlauer Allee 6, Prenzlauer Berg, (Mon–Thurs 10am–8pm; ☎4 42 55 42). First post-Wall women's centre in east Berlin offers courses and counselling, as well as various cultural events and computer and media facilities.

Frauentreff Brunnhilde, Rheinsberger Str. 61, Mitte (Mon & Wed 9am–6pm, Tues & Fri 9am–3pm, Thurs 1–6pm; ☎4 49 32 27; U-Bahn Bernauer Str.). Advice on various legal and tax issues, creative courses and cinema nights.

Frieda, Proskauer Str. 7, Friedrichshain (Mon 3–9pm, Tues & Thurs 9am–11pm, Fri 9am–midnight, Sun 11am–2pm & 3–6pm; ☎4 22 42 76). Women's centre in alternative Friedrichshain, with counselling, self-help groups, political and cultural events.

Schokofabrik, Mariannenstr. 6, Kreuzberg ☎6 15 29 99, (Mon–Fri & Sun 11am–10pm). One of Europe's largest women's centres, with a café/gallery, sports facilities (including a women-only Turkish bath, see p.276) and diverse events.

Weiberwirtschaft, Anklamer Str. 38, Mitte, ☎4 40 22 30; U-Bahn Bernauer Str. Building complex housing businesses or services owned by, and for, women.

Archives

FFBIZ (Archive of the Women's Research, Education and Information Centre), Danckelmannstr. 15 & 47, Charlottenburg ☎3 22 10 35 (Tues 2–6pm, Fri 3–10pm). The place to make contact with the Berlin Historians' Network, and for guided tours of Women's Berlin. On Tuesday between 10am and 1pm there's a breakfast served for women only.

See also Spinnboden archive in "Gay and lesbian Berlin", p.35.

Galleries and cultural centres

Begine, Potsdamer Str. 139, Schöneberg ☎2 15 43 25. Earnest lectures and films (Sept–May), and excellent performances by women musicians and dancers. Also runs a women's travel service, Frauen Unterwegs Reisen (☎215 1022).

Lärm und Lust, Schwedenstr. 14, Wedding ☎4 91 53 04. A venue for women musicians and bands.

Das Verborgene Museum, Schlüterstr. 70, Charlottenburg ☎3 13 36 56 (Wed & Fri 3–7pm, Sat & Sun noon–4pm). A gallery founded by women artists for research, documentation and exhibition of women's art.

Accommodation

Hotel Artemisia, Brandenburgische Str. 18, Wilmersdorf ☎8 73 89 05. The first women-only hotel in the city, with a roof garden and exhibitions. DM100 (€51.15) per person (includes breakfast); it's advisable to book in advance (see p.235).

Intermezzo, An der Kolonnade 14, Mitte, ☎22 48 90 96. Women's hotel near Potsdamer Platz with easy access for wheelchairs (see p.232).

Gay and lesbian Berlin

Despite the horrors of the past, Berlin has a good record for tolerating an open and energetic gay and lesbian scene. As far back as the 1920s, Christopher Isherwood and W.H. Auden both came here, drawn to a city where, in sharp contrast to the oppressiveness of London, there was a gay community who did not live in fear of harassment and legal persecution. Today, Berlin's gay and lesbian communities are among the most vibrant in the world.

The easy-going, easy-living attitude stretches into the straight community, too, and it's not uncommon to see transvestites at their glitziest dancing atop tables even at the most conservative of bashes. The best time to arrive and plunge yourself into the hurly-burly is during **Gay Pride Week**, centred around the gay pride **Christopher Street Day** parade on the last Saturday in June every year. The Love Parade held annually in July (see "Festivals and Events") also has a strong gay presence. For detailed **information** on the gay scene in Berlin, contact **Mann-o-Meter** (see "Contacts and information"), or pick up a copy of the German/English *Berlin von Hinten* (DM22.80/€11.65), the city's most useful gay guide. *Siegessäule*, a monthly gay magazine, has listings of events and an encyclopedic directory of gay contacts and groups. It's available free from all of the groups below and most gay bars (see *Cafés and Bars* in Listings), as well as at the Prinz Eisenherz bookshop.

For **hotels** friendly to gays, plus details of the accommodation services, see *Accommodation* in Listings.

Lesbian Berlin

As in many other large cities, **lesbians** in Berlin have a much lower profile than gay men. Perhaps because of this, there's no real distinction between bars and cafés for lesbians and straight women - see *Cafés and Bars* in Listings. *Blattgold* (DM8/€4.10), a monthly publication listing all lesbian groups and events, is the main newspaper, available from feminist meeting places and bookshops.

The most important event of the year is the annual **Lesbian Weeks**, a one-week internation-al festival of music, dance and political discussion held in October. For more information, call ☎6 91 29 71.

Contacts and information

Lesbenberatung Kommunikations und Beratungszentrum, Kulmer Str. 20a, 2nd Gartenhaus, 4th floor, Schöneberg (Mon–Thurs 5–8pm; ☎2 15 20 00). Lesbian advisory service for those coming out.

Lied-Strich Schwules Kulturbüro e.V., Kulmer Str. 30, Schöneberg (Mon–Fri 10am–6pm; ☎2 16 29 78). An organization that promotes gay art in the city, and arranges exhibitions specifically for gays and lesbians.

Mann-O-Meter Information und Treffpunkt für Schwule, Motzstr. 5, Schöneberg ☎2 16 80 08; *www.mann-o-meter.de*; U-Bahn Nollendorfplatz (Mon–Sat 5–10pm, Sun 4–10pm). An information centre, meeting point and very successful gay accommodation service.

SchwuZ, Mehringdamm 61, Kreuzberg ☎6 93 70 25; U-Bahn Mehringdamm. Evening meeting point that can get pretty wild, especially at weekends. During the week a venue for workshops and theatre groups. Highly recommended.

Sonntagsklub, Greifenhagener Str. 28, Prenzlauer Berg (daily 5pm–midnight; ☎4 49 75 90). Information and communication centre for gays and lesbians in emerging Prenzlauer Berg

Vorspiel Schwuler Sportverein (SSV) ☎3 32 17 77. Berlin's gay sports club, offering a variety of activities. Call for current details, since the address is not publicized.

Health and advice centres

Berliner AIDS-Hilfe, Meinekestr. 12, Wilmersdorf (Mon–Thurs 10am–6pm, Fri 10am–3pm; ☎8 85 64 00). Helpline (24hr), free consultations. Dispenses condoms and lubricants.

Deutsche AIDS-Hilfe e.V., Dieffenbachstr. 33, Kreuzberg ☎6 90 08 70 (Mon–Fri 10am–1pm). Constructive help and information on AIDS.

Kommunikations-und-Beratungszentrum homosexueller Frauen und Männer e.V., Kulmer Str. 20a, Schöneberg ☎ 2 15 37 42 (Mon, Wed & Thurs 5–8pm, Tues & Fri 3–6pm). Comprehensive advice and information centre, offering single and group consultations, a small café, a telephone advisory service and lists of gay bars, activities, doctors and therapists.

Bookshops and galleries

Chronika, Bergmannstr. 26, Kreuzberg ☎ 6 93 42 69. Contains the largest selection of lesbian literature in Berlin. They often present readings and literary events.

Galerie Janssen, Pariser Str. 45, Wilmersdorf ☎ 8 81 15 90 (on Ludwigkirch Platz; Mon–Fri 11am–6.30pm, Sat 11am–2pm). Men's art gallery, also selling posters, postcards and some art books. The building next door contains Janssen's photographic gallery, devoted to exhibiting "classical and contemporary" gay photography.

Prinz Eisenherz Buchladen GmbH, Bleibtreustr. 52, Charlottenburg ☎ 3 13 99 36. Friendly and informative gay bookstore with helpful assistants. Excellent for relaxed browsing and for free magazines, what's-on posters and leaflets about the current gay scene in the city.

Archives

Lesbisch-Schwules Pressearchiv, c/o SchwulZ, Mehringdamm 61 (by appointment only; ☎ 69 40 17 23). Newspaper cuttings reflecting the German-language media's attitude to homosexuality. Monthly samples of the latest snippets are available from the Prinz Eisenherz bookshop and some gay bars.

Lila Archiv e.V., c/o Ursula Sillge, Chorinerstr. 9, Prenzlauer Berg (by appointment only; ☎ 4 48 57 13). Information on the women's movement and gay and lesbian lifestyles, particularly within the former GDR and Eastern Europe as a whole.

Schwules Museum, Mehringdamm 61, Kreuzberg, 2nd Hinterhof ☎ 6 93 11 72 (Wed–Sun 2–6pm). An interesting and relatively unknown museum with changing exhibitions on local and international gay history. Library and archive material is also available to browse through.

Spinnboden ("Archive and Treasury for Womanlove"), Anklamer Str. 38, Mitte (Mon & Fri 2–9pm; ☎ 4 48 58 48; donation expected for each visit). A comprehensive archive of every aspect of lesbian experience, with a beautifully housed collection of 5000 books, videos, posters and magazines. Foreign visitors are welcome.

Staying on

Berlin acts as a magnet for young people from Germany and all over Europe. Its reputation as a politicized, happening city, with a high profile in the arts and a more relaxed and tolerant attitude than its parent state, means that many people come here to live and work. That the English-speaking community – Americans, Brits and Irish – is a large one will work to your advantage when it comes to finding out the latest situation for jobs and housing, and to your disadvantage in terms of competition.

An important **caveat** to the notes below is that things change quickly in this city, and with massive unemployment among former GDR citizens since unification, it seems likely that rules, regulations and openings will have changed at least subtly by the time you read this.

Work

If you don't mind what you do (or what hours you do it), and are prepared to work "black" (without a contract, taxes or insurance), finding **work** in Berlin shouldn't pose too much of a problem. **Work permits** aren't required for EU nationals, though everyone else will need one – and, theoretically, should not even look for a job without one.

However, the paperwork and bureaucracy are complicated and tedious. The following notes cover only the initial stages of the process you'll need to follow: it's essential to seek advice from an experienced friend, especially when completing official forms – writing the wrong thing could land you in a lot of unnecessary trouble. The best official place for advice is the **Ausländer Beauftragte des Senats** at Potsdamer Str. 65, Tiergarten ☎9 01 72 39.

If you're an **EU national** and want to stay in Berlin for longer than three months, you only need to prove that you have a roof over your head to satisfy the authorities. Do this by completing a *Polizeianmeldungsformular* ("registration document"), available from any newsagent for DM2 (€1). Then fill in the address details and get it signed by your landlord or equivalent – this is the tricky bit since not all lets are legal, especially if you find yourself subletting. You then go to your local police station and get the thing stamped. Providing they have a *Polizeianmeldungsformular*, EU nationals don't need a work permit either to look for or take up a job. The next stage is to get an **Aufenthaltserlaubnis** ("permission to stay") from the Landeseinwohneramt, Friedrich-Krause-Ufer 24, Tiergarten (☎90 15 80; Mon, Tues & Thurs 7.30am–1pm, Fri 7.30am–noon). Officially you can't get one until you have a job – but you can't get a job without one. The loophole to this Catch-22 situation is that most employers aren't too concerned about the *Aufenthaltserlaubnis* if you're an EU citizen – plus the fact that you can only get one six months after you've registered with the police.

For **non-EU nationals** – North Americans, Australasians and everybody else – finding legal work is much more difficult, unless you've secured the job legally before arriving in Germany. The best advice is to approach the German embassy or consulate in your own country.

Finding a job

Since long-term accommodation can work out quite cheap in Berlin, it's possible to live reasonably well on comparatively little here. Indeed, it's possible to get by on a take-home pay of DM1500–2000 (€770–1025) a month.

Numerous **job agencies** offer both temporary and permanent work – usually secretarial – but you'll obviously be expected to have a good command of German and fast typing speeds. Check the Yellow Pages under *Arbeitsvermittlung*. Other than that, there are also several cleaning agencies (look in the Yellow Pages under *Reinigungsbetriebe*) where only a minimal knowledge of the language is needed.

However, the best sources of both temporary and permanent work are certain **newspapers and magazines**: *Zweite Hand* (published on Tues, Thurs & Sat), *Tip* or *Zitty* (bimonthly on alternate weeks, first copies on sale Wed). Other than personal contacts, these are also the best places to find English-language **teaching work** – either privately or in a school. For private work, the normal rate is DM25–30 (€12.80–15.35) per hour – don't be beaten down to anything less than that. Previous experience is not always necessary (particularly for private lessons). You can place an advert for your services free in *Zweite Hand* or for a small fee in *Tip*, *Zitty* or *Prinz*. Or you can approach the city's many language schools directly; look in the above-mentioned magazines for names and addresses.

Otherwise, Berlin's innumerable **cafés and restaurants** often look for workers. You'll need to tramp around town a bit first, and they'll expect a decent working knowledge of German, but you can often work black. If you do sign a contract with them, it's likely that you'll need a *Gesundheitspass* (health certificate), information about which can be found at any local **Bezirksamt**. These local official information offices (they're listed in the front of the Yellow Pages, and are usually located in the local town hall) can also advise on claiming social security and unemployment benefit.

One last tip: pick up the Sunday *Berliner Morgenpost* late on Saturday evening around Zoo Station and scan the job (*Stelle*) section – some jobs are advertised in English, and the best ones always go quickly.

Accommodation

The influx of government workers from Bonn has put some pressure on the rental market, and **apartments** in Berlin are becoming increasingly expensive to rent and difficult to find. In addition, **permanent accommodation** often requires an illegal takeover fee known as an *Abstand*. This can range from DM4000 to DM30,000 (€2045–15,350) or even more, depending on

the fittings and the amount of decorating that has been carried out. (It can in turn, and again illegally, normally be extracted from the person who moves in when you leave.) A *Kaution* (deposit), usually in the form of three months' refundable rent, is also required.

Apartment hunting

Although *Tip*, *Zitty*, *Zweite Hand* and the Sunday *Berliner Morgenpost* advertise apartments and rooms, it's much quicker and less traumatic to sign on at one of the several **Mitwohnzentralen**, accommodation agencies that specialize in long-term sublets in apartments throughout the city. (For full details, see *Accommodation* in Listings.) Wherever you look, expect to pay between DM750 (€380) and DM1500 (€770) for a self-contained one- or two-roomed apartment, or between DM300 (€153.50) and DM600 (€310) for a room in a shared apartment. In listings or adverts, the word *Warm* means that the rent is inclusive of heating and other charges; *Kalt*, non-inclusive. Incidentally, Berlin is the only city in Germany with a large number of apartments that have coal-fuelled burners for heating (*Ofenheizung* in German). These are messy and inconvenient as they require constant stoking up – if you're out of the house for more than a few hours, be prepared to come back to Arctic temperatures during the bitterly cold Berlin winter.

Once you've been here a few months and made contact with people, **word of mouth** also works well if you're searching for somewhere better (or cheaper) to stay: tell everyone you meet you're on the lookout and something will usually become available surprisingly quickly – there's a high turnover in apartments here.

When you finally find a place to live, you need to buy an *Anmeldungsformular* (registration form; see opposite). Ask your landlord or landlady to complete this (if you don't have an apartment or room, friends will usually sign – illegally – that you're living at their home), take it to the local police station to be stamped, and you'll be able to apply for your resident's permit.

Squatting and communal living

The tolerant attitude of the 1980s is very much a thing of the past, and although one or two **radical squats** still exist, the hassle you're likely to get from the authorities isn't really worth it for the money saved. Squatting is more of a **political gesture** than a practical alternative. Best chances of finding somewhere are in Friedrichshain or outside the city in Potsdam – but you'll need luck and contacts.

Originating in the events of 1968, the **Wohngemeinschaften** (literally "communities") are now a firmly established part of the "alternative" scene in what used to be West Berlin. Nothing like the hippy communes of yore, they consist of four to eight people (often with a few children thrown in), who share rent, food and, supposedly, a few ideals. In the independently minded 1990s, however, the stringent requirements of being home every evening at a certain time to eat with "the family", cooking and cleaning to a strict weekly rota, the lack of privacy and heavy "talks" if you don't fulfil community expectations can be too much for some. Having said this, the **Wohngemeinschaften** often advertise rooms to rent and, once you're in, these can be as permanent as you like.

Finally, **council apartments** (*Sozialwohnungen*) are few and far between, have long waiting lists and, with the influx of GDR citizens that began in 1989, are now almost beyond hope. It's worth enquiring at your local Bezirksamt on arrival, though, particularly if you have a "social problem" (eg pregnancy), as they're then required to find something as soon as possible.

Part 2

Berlin: The City

Chapter 1

Introducing the city

No one in their right mind should come to Berlin for light-hearted sightseeing: in its western reaches especially, this is a profoundly scarred city. Even in the flashiest sections of the West End, around the Memorial Church, it still seems half-built, the modern buildings somehow making it look less finished and more ugly. Unlike Paris, Amsterdam or Munich, Berlin isn't a city where you can simply stroll and absorb the atmosphere. You need to plan your trips and target your points of interest, using the city's transport system (described in detail on p.47) to cover what can be longish distances. Those points of interest are, almost without exception, sombre: the Reichstag, looming symbol of the war years; the remains of the Wall, facet of its aftermath; and several museums which openly and intelligently try to make sense of twentieth-century German history. The eastern part of the city is, in fact, the real Berlin, cut off by the Wall for thirty years. The area east of the Brandenburg Gate, along Unter den Linden, is fast regaining its original place as centre of the city. This neighbourhood, and the eastern districts of Mitte and Prenzlauer Berg, have emerged as dynamic magnets for shopping and entertainment. Here especially, the rapid transformation of Berlin into capital city and, the city fathers hope, economic and cultural powerhouse, is evident.

Orientation

Unter den Linden (Chapter 2), a great strip of stately Neoclassical buildings that stretches east from the **Brandenburg Gate**, lies at the new centre of Berlin. Just north of the Gate is the restored seat of Germany's parliament, the **Reichstag**, while a few hundred metres east, Unter den Linden intersects with **Friedrichstrasse**, which cuts north–south across this part of the city. A left turn from here leads north to **Bahnhof Friedrichstrasse**, while heading south takes you down through a new luxury shopping avenue, built from scratch just a few years ago, to what used to be **Checkpoint Charlie**.

Orientation

Continuing along Unter den Linden from the Friedrichstrasse intersection leads, by way of some of Berlin's finest eighteenth- and nineteenth-century architecture, to **Schlossplatz and the Museum Island** (Chapter 3), home to eastern Berlin's leading museums. At the Museum Island, Unter den Linden becomes **Karl-Liebknecht-Strasse**, which leads to **Alexanderplatz** (Chapter 4), the eastern commercial and transport hub, from where rail, tram and bus links run out to the suburbs. North from here, the swathe of land of the **Scheunenviertel** (Chapter 5) contains what was once the heart of the city's Jewish community, and has some fascinating remainders from those days along Grosse Hamburger Strasse and Oranienburger Strasse.

Wartime damage has left the **West End** of Berlin (Chapter 6), with the appearance of a badly patched-up skeleton: beneath the surface the former street plan survives, but in a haphazard fashion and fractured by the erstwhile course of the Wall. The heart of the area is the **Zoologischer Garten**, or more properly, the adjacent combined U-Bahn, S-Bahn and train **Zoo Station**. A stone's throw from here is the district's single notable landmark, the rotting tusk of the **Kaiser-Wilhelm-Gedächtniskirche** (Kaiser Wilhelm Memorial Church); the **Kurfürstendamm**, an upmarket shopping boulevard, targets in on the church from the west. To the north and east of the Zoo is the **Tiergarten park** (Chapter 6), ending in the east back at the Brandenburg Gate. Just south of the park is one of Berlin's three important cultural collections, the **Kulturforum**.

Two districts make up the area described as **South of the centre** (Chapter 7): **Kreuzberg** is an enclave of immigrant workers, "alternative" living, and one of the most vibrant areas at night; **Schöneberg**, while being a mainly residential area, competes with Kreuzberg for nightlife – though the clubs, bars and restaurants here are that little bit smarter.

The area **West of the centre** (Chapter 8) is one of Berlin's most attractive – and most overlooked by visitors. A huge region stretching from the museums and gardens around **Schloss Charlottenburg** at the city's edge to the medieval town of **Spandau** 10km away, much of it comprises woodland (the Grunewald) and lakes (the Havel and Wannsee), a reminder that about a third of the western part of Berlin is either forest or park. It's also where, to the southwest, you'll find the **Dahlem museum complex** (displaying everything from German folk art to Polynesian huts); to the northwest is the **Olympic Stadium** and another grim reminder of the war years, **Plötzensee prison**.

The land to the **East of the centre** (Chapter 9) looks like an endless sprawl of prewar tenements punctuated by high-rise developments and heavy industry. However, much of the atmosphere of prewar Berlin has been preserved to the immediate northeast of the centre in the cobbled streets of **Prenzlauer Berg**, while **Friedrichshain** to the east offers some unusual architectural leftovers from the

1950s, and one of eastern Berlin's larger parks. Moving out to the northern edge of the city, the airy suburbs of **Pankow** and **Weissensee** contrast sharply with the inner-city tenement districts. Industrial grime and high-density living reassert themselves in **Lichtenberg**, east of Friedrichshain, but compensation is offered by riverside parkland and open spaces in **Treptow** to the south. **Köpenick**, at the city's southeastern edge, with its lakes and woodland, dotted with small suburban towns and villages, offers the truest break from the city, to the extent that it's easy to forget that this area still belongs to Greater Berlin. For further ventures out of the city **Potsdam** (Chapter 10) is the best target, where Frederick the Great's palace and gardens of **Sanssouci** have long been a major – and deserved – tourist draw.

Nowhere in the city is more than a stone's throw from a bar, be it a corner *Kneipe* or a slick upscale café – indeed, the variety of bars and restaurants is one of the city's great strengths. The **Listings** of our favourite places to stay, eat, drink and shop follows the Guide, along with chapters on nightlife and information on children's activities and sport.

Arrival

The major points of arrival in Berlin all lie within easy reach of the city centre by public transport. The most distant of the city's three airports is only about 35 minutes away by S-Bahn, and the main station for those arriving by train – Bahnhof Zoologischer Garten, or **Zoo Station** – lies at the heart of Berlin's West End and at the western hub of the city's U- and S-Bahn network. Using this, you can reach just about anywhere in the city.

By air

Chances are you'll arrive at **Tegel airport**, the city's largest: **Schönefeld airport**, on the eastern side of the city, is mainly used by flights from Eastern Europe and the Middle and Far East, while **Tempelhof airport** is largely, though not exclusively, for domestic flights.

The central information line for all three airports is ☎ 01805/00 01 86.

Tegel
Nearly all scheduled and charter flights arrive at the refreshingly small and manageable **Tegel Airport** (*www.tegel.de*). Here you'll find currency exchange facilities open till 10pm daily (at Berliner Bank, by Gate 1), left luggage (DM10/€5.10 per item), the usual car rental companies (except Eurorent) and, when you're leaving, scant duty-free shopping.

From Tegel, express #X9 or regular #109 **buses** (DM4/€2.05) run every five to fifteen minutes, depending on the time of day, directly to **Zoo Station** (see below) at the centre of the West End of the city. The JetExpressBus TXL provides a (relatively expensive) connection to **Unter den Linden** and the city's eastern hub (35min; DM9.90/€5). Alternatively, take bus #109 to Jakob-Kaiser-Platz or bus #128 to Walter Schreiber Platz and transfer to the U-Bahn system (the bus ticket is valid for the U-Bahn journey: see p.48). **Taxis** cover the distance in half the time (depending on the traffic) and cost DM30–40 (€15.35–20.45).

Schönefeld

Berlin's second airport, **Schönefeld** (*www.berlin-airport.de*), lies just beyond the southeastern edge of the city. It mainly serves Eastern Europe, Turkey, and the Middle and Far East. Take **bus #171** (DM4/€2.05, ticket also valid on S- and U-Bahn, see p.48) from the terminal building to S-Bahnhof Flughafen Schönefeld, from where S-Bahn line #9 provides a direct link to the city centre, running to Charlottenburg via the Ostbahnhof, Alexanderplatz, Friedrichstrasse and Zoo Station (journey time to Alexanderplatz approximately 35min). Alternatively, if you continue one stop further on bus #171 to Rudow U-Bahn station, U-Bahn line #7 also runs into town (change at Hermannplatz for trains to Alexanderplatz, or Berliner Strasse for trains to Zoo Station). If you're not going to the centre, S-Bahn line #45/#4 makes a complete loop around Berlin, connecting with all U-Bahn and S-Bahn lines along the way (the last northern section is still under construction at the time of writing).

A **taxi** into town (for example to Bahnhof Friedrichstrasse) from Schönefeld is prohibitively expensive, costing around DM60 (€30.60).

Tempelhof

Tempelhof (*www.berlin-airport.de*), the closest airport to the city centre, is currently used mainly by German domestic carriers, some European airlines and scheduled flights by very small operators. However, it's due to close sometime in the next few years and is gradually shutting down; flights are all being switched to Tegel. From the forecourt, **bus #119** links the airport with the Europa Center. A few minutes' walk west is Platz der Luftbrücke U-Bahn station, from where trains on line #6 take under ten minutes to reach Bahnhof Friedrichstrasse in the city centre (or change at Stadtmitte for Zoo Station). A taxi to Friedrichstrasse or Zoo Station would cost about DM20 (€10.25), and probably take longer.

By train

Trains from Western European destinations generally stop at both **Zoo Station** and **Ostbahnhof** (many trains from the west also stop at Wannsee and Spandau stations). Where you alight depends on where

you're staying – if your accommodation is pre-booked, check before
arrival. If you have not yet arranged anything, it's probably best to
get off at Zoo Station, which is handily located for the city's main
tourist office, and has excellent **U- and S-Bahn links** to all parts of
the city. Both principal stations have exchange offices and ATMs
(see Basics, p.22), while Zoo Station also has lockers and left luggage facilities (see *Directory*, p.317), plus the extremely helpful
EurAide office (see overleaf), located down the hall from the
Western Union office.

Trains from Eastern European destinations usually stop at
Bahnhof Lichtenberg, connected to the centre by S-Bahn lines
#5, #7 and #S75. This small station has lockers, an information
desk, and a couple of shops. A new major terminus is currently
under construction at Lehrter Stadtbahnhof, which, upon completion in 2005, will be Berlin's new rail hub for all train traffic,
superseding Zoo Station, and will include direct airport connections.

By bus

Most international **buses** and those from other German cities stop
at the **Zentraler Omnibus Bahnhof** or **ZOB** (central bus station),
Masurenallee, Charlottenburg, west of the centre, near the
Funkturm; regular #149 buses or U-Bahn line #2 from
Kaiserdamm station link it to the Ku'damm area, a journey of about
fifteen minutes. Alternatively, a few minutes' walk to the Westkreuz
S-Bahn station will get you there even faster. The bus station is a
poor introduction to the city, shopworn and uninviting, but you'll
find at least an information booth, a taxi stand, and a couple of
snack places.

By car

Getting into Berlin **by car** is relatively easy: Germany's famed autobahns (*Autobahnen*) take you quite close to the heart of the city. It
may, however, be a long trip – the autobahns are very congested and
delays are the norm. From the south you're most likely to approach
on autobahn #9, which will turn into #10 (the ringroad around
Berlin), from which you turn off onto #115, a highway that eases you
directly into Kaiserdamm and the west side of the city, just fifteen
minutes from Zoo Station. From the west you'll approach on autobahn #2, but the route once you hit the ringroad is the same. Drivers
coming from the Hamburg area will approach from the north on
#24, which also turns into #10, but this time you turn off on the
#111 road. Street **parking** can be tough in the city, but there are lots
of spaces in the neighbourhood around Kurfürstendamm. Parking
facilities are much scarcer on the eastern side of the city. However,
almost all the larger hotels have garages.

Information

Berlin's **tourist office**, Berlin Tourismus Marketing (*www.btm.de*), has several offices (see box below), but the largest, and the only one with an accommodation-booking facility, is the **Europa Center** office. BTM publishes a bilingual events magazine *Berlin: Das Magazin* (DM3.90/€2), three times a year, that details most of the mainstream cultural happenings in the city. In addition, they produce a very handy free map and a couple of brochures detailing hotels and some of the more expensive shopping and eating alternatives. All of the tourist offices feature racks of leaflets and flyers from various places and productions around town, a good way to get a quick feel for what's worthwhile. And they sell two special discount passes that may save you some money: the **Welcome Card** (DM35/€17.90), which gives half-price entry to most of the city's municipally held museums, plus unlimited travel on the public transport system for an adult and up to three children for three days; and the "**State Museum three-day tourist ticket**", which allows entry to all of Berlin's state museums, including those on Museum Island, and in Dahlem, the Kulturforum, Charlottenburg, and elsewhere, for three consecutive days. It costs DM16 (€8.20) and is available from the offices at Europa Center and Brandenburg Gate.

For travel information and bookings, as well as general tips and advice, there's also the helpful **EurAide** office in Zoo Station (daily: June–Sept 8am–noon & 1–6pm; Oct–May 8am–noon & 1–4.30pm; *www.euraide.de*), set up specifically for English-speaking travellers. The office has a wealth of information and knowledgeable staff and serves as something of an oasis. Additionally, Berlin has a couple of **cultural centres**: the British Council, at Hackescher Markt 1, Mitte (Mon & Thurs 1–8pm, Tues, Wed & Fri 11am–6pm, Sat 11am–2pm; ☎31 10 99 10; *www.britcoun.de*), has a new and very impressive information centre with magazines, books, videos, and more, while the Amerika Haus, Hardenbergstrasse 22–24, Charlottenburg (☎31 10 74 06; *www.usembassy.de*) is now under the jurisdiction of the US Embassy and its reference library accessible by appointment only.

Berlin has two essential **listings magazines** – *Tip* (*www.tip-berlin.de*; DM4.70/€2.40) and *Zitty* (*www.zitty.de*; DM4/€2.05) –

MAIN TOURIST OFFICES IN BERLIN

Europa Center (entrance on Budapester Str.), Tiergarten ☎25 00 25 (Mon–Sat 8.30am–8.30pm, Sun 10am–6.30pm).

Brandenburg Gate (south wing; daily 9.30am–6pm).

Info-Point Tegel airport (main hall) ☎41 01 34 26 (daily 5am–10.30pm).

Info-Point KaDeWe, Wittenbergplatz, Charlottenburg (Mon–Fri 9.30am–8pm, Sat 9am–4pm).

---

which come out on alternate weeks. *Zitty* is marginally the better of the two, with day-by-day details of gigs, concerts, events, TV and radio, theatre and film, alongside intelligent articles on politics, style and the Berlin in-crowd, and useful classified ads. Reading copies of these can be found in any bar. Alternatively, the free magazine, *(030)*, has sparse literary content but very good club, music and film listings – it comes out biweekly with a film update on the off-week. The monthly *Prinz* (DM2/€1) is unable to compete with the big two (its headquarters are in Munich, and it shows), and relies on titillating covers to entice readers; it's worth picking up only for its eating section. Berlin's diverse arts scene is covered by *Artery Berlin* (DM3.50/€1.80), a monthly English/German publication with full listings of what's happening in the city's many galleries. The monthly *Berlin Programm* (*www.berlin-programm.de*; DM3/€1.50) has more condensed listings, alongside information on opening times, and national and international train, bus and plane timetables.

City transport

Wartime bombing provided city planners with a chance to widen and straighten streets and modernize rail systems, and as a result Berlin is relatively easy to navigate. It is, however, a large city, and sooner or later you'll need to use its efficient, if expensive, **public transport network**; this, consisting of a metro system, suburban trains, buses and trams, is extensive, reaching just about everywhere. The city's boats are mostly for sightseeing purposes but there are some ferries traversing the larger lakes on the eastern and western edges of the city.

U-and S-Bahn, buses and trams

The mainstay of the transport system is the **U-Bahn** (*www.bvg.de*), which is clean, punctual and rarely overcrowded. Running both under and over ground, it covers much of the centre and stretches into the suburbs: trains run from 4am to between midnight and approximately 12.30am, an hour later on Friday and Saturday. U-Bahn lines #2 and #9 run throughout the night on Friday and Saturday. The **S-Bahn** system (*www.s-bahn-berlin.de*), a separate network of suburban trains, has been extended since unification and these days, though the service is still far less frequent than the U-Bahn, it's better for covering long distances fast – say for heading out to the Wannsee lakes or Potsdam.

You never seem to have to wait long for a **bus** in the city: timetables at the stops are uncannily accurate, and the city network covers most of the gaps in the U-Bahn system, with buses converging on Zoo Station and Alexanderplatz. Buses #100 and #200, which run between the two, are good for sightseeing purposes. **Night buses**

mostly run every half hour and routes often differ from daytime ones;
maps of the night bus routes can be picked up in most U-Bahn ticket booths.

Trams are found for the most part in the eastern section of the
city, the network surviving from prewar days; new cars have recently been introduced and the ride is always quiet and comfortable. The
main tram **terminus** in the centre of town is at **Hackescher Markt**,
and several lines now connect Alexanderplatz to the tram system.
Tickets are available from machines on the trams, at the termini or
from U-Bahn stations. There's talk, too, of reintroducing trams to
western Berlin, such are their environmental advantages.

For **more information** about Berlin's public transport system, and
a larger scale U- and S-Bahn map than the one in this guide, it's
worth getting hold of the excellent *BVG & S-Bahn Berlin Atlas*
(DM12/€6.15) from either the cubicle outside Zoo Station, the
Friedrichstrasse or Alexanderplatz transport information offices, or
from one of the larger U-Bahn stations (see box above). It contains
complete listings and timetables for the U- and S-Bahn systems, plus
bus, tram and ferry routes. Most U-Bahn stations also provide simple
free maps; ask at the kiosk on the platform.

Tickets

Tickets for the U- and S-Bahn system and the bus network can be
bought from the orange-coloured machines on the platforms of the
U-Bahn stations. These take all but the smallest coins, give change
and have a basic explanation of the ticketing system in English.
Though it's tempting to ride without a ticket, be warned that plain-
clothes inspectors frequently cruise the lines (particularly, for some
reason, at the beginning of the month), meting out on-the-spot **fines**
of DM60 (€30.60) for those without a valid ticket or pass. If you're

taking a bus after 8pm, you must board by the front door by the driver and purchase or show a ticket.

Single tickets (*Normaltarif*) common to the whole VBB system cost DM4 (€2.05), and allow you to travel in any two of the three tariff zones. If you're heading for the outskirts of town or Potsdam, it'll cost DM4.50 (€2.30) to travel through all three tariff zones. Tickets are valid for two hours, enabling you to transfer across the three networks to continue your journey, and to return within that time by a different route. A *Kurzstrecke*, or short-trip ticket, costs DM2.50 (€1.30) and allows you to travel up to three train or six bus stops (no return journeys). On the U- and S-Bahn, tickets other than the passes mentioned below are supposed to be punched before travelling; on the bus the driver may **check** your ticket.

It's possible to save a little money by buying a **day ticket** (*Tageskarte*) for DM8.70/€4.45 (2 zones) or DM9.90/€5.06 (3 zones) from any U-Bahn station or the transit authority office on Grunewaldestrasse, Schöneberg, next to Kleistpark U-Bahn station (Mon–Fri 8am–6pm, Sat 7am–2pm). These are valid until 3am of the day following your purchase. The small **group ticket** (*Kleingruppenkarten*) is available for a whole day's travel for up to five people; it costs DM21 (€10.74) for 2 zones and DM25 (€12.78) for three zones.

You can also buy a **seven-day ticket** (*Sieben-Tage-Karte*) for DM42–52 (€21.05–26.55), depending on the zones through which you travel, or a **monthly ticket** (*Monatskarte*, also known as an *Umweltkarte*) for DM105–130 (€53.70–66.50), from any kiosk. A **premium monthly ticket** (*Umweltkarte Premium*), costing DM120–150 (€61.35–76.70), allows unlimited travel through all three tariff zones and for one adult and up to three children to travel with you free after 8pm, all day Saturday and Sunday and on public holidays. The monthly cards obviously represent a considerable saving; although tickets begin on the first of each month, not on the date of purchase (however, they are transferable, so you could buy the ticket with someone else or sell it to a friend before leaving). There's also the **Welcome Card** (see p.46), which, in addition to tourist offices, you can buy from hotels and the larger U- and S-Bahn stations (see box opposite).

Taxis

Taxis are plentiful and always metered, but pricey: for the first 6km it's DM4 (€2.05), plus DM2.20 (€1.10) per kilometre, which rises to DM2.40 (€1.20) per kilometre from 11pm to 6am and all day Sunday. If you're travelling in small groups, however, it can work out to be not much more expensive than public transport. Taxis cruise the city day and night and congregate at useful locations, such as outside the KaDeWe store, on Savignyplatz and by Zoo Station in the West End; and in the east at the northern entrance to

Friedrichstrasse station, the entrance to Alexanderplatz S-Bahn station and in front of the nearby *Forum Hotel*. Short trips, known as *Kurzstrecke*, can be paid on a flat rate of DM5 (€2.50) for up to two kilometres, though this only works when you hail a moving cab, not one from a taxi stand. Drivers are generally polite and know their way around, but you will find one or two who are student part-timers or moonlighting second-jobbers, so don't expect them necessarily to have an infallible knowledge of the city. For a selection of taxi firms see *Directory*, p.318 – the car is nearly always a Mercedes, so you can count on a comfortable ride.

Driving

Though there's practically no need for a car within the city, you may want to tour around outside Berlin and one way of doing so is by **car**. The most important rules to bear in mind when driving in Berlin are simple. You drive on the right; main roads have a yellow diamond indicating who has priority; but if you are driving in built-up areas, traffic coming from the right normally has right of way. This is particularly important to remember in the former East Berlin, where **trams** always have the right of way. Unfamiliarity with the traffic system means that unwary visiting drivers are prone to cutting in front of turning trams at junctions – a frightening and potentially lethal error. Also, when trams halt at their designated stops, it's forbidden to overtake until the tram starts moving, to allow passengers time to cross the road and board.

Seatbelts are compulsory in front and rear seats; and children under twelve years must sit in the back. A surviving GDR traffic regulation is the "Grüner Pfeil", or green arrow attached to traffic lights at the right-hand turning lane at junctions: it means if the light is red, but no traffic is approaching from the left, you may proceed. The **speed limits** are 50km per hour in urban areas, 100km per hour out of built-up areas and 130km per hour on the motorways (except where different limits are specified). There are **on-the-spot-fines** for speeding and other offences; for speeding these are calculated on a sliding scale up to about DM75 (€38.35) – after a cutoff point of roughly 25km over the limit, you're charged and taken to court. For failing to wear seatbelts, the immediate fine is DM75 (€38.35). The maximum permitted **blood alcohol level** is 80mg per 100ml.

Thanks to a post-unification boom in car-ownership and extensive road construction projects, Berlin suffers **traffic snarl-ups** that can compete with the worst any other European city has to offer. The authorities seemingly have little clue as to how to control the rush-hour jams that start at around 5pm and are particularly bad on Friday afternoons: don't be surprised if a journey you'd allowed twenty minutes for takes three or four times as long during these periods.

The recent installation of **parking meters** seems to have aided your chances of finding a place to park. The meters, identifiable by their tall grey rectangular solar power umbrellas, generally cost DM1 (€0.50) per 30min, DM4 (€2.05) in places like Alexanderplatz. You're supposed to move after the hour, and stiff fines are handed out to those without tickets; if you drive a car with foreign plates you can expect it to be towed away.

Car rental

All the major **car rental** agencies are represented in Berlin, although the best deals are often found through local operators – for a selection of both see *Directory*, p.316. You can find local car rental firms in the Yellow Pages under *Autovermietung* (*PKW an Selbstfahrer*); phoning around should trawl in something for under DM60 (€30.70) a day, though watch out for hidden extras such as limited mileage. Most rental places do good-value Friday afternoon–Monday morning deals, and most expect to see a credit card and passport. Four-star unleaded fuel currently costs just over DM2 (€1) per litre.

Cycling

Cycling is a quick and convenient way of getting around the city, largely due to an extensive network of bike paths (which pedestrians should avoid at all costs – cyclists in Berlin move quickly and have little patience for those in their way.) You can also take your bike on the U- or S-Bahn should you wish to explore the countryside and lakes of the Grunewald and Wannsee areas. To take your bike on a train you'll need an extra ticket costing DM2.50 (€1.30), unless you've purchased a Premium monthly ticket.

For **bike rental** the cheapest is Bike City, headquartered in a mobile home unit just north of Zoo Station (daily 10am–6pm) – it's a kind of public works project that rents bikes for DM10 (€5.10) for 24 hours. The best place though is Fahrradstation (see *Directory*, p.316, for branches): prices for an ordinary bike start at DM20 (€10.25) for a day, DM49 (€25.05) for a weekend and DM70 (€35.80) for a week; for a mountain bike it's DM25 (€12.80), DM55 (€28.10) and DM100 (€51.10); and for a tandem, DM40 (€20.45), DM65 (€33.20) and DM175 (€89.50). They also run bike tours around the city, to Potsdam and the eastern lakes. If you're planning to stay for any length of time, it works out cheaper to **buy** a second-hand machine and sell it when you leave. Try any of the bike shops, or look under *Fahrräder* in the classified ads section of *Zweite Hand* (published Tues, Thurs & Sat), *Die Berliner Morgenpost* (Sun) or *Der Tagesspiegel* (Sun).

Boats

More an option for messing about on Berlin's numerous canals than a practical mode of transport, **boats** run regularly throughout the summer. From the centre of town, Reederei Heinz Riedel, Planufer 78, Kreuzberg (☎6 93 46 46) runs daily trips on the River Spree, taking in the Reichstag and the Landwehrkanal. Starting points are the Hansabrücke on the Spree in Moabit, Kottbusser Brücke on the Landwehrkanal in Kreuzberg, and Märkische Brücke in Mitte. Trips cost DM21 (€10.75) and last around three hours. The same company also runs trips out to the Pfaueninsel and the Wannsee in the west of the city, to the Müggelsee in the east, and on the lakes surrounding Berlin.

The Stern und Kreis Schiffahrt, Puschkinallee 16–17, Treptow (☎5 36 36 00; *www.sternundkreis.de*), offers a variety of city-centre trips with departures from Jannowitzbrücke, Treptower Hafen, the Berliner Dom and the Palastufer (tickets from DM14/€7.15); between April and mid-October they also run a number of tours around the lake systems in the Grunewald, including trips to Potsdam. A number of smaller companies also run cruises along the waterways in and around Berlin, ranging as far afield as **Spandau**, **Potsdam** and **Werder** – details available from the Reederverband der Berliner Personenschiffahrt, Kronprinzessinnenweg 5, Grunewald (☎8 03 87 03). Full details and timetables for all Berlin cruise companies are available from city tourist offices.

Guided tours

By far the best **walking tour** company is Original Berlin Walks (☎3 01 91 94; *www.berlinwalks.com*), which offers general English-language tours of the city, plus more specialized ones of Third Reich sites, Jewish life and Potsdam; their city tour leaves daily at 10am (April–Oct also 2.30pm) from the taxi stand outside Zoo Station. Insider Tour (☎6 92 31 49; *www.insidertour.com*) also offers regular English-language city walks daily at 10am and 2.30pm, starting out from the *McDonald's* across from Zoo Station.

A variety of **bicycle tours** are offered by Fahrradstation (see *Directory*, p.316, for branches); they can be from ten to twenty kilometres in length and last about 2–3 hours. You can pick up a schedule at any of their branches, and bikes can be rented beforehand.

Bus tours abound: most of them depart from points on Kurfürstendamm between Breitscheidplatz and Knesebeckstrasse, making the rounds several times every day, though schedules are curtailed in the winter. Companies include Severin + Kühn (☎8 80 41 90; *www.severin-kuehn-berlin.de*), and **Tempelhofer Reisen**, (☎7 52 40 57; *www.tempelhofer.de*. A basic two-hour tour from any company will cost about DM30/€15.35.

Chapter 2

Unter den Linden and around

U nter den Linden and the surrounding area formed the show-piece quarter of Hohenzollern Berlin, capital of Brandenburg-Prussia and later the German Empire, and now, with the city's regeneration as capital of unified Germany, the street once again constitutes its nucleus. The revival of Unter den Linden has not only returned an important historical district, but also provided the city with the coherent centre that it lacked for so long, with a set of cultural and political attractions befitting a capital – not least its parliament, the **Reichstag**.

Berlin had been a relative backwater until the seventeenth century, but with the rise of Prussia architects were commissioned to create the trappings of a capital city – churches, theatres, libraries, palaces and an opera house – which were all set down here. Safe **Baroque** and **Neoclassical** styles predominate, and there are no great flights of architectural fancy. These buildings were meant to project an image of solidity, permanence and power, perhaps to allay the latent insecurity of Brandenburg-Prussia as a relatively late arrival on the European stage. However, almost every one of these symbols of Hohenzollern might was left gutted by the bombing and shelling of World War II. Paradoxically, it was the postwar communist regime that resurrected them from the wartime rubble to adorn the capital of the German Democratic Republic. The result was a pleasing re-creation of the old city, though one of the motives behind this restoration was to import a sense of historical continuity to the East German state by tacitly linking it with Prussia. Whether anyone outside the Politbüro really bought into this particular conceit is doubtful, but central East Berlin always compared favourably with the haphazard, soulless jumble of central West Berlin.

So successful has the **restoration** been that, looking at these magnificent eighteenth- and nineteenth-century buildings, it's difficult to believe that as recently as the 1960s large patches of the centre lay in ruins. Like archeologists trying to picture a whole vase from a single fragment, the builders took a facade, or just a small fraction of one, and set about re-creating the whole. And even though much of what can be seen today is an imitation, it's often easy to suspend disbelief and imagine an unbroken continuity.

Unter den Linden remains impressive, with a surprising number of worthy buildings. The **Brandenburg Gate**, for long a forlorn symbol left stranded by the Wall, has regained some stature now that it's fulfilling its intended role as a gateway to something significant, and in just a few blocks you can stroll by museums, a cathedral, an opera house, a university, public squares like **Bebelplatz**, and several other notable sites, all enlivened by a new sense of vitality on the street. The rejuvenation continues south of Unter den Linden. **Potsdamer Platz**, the prewar life and soul of Berlin, has been reinvented as a temple to commercialism; while a different approach can be seen on the **Gendarmenmarkt**, where as recently as twelve years ago the twin Neoclassical churches that grace the square were bombed-out shells. Now restoration of the area is complete and Gendarmenmarkt has been returned to its position as one of Berlin's most striking corners. Less aesthetically impressive, but historically significant, is **Checkpoint Charlie**, further south on Friedrichstrasse; little is left of the Cold War border crossing, but the area nevertheless retains an echo of the tension that once pervaded it.

Unter den Linden

Unter den Linden itself is Berlin's grandest boulevard, rolling due east from the Brandenburg Gate towards Alexanderplatz. Once the

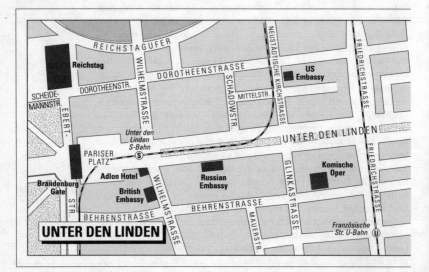

main east–west axis of Imperial Berlin and site of many of the city's
foreign embassies, it has been revitalized since 1989, reassuming its
old role as one of Berlin's most important streets. The street –
"beneath the lime trees" – was named after the trees that border its
central island. The first saplings were planted by Friedrich Wilhelm
the Great Elector during the seventeenth century to line the route
that ran from his palace to the hunting grounds in the Tiergarten.
The original trees were replaced by crude Nazi totem-poles during
the 1930s, and the present generation dates from a period of postwar planting.

Until 1989 the western extremity of Unter den Linden marked the
end of the road for East Berliners: a low barrier a hundred metres or
so short of the Brandenburg Gate cut it off from Charlottenburger
Chaussee (today known as Strasse des 17 Juni), its prewar continuation through the Tiergarten to the city's West End. From this vantage point it was possible to view the Brandenburg Gate, beyond
which the discreet presence of armed border guards and the sterile
white concrete of the Wall signalled the frontier with West Berlin.
During this period Unter den Linden was reduced to little more than
a grandiose blind alley, lined by infrequently visited embassies that
gave it a strangely decorative feel.

Now, however, the situation couldn't be more different. The
Brandenburg Gate and the **Reichstag**, once separated, form adjacent symbols of the city's unity; the embassies have been joined by
the offices of international companies and touristy shops; and traffic
is heavy, as tourists heading for architectural highlights such as the
Alte Bibliothek, and museums including the **Deutsche Guggenheim**

and the **Deutsches Historisches Museum**, compete for pavement space with civil servants and businesspeople.

The Brandenburg Gate and the Reichstag

At the head of Unter den Linden is the **Brandenburg Gate** (Brandenburger Tor; S-Bahn Unter den Linden), a building dense with meaning and historical associations. Originally built as a city gate-cum-triumphal arch in 1791, it was designed by Carl Gotthard Langhans and modelled after the Propylaea, the entrance to the Acropolis in Athens. The Gate became, like the Reichstag later, a symbol of German solidarity, looking out to the Siegessäule and guarding the city's grandest thoroughfare. In 1806 Napoleon marched under the arch and took home with him the **Quadriga**, the horse-drawn chariot that tops the Gate. It was returned a few years later, and the revolutionaries of 1848 and 1918 met under its form; later the Gate was a favoured rallying point for the Nazis' torch-lit marches.

After the building of the Wall placed the Gate in the Eastern sector, nearby observation posts became the place for visiting politicians to look over from the West in what was a handy photo-opportunity – the view was apparently emotive enough to reduce Margaret Thatcher to tears. With the opening of a border crossing here just before Christmas 1989, the east–west axis of the city was symbolically re-created and the post-Wall mood of eagerness for unification was strengthened. When the GDR authorities rebuilt the Quadriga following wartime damage, they removed the Prussian Iron Cross from the Goddess of Victory's laurel wreath, which topped her staff, on the grounds that it was "symbolic of Prussian–German militarism". When the border was reopened, the Iron Cross was replaced. Yet, despite the recent jubilation, it's easy to see why some, mindful of historical precedent, still view the Gate with a frisson of unease.

The Brandenburg Gate has been reopened to traffic, though there is talk in the administration of turning it into a pedestrianized zone.

A minute's walk north of the Gate up Ebert Strasse is the **Reichstag**, a stolid, looming structure that has never been considered particularly attractive, although its colonnaded Neoclassical

---

A chip off the Eastern bloc

If you're looking for the standard souvenir, a **chip of the Berlin Wall**, you'll find that Wall shards are hard to come by these days. Be warned that the pieces sold on the street by the Brandenburg Gate and Checkpoint Charlie are almost never the real thing. Despite official-looking "certificates of authentication" often given with a purchase, the only way you can be sure of getting the real thing is to look for a pale aggregate of flint, pebbles and other hard stones.

The Reichstag in ribbons

In 1995, after some twenty years of lobbying, wrangling and debate, the conceptual artist **Christo** and his wife Jeanne-Claude realized their long-held dream of wrapping up the Reichstag. For two weeks in June and July, the historic building was packaged in 100,000 square metres of shiny-grey polypropylene and tied with deep-blue rope. Several hundred people were involved in the massive project, many of them mountain climbers employed to scramble along the sides of the building laying rope and tying knots. Some one million visitors saw the artwork, and even most detractors had to admit that it was indeed impressive. The price tag was said to be around $9 million.

facade is suitably impressive. Its pivotal role in history, however, is unquestionable. Built in the late nineteenth century to house the German parliament, familiar from flickering newsreels as it burned in 1933, and the scene of Hitler's wresting of control of Germany in the same year, the Reichstag today seems lost in a sea of irony. Inscribed with the words *Dem Deutschen Volke* ("To the German People"), what was once the symbol of national unity for years stood hard by the border that underlined its division.

Until the Weimar Republic the Reichstag was home of a sham parliament – it had little power, since the Chancellor was an appointee of the Kaiser and answerable only to him. But in November 1918 Philipp Scheidemann declared the German Republic from a window here, and for the first time the building hosted a working democratic body, though this was to last just fourteen years before the Nazi Party was boosted to power. The **fire** that gutted the building in March 1933 allowed the Nazis to introduce emergency measures eliminating representative government in Germany; debate as to who actually started it began immediately after the incident and continues to this day. In a show trial, Göring, as minister of the interior for the State of Prussia, successfully accused an itinerant ex-Communist Dutch bricklayer, **Marius van der Lubbe**, of arson; he was executed the following year. It's equally likely, however, that members of the SA, the precursors of the SS, began the fire to allow the draconian measures to be brought in. By an emergency decree on the day after the fire, the basic civil rights guaranteed by the Weimar constitution were suspended and the death penalty was introduced for a range of political offences.

The Reichstag resumed its role as the permanent seat of the German parliament for the first time since the Third Reich on April 19, 1999. Outfitting the building to make way for the resumption of its governmental chores took several years – not only was the interior completely gutted and refashioned with a new plenary chamber and offices for the legislators, but a glass **dome**, supported by a soaring mirrored column, set atop as well. Designed by British architect Sir Norman Foster, the cupola aroused much controversy when ini-

*For more on
the Berlin Wall
see p.75.
Surviving
stretches can be
seen on
Niederkirchner-
strasse (see
p.71), compris-
ing the East
Side Gallery on
Mühlenstrasse
(see p. 180),
and at the
Berlin Wall
Memorial on
Bernauer-
strasse (see
p.117).*

tially proposed, but has since proven a popular success, with hoards of visitors winding their way up the circular ramp that spirals up the inside; the **viewing deck** (daily 8am–10pm; free) at the top offers a stunning view of the city.

Immediately behind the Reichstag, it's only just possible to make out the course of the **Berlin Wall**, marked in the street by a line of brick, which for 28 years divided the city; across the street, a poignant series of plaques marks the names (where known) of those killed trying to swim to the West across the nearby River Spree.

Pariser Platz to Bebelplatz

Pariser Platz is the square just to the east of the Brandenburg Gate, where symmetrical ornamental gardens have been restored, and several new office buildings erected, all with a view to reproducing the feel, if not the exact look, of the prewar square. Directly adjacent to the Brandenburg Gate on the north is the **Haus Liebermann**, patterned after the home of the Impressionist painter Max Liebermann that once stood here. It now features temporary art exhibitions (opening times and entrance fees vary). On the southeast corner of the Platz, the legendary **Adlon Hotel**, once one of Europe's grandest hotels, has been rebuilt. The original was host to luminaries from Charlie Chaplin to Lawrence of Arabia and Kaiser Wilhelm II, and was regarded throughout the continent as the acme of luxury and style. The building was destroyed in the closing days of the war, and this new version, modelled closely on its predecessor – the lobby fountain, for example, was salvaged from the original – attempts the same heights of opulence. Even if you can't afford a drink here, let alone a room, have a look at the lobby and imagine a time when Berlin was the cultural capital of Europe.

Among the first buildings you'll see as you head east down Unter den Linden from Pariser Platz is the massive **Russian Embassy** which rears up on the right. Built in 1950 on the site of the prewar (originally Tsarist) embassy, it's an example of the much-maligned *Zuckerbäckerstil* or "wedding-cake style" characteristic of Stalin-era Soviet architecture, and was the first postwar building to be erected on Unter den Linden. *Zuckerbäckerstil* is a kind of blunted, monumental Classicism, and Berlin has a number of such buildings, the most spectacular being those along Karl-Marx-Allee (see p.178).

The next block along from the embassy is a row of shops which also includes the box office for the **Komische Oper**, one of Berlin's leading opera companies. The actual entrance to the theatre itself is on the street behind at Behrenstrasse 55–57, and though the building doesn't look like much from the outside, the interior is a wonderful 1890s frenzy of red plush, gilt and statuary (see *The arts*). Just slightly further on from here Unter den Linden hits **Friedrichstrasse**; before the war this was one of the busiest crossroads in the city, a focal point for cafés and hotels, including the famous *Café Kranzler*. Like most of the rest of Weimar Berlin the café vanished in the debris of the war, although it was later re-established on the Kurfürstendamm in the west of the city.

The Deutsche Guggenheim Berlin Museum

At the southeast corner of Unter den Linden and Charlottenstrasse is the German branch of New York's **Guggenheim Museum** (daily 11am–8pm; *www.deutsche-guggenheim-berlin.de*; DM8/€4.10, concessions DM5/€2.50, Mon free; U-Bahn Französische Strasse), though it's a far cry from the museum's architectural landmarks in New York and Bilbao. Housed in a former bank building, this exhibition space shows rotating exhibitions focusing on top-drawer modern painters and important schools and movements. The galleries are modest in size, but comfortably laid out and well lit. There's a small museum shop and a sleek, quiet café on site.

The Staatsbibliothek and monument to Frederick the Great

A little further along Unter den Linden on the northern side is the **Staatsbibliothek zu Berlin** (Mon–Fri 9am–9pm, Sat 9am–5pm; free; tours every first Sat of the month at 10.30am (free); U-Bahn Französische Strasse), the former Prussian (and later GDR) state library, now twinned with the Staabi on Potsdamer Strasse (see p.132). It's a typically grandiose edifice dating from the turn of the twentieth century, with a facade extensively patched up after wartime shrapnel damage, and is now mainly the haunt of Humboldt University students. Visitors who don't feel like delving into the volumes within can sit in the ivy-clad courtyard by the fountain and have a drink or snack at the small café. As you do so, admire a GDR-era sculpture showing a member of the proletariat apparently reading a didactic Brecht poem on a relief at the other side of the fountain. The subject of the poem is the way in which the workers and soldiers who carry out the orders of kings and emperors are forgotten while the rulers themselves live on as historical figures.

Back on Unter den Linden is a statue commemorating just such a historical figure. Christian Rauch's equestrian **monument to Frederick the Great** dates from the nineteenth century and shows Frederick astride a charger. Around the plinth, about a quarter of the size of the monarch, are representations of his generals, mostly on foot and conferring animatedly. Frederick was the enlightened despot who laid the foundations of Prussian power.

After the war, the statue of *Der alte Fritz*, as Frederick the Great is popularly known, was removed from Unter den Linden and only restored to its city centre site in 1981 after a long exile in Potsdam. Its reinstatement reflected an odd revaluation by Erich Honecker's GDR of the pre-socialist past. No longer were figures like Frederick the Great, Blücher, Scharnhorst *et al* to be reviled as imperialistic

For more on the life of Frederick the Great, see "Park Sanssouci", pp.212–213.

militarists, but were to be accorded the status of historic figures worthy of commemoration. Even Bismarck, the Iron Chancellor of Wilhelmine Germany, was recognized as having "in his *Junker* way played a progressive historical role".

The Humboldt Universität

You don't need student ID to eat in the university mensa (turn left out of the main entrance hall and continue down the corridor).

Frederick the Great's monument is the vanguard of a whole host of historic buildings, survivors of nineteenth-century Berlin that were described by Christopher Isherwood as "so pompous, so very correct", and have been restored over the last 45 years or so from the postwar rubble. On the left-hand side of the street is the **Humboldt Universität**, a restrained Neoclassical building from 1748, originally built as a palace for Frederick the Great's brother. In 1809 the philologist, writer and diplomat Wilhelm Humboldt founded a school here that was to become the University of Berlin, and later be renamed in his honour. Flanking the entrance gate are statues of Wilhelm and his brother Alexander, famous for his exploration of Central and South America. Wilhelm is contemplating the passing traffic, book in hand, and Alexander is sitting on a globe above a dedication to the "second discoverer of Cuba" from the University of Havana. Alumni of the Humboldt Universität include Karl Marx, Friedrich Engels and Karl Liebknecht, the socialist leader and proclaimer of the first German republic who was murdered in 1919 (see p.81). The philologists Jacob and Wilhelm Grimm (better known as the Brothers Grimm) and Albert Einstein are some of the better-known former staff members.

Bebelplatz and around

Directly opposite the university is **Bebelplatz**, formerly Opernplatz, the scene on May 10, 1933, of the infamous **Büchverbrennung**, the burning of books that conflicted with Nazi ideology. On the orders of Hitler's propaganda minister, Joseph Goebbels, thousands of books went up in smoke, including the works of "un-German" authors like Erich Maria Remarque, Thomas Mann, Heinrich Mann, Stefan Zweig and Erich Kästner, along with volumes by countless foreign writers, H.G. Wells and Ernest Hemingway among them. The most fitting comment on this episode was made with accidental foresight by the Jewish poet Heinrich Heine during the previous century: "Where they start by burning books, they'll end by burning people." A recent and intriguing memorial to the book burning, "The Empty Library", incorporates these words on a plaque; to see it go to the middle of Bebelplatz and look through the glass pane set in the ground.

Bebelplatz was originally conceived by Frederick the Great as a tribute to the grandeur of ancient Rome and a monument to the greater glory of himself. He and the architect **Georg Wenzeslaus von Knobelsdorff** drew up plans for what was to be known as the Forum Fridericianum, a space that would recall the great open squares of the Classical city. It never fulfilled such lofty ambitions, and instead exhibits a rather humble and unimpressive mien.

The Alte Bibliothek and Staatsoper
On the western side of the square is the **Alte Bibliothek**, a former royal library known colloquially as the **Kommode** ("chest of drawers"), thanks to its curved Baroque facade. The design of the Kommode, which was built between 1775 and 1780, was based on that of the Michaelertrakt in Vienna's Hofburg. Lenin spent some time here poring over dusty tomes while waiting for the Russian Revolution, and despite the fact that only the building's facade survived the war, it's been immaculately restored. Knobelsdorff's Neoclassical **Staatsoper**, on the eastern side of the square, looks a little plain opposite the Kommode, though it represented the pinnacle of the architect's career and was Berlin's first theatre. The building is best viewed from Unter den Linden, where an imposing portico marks the main entrance. Just under two centuries after its construction it became the first major building to fall victim to World War II bombing, on the night of April 9–10, 1941. The Nazi authorities restored it for its bicentenary in 1943, but on February 3, 1945, it was gutted once again. Like virtually everything else around here it has been totally reconstructed and is now one of Berlin's leading opera houses (see *The arts*, p.285).

Sankt-Hedwigs-Kathedrale
Just behind is another Knobelsdorff creation, the stylistically incongruous **Sankt-Hedwigs-Kathedrale** (Mon–Sat 10am–5pm, Sun 1–5pm; free), which was built as a place of worship for the city's Catholic minority in 1747 and is still in use. According to popular legend it owes its circular shape and domed profile to Frederick the Great's demand that it be built in the form of an upturned teacup. This probably stems from the fact that the monarch "advised" Knobelsdorff, but the truth is that the building's shape was inspired by the Pantheon in Rome. Reduced to a shell on March 2, 1943, the cathedral was not reconstructed until 1963, a restoration that left it with a slightly altered dome and a modernized interior.

   The **interior**, past the hazy biblical reliefs of the entrance portico, is perhaps the most unusual aspect of the whole building. The greatest feature of the vast main hall is the split-level double altar – the upper one is used on Sundays and special occasions, while the sunken altar in the crypt, reached by a flight of broad stairs, is used for weekday Masses. All this is complemented by the stainless steel pipes of the ethereal-sounding organ above the entrance and 1970s-style globe-lamps hanging from the ceiling. If you've survived the combined effects of all this, the crypt with its eight grotto-like side chapels and near-abstract charcoal drawings is a further attraction.

The Opernpalais and Kronprinzenpalais

Back on Unter den Linden, just east of the Staatsoper, is a lawn dotted
with **statues of Prussian generals**. Scharnhorst stands at the front,
while Yorck, Blücher and Gneisenau bring up the rear. Blücher, whose
timely intervention turned the day at Waterloo, looks most warlike,
with his foot resting on a cannon barrel and a sabre in his hand.

Next door to this martial grouping is the eighteenth-century
Opernpalais, a Baroque palace known as the Prinzessinpalais
(Princess's Palace) before the war, in memory of its role as a swanky
town residence for the three daughters of Friedrich Wilhelm III. It's
now home to a couple of pricey restaurants and the genteel
Operncafé (see *Cafés and bars*, p.266).

The Opernpalais is really a wing of its neighbour opposite, the
Kronprinzenpalais (Mon, Tues & Thurs–Sun 10am–6pm;
www.dhm.de; free; U-Bahn Friedrichstrasse). Originally built in

---

Karl Friedrich Schinkel (1781–1841)

Karl Friedrich Schinkel was an incredibly prolific architect who quite literally transformed nineteenth-century Berlin, creating some of the city's
most famous Neoclassical buildings. His first ever design, the
Pomonatempel in Potsdam (see p.219), was completed while he was still
a nineteen-year-old student in Berlin. Despite this auspicious beginning,
his architectural career did not take off immediately and for a while he
worked as a landscape artist and set decorator for the theatre, later turning his hand to set design (an activity which he pursued even after he had
established himself as an architect). Towards the end of the first decade of
the nineteenth century he began submitting architectural designs for the
great public works of the time, and, in 1810, he secured a job with the
administration of Prussian buildings.

In 1815 he was given a position in the new Public Works Department, an
appointment which marked the beginning of the most productive phase of his
career. During the years between 1815 and 1830, when he was made head of
the department, he designed some of his most famous buildings.
Constructions like the Grecian-style **Neue Wache** (see p.64), the elegant
Schauspielhaus (see p.73), and the **Altes Museum** (p.87) with its striking
Doric columns were just what were needed to enhance the ever-expanding
capital of Brandenburg-Prussia. Other creations from this period include the
War Memorial Cross in Kreuzberg (see p.137) and the
Friedrichwerdersche Kirche (see opposite), both inspired by Neo-Gothic
styles that were all the rage in England at the time. Later in his career
Schinkel experimented with other architectural forms, a phase marked by the
Romanesque Charlottenhof and Römischer Bäder in Potsdam (see p.216).

By virtue of his own designs and the role he played in shaping
Brandenburg-Prussia's building policy, Schinkel remains, without doubt,
one of the most influential German architects of the nineteenth century.
Nearly every town in Brandenburg has a building that Schinkel had, at the
very least, some involvement in, and a lasting testimony to his importance
is the fact that even the identity of late twentieth-century Berlin was in part
defined by his works.

1663 and given a Baroque face-lift in 1732, this started life as a residence for Prussian crown princes, but was converted into a national art gallery after 1919, becoming a leading venue for modern art exhibitions. In 1933 the Nazis closed it, declaring hundreds of Expressionist and contemporary works housed here to be examples of *entartete Kunst* or "degenerate art". Most of these were either sold off abroad or destroyed, and a number were bought at knockdown prices by leading Nazis, Göring among them. The Kronprinzenpalais is now playing host to temporary exhibitions drawing on the collections from the Deutsches Historisches Museum, which is closed for renovation until 2002.

To the immediate east of the Kronprinzenpalais, behind an imposing statue of Freiherr vom Stein – a civic reformer of the early nineteenth century – is a grassy field, until a few years ago the site of the former **GDR Foreign Ministry**. A forgettable wedge of East German modernism empty since reunification, it was happily torn down by the government. It occupied the former site of Karl Friedrich Schinkel's architectural school. This was reckoned to be one of his finest creations and Schinkel even moved in here, occupying a top-floor apartment until his death in 1841. Inevitably, wartime bombing took its toll and in 1962 the remains were demolished in a departure from the GDR's usual policy of restoring the city's monuments wherever possible. It's been proposed that Schinkel's Bauakademie be rebuilt, and already, as a kind of advertisement and incentive, a corner section of the building has been reconstructed on its original site. A statue of Schinkel himself can be seen, looking a little lost, in the middle of the field.

The Friedrichwerdersche Kirche and Jungfernbrücke

Karl Friedrich Schinkel was the man who, more than anyone, gave nineteenth-century Berlin its distinctive Neoclassical stamp (see box), and on the western side of the field that once housed his Bauakademie is the architect's **Friedrichwerdersche Kirche**, on Am Werderschen Markt, which houses the **Schinkel Museum** (Tues–Sun 10am–6pm; *www.smb.spk-berlin.de*; DM4/€2.05, concessions DM2/€1; S-Bahn Hausvogteiplatz). The church itself is a rather plain Neo-Gothic affair, a stylistic departure for Schinkel, who was infatuated with the Classical styles he had encountered on trips to Italy. The inspiration for the Friedrichwerdersche Kirche came from churches Schinkel had seen on a visit to England in 1826.

The Schinkel Museum was opened in 1987 when postwar restoration of the building was completed to coincide with Berlin's 750th anniversary. A display in the church's upper gallery gives a full rundown of Schinkel's achievements, setting his work in the context of the times, and also details the history of the church. On the ground floor is a jumble of German Neoclassical statuary from the nineteenth century.

Opposite the church is one of the city's many new Federal government buildings, the **Foreign Ministry**. The structure, though massive, projects an unassuming aspect by means of its plain glass facade, through which you can see a serene covered courtyard, complete with trees and fountain. It illustrates one answer to a common problem facing architects for the new German capital: how to create large and significant civic buildings whilst avoiding any hints of Nazi monumentalism. A good example of such gigantism, in fact, lies directly behind – an immense and imposing structure built between 1934 and 1938 for the Central Bank. Having survived the war, it was later used as SED (Socialist Unity Party of Germany) Headquarters, one-time nerve centre of the East German communist party, and is now also occupied by the Foreign Office. Heading down Unterwasserstrasse, running alongside the Spree east of the ex-SED Headquarters, leads to the **Jungfernbrücke**, Berlin's oldest surviving bridge. It's actually a drawbridge and the creaky-looking winding gear is still used to raise it and allow passing boats by.

The Neue Wache and around

Berlin's most
spectacular
war memorial
– to Soviet
troops killed
liberating the
city – can be
found in the
suburb of
Treptow. See
p.181.

Schinkel's most famous surviving creation, the **Neue Wache**, is on Unter den Linden opposite the Opernpalais. Built between 1816 and 1818 as a guardhouse for the royal watch, it resembles a stylized Roman temple and served as a sort of Neoclassical police station until 1918. In 1930–31 it was converted into a memorial to the military dead of World War I, and in 1957 the GDR government extended this concept to include those killed by the Nazis, dedicating the building as a "Memorial to the Victims of Fascism and Militarism".

These days it serves as the "National Memorial to the Victims of War and Tyranny", and inside it a granite slab covers the tombs of an unknown soldier and an unknown concentration camp victim. At the head of this memorial stone is a statue, depicting a mother clutching her dying son, an enlargement of a small sculptural piece by Käthe Kollwitz. Until 1990 one of East Berlin's better-known ironies was played out in front of the Neue Wache with the regular changing of the Nationale Volksarmee (National People's Army – the GDR army) honour guard, a much-photographed goose-stepping ritual that ended with the demise of the East German state.

The Zeughaus

Across Hinter den Giesshaus, opposite the Neue Wache, is one of eastern Berlin's finest Baroque buildings, the old Prussian Arsenal or **Zeughaus**, which now houses the **Deutsches Historisches Museum**, Unter den Linden 2. The museum is closed until 2002 while it undergoes a major renovation, which will include an annexe designed by I.M. Pei, architect of the famous glass pyramid at the entrance to the Louvre in Paris. Until then, some of its collection is housed in the Kronprinzenpalais (see p.62).

The original plans for the Zeughaus were drawn up by François Blondel, but the building was completed by Andreas Schlüter, who was responsible for many of the decorative elements, notably the walls of the Schlüterhof, the museum's inner courtyard, which are lined by reliefs depicting the contorted faces of dying warriors. These are vivid, realistic depictions of agony and anguish, with nothing heroic about them; death is shown as cutting everyone down to size, and none are spared its indignities.

There was much excitement at the Zeughaus on June 14, 1848, when, during the revolutionary upheavals, the people of Berlin stormed the building looking for arms. A number of citizens were killed, and no weapons were found, but the incident gave the authorities an excuse to bring troops into the city and ban various democratic newspapers and organizations. Just over thirty years later the Zeughaus was turned into a museum devoted to the exploits of the Prussian army, and from 1953, though heavily damaged, the building was given over to the nascent Museum für Deutsche Geschichte, offering the GDR's version of German history. The highly political and subjective nature of its content was to cause problems for the directors and staff of the museum after the *Wende* (literally "turning" – see Contexts, p.344) and, despite attempts to redress the balance with a special exhibition about German victims of Stalinist persecution during the period, it was closed down just after reunification. The Deutsches Historisches Museum was then established in 1991, with an exhibition entitled "Pictures and Objects from German History" that presented a West German slant on those same historical events, but it too was found wanting. After renovations, a new exhibition will be installed, but the manner in which the museum will present the tangled history of Germany is still being debated.

Just behind the Neue Wache is the **Maxim-Gorki-Theater** (see *The arts*, p.287), a one-time singing academy converted into a theatre after World War II. The grand-looking building just to the east, the **Palais am Festungsgrab**, has had a chequered career. Originally built during the eighteenth century as a palace for a royal gentleman of the bedchamber, it later served as a residence for Prussian finance ministers, and during GDR days it was the Zentrale Haus der Deutsch-Sowjetischen Freundschaft or "Central House of German-Soviet Friendship". Today it houses the **Museum Mitte von Berlin** (Wed & Thurs 1–5pm, Fri 1–8pm, Sat 11am–8pm, Sun 11am–5pm; free; U-Bahn Friedrichstrasse), a modest local history museum, and the *Tadschikische Teestuben*, a tearoom serving Russian specialities (see *Restaurants*, p.254).

South of Unter den Linden

The network of streets south of Unter den Linden, cut in two by the north–south axis of Friedrichstrasse, is easy to explore on foot. On

CENTRAL BERLIN

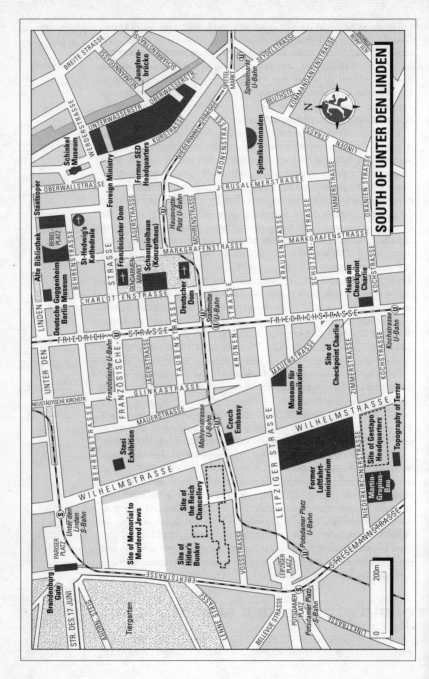

SOUTH OF UNTER DEN LINDEN

BREITE STRASSE

NEUMANNSGASSE

SCHARRENSTRASSE

Jungfern-brücke

OBERWASSERSTR.

UNTERWASSERSTR.

WERDERSTRASSE

Schinkel Museum

KURSTRASSE

Former SED Headquarters

Foreign Ministry

OBERWALLSTRASSE

NIEDERWALLSTRASSE

SPITTELMARKT STRASSE

Spittelmarkt U-Bahn

BEUTHSTR.

KOMMANDANTENSTRASSE

SEYDELSTRASSE

ALTE JAKOBSTRASSE

ALTE JAKOBSTRASSE

Spittelkolonnaden

JERUSALEMERSTRASSE

LINDENSTRASSE

Staatsoper

Alte Bibliothek

BEBEL-PLATZ

Deutsche Guggenheim Berlin Museum

St-Hedwig's Kathedrale

Französischer Dom

BEHRENSTRASSE

Schauspielhaus (Konzerthaus)

JÄGERSTRASSE

GENDARMEN-MARKT

Hausvogtei Platz U-Bahn

MOHRENSTRASSE

MARKGRAFENSTRASSE

KRONENSTRASSE

KRAUSENSTRASSE

SCHÜTZENSTRASSE

ZIMMERSTRASSE

ORANIENSTRASSE

KOCHSTRASSE

Haus am Checkpoint Charlie

LINDEN

LINDEN

STRASSE

CHARLOTTENSTRASSE

Deutscher Dom

Stadtmitte U-Bahn

F·R·I·E·D·R·I·C·H·S·T·R·A·S·S·E

Site of Checkpoint Charlie

Kochstrasse U-Bahn

UNTER DEN

Französische U-Bahn

F·R·I·E·D·R·I·C·H· S·T·R·A·S·S·E

JÄGERSTRASSE

TAUBENSTRASSE

KRONEN-STRASSE

MAUERSTRASSE

Museum für Kommunikation

NEUSTÄDTISCHE KIRCHSTR.

BEHRENSTRASSE

FRANZÖSISCHE STRASSE

GLINKASTRASSE

MAUERSTRASSE

Mohrenstrasse U-Bahn

Czech Embassy

WILHELMSTRASSE

Site of Gestapo Headquarters

Topography of Terror

Stasi Exhibition

WILHELMSTRASSE

Former Luftfahrt-ministerium

LEIPZIGER STRASSE

Martin-Gropius-Bau

NIEDERKIRCHNERSTRASSE

Site of the Reich Chancellery

Site of Memorial to Murdered Jews

VOSSSTRASSE

Site of Hitler's Bunker

LEIPZIGER PLATZ

Potsdamer Platz U-Bahn

STRESEMANNSTRASSE

PARISER PLATZ

Unter den Linden S-Bahn

WILHELMSTRASSE

EBERTSTRASSE

LENNÉSTRASSE

Potsdamer Platz S-Bahn

POTSDAMER PLATZ

LINKSTRASSE

Brandenburg Gate

STR. DES 17 JUNI

AHORN STEIG

Tiergarten

BELLEVUESTRASSE

N

200m

0

the western side of Friedrichstrasse the main points of interest are along Wilhelmstrasse, Berlin's prewar Regierungsviertel or "government quarter". Just southwest of here is **Potsdamer Platz**, which was the city's busiest corner until pulverized by the war and then effectively erased from the Berlin landscape by the building of the Wall. A huge commercial project has recently gone up here in an attempt to re-create the area's former liveliness. The area between Wilhelmstrasse and Potsdamer Platz was the site of **Hitler's Chancellery and Bunker**, where the final chapter of the Third Reich unfolded, and though little now remains, trying to figure out what was where can be a compelling activity.

More tangible evidence of the past survives in the grid-like street pattern of Friedrichstadt on the other side of Friedrichstrasse, one of a number of seventeenth-century city extensions that took Berlin beyond its original walled core. Although the war took its toll here too, much has survived or been rebuilt, including the immaculately restored **Gendarmenmarkt**, one of the architectural highlights of Berlin, with two attractive churches – the **Französischer Dom** and **Deutscher Dom**. At the far southern end of Friedrichstrasse is the site of **Checkpoint Charlie**, the principal gateway between East and West through the **Berlin Wall**.

Wilhelmstrasse to Potsdamer Platz

Wilhelmstrasse used to run parallel to the Wall, which lay just a couple of hundred metres beyond the late-period GDR housing development that sits on the western side of the street like a beached ocean liner. On the same side, below Behrenstrasse, is a large empty lot once part of the Wall's death strip and now slated to contain the National Memorial to the Murdered Jews of Europe, consisting of a number of stone stelae and a study centre. The project's design, proposed by American architect Peter Eisenmann, has been the subject of debate for a decade, and, though finally approved, there is certain to be more wrangling before the memorial is actually built.

On the opposite side of Wilhelmstrasse to the proposed memorial, along a pathway just below Behrenstrasse, is **Stasi: The Exhibition** at Mauerstrasse 38 (Mon–Sat 10am–6pm; *www.bstu.de*; free; U-Bahn Mohrenstrasse), a sobering look at the "Ministerium für Staatssicherheit", presented by the government commission responsible for sifting through and reconstructing Stasi files. It's a briefer look at the workings of the feared secret police than the similar exhibition at their former headquarters on Normannstrasse (see p.184), but it does nevertheless contain several intriguing intelligence devices, including hidden cameras, tiny tape recorders, a big toolbox for producing counterfeit documents and even the proverbial toothpaste tube with hidden compartment. Apart from these sometimes comical tools, however, the exhibit relates (in German only), just what a powerful and frightening organization the Stasi was, and the

South of Unter den Linden

amazing degree of observation, infiltration, and control they practised in the GDR.

Apart from the marooned apartment building, the only other
structure actually on Wilhelmstrasse that stands out is an apparent
airport control tower that turns out to be the **Czech Embassy**. But
it's really what you can't see that makes the street interesting; from
1871 onwards it was Imperial Berlin's Whitehall and Downing
Street rolled into one, lined by ministries and government buildings,
including the Chancellery and, after the Republic was established in
1918, the Presidential Palace. Historical markers have been placed
along the street, with photos and descriptions of the former buildings.

The site of Hitler's Chancellery and Bunker

The Nazis remodelled Wilhelmstrasse, replacing the original
Chancellery with a vast **new building** designed by Albert Speer in
1938. This gigantic complex, including Hitler's underground bunker
(see below), stood between Wilhelmstrasse and Ebertstrasse just
north of Vosstrasse. Today nothing remains, for, even though the
Chancellery building survived the war, it was torn down in a fit of
conquering revenge by the Soviet army, who used marble from the
site to fashion the memorial on Strasse des 17 Juni (see p.127) and
the huge war memorial at the Soviet military cemetery in Treptower
Park (see p.181).

Just above An der Kolonnade (slightly to the north of the
Chancellery site) is the site of **Hitler's Bunker**, where the Führer
spent his last days, issuing meaningless orders as the Battle of Berlin
raged above. Here Hitler married Eva Braun and wrote his final testament: he personally was responsible for nothing; he had been
betrayed by the German people, who had proved unequal to his leadership and deserved the future he could now envisage ahead of them.
On April 30, 1945, he shot himself, and his body was hurriedly
burned by loyal officers. In a 1992 postscript to the story, the KGB
released film showing a gaunt corpse with a toothbrush moustache,
allegedly Hitler, claiming that the dictator's body had in fact survived
destruction in the war's final days and fallen into Soviet hands.
Subsequently, so the tale went, the body was transported to Russia
where it exerted a near-obsessional fascination for Stalin and many
others who saw it. The corpse was ferried around various secret locations until the 1970s, when it was finally destroyed on the orders of
Leonid Brezhnev. Details were predictably sketchy and, given the
obvious hard currency-spinning potential of such a sensational reve-
lation, it's hard not to suspect a dollar-making scam on the part of
the former Soviet spy service.

For several years after reunification there was debate about what
to do with the remains of the bunker. Some said they should be preserved as a memorial; others claimed that they would become a

The uprising of June 1953

On June 16 and 17, 1953, Leipziger Strasse was the focal point of a **nationwide uprising** against the GDR's communist government. General dissatisfaction with economic and political conditions in the eastern half of the city came to a head when building workers (the traditional proletarian heroes of GDR mythology) constructing the prestigious Stalinallee project went on strike, protesting at having to work longer hours for the same pay. On June 16 they marched on the Haus der Ministerien, which was at that time the seat of the GDR government. Here they demanded to speak to GDR President Otto Grotewohl and SED General Secretary Walter Ulbricht. These two declined to make an appearance, so speakers from the crowd got up to demand the dissolution of the government and free elections. Thanks to western radio broadcasts, the news rapidly spread across the country, and in the morning of the following day, a wave of strikes and demonstrations took place throughout the GDR. Tools were abandoned, and traffic in East Berlin came to a standstill as 100,000 demonstrators marched on the Haus der Ministerien once again; clashes with the police followed as demonstrators attacked SED party offices and state food stores. The GDR authorities proved unequal to the situation, and at 1pm the Soviet military commandant of the city declared a state of emergency. It's estimated that several hundred people died as Soviet tanks rolled in to restore order. Afterwards, Bertolt Brecht sardonically suggested that the GDR government should "dissolve the people, and elect another".

shrine for rightists and neo-Nazi groups and should be destroyed. Finally it was decided to leave the bunker buried and unmarked. The large office buildings now going up on Leipziger Platz will soon obscure the site entirely.

The Luftfahrtministerium

One relic of the Nazi past that has survived very much intact is Hermann Göring's **Luftfahrtministerium**, or Air Ministry, a fortress-like structure on the southwest side of the Leipziger Strasse–Wilhelmstrasse junction. Göring promised Berliners that not a single bomb would fall on the city during the war; if this were to happen, the Reichsmarschal said, he would change his name to Meyer – a common Jewish surname. Ironically, the Air Ministry was one of the few buildings to emerge more or less unscathed from the bombing and Red Army shelling. After the establishment of the GDR it became the SED regime's Haus der Ministerien (House of Ministries), and was the venue for a mass demonstration on June 16, 1953 (see box above), that was to be a prelude for a general but short-lived uprising against the communist government the next day. There's a historical irony of sorts in the fact that the building became, for a number of years after reunification, the headquarters of the Treuhandanstalt, the agency responsible for the privatization of the former GDR's economy. It has again been tidied up and now houses the Federal Finance Ministry.

Potsdamer Platz and around

West of Göring's ministry, Leipziger Strasse runs into **Leipziger Platz**, which lies on former "Death-Strip" territory. Long an empty, derelict place, it's now the site of furious building as office towers and retail space surround this centrally located plot.

Potsdamer Platz

Beyond here is **Potsdamer Platz**, said to have been the busiest square in Europe in prewar days, with stores, bars and clubs pulsing with life day and night. The war left Potsdamer Platz severely battered, though it soon regained some of its vitality in the first chaotic postwar years as a black market centre at the junction of the Soviet, American and British occupation sectors. Later, West Berliners watched from their side of the dividing line as the Soviets put down the East Berlin uprising of 1953. During the rest of the decade the Cold War was played out here in words, with the Western authorities relaying their version of the news to East Berliners by means of an electronic newsboard – countered by an Eastern billboard exhorting West Berliners to shop in cheap East Berlin stores. This ended with the coming of the Wall, which finally put a physical seal on the ideological division of Potsdamer Platz. On the Eastern side all the buildings (which were mostly war vintage wrecks) were razed to give the GDR's border guards a clear field of fire, while in the West only a couple of battered survivors, including the hulk of the Hotel Esplanade, once one of the city's finest, were left as a reminder of the way things used to be. For many years tourists were able to gaze out at the East from a viewing platform here, and ponder the sight of prewar tramlines disappearing at the base of the Wall.

The dismantling of the Wall produced one of Europe's most valuable lots, a huge empty site smack in the middle of the city, and it was no surprise that the land was bought up by huge corporations, Sony and Daimler-Benz principally, with equally huge plans for sprawling **commercial complexes**. The construction of this mini-city from scratch represents an amazing feat of engineering: an entire infrastructure for power, water, and sewage was created; subway tunnels were drilled and new S- and U-Bahn stations built; the surviving Weinhaus Huth, a landmarked building, was picked up and trundled to another spot; and the remaining interior portions of the Hotel Esplanade were incorporated into a new restaurant. For several years the area, sporting a thicket of huge cranes and dominated by the incessant sounds of building, was touted as "Europe's largest construction site".

Daimler-Benz hired, among others, Renzo Piano and Richard Rogers to create an ensemble of disparate buildings that includes several restaurants, a stage theatre, a movie multiplex, a 3D big-screen movie theatre, and the obligatory shopping mall. The decision to use a variety of forms and facades was a good one, but inevitably the results on street level aren't all that stimulating. The **Sony Center**, designed by Helmut Jahn, is more uniform, with several similar glass-sheathed buildings grouped around a capacious, circular courtyard. It has the same touristy pulls as the Daimler-Benz complex, but does include a couple of worthwhile attractions. The **Filmmuseum Berlin** (Tues–Sun 10am–6pm; *www.filmmuseum-berlin.de*; DM12/€6.15, concessions DM8/€4.10) contains an excellent presentation on the history of the movies, concentrating on the German film industry, from *The Cabinet of Dr. Caligari* to *Run, Lola, Run*. No fewer than three rooms are devoted to artefacts – costumes, letters, photos, and the like – of Germany's biggest world star, Marlene Dietrich. The **"Music Box"** (Sun–Thurs 10am–8pm, Fri & Sat 10am–10pm; DM15/€7.70, concessions DM12/€6.15), is a kind of multimedia, interactive museum allowing visitors to experience music in various ways: you can "conduct" a performance of the philharmonic orchestra, for instance, or experiment with different drum sounds. The Sony Center's rotunda, topped by a conical glass roof, is perhaps the most impressive showpiece in the platz, open to the elements but at the same time providing a remove from the urban racket surrounding it.

Despite all the fuss however – and the huge amounts of money – the new Potsdamer Platz offers little that can't be found in Manchester, Pittsburg or even Frankfurt.

South and east from Potsdamer Platz

Heading south from Potsdamer Platz down Stresemannstrasse will take you to Niederkirchnerstrasse, where, slightly to the east, you'll find one of the few remaining stretches of the Wall. Protected from souvenir hunters, it's now illegal to chip a bit off.

The Martin-Gropius-Bau and the Topography of Terror

The magnificently restored building on the southern side of Niederkirchnerstrasse is the **Martin-Gropius-Bau** (times and prices vary – ring ☎2 54 86 05; bus #248, #341 & #129; S-Bahn Anhalter Bahnhof). Designed in 1877 by Martin Gropius, a pupil of Schinkel and the uncle of Bauhaus guru Walter (see p.143), the Gropius-Bau was, until its destruction in the war, home of the museum of applied art. In recent years it has been rebuilt and refurbished, and now houses changing exhibitions of art, photography and architecture. The *Gropius Restaurant* serves snacks and meals and is a useful stopping-off point and necessary pick-me-up before tackling an adjacent exhibition, **The Topography of Terror** (Tues–Sun 10am–6pm; *www.topographie.de*; free). This consists of an outdoor exhibition a little way from the Gropius-Bau, for nothing is left of the buildings that once stood around here: the Reich Security offices, including the headquarters of the Gestapo and SS. A numbered series of notice-

See also the
Jewish
Museum on
p.135; and the
note on p.168
on The
Wannsee
Conference.

boards with photographs and English texts indicate the sites of the most important buildings and reveal just how massive a machine the Nazi organization became: it was here that Himmler planned the Final Solution, the deportation and genocide of European Jews, and organized the Gestapo, the feared secret police. The ground underneath the exhibition once held the cellars of the Gestapo headquarters, which stood at Prinz-Albrecht-Str. 8 (now Niederkirchnerstrasse), where important prisoners were interrogated and tortured. The staff of the SS were based in the former *Hotel Prinz Albrecht* next door, and just around the corner in the Prinz-Albrecht-Palais (opposite the entrance to Kochstrasse) was the SS security service headquarters, where extensive records of all "enemies of the state", a category that included Jews and homosexuals, were kept.

The ruins of the Reich Security offices were destroyed after the war and the wasteland they once occupied, the empty space behind the Topography of Terror exhibit, is currently in the initial stages of development into larger facilities for a permanent museum.

From here it's a ten-minute walk (or two stops on the #129 bus) down Wilhelmstrasse, along Kochstrasse and up Friedrichstrasse to the site of Checkpoint Charlie – see p.75.

Gendarmenmarkt and around

To the east of Friedrichstrasse is **Gendarmenmarkt** (reached from Unter den Linden via Charlottenstrasse; bus #147 & #257; U-Bahn Stadtmitte), a square whose present appearance belies the fact that its historic buildings were almost obliterated during the war. It's now one of the most successfully restored parts of the city, but rebuilding lasted until well into the 1980s, and it's only really in the last few years that the area has re-emerged as one of Berlin's most attractive corners. Gendarmenmarkt's origins are prosaic. It was originally home to Berlin's main market until the Gendarme regiment, who gave the square its name (recently readopted after a long GDR-era hiatus as Platz der Akademie), set up their stables on the site. With the departure of the military, Gendarmenmarkt was transformed at the behest of Frederick the Great, who ordered an architectural revamp of the two churches that stood here, in an attempt to mimic the Piazza del Popolo in Rome.

Just a block west of Gendarmenmarkt, along Friedrichstrasse, there's an upmarket shopping district, which, like Potsdamer Platz, was constructed in the last few years, more or less from scratch. It offers the usual chichi stores, along with an eclectic mix of architecture.

The Französischer Dom

The results of Frederick's revamp are impressive, and are at their most eye-catching in the **Französischer Dom** at the northern end of the square. Originally built as a simple place of worship for Berlin's influential Huguenot community at the beginning of the eighteenth century, the building was transformed by the addition of a Baroque tower, turning it into one of Berlin's most appealing churches.

The tower (see below) is purely decorative and not actually consecrated, but it's so striking that a lot of visitors don't actually notice the church proper, the **Französischen Friedrichstadt Kirche** (French Church in Friedrichstadt; Tues–Sat noon–5pm, Sun 11am–5pm), which is so modest in appearance that it looks more like an ancillary building for the tower. The main entrance to the church is at the western end of the Dom, facing Charlottenstrasse. The church, reconsecrated in 1983 after years of restoration work, has a simple hall-like interior with few decorative features and only a plain table as an altar.

The Hugenottenmuseum and Dom Tower

At the base of the tower next door is the entrance to the **Hugenottenmuseum** (Tues–Sat noon–5pm, Sun 11am–5pm; DM3/€1.50, concessions DM1.50/€0.80), detailing the history of the Huguenots in France and Brandenburg. There are sections dealing with the theological background of the Reformation in France, the Revocation of the Edict of Nantes leading to the flight of the Huguenots from their native country, their settling in Berlin, and the influence of the new arrivals on trade, science and literature. The museum also has a short section on the destruction and rebuilding of the Dom.

A longish spiral of steps leads up to the Dom **tower**, which was built some eighty years after the church and only finally put to rights, after wartime damage, in 1987. Here you'll find a balcony (daily 10am–3.30pm; DM3/€1.50, concessions DM2/€1) running around the outside that offers good views of the surrounding construction sites. Another attraction are the tower bells, which ring out automatically every day at noon, 4pm and 7pm – a near deafening experience if you happen to be on the balcony at the time. At other times during the week concerts are performed by bell-ringers – ask for details.

The Deutscher Dom and the Schauspielhaus

At the southern end of the square, the **Deutscher Dom**, built for the city's Lutheran community, is the stylistic twin of the Französischer Dom. The Dom now hosts the "**Questions on German History**" exhibit (Tues–Sun 10am–6pm; free) formerly housed in the Reichstag, which chronicles the political movements and events that have characterized the last two hundred years of German history. The commentary to the rather wordy, document-based exhibition is in German only, but an inexpensive English-language guidebook (DM10/€5.10) is available in the bookstore on the top floor.

Between the two churches on Gendarmenmarkt stands Schinkel's Neoclassical **Schauspielhaus** (now renamed Konzerthaus Berlin).

Dating from 1817, it was built around the ruins of Langhans's burned-out National Theatre, retaining the latter's exterior walls and portico columns. A broad sweep of steps leads up to the main entrance and into an interior of incredible opulence, where chandeliers, marble, gilded plasterwork and pastel-hued wall paintings all compete for attention. Gutted during a raid in 1943, the building suffered further damage during heavy fighting as the Russians attempted to root out SS troops who had dug in here. Reopened in October 1984, it's now the home of the Berlin Symphony Orchestra (see "Live music" in *The arts*). At Christmas 1989 Leonard Bernstein conducted a performance of Beethoven's Ninth Symphony here to celebrate the *Wende*, with the word *Freiheit* ("Freedom") substituted for *Freude* ("Joy") in Schiller's choral finale.

A **statue of Schiller** stands outside the Schauspielhaus. It was repositioned here in 1988, having been removed by the Nazis over fifty years earlier, returned to what was then East Berlin from the West in exchange for reliefs originally from the Pfaueninsel (see p.167) and a statue from a Tiergarten villa. Outside Germany, Friedrich Schiller (1759–1805) is best known for the *Ode to Joy* that provides the words to the final movements of Beethoven's Ninth Symphony, but in his homeland he is venerated as one of the greatest German poets and dramatists of the Enlightenment. His works, from early *Sturm und Drang* dramas like *Die Räuber* ("The Thieves") to later historical plays like *Maria Stuart*, were primarily concerned with freedom – political, moral and personal – which was probably the main reason why the Nazis were so quick to bundle him off Gendarmenmarkt.

Leipziger Strasse and around

From Gendarmenmarkt, Charlottenstrasse continues south to **Leipziger Strasse**, once a main Berlin shopping street running from Alexanderplatz to Potsdamer Platz. For many years Leipziger Strasse was a lifeless housing and commercial development dating from the early 1970s "big is beautiful" phase of East Berlin town planning. The buildings on the south side of the street are higher than those on the north side – at this height they conveniently block off the huge offices of the late **Axel Springer**, extreme right-wing newspaper and publishing magnate (the newspaper *Bild* was his most notorious creation) just over the erstwhile border, which the wily old media mogul had built here to cause maximum irritation to the GDR authorities.

Until the late nineteenth century Leipziger Strasse was a quiet residential area, but by the turn of the twentieth century it had become one of Berlin's foremost shopping streets, with the establishment of Tietz and Wertheim's department stores, and a host of smaller operations and restaurants, including the celebrated Kempinski's. World War II put paid to all that (all three above-men-

tioned concerns were Jewish owned and run and were confiscated
by the Nazis), relegating the street's commercial glory to the history books. Leipziger Strasse is now once again a main route leading
from the heart of Berlin towards the city's West End, as thundering
traffic attests.

The Spittelkolonnaden and around

Virtually nothing remains of prewar Leipziger Strasse. The only
apparent survivor, the Spittelkolonnaden, a semicircular colonnade
on the right towards its eastern end, on the site of what used to be
Donhoffplatz, turns out to be a copy of part of an eighteenth-century structure formerly on the opposite side of the street. In front of
this replica is another copy – this time of a **milepost** that once stood
in the vicinity. A little further along is the **Spittelmarkt**, which marks
the site of a medieval hospital. To the left of the street is the
Spindlerbrunnen, a chocolate-coloured nineteenth-century fountain
that was erected here in 1891. It survived the war by virtue of the fact
that it was removed to the grounds of a suburban hospital in 1927
and only returned to its old site in 1980.

Museum für Kommunikation Berlin

Towards the western end of Leipziger Strasse, at the junction with
Mauerstrasse, is the former Imperial postal ministry, now home to
the **Museum für Kommunikation Berlin** (Tues–Fri 9am–5pm, Sat
& Sun 11am–7pm; *www.museumsstiftung.de*; free; U-Bahn
Mohrenstrasse). The museum traces its roots back to the world's
first postal museum, which opened in Berlin in 1872 and moved
into this Baroque palace to share space with the postal ministry in
1898. When the building was damaged in the war the collection dispersed, and only after reunification and several years of renovation
could it reopen in its historic home in March 2000. There's a lot
more here than just stamps, and if you have a keen interest in the
gadgets and devices that led us to the world of the Internet, you
should have a look. The interior itself, ornate Wilhelmine detailing
around a wonderful, light-filled central court, is worth checking out
too.

Checkpoint Charlie – and the legacy of the Wall

Erected overnight on August 13, 1961, to cordon off the Soviet sector and corral the British, American and French sectors of the city
some 200km inside the GDR, the **Berlin Wall** underlined the city's
schizophrenia and frenzy and for a generation marked the city's *rai-
son d'être* – the "stabilization of the impossible". Late in 1989 the
East German government, spurred by Gorbachev's *glasnost* and
confronted by a tense domestic climate, realized it could keep the
impossible stable no longer. To an initially disbelieving and then jubi-
lant Europe, travel restrictions for GDR citizens were lifted on

November 9, 1989 – effectively, the Wall had ceased to matter, and pictures of Berliners, East and West, hacking away at the detested symbol filled newspapers and TV bulletins around the world. Now the Wall has almost entirely vanished, and the few sections that remain are protected from the tourist chisels by barbed wire and by its official status as a "historic landmark".

A couple of hundred metres south of the Leipziger Strasse-Friedrichstrasse intersection is the site of **Checkpoint Charlie**, one of the most famous names associated with the Wall and Cold War-era Berlin. This allied military post on Friedrichstrasse marked the border between East and West Berlin until July 1990, when it was removed. It can now be seen in the Allied Museum (see p.157), although a replica has been installed at the original site. While it stood it was one of Berlin's more celebrated landmarks and the building lent its name informally to the adjacent GDR border crossing (official title Grenzübergang Friedrichstrasse), which, with its dramatic "YOU ARE NOW LEAVING THE AMERICAN SECTOR" signs and unsmiling border guards, used to be the archetypal movie-style Iron Curtain crossing. In the Cold War years it was the scene of repeated border incidents, including a stand-off between American and Soviet forces in October 1961, which culminated in tanks from both sides growling at each other for a few days.

The site of the border crossing itself is hardly recognizable now. The extensive **border installations** were torn down in 1991, having stood derelict since the spring of the previous year, and in their place an impromptu coach park set up. A high-profile complex of office buildings and retail shops called the American Business Center – part of it designed by American architect Philip Johnson – has gone up on the western side of Friedrichstrasse. All that remains of the border crossing is a former guard tower, now designated a historic monument.

The Museum Haus am Checkpoint Charlie

For tangible evidence of the trauma of the Wall, head for the **Museum Haus am Checkpoint Charlie** at Friedrichstr. 44 (daily 9am–10pm; DM8/€4.10, concessions DM5/€2.50; *museum-haus-am-.checkpointcharlie.org*; nearest U-Bahn Kochstrasse or bus #129). Here the history of the Wall is told in photos of escape tunnels and with the home-made aircraft and converted cars by which people attempted, succeeded, and sometimes tragically failed to break through the border. Films document the stories of some of the 230-odd people murdered by the East German border guards, and there's a section on human rights behind the Iron Curtain, but it's a scruffy, rather dated collection, and not quite the harrowing experience that some visitors seem to expect. For more details, pick up a copy of *It Happened at the Wall* or *The Wall Speaks*, both on sale here.

The Wall – some history

After the war, Berlin was split among its conquerors, as Stalin, Roosevelt and Churchill had agreed at Yalta. Each sector was administered by the relevant country, and was supposed to exist peacefully with its neighbours under a unified city council. But almost from the outset, antagonism between the Soviet and other sectors was high. Only three years after the war ended, the Soviet forces closed down the land access corridors to the city from the Western zones in what became known as the **Berlin Blockade**: it was successfully overcome by a massive Western **airlift** of food and supplies that lasted nearly a year. This, followed by the 1953 uprising, large-scale cross-border emigration (between 1949 and 1961, the year the Wall was built, when over three million East Germans fled to the Federal Republic – almost a fifth of the population) and innumerable "incidents", led to the building of what was known in the GDR as the "anti-Fascist protection wall".

When the four powers were deciding on sectors, one of the parish maps of Greater Berlin from 1920 was used to delineate them: the Wall followed the Soviet sector boundary implacably, cutting through houses, across squares and rivers with its own cool illogicality. An oddity of the Wall was that it was built a few metres inside GDR territory; the West Berlin authorities therefore had little control over the **graffiti** that covered it. The Wall was an ever-changing mixture of colours and slogans, with occasional bursts of bitterness: *"My friends are dying behind you"*; humour: *"Why not jump over and join the Party?"*; and stupidity: *"We shoulda nuked 'em in 45"*.

Over the years, at least two hundred people were **killed** endeavouring to cross the Wall. Initial escape attempts were straightforward, and often successful – hollowing out furniture, ramming checkpoint barriers and simple disguise brought many people over. However, the authorities quickly rose to the challenge, and would-be escapees became more resourceful, digging tunnels, and constructing gliders, one-man submarines and hot-air balloons. By the time the Wall came down, every escape method conceivable seemed to have been used – even down to passing through Checkpoint Charlie in the stomach of a pantomime cow – and those desperate to get out of the GDR preferred the long wait and complications of applying to leave officially to the risk of being gunned down by a border guard. The guards, known as Grepos, were under instructions to shoot anyone attempting to scale the Wall, and to shoot accurately: any guard suspected of deliberately missing was court-martialled, and his family could expect severe harassment from the authorities.

When the end came, it happened so quickly that Berliners, East and West, seemed not to believe it; but within days of the announcement that citizens of the GDR were free to travel, enterprising characters were renting out hammers and chisels so that souvenir hunters could take home their own chip of the Wall. Today, especially in the city centre, it's barely possible to tell exactly where the Wall ran: odd juxtapositions of dereliction against modernity, an unexpected swathe of erstwhile "Death Strip", are in most cases all that's left of one of the most hated borders the world ever knew.

One sad postscript to the story of the Wall hit the headlines in spring 1992. Two former **border guards** were tried for the murder of Chris Gueffroy, shot dead while illegally trying to cross the border at Neukölln in February 1989. Under the GDR government the guards had been treated to a meal by their superiors and given extra holiday for their patriotic actions; under the new regime, they received sentences for murder – while those ultimately responsible, the former leaders of the GDR, evaded punishment.

South of
Unter den
Linden

CENTRAL BERLIN

North of Unter den Linden

Heading north of Unter den Linden along Friedrichstrasse itself takes you towards Bahnhof Friedrichstrasse, once the biggest border crossing point for East Berlin-bound travellers. Before the war, Friedrichstrasse was a well-known prostitutes' haunt, lined by cafés, bars and restaurants. Nazi puritanism dealt the first blow to this thriving Vergnügungsviertel (Pleasure Quarter), and the work was finished by Allied bombers, which effectively razed the street. The destruction caused by bombing widened Friedrichstrasse considerably, turning what had once been a narrow, slightly claustrophobic street into a broad, desolate road that offered many visitors a first, uninspiring impression of East Berlin. Friedrichstrasse has now slipped back into its north–south axis role, though the stretch above the train station still seems lifeless when compared to the development south of Unter den Linden.

Around Bahnhof Friedrichstrasse

Just before the train station on Friedrichstrasse is a symbol of Honecker-era East Berlin in the shape of the Japanese-built **Internationales Handelszentrum**, a 93.5-metre-high piece of self-consciously modernist architecture whose main purpose was to show that West Berlin didn't have a monopoly on thrusting, com-

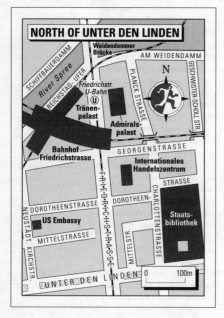

mercial dynamism. The station itself, once a tangle of checkpoints and guard posts, has been renovated and outfitted with a shopping arcade. Under the tracks to the east of the station, beside the Handelszentrum, is a delightful antiques market with a fascinating assemblage of old art, jewellery, books and curios.

Bahnhof Friedrichstrasse

Before the *Wende*, **Bahnhof Friedrichstrasse**, as one of the main border crossing points for Western visitors to East Berlin, was probably the most heavily guarded train station in Europe. There was always a regular flow of mainline and S-Bahn traffic between Friedrichstrasse and Zoo Station in West Berlin (except during the Berlin Blockade of 1948–49, see p.138), but until late 1989 the East German government did all it could to keep its own citizens from joining it. Customs and passport controls and, more discreetly, armed guards separated westbound platforms from the rest of the station.

The Tränenpalast

Between Bahnhof Friedrichstrasse itself and the River Spree is a glass and concrete construction that was, until 1990, the **border crossing entrance** for westbound travellers, with an estimated eight million people passing through its doors each year. Known as the Tränenpalast or "Palace of Tears", this is now a concert venue but during the days when the Berlin Wall was a very real barrier, visitors and tourists – and occasionally East German citizens who had been granted exit visas – queued inside to get through passport and customs controls before travelling by U- or S-Bahn to West Berlin.

Visitors to the East had to return to the West by midnight, and the functional entrance to the Tränenpalast was the scene of many a poignant farewell as people took leave of relatives, friends and lovers here. Within, a few reminders of its old role survive, including a cubicle with blackened glass windows overlooking the main hall, from which border guards watched those leaving the country.

Between the wars the site now occupied by the Tränenpalast was an unsightly vacant lot and, before the Nazis came to power, an architectural competition was held in search of a suitable design for a building to fill it. Some incredibly imaginative – and improbable – proposals were submitted, many of which were way ahead of their time. One entrant was Mies van der Rohe, who proposed an immense, tricornered glass and steel tower. History overtook the various proposals and the space remained unused until the construction of the Wall set the seal on the division of Berlin.

North of the station

Back on Friedrichstrasse, just north of the rail bridge, on the right at no. 101, is the Jugendstil **Admiralspalast**, a rare prewar survivor originally built as a variety theatre in 1910. Amid the predominantly concrete architecture of the immediate area, its partly gilded facade, divided by fluted columns and inset with bas-reliefs, comes as a real surprise. As one of the few buildings in the area to have survived the bombing, it became an important political meeting hall in the immediate postwar years and on April 22 and 23, 1946, was the venue for the forced union of the social democratic SPD with the prewar Communist Party, the KPD. This resulted in the birth of the SED (Sozialistische Einheitspartei Deutschlands), the GDR communist party that controlled the country until March 1990. The building houses Die Distel theatre, a satirical cabaret whose occasionally daring performances highlighted the paradoxes and frustrations of the pre-*Wende* GDR and provided Western journalists with good intro paragraphs for state-of-the-nation pieces in the autumn of 1989.

Chapter 3

Schlossplatz and the Museum Island

At the eastern end of Unter den Linden the Schlossbrücke leads onto **Schlossplatz** and the island in the middle of the River Spree that formed the core of the medieval twin town of Berlin-Cölln. By virtue of its defensive position, this island later became the site of the Hohenzollern *Residenz* – location of the fortress-cum-palace and church of the family who controlled Berlin and Brandenburg from the fifteenth century onwards. Centred roughly around present-day Schlossplatz, this was originally a martial, fortified affair, as much for protection from the perennially rebellious Berliners as from outside enemies, but over the years domestic stability resulted in the reshaping of the *Residenz* on a slightly more decorative basis. With the consolidation of their authority during the nineteenth century and the rise of Brandenburg-Prussia to great power, the Hohenzollerns decided it was time to add a museum quarter to their increasingly bombastic capital. This was duly done, over eighty years or so, on the northern tongue of the mid-Spree island, an area which became known as the Museumsinsel or **Museum Island**.

A few of the world's greatest museums reside here: the **Pergamonmuseum**, with a jaw-dropping collection of antiquities, the **Altes Museum**, with its selection of superlative Greek vases, and the **Altes Nationalgalerie**, boasting a world-class assortment of nineteenth-century European paintings. Perhaps it was to bask in the reflected glory of such cultural monuments that the GDR government felt impelled to build its most important civic buildings, the **Palast der Republik** and the **Staatsrat** nearby.

Schlossplatz and around

Schlossplatz (known as Marx-Engels-Platz until 1994) is reached from Unter den Linden via Schinkel's **Schlossbrücke**. When it was

CENTRAL BERLIN

opened on November 28, 1823, the bridge was not fully completed, lacking among other things a fixed balustrade, and 22 people drowned when temporary wooden barriers collapsed. Eventually cast-iron balustrades were installed, featuring graceful dolphin, merman and seahorse motifs designed by Schinkel. The very pristine-looking Classical statues of warriors and winged figures lining each side of the bridge represent scenes from ancient Greek mythology and earned the bridge the popular epithet of Puppenbrücke or "Puppet Bridge". Once wartime bombing started they were removed for safekeeping; after the division of the city they ended up in West Berlin, and were only returned to the East in 1981.

Schlossplatz

Beyond the bridge is **Schlossplatz** itself, former site of the Berliner Schloss, the old Imperial Palace, the remains of which were demolished by the communists after the war, and which, along with the Berliner Dom (see p.83), formed the Imperial *Residenz*. Work began on the palace in 1443 and the Hohenzollern family were to live there for nearly half a millennium. Over the centuries the Schloss was constantly extended and reshaped, the first major overhaul coming in the sixteenth century when it was transformed from a fortress into a Renaissance palace. Later it received a Baroque restyling, and subsequently virtually every German architect of note, including Schlüter, Schinkel and Schadow, was given the opportunity to add to it. For centuries the Schloss dominated the heart of Berlin, and until the 1930s no city centre building was allowed to stand any higher.

On November 9, 1918, the end of the Hohenzollern era came when Karl Liebknecht proclaimed a "Free Socialist Republic" from one of the palace balconies (now preserved in the facade of the Staatsrat building, see below), following the abdication of the Kaiser. Almost simultaneously the Social Democrat Phillip Scheidemann was proclaiming a democratic German republic from the Reichstag, and it was in fact the latter that prevailed, ushering in the pathologically unstable Weimar Republic of the 1920s.

After the war the Schloss, as a symbol of the still recent Imperial past, was an embarrassment to the SED authorities and they ordered the dynamiting of its ruins in 1950, despite the fact that it was no more badly damaged than a number of other structures subsequently rebuilt. Today the Berliner Schloss can only be appreciated in photographs and there is, predictably, great nostalgia for it, with some even calling for it to be re-created – despite the fact that its piecemeal construction and bombastic architectural style made it a rather unattractive building. Notwithstanding, during the summers of 1993 and 1994 the pro-Schloss lobby erected a spectacular scaffolding and canvas replica of the building here, to mobilize public support for their aims. Tepid response and a lack of money have put the project on the back burner.

The Palast der Republik

It was no coincidence that the GDR authorities chose the space formerly occupied by the Schloss for their **Palast der Republik**, which was built on the southeastern side of Schlossplatz during the early 1970s to house the Volkskammer, the GDR's parliament. Irreverently dubbed "Ballast der Republik", this huge angular building with its bronzed, reflecting windows was completed in less than a thousand days, and was a source of great pride to the Honecker regime. As well as the former Volkskammer, it also housed an entertainment complex, including restaurants, cafés, a theatre and a bowling alley. The interior is a masterpiece of tastelessness and the hundreds of lamps hanging from the ceiling of the main foyer gave rise to its other nickname, Erichs Lampenladen – "Erich's lamp shop". Shortly before unification an asbestos hazard was discovered in the building, and following October 3, 1990, it was closed indefinitely. Today it stands empty, an unmissable reminder of the old GDR and an embarrassment to the new Germany, its future – indeed its existence – uncertain.

The Staatsrat and Neue Marstall

A slightly less jarring reminder of the GDR is the former **Staatsrat**, or State Council, on the southern side of Schlossplatz, an early 1960s building with some stylistic affinities to the *Zuckerbäcker* architecture of the Stalin era. It's enhanced by the inclusion in its facade of a big chunk of the Berliner Schloss, notably the balcony from which Karl Liebknecht proclaimed the German revolution in 1918. Immediately to the east of the Staatsrat is the **Neue Marstall**, an

unimaginative turn-of-the-century construction, built to house the
hundreds of royal coaches and horses used to ferry the royal household around the city.

From this building revolutionary sailors and Spartacists beat off
government forces during the November Revolution of 1918, when
the building was headquarters of the revolutionary committee. A
couple of plaques commemorate this deed of rebellious derring-do
and Liebknecht's proclamation of the socialist republic. One shows
Liebknecht apparently suspended above a cheering crowd of sailors
and civilians, while the other, to the left of the entrance, has the head
of Marx hovering over some excited but purposeful-looking members of the proletariat. Just behind the Neue Marstall, at Breite
Strasse 25, is the delicately gabled **Ribbeckhaus**, a late-Renaissance
palace from the seventeenth century that's one of the city's oldest
surviving buildings. It now houses a part of Berlin's city library.

The Berliner Dom

On the northern side of Karl-Liebknecht-Strasse, opposite the Palast
der Republik, is a hulking symbol of Imperial Germany that managed
to survive the GDR era. The **Berliner Dom** (April–Sept Mon–Sat
9am–8pm, Sun noon–8pm; Oct–March Mon–Sat 9am–7pm, Sun
noon–7pm; DM5/€2.50, concessions DM3/€1.50) was built at the
turn of the twentieth century on the site of a more modest cathedral,
as a grand royal church for the Hohenzollern family. Fussily ornate
with a huge dome flanked by four smaller ones, its appearance was
meant to echo that of St Peter's in Rome, but somehow it comes
across as little more than a dowdy Neo-Baroque imitation.

The Berliner Dom served the House of Hohenzollern as a family
church until 1918, and its vault houses ninety sarcophagi containing
the remains of various members of the line. The building was badly
damaged during the war, but has undergone a long period of reconstruction, leaving it looking like a simpler version of its prewar self,
with various ornamental cupolas missing from the newly rounded-off
domes.

The main entrance leads into the extravagantly overstated
Predigtkirche, the octagonal main body of the church. From the
marbled pillars of the hall to the delicate plasterwork and gilt of the
cupola, there's a sense that it's all meant to reflect Hohenzollern
power rather than serve as a place of worship. As if to confirm this
impression six opulent Hohenzollern sarcophagi, including those
of Great Elector Wilhelm I, and his second wife, Dorothea, are
housed in galleries at the northern and southern ends of the
Predigtkirche. The spiritual underpinnings of the society they ruled
are less ostentatiously represented by statues of Luther,
Melanchthon, Calvin and Zwingli, along with four German princes
favourable to the Reformation, in the cornices above the pillars in
the main hall.

For an overhead view of all this, head for the **Kaiserliches
Treppenhaus** (Imperial Staircase), a grandiose marble staircase at
the southwest corner of the building, which leads past pleasantly
washed-out paintings of biblical scenes to a balcony looking out onto
the Predigtkirche. Here you'll also find a small exhibition on the history of the building. To the south of the Predigtkirche is the restored
Tauf- and Traukirche. At first sight this appears to be a marbled
souvenir shop, but it is in fact a side chapel used for baptism and
confirmation ceremonies.

The Lustgarten

Adjacent to the Dom is the **Lustgarten**, originally a garden built by
the Great Elector, and later turned into a parade ground by King
Friedrich Wilhelm I, Prussia's "Soldier-King", as part of his general
attempt to transform the city into a vast barracks. In 1942 resistance
fighters under the Jewish communist Herbert Baum set fire to an
anticommunist exhibition that was being held here, an action that
cost them their lives. It is commemorated by a stone cube on the
square which, despite the inscription "forever bound in friendship
with the Soviet Union", still attracts wreath-layers. At the northern
end of the square, at the foot of the steps leading up to the Altes
Museum (see p.87), is what looks like a large granite saucer. This
was carved from a huge glacier-deposited boulder found near
Fürstenwalde, just outside Berlin.

The Museum Island

Northwest of Schlossplatz, extending peninsula-like from the square,
is an area known as the **Museum Island** (Museumsinsel), location of
eastern Berlin's most important museums: the **Pergamonmuseum**,
the **Altes Museum**, the **Alte Nationalgalerie** and the **Bodemuseum**.
Their origins go back to 1810, when King Friedrich Wilhelm III
decided Berlin needed a museum to house the then rather scant collection of royal treasures. He ordered the reclamation of a patch of
Spree-side marsh and commissioned Schinkel to come up with a suitable building – the Altes Museum at the head of the Lustgarten.

Things really started to take off when German explorers and
archeologists began plundering the archeological sites of Egypt and
Asia Minor. The booty brought back from Egypt by the Egyptologist
Carl Richard Lepsius during the 1840s formed the core of what was
to become a huge collection, and the **Neues Museum** was built to
house it at the behest of King Friedrich Wilhelm IV. Later in the century the Imperial haul was augmented by treasures brought from
Turkey by Heinrich Schliemann, for which the vast
Pergamonmuseum was constructed.

During World War II the contents of the museums were stashed
away in bunkers and mine shafts for protection from bombing, and

in the confusion of 1945 and the immediate postwar years it proved difficult to recover the scattered exhibits. Some had been destroyed, others ended up in museums in the Western sector and others disappeared to the East with the Red Army. Gradually, though, the various pieces were tracked down and eventually most of what had survived was returned to the Museum Island, which has become a major Berlin tourist draw.

Unification has brought the opportunity – and confusion – of bringing together long-divided collections. Thus, for several years, while art works are reshuffled and galleries renovated, some museums will be closed and various collections inaccessible (see box below).

Visiting the museums

Entry to either the Pergamonmuseum or Altes Museum costs DM8 (€4.10), concessions DM4 (€2.05), and, on the same day, the ticket is valid for entry to any other state museum. Alternatively, the "three-day tourist ticket" allows entry to all of Berlin's state museums (see *Introducing the city*, p.46). Entry is free on the first Sunday of every month. Most exhibits are in German only, although some collections do provide explanations and information sheets in English. For the Pergamon, an English-language audio tour is included in the entry price. Note that all the museums are **closed** on Monday.

The nearest U- and S-Bahn station to the Museum Island is Friedrichstrasse; buses #100, #157 and #348 also pass nearby.

The new-look Museum Island

An ambitious plan is currently in progress to **restructure and renovate** Museum Island, which, by 2010, will result in one of the world's great museum complexes. In December 2001 the **Alte Nationalgalerie** will reopen as home to the city's collection of nineteenth-century European paintings, including the Galerie der Romantik currently housed at Schloss Charlottenburg. This will be followed in 2002 by the closure of the **Altes Museum** until 2005, when it will reopen with the collection of Greek and Roman art from the Department of Antiquities in the Pergamon. In October 2005 the **Bodemuseum** is also scheduled to reopen, with the Sculpture Collection and the Museum of Byzantine Art. The **Neues Museum**, a ruin since the war, is being renovated to accommodate the Egyptian Museum and the Museum for Pre- and Early History, both of which are currently residing in Charlottenburg – it's due to open in 2008. And finally the **Pergamonmuseum** will close sometime after 2005 and reopen five years later with its collections – Near Eastern Antiquities, Antiquities and Islamic Art – reunited and reordered, and its courtyard roofed over to allow for large architectural pieces.

In addition, the plans call for an interior corridor that will connect all the buildings on Museum Island, a central entrance to the island with its own exhibition space, and the removal of offices and workshops currently contained in the museums themselves, to a new structure across the street from the island.

The Pergamonmuseum

The **Pergamonmuseum** (Tues–Sun 10am–6pm; *www.smb
.spk-berlin.de*; DM8/€4.09, concessions DM4/€2.05; U-Bahn
Friedrichstrasse) is accessible from Am Kupfergraben on the south
bank of the River Spree. It's a massive structure, built in the early
part of this century in the style of a Babylonian temple, to house the
treasure trove of the German archeologists who were busy plundering the ancient world, packaging it up and sending it back to Berlin.

Department of Antiquities

The museum is divided into three sections, the most important of
which, the **Department of Antiquities** on the main floor, contains
the **Pergamon Altar**. A huge structure dedicated to Zeus and Athena,
dating from 180 to 160 BC, it was unearthed at Bergama in western
Turkey by the archeologist Carl Humann and brought to Berlin in
1903. The **frieze** shows a battle between the gods and giants and is
a tremendously forceful piece of work, with powerfully depicted figures writhing in a mass of sinew and muscle. To the rear of the Altar
is the **Telephos Frieze**, another amazing Pergamon find, which originally adorned the interior of the Pergamon Altar; its depiction of the
life story of Telephos, the legendary founder of Pergamon, is a bit
more sedate. The section also contains other pieces of Hellenistic
and classical architecture, including the two-storey **market gate**
from the Turkish town of Miletus. Built by the Romans in 120 AD, the
gate was destroyed by an earthquake just under a thousand years
later and brought to Berlin in fragmentary form for reconstruction
during the nineteenth century.

The Middle Eastern Section

The **Middle Eastern Section**, also on the main floor, has items going
back four thousand years to Babylonian times. The collection
includes the enormous **Ishtar Gate**, the **Processional Way** and the
facade of the **Throne Room** from Babylon, all of which date from the
reign of Nebuchadnezzar II in the sixth century BC. While it's impossible not to be awed by the size and remarkable state of preservation
of the deep-blue enamelled bricks of the Babylon finds, it's as well to
remember that much of what you see is a mock-up, built around the
original finds. Look out for the weird mythical creatures that adorn
the Ishtar Gate, and check the small model of the whole structure to
get some idea of its enormous scale.

The Islamic Section

Pride of place in the museum's **Islamic Section** goes to the relief-
decorated facade of a Jordanian **Prince's Palace** at Mshatta, from
743 AD, presented to Kaiser Wilhelm II by the sultan of Turkey. On
a slightly more modest scale is a thirteenth-century **prayer niche**

decorated with turquoise, black and gold tiles, from a mosque in Asia Minor. Also worth seeking out is the **Aleppo Room**, a reception chamber with carved wooden wall decorations, reassembled in Berlin after being removed from a merchant's house in present-day Syria. The section is also home to a host of smaller but no less impressive exhibits from Arabia and Persia, including carpets, ceramics, leatherwork, and wooden and ivory carvings.

The Alte Nationalgalerie

Roughly behind the Pergamonmuseum and Neues Museum is the **Alte Nationalgalerie** (Tues–Sun 10am–6pm; *www.smb.spk-berlin .de*; DM8/€4.09, concessions DM4/€2.05), a slightly exaggerated example of post-Schinkel Neoclassicism that contains the nineteenth-century section of Berlin's state art collection. The main body of the museum is a colonnaded, temple-like structure raised above the lower block where the main entrance is situated. A double flight of stairs leads up either side of the entrance to an equestrian statue of King Friedrich Wilhelm IV, commemorating his role in expanding the Museum Island during the mid-nineteenth century.

The museum is closed for renovations until December 2001. Highlights from its collection are currently on display at the neighbouring Altes Museum. It's worth taking a peek at the building, though, a grandiose interpretation of a Corinthian temple, built in 1876 and placed atop a huge pediment fronted by a statue of its royal patron, Friedrich Wilhelm IV. Subtle it's not. There's a pleasant little lawn in front punctuated by several sculptures, including *Centaur and Nymph* by Reinhold Begas, dating from around 1888, and Louis Tuaillon's 1895 *Amazon*.

The Altes Museum

At the head of the Lustgarten the **Altes Museum** (Tues–Sun 10am–6pm; *www.smb.spk-berlin.de*; DM8/€4.09, concessions DM4/€2.05; U-Bahn Friedrichstrasse) is perhaps Schinkel's most impressive surviving work, with an 87-metre-high facade fronted by an eighteen-column Ionic colonnade. Along with the Schauspielhaus (see p.73), this is one of Berlin's most striking Neoclassical buildings. Originally opened as a home for the royal collection of paintings in 1830, the Altes Museum is now host to highlights from the Alte Nationalgalerie's nineteenth-century art collection, as well as the Collection of Classical Antiquities.

Particularly noteworthy among the **Alte Nationalgalerie's collection** are several works of the "German Romans", mid-nineteenth-century artists like Anselm Feuerbach and Arnold Böcklin, who spent much of their working lives in Italy – Böcklin's eerie, dreamlike *Isle of the Dead* retains its power even today. A highlight of this school is the Casa Bartholdy **frescoes**, softly illuminated paintings by Peter

Cornelius, Wilhelm Veit and others that illustrate the story of Joseph. The broad canvases of Adoph von Menzel strike a rather different note: though chiefly known during his lifetime for his detailed depictions of court life under Frederick the Great, it's his interpretations of Berlin on the verge of the industrial age, such as *The Iron Foundry*, that make more interesting viewing today. Also on hand are several rooms containing **Impressionist** works by van Gogh, Degas, Monet and native son Max Liebermann, plus statues by Rodin.

One floor below is a permanent installation of objects from the **Collection of Classical Antiquities**, small sculpture and pottery from the city's famed Greek and Roman collections. These small works perhaps lack the power and drama of the huge pieces on view at the Pergamon, but there are some captivating items well presented here: *The Praying Boy*, a lithe and delicate bronze sculpture from Rhodes dating back to 300 BC, is the collection's pride and joy. Look too for the vase of Euphronios, decorated with an intimate painting of athletes in preparation – the series of Greek vases here is considered to be among the finest in the world. The Rotunda, filled with soft natural light and encircled by statues of Greek and Roman gods, forms an impressive centerpiece to the exhibition and can be visited free of charge.

The Bodemuseum

At the northeastern tip of the Museumsinsel is the **Bodemuseum**, housed in an intimidating, turn-of-the-century Neo-Baroque building. It is also presently closed (see p.85), but when restored, the impressive building will house the **Sculpture Collection**, an excellent, chiefly German collection of sculpture particularly authoritative in its sections detailing the Middle Ages – including work by the masters Tilman Riemenschneider, Nicolaus Gerhaert, Michael Erhart and Hans Multscher. Also finding a home here will be the **Museum for Byzantine Art**, with an extensive range of objects, mainly religious in nature, from the pre-medieval eastern Mediterranean.

The Neues Museum

Between the Altes Museum and the Pergamonmuseum is the **Neues Museum**, originally built to house the Egyptian Collection. Bombed out in the war, the building is slowly being rebuilt and is scheduled to open in 2008 as the new home of the Egyptian Museum and the Museum for Pre- and Early History.

Chapter 4

Alexanderplatz and around

Alexanderplatz, dominated by a huge TV tower and furnished almost exclusively in concrete, is an unmistakable product of the old East Germany. During East Berlin's forty-year existence, while Unter den Linden was allowed to represent the glories of past Berlin, Alexanderplatz and its environs were meant to represent the glories of a modern socialist capital city. It's hard to imagine, though, that the concrete gigantism of the GDR era will wear as well as the efforts of Schinkel and his contemporaries. This is one part of town where there's little point in trying to spot what remains of prewar Berlin by looking at old photos. Elsewhere at least a few buildings have made it through to the postwar period, but around Alexanderplatz there's almost no trace of the buildings that stood here before 1945. Whole streets have vanished – the open area around the base of the **TV tower**, for example, used to be a dense network of inner-city streets – and today only a few survivors like the **Marienkirche** and **Rotes Rathaus** remain standing amid the modernity.

This is not to say that Alexanderplatz should be passed up. If you can let your sensibilities take a back seat, it's worth exploring not only the area's handful of historic buildings but also the ugly East

---

The Berlin that never was

As you survey what has replaced the destroyed city centre around Alexanderplatz, ponder on a couple of paths that history nearly took: one school of thought considered that Berlin in 1945 was simply not worth rebuilding, and proposed to build a **new Berlin** from scratch, 60km away, as had been done at Stalingrad. More disturbing, though, was the wartime plan by the Allies to drop **anthrax bombs** on the city, which would have killed all the inhabitants but left the buildings standing. Had this happened, it would now be possible (presumably having donned protective gear) to wander the streets of a ghost city, completely unchanged since the day the bomb dropped.

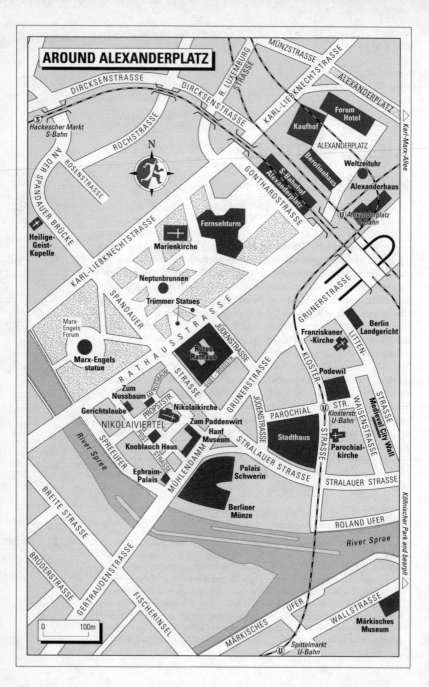

AROUND ALEXANDERPLATZ

MÜNZSTRASSE

DIRCKSENSTRASSE

DIRCKSENSTRASSE

R. LUXEMBURG STRASSE

KARL-LIEBKNECHTSTRASSE

ALEXANDERPLATZ

Karl-Marx-Allee

Hackescher Markt S-Bahn

ROCHSTRASSE

AN DER SPANDAUER BRÜCKE

ROSENSTRASSE

Forum Hotel

Kaufhof

ALEXANDERPLATZ

Berolinahaus

Weltzeituhr

S-Bahnhof Alexanderplatz

GONTHARDSTRASSE

Alexanderhaus

N

Alexanderplatz U-Bahn

Heilige-Geist-Kapelle

KARL-LIEBKNECHTSTRASSE

Fernsehturm

Marienkirche

SPANDAUER

Neptunbrunnen

Trümmer Statues

STRASSE

GRUNERSTRASSE

LITTEN-

Berlin Landgericht

Marx-Engels Forum

Marx-Engels statue

RATHAUSSTRASSE

RATHAUSSTRASSE

JÜDENSTRASSE

Rotes Rathaus

BUSI-BOSSSTR.

Franziskaner-Kirche

Podewil

KLOSTER-

GRUNERSTRASSE

STRASSE

WAISENSTRASSE

Medieval City Wall

Zum Nussbaum

RATHAUSMUSEUM

PROPSTSTR.

Gerichtslaube

Nikolaikirche

NIKOLAIVIERTEL

POST STRASSE

Zum Paddenwirt

Hanf Museum

JÜDENSTRASSE

PAROCHIAL

Stadthaus

STR.

Klosterstr. U-Bahn

Parochialkirche

STRALAUER STRASSE

River Spree

SPREEUFER

Knoblauch Haus

MÜHLENDAMM

Ephraim-Palais

Palais Schwerin

STRALAUER STRASSE

Berliner Münze

BREITE STRASSE

ROLAND UFER

River Spree

Köllnischer Park and bearpit

BRÜDERSTRASSE

GERTRAUDENSTRASSE

FISCHERINSEL

0   100m

MÄRKISCHES   UFER

WALLSTRASSE

Märkisches Museum

Spittelmarkt U-Bahn

German creations that have their own place in Berlin's architectural chronology.

If it all gets too much, relief from the concrete is on hand in the nearby **Nikolaiviertel**, an attempt to re-create the destroyed medieval heart of Berlin; and also in the area to the immediate east, which has a clutch of secluded old buildings and a stretch of Berlin's first wall – built to keep people out rather than in. Also close by are a few interesting museums, detailing the history of the city itself.

Marx-Engels-Forum to Alexanderplatz

CENTRAL BERLIN

Despite its apparent concrete aridity, this area has some rewarding corners. Most of the attractions are of GDR vintage, foremost among them being the gargantuan TV tower or **Fernsehturm** and Alexanderplatz itself. Surprisingly, one or two older landmarks have managed to cling to life amid the brutalist modernity, including the city's oldest church, the medieval **Marienkirche**, and the nineteenth-century **Rotes Rathaus**, now once again seat of Berlin's civic administration. The route to Alexanderplatz from Schlossplatz leads up **Karl-Liebknecht-Strasse**, a busy street of shops and restaurants.

Around the Marx-Engels-Forum

On the right-hand side of Karl-Liebknecht-Strasse, opposite the *Radisson SAS Hotel*, is the **Marx-Engels-Forum**, a severely well-ordered patch of city-centre greenery. At its heart sits a lumpen bronze representation of the founders of the "scientific world view of the working class", as pre-*Wende* guidebooks used to refer to Karl Marx and Friedrich Engels. Facing the monument are eight steel pillars bearing photogravure images of uplifting scenes from Soviet and East German life and events from various revolutionary struggles. These have been partly vandalized, and someone has made a determined effort to scratch out the face of Erich Honecker on one of them. Nearby are blurred bronze reliefs of men and women doing nothing in particular, and between the Marx-Engels statue and the Palast der Republik are similarly unclear stone reliefs showing muscular men standing around.

Heilige-Geist-Kapelle and Hackescher Markt Station

Just beyond the *Radisson*, it's worth taking a quick walk north along Spandauer Strasse, once one of the city's more important streets, though almost all its historic buildings were destroyed during the war. One of the few exceptions, a little way along on the left, is the quaintly incongruous fourteenth-century **Heilige-Geist-Kapelle**. Today this red-brick Gothic edifice is dwarfed by a larger, newer building (originally a trade school, now part of Humboldt

Universität) that was grafted onto it at the turn of the twentieth century. The original interior has not survived, and in many ways it's a
miracle the chapel is still standing: during the course of the last six
hundred years, it has survived a huge city fire in 1380, the enor-
mously destructive explosion of a nearby gunpowder magazine in
1720, and, above all, wartime bombing.

At its northern end Spandauer Strasse turns into An der Spandauer
Brücke. Nearby is **Hackescher Markt S-Bahn station**, a nineteenth-
century construction retaining its original red-tile facade, with mosaic decorative elements and rounded windows typical of the period.
It's now a protected building and its architectural features are best
appreciated by walking through the station itself and taking a look at
the northern facade. On both sides you'll see that the arches under
the S-Bahn tracks have now been renovated to house trendy restaurants, bars, and clothes shops. The station has undergone several
name changes this century. Until the *Wende* it was called S-Bahnhof
Marx-Engels-Platz: before the war it was known as Bahnhof Börse,
thanks to its proximity to Berlin's long-since-vanished Stock
Exchange. This stood behind the Humboldt Universität building on
Spandauer Strasse (the site is now occupied by the *Radisson*), was
gutted during the war and suffered an unlikely fate: it was demolished and its granite blocks were used to build the panorama wall of
East Berlin's zoo, behind the polar bear enclosure.

The Neptunbrunnen

Returning to Karl-Liebknecht-Strasse, head east past the Polish and
Hungarian cultural centres (full of folksy tack). Roughly opposite
these, on the other side of the street, is a large open space on which
stands the **Neptunbrunnen**, an extravagantly imaginative fountain
incorporating a statue of a trident-wielding Neptune sitting on a
shell. A serpent, seal and alligator spray the god of the sea with
water, and he is supported by strange fish and eel-draped aquatic
centaurs with webbed feet instead of hooves. Around the rim of the
fountain sit four female courtiers, symbolizing what were at the time
the four most important German rivers: the Rhine, the Vistula, the
Oder and the Elbe. The statue was built in 1891 and originally positioned on the Schlossplatz.

The Marienkirche

To the north of the Neptunbrunnen is the **Marienkirche** (Mon–Thurs
10am–4pm, Sat & Sun noon–4pm; free; U- & S-Bahn Alexanderplatz
or bus #100, #157, #200 or #348), Berlin's oldest parish church,
once hemmed in by buildings and now standing oddly isolated in the
shadow of the huge Fernsehturm (see opposite). The Gothic nave in
stone and brick dates back to about 1270, but the tower is more
recent, having been added in 1466, with the verdigris-coated upper
section tacked on towards the end of the eighteenth century by the

designer of the Brandenburg Gate, Carl Gotthard Langhans. This uncontrived combination of architectural styles somehow makes the Marienkirche one of Berlin's most appealing churches, its simplicity a reminder of the city's village origins.

The **interior** is an excellent place to escape the increasingly frenetic streetlife of the area and listen to a free organ recital (Sat 4.30pm). Near the main entrance at the western end of the church is a small cross erected by the citizens of Berlin and Cölln as penance to the pope, after a mob immolated a papal representative on a nearby marketplace. There are five holes in the cross and, according to tradition, during the Middle Ages convicted criminals wishing to prove their innocence could do so by inserting the fingers of one hand into the holes simultaneously – not too many escaped punishment, though, as the feat is virtually an anatomical impossibility. Just inside the entrance, look out for the fifteenth-century *Totentanz*, a 22-metre frieze showing the dance of death. It's very faded, but accompanied by a representation of how it once looked, with Death shown as a shroud-clad mummy popping up between people from all levels of society.

The vaulted nave is plain and white but enlivened by some opulent decorative touches. Foremost among these is Andreas Schlüter's magnificent **pulpit**, its canopy dripping with cherubs and backed by a cloud from which gilded sunrays radiate. Complementing this are the white marble altar with a huge triptych altarpiece and the eighteenth-century organ, a riot of gilded filigree and yet more cherubs, topped by a sunburst.

The Fernsehturm

The Marienkirche, like every other building in the vicinity, is overshadowed by the gigantic **Fernsehturm**, or TV tower, just to the east (daily: March–Oct 9am–1am; Nov–Feb 10am–midnight; *www.berlinerfernsehturm.de*; DM10/€5.10; U- & S-Bahn Alexanderplatz, bus #100, #142, #157, #200 or #257). This 365-metre-high transmitter is the second highest structure in Europe and dominates the eastern Berlin skyline like a displaced satellite sitting on top of a huge factory chimney. It was built during the isolationist 1960s, a period when the east part of the city was largely inaccessible to West Germans, and intended as a highly visible symbol of the permanence of East Berlin and the German Democratic Republic. Its construction was watched with dismay and derision by West Berliners (and many people in the East), but after completion in 1969 the tower soon became a popular stopoff on the East Berlin tourist circuit.

These days, having outlasted the regime that conceived it, the Fernsehturm has become part of the scenery, and though few would champion it on the grounds of architectural merit, it does have a certain retro appeal. It also makes an unmissable orientation point, and there's a tremendous **view** (40km on a rare clear day, although the summit is often shrouded in cloud) from the observation platform – reached by a very fast lift. Above the observation platform is the *Tele-Café* (see *Cafés and bars*, p.266), whose main attraction is that it revolves on its own axis twice an hour.

When the sun shines on the globe of the tower, the reflected light forms a cross visible even in western Berlin, much to the reported chagrin of the old GDR authorities and amusement of Berliners, who call it the "pope's revenge". If you want to go up, bear in mind that there are sometimes long queues (the evening is your best bet).

The Rotes Rathaus

Across Rathausstrasse from the Neptunbrunnen is a rare survivor of Hohenzollern-era Berlin in the shape of the **Rotes Rathaus**, Berlin's "Red Town Hall". So called because of the colour of its bricks rather than its politics, the Rotes Rathaus has a solid angularity that contrasts sharply with the finicky grandeur of contemporaries like the Dom (see p.83). This is perhaps because it's a symbol of the civic rather than the Imperial Berlin of the time: a city in the throes of rapid commercial expansion and industrial growth. The building has lost some of its impact now that it's been hemmed in by new structures, but it remains a grandiose, almost Venetian-looking structure – look out for the intricate bas-relief in terracotta, illustrating episodes from the history of Berlin, that runs around the building at first-floor level. The Rathaus was badly knocked around in 1945, but made a good comeback following restoration during the 1950s. During GDR days it was headquarters of the East Berlin city administration (West Berlin was administered from Schöneberg town hall, see p.148), but since October 1991 it's been the seat of the united Berlin city administration.

The reconstruction of the Rathaus and thousands of other Berlin buildings is largely due to the *Trümmerfrauen* or "rubble women", who set to work in 1945 clearing up the 100 million tons of rubble created by wartime bombing and shelling. Their deeds are commemorated by the **statue** of a robust-looking woman facing the eastern entrance to the Rathaus on Rathausstrasse. Women of all ages carried out the bulk of the early rebuilding work, since most of Berlin's adult male population was dead, disabled or being held in PoW camps by the Allies. Despite this, the male contribution to the work is also marked by a statue of a man looking wistfully towards his *Trümmerfrau* counterpart from the western end of the Rathaus.

From the Rathaus the pedestrianized Rathausstrasse leads northeast up towards Alexanderplatz, past a series of largely missable shops and cafés. At the end of the street the arched canopy of **S-Bahnhof Alexanderplatz** rises above *Imbiss* stands. The station is one of the few buildings around here bearing any resemblance to its prewar appearance (though it's actually a 1960s rebuild).

Alexanderplatz

Just to the southeast of the station entrance, Rathausstrasse passes under the rail tracks onto **Alexanderplatz** itself, a huge, windswept, pedestrianized plaza surrounded by high-rises. Alexanderplatz has long been an important business and traffic centre. During the eighteenth century routes to all parts of Germany radiated out from here, and a cattle and wool market stood on the site. It acquired its present name after the Russian tsar Alexander I visited Berlin in 1805, and was made famous beyond the city by Alfred Döblin's unreadable novel of life in the Weimar era, *Berlin Alexanderplatz* (subsequently filmed by Fassbinder). Today, in addition to the S-Bahn line running overhead, three underground lines cross beneath the Platz, various bus routes converge on the area, and several tram lines course through it, making it one of central Berlin's busiest corners.

The route onto "Alex" leads through a gap between a couple of prewar survivors: the **Alexanderhaus** and the **Berolinahaus**, two buildings designed at the beginning of the 1930s by the architect and designer Peter Behrens, whose ideas influenced the founders of the Bauhaus. These two buildings are the only Alexanderplatz buildings not to have been destroyed in the war. Today Behrens' buildings, once the tallest in the area, have been put in the shade by the ugly *Forum Hotel* and various other local high-rises. At the centre of things is the sorry-looking **Brunnen der Völkerfreundschaft** ("Friendship of the Peoples Fountain"), which used to be a hangout for prostitutes and is now covered in graffiti. A more renowned monument is the **Weltzeituhr** (World Clock) in front of the Alexanderhaus. Central Berlin's best-known rendezvous point, it tells the time in different cities throughout the world, and looks like a product of the same architectural school responsible for the Fernsehturm.

Despite its drab contemporary appearance, Alexanderplatz has figured prominently in city upheavals ever since revolutionaries (including the writer Theodor Fontane) set up barricades here in 1848. In 1872 it was the site of a demonstration by an army of homeless women and children, and half a century later, during the revolution of 1918, sailors occupied the Alexanderplatz police headquarters (a feared local landmark that lay just to the southeast of the Platz – a plaque marks the spot) and freed the prisoners. More recently, Alexanderplatz was the focal point of the million-strong city-wide **demonstration** of November 4, 1989, which formed a prelude to the events of November 9. Hundreds of thousands of people crammed into the square to hear opposition leaders speak. Veteran writer Stefan Heym summed up the mood in his speech to the crowd: "Power belongs not to one, not to a few, not to the Party and not to the State. The whole people must have a share."

Before the war, Alexanderplatz was one of the city's main shopping centres with two expensive department stores in the vicinity:

Hermann Tietz, a Neo-Baroque palace between the Berolinahaus and what is now the *Forum Hotel*, and Wertheim, the biggest department store in Germany, which stood on the opposite side of the S-Bahn tracks to the Alexanderhaus. Both were Jewish-owned until "Aryanized" by the Nazis. The Kaufhof department store facing the fountain was, as Centrum, one of the best-stocked shops in East Germany, though these days it's just another run-of-the-mill big store. Today commercial life on Alexanderplatz seems to happen more at street level, with stalls and snack bars jostling for space in the plaza.

Throughout its existence the face of Alexanderplatz has undergone many transformations. A major reshaping at the end of the 1920s cleaned up what had turned into a rather sleazy corner of the city, and during the early 1960s the GDR-era city authorities decided to realize their vision of what a modern, socialist metropolis should look like by giving the then still war-damaged area the form it retains today. Further major changes are afoot and over the next decade or so, if plans under discussion are implemented, Alexanderplatz looks set to be transformed into a US-style "downtown", dominated by a dozen or so high-rise office and apartment buildings.

Alexanderplatz to Strausberger Platz

From Alexanderplatz, a short walk takes you southeast down **Karl-Marx-Allee** towards the district of Friedrichshain. The section of Karl-Marx-Allee running between Alexanderplatz and **Strausberger Platz** went up during the early to mid-1960s and is predictably stark and angular; this is where the GDR Politbüro and Eastern Bloc dignitaries took the salute during the military parades held every year to mark the GDR's anniversary. The last such occasion was on October 7, 1989, when Mikhail Gorbachev warned that "Life punishes those who arrive late" – a pointed reference to the East German leadership's rejection of his liberalization plans. It was already too late for Honecker and his Politbüro though, and the event sparked a series of demonstrations across the country that led to the downfall of the SED regime and subsequent collapse of the GDR. From Strausberger Platz onwards, where the district of Friedrichshain begins, the architecture recalls an earlier era and things get more interesting (see p.178).

Nikolaiviertel and around

CENTRAL BERLIN

Slightly to the southwest of the Rotes Rathaus lies the **Nikolaiviertel**, a recent development that attempts to re-create the old prewar heart of Berlin on the site of the city's **medieval** core, which was razed overnight on June 16, 1944.

To the east of here, in a quiet quarter cut off from the rest of the city centre by the speeding traffic of Grunerstrasse, a few historic buildings and one of the city's oldest *Gaststätten* survive. It's also worth heading south across the River Spree, to where a couple of museums, including the **Märkisches Museum**, have some excellent material on the history of the city.

The Nikolaiviertel

The compact network of streets that forms the **Nikolaiviertel** was a radical architectural departure for the old-style GDR. No longer, it seems, did the city planners feel compelled to build enormous monuments to the concrete-pourer's art; most of the Nikolaiviertel buildings are no more than four or five storeys high, and a concerted effort was made to inject a bit of vernacular individuality into the designs. One or two original buildings aside, the Nikolaiviertel consists partly of exact replicas of historic Berlin buildings that didn't make it through to the postwar era and partly of stylized buildings not based on anything in particular, but with a vaguely "old Berlin" feel. Sometimes it doesn't quite come off, and in places the use of typical East German *Plattenbau* construction techniques, with prefabricated pillars and gables, isn't too convincing, but all in all the Nikolaiviertel represents a commendable effort to get away from the monumentalism of earlier postwar construction projects. It also represents an attempt to attract big-spending tourists, with a series of expensive restaurants, cafés and *Gaststätten* (see *Cafés and bars* and *Restaurants*).

The nearest U-Bahn station to the Nikolaiviertel is Klosterstrasse; buses #142 and #257 also pass nearby.

Around the Nikolaikirche

At the centre of it all, on Nikolaikirchplatz, just off Propststrasse, is the Gothic **Nikolaikirche** (Tues–Sun 10am–6pm; *www.stadtmuseum .com*; DM5/€2.50 combined ticket with Knoblauchhaus and Ephraim Palais, concessions DM2.50/€1.30, Wed free), a thirteenth-century church, restored to its twin-towered prewar glory. The Nikolaikirche is one of the city's oldest churches and it was from here on November 2, 1539, that news of the Reformation was proclaimed to the citizens of Berlin. The distinctive needle-like spires date from a nineteenth-century restoration of the church, or rather their design does – the building was thoroughly wrecked during the war, and what you see today is largely a rebuild, as extensive patches of lighter, obviously modern masonry show.

The church is now a **museum** that traces the building's history, although it is often given over to temporary exhibitions. An unusual feature of its interior is the bright colouring of the vault ribbings: the orange, purple, green, and other vivid lines look like a Sixties Pop Art addition, but actually follow a medieval pattern discovered by a restorer in the 1980s. There are also a number of intricately carved tombs inside, most notably those of Daniel Männlich and Johann Andreas von Kraut, the former designed by Andreas Schüter.

Some of the **best Nikolaiviertel houses** are around the Nikolaikirche, along Propststrasse and on the southern side of Nikolaikirchplatz, behind the church itself. The last are particularly convincing – it's hard to believe that these pastel-facaded townhouses are fakes dating back only as far as the beginning of the 1980s.

For details of Zum Nussbaum and other eating places in this area, see Cafés and bars and Restaurants in Listings.

For a little light relief head for **Zum Nussbaum** on the corner of Propststrasse and Am Nussbaum, a handily located copy of a celebrated sixteenth-century *Gaststätte* that stood on the nearby Fischerinsel until destroyed during the bombing. The original is said to have been the local haunt of Berlin artists Heinrich Zille and Otto Nagel, and the replica is a faithful copy, right down to the walnut tree in the tiny garden. It's a little touristy but still a good place for a beer, particularly in summer if you can get a table outside.

Propststrasse runs all the way down to the River Spree and a rather clichéd statue of St George and the Dragon. Before here a right turn into Poststrasse will take you past the **Gerichtslaube**, another Nikolaiviertel replica, this time of Berlin's medieval courthouse. The original was dismantled in 1870 in order to create the space needed for the building of the Rotes Rathaus, and was removed to the grounds of Schloss Babelsberg in Potsdam where it can still be seen (see p.222). The copy houses a couple of pricey tourist restaurants.

The Knoblauch-Haus

A left turn at the Propststrasse–Poststrasse intersection is more rewarding, leading to the **Knoblauch-Haus**, Poststrasse 23 (Tues–Sun 10am–6pm; *www.stadtmuseum.com*; DM5/€2.50 combined ticket with Nikolaikirche and Ephraim Palais, concessions DM2.50/€1.30, Wed free), a Neoclassical townhouse built in 1759 and a rare survivor of the war. It was home to the patrician Knoblauch family, who played an important role in the commercial and cultural life of eighteenth- and nineteenth-century Berlin, and now contains an exhibition about their activities. While the careers of Eduard Knoblauch, Berlin's first freelance architect, and Armand Knoblauch, founder of a major city brewery, are mildly interesting, the real appeal here is the **interior** of the house, furnished in the grand-bourgeois style of the times, which gives a good impression of upper middle-class life in Hohenzollern-era Berlin. The ground floor and vaulted basement of the Knoblauch-Haus are home to the *Historische Weinstuben* (see *Restaurants*, p.251), a reconstruction of a nineteenth-century wine-restaurant once favoured by the playwrights Gerhart Hauptmann, August Strindberg and Henrik Ibsen.

The Ephraim-Palais

There's another relic of Berlin bourgeois high life at the southern end of Poststrasse, where the elegant Rococo facade of the **Ephraim-**

Palais, Poststrasse 16 (Tues–Sun 10am–6pm; *www.stadtmuseum
.com*; DM5/€2.50 combined ticket with Nikolaikirche and
Knoblauch-Haus, concessions DM2.50/€1.30, Wed free), curves
round onto Mühlendamm. A rebuild of an eighteenth-century merchant's mansion, this now houses a museum of Berlin-related art
from the seventeenth to the beginning of the nineteenth centuries,
with numerous pictures, prints and maps giving a good impression
of how the city looked in its glory days.

The Ephraim-Palais was built by Veitel Heine Ephraim, court jew-
eller and mint master to Frederick the Great, and all-round wheeler-
dealer. He owed his lavish lifestyle primarily to the fact that he
steadily reduced the silver content of the Prussian *thaler*. This
earned a great deal of money for Frederick and Ephraim himself but
ruined the purchasing power of the currency. Ephraim's palace
housed a museum of sport from 1925 to 1934, before being dismantled in 1935 as part of a road-broadening scheme; much of the
facade, however, was preserved and later turned up in West Berlin,
whence it was returned to be incorporated into the 1980s rebuild.

The Hanf Museum

Nearby, in another reconstructed Berlin house, is the **Hanf Museum**
(Hemp Museum), Mühlendamm 5 (Tues–Fri 10am–8pm, Sat & Sun
noon–8pm; *www.hanflobby.de/hanfmuseum*; DM5/€2.50),
Germany's only museum dedicated to cannabis. It's somewhat amateurish, filled with an odd assortment of glass cases and ill-framed
exhibits, but there is a surprisingly large amount of information
about the history, uses and cultural significance of the plant.
Devotees may find it interesting, but all exhibits are in German. A
small shop offers the usual paraphernalia, and there's a café in the
basement. Alternatively, next door is *Zur Rippe*, an old-style
Gaststätte where you can slake your thirst and dine on traditional
Berlin specialities.

Around the Molkenmarkt

The area where Mühlendamm meets Stralauer Strasse is known as
the **Molkenmarkt**, one of the oldest public spaces in Berlin. The two
pompous and dull buildings on the southern side of Mühlendamm are
the **Berliner Münze** (Berlin Mint) and the former **Palais Schwerin**
(built for Otto Schwerin, a minister of Friedrich I of Prussia). The latter is completely missable and the only redeeming feature of the former is a replica of a frieze depicting coining techniques by Gottfried
Schadow, designer of the Brandenburg Gate Quadriga.

The Stadthaus and around

Bypass them both and head for Jüdenstrasse –"Jews' Street" – running north from Stralauer Strasse in the shadow of the domed
Stadthaus. Reminiscent of the Französischer Dom but dating from

as recently as 1911, this building is a relic of the area's days as an administrative district of Wilhelmine Berlin and now houses federal government offices. The area around Jüdenstrasse was Berlin's original ghetto, a role that ended when the Jews were driven out of Brandenburg in 1573. When the Jews were allowed back into Berlin in 1671 they settled mainly around what is now Oranienburger Strasse (see p.109).

A right turn midway along Jüdenstrasse leads into Parochialstrasse, where the first stone of communist control over postwar eastern Berlin was laid at **Parochialstrasse 1**. The building hosted the opening meeting of Berlin's post-Nazi town council, headed by future SED chief Walter Ulbricht, even as fighting still raged a little to the west. Ulbricht and his comrades had been specially flown in from Soviet exile to sow the seeds for a future communist civil administration and moved in here, having been unable to set up shop in the still-burning Rotes Rathaus. Further along the street and right into Klosterstrasse brings you to the **Parochialkirche**, a Baroque church that dates back to the sixteenth century. The bare brick interior (legacy of the usual wartime gutting) is a venue for changing art exhibitions (free) of the worthy-but-dull kind usually found in churches.

Around Klosterstrasse

On the northeastern side of the Parochialstrasse–Klosterstrasse (named after a long-vanished local monastery) junction is **Podewil**, an eighteenth-century residence that's now home to an arts centre, music venue (see *Clubs and live venues*) and pleasant café. Not far away at the top of Klosterstrasse is the gutted thirteenth-century **Franziskaner-Kirche**, destroyed by a land mine in 1945 and left a ruin as a warning against war and fascism. Behind here, at Littenstrasse 14–15, is the **Berlin Landgericht**, a courthouse whose Neo-Baroque facade conceals a wonderful Jugendstil interior of strange interlocking stairwells that seem to owe their structure to organic processes rather than the work of an architect. A rather more functional piece of Berlin architectural history can be seen towards the southern end of Littenstrasse in the shape of a fragment of Berlin's medieval Stadtmauer or city wall.

If you're thirsty or hungry, try Berlin's oldest pub, Zur letzten Instanz (see p.266) on nearby Waisenstrasse.

South of the Spree

From Klosterstrasse it's a short U-Bahn hop to Märkisches Museum station on the **southern side of the Spree** (you can also walk via Mühlendamm and along Fischerinsel, a shoddy GDR-era showpiece housing development), where you'll find the Märkisches Museum, an institution dating from before reunification. There is little else in the neighbourhood to attract attention. East of the museum, old factories and large industrial yards line the banks of the Spree. Southwards lies a swath of residential buildings.

The Märkisches Museum

Looking like a red-brick Neo-Gothic cathedral, the **Märkisches Museum**, Am Köllnischen Park 5 (Tues–Sun 10am–6pm; *www.stadtmuseum.com*; DM8/€4.10, concessions DM4/€2.05, Wed free; U-Bahn Märkisches Museum or bus #147/#240), covers the history of Berlin and the Mark Brandenburg. Although the exhibition expanded when the former Berlin Museum in Kreuzberg became part of the Jewish Museum Berlin (see p.135) and its collection was integrated into the holdings here, it nevertheless remains episodic; eighteenth- and nineteenth- century culture is definitely its forte, while coverage of the Third Reich and postwar years is inadequate.

The museum has an old-fashioned flavour to it, with lots of small rooms crammed with paintings, gadgets and glass vitrines. The **ground floor** covers early history, starting with pottery pieces from the first prehistoric settlers and ending with copies of royal proclamations from Friedrich William, the Great Elector, who died in 1688 – but is the least rewarding section. The two **upper floors** are more engaging, with rooms devoted to themes such as "Industrialization", "Intellectual Life", "Woman", and "the Military". Particularly noteworthy is the **Gottische Kapelle**, a room resembling a small chapel and filled with wonderful pieces of medieval sacred art from (usually) unknown local artisans, including the expressive sculpture, *Spandauer Madonna*. Slightly more secular in theme is the room devoted to the "Panorama", a huge arcade-like machine, built over a hundred years ago: as you peer through the eyepiece, a huge drum rotates to show you in turn dozens of fascinating 3D photographs of old Berlin.

In the late nineteenth century, Berlin was a centre of **barrel organ** production, an industry established by Italian immigrants, and many examples of these music-makers are on display in the museum, as well as their increasingly large and more intricate progeny. Organ-grinding performances are given every Sunday at 3pm in the exhibition room devoted to the devices.

Another bit of Berliniana is on view outside the museum: a **statue** of **Heinrich Zille**, the Berlin artist who produced earthy satirical drawings of Berlin life around the turn of the twentieth century. Behind him is a leafy park, the Kollnischer, with a **bearpit**, home to a couple of sleepy brown bears. Nearby, at Märkisches Ufer 10, is the Baroque **Ermeler Haus**, an eighteenth-century mansion transplanted here from nearby Breite Strasse – these days it houses a couple of decent restaurants (see *Restaurants*).

Chapter 5

The Scheunenviertel
and around

T he **Scheunenviertel** is the name commonly given to the northern periphery of central Berlin, a crescent-shaped area running roughly from Weidendammer Brücke (which crosses the

River Spree just north of Bahnhof Friedrichstrasse) to Rosa-Luxemburg-Platz. After the *Wende* this emerged as one of the most intriguing parts of the unified city, its appeal based on both its history as Berlin's prewar **Jewish quarter** and a contemporary nightlife boom that makes it one of the city's essential after-hours destinations.

The district has its origins in the Spandauer Vorstadt, one of a number of suburbs built beyond Berlin's walled centre during the seventeenth century. *Scheunenviertel*, meaning "barn quarter", originally just described what is now Rosa-Luxemburg-Platz and its environs, where barns were built following a decree that flammable hay and straw could no longer be stored in the city centre. However, the term has since become common usage to describe most of the area covered in this chapter.

The Jews moved in after they were permitted to return to Berlin in 1671, following the expulsion orders a century before. From that point on the area became a refuge for Jews fleeing persecution and pogroms in eastern Europe and Russia, and by the nineteenth century the Scheunenviertel was the cultural and spiritual centre of

Berlin's by now well-established and influential Jewish community.

The melting-pot atmosphere made the area an ideal refuge for those at odds with the Prussian and later the Imperial German establishment, and it became a notorious centre of revolutionary and criminal activity, so much so that the authorities were constantly trying to find ways to justify pulling it down. At one point they refused to put down cobblestones in the heart of the Scheunenviertel for fear that the inhabitants would rip them up and use them to build barricades.

The Scheunenviertel's vibrant nature also attracted **artists** and **writers** who created their own bohemian enclave here, and during the 1920s local bars and dives numbered personalities like Bertolt Brecht, Marlene Dietrich and the actor Gustav Gründgens among their patrons. During these years the Scheunenviertel became a regular battleground for the street gangs of the left and right, who had their own *Kneipen* and meeting halls in the area.

Deportation of the Jews under the Nazis did much to take the soul out of the Scheunenviertel; this was followed in the GDR-era by a general shutting down of what little business life remained. From the 1950s until the *Wende* the quarter was little more than a network of decrepit prewar streets punctuated by the occasional slab of GDR-era housing. Few visitors strayed here from Unter den Linden, and apart from a couple of pockets of restoration the area was allowed to decay quietly – forgotten almost as much by the authorities as by visitors to East Berlin. Today the Scheunenviertel has undergone a dramatic revival, with renovation projects putting the infrastructure to rights and new bars and restaurants appearing almost every week. Though the brightly painted squatted houses in the backstreets are giving way to the ever-encroaching forces of renovation, it's still one of the more rewarding corners of the city to explore.

For the visitor the main points of interest are centred around the neat segment formed by Oranienburger Strasse, Auguststrasse and Rosenthalerstrasse. **Oranienburger Strasse** itself is home to countless bars and restaurants, as well as the **Neue Synagoge**, with its exhibitions on Jewish culture, while just to the east is the newly renovated **Hackesche Höfe**, a sort of "art mall" and a major hub of activity for both tourists and locals. The whole area is now the centre of a rapidly expanding café, gallery and upmarket shopping scene.

Upper Friedrichstrasse

These days the streets around **Upper Friedrichstrasse**, across the Spree just north of Bahnhof Friedrichstrasse, are home largely to shops and apartments, belying the fact that this is where the industrial revolution first hit Berlin. The main attractions have artistic associations, like the **Berliner Ensemble**, where Brecht worked upon his postwar return to Berlin; and the nearby **Deutsches Theater**, which is shaping up as one of the city's, if not the country's, best contemporary theatres. The Brecht connection also takes in the playwright's home and workplace – the **Brecht-Haus** – and, not far away, his grave.

The Berliner Ensemble

Friedrichstrasse runs north via the handsome wrought-iron Weidendammer Brücke into central Berlin's theatreland. Immediately to the left on Bertolt-Brecht-Platz is the **Berliner Ensemble** theatre (see *The arts*, p.287), generally thought of as Berlin's "Brecht theatre", complete with a statue of the man himself in front. The theatre is still trying to live down its reputation of GDR days, when its stock in trade was slightly lacklustre productions of Brecht's work, performed in ritualistic tribute to one of the few world-renowned German writers East Germany could claim as its own.

The building, which dates from the early 1890s, is rather austere from the outside but boasts an opulent Neo-Baroque interior. Originally known as the Theater am Schiffbauerdamm (after the street on which it stands), the Brecht connection goes back to the 1920s: on August 31, 1928, the world premiere of his *Dreigroschenoper* ("The Threepenny Opera") was staged here, the first of 250 consecutive performances. After spending much of the Nazi era in American exile, Brecht returned in 1949 with his wife, Helene Weigel, to take over direction of the theatre, marking his return by painting a still-visible red cross through the coat of arms on the royal box.

The Deutsches Theater

A few streets to the northwest at Schumannstrasse 13a (turn right by the war-era bunker on Reinhardtstrasse) is the elegant **Deutsches Theater** (see *The arts*, p.287), founded in 1883. In 1905 Max Reinhardt, who was to dominate the theatre scene for nearly three decades, took over as director (moving on from the Theater am Schiffbauerdamm); and in 1922 a young and unknown Marlene Dietrich made her stage debut here. A couple of years later Bertolt Brecht arrived from Munich and began his energetic conquest of Berlin's theatre world. In time for its 1983 centenary, millions were spent on restoring the interior to its turn-of-the-century splendour; and in contrast to the Berliner Ensemble, the Deutsches Theater is going from strength to strength, and is now widely regarded as one of the city's best.

At its western end Reinhardtstrasse passes under a low S-Bahn bridge, which was bricked off by the Wall until 1989. Now that there are no more guards lurking in the shadows, you're free to wander around on a piece of land which, for over 28 years, was part of the *Todesstreife* or "death strip" of the Wall fortifications. To the south is the Spree and an impressive view of the Reichstag on the opposite bank, while to the west looms what is, at the time of writing, still a huge construction site, soon to house government bureaucrats.

Around Oranienburger Tor

Returning to the junction of Reinhardtstrasse and Friedrichstrasse, the clumsy GDR-era Jugendstil pastiche of the **Friedrichstadt Palast** theatre (again, see *The arts*) rears up opposite; it's perfect if you're into big, splashy, scantily clad revues, but otherwise eminently miss-able. Things start to get more interesting a little further to the north along Friedrichstrasse, around **Oranienburger Tor**. During the nine-

---

Bertolt Brecht (1898–1956)

Bertolt Brecht is widely regarded as one of the leading German dramatists of the twentieth century. Born in Augsburg, the son of a paper-mill manager, he studied medicine, mainly to avoid full military service in World War I. Working as an army medical orderly in 1918, his experiences helped shape his passionate anti-militarism. Soon he drifted away from medicine onto the fringes of the theatrical world, eventually winding up as a dramatura at the Munich Kammerspiele in 1921. Increasingly he was drawn to Berlin, and a few years later took up a similar position at the Deutsches Theater under Erwin Piscator, where he began his speedy ascent to the heights of German theatre. Brecht's earliest plays were anarchic semi-Expressionistic pieces: his first work, *Baal*, depicted life as an intensely sensual yet ultimately futile and doomed experience. Although his work attracted the attention of the critics and his first performed play, *Trommeln in der Nacht* ("Drums in the Night"), won the prestigious Kleist prize in 1922, it wasn't until the premiere of the *Dreigroschenoper* ("The Threepenny Opera") co-written with the composer Kurt Weill, six years later, that Brecht's real breakthrough came.

The *Dreigroschenoper* marked the beginning of a new phase in Brecht's work. A couple of years earlier he had embraced Marxism, an ideological step that had a profound effect on his literary output, leading him to espouse a didactic "epic" form of theatre. The aim was to provoke the audience, perhaps even move them to revolutionary activity. To this end he developed the technique of **Verfremdung** ("alienation") to create a sense of distance between spectators and the action unfolding before them. By using effects such as obviously fake scenery, monotone lighting, and jarring music to expose the sham sentimentality of love songs, he hoped constantly to remind the audience that what they were doing was watching a play – in order to make them judge, rather than be drawn into, the action on stage. The result was a series of works that were pretty heavy-going, though the opera *Aufstieg und Fall der Stadt Mahagonny* ("Rise and Fall of the City of Mahagonny") and *Die Heilige Johanna der Schlachthöfe* ("St Joan of the Stockyards") from this period are reasonably accessible.

---

teenth century this area was the location of one of Berlin's densest concentrations of heavy industry. Development had begun during the 1820s with the establishment of a steam-engine factory and iron foundry in Chausseestrasse. In 1837 August Borsig built his first factory, and by the 1870s his successors were churning out hundreds of steam engines and railway locomotives each year.

Other industrial concerns were also drawn to the area, earning it the nickname Feuerland – "Fireland". However, by the end of the century most had outgrown their roots and relocated en masse at the edges of the rapidly expanding city. A reminder of the past, and of Borsig's local influence, is the **Borsighaus** at Chausseestrasse 9. Once the central administration block of the Borsig factories, this sandstone building, its facade richly decorated with bronze figures, looks like a displaced country residence.

In 1933, unsurprisingly, Brecht went into exile, eventually ending up in the States. His years away from Germany were among his most productive. During this time he wrote some of his greatest parable-plays, works that benefited from a tempering of the writer's more overt didactic intent: *Leben des Galilei* ("The Life of Galileo"), *Der gute Mensch von Sezuan* ("The Good Woman of Szechuan"), *Mutter Courage und ihre Kinder* ("Mother Courage and her Children"), *Der Kaukasische Kreidekreis* ("The Caucasian Chalk Circle"). The political message was still very much present in his work, but somehow the dynamic and lyrical force of his writing meant that it was often largely lost on his audience – at the Zürich premiere of *Mutter Courage* in 1941, Brecht was dismayed to learn that the audience in fact identified with his heroine, whom he had intended to serve as an unsympathetic symbol of the senselessness of wartime sacrifice.

In America Brecht had tried to make a living as a Hollywood scriptwriter, though not with much success – only one film made it to the screen, *Hangmen Also Die*, directed by another German-in-exile, Fritz Lang. In 1947 Brecht came before the Committee for Un-American Activities, but was able to defend himself without implicating any of his friends. Returning to Europe, he finally settled in East Berlin in 1949, after a brief period in Switzerland. His decision to try his luck in the Soviet-dominated Eastern sector of Germany was influenced by the offer of the chance to take over at the Theater am Schiffbauerdamm, the theatre where the *Dreigroschenoper* had been premiered more than twenty years earlier. However, before heading east, Brecht first took the precaution of gaining Austrian citizenship and lodging the copyright of his works with a West German publisher.

The remainder of Brecht's life was largely devoted to the running of what is now known as the Berliner Ensemble and facing up to his own role in the fledgling GDR. The workers' uprising of 1953 prompted a private ironic outpouring (see p.69), but did not prevent him from accepting the Stalin Peace Prize the following year. Two years later Brecht died, and though he never did break with the workers' and peasants' state, it's interesting to reflect on what might have happened had he lived a few years longer.

The Dorotheenstädtische Friedhof

Roughly opposite here is the **Dorotheenstädtische Friedhof** (daily:
April–Sept 8am–7pm; Oct–March 8am–4pm; U-Bahn Oranienburger
Tor, bus #140, trams #1 & #13), eastern Berlin's VIP cemetery.
Here you'll find the graves of Bertolt Brecht and Helene Weigel; the
architect Karl Friedrich Schinkel, his last resting place topped by an
appropriately florid monument; John Heartfield, the Dada luminary
and interwar photomontage exponent, under a headstone decorated
with a runic H; the philosopher Georg Hegel, whose ideas influenced
Marx; the author Heinrich Mann, and many other Berlin worthies. A
leaflet detailing who lies where is available from the cemetery administration offices (on the right at the end of the entrance alley) for
DM2 (€1). The Dorotheenstädtische Friedhof also encloses the
Französischer Friedhof (entrance on Chausseestrasse), originally
built to serve Berlin's Huguenot community and now rather overgrown.

The Brecht-Haus

Just past the Dorotheenstädtische Friedhof entrance is the **Brecht-
Haus**, Chausseestrasse 125 (guided tours every 30min: Tues–Fri
10am–noon, Thurs also 5–7pm, Sat 9.30am–2pm, Sun 11am–6pm,
last entrance 30min before closing; DM4/€2.05, concessions
DM2/€1; afternoon tours can be booked in advance – call ☎2 82 99
16; U-Bahn Oranienburger Tor, bus #157, trams #1 & #13), final
home and workplace of Brecht and Helene Weigel, his wife and col-
laborator. The guided tours take in the seven simply furnished rooms
– an absolute must for Brecht fans, but not so fascinating if you're
only casually acquainted with his works. The Brecht-Haus also has a
Bertolt Brecht **archive** (Tues–Fri 8am–4pm) and the basement is
home to the *Kellerrestaurant im Brechthaus* (see *Restaurants*),
which dishes up Viennese specialities, supposedly according to
Weigel's recipes.

A little way past the Brecht-Haus stands a brutalist **pillar commemorating the Spartakusbund**, the breakaway antiwar faction of
the SPD formed by Karl Liebknecht in 1916, which later evolved into
the KPD, Germany's Communist Party. The inscription, a quote from
Liebknecht, says, "Spartakus means the fire and spirit, the heart and
soul, the will and deed of the revolution of the proletariat." The modern-day proletariat, however, seems little interested in this relic of its
revolutionary past.

Museum für Naturkunde

Continuing northwest on Chausseestrasse, a left turn into
Invalidenstrasse leads to the **Museum für Naturkunde** at no. 43
(Tues–Sun 9.30am–5pm; DM5/€2.50, concessions DM2.50/€1.30;
U-Bahn Zinnowitzer Strasse, tram #8, #13 or #50, bus #157, #245

or #340), one of the world's largest natural history museums. The museum's origins go back to 1716 though the present building, and the nucleus of the collection it houses, date from the 1880s.

High point of the sixteen-room display (exhibits are not labelled in English) is the reconstructed brachiosaurus skeleton in the main hall. The museum is also home to the fossil remains of an archaeopteryx, the oldest known bird. Elsewhere, amid the endless glass cases containing stuffed animals, fossils, and insects pinned on card, the rooms devoted to the evolution of vertebrates and the ape family stand out, as does the interesting if slightly ghoulish section on how the numerous stuffed animals were "prepared for exhibition", as the commentary delicately puts it. The museum also boasts a vast mineralogy collection including a number of meteorites.

Oranienburger Strasse to Sophienstrasse

The area around Oranienburger Strasse, which runs southeast from Friedrichstrasse just below Oranienburger Tor, is the start of the Scheunenviertel proper and heart of Berlin's prewar **Jewish district**. Although Berlin's Jewish population numbers only around twelve thousand today, it has an enduring symbol in the shape of the **Neue Synagoge**, which over the last couple of years has been restored and is now a museum. With the opening of a number of Jewish cafés and a cultural centre, Oranienburger Strasse has regained a little of its pre-Nazi identity.

A few streets away on **Grosse Hamburger Strasse** are further reminders of Jewish Berlin, although here the past is recalled more by the absence of certain landmarks than by their presence. Just behind Grosse Hamburger Strasse, **Sophienstrasse** ranks as one of Berlin's best-restored nineteenth-century streets, taking its name from the nearby **Sophienkirche**, the city's finest Baroque church. The big draw here, however, is the **Hackesche Höfe**, a restored series of turn-of-the century courtyards.

Oranienburger Strasse

Until 1989 **Oranienburger Strasse** was one of central Berlin's more desolate streets, but since the *Wende* it has been through a phase as an atmospheric bar-crawling strip, and is now principally known for its upscale **restaurants**. With a host of stylish watering-holes both here and on the surrounding streets, it is as much a trendy tourist haunt as part of the new eastern Berlin *Szene* (see p.134). Prostitutes do still openly solicit passing motorists along the stretch bordering on Monbijou Park (see below), but their "patch" is slowly receding as the area succumbs to the lights of nouveau restaurants and cafés springing up around the Hackescher Markt S-Bahn station.

The revitalization of Oranienburger Strasse began with **Tacheles** (*www.tacheles.de*), a group of young international artists who took over a spectacularly ruined building on the southern side of the street, just beyond the Oranienburger Tor junction, in early 1990. The exterior is usually festooned with works-in-progress, and the building has become home and workplace to an ever-changing band of painters, sculptors, kindred spirits and hangers-on. Inside is a café/bar (see *Cafés and bars*, p.263) and regular gigs and events take place here (see *Clubs and live venues*, p.282).

The Tacheles building itself has an interesting past, reflecting the history of the city in which it stands. Built in 1907, it was one of the first reinforced concrete structures in Europe, originally housing the Friedrichstrassepassagen shopping centre, then between the wars the AEG's exhibition hall for all its electrical products. From 1934 onwards the building was used by the SS and the Deutsche Arbeitsfront, a Nazi labour organization. After the war it housed a cinema and work space for art students before suffering partial demolition and standing vacant for many years until the Tacheles collective moved in. Rumours of its demise have been rampant in the last few years, as speculators eager to swallow up a big chunk of prime real estate (which it helped bring to life) have zoned in on the building, but, after much political wrangling, it seems that Tacheles has ensured its future as a permanent fixture in the cultural land-scape. Indeed, it's come a long way since its anarchic beginnings, much to the disappointment of those involved in the early days, who inevitably claim the new-look Tacheles with its plate-glass windows is not the place it once was.

A little way along from Tacheles, on the opposite side of the street, is an important-looking building that turns out to be a nineteenth-century **post office administration building**. It's built in the mock-Moorish style so favoured by Berlin civic architects during the nineteenth century. They decked out everything from stations to breweries in alternating bands of orange and yellow brick, with generously arched doorways and windows and fanciful turrets with decorative cupolas. These days it's home to a yearly festival of new experimental art, held in May (see *The arts*, p.291).

The Neue Synagoge and around

Before the war Oranienburger Strasse and its immediate environs were at the heart of Berlin's main **Jewish quarter**. During the initial waves of Jewish immigration from the seventeenth century onwards the area was a densely populated and desperately poor ghetto, but by the nineteenth century Berlin's Jews had achieved a high degree of prosperity and assimilation. This was reflected in the building of the grand **Neue Synagoge**, to a design by Eduard Knoblauch, halfway down Oranienburger Strasse just off the corner of

Krausnickstrasse. The synagogue was inaugurated in the presence of Bismarck in 1866, a gesture of official recognition which, coming at a time when Jews in Russia were still enduring officially sanctioned pogroms, must have made many Jews feel that their position in German society was finally secure. The acceptance that they had enjoyed in Wilhelmine Germany contributed to the sense of disbelief many Jews felt at the rise of Nazism during the 1920s and 1930s.

Like the post office building near the Tacheles, the Neue Synagoge was built in mock-Moorish style, with the conspicuous addition of a bulbous gilt and turquoise dome. It was Berlin's central synagogue for over sixty years, serving also as a venue for concerts, including one in 1930 by Albert Einstein in his lesser-known role as a violinist. A Jewish museum was opened next door on January 24, 1933, just six days before the Nazi takeover. Neither museum nor synagogue survived the Third Reich: both were damaged on Kristallnacht (see pp.112–113). The synagogue wasn't actually destroyed thanks to the intervention of the local police chief who chased off SA arsonists and called the fire brigade to extinguish the flames. It remained in use as a place of worship until 1940 when it was handed over to the Wehrmacht, who used it as a warehouse until it was gutted by bombs on the night of November 22, 1943.

After the war the synagogue remained a ruin and in 1958 the main hall, which was thought to be on the verge of collapse, was demolished, leaving only the building's facade and entrance rooms intact. For many years these stood here largely overlooked, a plaque on the shattered frontage exhorting the few passers-by to: *Vergesst es nie* – "Never forget". The Jewish community pressed for what was left to be turned into a museum, but the authorities did not respond until 1988, when it was decided to resurrect the shell as a "centre for the promotion and preservation of Jewish culture".

A new plaque was affixed to the building amid much official pomp and ceremony on November 9, 1988, the fiftieth anniversary of Kristallnacht, and work began on restoration of the facade and the reconstruction of the gilded dome. In 1995, the extensive renovation work was completed and the building was reopened as a museum and cultural centre, officially called **Centrum Judaicum – Neue Synagoge** (Mon–Thurs & Sun 10am–6pm, Fri 10am–2pm; entry free except for special exhibitions). Inside there are two permanent exhibitions: one on the history and restoration of the synagogue itself, and another on the Jewish life and culture that could once be found in the surrounding area. Already the synagogue's dome, visible from far and wide, has become a Berlin landmark once again.

The offices next door to the synagogue at Oranienburger Strasse 28–29 are the **headquarters** of Berlin's Jewish community (Mon–Thurs 9am–4.30pm, Fri 9am–1.30pm), and it's worth drop-

Kristallnacht and Berlin's Jews

Kristallnacht ("Crystal Night"), so called after the sound of breaking glass
as Jewish businesses and institutions were wrecked, marked an intensifi-
cation of Nazi attacks on the Jews. The murder of Ernst vom Rath, a
German official in Paris, by Herschel Grynszpan, a young German-Jewish
refugee protesting at his parents' forced deportation to Poland with ten
thousand other Jews, gave the Nazis the excuse they had been waiting for
to unleash a general pogrom on German Jews. (Ironically, vom Rath was
an anti-Nazi whom Grynszpan had mistaken for his intended target, the
German ambassador.) At a party meeting on November 9, 1938, Nazi propaganda minister Joseph Goebbels, having broken the news of the assassination, ordered Reinhard Heydrich, chief of the Reich's Security Head
Office, to organize "spontaneous" anti-Jewish demonstrations. Heydrich
directed the police to ensure that attacks on the German Jewish community, mainly instigated by SA men in civilian clothes, were not hindered.
Kristallnacht resulted in the deaths of at least 36 Jews and the destruction
of 23 of the city's 29 synagogues, with hundreds of shops and businesses
wrecked. After the attacks the Nazi government fined the German Jewish
community one billion marks, ostensibly to pay for the damage, and enact-
ed new laws confiscating Jewish property.

Kristallnacht was the violent public culmination of a process of state-
backed persecution of German Jews that had started when the Nazis
assumed power in 1933. The first step was the SA-enforced boycott of
Jewish shops, businesses, and medical and legal practices that began on
April 1 of that year. A series of laws passed in the years that followed
banned Jews from most of the professions, and in September 1935 the
Nürnberg laws effectively deprived Jews of their German citizenship,

ping in to pick up literature about the synagogue and a map (English-
language versions of both available) showing important Jewish sites
in the city past and present. In order to get in (the offices and the
museum share an entrance) you'll have to pass through airport-type
magnetic detectors – a sad reflection of the continuing threat to
Jewish institutions from terrorist attack and the homegrown far
right.

*See
Restaurants
and Cafés and
bars in
Listings for
more details.*

There's a clutch of **cafés**, **bars** and **restaurants** in the vicinity of
the synagogue on Oranienburger Strasse, including the kosher vegetarian *Oren* next door, full of city intellectuals in wire-rimmed glasses, *Café Silberstein* with its famous crazy chairs, and the studenty
cellar-bar *Assel* further down the street.

Towards the southern end of Oranienburger Strasse is
Monbijoupark, once the grounds of a Rococo royal palace, reduced
to rubble by the war and, like so many Hohenzollern relics, never
rebuilt. Today this park makes an unexpected and shady refuge from
the unrelentingly urban landscape of the area. A footbridge at its
southwestern corner links it to the Museumsinsel. Just after it meets
the park, Oranienburger Strasse veers off to the left to become a
strip of small and trendy clothes shops.

introducing apartheid-like classifications of "racial purity". There was a brief respite in 1936 when Berlin hosted the Olympic Games and the Nazis, wishing to show an acceptable face to the outside world, eased up on overt anti-Semitism, but by the following year large-scale expropriation of Jewish businesses had begun. After Kristallnacht all remaining Jewish businesses were forcibly "Aryanized", effectively excluding Jews from German economic life. With the outbreak of war in September 1939, Jews were forced to observe a night-time curfew and were forbidden to own radios. Forced transport of Jews to the east (mainly occupied Poland) began as early as February 1940, and September 1941 saw the introduction of a law requiring Jews to wear the yellow Star of David, heralding the beginning of mass deportations.

In January 1942, the **Wannsee Conference** held in a western suburb of Berlin (see p.168) discussed the Endlösung or "Final Solution" to the "Jewish Question", drawing up plans for the removal of all Jews to the east and, implicitly, their eventual extermination. As the Final Solution began to be put into effect, daily life for Berlin's Jews grew ever more unbearable: in April they were banned from public transport, and in September their food rations were reduced. By the beginning of 1943 the only Jews remaining legally in Berlin were highly skilled workers in the city's armaments factories, and in February deportation orders began to be enforced for this group, too. Most Berlin Jews were sent to Auschwitz and Theresienstadt concentration camps, and only a handful survived the war. By the end of the war Berlin's 160,564-strong Jewish population (1933 figure) had been reduced to about 6500; 1400 survived as "U-boats", hidden by Gentile families at great personal risk, and the rest had somehow managed to evade the final round-ups, usually as a result of having irreplaceable skills vital to the war effort.

Auguststrasse

Auguststrasse, which branches off from Oranienburger Strasse opposite Tacheles, is another street that's undergone a breathtaking transformation since 1989, and is now the centre of a thriving arts scene. The galleries on and around Auguststrasse attract artists from all around the world and feature some of the most interesting and controversial work you're likely to see in Berlin. The city authorities have provided an enviable level of financial support. In June 1992 they stumped up for the "37 Rooms Exhibition", in which the whole of Auguststrasse was turned into a giant gallery, an event widely viewed as having given artistic life on the street an air of legitimacy.

A good starting point is Galerie EIGEN + Art, at no. 26, an excellent place to pick up information about what's going on in other venues along the street (see *The arts*).

Around Grosse Hamburger Strasse

At the eastern end of Oranienburger Strasse, a left turn leads into Grosse Hamburger Strasse, site of some poignant reminders of the area's Jewish past. It also offers access to one of Berlin's prettiest churches and an attractive restored street.

The Jewish Cemetery and around

On the immediate right, just into Grosse Hamburger Strasse, is the location of Berlin's oldest **Jewish cemetery**, established in 1672, and the first **Jewish old people's home** to be founded in the city. The Nazis used the building as a detention centre for Jews, and 55,000 people were held here before being shipped off to the camps. A memorial tablet, on which pebbles have been placed as a mark of respect (following the Jewish practice for grave-site visits), and a sculpted group of haggard-looking figures, representing deportees, mark the spot where the home stood.

The grassed-over open space behind is the site of the cemetery itself. In 1943 the Gestapo smashed most of the headstones and dug up the remains of those buried here, using gravestones to shore up a trench they had excavated through the site. A few cracked headstones with Hebrew inscriptions line the graveyard walls. The only freestanding monument was erected after the war to commemorate Moses Mendelssohn, the philosopher and German Enlightenment figure. Also adorned with pebbles, it's on the spot where he is thought to have been buried, with an inscription in German on one side and in Hebrew on the other. Just to the north of the cemetery at **Grosse Hamburger Strasse 27** is a former Jewish boys' school, recently reopened as a Jewish secondary school for both sexes. Above its entrance a still-visible sign from prewar days reads, in German, "Jewish Community Boys' School". On the facade a plaque pays homage to Mendelssohn, who was a founder of Berlin's first Jewish school here in 1778, and who, until 1938, was commemorated by a bust in the school garden.

On the other side of the street is the **Missing House**, a unique and effective monument to the wartime destruction of Berlin. A gap in the tenements marks where house number 15–16 stood until destroyed by a direct hit during an air raid. In the autumn of 1990 the French artist Christian Boltanski put plaques on the side walls of the surviving buildings on either side as part of an installation, recalling the names, dates and professions of the former inhabitants of the vanished house.

Wartime scars

Like the old houses around Grosse Hamburger Strasse, nearly all buildings that remain from the war, and which have not had their facades redone since the *Wende*, show the damage inflicted during the Battle of Berlin: take a look at Krausnickstrasse, Auguststrasse, or on the sidestreets of Prenzlauer Berg (see Chapter 9), and you'll see scores of bullet and shell marks.

The Sophienkirche

Continuing north along the street, past turn-of-the-century Neo-
Baroque apartment buildings, brings you to the entrance gateway of
the **Sophienkirche** on the right-hand side.

Dating back to 1712, this is one of the city's finest Baroque
churches, and was the only central Berlin church to survive the war
more or less undamaged. Its clear, simple lines come as a welcome
change after the monumental Neoclassicism and fussy Gothic
revivalism of so much of Berlin's architecture. The church's seventy-
metre-high tiered tower is one of the area's most prominent landmarks and was added during the 1730s.

The ground on which the church was built was a gift from the
Jewish community to the Protestant community, who at the time
were slightly financially embarrassed. The church itself was paid
for by Princess Sophie Louise, in order to provide a parish church
for the neighbourhood, then an outlying area known as the
Spandauer Vorstadt. The **interior**, in washed-out shades of green
and grey, is a simple but pleasing affair, and you can't help but feel
that this is one church where restoration could only have a detri-
mental effect. The one note of aesthetic exuberance is a pulpit with
a crown-like canopy, set on a spiral pillar, which makes it look
exactly like a chalice.

Sophienstrasse and the Hackesche Höfe

Just beyond the Sophienkirche, a sharp turn to the right takes you
into **Sophienstrasse**, first settled at the end of the seventeenth century and once the Spandauer Vorstadt's main street.

During the 1980s the street was extensively restored and its buildings now house a mix of retailers and arts and crafts workshops. In
places, however, the restoration is only skin deep and the pastel
frontages of the old apartment houses conceal squalid, crumbling
courtyards. House no. 11 dates back to 1780, and the vaguely
Gothic-looking **Handwerkervereinshaus** at no. 18 used to be the
headquarters of the old Craftsmens' Guild. Until the founding of the
German Social Democrat Party (SPD), this had been the main focus
of the Berlin workers' movement, and thereafter its headquarters
continued to play an important role as a frequent venue for political
meetings, including, on November 14, 1918, the first public gathering of the Spartakusbund (Spartacus League), the breakaway antiwar faction of the SPD that later evolved into the KPD (Communist
Party of Germany).

At Sophienstrasse 21, a doorway leads to the **Sophie-Gips Höfe**, a
recently renovated retail and office complex that houses the
Sammlung Hoffman, a private art collection some of the larger
pieces of which are on display outside, and *Barcomi's Delicatessen*,
a trendy coffee and cake establishment representative of the current
climate of the neighbourhood. A walk through the colourful, neon-lit

passageway brings you to neighbouring Gipsstrasse, a rather quiet side street but a night-time favourite, with a couple of trendy bars as well as the fashionable *Fournier's* restaurant (see *Restaurants*, p.251).

The Hackesche Höfe

Further down Sophienstrasse, just past the *Sophienclub* at no. 8, is the latest significant force of revitalization in the area, the **Hackesche Höfe**, a series of nine courtyards built between 1905 and 1907 to house businesses, flats and places of entertainment. Restored to their former Art Deco glory, the *Höfe* (courtyards) bustle with crowds visiting the several cafés, stores, galleries, theatres and cinemas within. The *Höfe* were originally intended as a centre for the city's emerging artists but the result is all a bit too premeditated to be of any use to up-and-coming talent, most of whom gravitate to the network of galleries on and around Auguststrasse. That said, it's one of the main draws of the neighbourhood, and definitely worth a look-in, if nothing else for the architecture and people-watching opportunities. The first courtyard, decorated with blue mosaic tiles, is home to the **Chamaleon Varieté**, a venue at the forefront of the revival of the city's interwar cabaret tradition (see *The arts*). The second courtyard contains the **Hackesche Höfe Theater**, which regularly plays host to *klezmer* concerts and Jewish-themed theatre pieces.

Directly opposite Sophienstrasse is Neue Schönhauserstrasse, another street with a concentration of shops displaying a young and fashionable assortment of clothing and footwear, in addition to a couple of sleek and rather expensive restaurants – all a very long way from the old GDR.

CENTRAL BERLIN

North and east of Sophienstrasse

North of Sophienstrasse are a few lesser-known attractions, worth seeking out if you've developed a taste for wandering the backstreets of central Berlin. Further out, at the very northern boundary of the district, is one of the few remaining sections of the Wall – now the **Berlin Wall Memorial**. East of Sophienstrasse, between Alte Schönhauser Strasse and Karl-Liebknecht-Strasse, is the traditional heart of the old Scheunenviertel quarter, and one-time centre of the city's scrap-iron and rag-and-bone trades. The obvious attraction here is the **Volksbühne** theatre.

The Garnisonsfriedhof and Volkspark am Weinberg

The leafy **Garnisonsfriedhof** on Kleine Rosenthaler Strasse is a neglected military cemetery dating from the eighteenth century, full of rusting cast-iron crosses with near-obliterated inscriptions commemorating the officers and men of the Prussian army. Also here is the rather grander tomb of Adolph von Lützow, a general who found fame during the Napoleonic Wars, contrasting sharply with the overgrown wooden crosses commemorating victims of the Battle of Berlin, hidden away in a far corner. Information about the history of the cemetery is available from the administration offices near the entrance, which also house a small **exhibition** (Mon–Thurs 10am–5.50pm, Fri 10am–3.30pm; free). There's more innercity greenery a few streets to the northwest in the **Volkspark am Weinberg**, a sloping park on the site of a former vineyard at the corner of Brunnenstrasse and Veteranenstrasse.

The Berlin Wall Memorial

Northwest again from the park, right on the edge of the district, is **Bernauerstrasse** (U-Bahn Bernauerstrasse or S-Bahn Nordbahnhof), a street that was literally bisected by the Wall. Before the Wall was erected you could enter or exit the Soviet Zone just by going through the door of one of the buildings on this street, which is why, on August 13, 1961, some citizens who woke up to find themselves on the wrong side of the newly established "national border" leapt out of windows to get to the West. Over the years, the facades of these buildings were cemented up and incorporated into the partition itself, until they were knocked down and replaced by the Wall proper in 1979. A short section of it, now the **Berlin Wall Memorial** (Berliner Mauer Gedenkstätte) remains at the corner of Bernauerstrasse and Ackerstrasse, enclosed at both ends by a newly erected "sculpture" of rusted metal barriers. Across the street at Bernauerstrasse 111 is the **Wall Documentation Centre** (Wed–Sun 10am–5pm; free), where photos, sound recordings and info-terminals keep alive the story of the Wall. Diagonally across the street is the site of the **Versöhnungskirche** (Church of Reconciliation), blown up by the GDR border patrol in 1985 and now in the process of being rebuilt, using various salvaged relics from the old building. Originally built in 1894, its new incarnation is intended to symbolize a reconciliation of East and West.

The Volksbühne and around

On Rosa-Luxemburg-Platz the most prominent landmark is the **Volksbühne** theatre, built in 1913 with money raised by public subscription. Under the directorship of the ubiquitous Max Reinhardt, it became Berlin's people's theatre and, daringly for that time, put on plays by Hauptmann, Strindberg and Ibsen. Erwin Piscator continued the revolutionary tradition from 1924 to 1927, and immediately after the war in September 1945 a production of Lessing's plea for tolerance, *Nathan the Wise*, was put on here. The theatre was offi-

cially reopened in 1954 and became one of the ex-GDR capital's best
theatres. These days it's still one of the most exciting and innovative
theatres in the city, under director Frank Castorf (see *The arts*).

Nearby, at Weydingerstrasse 14 and Kleine Alexanderstrasse 28,
is the **Karl-Liebknecht-Haus**, the former KPD central committee
headquarters, which also housed the editorial offices of the
Communist newspaper *Rote Fahne* ("Red Flag"). From the late
1920s onwards this was an important centre of resistance to the
increasingly powerful Nazis: 100,000 pro-Communist workers
demonstrated here on January 25, 1933, just a few days before Hitler
came to power. After the Reichstag fire in February 1933 the KPD
was broken up and its headquarters ransacked.

A couple of nearby streets, Almstadtstrasse and Mulackstrasse,
though fairly unremarkable today, were important parts of the
Scheunenviertel scene during its heyday. **Almstadtstrasse**, formerly
known as Grenadierstrasse, became a magnet for Jewish migrants
from eastern Europe and Russia at the end of the nineteenth century
and it was here that a bustling street market grew up, echoing the
Schtetl districts where Jewish traders did business in eastern
European and Russian towns. During the inflationary period of
1923–24 the street gained notoriety as a black-market centre, with
dealers trading illegally in everything from currency to precious
stones.

Mulackstrasse was home to a famous Scheunenviertel *Gaststätte*,
the *Mulack-Ritz*, whose clientele encompassed pimps, prostitutes
and small-time gangsters, as well as artists and actors. The establishment survived until the general closing down enforced by the
GDR authorities in the 1960s, though the interior has been preserved
in the Gründerzeitmuseum in Mahlsdorf (see p.189).

Chapter 6

The West End, Tiergarten and around

L atterly regarded as the centre of West Berlin, the area around Zoo Station is gradually reverting to its prewar role. In Wilhelmine and Weimar Berlin, this was the city's **WEST END**. Far from the municipal grandeur of the poorer working-class residential neighbourhoods to the south and east, the West End was based, then as now, on the slick shops of the **Kurfürstendamm**. It was a centre for cinemas, cabaret and clubs by night, cafés and shops by day: even in the grim first few years after the war, a few shops managed to struggle on here. With the coming of the Berlin Wall, the West End had a new role forced upon it, one it played poorly. West Berlin was a city without a true centre, and no amount of showcase building could transform the area into the heart of a great late twentieth-century metropolis. Now, with the balance of the city restored, the West End should regain its proper role as complement to the new centre further to the east.

While no one could call the area immediately around Zoo Station attractive, and first impressions suggest little more than a glorified (though scruffy) shopping precinct run up against third-rate modern architecture, there's plenty to explore – once you've scratched below the surface.

On the eastern side of Zoo Station the zoo itself, the Zoologischer Garten, occupies the westernmost portion of the **Tiergarten** – Berlin's central park. Stretching over to the Brandenburg Gate and Reichstag in the east, the Tiergarten offers a welcome contrast to the development surrounding it and has some very pretty spots, especially in spring and summer. Just south of the central portion of the park, and west of the Potsdamer Platz complex, is the **Kulturforum**, one of the city's pockets of cultural interest. Highlight of the superb agglomeration of museums, exhibition spaces and venues is the **Gemäldegalerie**, with its internationally renowned collection of European art.

Around Zoo Station

Whether you come by train, or on the bus from Tegel airport, chances are you'll arrive at Bahnhof Zoologischer Garten – **Zoo Station**. Perched high above the street, and with views across to the zoo itself, the train station conjures up memories of prewar steam trains as you pull in under its glassy roof. Unfortunately, that's as far as the nostalgia goes: Zoo Station is comparatively small, without a large lobby or grand entrance portal, so overall it rather lacks presence. More importantly though, at street level it has been smartened up quite a bit, and despite the retinue of urban casualties permanently posted by the entrance, it's a far cry from the days, a decade or so ago, when it was a marketplace for heroin dealing and child prostitution. A few glossy, late-opening stores like Body Shop and Internationale Presse contribute to the new look, while better signposting, a prominent new information kiosk in the lobby, and the presence of EurAide, a company providing English-language travel information (see p.46), make the whole place a lot more traveller-friendly.

South to the Ku'damm

Step out east from Zoo Station and you're in the centre of the West End's maelstrom of bright lights, traffic and high-rise buildings. Walk a block south along Joachimstalerstrasse to Kantstrasse, and on the corner you can't miss the **Erotik-Museum** (daily 9am–midnight; *www.erotikmuseum.com*; DM10/€5.10). The museum is run by Beate Uhse, a household name in Germany; once a Luftwaffe test pilot she began selling sex education pamphlets after the war and now heads a multimillion-mark corporation dedicated to all things sexual. Located on three floors above her sex shop, the museum is really an assemblage rather than an organized exhibition, but it does present a surprisingly extensive collection of prints, paintings and objects – including Japanese silk paintings, Balinese fertility shrines, Indian reliefs in wood and Chinese bordello tokens, to name but a few. The assortment of 1920s and 1930s artwork from Europe, including charcoal sketches of cabaretist Anita Berber, and pieces by George Grosz and local favorite Heinrich Zille, are particularly good, suggesting – albeit faintly – something of the atmosphere of Weimar Berlin.

For more on shopping around Zoo Station and along the Ku'damm, see Shopping in Listings.

Another block south and you're at the eastern end of the **Kurfürstendamm** (universally known as the **Ku'damm**), a 3.5-kilometre strip of ritzy shops, cinemas, bars and cafés that homes in on the centre like the spoke of a broken wheel. The great landmark here, the one that's on all the postcards, is the **Kaiser-Wilhelm-Gedächtniskirche** (Kaiser Wilhelm Memorial Church), built at the end of the nineteenth century and destroyed by British bombing in November 1943. Left as a reminder, it's a strangely effective memori-

KaDeWe

Zoologischer
Garten
(Zoo)

BUDAPESTER STRASSE

NÜRNBERGER STRASSE

PASSAUER STRASSE

Tourist
Office

Europa Center

TAUENTZIENSTRASSE

NÜRNBERGER STRASSE

Late-night
Post Office

Augsburger Str.
U-Bahn

MARBURGER STRASSE

BREITSCHEID-
PLATZ

HARDENBERGSTR.

LOS ANGELES PLATZ

STRASSE

ISLEBENER STRASSE

Zoo
Station

Zoologischer
Garten
U-Bahn

Kaiser-Wilhelm-
Gedächtniskirche

Chapel

KURFÜRSTENDAMM

AUGSBURGER

RANKE

STRASSE

EurAide
Office

Erotik
Museum

JOACHIMSTALER STR.

JOACHIMSTALER STRASSE

MEINEKESTRASSE

LIETZENBURGER STRASSE

HARDENBERGSTRASSE

Jüdisches
Gemeindehaus

Kurfürstendamm
U-Bahn

KURFÜRSTENDAMM

STRASSE

FASANENSTRASSE

FASANENSTRASSE

KANTSTRASSE

UHLANDSTRASSE

Käthe
Kollwitz
Museum

FASANENSTRASSE

MEINEKESTRASSE

STEIN
PLATZ

UHLANDSTRASSE

UHLANDSTRASSE

GOETHESTRASSE

CARMENSTRASSE

GROLMANSTRASSE

Uhlandstrasse
U-Bahn

Story of
Berlin

KURFÜRSTENDAMM

KNESEBECKSTRASSE

SAVIGNY
PLATZ

KNESEBECKSTRASSE

KANTSTRASSE

GROLMANSTRASSE

PESTALOZZISTRASSE

Savignyplatz
S-Bahn

NIEBUHRSTRASSE

BLEIBTREUSTRASSE

MOMMSENSTRASSE

KURFÜRSTENDAMM

AROUND ZOO STATION

0   100m

△ Technische Universität

▽ Adenauerplatz

al, the crumbling tower providing a hint of the old city. It's possible to
go inside what remains of the nave (Mon–Sat 10am–4pm): there's a
small exhibit showing wartime destruction and a "before and after"
model of the city centre. Adjacent, a modern **chapel** contains the tender, sad charcoal sketch, *Stalingrad Madonna*, while at the back the
blue-glass campanile of the chapel has gained the nickname of the
"Lipstick" or the "Soul-Silo" because of its tubular shape: its base contains a shop selling Third World gifts. The area around the church acts
as a magnet for vendors, caricaturists, and street musicians, while
Breitscheidplatz, the square behind, often hosts fairs or festivals in
the summer that feature much the same cast of characters – otherwise
it serves as an outdoor annexe to the Europa Center shopping mall.

The Europa Center and around

Breitscheidplatz marks the beginning of Tauentzienstrasse, with the
Europa Center, a huge shopping centre that contains the Berlin
Tourismus Marketing **tourist office** (Mon–Sat 8.30am–8.30pm, Sun
10am–6.30pm; *www.btm.de*) on its northern side. There's nothing
much of interest in this rather generic mall, which was built in the
1960s as a capitalist showcase for West Berlin, topped by a huge,
rotating Mercedes-Benz symbol. An intriguing sculpture entitled the
"Flow of Time", an alternative clock consisting of an elaborate series
of liquid-filled glass pipes, does however attract some attention down
in the lobby. Further down Tauentzienstrasse, and claiming to be the
largest store on the continent, is the **KaDeWe**, an abbreviation of
Kaufhaus Des Westens – "the Department Store of the West". It's an
impressive statement of the city's standard of living, and the sixth-
floor food hall is a mouthwatering inducement to sample the many
exotic snacks sold there. A little further down, **Wittenbergplatz U-
Bahn station** has been likeably restored to its prewar condition both
inside (1920s kitsch) and out (Neoclassical pavilion). Near the
entrance, a tall sign reminds passers-by of the wartime concentration
camps: it states that the German people must never be allowed to
forget the atrocities that were carried out there, and lists the names
of the camps. It's an odd memorial, and one that goes largely unnoticed by Ku'damm shoppers.

West along the Ku'damm

West of the Europa Center, the Ku'damm begins its stretch of shops
and cafés, which tend to be less expensive the further west you go,
blazing a trail at night in a dazzle of neon. The Ku'damm was built
under Bismarck in the nineteenth century, and Thomas Wolfe called
it "the largest coffee-house in Europe" when spending time here in
the 1920s; these days there's little left from either man's time. If the
shops are beyond your budget, some of the street vendors selling
clothes and jewellery are fun places to find trinkets.

The Jüdisches Gemeindehaus and Zille-Hof

There's little to do on the Ku'damm other than spend money, but
you'll find a couple of places of interest on Fasanenstrasse, which
traverses it about 200m from the Ku'damm U-Bahn. On the north
side, at nos. 79–80, the **Jüdisches Gemeindehaus** (Jewish
Community House) incorporates parts of a former synagogue
attacked by the Nazis on the night of November 9, 1938, when synagogues, Jewish-owned shops and homes throughout the country
were destroyed – the Kristallnacht or "Crystal Night", so-named
because of the mass of broken glass that resulted (see p.112–113).
A wall in the front courtyard is inscribed with the names of the concentration camps and wartime ghettos. Opposite the Gemeindehaus
(just under the rail bridge) is the **Zille-Hof** flea market-cum-
junk/antique shop – there's plenty of interesting stuff among the rub-
bish, but the pleasure is in rummaging as much as in buying.

The Käthe Kollwitz Museum and The Berlin Story

Fasanenstrasse continues on the other side of the Ku'damm, where the
one cultural attraction, the **Käthe Kollwitz Museum**, is at no. 24 (daily
except Tues 11am–6pm; *www.kaethe-kollwitz.de*; DM8/€4.10, concessions DM4/€2.05; U-Bahn Uhlandstrasse, bus #109, #119, #129
& #219). The drawings and prints of Käthe Kollwitz are among the
most moving works from the first half of the twentieth century. Born
in 1867, she lived for almost all her life in Prenzlauer Berg in the eastern part of the city (see Chapter 9), where her work evolved a radical
left-wing perspective. Following the death of her son in World War I,
her woodcuts, lithographs and prints became explicitly pacifist, often
dwelling on the theme of mother and child – her most famous print, *No
More War*, a stark, furious work depicting a protesting mother, is a
perfect example. Her sculptures too, often deal with this subject: two
of her bronzes, *Tower of Women* and the pietà *Mother with Dead
Son*, can be seen here. When her grandson was killed in World War II
her work became even sadder and more poignant. The museum's comprehensive collection of her work makes it possible to trace its development, culminating in the tragic sculptures on the top floor.

While it can't really be called a cultural attraction, **The Berlin
Story**, just down from the Uhlandstrasse U-Bahn at Kurfürstendamm
207–208 (daily 10am–8pm; *www.story-of-berlin.de*; DM18/€9.20,
concessions DM14/€7.15) might have some appeal for those seeking a basic grounding in the history of the city. It's a privately run
multimedia exhibition, with life-size dioramas accompanied by film
clips, loud noises, flashing lights, smoke and smells, that takes view-
ers through some of the highs and lows of the city's turbulent past.

Adenauerplatz and Savignyplatz

By the time you reach **Adenauerplatz**, the slick showrooms of the
Ku'damm have died out and the bars become affordable: although

the clientele tends to consist of loud and brash teenagers, it's not a
bad starting point for an evening's boozing. Best of all for eating,
drinking and nightlife, though, is the squashed rectangle of streets
south and west of Zoo Station, roughly bordered by Kantstrasse,
Hardenbergstrasse and Leibnizstrasse, and focusing on
Savignyplatz.

Hardenbergstrasse itself runs from Zoo Station to Ernst-Reuter-
Platz, a blandly modern oval named after the city's first postwar gov-
erning mayor. To the east, the **Technische Universität** (most striking of whose buildings is the huge, brilliantly painted **Umlauftank**, a
hydraulics research centre at the edge of the Tiergarten) marks an
uncompromisingly modern start to Strasse des 17 Juni; a collection
of old clothes and new crafts makes the weekend **flea market** on the
north side of the street a good place to browse.

CENTRAL BERLIN

The Tiergarten and Kulturforum

The **Tiergarten**, a huge swathe of peaceful green smack in the middle of Berlin, has some beautifully landscaped meadows, gardens
and woodlands that serve as a great antidote to the bustle and noise
of the city, yet at the same time contain a number of attractions. Just
to the south is the **Kulturforum** museum complex, the highpoints of
which, in addition to the **Gemäldegalerie**, include the **Neue
Nationalgalerie**'s collection of twentieth-century art and the
Kunstgewerbemuseum's superb applied arts exhibition.

The Tiergarten and around

Immediately to the east of Zoo Station the **Zoologischer Garten**
(daily: summer 9am–6.30pm; winter 9am–5pm; *www.zoo-berlin.de*;
DM14/€7.15, under-15s DM7/€3.60; aquarium same prices; combined ticket DM22.50/€11, under-15s DM11.50/€5.60) forms the
beginning of the **Tiergarten**, a restful expanse of woodland and lakes.
Designed by Peter Lenné, the park was laid out under Elector
Friedrich III as a hunting ground and destroyed during the Battle of
Berlin in 1945 – though so successful has its replanting been that
these days it's hard to tell it's not original. The zoo and its aquarium
are like any the world over, and expensive to boot (see *Children's
Berlin*): better to wander through the Tiergarten, tracing the course
of the **Landwehrkanal**, an inland waterway off the River Spree.

Near the Corneliusbrücke, a small, odd sculpture commemorates
the radical leader **Rosa Luxemburg**. In 1918, along with fellow revolutionary Karl Liebknecht (see p.81), she reacted against the
newly formed Weimar Republic and especially the terms of the
Treaty of Versailles, declaring a new Socialist Republic in Berlin
along the lines of Soviet Russia (she had played an important part
in the abortive 1905 revolution). The pair were kidnapped by mem-

THE TIERGARTEN AND AROUND

Former course of Wall

Reichstag
Brandenburg Gate
Site of Hitler's Bunker
Luftfahrts-ministerium
Topography of Terror
Potsdamer-Platz U-Bahn
Gropius-Bau
Soviet War Memorial
Philharmonie & Musikinstrumenten-Museum
Kupferstichkabinett
Staatsbibliothek
Matthäikirche
Kunstgewerbe-museum
Neue Nationalgalerie
Gemäldegalerie
Resistance Exhibition
Haus der Kulturen der Welt
Tiergarten
Bauhaus Archive
Siegessäule
Schloss Bellevue
Cornelius-brücke
Neuer See
Aquarium
Europa Center
Tourist Office
Zoologischer Garten (Zoo)
Zoo Station
Erotik Museum
Kaiser-Wilhelm-Gedächtniskirche

0   200m

River Spree

N

bers of the elite First Cavalry Guards: Liebknecht was gunned down while "attempting to escape", Luxemburg was knocked unconscious and shot, her body dumped in the Landwehrkanal at this point.

Just to the north, a pretty little group of ponds makes up the grand-sounding **Neuer See**; in summer there's a popular beer garden here, the *Café am Neuen See* (see *Cafés and bars*, p.273) and it's possible to rent **boats** by the hour.

The broad avenue that cuts through the Tiergarten to form the continuation of Unter den Linden's triumphal way was originally named Charlottenburger Chaussee. Once known as the **East–West Axis**, it was a favourite strip for Nazi processions: indeed Hitler had the stretch from the Brandenburg Gate to Theodor-Heuss-Platz (formerly Adolf-Hitler-Platz) widened in order to accommodate these mass displays of military might and Nazi power; on his birthday in 1938, 40,000 men and 600 tanks took four hours to parade past the Führer. Later, in the final days of the war, Charlottenburger Chaussee became a makeshift runway for aeroplanes ferrying Nazi notables to and from the besieged capital. Now called Strasse des 17 Juni, its name commemorates the day in 1953 when workers in the East rose in revolt against the occupying Soviet powers, demanding free elections, the removal of all borders separating the two Germanys, and freedom for political prisoners. Soviet forces were quickly mobilized, and between two and four hundred people died; the authorities also ordered the execution of twenty-one East Berliners and eighteen Soviet soldiers – for "moral capitulation to the demonstrators".

The Siegessäule

By night, the area around the Siegessäule is one of the city's principal cruising points for gay men. See Gay and lesbian Berlin in Basics.

At the centre of Strasse des 17 Juni is the **Siegessäule** (daily: summer 9.30am–6.30pm; winter 9.30am–5.30pm; DM2/€1, concessions DM1/€0.25); U-Bahn Hansaplatz, bus #100, #187 & #341), the victory column celebrating Prussia's military victories (chiefly that over France in 1871). It was shifted to this spot on Hitler's orders in 1938 from what is today known as Platz der Republik. Though the boulevard approaches exaggerate its size, it's still an eye-catching monument: 67m high and topped with a gilded winged victory that symbolically faces France. The summit offers a good view of the surrounding area, but climbing the 585 steps to the top is no mean feat. Have a look, too, at the mosaics at the column's base, which show the unification of the German peoples and incidents from the Franco-Prussian War: they were removed after 1945 and taken to Paris, only to be returned when the lust for war spoils had subsided. Dotted around the Siegessäule are **statues** of other German notables, the most imposing being that of Bismarck, the "Iron Chancellor", under whom the country was united in the late nineteenth century. He's surrounded by figures symbolizing his achievements; walk around the back for the most powerful.

East from the Siegessäule

From the Siegessäule it's a long hike down to the Brandenburg Gate and Reichstag, and most visitors take the #100 or #200 bus from Zoo Station or the Europa Center. If you do come this way, it's worth looking out for **Schloss Bellevue**, an eighteenth-century building that was once a guesthouse for the Third Reich and is today the Berlin home of the Federal President – and only visitable when he's not in residence. Further east, on John-Foster-Dulles-Allee, sits the upturned banana of the **Kongresshalle**, an exhibition centre whose concept couldn't be matched by available technology: its roof collapsed in 1980, and it has since been rebuilt and reopened as the **Haus der Kulturen der Welt**, a venue for theatre, music, performance art and exhibitions from the Third World and Far East (see *Clubs and live venues*). South from here, on the north side of Strasse des 17 Juni, is the **Soviet War Memorial** to the Red Army troops who died in the Battle of Berlin. Built from the marble of Hitler's destroyed Berlin HQ, the Reich's Chancellery, it's flanked by two tanks that were supposedly the first to reach the city.

Around the Tiergarten

On the southeast side of the park, the **Kulturforum**, a complex of art museums, offers a variety of cultural delights (see below). Few visitors venture north into **Wedding**, an industrial/working-class residential suburb whose charms are few, despite its prewar fame as a socialist heartland known as "Red Wedding". But it's worth pushing north from the park for the **Hamburger Bahnhof** at Invalidenstrasse 50–51 (Tues–Fri 10am–6pm, Sat & Sun 11am–6pm; *www.smb.spk-berlin.de*; DM8/€4.10, concessions DM4/€2.05), free first Sun of each month; U-Bahn Zinnowitzer Strasse or S-Bahn Lehrter Stadtbahnhof). Like the Anhalter Bahnhof to the south (see p.134), the Hamburger station was damaged in the war, though it had ceased functioning as a station as early as 1906. Fortunately, it didn't suffer its twin's fate in postwar redevelopment, and is today the home of the new **Museum for Contemporary Art**. The collection here represents a thorough survey of postwar art: Rauschenberg, Twombly, Warhol, Beuys, Lichtenstein, right on up to Keith Haring and Donald Judd. And the old railway station makes a spacious, effective setting, particularly the main hall, where large sculptures by Judd, Anselm Kiefer and Richard Long, among others, are displayed. It's well worth a visit, though there are disappointingly few surprises. When you need a break, there's a good bookstore and café on the premises.

The Kulturforum

To the west of Potsdamer Platz, the **Kulturforum** (U- or S-Bahn Potsdamer Platz) is a mixture of museums and cultural spaces that could easily fill a day of your time. Along with the Dahlem museum complex and the collections on the Museum Island, it's one of

Berlin's cultural focal points. With the completion of the Gemäldegalerie, which brings together a world-class collection of early European paintings formerly split between museums in the East and West, this complex has finally achieved the prominent status intended for it when construction began in a still-divided city.

The Neue Nationalgalerie

By far the finest building here – architecturally speaking – is the **Neue Nationalgalerie**, Potsdamer Strasse 50 (Tues–Fri 10am–6pm, Sat & Sun 11am–6pm; *www.smb.spk-berlin.de*; DM8/€4.10, concessions DM4/€2.05, free first Sun of month), a black-rimmed glass box that seems almost suspended above the ground, its clarity of line and detail having all the intelligent simplicity of the Parthenon. Designed by Mies van der Rohe in 1965, the upper section is used for temporary exhibits, often of contemporary art, while the underground galleries contain paintings from the beginning of the twentieth century onwards. Included among the permanent collection are the paintings of the "Brücke" group, such as Ernst Kirchner and Karl Schmidt-Rottluff. **Kirchner** spent time in Berlin before World War I, and his *Potsdamer Platz* dates from 1914, though it might as well be in another country instead of just down the road. The galleries move on to the portraits and Berlin cityscapes of **Grosz** and **Dix**, notably Grosz's *Gray Day* and Dix's *Maler Family*. Cubism is represented by work from **Braque**, **Gris** and **Picasso** (though the latter is seen in greater number and to better effect in the Berggruen Collection in Charlottenburg; see p.155). There are also pieces by, among others, Klee, Max Beckmann and Lyonel Feininger.

The Gemäldegalerie

The real jewel of the Kulturforum is the **Gemäldegalerie** (Picture Gallery; Tues–Fri 10am–6pm, Sat & Sun 11am–6pm; *www.smb .spk-berlin.de*; DM8/€4.10, concessions DM4/€2.05, free first Sun of month), which holds a stupendous collection of early European paintings. Originally housed in the prewar Kaiser-Friedrich Museum, the gallery's paintings were stashed in various places throughout the city for safekeeping during the war years, with the result that after the division of Berlin the collection was split between the Bode Museum in the East and the Dahlem complex in the West. The gallery's holdings have now been reunited in a new custom-built structure.

Almost nine hundred paintings are on display, arranged in chronological order, and subdivided by region, beginning on the north side of the building with **German works** of the middle ages and Renaissance. Highlights include the large *Wurzach Altar* of 1437, made in the workshop of the great Ulm sculptor Hans Multscher; its exaggerated gestures and facial distortions mark it out as an ancient precursor of Expressionist painting. An interesting contrast is offered by the far more subtle *Solomon before the Queen of Sheba*, painted in the same year by Konrad Witz, while the exquisite *Nativity* by Martin Schongauer is the most important surviving panel by the father-figure of the German Renaissance.

These apart, the best works here are by Albrecht Altdorfer, one of the first fully realized German landscape painters, and Albrecht Dürer – among others, *The Madonna with the Siskin* and *Hieronymous Holzschuher* – with an impressive group of works by Dürer's eccentric pupil Hans Baldung, notably an exotic *Adoration of the Magi* triptych. Holbein the Younger is represented by several superbly observed portraits, the most celebrated being *The Danzig Merchant Georg Gisze*, with a still-life background that's a real tour-de-force of artistic virtuosity. Notable among the many examples of Cranach are his tongue-in-cheek *The Fountain of Youth*, and his free reinterpretation of Bosch's famous triptych *The Garden of Earthly Delights*.

The Netherlandish section
A lighter, less crude treatment of religious subjects is apparent in the **Netherlandish section**. Particularly illustrative is Jan van Eyck's beautifully lit *Madonna in the Church*, crammed with architectural detail and with the Virgin lifted in the perspective for gentle emphasis. Petrus Christus is thought to have been a pupil of van Eyck, and certainly knew his work, as *The Virgin and Child with St Barbara and a Carthusian Monk* reveals: in the background are tiny Flemish houses and street scenes, the artist carefully locating the event in his native Bruges. Dieric Bouts' figures tend to be stiff and rather formalized, but his *Christ in the House of Simon the Pharisee* is filled with gesture, expression and carefully drawn detail.

Also on show are some pieces by Rogier van der Weyden, which show the development of the Eyckian technique to a warmer, much more emotional treatment of religious subjects. The figures in his *Middelburg Altar* reveal a delicacy of poise and an approachable humanity that was to greatly influence German painting in the fifteenth century. Albert van Ouwater was also influential, although his *Raising of Lazarus* is the only complete work to have survived; it's a daring picture, the richly dressed merchants on the right contrasting strongly with the simplicity of the Holy Family on the left. Geertgen tot Sint Jans was Ouwater's pupil, though his *St John the Baptist* is quite different from his master's painting – the saint sits almost comically impassive against a rich backdrop of intricately constructed landscape. Two other major paintings nearby are both by Hugo van der Goes: the *Adoration of the Shepherds* (painted when the artist was in the first throes of madness) has the scene unveiled by two characters representing the prophets, while the shepherds stumble into the frame; the *Adoration of the Magi* – also known as the *Monforte Altarpiece* – has a superbly drawn realism that marks a new development in Netherlandish art, carrying precision over into a large-scale work with a deftly executed, complex perspective. The small altarpiece *Triptych with the Adoration of the Magi* by Joos van Cleve reveals how these techniques were absorbed by Goes' successors. The collection then moves into the sixteenth century and the works of Jan Gossaert, Quentin Massys and Bruegel the Elder, whose *Netherlandish Proverbs* is an amusing, if hard-to-grasp, illustration of over a hundred sixteenth-century proverbs and maxims – a key and English translation help you pick out a man armed to the teeth, banging his head against a brick wall and casting pearls before swine.

The Dutch and Flemish collections
The next section reveals the gallery's second strength in the **Dutch and Flemish collections**. This contains the large portraits of Van Dyck and the fleshy canvases of Rubens, as well as a fine group of Dutch interiors. The paintings of Vermeer are the most easily identifiable, though his *Woman with a Pearl Necklace* is not one of his greater works. Better is *Man and Woman Drinking Wine*, which displays his usual technique of placing furniture obliquely in the centre of the canvas, the scene illuminated by window light. His contemporary Pieter de Hooch is represented by *The Mother*, a masterly example of Dutch interior painting. Other rooms trace the development of Dutch art through the works of Nicholas Maes, Gerrit Dou, Jan Steen and Frans Hals.

The highpoint of this section, hung in a large octagonal room, are the paintings of **Rembrandt**. The most famous picture here, *The Man in the Golden Helmet*, was recently proved to be the work of his studio rather than the artist himself, though this does little to detract from the elegance and power of the portrait, its reflective sorrow relieved by the bright helmet. Other (verified) works include a 1634 *Self-Portrait*, painted at the height of the artist's wealth and fame; *The Mennonite Preacher Anslo and His Wife*, from 1641; a beautifully warm and loving *Portrait of Hendrickje Stoffels*, the artist's later, common-law wife; and several other religious paintings.

Interruping the chronology somewhat are three rooms in the southwest corner displaying, respectively, eighteenth-century French, English (including several Gainsborough portraits) and German paintings.

Italian paintings
The galleries on the museum's southern side contain, for the most part, **Italian paintings** from the Renaissance to the eighteenth century. This collection is particularly strong on works from the Florentine Renaissance: Fra Filippo Lippi's *The Adoration in the Forest* is a mystical image of unusual grace and beauty, rightly one of the most admired paintings of the period, while Correggio's play-

fully suggestive *Leda with the Swan* is a good example of the Classical preoccupations of the period. Classical themes again crop up in Piero de Cosimo's *Venus, Mars, and Cupid*, completed about two decades before Correggio's painting; though not one of the eccentric artist's better-known works, it is an intimate rendering of a popular scenario. There's work here, too, by Giotto, Verrocchio, Masaccio, Mantegna, Raphael and Titian, and, most importantly, two by Botticelli: *Madonna wth Saints* and *Mary with the Child and Singing Angels*.

Other noteworthy painters represented in the museum include Caravaggio (*Cupid Victorious*, heavy with symbolism and homoeroticism), Poussin (the important *Self-Portrait*), Claude and Canaletto.

The Philharmonie and Musikinstrumenten museum

North of the Nationalgalerie, the **Matthäikirche** (Matthias Church) is the only survivor from the war in this area. Opposite is the **Philharmonie**, home of the Berlin Philharmonic and, until he retired and subsequently died in 1989, its renowned conductor **Herbert von Karajan** (see below). Looking at the gold-clad ugliness of the building, designed in the 1960s by Hans Scharoun, and bearing in mind von Karajan's famously short temper with artists, it's easy to see how it got its nickname among Berliners of "Karajan's circus". Should you wish to reserve a seat the box office is open Monday to Friday from 3.30pm to 6pm, Saturday and Sunday 11am to 2pm (☎25 48 81 32): the chances of getting a ticket for major concerts are slim unless you've booked months in advance, but it's worth trying your luck for other performances under guest conductors.

Continuing the musical theme, the **Musikinstrumenten museum** (Tues–Fri 9am–5pm, Sat & Sun 10am–5pm; DM4/€2.05, concessions DM2/€1, free on first Sun of month) at Tiergartenstrasse 1, in the same building as the Philharmonie, comes as something of a dis-

For more on classical music and the performing arts, see The arts in Listings.

Herbert von Karajan (1908–89)

The success of Austrian conductor **Herbert von Karajan** in the postwar years obscured a murky past that included a close association with the Nazi Party. Exactly what this association was is unclear, though his organizing of concerts for the Führer – including an occasion when he had the audience seating arranged in the form of a swastika – is well documented, and in later years few of the world's great Jewish soloists ever performed or recorded with him.

From the 1960s to the 1980s von Karajan ruled the Berlin Philharmonic with a rigid discipline that alienated many who worked under him, but proved fabulously successful in the field of popularizing classical music. Under the Deutsche Grammophon label, they recorded just about everything that had a chance of selling, all in the highly polished von Karajan style – a style as distinctive (and to some as likeable) as that of Mantovani.

The Tiergarten and Kulturforum

appointment. Its collection of (mostly European) keyboards, wind and string instruments from the fifteenth century to the present day is comprehensive and impressively laid out, but it's all strictly look-don't-touch stuff, with guards vigilant for the slightest tinkle. Content yourself with the prerecorded tapes that give a taste of the weird and wonderful sounds of the instruments, which include a seventeenth-century cembalo, a nineteenth-century glass harmonica, consisting of liquid-filled glasses, and a three-storey-high 1929 Wurlitzer organ.

The Kunstgewerbemuseum

Much better is the **Kunstgewerbemuseum** (Museum of Applied Arts; Tues–Fri 10am–6pm, Sat & Sun 11am–6pm; DM4/€2.05, concessions DM2/€1, free first Sun of month) at Matthäikirchplatz 10, an encyclopedic but seldom dull collection of European arts and crafts. The top floor contains the Renaissance, Baroque and Rococo pieces (wonderful silver and ceramics), along with Jugendstil and Art Deco objects, particularly furniture. Among the many impressive pieces is a massive silver buffet that once resided in the Berlin City Palace, one of the very few surviving artefacts from that residence, and, of course, the museum has a superb collection of Meissenware and KPM porcelain. The ground floor holds the Middle Ages to Early Renaissance collections, with some sumptuous gold pieces. The highlights are Lüneburg's municipal silver and the treasures from the Stiftskirche in Enger and, in the basement, a small but great assembly of Bauhaus furniture, glittering contemporary jewellery, and a display on the evolution of product design.

The Kupferstichkabinett and Staatsbibliothek

The **Kupferstichkabinett** (Engraving Cabinet; Tues–Fri 10am–6pm, Sat & Sun 11am–6pm; DM4/€2.05, concessions DM2/€1, free first Sun of month) at Matthäikirchplatz 4 holds an extensive collection of European medieval and Renaissance prints, drawings and engravings, many kept under protective lighting. Founded by William Humboldt in 1831, the collection includes Botticelli's exquisite drawings for Dante's *Divine Comedy* (until recently divided between the Altes Museum and the Dahlem museum complex). The museum organizes exhibitions on all aspects of print-making, drawing and related design.

Lastly, the **Staatsbibliothek** (Mon–Fri 10am–8pm, Sat 10am–7pm; free), across Potsdamer Strasse from the other buildings, has over three and a half million books, occasional exhibitions, a small concert hall, a reasonable café and a wide selection of British newspapers. As the final building to be designed by Hans Scharoun, and the most popular of his works among his fans, the *Staabi*'s most recent claim to fame came when it was used as an important backdrop in Wim Wenders' poetic film elegy to the city, *Wings of Desire*.

Chapter 7

South of the centre

D irectly south of the centre and the Tiergarten lie the *Bezirke*, or districts of **Kreuzberg** and **Schöneberg** respectively. Both are, in the main, residential: by day, Kreuzberg is the more unkempt and less immediately likeable of the two; Schöneberg is more middle class and less ethnically mixed. If you've taken pension accommodation or found a private room via the tourist office, chances are that you'll end up in one of these areas, and while not crammed with things to see, both have their attractions. **Nightlife** in both is excellent, with the bars and clubs around Schöneberg's Nollendorfplatz being the place where smart people (and particularly smart gay people) hang out; Kreuzberg's reputation as home to

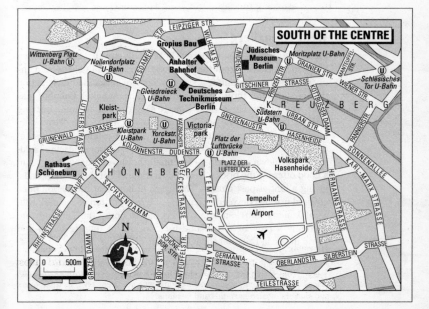

some of the city's more avant-garde nightspots still rings true, even if it's no longer at the cutting edge of Berlin's *Szene**.

Kreuzberg

The area directly south of Berlin's centre, bounded to the east by the River Spree and to the south by the *Bezirk* of Tempelhof, is **KREUZBERG**, famed for its large immigrant community and self-styled "alternative" inhabitants, nightlife and goings on. Effectively there are two Kreuzbergs: the **west**, the area bounded by Schöneberger Strasse in the west, Viktoriapark in south and Südstern in the east, is a richer, fancier, more sedate area than its neighbour to the **east**, which is sometimes referred to as **SO 36** after its old postal code. East Kreuzberg was the former West Berlin's "happening" quarter, a mix of punks and old hippies, and the place to hang out and hit the raucous nightspots. Throughout the 1970s and 1980s, this was where the youth of the Federal Republic came to get involved in alternative politics and (until the loophole was abolished; see box opposite) avoid national service. Though there's precious little in the way of things to see, next to Prenzlauer Berg (see p.171) it's the city's liveliest neighbourhood.

There's a detailed **map of Kreuzberg** in the colour section at the back of this book.

West Kreuzberg

First **the west**. It's only a short walk south, cutting down Stresemannstrasse, from the Gropius-Bau (see p.71) to the remains of the **Anhalter Bahnhof**, a sad reminder of misguided civic action that some would term civic vandalism. The Anhalter Bahnhof was once one of the city's (and Europe's) great rail termini, forming Berlin's gateway to the south. Completed in 1870, it received only mild damage during World War II and was left roofless but substantial in 1945. Despite attempts to preserve it as a future museum building, it was blown up in 1952 – essentially because someone had put in a good offer for the bricks. Now only a fragment of the facade stands, giving a hint at past glories. The patch of land that the station once covered is today devoted to a park – the rear portion of the park will, as of January 2001, sport a concert hall to house the **Tempodrom**, currently a popular tent venue for concerts of touring bands and world music in Friedrichshain (see *Clubs and live venues*).

---

* The term *Szene* ("the scene") is commonly used to refer to the happening places of the moment, and to those people who see themselves as the movers and shakers in current trends and fashions.

The Gruselkabinett and S-Bahn

Kreuzberg

If you look to one side of the Anhalter Bahnhof, you'll see a blunt and featureless building, a fortified bunker-storehouse built during the war and one of a handful of Nazi buildings that remain in the city. It's now given over to the **Gruselkabinett** (Mon, Tues, Thurs & Sun 10am–7pm, Fri 10am–8pm, Sat noon–8pm; DM12/€6.15, S-Bahn Anhalter Bahnhof), an amateurish "chamber of horrors" type of exhibit, of which the only vaguely interesting part is that given over to the bunker itself, with a few odd artefacts found there and in Hitler's bunker further north.

The Nazis also excavated the stretch of the **S-Bahn** that runs underground south of the Anhalter Bahnhof and heads north below Potsdamer Platz to Bahnhof Friedrichstrasse. It was built in 1935 and supposed to be ready in time for the 1936 Olympics; however, the furious pace at which it was excavated meant that safety measures were skimped: when part of the tunnel between Potsdamer Platz and the Brandenburg Gate collapsed, nineteen workers were killed, and the line was only finally completed in 1939. The tunnel passes under the River Spree, the Landwehrkanal and the U-Bahn line #2, which, during the war, sheltered Berliners from bombing raids. When on May 2, 1945, it was thought that the Soviets were preparing to use the S- and U-Bahn systems to send shock troops directly into the city centre, the Nazis blew up the bulkheads where the tunnel passes under the Landwehrkanal, flooding the tunnel and the local U-Bahn system. As a result, many civilians sheltering in the U-Bahn died horrific deaths, drowning in the choking muddy waters that surged through the tunnels.

The Jüdisches Museum Berlin

A brisk twenty-minute walk east from here, through streets levelled during wartime bombing, takes you to another Kreuzberg high spot, the **Jüdisches Museum Berlin** (Jewish Museum Berlin; ☎25 99 33 00; *www.jmberlin.de*; U-Bahn Hallesches Tor) at Lindenstrasse 14. The museum is housed in an extraordinary building by Daniel Libeskind: the ground plan is in the form of a compressed lightning bolt (intended to be a deconstructed Star of David) while the struc-

---

How Berliners avoided national service

Because of Berlin's erstwhile position as an "occupied" city, it was the only place in Germany where permanent residence meant that the compulsory eighteen months' **national service**, which all males between the ages of 18 and 32 are obliged to do, could be avoided. Throughout the 1960s, 1970s and 1980s, especially when antiwar feelings were running high, the city thus became a haven for those who refused to do their service. With unification, the anomaly was abolished – and many of those who thought they'd escaped doing their stint found themselves called up.

ture itself is sheathed in polished metallic facing, with windows – or rather thin angular slits – that trace geometric patterns on the exterior.

The **interior** is just as unusual, manifesting Libeskind's ideas about symbolic architecture, whilst retaining a sculptural symmetry: a "void" – an empty and inaccessible diagonal shaft – cuts through the structure, while three long intersecting corridors, each representing an element of Jewish experience, comprise the basement – the "axis of continuity", leading to the planned exhibition space (see below), the "axis of exile", which leads outside to a garden of stelae, and the "axis of the Holocaust", connecting with the Holocaust Tower, dimly lit and, again, completely empty. There's no front door – entry is through an underground tunnel connected to the Baroque building next door, the Kollegienhaus. That building, which once held Berlin's Superior Court, became the home of the Berlin Museum in the 1960s, and the Jewish Museum was originally intended to be only an annexe of that. The fall of the Wall, however, as well as the sheer force of Libeskind's stunning building, eventually turned the Jewish Museum into an independent foundation and shunted the Berlin Museum back to its original home, the Märkisches Museum in Mitte (see p.101).

Set to officially open in October 2001, the Jewish Museum will portray the history and culture of German-speaking Jewry and its relation to German history in general – no easy task, given the sensitive nature of the latter.

The Deutsche Technikmuseum Berlin

The German Technology Museum will absorb children's interest for hours – see Children's Berlin for more ideas.

A fifteen-minute walk south from the Anhalter Bahnhof, down Stresemannstrasse and Möckenstrasse, leads to the **Deutsche Technikmuseum Museum Berlin** at Trebbiner Strasse 9 (German Technology Museum of Berlin; Tues–Fri 9am–5.30pm, Sat & Sun 10am–6pm; *www.dtmb.de*; DM5/€2.50, concessions DM2/€1; U-Bahn Möckernbrücke, bus #129 or #248). This is one of the city's most entertaining museums and a children's and button-pushers' delight. The technology section has plenty of experiments, antiquated machinery and computers to play with, alongside some elegant old cars and planes. The transport museum, a superb collection of ancient steam trains and carriages, is even more impressive; the polished behemoths have been brought to rest in what was once a workshop of the old Anhalter Bahnhof.

The Viktoriapark and around

Reaching the **Viktoriapark** (the "Kreuzberg", as it's popularly known) from here means a half-hour's walk, retracing your steps to the U-Bahn and heading south down Grossbeerenstrasse. On the slopes of a hill, the park is one of the city's most likeable, a relaxed ramble of trees and green space with a pretty brook running down the middle. To one side is the *Golgotha Café* and disco (see *Cafés and bars*), packed on summer evenings; on another side is what claims to be Germany's northernmost vineyard; and atop the hill is the **Cross** (though it's more of a Neoclassical spire) from which Kreuzberg gets its name, designed by Schinkel to commemorate the Napoleonic Wars. The view is a good one too.

The well-restored streets around the hill, along with Yorckstrasse to the north, have a scattering of cafés, their tone and clientele reflecting the residents of the neighbourhood, who are on the whole slightly older than those of East Kreuzberg. Between Hagelbergerstrasse and Yorckstrasse, the **Riehmer's Hofgarten** is an impressive turn-of-the-century bourgeois residential building, though the steel and glass Yorck Cinema doesn't fit well in the ensemble.

East of the park, the area around **Bergmannstrasse**, filled with *Trödelläden* (junk shops, though with a few antiques), is worth a wander, as is **Chamissoplatz** for its well-preserved, tidily balconied nineteenth-century houses and, a block south, water tower. The square also boasts one of Berlin's few remaining Wilhelmine *pissoirs* – ornate public toilets, characteristically dark green in colour, erected in an early attempt at sanitation. This one has been recently renovated, and gents can pop in for a Bismarckian moment of relief.

The buildings around here are among the few that housed working-class families at the end of the nineteenth century to have survived in what was West Berlin: restoring them to their original design has been painstaking, and though the area is now thoroughly gentrified, there's no denying that it's a pleasant place to live. About halfway along Bergmannstrasse the **Marheineke market hall** has a little of everything, including some real bargains amid the dross. Keep walking and you reach the eighteenth- and nineteenth-century **cemeteries** along the eastern stretches of Bergmannstrasse. They're full of forgotten Berlin worthies, the only name of any real note being Gustav Stresemann, chancellor and foreign minister in the Weimar years – he's in Luisenstädtischen Kirchhof, the most southeasterly of the four cemeteries here.

Just to the west, intersecting Bergmannstrasse, is Mehringdamm, location of the Schwules Museum (Gay Museum) at Mehringdamm 61: see p.35.

Tempelhof Airport

South and east of the Viktoriapark, the housing fades away to the flatlands containing **Tempelhof Airport** (not actually in Kreuzberg but in the neighbouring *Bezirk* of Tempelhof). The airport was opened in the 1920s and was once Germany's largest; the present complex was built in 1936–41 and is one of the best surviving examples of Nazi architecture. A huge bronze eagle that surmounted the building was removed in the 1960s, ostensibly to make way for a radar installation (the eagle's head can still be seen at the entrance to the airport), but you can't help thinking that its removal probably had more to do with its being an ugly reminder of the Nazi past. Until

Kreuzberg

recently the airport was used only for visiting dignitaries and the military, but today it handles only a light load of small carrier flights. Sadly, the airport is scheduled to close in a few years' time; what will become of the land is a matter for heated debate.

It was to Tempelhof that the Allies flew in supplies to beat the **Berlin Blockade** of 1948–49 (see box below) – an act that was to strengthen anti-Soviet feeling among West Berliners and increase the popularity of the occupying forces. At the height of the airlift a plane landed here every minute and the **Luftbrückendenkmal**, a memorial at the entrance to the airport, commemorates the seventy airmen and eight ground crew who died in crashes while attempting to land. The memorial represents the three air corridors used, and forms half of a bridge: the other half, "joined by air", is in Frankfurt. Inside the airport a small exhibition shows photographs of its building and the Blockade – mostly publicity shots of gleaming USAF pilots and scruffy kids, with little on the role of Tempelhof in the war years.

Other than the airport there's little to detain you here. The **Polizeihistorische Sammlung** at Platz der Luftbrücke 6 (Police History Collection; Mon–Wed 9am–3pm, Thurs & Fri by appointment; free; U-Bahn Platz der Luftbrücke, bus #104, #119, #184 or

---

The Berlin Blockade (1948–49)

The **Berlin Blockade** was the result of an escalation in tensions between East and West in the late 1940s. These came to a head when the Western zone introduced the Deutschmark as currency in June 1948: the Soviets demanded that their own Ostmark be accepted as Berlin's currency, a move that was rejected by the city's parliament. Moscow's answer to this was an attempt to bring West Berlin to its knees by severing all road and rail links to the Western zones and cutting off the power provided by plants on the Eastern side. West Berlin had to "import" almost all of its food and fuel: when the Soviets pulled the plugs, the city had only a month's supply of food and ten days' of coal.

Rather than use military force, it was decided to try and supply the city by air: the Soviets, it was gambled, would not dare risk an international incident – possibly even war – by shooting down Western aircraft. The airlift thus began on June 26, 1948, and at its height nine months later, planes were landing or taking off every thirty seconds and bringing 8000 tons of supplies to the city each day.

The Soviets called off the Blockade in May 1949, but they had been defeated in more ways than one. For the occupying British and American forces, the propaganda value was enormous: aircrews who a few years previously had been dropping bombs on the city now provided its lifeline. Photographs of the "candy bomber" – a USAF captain who dropped chocolate bars and sweets from his plane on small parachutes for the city's children – went around the world. No longer were the occupiers seen as enemies, but rather as allies against the Soviet threat. The Blockade considerably eased the birth pangs of the Federal Republic, which took place the same year.

#341) is worth dipping into for its nineteenth-century uniforms and illustrations intended to help police determine "typical criminal types".

East Kreuzberg

In the 1830s, Berlin's industries started recruiting peasants from the outlying countryside to work in their factories and machine shops. It was to the small village of Kreuzberg that many came, to work in the east of the city and live in buildings that were thrown up by speculators as low-rent accommodation. Kreuzberg was thus established as a solidly working-class area and, in time, a suburb of Greater Berlin. Siemens, the electrical engineering giant, began life in one of Kreuzberg's rear courtyards. In the 1930s local trade unionists and workers fought street battles with the Nazis, and during the war it was one of the very few areas to avoid total destruction, and among the quickest to revive in the 1950s. When the Wall was built in 1961, things changed: Kreuzberg became an eastern outpost of West Berlin, severed from its natural hinterland in the East. Families moved out, houses were boarded up, and Kreuzberg began to die. At the same time, the city, deprived of cheap East Berlin labour to work in its factories, began to look further afield for the migratory workers who have come to be known as *Gastarbeiter*. Turks began to move to the city in large numbers, in time bringing their families and Islamic customs; few landlords welcomed the new workers, who gradually began to found a community in the area with the cheapest rentable property: Kreuzberg.

Throughout the 1960s and 1970s, Kreuzberg developed as West Berlin's Turkish enclave, with other *Gastarbeiter* from Yugoslavia, Greece, Spain and Italy joining them. Along, too, came the radicals, students and dropouts of the 1968 generation – attracted to the city because of the national service loophole (see box on p.135), and to Kreuzberg because it offered vast potential for **squatting**. The ruling that pre-1950s-built apartments were subject to rent restrictions meant that speculators often allowed them to fall into disrepair so that they could erect new buildings and charge whatever rent they pleased; squatters who maintained and developed these old apartments thus saved some of the city's old architecture.

In the 1980s Kreuzberg became the focus and point of reference for squatters throughout the Federal Republic, and the Social Democratic city government adopted a liberal approach to them, offering subsidies to well-organized squats and giving them some security of tenure. Projects like the **Mehringhof**, a home for alternative industries and arts (actually just in west Kreuzberg at Gneisenaustrasse 2), flourished.

All went well until the Christian Democrats took over the city. Using arguments over the role of city property – many of the buildings here are owned by the government – and the growing problems of crime and drug dealing, the right-wing minister of the interior ordered the riot police to enter Kreuzberg and forcibly close down the squats. There were riots in the streets, demonstrations all over the city, and intense political protest, which reached its peak with the death of a fifteen-year-old boy who was hit by a bus during a demonstration. Activists called a strike and the city government had to back down.

Over the last half-decade, the squatter movement has died a natural death. The city government occasionally clears out a building, but generally the squatters themselves haved moved on or up of their own volition, and less than a handful of squats remain. The Turks and other immigrant communities are thriving; and slowly, though perhaps inevitably, signs of gentrification are appearing, as astute Berliners (with an eye to their political profiles) move to the area. To say you lived in Kreuzberg was, until the Wall came down, a way of making a statement. At one time, if you wanted to gauge the political temperature of West Berlin, you had only to see what was happening on the streets here. In 1988, Kreuzberg constituted enough of a threat for the authorities to seal off the area during the annual conference of the IMF. Despite the provocation, things – perhaps surprisingly – remained calm. With the end of the Wall only the occasional uprising still occurs, usually on May Day, when an annual demonstration ritually turns into a riot, and the atmosphere is more subdued and less political than it was pre-*Wende*. It remains to be seen to what extent activists here will again turn their attention away from local matters towards national issues.

You don't, however, need any interest in revolution or city machinations to enjoy Kreuzberg. The **nightlife** here is among the city's wildest (see *Clubs and live venues*), and it's an enjoyable area to wander through by day, stopping off at one of the innumerable Turkish snack bars for a kebab, breakfasting on a 9am vodka-and-beer special at a café (see *Cafés and bars*), or just taking in the feel of the place – which is much like an Istanbul market in an Eastern bloc housing development.

Around Oranienstrasse

Catching U-Bahn line #1 (unkindly named the "Istanbul Express" in this stretch) to **Kottbusser Tor** or Schlesisches Tor stations is a good introduction to eastern Kreuzberg.

The area around Kottbusser Tor is typical: a scruffy, earthy shambles of Turkish street vendors and cafés, the air filled with the aromas of southeast European cooking. Cutting through Dresdener Strasse, past the Babylon Cinema (a venue, incidentally, that often shows films in English; see *The arts*), takes you to Kreuzberg's main strip, **Oranienstrasse**, which from Moritzplatz east is lined with café-bars, art galleries and clothes shops, and in a way forms an "alternative" Kurfürstendamm.

South of Kottbusser Tor U-Bahn, it's less than ten minutes' walk down Kottbusser Damm to the Landwehrkanal. Turning left here and walking along Paul-Lincke-Ufer in an eastward direction, you'll find the food **market** that brings Maybachufer, on the opposite side of the canal, alive in a myriad of colours and a babble of noise and excitement on Tuesday and Friday afternoons.

Around the Schlesisches Tor

Around the **Schlesisches Tor** (the "Silesian Gate", which gave the station its name, was the former entrance to the city for immigrants from Silesia) things are more residential, although for years the nearness of the Wall heightened the tension of the area. The River Spree here was in GDR territory, a strange situation for those residents of West Berlin whose apartments backed directly onto it. A reminder of those days exists in the **Museum der Verbotenen Kunst** (Museum of Prohibited Art; Sat & Sun noon–6pm; free; U-Bahn Schlesisches Tor), just a five minute walk down Schlesische Strasse and across the Landwehrkanal. This small art museum occupies one of the last remaining GDR guard towers in Berlin, now stranded in a park that once was part of the Wall's death strip; unfortunately the building is more provocative than the very modest exhibition it houses. At night the areas around both the Schlesisches Tor and the Kottbusser Tor seem a little sharper, darkness giving them an edge of danger and a sense of concealed, forbidden pleasures.

Schlesisches Tor is only ten minutes' walk, or a few stops away from Treptower Park and the remarkable memorial to Soviet troops killed in the Battle of Berlin – see p.181 for details.

The Landwehrkanal runs south of Oranienstrasse, and below that the broad path of Hasenheide-Gneisenaustrasse, marking the transition from east to west Kreuzberg. Here you'll find the **Südstern**, a church situated at the convergence of several streets which lends its name to this area (there's a convenient U-Bahn station). Around the church is another clutch of café-bars, and Gneisenaustrasse has some good restaurants; but the flavour of east Kreuzberg has gone, and things feel (and are) a lot tamer.

Schöneberg

Like Kreuzberg, **SCHÖNEBERG** was once a separate suburb, one that was swallowed up by Greater Berlin as the city expanded in the late eighteenth and nineteenth centuries. Blown to pieces during the war, it's now a mostly middle-class residential area, stretching below the Tiergarten and sandwiched between Kreuzberg to the east and Wilmersdorf to the west. Things to see are few, but what is here is both fascinating and moving.

The Bauhaus Archive

Although Schöneberg officially begins south of Kurfürstenstrasse, on the edge of the Tiergarten at Klingelhöferstrasse 14 is the

Bauhaus Archive (Mon & Wed–Sun 10am–5pm; *www.bauhaus.de*; DM5/€2.50, concessions DM2.50/€1.30; bus #129 to Lützowplatz). The Bauhaus school of design, crafts and architecture was founded in 1919 in Weimar by Walter Gropius. It moved to Dessau in 1925 and then to Berlin, to be closed by the Nazis in 1933. The influence of Bauhaus has been tremendous, and you do get some idea of this from the small collection here. Marcel Breuer's seminal chair is still (with minor variations) in production today, and former Bauhaus director Mies van der Rohe's designs and models for buildings show how the modernist Bauhaus style has changed the face of today's cities. There's work, too, by Kandinsky, Moholy-Nagy, Schlemmer and Klee, all of whom worked at the Bauhaus. The building, incidentally, was designed by Gropius himself.

The diplomatic district

East of the Archive, Reichspietschufer, which in the late 1930s was the centre of Berlin's **diplomatic district**, follows the leafy course of the Landwehrkanal towards the Neue Nationalgalerie. The next

The Bauhaus

Bauhaus, a German word whose literal meaning is "building-house", has become a generic term for the aesthetically functional design style that grew out of the art and design philosophy developed at the Dessau school. The origins of the Bauhaus movement lie in the Novembergruppe, a grouping of artists founded in 1918 by the Expressionist painter Max Pechstein with the aim of utilizing art for revolutionary purposes. Members included Bertolt Brecht and Kurt Weill, Emil Nolde, Eric Mendelssohn and the architect **Walter Gropius**. In 1919 Gropius was invited by the new republican government of Germany to oversee the amalgamation of the School of Arts and Crafts and the Academy of Fine Arts in Weimar into the **Staatliche Bauhaus Weimar**. It was hoped that this new institution would break down the barriers between art and craft, creating a new form of applied art. It attracted over two hundred students who studied typography, furniture design, ceramics, wood-, glass- and metalworking under exponents like Paul Klee, Wassily Kandinsky and Laszlo Moholy-Nagy.

Financial problems and opposition from the conservative administration in Weimar eventually forced Gropius to relocate to Dessau, chosen after the town authorities offered financial and material support and because it was home to a number of modern industrial concerns, notably an aeroplane factory and a chemical works. Dessau's **Bauhausgebäude**, designed by Gropius and inaugurated on December 4, 1926, is one of the classic buildings of modern times – a forerunner of architectural styles that would not come into their own until the 1950s and 1960s.

Towards the end of the 1920s the staff and students of the Bauhaus school became increasingly embroiled in the political battles of the time. As a result, Gropius was pressurized into resigning by the authorities and replaced by the Swiss architect Hannes Meyer. He, in turn, was dismissed in 1930 because of the increasingly left-wing orientation of the school. His successor **Ludwig Mies van der Rohe** tried to establish an apolitical atmosphere, but throughout the early 1930s Nazi members of Dessau town council called for an end to subsidies for the Bauhaus. Their efforts finally succeeded in the summer of 1932, forcing the school to close down. The Bauhaus relocated to the more liberal atmosphere of Berlin, setting up in a disused telephone factory in Birkbuschstrasse, in the Steglitz district. However, after the Nazis came to power, police harassment reached such a pitch that on July 20, 1933, Mies van der Rohe took the decision to shut up shop for good. He and many of his staff and students subsequently went into exile in the United States.

left turn off Reichspietschufer, **Stauffenbergstrasse**, takes its name from one of the instigators of the July Bomb Plot to assassinate Hitler, **Count Claus Schenk von Stauffenberg**. Stauffenberg (see below) was chief of staff at the German Army Office that once stood on this street, formerly known as Bendlerstrasse; today, the site of the building where he worked and died is occupied by the permanent exhibition **Resistance to National Socialism**, Stauffenbergstrasse 13–14 (Mon–Fri 9am–6pm, Sat & Sun

10am–6pm; free; bus #129), a well-mounted collection of photos and documents covering the surprisingly wide range of groups opposed to the Third Reich. This absorbing exhibition is a little off the beaten track, though translation of the main exhibits makes it highly accessible.

The July Bomb Plot

The **July Bomb Plot** that took place in the summer of 1944 at Hitler's Polish HQ, the "Wolf's Lair" in Rastenburg, was the assassination attempt that came closest to success. The plot, led by **Count Claus Schenk von Stauffenberg**, an aristocratic officer and member of the General Staff, had gained the support of several high-ranking members of the German army. Sickened by atrocities on the eastern front, and rapidly realizing that the Wehrmacht was fighting a war that could not possibly be won, von Stauffenberg and his fellow conspirators decided to kill the Führer, seize control of army headquarters on Bendlerstrasse and sue for peace with the Allies. Germany was on the precipice of total destruction by the Allies; only such a desperate act, reasoned the plotters, could save the Fatherland.

On July 20, Stauffenberg was summoned to the Wolf's Lair to brief Hitler on troop movements on the eastern front. In his briefcase was a small bomb, packed with high explosive: once triggered, it would explode in under ten minutes. As Stauffenberg approached the specially built conference hut, he triggered the device. Taking his place a few feet from Hitler, Stauffenberg positioned the briefcase under the table, leaning it against one of the table's stout legs, no more than six feet away from the Führer. Five minutes before the bomb exploded, the Count quietly slipped from the room unnoticed by the generals and advisers, who were absorbed in listening to a report on the central Russian front. One of the officers moved closer to the table to get a better look at the campaign maps and, finding the briefcase in the way of his feet under the table, picked it up and moved it to the other side of the table leg. Now, the very solid support of the table leg lay between the briefcase and Hitler.

At 12.42pm the bomb went off. Stauffenberg, watching the hut from a few hundred yards away, was shocked by the force of the explosion. It was, he said, as if the hut had been hit by a 155mm shell; there was no doubt that the Führer, along with everyone else in the room, was dead.

Stauffenberg hurried off to a waiting plane and made his way to Berlin to join the other conspirators. Meanwhile, back in the wreckage of the conference hut, Hitler and the survivors staggered out into the daylight: four people had been killed or were dying from their wounds, including Colonel Brandt, who had moved Stauffenberg's briefcase and thus unwittingly saved the Führer's life. Hitler himself, despite being badly shaken, suffered no more than a perforated eardrum and minor injuries. After being attended to, he prepared himself for a meeting with Mussolini later that afternoon.

It quickly became apparent what had happened, and the hunt for Stauffenberg was on. Hitler issued orders to the SS in Berlin to summarily execute anyone who was slightly suspect, and dispatched Himmler to the city to quell the rebellion.

The Shell-Haus

On the corner of Reichspietschufer and Stauffenbergstrasse, the Shell-Haus – now known as the Bewag building – is one of Berlin's great edifices that substantially survived World War II. A procession of tiered levels, this office building was designed by Emil

Back in the military Supreme Command headquarters in Bendlerstrasse, the conspiracy was in chaos. Word reached Stauffenberg and the two main army conspirators, generals Beck and Witzleben, that the Führer was still alive. They had already lost hours of essential time by failing to issue the carefully planned order to mobilize their sympathizers in the city and elsewhere, and had even failed to carry out the obvious precaution of severing all communications out of the city. After a few hours of tragicomic scenes as the conspirators tried to persuade high-ranking officials to join them, the Bendlerstrasse HQ was surrounded by SS troops, and it was announced that the Führer would broadcast to the nation later that evening. The coup was over.

The conspirators were gathered together, given paper to write farewell messages to their wives, taken to the courtyard of the HQ and, under the orders of one General Fromm, shot by firing squad. Stauffenberg's last words were "Long live our sacred Germany!"

Fromm had known about the plot almost from the beginning, but had refused to join it. By executing the leaders he hoped to save his own skin – and, it must be added, save them from the torturers of the SS.

Hitler's ruthless revenge on the conspirators was without parallel even in the bloody annals of the Third Reich. All the colleagues, friends and immediate relatives of Stauffenberg and the other conspirators were rounded up, tortured and taken before the "People's Court" (the building where the court convened, the Kammergericht building, still stands – see below), where they were humiliated and given more or less automatic death sentences, most of which were brutally carried out at **Plötzensee prison** to the northwest of the city centre (see p.158). Many of those executed knew nothing of the plot and were found guilty merely by association. As the bloodlust grew, the Nazi Party used the plot as a pretext for settling old scores, and eradicated anyone who had the slightest hint of anything less than total dedication to the Führer. General Fromm, who had ordered the execution of the Bendlerstrasse conspirators, was among those tried, found guilty of cowardice and shot by firing squad. Those whose names were blurted under torture were quickly arrested, the most notable being Field Marshal Rommel, who, because of his popularity, was given the choice of a trial in the People's Court – or suicide and a state funeral.

The July Bomb Plot caused the deaths of at least five thousand people, including some of Germany's most brilliant military thinkers and almost all of those who would have been best qualified to run the postwar German government. Within six months the country lay in ruins as the Allies advanced; had events at Rastenburg been only a little different, the entire course of the war – and European history – would have been altered incalculably.

Fahrenkamp in 1931 and was a leading piece of modernist architecture. Have a look at James Stirling's blue and pink monstrosity of a residential building, just to the east, if you're in any doubt about the Shell-Haus's credentials.

Down Potsdamer Strasse

Potsdamer Strasse itself leads south into Schöneberg proper, quickly becoming a broad, untidy strip of Turkish cafés, restaurants and wholesalers. By night the junction of Potsdamer Strasse and Kurfürstenstrasse is a gathering place for the city's heroin addicts and dealers: conspiratorial little groups form and quickly disperse, deals having been done. It's fairly unpleasant, but not perhaps as bad as the prostitution that goes on further along Kurfürstenstrasse. Many of the women are also drug addicts, which accounts for the dealing on the street corner.

A little further south on Potsdamer Strasse is the *Begine* café at no. 139 – part of a cluster of women's groups here and about the only thing on the street to which even money can't buy access for men.

The Sportpalast

Continuing south, it's worth turning off Potsdamer Strasse at Pallasstrasse and heading west for a block. This was the site of the famed **Sportpalast**, a sports centre that was the main venue for Nazi rallies in the 1930s. Hitler delivered some of his most famous speeches in the Sportpalast: most of the old newsreels showing the Führer working himself up into an oratorical fever were filmed here, and it was also the place where Goebbels asked the German people if they wanted "total war" – the affirmative reply failing to comprehend the force of destruction that would be unleashed on the city.

The Sportpalast was demolished in 1974 to make way for the huge and undistinguished apartment building that straddles the road. Beneath it, on the south side of the road, is one of the city's remaining **flak towers**. Several of these were built to defend the city from Allied raids: the largest, the Tiergarten tower, was severely damaged by bombing (the raid also destroyed the best of the city's collection of Egyptian ceramics, which had been stored in the tower for safekeeping). After the war, the Pallasstrasse tower proved impervious to demolition attempts, and the lower levels, which had been air-raid shelters, were used by NATO troops to store food and provisions in case of a Soviet invasion. Ironically, from the Cold War years until recently, supplies that were reaching the end of their shelf life were sold off – usually on the cheap to the Soviet Union.

Around the Kleistpark

South of Pallasstrasse is the **Kleistpark**, which, fronted by the **Königskolonnaden**, a colonnade from 1780 that originally stood on Alexanderplatz, gives this stretch of Potsdamer Strasse a touch of dignity: on a misty morning you might be fooled into thinking you were in Paris. The **Kammergericht building** behind the park was once the Supreme Court of Justice. Here the Nazi courts under the infamous Judge Freisler held the "People's Court" following the July Bomb Plot, as well as show trials of their political opponents, a prelude to the inevitable executions – which often took place in Plötzensee prison (see p.158). Freisler met his unlamented end here in the final few weeks of the war: on his way from the courtroom a bomb from an American aircraft fell on the building, dislodging a beam that crushed Freisler's skull. Today much restored, only thirty of the building's 486 rooms are in use, formerly as a meeting place of the Allied Air Control, which oversaw safety in the air corridors leading to the city. Until the meetings came to an end with unification, a place was always set for Soviet representatives – even though they ceased to attend meetings in 1948. The building is now used by NATO.

Over Potsdamer Strasse from the Kleistpark, at the end of Grossgörschenstrasse, lies the **Sankt-Matthäus-Kirchhof**, a graveyard that contains the bodies of the Brothers Grimm, united in death as they were in copyright. The bodies of Stauffenberg and his co-conspirators were also buried here following the July Bomb Plot, only to be exhumed a few days later and burned by Nazi thugs.

Around Nollendorfplatz

Back in the middle of Potsdamer Strasse, it's a short detour west along Bülowstrasse to **Nollendorfplatz**. In the Weimar Berlin of the 1920s and early 1930s, Nollendorfplatz was the centre of the city's large **gay and lesbian community**. Even by contemporary standards, Berlin's gay scene in those days was prodigious: there were around forty gay bars on and near this square alone, and gay life in the city was open, fashionable and well organized, with its own newspapers, community associations and art. The city's theatres were filled with plays exploring gay themes, homosexuality in the Prussian army was little short of institutionalized, and gay bars, nightclubs and brothels proudly advertised their attractions – there were even gay working men's clubs. All this happened at a time when the rest of Europe was smothered under a welter of homophobia and repression, when to be "discovered" as a homosexual or lesbian meant total social ostracism. Under the Third Reich, homosexuality was quickly and brutally outlawed: gays and lesbians were rounded up and taken to concentration camps, branded for their "perversion" by being forced to wear (respectively) pink or black triangles. (The black triangle represented "antisocial" offenders: in an attempt to ignore the existence of lesbianism, lesbians were arrested on pretexts such as swearing at the Führer's name. As homosexuality was, at the time, still illegal in Allied countries, no Nazis were tried for crimes against gays or lesbians at Nürnberg.) A red granite plaque in the shape of a triangle at

Schöneberg

Nollendorfplatz U-Bahn station commemorates the thousands of men and women who were murdered in the camps. Today, the area around Nollendorfplatz remains the focus of western Berlin's gay nightlife and especially its bars (see "Gay Cafés and bars", p.274).

As well as its first-rate nightlife, Nollendorfplatz holds a couple of offbeat attractions by day. Walk past the proto-Deco **Metropol Theater**, and down Maassenstrasse, which leads on to Nollendorfstrasse, where at no. 17 stands the building in which **Christopher Isherwood** lived during his years in prewar Berlin, a time that was to be elegantly recounted in perhaps the most famous collection of stories about the city ever written – *Goodbye to Berlin*:

> *From my window, the deep solemn massive street. Cellar shops where lamps burn all day, under the shadow of top-heavy balconied façades, dirty plaster frontages embossed with scroll work and heraldic devices. The whole district is like this: street leading into street of houses like shabby monumental safes crammed with the tarnished valuables and secondhand furniture of a bankrupt middle class.*

Schöneberg has since been reborn as a fancy, even chic neighbourhood; the would-be Isherwoods of the moment hang out in East Kreuzberg, or Prenzlauer Berg (see p.171) in eastern Berlin. At night, this part of Schöneberg, particularly the area around **Winterfeldtplatz**, is good for eating and especially drinking: tidily bohemian, less sniffy than Savignyplatz (see p.124), and much more middle-of-the-road than East Kreuzberg. On Wednesday and Saturday mornings the square holds an excellent **market** – see *Shopping*.

Rathaus Schöneberg

Schöneberg's most famous attraction actually has the least to see: the **Rathaus Schöneberg** on Martin-Luther-Strasse, the penultimate stop on U-Bahn line #4. Built just before World War I, the Rathaus became the seat of the West Berlin parliament and senate after the last war, and it was outside here in 1963 that **John F. Kennedy** made his celebrated speech on the Cold War political situation, just a few months after the Cuban missile crisis:

> *There are many people in the world who really don't understand, or say they don't, what is the great issue between the free world and the Communist world. Let them come to Berlin. There are some who say that Communism is the wave of the future. Let them come to Berlin. And there are some who say in Europe and elsewhere we can work with the Communists. Let them come to Berlin. And there are even a few who say it is true that Communism is an evil system, but it permits us to make economic progress. Lässt sie nach Berlin kommen. Let them come to Berlin . . . All free men, wherever they may live, are citizens of Berlin, and, therefore, as a free man, I take pride in the words "Ich bin ein Berliner".*

Rousing stuff. But what the president hadn't realized as he read from his phonetically written text was that he had actually said "I am a small doughnut", since *Berliner* is a name for jam doughnuts. The day after Kennedy was assassinated, the square in front of the Rathaus was given his name – a move apparently instigated by the city's students, among whom the president was highly popular.

If you've time and interest you can climb the Rathaus tower (daily 10am–5pm) and see the replica **Liberty bell** donated to the city by the US in 1950, though it's more pleasant, and certainly less strenuous, to take a stroll in the small **Volkspark**, a thin ribbon of greenery that runs southwest from here.

Chapter 8

West of the centre

While there's more than enough to detain you in Berlin's centre, the **western suburbs** hold a disparate group of attractions of considerable cultural and historical interest. **Schloss Charlottenburg** is the prettiest point here – Berlin's pocket Versailles – with fine collections of paintings inside and wanderable gardens out. Another important target, though, is the **Dahlem museum complex**, which contains a world-class ethnological museum as well as museums of Indian and East Asian Art. The **Olympic Stadium** and **Plötzensee Prison Memorial** are strong reminders of the 1930s and wartime Berlin.

Further west still are the lakes and woodlands of the **Grunewald** – the city's very own eco-friendly playpen. Once you're out of the claustrophobic city, the verdant **countryside** and **lakes** come as a surprise, a reminder of Berlin's position in Mitteleuropa – and of the fact that one-third of the city is greenery and parkland. Thanks to the efficient U- and S-Bahn systems it's possible to reach Berlin's western edges in under three-quarters of an hour, making the contrast between inner-city excitement and rural relaxation all the stronger.

Charlottenburg: the Schloss and museums

The district of **CHARLOTTENBURG** stretches north and west of the centre of town, reaching as far south as the forests of the Grunewald. The most significant attraction here, one that needs half a day at least to cover, is the **Schloss Charlottenburg and museum complex** on Spandauer Damm, while you can round off a day here with a visit to one of the other museums across the way, notably the **Ägyptisches Museum**. If, however, museums aren't to your taste, there are few better ways to idle away a morning in Berlin, or take a break from sightseeing, than to explore the surrounding **Schloss Gardens**. The nearest U-Bahn stations are five to ten minutes away by foot: Richard-Wagner-Platz on the #7 line or Sophie-Charlotte-Platz on

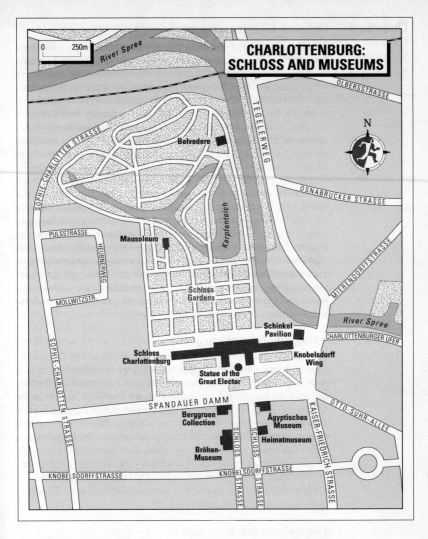

the #2 line. The nearest bus routes are the #X21, #X26, #109, #110 and #145. The Schloss is open Tuesday to Friday from 9am to 5pm, and Saturday and Sunday from 10am to 5pm; combined tickets, which are the best value and include entrance to all other Schloss buildings, cost DM15 (€7.70), concessions DM10 (€5.10); entry costs for individual galleries and buildings are given in the text.

Continuing westwards, Charlottenburg breaks out into open country and forest, with the Olympic stadium and tower the main draws (see p.159).

Schloss Charlottenburg

Schloss Charlottenburg comes as a surprise after the unrelieved
modernity of the city streets. Commissioned as a country house by
the future Queen Sophie Charlotte in 1695 (she also gave her name
to the district), the Schloss was expanded and added to throughout
the eighteenth and early nineteenth centuries to provide a summer
residence for the Prussian kings, the master builder Karl Friedrich
Schinkel providing the final touches. Approaching the sandy elabo-
rateness of the Schloss through the main courtyard, you're confronted with Andreas Schlüter's **statue** of Friedrich Wilhelm, the Great
Elector, cast as a single piece in 1700. It's in superb condition,
despite (or perhaps because of) spending the war years sunk at the
bottom of the Tegeler See for safekeeping. Immediately behind is the
entrance to the Schloss. To view its central section, which includes
the restored residential quarters, you're obliged to go on the conducted **tour** that's in German only, which makes it worth buying the
detailed (English) guidebook before you start. The tour
(DM8/€4.10, concessions DM4/€2.05) is a traipse through increasingly sumptuous chambers and bedrooms, filled with gilt and carv-
ing. Look out for the **porcelain room**, packed to the ceiling with
china, and the **chapel**, which includes a portrait of Sophie Charlotte
as the Virgin ascending to heaven.

The Knobelsdorff Wing

It's just as well to remember that much of the Schloss is in fact a fake,
a reconstruction of the buildings following wartime damage. This is
most apparent in the **Knobelsdorff Wing** to the right of the Schloss
entrance as you face it; the upper rooms, such as the elegantly
designed Golden Gallery, are too breathlessly perfect, the result of
intensive restoration. Better is the adjacent White Hall, whose
destroyed eighteenth-century ceiling painting has been replaced by a
witty contemporary pastiche. Next door, the Concert Room contains
a superb collection of works by **Watteau**, including one of his greatest paintings, *The Embarcation for Cythera*, a delicate Rococo
frippery tinged with sympathy and sadness. Also here is his *The Shop
Sign*, painted for an art dealer in 1720.

The Galerie der Romantik

Downstairs, the Knobelsdorff Wing currently contains the **Galerie
der Romantik** (Tues–Fri 10am–6pm, Sat & Sun 11am–6pm;
DM4/€2.05, concessions DM2/€1, free first Sun of month), a collection of nineteenth-century paintings from the German
Romantic, Classical and Biedermeier movements. The gallery is
soon to be integrated into the collection of the Alte Nationalgalerie
on Museum Island, which will reopen in December 2001 (see
p.85). Most dramatic are the works of **Caspar David Friedrich**, all
of which express a powerful elemental and religious approach to

landscape. This is particularly evident in *Morning in the Riesengebirge* and *Der Watzmann*, where it seems as if some massive, primeval force is about to leap forth from the earth. Typical of the brooding and drama of his Romantic sensibility is the *Monastery Among Oak Trees* of 1809, perhaps the best known of his works. In the next room, *Moonrise at Sea* reveals something of Friedrich's philosophy: initially a straightforward seascape, on closer study the painting unfolds its deeper meaning: the moon that illuminates the scene and guides the ships represents Christ; the rock on which the figures sit is a symbol of the constancy of Christian faith.

This room also contains works by **Karl Friedrich Schinkel**, the architect responsible for the war memorial in Kreuzberg and, more notably, the Neoclassical design of the Altes Museum and many other buildings standing today in eastern Berlin. His paintings are meticulously drawn Gothic fantasies, often with sea settings. *Gothic Church on a Seaside Bluff* is the most moodily dramatic and didactic in purpose: the medieval knights in the foreground stand next to a prayer tablet – Schinkel believed that a rekindling of medieval piety would bring about the moral regeneration of the German nation. His *Medieval City on a River*, painted shortly after the end of France's domination of Schinkel's native Prussia, is even more overt in its religious and political overtones. The unfinished spire of the cathedral is topped by a flag bearing the imperial eagle; the king, at first barely noticeable beneath the cathedral, is returning home in triumph; and the storm clouds, symbol of French dominance, are clearing. Look out, too, for the topographical paintings of **Eduard Gaertner**, which show the Berlin of the early nineteenth century – and reveal just how good a restoration job the GDR authorities made of Unter den Linden. Check out Gaertner's 1853 painting of that name for evidence.

The Museum für Vor- und Frühgeschichte

The western wing of the Schloss once sided an orangerie (much depleted after the war) and the **gallery** there now houses major exhibitions. Also in the west wing is the **Museum für Vor- und Frühgeschichte** (Museum of Pre- and Early History; Tues–Fri 10am–6pm, Sat & Sun 11am–6pm; DM4/€2.05, concessions DM2/€1, free first Sun of month), an unexciting collection of archeological finds from the Berlin area, along with general European prehistoric finds. There are, though, some interesting pieces from the Schliemann excavations of Troy, though the best finds (some represented here in reproductions) remain in Russia, carted away as spoils of war. Delicate negotiations for the return of the Schliemann treasures continue, with the German authorities hoping that they will have them back in Berlin by the time this collection moves to the Neues Museum on Museum Island in 2008.

Around the Schloss Gardens

Laid out in the French style in 1697, the **Schloss Gardens** (usually open daily 9am–5pm, till 9pm in the summer months – check at the Schloss complex) were transformed into an English-style landscaped park in the early nineteenth century; after severe damage in the war, they were mostly restored to their Baroque form. Though it's possible to buy a map in the Schloss, it's easy enough to wander through the garden to the lake and on to the grounds behind, which do indeed have the feel of an English park. The first place to head for, before hitting the gardens proper, is the **Schinkel Pavilion**, just to the east of the Schloss (Tues–Sun 10am–5pm; DM4/€2.05, concessions DM2/€1), which was designed by the architect for Friedrich Wilhelm III, and where the king preferred to live, away from the excesses of the main building. Square and simple, it today houses Schinkel's drawings and plans. Deeper into the gardens, on the north side of the lake, is the **Belvedere** (April–Oct Tues–Sun 10am–5pm; Nov–March Sat & Sun only noon–4pm; DM3/€1.55, concessions DM2/€1), built as a teahouse in 1788 and today housing a missable collection of Berlin porcelain.

On the western side of the gardens a long tree-lined avenue leads to the hushed and shadowy **Mausoleum** (April–Oct Tues–Sun 10am–5pm; DM2/€1, concessions DM1/€0.50), where Friedrich Wilhelm III is buried: his sarcophagus, carved with his image, makes him seem a good deal younger than his seventy years. Friedrich Wilhelm had commissioned the mausoleum to be built thirty years earlier for his wife, Queen Luise, whose own delicate sarcophagus depicts her not dead but sleeping. Later burials here include Kaiser Wilhelm I, looking every inch a Prussian king.

Other museums

Though you could happily spend a whole day wandering around the Schloss and its gardens, just across the way another group of excellent museums beckons. These in themselves could easily take an afternoon of your time; it's best to come on Sunday when all are open – preferably on the first Sunday of the month, when most are free.

The Ägyptisches Museum

The best of the museums opposite the Schloss is the **Ägyptisches Museum**, Schlossstrasse 70 (Egyptian Museum; Mon–Fri 10am–6pm, Sat & Sun 10am–6pm; DM8/€4.10, concessions DM4/€2.05, free first Sun of month), the result of innumerable German excavations in Egypt from the early part of the century. The museum's pride and joy is the *Bust of Nefertiti* on the first floor, a treasure that has become a symbol for the city as a cultural capital. There's no questioning its beauty – the queen has a perfect bone structure and gracefully sculpted lips – and the history of the piece is equally interesting. Created around 1350 BC, the bust probably never left the studio in Akhetaten in which it was created, acting as a model for other portraits of the queen (its use as a model explains why the left eye was never drawn in). When the studio was deserted, the bust was left there, to be discovered some 3000 years later in 1912. In the last few days of the war, the bust was "removed" from the Soviet sector of Berlin, and until recently wrangles continued over its return. Elsewhere in the museum, atmospheric lighting focuses attention on the exhibits, which are of a uniformly high standard. Look out for the Expressionistic, almost Futuristic *Berlin Green Head* of the Ptolemaic period, and the Kalabsha Monumental Gate, given to the museum by the Egyptian government in 1973.

The Heimatmuseum Charlottenburg and the Berggruen Collection

Immediately south of the Ägyptisches Museum at Schlossstrasse 69, the **Heimatmuseum Charlottenburg** (Tues–Fri 10am–5pm, Sun 11am–5pm; free) isn't anything special except for a few photos of Charlottenburg from the Weimar and wartime eras. Across Schlossstrasse, however, is a wonderful museum, the **Berggruen Collection: Picasso and His Age** (Tues–Fri 10am–6pm, Sat & Sun 11am–6pm; DM8/€4.10, concessions DM4/€2.05, free first Sun of month). Heinz Berggruen, a young Jew forced to flee Berlin in 1936, wound up as an art dealer in Paris, where he got to know Picasso and his circle and assembled a collection of personal favourites. In 1996 the city gave him this building to show off, in a comfortable, uncrowded setting, dozens of his Picassos. The Picassos, most of them rarely seen before, steal the show, of course – highlights include the richly textured Cubist work *The Yellow Sweater* and large-scale *Reclining Nude* – but the collection also boasts a handful of Cézannes and Giacomettis and a pair of van Goghs – all highly recommendable.

The Bröhan-Museum

Just south of the Berggruen Collection, the **Bröhan-Museum** at Schlossstrasse 1a (Tues–Sun 10am–6pm; DM6/€3.10, concessions DM3/€1.50) houses a great collection of Art Deco and Jugendstil ceramics and furniture, laid out in period rooms dedicated to a particular designer and hung with contemporary paintings – worthiest of which are the pastels of Willy Jaeckel and the resolutely modern works of Jean Lambert-Rucki. Small, compact and easily taken in, the Bröhan forms a likeable alternative to the more extensive Ägyptisches Museum or the Schloss collections.

The Dahlem museum complex

The suburb of **Dahlem** lies to the southwest of central Berlin in the district of Zehlendorf, a neat village-like enclave that feels a world away from the technoflash city centre. Mostly residential, it's home to the Free University, the better-off bourgeoisie and an excellent

To reach the
museums, take
U-Bahn line
#1 to Dahlem-
Dorf and fol-
low the signs;
the main
entrance is on
Lansstrasse.

For a run-
down of the
collection
transfers tak-
ing place
between muse-
ums in the
east and west
see the box on
p.85.

museum complex (*www.smb.spk-berlin.de*). The recent transfer of the Gemäldegalerie to the Kulturforum (see p.128) has removed the star attraction but at the same time brought some of the other fine collections, which were undeservedly overshadowed by the Picture Gallery's famous paintings, into the light: the **Museum of Ethnology**, the **Museum of Indian Art**, the **Museum of East Asian Art**, and, a block away, the **Museum of European Cultures**. All the museums are open from Tuesday to Friday 10am to 6pm, Saturday and Sunday 11am to 6pm; entrance for the first three is on Lansstrasse, but at Im Winkel 6/8 for the Museum of European Cultures. Admission to each museum is DM4 (€2.05), concessions DM2 (€1); on the first Sunday of the month entry is free.

The Museum of Ethnology

On display at the **Museum of Ethnology** is a small portion – imaginatively and strikingly laid out – of one of the world's most extensive collections of ethnological artefacts. Covering three continents – Asia, Africa and the Americas, plus the Pacific and South Sea Islands – the museum details the varying cultures of dozens of civilizations and ethnic groups, each with their own traditions, religious beliefs and artistic forms. In particular, look out for the group of sailing boats from the South Sea Islands, dramatically lit and eminently touchable; the huge and macabre engraved stone stele from Guatemala; and the thoughtful exhibition on North American Indians, which not only contains artefacts such as clothing and weapons, but also examples of the non-Indian literature and ephemera – dime novels, advertising signs, rodeo posters and the like – that created many of our myths of indigenous American life. Equally imposing is a wall of painted ceremonial masks from South Asia and an exhibit of huts from Polynesia, Micronesia, New Guinea and New Zealand. But many of the smaller pieces, such as bronzes from Benin and carved figures from Central America, are also captivating.

The Museums of Indian Art and East Asian Art

The **Museum of Indian Art** is another standout, with its assortment of intricate bronze, wood or jade religious sculptures. Many of these crafted pieces are from the Buddhist temples and monastaries that lined the northern Silk Route, and indeed religious art naturally comprises the great bulk of the collection. There is however an intriguing series of miniature paintings on display, in which the artists were clearly free to explore more secular themes; with subjects such as court scenes and nature studies, the works are characterized by a certain informality and playfulness.

The **Museum of East Asian Art** concentrates on art from China, Japan and Korea, devoting separate sections to each of these countries. The collections of calligraphy from China and Japanese woodcuts are particularly impressive, but other exhibits worth seeking out are a stunning seventeenth-century gold and lacquer throne inlaid with mother-of-pearl, and a Japanese tearoom, built by Japanese carpenters as part of the museum's recent renovations.

The Museum of European Cultures and the Geheimes Staatsarchiv

At Im Winkel 6, a short signposted walk directly north from the main complex, is the **Museum of European Cultures**, formerly the Museum of Folklore (Museum Europäischer Kulturen; Tues–Fri 10am–6pm, Sat & Sun 11am–6pm; DM4/€2.05, concessions DM2/€1, free first Sun of month), a modest museum using its collection of handicrafts, paintings, prints and the like to put together changing exhibitions on various aspects, including religious practices, handicrafts, modernization and commerce, of the regional and national cultures of the continent. Of much more specialized interest, the **Geheimes Staatsarchiv**, in the next street to the west (Secret State Archive; Archivstrasse 12–14; reading room Mon–Fri 8am–3.30pm, Tues until 7.30pm), holds the once-secret Prussian State Archive, a mass of state documents, records and files now chiefly used as a resource for academic study.

The Domäne Dahlem and Dorfkirche St Annen

Further west (turn left out of the U-Bahn station and continue along Königin-Luise-Strasse to no. 49) is the **Domäne Dahlem** (Mon & Wed–Sun 10am–6pm; ☎8 32 50 00; *www.snafu .de/~domaene-dahlem*; DM3/€1.50, concessions DM1.50/€.80), a working farm and handicrafts centre that attempts to show the skills and crafts of the preindustrial age. The old estate house has a few odds and ends, most interesting of which are the thirteenth-century swastikas, but the collection of agricultural instruments in an outbuilding is better, with some good turn-of-the-century inducements to farmers from grain manufacturers. Elsewhere are demonstrations of woodcarving, wool and cotton spinning and various other farm crafts, but it's best to come at the weekend, when some of the old agricultural machinery is fired up and the animals are paraded round – phone up first to see what's on.

A little further down Königin-Luise-Strasse, at no. 55, is the **Dorfkirche St Annen**, a pretty little brick-built church that dates back to 1220. If it's open (officially Mon, Wed & Sat 2–5pm, but seemingly random), pop in for a glimpse of the Baroque pulpit and gallery, and carved wooden altar. If not, content yourself with the old gravestones.

The Allied Museum and the Botanical Gardens

If, after all that, you have the stamina for another museum, and an interest in Cold War Berlin, take the #183 bus west to the **Allied**

The Dahlem museum complex	**Museum** at Clayallee 135 (Mon, Tues & Thurs–Sun 10am–6pm; *www.alliiertenmuseum.de*; free). The highlights here are a segment of the Wall, a guardtower, and, most impressively, the original Checkpoint Charlie guardpost. The rest of the museum delivers a well-presented, but nevertheless somewhat turgid exhibition on Cold War Berlin, enlivened only occasionally by a spy story.

Alternatively, as an escape from cultural overload, catch the #183 bus in the opposite direction to the **Botanical Gardens**, Königin-Luise-Strasse 6–8 (daily: May–July 9am–9pm; April & Aug 9am–8pm; Sept 9am–7pm; March & Oct 9am–6pm; Feb 9am–5pm; Nov–Jan 9am–4pm; greenhouse closes 30min before garden; *www.bgbm.fu-berlin.de/bgbm*; DM6/€3.10, concessions DM3/€1.50; also S-Bahn Botanischer Garten or bus #101 from the city centre), where you'll find palatial, sticky hothouses sprouting every plant you've ever wondered about (some 18,000 species, including several gruesome fly-eating plants, lots of vicious looking cacti, and a huge variety of tulips), enticingly laid-out gardens and an uninspiring **Botanical Museum** (daily 10am–5pm; DM2/€1, concessions DM1/€.50).

The Plötzensee Prison Memorial

Berlin sometimes has the feel of a city that has tried, unsuccessfully, to sweep its past under the carpet of the present. When concrete reminders of the Third Reich can be seen, their presence in today's postwar city becomes all the more powerful. Nowhere is this more true than in the buildings where the Nazi powers brought dissidents and political opponents for imprisonment and execution – what is today the **Plötzensee Prison Memorial** (daily: March–Sept 8.30am–6pm; Feb & Oct 8.30am–5.30pm; Jan & Nov 8.30am–4.30pm; Dec 8.30am–4pm).

Plötzensee stands in the northwest of the city, on the border between the boroughs of Charlottenburg and Wedding. To get there, take bus #123 from Tiergarten S-Bahn station to the beginning of Saatwinkler Damm (ask for the "Gedenkstatte Plötzensee" stop; the journey takes 30min), and walk away from the canal along the wall-sided path of Hüttigpfad.

The former prison buildings have been refurbished as a juvenile detention centre, and the memorial consists of the buildings where the executions took place. Over 2500 people were hanged or guillotined here between 1933 and 1945, usually those sentenced in the Supreme Court of Justice in the city. Following the July Bomb Plot (see pp.144–145), 89 of the 200 people condemned were executed here in the space of a few days. The hangings were carried out with piano wire, so that the victims would slowly strangle rather than die from broken necks, and it is claimed (though there is no evidence to support this) that Hitler spent his evenings watching movie footage of the executions. Today the execution chamber has been restored to its wartime condition: on occasion, victims were hanged eight at a time, and the hanging beam, complete with hooks, still stands. Though decked with wreaths and flowers, the atmosphere in the chamber is chilling, and in a further reminder of Nazi atrocities an urn in the courtyard contains soil from each of the concentration camps. Perhaps more than at any other wartime site in Berlin, it is at Plötzensee that the horror of senseless, brutal murder is most palpably felt.

The Maria Regina Martyrum church

Ask at the memorial and you'll be given a map that shows you how to reach the church of **Maria Regina Martyrum** at Heckerdamm 230, a purposefully sombre memorial church dedicated to those who died in the Nazi years (alternatively, you can hop back on the #123 bus and save yourself the 3.5km walk). Completed in 1963, the church's brutally plain exterior is surrounded by a wide courtyard whose wall's are flanked by abstract *Stations of the Cross* modelled in bronze. The interior is a plain concrete shoebox, adorned only with an abstract altarpiece that fills the entire eastern wall. It's a strikingly unusual design, and one that has stood the test of time well.

Points west: the Funkturm, Olympic Stadium and beyond

To reach the **Funkturm**, the skeletal transmission mast that lies to the west of Charlottenburg, it's an easy matter of catching U-Bahn line #2 to Kaiserdamm, then travelling one stop south on bus #204, or catching bus #149 from Zoo Station. The Funkturm was built in 1928 as a radio and, eventually, a TV transmitter. One of Dr Goebbels's lesser-known achievements was to create the world's first regular TV service in 1941. Transmitted from the Funkturm, the weekly programme could only be received in Berlin; the service continued until just a few months before the end of the war. Today the Funkturm only serves police and taxi frequencies, but the mast remains popular with Berliners for the toe-curling views from its 126-metre-high **observation platform** (daily 10am–11pm; DM6/€3.10, concessions DM3/€1.50). With the aluminium-clad monolith of the **International Congress Centre** immediately below, it's possible to look out across deserted, overgrown S-Bahn tracks to the gleaming city in the distance – a sight equally mesmerizing at night.

The Olympic Stadium

To reach the **Olympic Stadium** (daily 8am–sunset; ☎30 06 33; DM2/€0.80, concessions DM1/€0.50) from the Funkturm, catch the U-Bahn line #2 three stops westwards to the Olympia-Stadion (Ost) station. From there, it's a fifteen-minute signposted walk to the stadium itself. If you take the (less convenient) #149 bus up Heerstrasse,

Points west:
the
Funkturm,
Olympic
Stadium
and beyond

*For more on
activities in
the stadium,
see Sport in
Listings.*

you cross **Theodor-Heuss-Platz**, a huge square formerly known as Adolf-Hitler-Platz: in the centre of the square is an eternal flame that used to be dedicated to the reunification of East and West Germany – and which is still, rather oddly, alight. The #A18 bus, starting at Theodor-Heuss-Platz, goes slightly nearer the stadium entrance than the #149. The stadium is sometimes closed for sporting events or team practice, so it's best to call before trudging out.

Built for the 1936 Olympic Games, the Olympic Stadium is one of the few fascist-era buildings left intact in the city, and remains very much in use. Whatever your feelings about it, the building is still impressive, the huge Neoclassical space a deliberate rejection of the modernist architecture then prevalent elsewhere.

It's possible to walk around inside the stadium: as you come in at the main (eastern) entrance, the sheer size of it comes as a surprise, since the seating falls away below ground level to reveal a much deeper auditorium than you'd imagined. Walk around to the western side, where the Olympic flame was kept and where medal winners are listed on the walls, and it's easy to see how this monumental architecture, and the massive sculptures dotting the grounds outside, some of which are still extant, could inspire the crowds. During the Olympics, Berliners were kept up to date with commentary on the games, interspersed with stirring music, from hundreds of loud-

---

The 1936 Olympic Games

Hitler used the international attention the 1936 **Olympics** attracted to show the "New Order" in Germany in the best possible light. Anti-Semitic propaganda and posters were suppressed in the city, German half-Jewish competitors were allowed to compete, and when (for the first time in the history of the games) the Olympic flame was relayed from Athens, the newsreels and the world saw the road lined with thousands wearing swastikas and waving Nazi flags. To the outside world, it seemed that the new Germany was rich, content, and firmly behind the Führer.

Though the games themselves were stage-managed with considerable brilliance – a fact recorded in Leni Riefenstahl's poetic and frighteningly beautiful film of the events, *Olympia* – not everything went according to official National Socialist doctrine. Black American athletes did supremely well in the games, **Jesse Owens** alone winning four gold medals, disproving the Nazi theory that blacks were "subhuman" and the Aryan race all-powerful. But eventually Germany won the most gold, silver and bronze medals (there's a memorial at the western end of the stadium), and the games were deemed a great success.

At the medal ceremony Hitler did not shake Owens's hand, not, as is usually stated, because of any racist reasons (though they were undoubtedly there), but because, as patron of the games, he had been told that he must either congratulate all the medal winners (which would have been impractical) or none. Owens must have been even more upset when he got back to the States, since President Roosevelt also refused to shake his hand.

---

speakers that ran all the way from the Museum Island via Unter den Linden and the Brandenburg Gate, through the Tiergarten and out to the stadium. Standing here, looking back out to the city, you realize what an achievement this was.

Around the Olympic Stadium

The area in which the stadium stands was under the control of the British: the army had its HQ and hospital nearby, and the fields around were used for drilling teenage recruits into shape. This meant that much of the stadium's environs were out of bounds, and probably explains its survival – the British being less eager to demolish

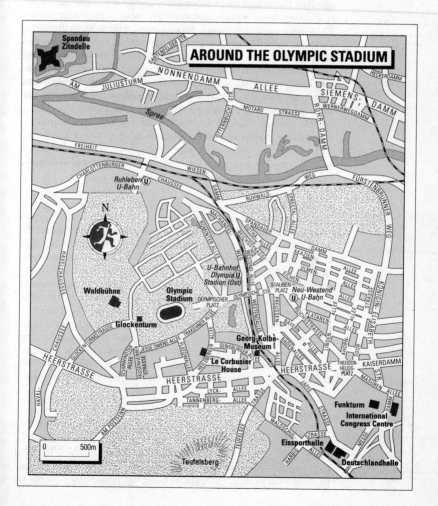

Points west:
the
Funkturm,
Olympic
Stadium
and beyond

interesting structures than the other Allies. Now, with the British army merely a memory, the land around the stadium is one of the most attractive and sought-after pieces of real estate in the city.

If you cut south and west around the stadium, down the road named after Jesse Owens, and take a right into Passenheimer Strasse, you reach the **Glockenturm** or bell tower (April–Oct daily 9am–6pm; DM4/€2.05, concessions DM1.50/€.80), the spot where Hitler would enter the stadium each morning, state business permitting. Rebuilt after wartime damage, it's chiefly interesting for the stupendous view it gives, not only over the stadium but also north to the natural amphitheatre that forms the Waldbühne, an open-air concert site (see *Clubs and live venues*), and across the beginnings of the Grunewald to the south. Also easy to spot is the **Teufelsberg** (Devil's Mountain), a massive mound that's topped with a faintly terrifying fairytale castle that used to be a US signals and radar base, built to listen in to Eastern bloc radio signals; no longer needed, it's scheduled to be dismantled – though no one seems in a hurry. The mountain itself is artificial: at the end of the war, the mass of debris that was once Berlin was carted to several sites around the city, most of the work being carried out by women known as *Trümmerfrauen* – "rubble women" (see p.94). Beneath the poplars, maples and ski runs lies the old Berlin, about 25 million cubic metres of it, presumably awaiting the attention of some future archeologist. In the meantime, it's popular as a place for weekend kite flying, and skiing and tobogganing in winter (see *Children's Berlin*).

Le Corbusier house and Georg-Kolbe-Museum

If you're a fan of the French architect Le Corbusier, you may want to make a pilgrimage to the **Le Corbusier house**, between Flatowallee, the street leading directly south of the stadium, and Heilsberger Allee. Built as part of the International Building exhibition in 1957, it contains more than five hundred apartments. Once heralded as a modernist vision of the ideal living environment, it now seems similar to all the other depressing concrete boxes thrown up in the 1960s. More interesting is the **Georg-Kolbe-Museum** at Sensburger Allee 25 (Tues–Sun 10am–5pm; *www.dhm.de/museen/kolbe*; DM5/€2.50, concessions DM3/€1.50; bus #149). Kolbe, a sculptor who died in 1947, never achieved the eminence of his contemporary Ernst Barlach – a judgement that perhaps seems reasonable when you view some of the 180 bronze figures and numerous drawings in what was the artist's home.

Spandau

SPANDAU, situated on the confluence of the Spree and Havel rivers, about 10km as the crow flies northwest of the city centre, is Berlin's oldest suburb – it was granted a town charter in 1232, and managed to escape the worst of the wartime bombing, preserving a couple of

SPANDAU

Havelsee

Bastion Kronprinz

Bastion Brandenburg

Zitadelle

Bastion Königin

Juliusturm   Museum

FALKENSEER DAMM

GALEN STR.

FALKENSEER PLATZ

NEUENDORFER STRASSE

U-Bahn Altstadt Spandau

Nicolaikirche

JULIUSTURM

ZITADELLENWEG

AM JULIUSTURM

U-Bahn Zitadelle

ALTSTADT

CARL-SCHURZ-STRASSE

River Spree

U-Bahn Rathaus Spandau

River Havel

N

S-Bahn Spandau

AM SCHLANGENGRABEN

FREIHEIT STRASSE

RUHLEBENER STRASSE

0   250m

old streets and an ancient moated fort, the **Zitadelle**. But the word Spandau immediately brings to mind the name of its jail's most famous – indeed in later years only – prisoner, **Rudolf Hess**.

The Zitadelle

However, there's little connection between Hess and Spandau itself. The jail, 4km away from the centre on Wilhelmstrasse, was demolished to make way for a supermarket for the British armed forces, and the chief reason to come here today is to escape the city centre, wander Spandau's village-like streets, and to visit the **Zitadelle** at Am Juliusturm 33 (Tues–Fri 9am–5pm; DM4/€2.05, concessions DM2/€1), a fort established in the twelfth century to defend the town. Postcard-pretty from the outside, with its moat and russet walls built during the Renaissance by an Italian architect, it is explorable, if not totally engrossing. There's a small local history

To get to the Zitadelle take U-Bahn line #7 to Zitadelle station. Spandau town is a ten-minute walk from the Zitadelle or one stop further on the U-Bahn to Altstadt Spandau.

Rudolf Hess (1894–1987)

Rudolf Hess marched in the Munich Beer Hall *Putsch* of 1923 and was subsequently imprisoned with Hitler in Landsberg jail, where he took the dictation of *Mein Kampf*. For a time he was the **deputy leader** of the Nazi party, second only to the Führer himself. He flew to Scotland in 1941, ostensibly in an attempt to sue for peace with King George VI and ally Great Britain with Germany against the Soviet Union. Perhaps because there seems no sane reason why Hess, who was immediately arrested and held until the Nürnberg trials, should have attempted his flight, various sources have claimed that the man held in jail until his suicide in 1987 was not actually Hess – and that it would have been impossible for a 93-year-old man to have hanged himself on a short piece of lamp flex. The basis of this story came from the doctor who examined Hess's corpse; he could find no trace of the serious wounds Hess had acquired in World War I. But it's recently been proved that Hess could indeed have killed himself using the lamp flex, and diligent research in archives in Munich has revealed that Hess's wartime wounds were in fact minor enough to have healed over the years – so putting to rest a colourful (and headline-grabbing) piece of conspiracy theory.

museum (*Heimatmuseum*), a pricey restaurant and the **Juliusturm**, from which there's a good view over the ramshackle Zitadelle interior and the surrounding countryside. If nothing else, it's a pleasant spot to picnic away a hot summer's day.

Spandau town

Aside from the Zitadelle, **Spandau town** is of minor interest, at its best around the **Nikolaikirche**, which dates from the Middle Ages, and Reformationsplatz (where there's a good *Konditorei*), in the playful sculptures of its modern marketplace, and in the restored street called **Kolk** (turn right off Am Juliusturm, opposite Breite Strasse). Also here is the **Brauhaus**, Neuendorfer Strasse 1, a nineteenth-century brewery that produces beer to a medieval recipe, and has tours explaining the brewing process. It's also possible in the summer months to catch **boats** from Spandau to Tegel, Wannsee and elsewhere; see *Introducing the city*.

Woodlands and lakes: the Grunewald, Havel and Wannsee

Few people associate Berlin with hikes through dense woodland or swimming from crowded beaches, though that's just what the **Grunewald** forests and the Havel lakes have to offer. The Grunewald is 32 square kilometres of mixed woodland between the suburbs of Dahlem and Wilmersdorf and the Havel lakes to the west; it's popular with Berliners for its bracing air and walks. Seventy percent of the

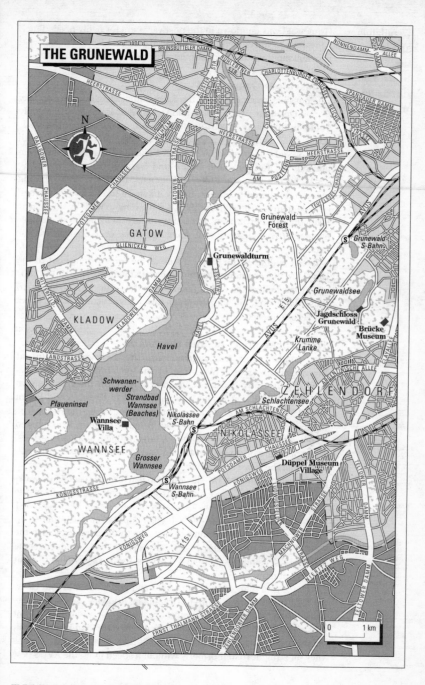

THE GRUNEWALD

NONNENDAMM-ALLEE

BRUNSBÜTTELER DAMM

CHARLOTTENBURGER CHAUSSEE

SPANDAUER DAMM

HEERSTRASSE

RUHLEBENER STR.

KLOSTER STR.

WEINMEISTER STRASSE

HAVEL CHAUSSEE

HEERSTRASSE

HEERSTRASSE

AM POSTFENN

TEUFELSSEE CHAUSSEE

AVUS

N

POTSDAMER CHAUSSEE

GATOWER DAMM

GATOW

GLIENICKER WEG

Grunewald Forest

Grunewald S-Bahn

Grunewaldturm

HAVEL CHAUSSEE

E 15

AVUS

Grunewaldsee

Jagdschloss Grunewald

Brücke Museum

CLAYALLEE

KLADOW

KLADOWER DAMM

Krumme Lanke

Havel

CLAYALLEE

ARGENTINISCHE ALLEE

LANDSTRASSE

ZEHLENDORF

Schwanen-werder

Schlachtensee

AM SCHLACHTENSEE

Pfaueninsel

Strandbad Wannsee (Beaches)

Nikolassee S-Bahn

Wannsee Villa

NIKOLASSEE

POTSDAMER CHAUSSEE

WANNSEE

Düppel Museum Village

TELTOWER DAMM

Grosser Wannsee

KONIGSWEG

Wannsee S-Bahn

KONIGSSTRASSE

POTSDAMER DAMM

POTSDAMER STR.

MACHNOWER STRASSE

MARTIN BUCHER STRASSE

KONIGSWEG

115

TELTOWER DAMM

ERNST THÄLMANN STRASSE

ERNST REUTER DAMM

NEUE BLITZ WEG

0   1 km

Woodlands
and lakes:
the
Grunewald,
Havel and
Wannsee

Grunewald was cut down in the postwar years for badly needed fuel, and subsequent replanting has replaced pine and birch with oak and ash, making it all the more popular.

Jagdschloss Grunewald

One possible starting point is the **Jagdschloss Grunewald** (mid-May to mid-Oct daily 10am–5pm; mid-Oct to mid-May Sat & Sun only 10am–6pm; *www.spsg.de*; DM4/€2.05, concessions DM2/€1; buses #115 and #183), a royal hunting lodge built in the sixteenth century and enlarged by Friedrichs I and II. Today it's a museum housing old furniture and Dutch and German painting, including works by Cranach the Elder and Rubens; there's a small hunting museum in the outbuildings. Really it's more fun to wander around outside than see the collections: it's refreshing to walk by the nearby lake, the **Grunewaldsee**, and concerts are held here on summer evenings (usually starting at 6pm; see *Zitty* or *Tip* magazine for details).

In the middle of the western side of the forest, right next to the Havel, is the **Grunewaldturm** (daily 10am–dusk; DM1.50/€0.80) which was built at the end of the nineteenth century as a memorial to Kaiser Wilhelm I; the 55-metre-high tower has a restaurant and views out across the lakes.

The Brücke Museum and the AVUS

Just southeast of the Jagdschloss, the **Brücke Museum** at Bussardsteig 9 (Mon & Wed–Sun 11am–5pm; DM7/€3.60, concessions DM3/€1.50), houses a collection of works by the group known as Die Brücke ("The Bridge"), who worked in Dresden and Berlin from 1905 to 1913, and whose work was banned by the Nazis. The big names are Kirchner, Heckel and Schmidt-Rottluff, who painted Expressionist cityscapes and had a large influence on later artists. Many of their works were destroyed during the war, making this collection all the more interesting.

Jagdschloss and the Brücke Museum can also be reached by walking, if you have a good map and a stout pair of legs, from the Grunewald S-Bahn station. It was from here, from October 1941 onwards, that much of the city's **Jewish population** was rounded up and loaded onto freight trains, to be taken to the death camps in the east. Previous round-ups in the city centre had offended some Berliners' sensibilities: here in the woods, the Jews were out of sight and out of mind.

Glance at a map of the Grunewald and you'll see a broad, ruler-straight road that runs down to Dreilinden. Known as the **AVUS**, this once formed part of a prewar motor racing circuit; today it fills a not dissimilar function, as motorists, bored with the 80km/h speed limit on the entry roads into the city, take out their frustration as soon as they hit straight road. Formerly without a speed limit, the AVUS now has a 100km/h maximum, introduced in 1990 after much environmental pressure.

Strandbad Wannsee

An alternative approach to the Grunewald, and to the start of a strip of **beaches**, is to take the S-Bahn, lines #1 or #7, to Nikolassee Station, from where it's a ten-minute walk or a quick bus ride to **Strandbad Wannsee**, a kilometre-long strip of pale sand that's the largest inland beach in Europe, and one which is packed as soon as the sun comes out. From here it's easy to wander into the forests. Travel one station further on the S-Bahn, to Wannsee, and you can catch one of several **ferries** that leave a little way from the S-Bahn station (ask there for directions).

From Strandbad Wannsee, it's possible to sail across the lake to Kladow on the F10 (your S-Bahn ticket is valid, otherwise it's DM4/€2.05); south to Potsdam and north to Spandau by other seasonal (or private) services; and to the **Pfaueninsel** (Peacock Island; daily: May–Aug 8am–8pm; April & Sept 9am–6pm; March & Oct 9am–5pm; Nov–Feb 10am–4pm; *www.spsg.de*; ferry DM2/€1). The attractions here include a mini-Schloss, built by Friedrich Wilhelm II for his mistress and today containing a small **museum** (April–Oct Tues–Sun 10am–5pm; DM4/€2.05, concessions DM2/€1). Most enjoyable, though, are the gardens, landscaped by Peter Lenné, the original designer of the Tiergarten. No cars are allowed on the island (nor, incidentally, are dogs, ghetto-blasters or smoking), which has been designated a conservation zone and is home to a flock of peacocks. The Pfaueninsel was a favourite party venue for the Nazis: in the 1930s, Joseph Goebbels, minister of propaganda, hosted a massive "Italian evening" here for over a thousand guests, including many famous German film stars and celebrities of the day.

Düppel Museum Village

Otherwise, the Grunewald area is ideal for walking. Targets include the **Düppel Museum Village** (Museumsdorf Düppel; 6km to the east of Wannsee U-Bahn at Clauertstr. 11; Easter to mid-Oct Thurs 3–7pm, Sun & holidays Sun 10am–5pm; phone to confirm ☏8 02 66 71; *www.düppel.de*; DM3/€1.50, concessions DM1.50/€0.80; bus #115), a reconstructed medieval country village, with demonstrations of contemporary handicrafts and farming techniques; and the surrounding, little-visited **Düppel Forest**.

The Wannsee villa

While it can't be described as the most enjoyable of sights, the one place that should on no account be missed on a trip here is the house overlooking the lake, where on January 20, 1942, the fate of European Jewry was decided: the **Wannsee villa** at Am Grossen Wannsee 56–58 (Mon–Fri 10am–6pm, Sat & Sun 2–6pm; free). To

Woodlands
and lakes:
the
Grunewald,
Havel and
Wannsee

*Several boat
companies run
trips around
the Grunewald
lakes: see
Introducing the
city for more
details.*

Woodlands
and lakes:
the
Grunewald,
Havel and
Wannsee

The Wannsee Conference

The conference at the **Wannsee villa** on January 20, 1942, was held at the instigation of Reinhard Heydrich, Chief of Reich Security Head Office and second only to Himmler. Göring had ordered Heydrich to submit plans for the rounding up, deportation and destruction of the Jews in Reich territory. Heydrich summoned SS and government officials, including Adolf Eichmann and Roland Freisler, later to gain infamy as the judge at the Volksgerichthof. Eichmann kept a complete set of minutes of the meeting, and these documents, discovered after the war, were to play an important part in the later Nürnberg trials of war criminals.

The problem Heydrich delineated was that Poland, France and the USSR contained ten million Jews: the "Final Solution" to the "Jewish Question" was that these people should be taken to camps and worked to death. Those who survived should be executed, since, under Nazi principles of natural selection, they would be the toughest, and in Heydrich's words could be "regarded as the germ cell of a new Jewish development". In these early stages the systematic killing machines like Auschwitz and Bergen-Belsen were not yet envisaged. More discussion was spent on how the Jews should be rounded up: great deception was to be used to prevent panic and revolt, and the pretence that Jews were being moved for "resettlement" was extremely important. Heydrich charged Eichmann with this task, a job that would eventually cost him his life when he was sentenced to death for war crimes in Israel in 1960.

At no time during the conference were the words "murder" or "killing" used, only careful euphemisms to shield the enormity of what was being planned. Reading through the minutes (copies are kept in the villa's library), it's difficult not to be shocked by the matter-of-fact manner in which the day's business was discussed, the way in which German politeness and efficiency absorb and absolve all concerned. When sterilization was suggested as one "solution" it was rejected as "unethical" by a doctor present; and there was much self-congratulation as various officials described their areas as "Judenfrei".

Heydrich himself died following an assassination attempt in Prague: some of the others present did not survive the war either, but, in contrast to the millions who were destroyed by their organizational genius, many of the Wannsee delegation lived on to gain a pension from the German state.

get here, take the S-Bahn to Wannsee, then catch a #114 bus (about a 5min journey) and get off at "Haus der Wannsee-Konferenz".

The villa, which is entered through strong security gates, contains an exhibition showing the entire process of the Holocaust, from segregation and persecution to the deportation and eventual murder of the Jews from Germany and all the lands the Third Reich conquered. Each room examines a different part of the process, and there's an English-language translation of the exhibits available from the ticket desk. Inevitably, it's deeply moving: many of the photographs and accounts are horrific, and the events they describe seem part of a world far removed from the quiet suburban backwater of Wannsee – which, in a way, underlines the tragedy. Particularly disturbing is the photograph of four generations of a single family – babe-in-arms, young mother, grandmother and ancient great-grandmother – moments before their executions.

The room where the conference took place is kept as it was, with documents from the meeting on the table and photographs of participants ranged around the walls, their biographies showing that most lived on to comfortable old age. Even fifty years after the event, to stand in the room where the decision was taken to coldly and systematically annihilate a race of people brings a shiver of fear and rage. The vast scale of the Holocaust sometimes makes it hard to grasp the full enormity of the crime: looking into the faces of the guilty, and then of those they destroyed, brings across the evil in a very real way.

The villa also has a library containing reference material such as autobiographies, first-hand accounts, slides, newspapers and much else concerning the Holocaust and the rise of neofascist groups.

Chapter 9

East of the centre

In the ten years since the *Wende*, rebuilding has significantly changed the face of the **eastern** side of Berlin – and continues to do so. Projects designed to iron out the differences between the two sides of the city have, somewhat inevitably, resulted in a strange mixture of past and present here: old GDR-style socialist architecture sits alongside the clean-cut lines and flashy design of new buildings, while bars practically unchanged since the fall of the Wall compete with slick and trendy dance clubs a few doors away. These elements have settled into a state of coexistence, even if they don't quite jell; often, of course, it's the incongruousness that appeals. There's much to see, including some decidedly offbeat attractions, and to experience these eastern *Bezirke* is an important part of getting the true flavour of Berlin.

Your first goal should be the streets of **Prenzlauer Berg**, a part working-class, part bohemian district that fans out northeast of the city centre, and has long been a centre of "alternative" culture and lifestyle. This area is also home to some of the best cafés, bars and nightlife in the eastern part of the city. **Friedrichshain**, immediately to the east of the centre, has some fascinating examples of GDR architecture, and one of the city's oldest and best parks. It has also become, in the last few years, a new frontier for the city's clubbers and bar-hoppers. If you've enough time, head out southeast to **Treptow** and its massive Soviet war memorial and riverside parks, and to **Lichtenberg**, with eastern Berlin's sprawling zoo, and, nearby, the building where the German army surrendered to the Soviets at the end of World War II.

Moving north away from the inner city, **Pankow**, once home to the GDR capital's elite, and the tidy district of **Weissensee**, where you'll find the city's largest Jewish cemetery, offer a break from urban grime. For a real escape from the city, head south for the lakes and woods around **Köpenick**, which are surprisingly unspoiled. All of the places described in this chapter are easily reached by S- and U-Bahn, tram or bus, and are as much an essential part of Berlin's identity as the better-known sights.

Prenzlauer Berg

The old working-class district of **PRENZLAUER BERG** radiates out from the city centre in a network of tenement-lined cobbled streets, and has effectively usurped Kreuzberg's role as home of the Berlin *Szene*. But then, even in GDR days it was a uniquely vibrant and exciting corner of East Berlin, home to large numbers of artists and young people seeking an alternative lifestyle who chose to live here on the edge of established East German society (literally as well as figuratively – the western boundary of Prenzlauer Berg was marked by the Berlin Wall). Given the all-embracing nature of the state, this was not as easy as in "alternative" West Berlin: in the GDR even minor acts of nonconformism, or actions that wouldn't have been regarded as out of the ordinary at all in the West, such as organizing an unofficial art exhibition or concert, could result in a run-in with the police or attract the unwelcome attentions of the Stasi.

Since 1989 countless new bars, restaurants and clothes shops have opened, particularly in the streets around Kollwitzplatz, thriving partly because the area's original inhabitants have been joined by an influx of people (often students) drawn from the west by cheap accommodation and **squatting** opportunities; though with many buildings reclaimed by their original owners, the days for breaking into the squat scene, or, in most cases, even finding a cheap apartment, are over. Gentrifying forces are on the move, but the area's venues still have a sense of freshness and energy that supersedes the more established, but faded, equivalent Kreuzberg and Schöneberg haunts.

Historically, Prenzlauer Berg is a relatively new *Bezirk*. It's set on a gently sloping hill that served as a wooded hunting ground for the local aristocracy until the first farmers moved in towards the end of the eighteenth century, clearing the trees and building windmills to take advantage of the exposed position. For the next fifty years or so the area was rural, lying outside the city limits. Industrialization resulted in an explosion of building, and by the turn of the twentieth century Prenzlauer Berg had become one of Berlin's most densely populated tenement districts. During the war it was fought over (bullet holes and shrapnel scars on the building facades testify to this) but not flattened, and most of the *Mietskaserne* (tenement blocks) put up in the late nineteenth and early twentieth centuries to house the city's rapidly expanding factory worker population are still standing. There are still a number of blackened buildings, with their overgrown *Hinterhöfe* (courtyards), which look as if they haven't been renovated since the war, and in many cases this is probably so. Restoration, however, is rapidly transforming the district.

The quickest way to **get to Prenzlauer Berg** is to take the U-Bahn from Alexanderplatz to either Eberswalder Strasse or Schönhauser Allee stations. For a more atmospheric approach, take tram #1 from Hackescher Markt, which, going up Prenzlauer Allee, is the most direct route to the Kollwitzplatz area, or try tram #13 or #53, which will take you through some of eastern Berlin's lesser-known backstreets and past the Volkspark am Weinberg (see p.117). Walking to Prenzlauer Berg from Rosa-Luxemburg-Platz involves a steepish hill but takes in a couple of interesting sights (see below).

Schönhauser Allee and around

It's a fairly easy walk to Prenzlauer Berg from central Berlin. The district starts just north of Rosa-Luxemburg-Platz at the beginning of **Schönhauser Allee**, and if you follow this street for about 600m you'll find yourself on **Senefelderplatz**, previously known as Pfefferberg (Pepper Hill), but later renamed after the inventor of the

lithographic process (printing from engraved stone), Alois
Senefelder. A statue of Senefelder stands on the square, with his
name appearing on the base in mirror script, as on a lithographic
block. The name Pfefferberg, incidentally, is still in use, and applies
to a former factory complex just below Senefelderplatz that features
a nightclub and *Biergarten* – a favourite spot in summer for late-
night drinking, snacking or just hanging out (see *Clubs and live
venues*).

The Jewish Cemetery

A little further along Schönhauser Allee, just past the police station,
is the **Jüdischer Friedhof**, Schönhauser Allee 23–25 (Mon–Thurs
10am–4pm, Fri 10am–1pm; male visitors are requested to keep their
heads covered), Prenzlauer Berg's Jewish cemetery, which opened
when space ran out at the Grosse Hamburger Strasse cemetery. Over
20,000 people are buried here, but for most this last resting place is
an anonymous one; in 1943 many of the gravestones were smashed
and a couple of years later the trees under which they had stood were
used by the SS to hang deserters found hiding in the cemetery during
the final days of war. Today many of the stones have been restored
and repositioned, and a memorial stone near the cemetery entrance
entreats visitors: "You stand here in silence, but when you turn away
do not remain silent."

Along and around Schönhauser Allee

Further along Schönhauser Allee, on the left near the junction with
Wörtherstrasse, is the confused **Segenskirche**, a bizarre mix of
Gothic and neo-Renaissance styles. About 500m or so north of here
is Eberswalder Strasse U-Bahn station, and the busy junction of
Schönhauser Allee, Danziger Strasse, Kastanienallee and
Eberswalder Strasse. Beyond the junction, **Schönhauser Allee**
assumes its true identity as Prenzlauer Berg's main drag, an old-fashioned shopping street which, thanks to its cobbled streets and narrow shop facades, still retains a vaguely pre-*Wende* (or perhaps even
prewar) feel. This effect is enhanced by the U-Bahn, which runs over-
ground and becomes an elevated railway. Supported by ornate steel
pillars, it leaves much of Schönhauser Allee in the shadows and was
nicknamed the *Magistratschirm* or "municipal umbrella" at the time
of its construction.

Schönhauser Allee extends northwards for a couple of kilometres
towards Pankow, lined by shops and street stalls. Just to the southeast of Schönhauser Allee U-Bahn station, at the intersection of
Stargarder Strasse and Greifenhagener Strasse, is the
Gethsemanekirche, which was a focal point for reformist activities
during the summer 1989 exodus from the GDR, and in the months
leading up to the *Wende*. Given the peaceful nature of Schönhauser
Allee today, it's hard to imagine that on October 7, 1989, the police

---

Nightlife in Prenzlauer Berg

Directly after the *Wende*, bars and cafés sprang up in the area around Kollwitzplatz and at the junction of Knaackstrasse and Rykestrasse (in the shadow of the nineteenth-century Wasserturm). Within a few years the scene spread out along Husemannstrasse, Sredzkistrasse and, to the west, Oderbergerstrasse. Lately the trend has been decidedly upscale, with pricey restaurants replacing primitive and popular *Szene* haunts. The area, however, remains lively, with diverse dining possibilities, and plenty of cafés and bars to work your way through. Not surprisingly, these tend on the whole to attract visitors from the western part of the city and hip tourists, so if you're looking to meet locals, head north for streets like Lychener Strasse and Dunckerstrasse on the other side of Danziger Strasse. See *Cafés and bars* in Listings.

---

were beating nonviolent demonstrators here, during the anti-government street protests that followed the celebrations of the GDR's fortieth anniversary. Just over a month later, however, the nightmare was over, and it was in Prenzlauer Berg that ordinary East Germans first experienced the reality of the passing of the old order. At 9.15pm on November 9, 1989, a couple walked through the nearby Bornholmer Strasse border crossing into West Berlin, becoming the first East Berliners to take advantage of the opening of the Wall (see "*Die Wende* to the present" in Contexts).

It's in the maze of streets on either side of Schönhauser Allee that Prenzlauer Berg's real attractions lie: here, you'll find some of the best **cafés**, **bars** and **restaurants** in the eastern part of Berlin (see box above). Starting at the intersection just north of the Segenskirche, a turn left into Oderbergerstrasse leads you to **Kastanienalle**, a lively area of bars and shops, or you could continue along Oderbergerstrasse and find a strip buzzing with eating and drinking joints. Alternatively, you can turn right into Sredzkistrasse from Schönhauser Alle and find the former **Schultheiss Brauerei**, an 1890s brewery built in the pseudo-Byzantine style much favoured by Berlin's architects during the late nineteenth century. The grounds of the former brewery have been transformed into the **Kultur Brauerei**, which, despite a recent facelift involving the addition of a movie multiplex, supermarket and family restaurants, remains a cultural centre with an alternative slant. Passing through the entrance around the corner at Knaackstrasse 97, you'll discover an inner courtyard with a live-music venue, a theatre and various exhibition spaces where there's almost always something – cultural, political or just entertaining – going on.

Kollwitzplatz and around

A right turn from Sredzkistrasse into Knaackstrasse leads to **Kollwitzplatz**, focal point for Prenzlauer Berg's main sights. It is

named after the artist **Käthe Kollwitz**, who lived in nearby
Weissenburgerstrasse (now called Kollwitzstrasse) from 1891 to
1943. Her work embraced political and pacifist themes and can be
best appreciated in the Käthe Kollwitz Museum in Charlottenburg
(see p.123). There's also an unflattering statue of Kollwitz in the little park on the square.

Along Husemannstrasse

Running north from Kollwitzplatz is **Husemannstrasse**, a nineteenth-century tenement street that was restored to its former glory
in late-GDR days and turned into a kind of living museum in an
attempt to recall the grandeur of old Berlin. Since the *Wende*,
restoration projects have transformed neighbouring streets too, covering raddled facades with fresh stucco and installing new wrought-
iron balconies.

Husemannstrasse is now home to a lively restaurant and bar
scene, anchored by the well-known and well-regarded *Restauration
1900*, which was established long before the Wall came down (see
Restaurants).

South of Kollwitzplatz

A left turn at the southern corner of Kollwitzplatz will land you on
Knaackstrasse, where, after 50m or so, the huge red-brick
Wasserturm (water tower) looms over the surrounding streets. Built
in 1875 on the site of a preindustrial windmill, the tower has been
designated a historic monument and converted into apartments with
room plans that follow the circular shape of the building. After the
Nazis came to power the SA turned the basement into a torture chamber, and later the bodies of 28 of their victims were found in the
underground pipe network. A memorial stone on Knaackstrasse
commemorates them: "On this spot in 1933 decent German resistance fighters became the victims of fascist murderers. Honour the
dead by striving for a peaceful world." Before the construction of the
Wasserturm, Prenzlauer Berg's water requirements had been provided by the slim tower at the southern end of the square. Before that
people had had to lug their water up from city centre wells, and open
sewers had taken their waste back downhill to the Spree, with the
unsurprising result that disease was rife.

From Knaackstrasse, a left turn into Rykestrasse brings you to
eastern Berlin's only functioning **synagogue**, an ornate edifice in the
courtyard of house no. 53. Originally built in 1904–5, this survived
both Kristallnacht and use as a stables by the SA. It was designated a
"Temple of Peace" in 1953 but today, poignantly, its capacity
exceeds the Jewish population of the eastern part of the city.

On the southwestern side of the water tower is Belforter Strasse,
where at no. 15 you'll find the **BAT** or **Studiotheater der
Hochschule für Schauspielkunst Ernst Busch**, which is part of the

School of Dramatic Art (see *The arts* in Listings). At the end of Belforter Strasse, cross Prenzlauer Allee into Heinrich-Roller-Strasse, which leads down to Greifswalder Strasse. On the right is a venerable and overgrown cemetery dating back to the early nineteenth century (access from Greifswalder Strasse), with some elaborate tombstones and vaults. Many of the memorials bear shrapnel and bullet scars, an indication of just how intense the fighting during the Battle for Berlin must have been; even the city's graveyards were fought for inch by inch. **Greifswalder Strasse** itself is a main route out of the city and looks very neat with its freshly painted facades. In pre-*Wende* days traffic came to a standstill along the side streets a couple of times a day as a convoy of black Citroëns and Volvos sped by, whisking high-ranking government members (notably Erich Honecker himself) from the Palast der Republik to their homes in the now infamous lakeside town of Wandlitz to the north of Berlin. But behind the immaculate facades, the *Hinterhöfe* of Greifswalder Strasse were just as run-down as those in the backstreets.

Ernst-Thälmann-Park and around

At the northeastern end of Greifswalder Strasse is another example of former-GDR civic window-dressing in the shape of the **Ernst-Thälmann-Park** (walkable from the Heinrich-Roller-Strasse and Greifswalder Strasse intersection or, if you're feeling lazy, take tram #2, #3 or #4). This is a model housing development, set in a small park and fronted by a gigantic marble sculpture of the head and clenched fist of Ernst Thälmann, the pre-1933 Communist leader who was imprisoned and later murdered by the Nazis. Floodlit and guarded round the clock by police in pre-*Wende* days, his likeness is now daubed with graffiti, and the concrete terrace on which it stands is favoured by local skateboarders. About 4000 people, mostly from the ex-GDR elite, live here in high-rise buildings with restaurants, shops, nurseries and a swimming pool all immediately at hand.

Behind the Ernst-Thälmann-Park on Prenzlauer Allee is the silver-domed **Zeiss Planetarium** (Mon & Tues 10am–noon, Wed & Sat 10am–noon & 1.30–9pm, Thurs & Fri 6–10pm, Sun 1.30–6pm; DM8/€4.10, concessions DM6/€3.10; ☎42 18 45 12), with an assortment of German-only displays on the universe around us. Nearby is Prenzlauer Allee's distinctive, yellow-brick 1890s S-Bahn station, one of the best-looking in the city, and just northeast of here, between Sültstrasse and Sodtkestrasse, is the so-called **Flamensiedlung**, a model housing development built in 1929–30 according to plans by the architect Bruno Taut. With his associate Franz Hillinger, Taut wanted to create mass housing that broke away from the tenement-house concept. Basing their design on work already done in Holland, they diffused the angularity of their apartment blocks with corner windows and balconies, and left open areas between them to create an environment far removed from the gloom of the tenement *Hinterhof*.

Friedrichshain

Spreading out east from the city centre, **FRIEDRICHSHAIN** is mainly residential in the north, but given over to extensive goods yards and moribund industry around the Hauptbahnhof and down towards the River Spree in the south. Friedrichshain's longest-established attractions are the Stalinist architecture of **Karl-Marx-Allee**, and the **Volkspark Friedrichshain**, resting place of the victims of the 1848 revolution. Since 1989 these attractions have been augmented by a museum in the former headquarters of the Stasi (see p.184), and the **East Side gallery**, a surviving stretch of Wall that has been transformed into a unique open-air art gallery. For those who find the club and café scene of Prenzlauer Berg already too gentrified, the area to the east of Warschauerstrasse U-Bahn station provides some new territory to explore.

Karl-Marx-Allee

Heading east along **Karl-Marx-Allee** from Strausberger Platz, the
prefabricated blocks of the 1960s give way to the *Zuckerbäckerstil*
(wedding-cake style) of the previous decade (see below). In
September 1951, work began on a scheme to turn Karl-Marx-Allee,
then known as Stalinallee, into "Germany's first socialist street", providing modern flats that would be "palaces for the people". The first
foundation stone of what was to become an ornate high-rise apartment building, the **Hochhaus an der Weberwiese**, was laid at
Marchlewskistrasse 25, just south of Weberwiese U-Bahn station.
Over the next few years similar buildings were constructed from
Strausberger Platz to the Frankfurter Tor U-Bahn station, which
marked the eastern limit of the old Stalinallee. At **Strausberger Platz**
itself, huge twin-tiered towers flank the route into central Berlin,
while 1500m further east two similarly grandiose structures at
Rathaus Friedrichshain, topped by ecclesiastical-looking domes,
stand on the site of an earlier customs gate.

These buildings epitomize the *Zuckerbäckerstil*, a mutated
Classicism that was repeated across the Soviet bloc throughout the
1950s, most famously in Warsaw's Palace of Culture and Moscow's
university and foreign ministry. Though the style was and is much
derided in the west, the buildings of Stalinallee were a well-thought-
out and relatively soundly constructed attempt at housing that would
live up to the great architectural tradition of Berlin. The Stalinallee
apartments with their central heating and parquet floors also provided an enviable level of comfort at a time when most Berliners were
crowded into bomb-shattered tenement blocks or makeshift temporary housing.

Ironically, it was striking workers from the Stalinallee construction project, angered by increased work norms, who sparked off the
uprising of June 1953 (see p.69). Later, when the project was completed, the apartments were given over mainly to SED functionaries
and high-ranking members of the security services. Most tenants are
now old and the whole street has been bought by a Wiesbaden-based
property company that's begun a much-needed renovation of the
blocks. The inhabitants have been assured that no one will be thrown
out but many fear that sooner or later the former Stalinallee housing
will be transformed into up-market apartments conveniently located
for city-centre offices, institutions and ministries.

The best way to appreciate the scale of Karl-Marx-Allee is by car;
it's worth taking a taxi trip up and down the length of this huge
boulevard. Beyond Frankfurter Tor, Karl-Marx-Allee becomes
Frankfurter Allee, a bleak arterial road lined by high-rises, rolling out
into the suburbs in the direction of Frankfurt an der Oder and
Poland. The only real attraction anywhere along its length is the former Stasi Headquarters in the neighbouring Bezirk of Lichtenberg –
to get there take the U-Bahn to Magdalenenstrasse station. On either

side of Frankfurter Allee however – just after the Frankfurter Tor –
the kind of eclectic **bar scene** that sprang up in Prenzlauer Berg and
Mitte in the early 1990s still blooms: on Simon-Dach-Strasse and
around Boxhagener Platz to the south, and around Rigaer Strasse to
the north (see *Cafés and bars*).

Volkspark Friedrichshain

Fifteen minutes' walk north of Karl-Marx-Allee is **Volkspark
Friedrichshain**, one of the city's oldest and largest parks (and a well-
known gay cruising area). At the western entrance to the park, where
Friedenstrasse and Am Friedrichshain meet, is the **Märchenbrunnen**
(Fairytale Fountain), a Neo-Baroque arcade and fountain with statues of characters from Brothers Grimm stories. Intended as a gift to
tenement-dwelling workers, it was put up in 1913 at the instigation
of Social Democratic members of the city council, in direct contra-
vention of the Kaiser's wishes.

A detour to a monument and a graveyard

A few hundred metres to the southeast of the Märchenbrunnen is the
Gedenkstätte für die Deutschen Interbrigadisten, a monument to
the German members of the International Brigades who fought
against the Fascists in Spain in the Spanish Civil War. Of the five
thousand Germans (including many leading Communists) who went
to Spain, only two thousand returned. There's another monument to
the east of here (just off Landsberger Allee), this time to victims of
an upheaval closer to home. The **Friedhof der Märzgefallenen** is
where many of the 183 Berliners killed by the soldiers of King
Friedrich Wilhelm IV during the revolution of March 1848 were
buried, their interment attended by 80,000 of their fellow citizens.
Only a few of the original gravestones survive, but the dead of 1848
have been joined by 33 of those killed in the November Revolution of
1918, commemorated by a statue of a *Rote Matrose* or "Red Sailor"
at the cemetery entrance, reflecting the role played in the revolution
by Imperial Navy sailors.

The Bunkerbergs

The final resting place of the revolutionaries is overshadowed by the
Grosser Bunkerberg and **Kleiner Bunkerberg**, two artificial hills
created when a million cubic metres of rubble from bombed-out
Berlin were dumped over a couple of wartime bunkers. In between
the two is a small, tree-shaded lake, and nearby you'll find the kind
of worthy sporting amenities and giant outdoor chess sets that keep
many Germans amused during their free hours. Set on a grassy slope
a little to the east is a **monument** commemorating the joint fight of
the Polish army and German resistance against the Nazis. Given the
feelings most Germans and Poles have for each other, the sentiments
expressed seem rather unconvincing.

In the area to the immediate east of the park is the **Sport und Erholungszentrum**, Landsberger Allee 77, a big modern leisure centre with several swimming pools, a wave machine, an ice- and roller-skating rink, a sauna, a bowling alley and various cafés (see *Sport* in Listings). The entrance is near the junction of Danziger Strasse and Landsberger Allee.

The East Side Gallery and Ostbahnhof

The **East Side Gallery** is a surviving stretch of Wall that has been turned into an open-air art gallery. Running along Mühlenstrasse, between the Hauptbahnhof and the Oberbaumbrücke in the south of the district, it's been daubed with various political/satirical images, some imaginative, some trite and some impenetrable. One of the most telling images shows Brezhnev and Honecker locked in a passionate kiss, with the inscription, "God, help me survive this deadly love." The gallery can also be reached from the Kreuzberg side over a pedestrian bridge just north of Schlesisches Tor U-Bahn station, or even glimpsed from a subway car as the train crosses the Oberbaumbrücke, once a lonely border crossing, now a busy thoroughfare spanning the Spree River, at the far southern edge of the district.

The old industrial area surrounding the bridge has become the new home for the techno scene as **clubs** have moved into warehouse and factory spaces. The bleak-looking area around the **Ostbahnhof** in particular comes alive at night at *Maria Am Ostbahnhof* and the neighbouring current headquarters of the *Tempodrom* (see *Clubs and live venues*).

Treptow

TREPTOW stretches out 8km southeast from the city centre between the River Spree and what used to be the border with West Berlin. A mainly residential district with a few industrial pockets, the once low-key landscape is now dominated by a recently completed waterside housing complex. The major attraction for visitors is the large Spree-side **Treptower Park** with its huge and sobering **Soviet war memorial**. The area is best reached from Treptower Park S-Bahn station, or by buses #104, #166, #167, #194 and #265.

Treptower Park

As Berlin expanded rapidly during the nineteenth century, **Treptower Park** was one of the places where the city's tenement-dwellers could let off steam, and by 1908 there were thirty-odd dance halls and restaurants here. Later, during the interwar years, the park became a well-known assembly point for revolutionary workers about to embark on demonstrations or go off to do battle with the

Brownshirts. Today, things are very different, since it's here that many of the Soviet casualties from the Battle of Berlin are buried.

The Soviet Memorial

At the heart of the park, the **Soviet Memorial** (Sowjetisches Ehrenmal) commemorates the Soviet Union's 305,000 estimated casualties during the Battle of Berlin in April and May 1945 and is the burial place of 5000 of them. It's best approached from the arched entrance on the south side of Puschkinallee. A little way to the south of here is a sculpture of a grieving woman representing the Motherland, to the left of which a broad concourse slopes up towards a viewing point flanked by two vast triangles of red granite, fashioned from stone bought from Sweden by the Nazis to furnish Berlin with projected victory monuments. From the viewing point the vista is dominated by a vast symbolic statue, a typical Soviet piece of gigantism using marble from Hitler's Chancellery. Over eleven

*One of the
interesting
things about
the memorial
is the complete
lack of any
religious
iconography –
eschewed by
the Soviet state
– showing that
grandiose
memorials
needn't depend
on pious
objects in
order to have
spiritual
power.*

metres high, and set on top of a hill modelled on a *kurgan* or traditional warriors' grave of the Don region, it shows an idealized Russian soldier clutching a saved child and resting his sword on a shattered swastika. Inside the plinth is a memorial crypt with a mosaic in true Socialist Realist style, showing Soviet citizens (soldiers, mother, worker, peasant, and what looks like an old age pensioner) honouring the dead. In the long sunken park area that leads up to the statue are the mass graves of the Red Army troops, lined by sculpted frescoes of stylized scenes from the Great Patriotic War.

In January 1990 the monument hit the headlines briefly when it was defaced, allegedly by neo-Nazis, despite the fact that the place was guarded around the clock. Many East Berliners suspected a put-up job, engineered by the still-communist government or its supporters, ostensibly to combat rising neo-Nazism. Until the *Wende* most of the visitors to the monument were Soviet citizens who came here by the busload to pay their respects, but since the beginning of the 1990s increasing numbers of former West Berliners have discovered the place, and it's become a popular Sunday promenade destination for the space-starved inhabitants of Neukölln and Kreuzberg. It remains an important part of the Berlin cityscape, its sheer scale imparting a sense of the Soviet Union's colossal losses during World War II, losses that shaped postwar Soviet defence and foreign policy, and explain as much as anything why history unfolded as it did in postwar Berlin.

Around the rest of the park

The rest of the park conceals a couple of low-key attractions, including the **Karpfenteich**, a large carp pool just south of the memorial, and, a little to the east of here, the **Archenhold Sternwarte** (Alt-Treptow 1; ☎5 34 80 80; shows Wed 6pm, Sat & Sun 3pm; DM6/€3.10, concessions DM4/€2.05), an observatory with the longest refracting telescope in the world.

The park continues north of Puschkinallee, where you'll also find the *Eierschale-Zenner* (see *Cafés and bars*), a riverside *Gaststätte* whose origins go back to the eighteenth century. Just to the east is the **Insel der Jugend**, a small island in the Spree reached via the **Abteibrücke**, an ornamental footbridge built by French prisoners of war in 1916 to link the island to the mainland. The end of Treptow's summer festival is marked by a firework display from this bridge, an event known as Treptow in Flammen or "Treptow in Flames". The island was originally the location of an abbey, but now the main attraction is *Die Insel*, a tower-like clubhouse that houses a café, cinema and gallery and is a regular venue for club nights and gigs, with occasional outdoor raves in summer (see *Clubs and live venues*). Returning across the bridge, walk northwest back to the S-Bahn station via a grass-lined boardwalk good for picnicking or just relaxing by the water – there's boat rental nearby, providing rowing boats and paddle boats (from DM10/€5.10 per hour). At the beginning of the boardwalk, you'll find a very tasty *Imbiss* stand serving fresh smoked fish.

For something a bit more frenetic, head southeast from the bridge to the **Spreepark**, a popular amusement park in the GDR days and recently refurbished, featuring the usual rides, *Bockwurst* stands and a big wheel. It's all part of the Plänterwald woods, which cover a couple of square kilometres and offer good, untaxing strolling. Just to the southwest of Neue Krug is the *Plänterwald*, a largish *Gaststätte* that makes a good place to interrupt your wanderings.

Gartenstadt Falkenberg

About 8km away, at the southeastern edge of Treptow, is the **Gartenstadt Falkenberg**, a settlement of model housing designed by Bruno Taut in response to slum conditions in the city-centre tenements. To get there, take the S-Bahn to Grünau station, from where it's a short walk southwest along Bruno-Taut-Strasse to the houses on the western end of that street and Akazienhof. The best examples are along Akazienhof: pastel-painted, cottage-like dwellings that must have seemed paradise to their first inhabitants, newly escaped from the filth and industry of the inner *Bezirke*. A plaque at Akazienhof used to state, without irony: "Many of the founder members [of the settlement] were active opponents of war and fascism. Their ideals have become reality in the German Democratic Republic."

Lichtenberg and Marzahn

North of Treptow is the *Bezirk* of **Lichtenberg**, a sprawling working-class district, part prefabricated postwar mass dwellings and part traditional tenement blocks, with heavy concentrations of industry in the north and south. Until the mid-nineteenth century Lichtenberg was little more than a country town and popular Sunday-outing destination for Berliners. With industrialization, however, the familiar Berlin tenements sprang up and the area's rustic past was soon forgotten. In these post-unification days Lichtenberg has been hard hit by the collapse of the old order, with unemployment running high. A nasty side-effect of all this is a reputation for mindless, often racially motivated violence, making it a place to avoid at night. By day, however, head here for the excellent **zoo** in Friedrichsfelde, in the eastern sector of the *Bezirk*. Of more esoteric appeal are the memorial to various figures from the socialist past in Lichtenberg proper, and the museum in Karlshorst, in the building where the Wehrmacht surrendered to the Soviet armed forces in 1945.

East and north of Lichtenberg is **Marzahn**, a mid-1970s satellite town which is not perhaps the most obvious sightseeing destination.

If you're in the mood for something more elaborate, you can take a cruise around the surrounding waterways (see Boats in Introducing the city).

| Lichtenberg and Marzahn | Silo-like apartment blocks and soulless shopping precincts stretch for miles out towards the edge of the city in what has to be one of the most desolate of the city's *Bezirke*. However, this *is* Berlin for tens of thousands of Berliners, and is worth a look for this reason alone. |

Lichtenberg

There's not much to write home about in **LICHTENBERG** proper. The only real reason to come here is to visit the former headquarters of the Stasi, the GDR's all-pervasive secret police, which has been turned into a slightly ghoulish tourist attraction, just a couple of minutes' walk from Magdalenenstrasse U-Bahn station.

The Stasi headquarters and around

The former **Stasi headquarters** is a huge complex bounded by Frankfurter Allee, Ruschestrasse, Normannenstrasse and Magdalenenstrasse – an area approximately the size of London's Whitehall – with another slightly smaller complex a few streets to the north. From here East Germany's infamous **Staatssicherheitsdienst** (State Security Service), or Stasi, kept tabs on everything that happened in the GDR. It was its job to ensure the security of the country's borders, carry out surveillance operations on foreign diplomats, business people and journalists, and monitor domestic and foreign media. It was, however, in surveillance of East Germany's own population that the organization truly excelled. Very little happened in the GDR without the Stasi knowing about it; files were kept on millions of innocent citizens and insidious operations were orchestrated against dissidents, real and imagined.

Part of the building from which all this was controlled now houses a museum with an unwieldy title, the **Forschungs- und Gedenkstätte Normannenstrasse** (Normannenstrasse Research and Memorial Centre, Ruschestrasse 103, Haus 1 (Tues–Fri 11am–6pm, Sat & Sun 2–6pm; *www.Stasi-Museum.de*; DM5/€2.50; U-Bahn Magdalenenstrasse), covering the GDR political system and the way in which the massive surveillance apparatus of the Stasi helped maintain it. Walking along the bare, red-carpeted corridors and looking at the busts of Lenin and Felix Dzerzhinsky – founder of the Soviet Cheka, forerunner of the KGB and model for the Stasi – it all seems to belong to a much more distant past, rather than an era which came to an end only at the beginning of 1990. But then the obsessively neat office and apartment of **Erich Mielke**, the minister of state security who oversaw Stasi operations from 1957 to October 1989, somehow makes it all the more immediate. Everything is just as he left it: white and black telephones stand on the varnished wooden desk as though awaiting incoming calls, and Mielke's white dress uniform hangs in a wardrobe. The only vaguely personal touch is the assortment of clay animal figures made by kindergarten children, so incongruous that the effect is almost grotesque.

The Stasi

The **Stasi** was the so-called *Schild und Schwert* – "sword and shield" – of the German Democratic Republic. It had around 85,000 full-time employees, all of whom held military ranks, and in 1989, the final year of its existence, its budget was about £1 billion. Though the Stasi was also responsible for external espionage and counterespionage, it's thought that about 95 percent of its budget was spent on spying on the East German people. The Stasi mounted what was probably the most comprehensive and long-lasting surveillance of its own population by any state: phones were tapped, mail intercepted, people followed, photographed and filmed. Much of the surveillance legwork was done by a 180,000-strong army of *Informeller Mitarbeiter* or *IM* ("unofficial co-workers"). These were, in effect, paid informers, and every factory, school, institute and military unit had at least one person in this category among its personnel. Most people in the GDR reckoned that their circle of friends and acquaintances would also include at least one *IM*.

The *Informeller Mitarbeiter* gathered material for the exhaustive files the GDR kept on about six million of its citizens (out of a total population of 16 million). As well as detailing anti-regime activities or comments, these files also recorded things like drinking habits, debts and sexual preferences – all useful material for possible blackmail. When details of some files emerged, the level of banality was scarcely believable – the most minute movements of subjects under observation were recorded, right down to visits to the bathroom and walks with the family dog. Stasi-chief Mielke felt that everyone was a potential enemy of the state and that it was thus of vital importance to know everything about everyone.

One result of this obsessive information gathering was that the Stasi was always well informed about the true state of affairs in the GDR. During 1989, according to Mielke, in an interview carried out in his jail cell with the news magazine *Spiegel*, the Stasi kept the government closely informed about the growing crisis. It was fully aware of popular discontent about shortages, crumbling infrastructure, poor working conditions, and anger at the totalitarian nature of the regime, and reported its findings assiduously and impartially. It all made no difference in the end though; when the GDR finally went under, the Stasi went with it, though not without a struggle.

On November 17, 1989, the Ministry for State Security was officially turned into the supposedly government-accountable Office for State Security. However, the first thing this ostensibly new organization did was order the destruction of Stasi files, an act which generated widespread popular outrage. In January 1990 the GDR government proposed a reorganization of its security service to counter an alleged neo-Nazi threat (not quite as absurd now as it seemed to many at the time). By now public patience was at an end and on January 15 the Stasi HQ was attacked by a mob. No one was lynched, though in the confusion some files were destroyed, but it was obvious that the Stasi as a cohesive organization was finished. Its operatives did their best to disappear and cover their tracks.

At the beginning of 1991 former citizens of the GDR were given the right to apply to see their Stasi files. Tens of thousands availed themselves of the opportunity to find out what the organization had recorded about them, and more importantly who had provided the information; many a friendship, and not a few marriages, have come to an end as a result.

On the floor above Mielke's offices various rooms are devoted to different aspects of the history of the Stasi and the GDR. The commentary is in German only, but the displays of Stasi surveillance apparatus, most of it surprisingly primitive, speak for themselves. The extensive array of bugging devices and cameras reveals the absurd lengths the GDR went to in order to keep tabs on what its citizens were doing – included in the display are watering cans and plant pots concealing toylike cameras. You'll also find a couple of rooms stuffed with medals, badges, flags and other items of GDR kitsch. For German-speakers the sections on political terror during the Stalin years and forced resettlement from border zones throw light on otherwise little-known aspects of GDR history.

Elsewhere in Lichtenberg

A rather sinister-looking **Rathaus** looms over Möllendorffstrasse a few streets to the west, and just north of here, marooned amid the traffic, is an improbably rustic **Dorfkirche**, dating back to Lichtenberg's village origins. The stone walls date from the original thirteenth-century structure, but the rest is more modern, the spire having been tacked on as recently as 1965. The only other attraction in Lichtenberg itself is the **Gedenkstätte der Sozialisten** or "Memorial to the Socialists", a kilometre or so northeast of Lichtenberg U- and S-Bahn station, at the end of Gudrunstrasse, and perhaps only for die-hard fans of GDR arcana. Its centrepiece is a four-metre chunk of red porphyry bearing the inscription *Die Toten mahnen uns* – "The dead remind us", commemorating the GDR's socialist hall of fame from Karl Liebknecht and Rosa Luxemburg onwards. A tablet bears a list of names that reads like the street directory of virtually any town in pre-*Wende* East Germany, recording the esoteric cult-figures of the workers' and peasants' state in alphabetical order, and until 1989 the East Berlin public were cajoled and coerced into attending hundred-thousand-strong mass demonstrations here. The whole thing actually replaced a much more interesting Mies van der Rohe-designed memorial that stood here from 1926 until the Nazis destroyed it in 1935. Altogether much more uncompromising, featuring a huge star and hammer and sickle, the original memorial caused problems for Mies van der Rohe when he came before Joseph McCarthy's Un-American Activities Committee in 1951. The Gedenkstätte is also the burial place of Walter Ulbricht, the man who took the decision to build the Wall, and Wilhelm Pieck, the first president of the GDR.

The Tierpark

To reach Lichtenberg's sprawling **Tierpark** or zoo (daily 9am–sunset or 7pm at the latest; DM14/€7.15, concessions DM11.50/€5.90; *www.tierpark.de*) in Friedrichsfelde, take the U-Bahn to Tierpark station (the zoo entrances are on the eastern side of Am Tierpark).

The Tierpark ranks as one of the largest zoos in Europe and a thorough exploration of its wooded grounds could easily absorb the better part of a day. It's an ideal destination for families, though some visitors may balk at the traditional nature of the place and the fact that some of the animals are kept in very small cages. However, others have much more space to roam around and virtually every species imaginable, from alpaca to wisent, can be found here, including rare Przewalski horses, which have been bred in the zoo in great numbers over the years, bringing the breed back from the edge of extinction.

Hidden away in the grounds of the zoo, just beyond an enclosure of lumbering pelicans, is **Schloss Friedrichsfelde** (Tues–Sun 10am–6pm; *www.stadtmuseum.com*; DM2/€1), a Baroque palace housing an exhibition of eighteenth- and nineteenth-century interior decor. Theodor Fontane described it as the Schloss Charlottenburg of the East, but he was exaggerating – the best thing about it is its pretty ornamental grounds.

Karlshorst

From the Tierpark, a stroll south down Am Tierpark, bearing left along Treskowerallee for about a kilometre, will bring you to **Karlshorst** (alternatively take the S-Bahn from Alexanderplatz, changing at Ostkreuz). For many years you were more likely to hear Russian than German spoken on the streets around here, as the area was effectively a Russian quarter, thanks to the presence of large numbers of Soviet soldiers and their dependants. The Russians accepted the unconditional surrender of the German armed forces in a Wehrmacht engineer's school here on May 8, 1945, and went on to establish their Berlin headquarters nearby. For many years after Karlshorst was a closed area, fenced off and under armed guard, out of bounds to ordinary East Germans. Later, they were allowed back into parts of the area, but Karlshorst retained an exclusive cachet, its villas given over to the elite of GDR society – scientists and writers – or used as foreign embassy residences.

The Russians finally left in the summer of 1994 but a reminder of their presence endures in the shape of the **Museum Berlin-Karlshorst** in Rheinsteinstrasse (corner of Zwieseler Strasse; Tues–Sun 10am–6pm; free), the building where the German surrender was signed. When the GDR still existed, this museum was officially known as the "Museum of the Unconditional Surrender of Fascist Germany in the Great Patriotic War 1941–45". Since then it has been renamed and rearranged to suit post-Cold War sensibilities. It features an exhibition on the long and tumultuous German-Russian relationship, obviously focusing on the treaty that ended the war.

Another unusual Karlshorst attraction is the **Trabrennbahn Karlshorst**, Treskowerallee 129, where you can enjoy a day at the races Berlin-style, watching trap and dog racing (Sat 2pm & Tues

6pm; price varies). The racetrack is to the left of Treskowerallee, just south of the S-Bahn bridge.

Marzahn

To see the real legacy of East Berlin – **MARZAHN** – it's probably best to go by day and preferably not looking too much like a tourist, as the area has a reputation for violence. It's in such places as Marzahn, all across the former GDR, that people are bearing the economic brunt of reunification's downside – unemployment, *Kurzarbeit* or "short-time working", and low wages – and where you'll see the worst effects caused by the collapse of a state that, for all its faults, ensured a certain level of social security for its citizens. Ironically, Marzahn was one of the GDR's model new towns of the 1970s, part of Honecker's efforts to solve his country's endemic housing shortage by providing modern apartments in purpose-built blocks with shopping facilities and social amenities to hand. But like similar developments in Western countries, it never quite worked out according to plan, with the usual crime and drugs (in this case alcohol and prescribed tranquillizers) surfacing.

Springpfuhl to Marzahner Promenade

Most of Marzahn dates from the 1970s, when it was built with an attendant industrial zone just to the west. Over 150,000 people live in a six-kilometre by two-kilometre strip of high-rise developments stretching from Springpfuhl in the south to Ahrensfelde in the north. For a brief taste, head for the **Wohngebiet am Springpfuhl** (Springpfuhl S-Bahn station), a representative development between Märkische Allee and Allee der Kosmonauten. There's little to do other than wander, trying to take in the immensity of it all, amid the blocks and windblown shopping precincts.

To the north of here is Alt-Marzahn (tram #18 for four stops from Helene-Weigel-Platz), where something of the area's village past survives. Admittedly it's not a very pleasant past; from 1866 the fields of the area were used as *Rieselfelder*, specially designated for the disposal of Berlin's sewage. Despite this malodorous development, Marzahn acquired a **Dorfkirche** in Neo-Gothic style a few years later, built by Schinkel's pupil Friedrich August Stüler. Nearby, at Alt-Marzahn 31, is the somewhat curious **Handwerksmuseum und Friseurmuseum** (Handicrafts Museum and Barber Museum, Tues–Sun 10am–6pm; *www.stadtmuseum.com*; DM4/€2.05, concessions DM2/€1). The former is devoted mainly to an exhibit of woodworking tools and a huge collection of locks and keys, while the latter consists of the many and varied haircutting, shaving and surgical tools employed by barbers throughout history. From Alt-Marzahn, head for **Marzahner Promenade** (bus #192 for three stops), which is more or less in the middle of things, and from where endless blocks stretch out north and south. By now you'll probably want to leave it all behind, and the S-Bahn, located at the southeastern end of the promenade, will whisk you back into town from S-Bahnhof Marzahn.

The Gründerzeitmuseum Mahlsdorf

Alternatively, take tram #62 from Mahlsdorf's S-Bahn station two stops south along Honower Damm, or walk for about ten minutes. The suburb of **Mahlsdorf** (in the neighbouring *Bezirk* of Hellersdorf), about 5km southeast of Marzahn, is no cultural centre, but it does boast one of the city's most notable museums, the excellent **Gründerzeitmuseum Mahlsdorf**, Hultschiner Damm 333 (Wed & Sun 10am–6pm; DM7/€3.60, concessions DM5/€2.50), a collection of furniture and household gear from 1880–1900, the period known as the *Gründerzeit* or "foundation time" when the newly united Germany was at its Imperial peak. The founder of the museum, Lothar Berfelde (better known in Germany as a writer under his pseudonym, Charlotte von Mahlsdorf), got the collection together during GDR days when such an undertaking was by no means an easy task, creating a representative *Gründerzeit* apartment by taking the complete contents of rooms and relocating them in this eighteenth-century manor house. Depending on your tastes the result is either exquisite or over-the-top, but either way the museum is fascinating and certainly worth the long haul out to the suburbs. In the basement are furnishings from the *Mulack-Ritz*, a famous turn-of-the-century Berlin *Kneipe* that originally stood on Mulackstrasse in the Scheunenviertel (see p.118). Lothar Berfelde was awarded the Bundesverdienstkreuz, Germany's equivalent of the OBE, in the summer of 1992 for his services to the preservation of the city's cultural and social heritage; he is, incidentally, one of Berlin's better-known transvestites.

Pankow and Weissensee

Pankow, the northernmost eastern Berlin *Bezirk* before the city gives way to open countryside, has a slightly different atmosphere to other Berlin suburbs. It has an almost village-like feel, contrasting sharply with the grime and decay of inner-city *Bezirke* like Prenzlauer Berg, and though there's not much in the way of sights, its broad streets and parks make for an hour or two's pleasant strolling. The neighbouring *Bezirk* of **Weissensee** is also largely residential, though as home to Germany's largest Jewish cemetery its attractions are perhaps a little more tangible than those of Pankow.

Pankow

PANKOW was always more than just another East Berlin suburb. For years its villas and well-maintained flats were home mainly to

members of the upper reaches of East Berlin society: state-approved
artists and writers, scientists, East Berlin resident diplomats and the
Parteibonzen (party bigwigs) of the old regime. Up until the 1960s
the area was perceived in the West as being the real centre of power
in the old GDR; Schloss Niederschönhausen, an eighteenth-century
palace on the edge of the *Bezirk*, was the official residence of the
GDR's first president, Wilhelm Pieck, and later of SED General
Secretary Walter Ulbricht, the man who took the decision to build the
Wall. The name of the suburb was also appropriated by one of the ex-
GDR's best-known rock bands, in a satirical dig at the social hierarchy of the workers' and peasants' state.

Pankow's main street is **Breite Strasse**, best reached by taking the
S-Bahn to Pankow station. Between Schönhauser Allee and Pankow
the train passes through what used to be the Todesstreifen or "Death
Strip", which separated East Berliners from the Wall proper. Though
you'd hardly know it now, until November 9, 1989, this was the clos-
est most East Berliners were ever likely to get to the West. From
Pankow station it's a short walk north along Berliner Strasse to
Breite Strasse. Alternatively, tram #53 from Hackescher Markt will

take you directly there, and give you a great view of the streets of Prenzlauer Berg.

Breite Strasse and around

At the junction of Berliner Strasse and Breite Strasse, on a mid-road island that used to be the village green, is the **Alte Pfarrkirche**, Pankow's parish church and oldest building. It dates back to the fifteenth century but was extensively restored in 1832, a project in which Schinkel had a hand, resulting in an unusual-looking Neo-Gothic jumble. At the western end of Breite Strasse is the turn-of-the-century Neo-Baroque Rathaus, a red-brick affair of fanciful gables, towers and cupolas, with a good *Ratskeller* in its basement.

Beyond the Rathaus, Wilhelm-Kuhr-Strasse leads to the neat **Bürgerpark**, a one-time private park with an impressive entrance portal symbolic of nineteenth-century Pankow's status as a villa quarter for Berlin's more well-to-do citizens. The Panke, a small river that lent its name to the settlement, flows through the park, and its willow-lined banks are popular with promenaders. West of the Bürgerpark is the heath-like **Volkspark Schönholzer Heide** (entrance from Herman-Hesse-Strasse), in the northwestern corner of which is a huge **Soviet cemetery**, where dozens of communal graves contain the remains of 13,200 soldiers killed during the Battle of Berlin.

The Schlosspark and around

A less gloomy possibility is the **Schlosspark**, to the north of Breite Strasse, in whose leafy grounds lurks **Schloss Niederschönhausen**, former home of Elisabeth Christine, the estranged wife of Frederick the Great. The Schloss was built at the beginning of the eighteenth century and given an extensive but run-of-the-mill face-lift in 1764. During GDR days it could only be admired from a distance, as it served first as official residence of the GDR president, from 1949 to 1960, and then as the old regime's most prestigious state guesthouse; these days you're free to wander the slightly dreary grounds from 9am until 7pm (9pm in summer). A few streets to the north of the park on Platanenstrasse is Pankow's most unusual building, the **Maria-Magdalenenkirche**, an Expressionist church from 1930, with a bizarre slab of a tower topped by three giant crucifixes.

Weissensee

WEISSENSEE, directly to the east of Pankow, is a predominantly middle-class area with a slightly sleepy atmosphere, hinting at the open countryside only a few kilometres away. The main attraction here is Berlin's largest **Jewish cemetery**, another indicator of the high profile of the all-but-vanished Jewish community. Tram #2, #3 or #4 from Hackescher Markt stops near the junction of Berliner Allee and Albertinenstrasse.

The Jewish Cemetery

The **Jüdischer Friedhof Weissensee** (Mon–Thurs & Sun 7am–5pm, Fri 7am–3pm) lies at the end of Herbert-Baum-Strasse (named after the Jewish resistance hero executed for his part in an attack on a Nazi propaganda exhibition in the Lustgarten in 1942, see p.84), ten minutes south of Berliner Strasse. Opened in 1880, when the Schönhauser Allee cemetery had finally been filled to capacity, this is one of Europe's largest Jewish cemeteries, and certainly the biggest in Germany.

At the entrance to the cemetery a sign requests that male visitors cover their heads before entering; this you are firmly expected to do. You may borrow a skullcap from the cemetery office to the right.

Immediately beyond the entrance is a memorial "to our murdered brothers and sisters 1933–45" from Berlin's Jewish community. It takes the form of a circle of tablets bearing the names of all the large concentration camps. Like many memorials to the war years in the city, it's a poignant monument to the horrors that occurred, and succeeds in being less inflated and militaristic than many others. Nearby is a memorial to Herbert Baum.

Beyond here are the cemetery administration buildings (information about the cemetery is available from here), constructed in similar mock-Moorish style to the synagogue on Oranienburger Strasse. The cemetery itself stretches back from the entrance for about a kilometre: row upon row of headstones, with the occasional extravagant family monument in between, a muted roll call of families systematically wiped out by the Final Solution.

A handful of well-tended postwar graves near the administration buildings are, paradoxically, symbols of survival, witness to the fact that a few thousand Berlin Jews did escape the Holocaust and that the city still has a small Jewish community of around ten thousand people.

The Weisser See and around

Back on Berliner Allee, it's only a few minutes' walk to the shady park containing the **Weisser See**, the lake that gives the district its name. Near the park entrance is a **monument** commemorating the struggle against fascism. The communist authorities tried to foster a tradition whereby newly engaged couples would lay flowers at the memorial, but this is an activity that has declined drastically in popularity since 1989. In the park itself it's possible to rent boats on the lake (which features a fairly unspectacular fountain), and there's an open-air stage and a *Gaststätte* nearby. Adjacent to the lake is a swimming pool, which is fed by an underground spring. To the north of the park, off Radrennbahnstrasse, is the **Radrennbahn Weissensee**, a cycle track where rock concerts were occasionally held. In the old days the SED administration brought in biggish-name Western acts like James Brown and ZZ Top at great expense, as a sop to the nation's disaffected youth. The initial impetus for this came after young people clashed with police who had attempted to move them on from streets near the Wall in the city centre, where they had been listening to a Eurythmics concert going on just over the border in West Berlin.

Along Pistoriusstrasse

After Berliner Allee, Weissensee's main street is the mostly residential **Pistoriusstrasse**, which branches off northwest from the former just before the Weisser See itself. Roughly halfway along it is Pistoriusplatz, site of a weekend market and prelude to another Berlin architectural experiment, the **Gemeindeforum Kreuzpfuhl**, which lies just to the right of the street, set around a small lake called the **Kreuzpfuhl**. It looks like no other development in the city, benefiting heavily from its position on the tree-lined lake shore, and is perhaps the most aesthetically successful of the many attempts to break away from the dreadful housing conditions of the *Mietskaserne*. These four-storey apartment blocks with their decorative red-brick facades and distinctive gabled roofs were built in 1908 and have been officially designated a "valuable monument of social history".

Köpenick and around

Köpenick is one of eastern Berlin's more pleasant *Bezirke*, located on the banks of the River Spree towards the southeast edge of the city, and easily reached by S-Bahn line #3 from Alexanderplatz, Friedrichstrasse Station and Zoo Station. The town of Köpenick is a slow-moving little place, but ideal to visit as an escape from the city centre. It also makes a convenient base for exploring Berlin's southeastern lakes, in particular the **Müggelsee**, with its appealing shoreline towns of Friedrichshagen and Rahnsdorf. Also easily accessible are the **Müggelberge**, Berlin's 150-metre-high "mountains", and the towns of **Grünau** and **Schmöckwitz** on the banks of the Lange See, which gives access to the Zeuthener See and Krossinsee.

Köpenick

KÖPENICK itself was a town in its own right during medieval times, and though it has since been swallowed up by Greater Berlin, it still retains a distinct identity. The presence of a number of major factories in the area meant that Köpenick always had a reputation as a "red" town. In March 1920, during the Kapp putsch attempt, workers from Köpenick took on and temporarily drove back army units who were marching on Berlin in support of the coup. The army later returned, but its success was short-lived as the putsch foundered – thanks mainly to a highly effective general strike. This militancy was to continue into the Nazi era: on January 30, 1933, the day Hitler came to power, the red flag could be seen flying from the chimney of the brewery in the suburb of Friedrichshagen. This defiance was

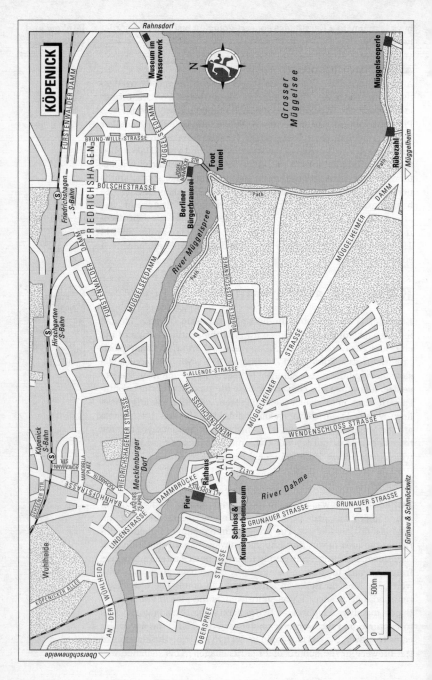

KÖPENICK

Museum im
Wasserwerk

Grosser
Müggelsee

Müggelseeperle

Rübezahl

▷ Müggelheim

FÜRSTENWALDER DAMM

BRUNO-WILLE-STRASSE

MÜGGELSEEDAMM

Friedrichshagen
S-Bahn

FRIEDRICHSHAGEN

BÖLSCHESTRASSE

JOSEF-NAWROCKI-STR

Foot
Tunnel

Berliner
Bürgerbrauerei

Path

River Müggelspree

FÜRSTENWALDER DAMM

MÜGGELSEEDAMM

Path

MÜGGELSCHLOSSENWEG

MÜGGELHEIMER

DAMM

Hirschgarten
S-Bahn

Path

MÜGGELSCHLOSS-STR

S-ALLENDE-STRASSE

MÜGGELHEIMER STRASSE

WENDENSCHLOSS STRASSE

Köpenick
S-Bahn

FRIEDRICHSHAGENER STRASSE

Mecklenburger
Dorf

BORNMANN STR

BAHNSTR

MANDRELLA PLATZ

DATE DER 23 APRIL

WENDENSCHLOSS STR

KIETZ

Rathaus

ALT
STADT

GEHSENER STR

BAHNHOFSTRASSE

LINDENSTRASSE

DAMMBRÜCKE

Pier

ALT KÖPENICK

Schloss &
Kunstgewerbemuseum

River Dahme

GRUNAUER STRASSE

GRUNAUER STRASSE

▷ Grünau & Schmöckwitz

Wuhlheide

KÖPENICKER ALLEE

AN DER WUHLHEIDE

STRASSE

OBERSPREE

500m

0

punished during the Köpenicker Blutwoche ("Köpenick Week of Blood") in June, during which the SA swooped on Social Democrats and Communists. Five hundred people were imprisoned and 91 murdered.

At the heart of Köpenick is the Altstadt or old town. To walk there from the S-Bahn station, follow Borgamannstrasse to Mandrellaplatz, location of Köpenick's **Amtsgericht** (District Court), in whose execution chamber the victims of the Köpenicker Blutwoche were killed. From Mandrellaplatz, Puchanstrasse leads to Am Generalshof and the Platz des 23 April, which commemorates the arrival in Köpenick of the Soviet army – liberators or conquerors, depending on your point of view. On the Platz a sculpted clenched fist on top of a stone tablet honours those killed by the Nazis in 1933.

The Altstadt

From the Platz, the Dammbrücke (you can rent boats by the foot of the bridge from DM5/€2.50 per hour) leads across the Spree into Köpenick's **Altstadt** (if you want to avoid the places mentioned above, there's a direct link from the S-Bahn station on tram #60 or #62, or bus #169). Situated on an island between the Spree and Dahme rivers, the Altstadt's streets run more or less true to the medieval town plan.

The most prominent building is the turn-of-the-century Neo-Gothic **Rathaus** on Alt Köpenick, a typically over-the-top gabled affair with an imposing clock tower. Eight years before World War I, an incident took place here that would capture the imagination of the world's press and provide the inspiration for a play that would make Köpenick famous far beyond the city limits of Berlin. On October 16, 1906, an unemployed shoemaker named **Wilhelm Voigt**, who had spent some time in prison, disguised himself as an army officer and commandeered a troop of soldiers. He marched them to the Köpenick Rathaus and, with their assistance, requisitioned the contents of the municipal safe. Having ordered his detachment to take Köpenick's mayor and book-keeper to the Neue Wache guardhouse in the city centre, he disappeared. Although Voigt was soon caught, the story was seized on abroad as an example of the Prussian propensity to blindly follow anyone wearing uniform. Later, the playwright Carl Zuckmeyer turned Voigt's exploits into a play, *Der Hauptmann von Köpenick* ("The Captain of Köpenick"). The robbery is re-enacted every summer in the second half of June during the Köpenick summer festival and a statue of Voigt now stands by the entrance of the Rathaus.

In **Grünstrasse** and **Böttcherstrasse** are a number of typical nineteenth-century *Bürgerhäuser* with restored facades, and given the sometimes down-at-heel nature of the Altstadt it's not hard to picture this area as it must have been a century or so ago.

The Schloss

At the southern end of the Altstadt island a footbridge leads to the Schlossinsel, site of Köpenick's Baroque **Schloss**, which is more of a fortified manor house dating back to the seventeenth century. The Schloss houses the **Kunstgewerbemuseum** (Museum of Applied Art; Tues–Sun 10am–6pm; *www.smb.spk-berlin.de*; DM4/€2.05, concessions DM2/€1), currently undergoing renovations until May 2002, at which time it will reopen with a collection of interior decorations from the sixteenth to eighteenth centuries. Although the pieces in its collection are not quite as impressive as those in the Kulturforum's Kunstgewerbemuseum (see p.132), the museum plans to take advantage of its setting by integrating the pieces into the original interiors of the Baroque manor, rather than tucking them behind glass display cabinets. The first floor, for example, will contain a complete festival hall, with the original ceiling and wall stucco decorations restored, and silverware and porcelain laid out on a huge banquet table; the highlight of the room will be a silver buffet originally found in the ruling Hohenzollern family's Berliner Schloss – one of the few pieces surviving intact from that castle.

The Kietz

Just to the southeast of the Altstadt is the **Kietz**, a cobbled street of fishing cottages whose origins go back to the early thirteenth century. The houses, with their painted shutters and whitewashed facades, back onto the **Frauentog**, a bay that separates the Schlossinsel from the mainland, where Köpenick's fishermen used to cast their nets. As in the Altstadt, renovation over the past several years has brightened up most of the cottages, and it's a pleasant stroll along the street.

FEZ Wuhlheide and Oberschöneweide

From Köpenick Altstadt, you can take tram #67 a few stops northwest to the **Freizeit- und Erholungszentrum (FEZ) Wuhlheide** (Mon–Fri 10am–5pm, Sat & Sun 10am–6pm; free), a large amusement park for children which takes up a sizeable chunk of the Wuhlheide woods. It's all a bit worthy, with workshops, open-air stages and sports facilities, but the main attraction seems to be the seven-kilometre-long **Berliner Parkeisenbahn**, a narrow-gauge rail line operated by children. For details on what's going on drop in at the information centre in the **FEZ-Palast** at the heart of it all.

For architecture fans **Oberschöneweide**, a little to the west of the FEZ, boasts some impressive modernist buildings designed by the architect Peter Behrens during the early part of the twentieth century. The first, opposite the FEZ itself at An der Wuhlheide 192–194, is a boathouse which used to be owned by AEG, and there are a couple of Behrens' factory buildings at Wilhelminenhofstrasse 83–85 (on the route of trams #26 or #61). Nearby, Zeppelinstrasse 11–71, Roedernstrasse 8–14b and Fontanestrasse 8a–12c are all examples of Behrens-designed residential housing.

The Grosser Müggelsee and around

From Luisenhain, opposite the Rathaus in Köpenick Altstadt, it's possible to take a Stern und Kreisschiffahrt boat trip around the nearby **Grosser Müggelsee**, one of Berlin's main lakes, just a few kilometres east of Köpenick itself. Although the lake lies within the city limits of Berlin, the atmosphere of suburbs like Friedrichshagen and Rahnsdorf is distinctly small-town, and wandering the shores of the lake and the surrounding woods is a welcome relief from pounding Berlin's relentless urban streets. Beware, though: the Müggelsee area gets very crowded at all times of the year – in summer, people swarm here for sun and sailing, and in winter to ice skate.

Friedrichshagen and the Müggelsee shore

Another way of reaching the Grosser Müggelsee is to take the S-Bahn to **FRIEDRICHSHAGEN**, a small town founded in 1753 as a settlement for Bohemian cotton spinners who, as a condition of their being allowed to live here, were required by law to plant mulberry trees for the rearing of silkworms. Leading down from the S-Bahn station is Friedrichshagen's main drag, **Bölschestrasse**, where a number of single-storey houses survive from the original eighteenth-century settlement, dwarfed by later nineteenth-century blocks, and a few vestigial mulberry trees still cling to life at the roadside. About halfway down this otherwise attractive street the **Christophoruskirche**, a gloomy Neo-Gothic church in red brick, puts a Lutheran damper on things.

To get away from it, make for the lake, which is reached via Josef-Nawrocki-Strasse, passing the extensive buildings of the **Berliner Bürgerbrauerei**, from whose chimney the red flag flew provocatively the day Hitler was sworn in as chancellor. Following the road around leads to a small park at the point where the Spree flows into the Grosser Müggelsee. Here there's a cruise-ship pier and a foot tunnel that takes you under the river. At the other side a path through the woods follows the lakeshore to two *Gaststätten*: *Rübezahl* and then *Müggelseeperle* (both of these can be reached on the cruise boats that run out here from the city – see *Introducing the city*). The first is a real architectural eyesore, looking like a transplant from Alexanderplatz, and the food isn't much better, but stopping off for a quick drink entails no major gastronomic risks.

Halfway between Friedrichshagen and Rahnsdorf is the **Museum im Wasserwerk**, Müggelseedamm 307 (April–Oct Wed–Fri 10am–4pm, Sat & Sun 10am–5pm; Nov–March Wed–Sun 10am–3pm; DM4/€2.05, concessions DM2/€1), an old waterworks building that's been turned into a museum detailing the history of

Berlin's water supply. Take tram #60 for six stops from Friedrichshagen S-Bahn station.

The Müggelberge

A little to the south of the *Rübezahl* is the main road and the bus stop from where bus #169 runs to Köpenick S-Bahn station. Opposite the bus stop is a path leading through the woods up to the summit of the **Müggelberge** hills. Around about the halfway mark is the **Teufelsee** (Devil's Lake), a small pool with a glass-smooth surface, which acts as a focus for various nature trails. More information on these, and on the flora and fauna of the area, can be obtained at the nearby **Lehrkabinett** information centre (May–Sept Wed–Fri 10am–4pm, Sat & Sun 10am–5pm; Oct–April Wed, Thurs, Sat & Sun 10am–4pm). Pushing on and up through the woods leads to the **Müggelturm** (daily 9am–5pm; DM2.50/€1.30, concessions DM1.50/€0.80), a functional-looking observation tower offering great views of the lake and woods, plus a café, bar and restaurant (see *Cafés and bars*). Incidentally, both the Teufelsee and Müggelturm are accessible by car and bike (if you've got the stamina) along reasonably well-surfaced tracks from the main road. Also accessible by car, but more pleasantly reached on foot, are the *Schmetterlingshorst* and the *Marienlust*, a couple of *Gaststätten* on the shore of the Langer See about 500m south of the Müggelturm.

Rahnsdorf

At the east end of the Grosser Müggelsee, the little town of **RAHNS-DORF** can be reached by S-Bahn or by tram #61 from Friedrichshagen. Rahnsdorf itself is one of eastern Berlin's more delightful hidden corners, a sprawl of tree-shaded lakeside houses with an old fishing village at its core. Head for **Dorfstrasse**, a cobbled street at the southern end of the village (bus #161 from the S-Bahn station for six stops, then follow the signs for Altes Fischerdorf or ask directions), lined by fishermen's cottages and centred around a small parish church. The best way to explore Rahnsdorf is to simply wander the lakeside and soak up the atmosphere. Just off Fürstenwalder Damm, on the western edge of town, there's an FKK (Freikörperkultur) **nudist beach** for hardy souls.

Grünau

Another possible local destination is **GRÜNAU** on the River Dahme, just to the south of Köpenick (tram #68 runs directly from Köpenick, and there's an S-Bahn station). There isn't a great deal in terms of sights, but you could do worse than go for a walk along the quiet banks of the Langer See, as the Dahme is called beyond Grünau.

The Langer See itself is a watersports centre, and the **Strandbad Grünau**, a beach of sorts, lies just outside town, with numerous *Gaststätten* nearby. To reach it, head along Regattastrasse past the

Regattatribüne, starting point for boat races along this stretch and venue for part of the 1936 Olympics.

Köpenick
and around

Schmöckwitz

Tram #68 passes through the tranquil villa settlement of Karolinenhof to **SCHMÖCKWITZ**, which has been inhabited since prehistoric times. Again, there aren't any real sights, but you can spend a pleasant hour or two wandering through the **Schmöckwitzer Werder**, a woodland area occupying a finger of land several kilometres square between the Zeuthener See and Krossinsee, southeast of Schmöckwitz. On the shores of the Krossinsee (and accessible by occasional buses from Schmöckwitz) are a couple of decent **campsites** (see *Accommodation*).

EAST OF THE CENTRE

199

Chapter 10

Potsdam and Sanssouci

66 "T he first fine day should be devoted to Potsdam, without which a complete impression of Berlin can scarcely be obtained," claims the prewar Baedeker, a nod to the fact that **Potsdam**, although not officially part of Berlin, was the natural completion of the Hohenzollern city, forming a unity with Charlottenburg and the old centre along Unter den Linden.

Above all, Potsdam means **Sanssouci**, Frederick the Great's splendid landscaped park of architectural treasures, including Schloss Sanssouci, the king's palace retreat. There is, however, much more to Potsdam: in the town itself, despite the depredations of Allied bombing and insensitive, politically motivated GDR planners, much of the historic centre remains intact, with grandiose city gates and an eighteenth-century **Baroque quarter** recalling the atmosphere of a *Residenzstadt* or royal residence. Other sights include **Cecilienhof**, where the fate of postwar Europe was sealed at the Potsdam conference; **Russische Kolonie Alexandrowka**, a nineteenth-century Russian colony of timber houses overlooked by an Orthodox chapel; the **Pfingstberg**, with its forlorn Jewish cemetery and ruined Belvedere; another Schloss across the River Havel in **Babelsberg**, which also boasts a film studio prominent in the history of German cinema; and myriad smaller attractions in between.

> There's a **map of Potsdam and Sanssouci** in the colour section at the back of this book.

Despite the fact that it lies just to the southwest of Berlin, until 1990 it was difficult to reach Potsdam: visa regulations made visiting a complicated affair and many people left it off their itineraries. Since the withering away of the border, however, the town has enjoyed an enormous influx of visitors from the West. Although Potsdam makes for a good day out from the city, you'll probably find that you need two or three days to take everything in, so practical details and listings are included in this chapter.

Potsdam

Like most towns in the Berlin area, **POTSDAM**'s origins are Slavonic and its first documented mention was as Poztupimi during the tenth century, making it older than Berlin by a couple of hundred years. In 1160 a castle was built here, marking the first step in the town's gradual transformation from fishing backwater, though for the next couple of centuries it remained a relatively sleepy place.

Under the Hohenzollerns, Potsdam became a **royal residence** and **garrison town**, roles which it enjoyed right up until the abdication of Kaiser Wilhelm II in 1918. World War II left Potsdam badly damaged: on April 14, 1945, a bombing raid killed four thousand people and reduced the town centre to ruins, destroying many fine Baroque buildings (the raid was so heavy that it could be heard and seen from Bernau, over 40km to the northeast). Immediately after the war, Potsdam was chosen by the victorious Allies as the venue for a conference where, on August 2, 1945, the division of Germany and Europe was confirmed. Subsequently, under the SED regime, it was decided to demolish the ruins of much of the old town and undertake extensive modern building programmes in pursuit of a "new, socialist Potsdam". These account for the unattractive and confused appearance of the eastern half of the town centre, and although attempts were made to preserve the architectural integrity of the town during the 1980s, the communists always felt ill at ease with its historical role and Imperial associations.

With the opening of the border in 1989, Potsdam's links with the rest of Berlin were once again revived, and it has since traded well on its tourist appeal. The influx of cash has allowed the town to be polished up considerably, not least through the destruction of the surrounding red-brick *Uhlan* barracks that used to house Russian soldiers. Nevertheless, it's surprising how many dilapidated buildings remain; capitalist elan will no doubt soon refurbish – or remove – even these structures, but for now they stand as reminders of the long historical road trodden by the city.

Arrival, information and accommodation

Visiting Potsdam couldn't be easier. There are excellent transport links from Berlin, and the local tourist office can arrange accommodation in either private rooms or hotels (due to the large volume of visitors, local accommodation is harder to come by in summer).

There is a direct S-Bahn link (line #7) from Berlin's Bahnhof Friedrichstrasse and Zoo Station to **Potsdam Hauptbahnhof**, from where it's just a few minutes' walk north across the Lange Brücke into the centre of town. Coming in by road from western Berlin, bus

#116 from S-Bahnhof Wannsee will deposit you on the Potsdam side of the **Glienicker Bridge**, just east of the centre. From here you can catch tram #93 to the **Platz der Einheit** in the centre of town. A more atmospheric approach is provided by the cruise boats from Wannsee (see p.52).

Just south of the Platz der Einheit is Potsdam's **tourist office**, at Friedrich-Ebert-Strasse 5 (April–Oct Mon–Fri 9am–8pm, Sat 9am–6pm, Sun 9am–4pm; Nov–March Mon–Fri 10am–6pm, Sat & Sun 10am–2pm; ☎27 55 80; *www.potsdam.de*). It's well equipped with maps and will book rooms in private accommodation. There's also a smaller office in the Hauptbahnhof.

The telephone code for Potsdam is ☎0331.

Accommodation

For details of accommodation price codes see Accommodation in Listings.

Ideally, you should spend at least a couple of days in Potsdam. If you're on a budget the best bet is to book a **private room** (around DM60–100/€30.70–51) through the tourist office (see above). Alternatively there's a large **hostel**, *Jugendgästehaus Siebenschläfer*, located on the Babelsberg side of the Havel but close to public transport, at Lotte-Puewka-Str. 43 (☎74 11 25) – dorms are DM30 (€15.35) per night. The closest **campsite** is *Camping Sanssouci Gaisberg*, An der Pirschheide 1 (☎03327 556 80), just south of Potsdam and connected to the city centre by tram #94 and to Sanssouci by bus #695. For other camping grounds, call the tourist office or the German Camping Club, in Berlin on ☎03 02 18 60 71.

Hotels

Apartment-Hotel Bornimer Hof, Rückerstr. 31 ☎54 96 60. A hotel complex offering two-room suites and bungalows, some quite spacious, in a very quiet wooded setting north of town. Wide range of prices depending on size of apartment and its facilities. ①–⑤.

art'otel potsdam, Zeppelinstr. 136 ☎9 81 50. A bright and colourful luxury hotel, part of it within a historic building. ⑥.

Babelsberg, Stahnsdorfer Str. 68 ☎7 88 89. An old-fashioned, value-for-money hotel in Babelsberg. ①.

Mercure Potsdam, Lange Brücke ☎27 22. A typical GDR-era plush hotel in the heart of town. ⑤.

Reinhold, Dortusstr. 8 ☎28 49 90; *www.hotel.reinhold.de*. Comfortable, small hotel over a restaurant and located in the middle of the Altstadt. ④.

Schiffs Pension Luise, Heinrich-Mann-Allee 1 ☎270 6229. A boat moored by the Lange Brücke, offering five small rooms with close-up views of the Havel. ①.

Schloss Cecilienhof, Im neuen Garten ☎3 70 50; *www.castle-cecilienhof.com*. Housed in a wing of Schloss Cecilienhof, this is the place to head for if you want a little luxury. ⑤.

Schlossgarten Hotel, Geschwister-Scholl-Str. 41a ☎97 17 00. Plain but pleasant new hotel right next to Sanssouci Park. ③.

Zum Hummer, Im Park Babelsberg 2 ☎61 95 49. A good-value place, pleasantly located in Babelsberg Park. ③.

The Altstadt

Platz der Einheit makes a good starting point for any exploration of the **Altstadt**, although only a few non-concrete buildings survive in its immediate vicinity, hinting at a world long since vanished. The fancy-looking building at the southeast corner of the square is a Neo-Baroque **post office**, to the immediate north of which stood the Wilhelm III Synagoge until it was wrecked on Kristallnacht, and later completely demolished – a plaque marks the spot. Southeast of the post office **Am alten Markt** branches off Am Kanal, leading to the **Nikolaikirche** (Mon 2–5pm, Tues–Sat 10am–5pm, Sun noon–5pm). This stately domed building, its Neoclassical lines at odds with its surroundings, will probably have attracted your attention already if you've come into town from the S-Bahn station. It was originally built according to plans drawn up by Schinkel, and the impact of its exterior is echoed within – the walls are decorated with paintings of New Testament scenes and the effect of the dome is, if anything, more impressive than from the outside. Much of what can be seen, however, is a restoration, as the church was very badly damaged during the war.

Diagonally opposite the Nikolaikirche is another survivor, Potsdam's former **Rathaus** (daily Tues–Sun 10am–6pm; free), which was built in Palladian Classical style during the mid-eighteenth century, when it must have represented something of a departure for Brandenburg's municipal architecture. Until 1875 the circular Rathaus tower, on top of which a gilded Atlas supports the globe, served as the town jail. The Rathaus lost its town-hall function in 1885, and was taken over by a bank, which remained there until the bombs came. Under the old authorities the building became a *Kulturhaus* or arts centre, a role it retains to this day. The **obelisk** in front of the Rathaus was designed by Knobelsdorff and in its original form bore four reliefs depicting the Great Elector and his successors. When it was re-erected during the 1970s these were replaced with reliefs of architects whose work did much to shape Potsdam: Schinkel, Knobelsdorff, Gontard and Persius.

East of the Platz der Einheit only a few ailing eighteenth-century townhouses survive on Am Kanal, although this area is the oldest part of Potsdam: at the southern end of Fischerstrasse is the site of what was once the Slavonic island settlement of Poztupimi, the forerunner of the modern town. Just to the southeast lies the **Freundschafts Insel**, a leafy mid-Havel island that makes a good place to take a break from street-pounding, with its ornamental garden and boat rental facilities.

West of the Platz der Einheit

Slightly more tangible vestiges of old Potsdam survive in a few of the streets west of the Platz der Einheit. **Yorckstrasse** boasts a number of fine **Baroque houses**, as does Wilhelm-Staab-Strasse. **Am Neuen Markt**, just to the south of Yorckstrasse, also has a couple of good-looking survivors, including, on the west side behind the *Waage* restaurant, some improbably grand (but decrepit) eighteenth-century coaching stables with an entrance in the form of a triumphal arch, which are now home to a haulage firm. At Am neuen Markt 1 is the **Kabinetthaus**, a small mansion that was the birthplace of Friedrich Wilhelm II, the only member of the Hohenzollern family actually born in Potsdam. Take a look too at Werner-Seelenbinder-Strasse, at the southern end of Am Neuen Markt. The Baroque buildings on the north side of the street are stunning, especially so in contrast to the dreary modern structures on the south side: old and new Potsdam in microcosm.

The large modern building to the immediate west of the Nikolaikirche is a teacher training institute on whose ground floor you'll find Potsdam's **tourist office** (entrance in Friedrich-Ebert-Strasse – see p.202). This uniformly dull colossus forms a neat ensemble, representative of the high-rise chicken-coop school of GDR architecture, with the startlingly unattractive and even more gargantuan *Hotel Mercure* opposite.

The hotel stands on the site of the **Stadtschloss**, a Baroque residence built at the behest of the Great Elector between 1662 and 1669. It was reduced to a bare, roofless shell in 1945 and the demolition of its skeletal remains in 1960 removed the last vestiges of what, judging by prewar photographs, was a not unappealing building, although a number of its statues were recently discovered languishing in a local wood. Like the royal palace in eastern Berlin, the Stadtschloss, with its Hohenzollern connections, was an embarrassment to the communist authorities – so they quite simply erased it.

The Marstall and around

North of the hotel across Breite Strasse is the former palace **Marstall** or royal stables, the oldest town-centre survivor. Originally built as an orangerie towards the end of the eighteenth century and converted into a stables by that scourge of frivolity, Friedrich Wilhelm I, the building owes its subsequent appearance to Knobelsdorff, who extended and prettified it during the eighteenth century. Today the Marstall houses Potsdam's **Filmmuseum**, Schlossstrasse 1 (Tues–Sun 10am–6pm; *www.brandenburg.de/filmmuseum*; DM4/€2.05, concessions DM2/€1; special exhibits DM10/€5.10, concessions DM6/€3.10).

This makes for an interesting hour or so's visit. Drawing on material from the UFA studios in nearby Babelsberg (later DEFA, the GDR state film company), the museum presents both a technical and

artistic history of German film from 1895 to 1980, with some particularly fascinating material concerning the genres of the immediate
postwar period. There's a vaguely hands-on feel, with a few visitor-
operated Bioscopes and numerous screens playing clips. The museum **cinema** is the best in Potsdam and there's also a good **café**.

A little to the west of the Marstall, a prefabricated office building
occupies the site of the **Garnisonkirche**, Potsdam's Baroque garrison church, last resting place of many prominent members of the
Hohenzollern family. On March 23, 1933, the Reichstag was recon-
vened here following the fire and the subsequent elections that had
given the Nazis a small majority (see p.157). The building was later
wrecked during the bombing, and its burnt-out shell finally demolished in 1968, despite protest from both home and abroad – another
victim of the old regime's discomfort with relics of the Prussian and
Imperial German past. The elimination of the Garnisonkirche and
Schloss transformed this part of the town, destroying its atmosphere
– it's hard to imagine that the bleak Breite Strasse was the main
promenade of the prewar town.

Also vanished from the town plan is the **Stadtkanal** or city canal,
tree-lined remnant of a fortification system that once ran around the
core of old Potsdam, following modern Dortustrasse, turning east
into Yorckstrasse, and then running the length of Am Kanal. An
address here was highly desirable, despite the stench from the stag-
nant waters, but in 1972 public hygiene won the day and the canal
was filled in. Just west of the point where Breite Strasse intersects
with Dortustrasse is the **Militärwaisenhaus**, a late eighteenth-century military orphanage that looks positively palatial, despite the fact
that it's obviously lost its dome. The present building replaced an
earlier half-timbered one and its main purpose was to provide a
home for the illegitimate offspring of grenadiers and local girls.

A little further along is the **Potsdam-Museum**, Breite Str. 8–12
(Tues–Sun & first Mon of each month 9am–5pm; DM4/€2.05, concessions DM2/€1, free first Mon of each month), which hosts changing exhibits on local history. The museum building was constructed
in 1769 with the architecture of Whitehall in London as its model, at
the instigation of Friedrich II. An annexe to the museum is housed at
Breite Str. 13.

From here it's worth making a quick detour down **Kiezstrasse**,
where a number of eighteenth-century Rococo houses have been
beautifully restored, including no. 4 which houses *Der
Froschkasten*, a traditional, and recommended, *Kneipe*. The nearby
high-rises on the Neustädter Havelbucht don't compare very
favourably, but do hide in their midst the **Dampfmaschinenhaus**
(guided tours mid-May to mid-Oct Sat & Sun 10am–5pm;
www.spsg.de; DM4/€2.05, concessions DM2/€1), which ranks as
the most imaginative pump house in Germany. At first sight it looks
like a mosque, and that's what the architect, Ludwig Persius, intend-

ed when he built it at the beginning of the 1840s. The chimney takes the form of a minaret, and the striped stonework and tiling look wildly incongruous. The pump originally supplied water to a reservoir on the Ruinenberg hill near Sanssouci.

The Baroque quarter and the Holländisches Viertel

North of the Platz der Einheit, the area bounded by Schopenhauerstrasse, Hegelallee, Hebbelstrasse and Charlottenstrasse is Potsdam's **Baroque quarter**, built between 1732 and 1742 on the orders of Friedrich Wilhelm I. **Bassinplatz**, though disfigured by a huge modern bus station, offers the best introduction to this episode of Potsdam's architectural history. At the southeastern corner of the square is the **Französische Kirche**, completed according to plans by Knobelsdorff in 1753, in imitation of the Pantheon in Rome, a recurring theme in German architecture of the period. At its western end, Bassinplatz is graced by the nineteenth-century **Peter-Pauls-Kirche**, a replica of the campanile of San Zeno Maggiore in Verona, and the first large Catholic church to be built in the town.

The main concentration of ornate Baroque houses, built with slight variations in detail to avoid monotony, lies to the west of here, on and around **Brandenburger Strasse**, Potsdam's pedestrianized main shopping street. The whole quarter was intended as a settlement for tradespeople in the then rapidly expanding town. Some 584 houses were built in all, and this area, unlike the Altstadt, survived the war substantially intact. Turning into Lindenstrasse from Brandenburger Strasse, the Dutch-style former **Kommandantehaus**, at nos. 54–55 (Tues, Thurs & first and third Sat of the month 9am–5pm, DM1/€0.50), is a building with uncomfortably recent historical associations; until the *Wende* it served as a Stasi detention centre, known as the "Lindenhotel". Handed over to the embryonic political opposition groups in November 1989, it is now part of the Potsdam Museum, with an exhibition on the history of the building: it was used as a Nazi "hereditary-health court", which made decisions about compulsory sterilization, and a prison for the Nazi "Peoples' Court", before its final function – viewing the cells in the back building is a chilling experience.

To the north and west of the Baroque quarter are the most impressive of Potsdam's three surviving town gates – the **Jägertor** or "Hunter's Gate" (at the end of Lindenstrasse), surmounted by a sculpture of a stag succumbing to a pack of baying hounds, and the **Brandenburger Tor** (at the western end of Brandenburger Strasse), a triumphal arch built by Gontard in 1733, with a playfulness lacking in its Berlin namesake.

The Holländisches Viertel

Just to the north of Bassinplatz is the **Holländisches Viertel** or "Dutch quarter", the best-known and most appealing part of

Friedrich Wilhelm I's town extension. In the area bounded by Gutenbergstrasse, Kurfürstenstrasse, Friedrich-Ebert-Strasse and Hebbelstrasse are 134 gabled, red-brick houses put up by Dutch builders for the immigrants from Holland who were invited to work in Potsdam by the king. In fact, not many Dutch took up the invitation, and many of those who did returned home when the promised employment dried up following Friedrich Wilhelm's death, allowing Germans to move into their houses.

Under the old regime it was decided to renovate the quarter, which even at the time of its building was recognized as one of the most attractive in the town. Restoration work has so far been only a partial success: modern builders lacked the skills to restore the carved gables, and bad planning meant that in some cases inhabitants were moved out but work was never started. As a result, a few of the houses look derelict, but some excellent restored examples can be found along **Mittelstrasse**, particularly at the junction with Benkertstrasse. Mittelstrasse has been gentrified to a large extent, with a number of trendy shops and cafés attracting both locals and tourists. Finally, at the top of Friedrich-Ebert-Strasse, at the northwestern corner of the Holländisches Viertel, is the **Nauener Tor**, a stylistically messy-looking town gate inspired by English architectural trends of the mid-eighteenth century.

Eating, drinking and nightlife

Eating and drinking pose few problems in Potsdam. There's a good array of **restaurants**, and most places are pleasant enough, though few would gain any stars in a gourmet's guide to the Berlin area. In town, the major and most convenient concentration of possibilities is along Brandenburger Strasse, although it pays to go a little further afield.

Restaurants

Arco, Friedrich-Ebert-Str., in the Nauener Tor ☎2 70 16 90. Occupying the east wing of the Nauener Tor, a small café that serves excellent Continental food. Outdoor seating in summer.

Brauerhaus, Kurfürstenstr. 52 ☎2 70 94 53. In a restored, Freemasons' building, this moderately priced pub-restaurant features German food and its own brew.

Hafthorn, Friedrich-Ebert-Strasse 90 ☎2 80 08 20. Large and lively restaurant offering Swabian specialities for surprisingly little money.

Kleines Schloss, Park Babelsberg ☎70 51 56. A traditionally minded lakeside place far from the hubbub of the city. Standard German dishes. Wed–Sun 11am–9pm.

Luise Restaurant, Luisenplatz 6 ☎90 36 63. Mid-priced German and Continental food in casual surroundings. The perfect place to eat before tackling Sanssouci, just up the road.

Terrassenrestaurant-Minsk, Max-Planck-Str. 10, am Brauhausberg ☎29 36 36. This ugly-looking modern establishment on the Babelsberg side of the

Potsdam

Havel serves surprisingly good pseudo-Belarussian cuisine. Clear views across to Potsdam are an additional attraction.

Waage, am Neuen Markt 12 ☎2 70 96 75. Inventive dishes with local ingredients. A little on the pricey side.

Zum Laubenpieper, am Pfingstberg 25 ☎50 21 50. Rustic restaurant offering huge servings of old-fashioned German food. Hilltop beer garden open during the summer.

Zur Linde, Lindenstr. 50 ☎2 80 50 31. No scene-maker, but a personable and relaxing restaurant with typical German food.

Cafés and bars

Babette, Brandenburger Str. 71 ☎29 16 48. Pleasant little café, also open as a cocktail bar Wed–Sun until 1am.

Café im Filmmuseum, Schlossstr. 1 ☎2 70 20 41. One of Potsdam's best cafés, and a good place to take a break after visiting the museum.

Deli Frizz, Friedrich-Ebert-Str. 35 ☎2 81 00 90. Alternative bistro serving light snacks, and natural food store.

Drachenhaus, Maulbeerallee ☎5 05 38 08. A pleasant and genteel little café in the grounds of Schloss Sanssouci itself, housed in a pagoda-style building once used by royal vintners. You can also eat well here.

Froschkasten, Kiezstr. 4 ☎29 13 15. One of the best and oldest bars in Potsdam, a *Kneipe* that also serves good food.

Galerie Mittelstrasse, Mittelstr. 18 ☎2 70 18 18. An arty but friendly café, bar and gallery in a venerable Dutch house. One of the best cafés in town. Cheap food with an outdoor barbecue in summer.

La Leander Benkertstr. 1 ☎2 70 65 76. In the Holländisches Viertel, a dark and relaxing café with a short menu.

La Madeleine, Lindenstr. 9 ☎2 70 54 00. A small creperie featuring over thirty variations – some decidedly odd – of the French speciality.

Langer Kerl, Brandenburger Str. 37; ☎29 68 78. Straightforward beer joint in an eighteenth-century town house. Closed Sun & Mon, and usually shut by 7pm.

Lapis Lazuli, Benkertstr. 21 ☎2 80 23 71. Hippy-ish café with old wooden tables and candles. Light snacks only.

Matschkes Galerie Café, Alleestrasse 10 ☎2 80 03 59. A quiet, leafy courtyard provides a wonderfully restful spot to enjoy authentic Russian cuisine.

Pub à la pub, Breite Str. 1 ☎24 07 26. A student hangout and bar in a classic GDR concrete hulk – check out the socialist mosaic on the far end.

Die Rebe, Feuerbachstr. 1 ☎96 48 47. A very pleasant wine-*Kneipe* serving food, just southwest of the Brandenburger Tor. Open until midnight but closed Sun & Mon.

Seerose, Breite Str. 24 ☎97 41 17. Housed in a bizarre-looking modern building, this popular bar offers good views across the Neustädter Havelbucht.

Souterrain, Allee nach Sanssouci 4 ☎90 38 74. Away from the centre on the road to Sanssouci, this lively café-bar is worth dropping into.

Nightlife

For **nightlife** the best bet is the *Lindenpark*, Stahnsdorfer Str. 76–78 (☎74 79 70), over in Babelsberg, with regular "alternative" discos and live bands. Also recommendable is the *Waschhaus*, Schiffbauergasse 1 (☎2 71 56 26; *www.waschhaus.de*), just off Berliner Strasse on the way into town from the Glienicker Brücke, a large complex with live music, galleries and an open-air cinema, often hosting various parties and events. At the same address is *Fabrik* (☎2 80 03 14), a theatre for contemporary dance and music. The *Altes Rathaus* (☎29 20 79) offers local live bands on occasional weekends, while a decent mainstream disco is *Art Speicher*, Zeppelinstrasse 136 (Thurs–Sat from 9pm; ☎9 81 50; *www.artspeicher.de*). For German-speakers the Hans-Otto-Theater, Zimmerstrasse 10 (☎2 30 38), is Potsdam's main theatre, with a programme worth investigating. The town also boasts a cabaret, the "Kabarett Obelisk", Schopenhauerstrasse 27 (☎29 10 69).

Listings

Bike rental City Rad Potsdam, in the Hauptbahnhof ☎61 90 52 (May–Oct).

Boat rental Grosse Fischer 11 ☎61 90 26.

Boat trips Weisse Flotte, Lange Brücke (tickets and information daily: May–Sept 8–11am & 11.30am–5.45pm; April & Oct 10am–3.30pm; ☎2 75 92 10; *www.weisse-flotte-potsdam.de*). Regular sailings to Wannsee, Caputh, Werder, Ferch and Templin.

Car rental Europcar, Lange Brücke ☎29 82 40; Ahrens & Merkle, Am Buchhorst 40 ☎8 68 02 98.

Gay info Homosexuellen-Integrations-Projekt, Berliner Str. 49 ☎29 20 65.

Lost property Friedrich-Ebert-Str. 79–81 ☎2 89 15 87.

Petrol stations Horstweg 2, Babelsberg (24hr); Potsdamerstr. 164; Fritz-Zubeil-Str.; Drewitzer Str. 2.

Police Henning-von-Treskow-Str. 9–13 ☎2 83 02.

Post office Main post office: Am Kanal 16–18 ☎23 80.

Public transport information Verkehrsbetrieb Potsdam (ViP) Customer Centre in the Hauptbahnhof ☎2 37 52 75; *www.vip-potsdam.de*. Deutsche Bahn Travel Centre in the Hauptbahnhof ☎01803/19 41 95; *www.bahn.de*.

Swimming Indoor pools "Am Brauhausberg", Max-Planck-Strasse ☎24 46 91; and "Am Stern", Newtonstr. 12 ☎62 11 29. For outdoor bathing head for the beaches at Babelsberg in Park Babelsberg and Templin (also for naturists) at Templiner Str. 102 (information on ☎2 70 15 21).

Taxis ☎29 29 29. Taxi ranks at Am Bassinplatz, the Hauptbahnhof, Platz der Einheit, Luisenplatz, and Bahnhof Babelsberg.

Women's centre Frauenzentrum, Zeppelinstr. 189 ☎90 13 13, with café on Fri & Sat.

Park Sanssouci

Park Sanssouci (*www.spsg.de*), Frederick the Great's fabled retreat, stretches out for two kilometres west of Potsdam town centre, and its gardens and palaces are what draw most visitors to the

Park Sanssouci

town. In 1744 Frederick ordered the construction of a residence where he would be able to live "without cares" – "sans souci" in the French spoken in court. The task was entrusted to the architect Georg von Knobelsdorff, who had already proved himself on other projects in Potsdam and Berlin. **Schloss Sanssouci**, on a hill overlooking the town, took three years to complete, while the extensive parklands to the west – the **Rehgarten** – were laid out over the following five years. As a finishing touch Frederick ordered the construction of the **Neues Palais** at the western end of the park, to mark the end of the Seven Years' War. Over the following 150 years or so, numerous additions were made, including the **Orangerie** and the laying of Jubiläumstrasse (now known as Maulbeerallee) just south of the Orangerie in 1913. The park is at its most beautiful in spring, when the trees are in leaf and the flowers in bloom, but these days it's usually overrun by visitors. To avoid the crowds, visit on a weekday, preferably outside summer, when you'll be better able to appreciate the place. The main **visitors' centre** (daily: April–Oct 8.30am–5pm; Nov–March 9am–4pm) is by the historic windmill (see p.214).

Schloss Sanssouci

To approach **Schloss Sanssouci** as Frederick the Great might have done, make for the eighteenth-century **obelisk** on Schopenhauerstrasse, which marks the main entrance to the park. Beyond, Hauptallee runs through the ornate Knobelsdorff-designed **Obelisk-Portal** – two clusters of pillars flanked by the goddesses Flora and Pomona – to the **Grosse Fontäne**, the biggest of the park's many fountains, around which stand a host of Classical statues, notably those of Venus and Mercury. The approach to the Schloss itself leads up through the Weinbergterrassen, whose terraced ranks of vines are among the northernmost in Germany.

Schloss Sanssouci opening times and prices

The Schloss can only be visited as part of a **guided tour**. These take place every twenty minutes and tickets for the whole day go on sale at 9am – get there as early as possible as demand is high.

The Schloss is open Tues–Sun: April–Oct 9am–5pm; Nov–March 9am–12.30pm & 1–4pm; DM10/€5.10, concessions DM5/€2.50.

Frederick had very definite ideas about what he wanted and worked closely with Knobelsdorff on the design of his palace, which was to be a place where the king, who had no great love for his capital, Berlin, or his wife Elizabeth Christine, could escape both. It's a surprisingly modest one-storey Baroque affair, topped by an oxidized green dome and ornamental statues, looking out over the vine terraces towards the high-rises of the Neustädter Havelbucht. Frederick loved the Schloss so much that he intended to be buried here, and had a tomb excavated for himself in front of the eastern wing, near the graves of his Italian greyhounds, animals whose company he preferred to that of human beings during the last, increasingly eccentric years of his life. When he died, however, his nephew Friedrich Wilhelm II had him interred in the Garnisonkirche in Potsdam itself, next to the father Frederick hated. Towards the end of World War II, the remains of Frederick and his father were exhumed and eventually taken to Schloss Hohenzollern in Swabia for safekeeping from the approaching Soviet army. Only in August 1991, after reunification, were the remains returned and buried with much pomp at the site Frederick had chosen. He lies there now, his last resting place marked by a simple stone bearing the terse inscription *Friedrich der Grosse*.

The interior

Inside, the Schloss is a frenzy of Rococo, spread through the twelve rooms where Frederick lived and entertained his guests – a process that usually entailed quarrelling with them. The most eye-catching rooms are the opulent **Marmorsaal** (Marble Hall) and the **Konzertzimmer** (Concert Room), where the flute-playing king forced eminent musicians to play his own works on concert evenings. Frederick's favourite haunt was his library where, surrounded by his two thousand volumes – mainly French translations of the classics and a sprinkling of contemporary French writings – he could oversee the work on his tomb. One of Frederick's most celebrated house guests was Voltaire, who lived here from 1750 to 1753, acting as a kind of private tutor to the king, finally leaving when he'd had enough of Frederick's bizarre behaviour, damning the king's intellect with faint praise and accusing him of treating "the whole world as slaves". In revenge Frederick ordered that Voltaire's former room be decorated with carvings of apes and parrots.

The **Damenflügel**, the west wing of the Schloss (mid-May to mid-Oct Sat & Sun only 10am–5pm; DM3/€1.50) was added in 1840, and its thirteen rooms housed ladies and gentlemen of the court. Nearby on the terrace is a wrought-iron summerhouse protecting a weather-beaten copy of a Classical statue, while just to the south an eighteenth-century sculpture of Cleopatra looks over the graves of Frederick's horses.

Frederick the Great

Frederick (1740–1786) had the great misfortune to be born the son of Friedrich Wilhelm I, Brandenburg-Prussia's "Soldier King", a stern militarist whose attitude to his children seems to have been much the same as his attitude to the conscripts in his army. Frederick was subjected to a strict and unforgiving regime from the earliest age. His education included the Lutheran catechism and military drill but precious little else, certainly no hint of the arts or humanities.

Frederick's interest in the latter emerged despite his father's best efforts, leading to conflict between the king and the young crown prince. Friedrich Wilhelm I's odious treatment of his son – he frequently thrashed him and forced him to kiss his boots in public – eventually prompted Frederick to try to flee the country in 1730, enlisting the aid of two friends, Hans Hermann von Katte and Karl Christoph von Keith. At the last moment von Keith hesitated, betraying the conspiracy before escaping himself. Frederick and Katte (with whom the prince had a very close, possibly homosexual, relationship) were arrested and stripped of rank and privileges. Both were court-martialled; Katte was sentenced to two years' imprisonment but the court declared itself unable to sit in judgement over a crown prince.

At this point the old king intervened to drastic effect. Katte was sentenced to death and Frederick was forced to watch his beheading from his cell, having been led to understand that he too was under sentence of death. When news of his shattered state was conveyed to the king by a priest, the monarch, having achieved his intended effect, granted Frederick a conditional pardon.

As penance and a test of his remorse Frederick had to serve in his father's civil administration pending restitution of rank and freedom. There was a marked improvement in his circumstances when in 1733 he was sent to the north Brandenburg town of Rheinsberg where, away from his father's hypercritical eyes, he was able to renew his interest in the arts. Only an arranged marriage to Elizabeth Christine, daughter of the Duke of Brunswick-Bevern, blighted what had become a relatively idyllic existence.

Around the Schloss

East of Schloss Sanssouci, overlooking the ornamental Holländischer Garten or Dutch Garden, is the **Bildergalerie** (mid-May to mid-Oct Tues–Sun 10am–5pm; DM4/€2.05, concessions DM2/€1), a restrained Baroque creation, which, it's claimed, was the first building in Europe to be erected specifically as a museum. Unfortunately, wartime destruction and looting scattered the contents, but a new collection was put together after the war, comprising paintings from around the GDR that had survived, including Caravaggio's wonderful *Incredulity of St Thomas* and several works by Rubens and Van Dyck.

Just to the right of the Holländischer Garten is the **Neptungrotte**, a Knobelsdorff-designed architectural oddity: a grotto with a Rococo entrance and a ring of empty statue pediments in front. The statues,

In 1740 the king died and Frederick acceded to the throne, much to the delight of the populace, who had been worn down by Friedrich Wilhelm I's austere style of rule. Initially Frederick lived up to early expectations, abolishing torture and censorship, establishing ostensible freedom of worship, and recalling exiled scholars. With the aid of Voltaire he published his **Antimachiavel**, a treatise expounding a princely ethic based on virtue, justice and responsibility. However, Frederick inclined towards enlightened despotism, and as his rule progressed he introduced increasingly unpopular measures such as the establishment of state monopolies for certain commodities. His first notably un-progressive act, however – the invasion of and subsequent annexation of Silesia – came in 1740 at the very beginning of his reign.

In 1756 Austria, Saxony, France and Russia, alarmed at the growing strength of Prussia, began squaring up for the **Seven Years' War**. Frederick struck first, attacking Saxony and, though initially successful, was later beaten at the Battle of Kolin. Encouraged, the French invaded Prussia and, though able to beat them back, Frederick could not prevent military defeat at the Battle of Kunersdorf, after which the Russian army occupied Berlin. With British aid Frederick was able to push out the invaders, gaining important victories in 1760 and 1761, but eventually the war fizzled out with all sides exhausted, and a general peace was concluded in 1763.

Frederick's 1740–1745 acquisitions were confirmed, the Habsburg hold on the now-crumbling Holy Roman Empire had been lessened and Prussia was the leading German state. The remaining 23 years of Frederick's reign were a period of reconstruction, marked by increasing eccentricity on the part of the monarch, who during this period came to be known as **Der alte Fritz** ("Old Fritz"). He retreated to Schloss Sanssouci and, in the company of Voltaire, honed his Francophile tendencies while overseeing the upkeep of his army (and extraction of punitive taxes from his people to finance it).

In 1772 he successfully secured a chunk of Poland for Prussia during the First Partition of that country and in 1777 launched his final military action, an unsuccessful campaign against Bavaria. When he died in 1786, he was, like his father, not mourned.

representing Moorish figures, are currently in Schloss Sanssouci awaiting renovation.

The Neue Kammern and gardens

On the opposite side of the Schloss, from a point near the Cleopatra statue, steps lead down to the **Neue Kammern** (April to mid-May Sat & Sun 10am–5pm; mid-May to mid-Oct Tues–Sun 10am–5pm; DM5/€2.50, concessions DM2/€1), the architectural twin of the Bildergalerie, originally used as an orangerie and later as a guesthouse. Immediately to the west of the Neue Kammern is the prim **Sizilianischer Garten** or Sicilian Garden, crammed with coniferous trees and subtropical plants, complementing the **Nordischer Garten**, another ornamental garden just to the north, whose most interesting feature is the strange-looking **Felsentor** or Rock Gate, a

gateway fashioned out of uncut stones and topped by a lumpen-look-
ing eagle with outstretched wings.

Frederick was prepared to go to some lengths to achieve the
desired carefree rural ambience for Sanssouci and retained an old
wooden windmill as an ornament just north of the Neue Kammern.
Four years after his death, this was replaced by a rustic-looking stone
construction, the **Historische Mühle**, which is now a restaurant.

The Ruinenberg

The **Ruinenberg**, rising to the north of Schloss Sanssouci, looks like
a cluster of Classical ruins, but in fact these fragments are artificial,
designed to render a little more interesting a small reservoir built
during the eighteenth century to feed the fountains in the park.
However, it was a long time before this reservoir fulfilled its purpose,
as attempts to fill it with water from the Havel proved fruitless. It
worked briefly in 1754 when Frederick the Great (in a characteristic
fit of manic inventiveness) allowed it to be filled with snow. When the
snow melted the locks were opened and water coursed through the
system, giving the fountains in the park a few minutes' life. It wasn't
until the building of the mosque-shaped pump house in the town centre that the problem was solved.

The Orangerie to the Neues Palais

From the western corner of the Sizilianischer Garten, **Maulbeerallee**
(Mulberry Alley), a road open to traffic, cuts through the park to the
ascent to the **Orangerie** (mid-May to mid-Oct Tues–Sun 10am–5pm;
DM5/€2.50, concessions DM3/€1.50).

This Italianate Renaissance-style structure with its belvedere towers is perhaps the most visually impressive building in the park, and
is certainly more outwardly imposing than the Schloss. A series of
terraces, with curved retaining walls sporting water spouts in the
shape of lions' heads, lead up to the sandy-coloured building, whose
slightly down-at-heel appearance lends it added character.

It was built at the behest of Friedrich IV and, like the
Friedenskirche (see p.222), inspired by the architecture seen on his
travels in Italy. The facade is lined with allegorical statues set in niches, depicting figures like "Industry" holding a cog wheel. The western
wing of the building is still used for its original purpose, as a refuge
for tropical plants in winter, and during the summer it's possible to
ascend the western tower, from where there are great views of the
Neues Palais and depressing vistas of Potsdam's high-rises to the
east. The Orangerie also houses a gallery, the Raphaelsaal, with
copies of paintings looted by Napoleon. Part of the Orangerie is
given over to private flats, occupied by members of the park staff –
which must be just about the best address in Potsdam.

Below the Orangerie, south of Maulbeerallee, is the
Jubiläumsterrasse with a large goldfish-inhabited pool, beyond

which are statues of Mercury and an equestrian Frederick the Great, a replica of the bronze one on Unter den Linden (which incidentally stood for many years in Potsdam).

The Belvedere, Drachenhaus and Antikentempel

From the western wing of the Orangerie, the arrow-straight Krimlindenallee, lined with lime trees, leads up towards a Rococo **Belvedere**, the last building to be built under Frederick the Great. It was the only building in the whole park to suffer serious war damage, but has recently been restored to its former glory. A couple of hundred metres short of the belvedere a path branches off to the left, leading to the **Drachenhaus**, a one-time vintner's house built in the style of a Chinese pagoda for the small vineyard nearby. Today there's a genteel café inside, an ideal point to interrupt your wanderings. Southwest of the Drachenhaus, a pathway leads across the park to the **Antikentempel**, originally built in 1768 to house part of the art collection of Frederick the Great. This domed rotunda is now the last resting place of a number of members of the Hohenzollern family, including the Empress Auguste Victoria, and Hermine, the woman Wilhelm II married in exile, who came to be known as the "last Empress".

The Neues Palais

To the west through the trees rises the **Neues Palais** (April–Oct Mon & Wed–Sun 9am–5pm; Nov–March Mon–Thurs, Sat & Sun 9am–4pm; DM8/€4.10, concessions DM4/€2.05), another massive Rococo extravaganza from Frederick the Great's time, built between 1763 and 1769 to reaffirm the might of Prussia and its king after the Seven Years' War. At the centre of the palace is a huge green-weathered dome, topped by a crown. It must have been the Neues Palais that inspired Lewis Carroll to note in his diary when visiting the town: "The amount of art lavished on the whole region of Potsdam is marvellous; some of the tops of the palaces were like forests of statues." The Classical figures adorning the roof were specially mass-produced by a team of sculptors to adorn Frederick's new creation.

The main entrance to the palace is in the western facade, approached via gates flanked by stone sentry boxes. Theoretically you have to join a guided tour, but once inside you can pretty much take things at your own pace. The interior is predictably opulent, though a couple of highlights stand out: the vast and startling **Grottensaal** on the ground floor, decorated entirely with shells and semiprecious stones to form images of lizards and dragons, and the equally huge **Marmorsaal**, with its beautiful floor of patterned marble slabs. The southern wing contains Frederick's apartments and the theatre where the king enjoyed Italian opera and French plays. A Francophile to the point of near mania, Frederick believed that the Germans were philistines incapable of producing great art. It was said that he'd "rather a horse sang him an aria, than allow a German in his opera". The last Imperial resident of the Neues Palais was Kaiser Wilhelm II, who packed sixty train carriages with the contents of the palace when he and his family fled in November 1918, following the revolution and abdication. Facing the Neues Palais entrance are the **Communs**, a couple of pointless Rococo fantasies joined by a curved colonnade. They look grandiose, but their purpose was mundane: they were built for the serving and maintenance staff of the palace.

The Rehgarten and Charlottenhof

From the Neues Palais, Ökonomieweg leads east through the **Rehgarten** or Deer Garden, the former court hunting ground (and still home to a few deer), where you'll find the slightly kitsch-looking **Chinesisches Teehaus** (mid-May to mid-Oct Tues–Sun 10am–5pm; DM2/€1, concessions DM1/€0.50), a kind of Rococo pagoda housing a small museum of Chinese and Meissen porcelain and surrounded by eerily lifelike statues of Oriental figures.

The broad expanse of rough parkland to the south of Ökonomieweg is **Charlottenhof**, a park created by Friedrich Wilhelm III as a Christmas present for his son, and today one of Sanssouci's quieter corners. A path leads over a bridge past a small farm building to the **Römische Bäder** (mid-May to mid-Oct Tues–Sun 10am–5pm; DM3/€1.50, concessions DM2/€1, or combined ticket with Schloss Charlottenhof DM7.50/€3.80, concessions DM4/€2.05), built by Schinkel and Persius in convincing imitation of a Roman villa.

Across the lawns to the south is **Schloss Charlottenhof** (mid-May to mid-Oct Tues–Sun 10am–5pm; DM7.50/€3.80, concessions DM4/€2.05, includes entry to Römische Bäder), another Roman-style building, once again designed by Schinkel and Persius for Friedrich IV. Though designated a palace it is, in reality, little more than a glorified villa, but its interior, unlike most Sanssouci buildings, is original. The effect is impressive: the hallway is bathed in blue light filtered through coloured glass decorated with stars, a prelude to the **Kupferstichzimmer**, or print room, whose walls are now covered in copies of Italian Renaissance paintings. Immediately east of Schloss Charlottenhof is the **Dichterhain** (Poets' Grove), an open space dotted with busts of Goethe, Schiller and Herder, among others. West of here through the woods and across a racetrack-shaped clearing called the **Hippodrom** is the **Fasanerie**, another Italian-style edifice built between 1842 and 1844.

The Grünes Gitter and around

At the southeastern corner of Sanssouci is the **Grünes Gitter** or Green Gateway entrance to the grounds, where there's an **informa-**

tion kiosk with a few leaflets about the park and its environs. Immediately to the north of here is the Italianate **Friedenskirche** (mid-May to mid-Oct daily 10am–6pm), designed by Persius for Friedrich Wilhelm IV and completed in 1850. With its 39-metre-high campanile and lakeside setting, it conjures up the southern European atmosphere that Friedrich Wilhelm was striving to create when he ordered the construction of the church using the St Clemente Basilica in Rome as a model, with the design centred on the magnificent Byzantine apse mosaic that was brought here from Murano. Adjoining the church is a domed Hohenzollern mausoleum containing the tombs of Friedrich Wilhelm IV and his wife Elizabeth, and Friedrich III and his wife Victoria. Directly to the west of the Friedenskirche is the **Marly-Garten**, once the kitchen garden of Friedrich I, who named it, with intentional irony, after Louis XIV's luxurious Marly park.

North of the centre

Heading north from along Friedrich-Ebert-Strasse will bring you to some of Potsdam's most fascinating, yet least-known corners, set in and around the woodland areas of **Pfingstberg** and, just to the east, the **Neuer Garten**. Architectural curiosities hereabouts include the **Alexander Newski Kapelle**, but the real crowd-puller is the **Schloss Cecilienhof**, scene of the postwar Potsdam conference.

Russische Kolonie Alexandrowka

The beginnings are inauspicious as you head north from Nauener Tor – on the left is a mid-nineteenth-century Italianate villa, once the residence of a royal gardener, behind which the former district headquarters of the Stasi rise up, while the Neo-Baroque affair a little to the north is a turn-of-the-century local government office. However, after about fifteen minutes' walking you'll reach **Russische Kolonie Alexandrowka**, a settlement of Russian-style wooden houses, built for a group of Russian military musicians who found themselves marooned here after the Napoleonic Wars. Its incongruity makes it one of the most intriguing sights in town, a collection of two-storey dwellings with steeply pitched roofs laid out in the form of a St Andrew's cross. The buildings are in fact half-timbered, but plank cladding gives them the look of birch-log cabins.

Their inhabitants were originally prisoners of war, among five hundred captured when the Prussians were fighting with the French in Kurland (part of modern Latvia). Sixty-two of these men were selected to form a Russian choir for the entertainment of the troops, and after the Prussians joined forces with the Russians to combat Napoleon's armies, their services were retained. At the end of the Napoleonic Wars they were stationed in Potsdam, consumed by homesickness but forbidden to return to Russia.

Eventually, in 1826, Friedrich Wilhelm III gave the order that
houses should be built for these men and their families. Eight houses were constructed on the arms of the cross, four more at the semicircular linking roads at each end, with an overseer's residence in the
middle. The names of the original occupants and subsequent inhabitants (a few of them descendants of the Russians, even today) are
carved into the housefronts. Some of the oldest inscriptions are in
Cyrillic script.

For many years this whole area was the focus of the Russian presence in Potsdam. The Red Army occupied huge barrack buildings
along Voltaireweg and Pappelallee, formerly the property of the
Wehrmacht and before that the Imperial German army, while Soviet
officers and their families lived in the nearby flats.

The Alexander Newski Kapelle

Directly to the north of the settlement is the **Kapelle des heiligen
Alexander Newski**, a church built for the Russians in 1829, set on
top of the closely wooded Kapellenberg hill. Access is either by
scrambling up the hillside, or via a track branching to the right off
Nedlitzer Strasse, which leads to a rudimentary car park. The chapel
is a fragment of Russia transplanted to Brandenburg: a compact
building in pink stucco edged with white, topped by a central onion-
domed tower, with smaller domes at each corner.

The chapel is usually accessible at weekends, but if there's anyone
about during the week it's often possible to take a look around. The
interior is festooned with icons, many of them gifts from the Tsarina
Alexandra, who started life as Princess Charlotte of Prussia. The
priest's wife oversees a little stall selling replica icons and holy
medals, and often plays Russian Orthodox choir tapes, which
enhance the already ethereal effect.

The first service held here, in 1829, was attended by Tsar Nicholas
I, and the chapel remained in use for well over a century, boosted by
the arrival in Berlin of thousands of Russian emigrés after the
Russian Revolution of 1917. During the 1960s the chapel lost its
priest, but in 1986 the patriarchate of Moscow sent a new one, and
regular church services are held for Potsdam's handful of Orthodox
families.

The Pfingstberg

Immediately to the north of the Kapellenberg is the wooded
Pfingstberg, another little-known Potsdam curiosity which, like the
Russian settlement and the Kapellenberg, has been rediscovered
over the past few years. At the foot of the Pfingstberg is the walled
Jüdischer Friedhof or Jewish cemetery. Only organized visits are
possible, every Sunday at 10am – enquire at the tourist office in town
for details. The cemetery was given by the town to Potsdam's growing Jewish population in 1763 – until then they had had to bury their

dead in Berlin. As recently as 1933 the Jewish community of
Potsdam numbered several hundred, of whom just two returned after
the war.

From the cemetery the path leads on up the hill to the ruined nineteenth-century **Belvedere**, a vast and improbable-looking edifice,
built to plans drawn up from Friedrich Wilhelm IV's sketches of the
folly-like castles constructed in Italy during the Renaissance. As the
name suggests, this unusual building was erected as a kind of viewing terrace for the royal inhabitants of nineteenth-century Potsdam
and their guests. Its walkways and towers give great views of
Potsdam itself, and of the landscape north as far as Spandau and
Charlottenburg, and west as far as the town of Brandenburg.

Although virtually undamaged by the war, the belvedere was
allowed to collapse into ruin by the pre-*Wende* city authorities,
because (according to some Potsdamers) it afforded such good
views of the border and West Berlin – renovation of the structure is
only now going ahead. The small building just to the southeast of the
belvedere is the **Pomonatempel**, Schinkel's first-ever finished building, constructed in 1800 when he was a nineteen-year-old student of
architecture. The neat Neoclassical temple, fronted by a four-
columned portico, is open at weekends from Easter to October.

The Neuer Garten

To the east of the Pfingstberg is the **Neuer Garten** (*www.spsg.de*),
another large park complex – the main entrance is at the eastern end
of Alleestrasse (which branches off Friedrich Ebert-Strasse at the
southern end of the Alexandrowka settlement), beyond which a road
snakes through the park. A couple of hundred metres east of the
road, overlooking the Heiliger See, stands the **Marmorpalais** or
Marble Palace (April–Oct Tues–Sun 10am–5pm; Nov–March Sat &
Sun 10am–4pm; DM6/€3.10, concessions DM3/€1.50) built for
Friedrich Wilhelm II, who died a premature death here in 1797,
allegedly as a consequence of his dissolute lifestyle. In more recent
years it was home to the GDR's main military museum, and until
1990 visitors were greeted by the incongruous sight of a MIG-17
parked in the palace grounds. It has now been restored to an approx-
imation of its original royal condition and the sumptuous rooms can
be seen once again.

Schloss Cecilienhof

Towards the end of the road through the wooded grounds of the
Neuer Garten is **Schloss Cecilienhof** (April–Oct Tues–Sun
9am–5pm; Nov–March Tues–Sun 9am–4pm; *www.spsg.de*; with
guided tour DM8/€4.10, concessions DM4/€2.05; without guided
tour DM6/€3.10, concessions DM4/€2.05), which looks like a mock-
Elizabethan mansion transplanted from the English Home Counties.
Building work on this, the last palace to be commissioned by the

Hohenzollerns, began in 1913 and was completed in 1917, the war having evidently done nothing to change the architectural style. Cecilienhof would only rate a mention in passing, were it not for the fact that the **Potsdam Conference**, confirming the decisions made earlier that year at Yalta about the postwar European order, was held here from July 17 to August 2, 1945. The conference was as much symbolic as anything else, providing a chance for Truman, Stalin and Churchill (replaced mid-conference by Clement Attlee) to show the world that they had truly won the war by meeting in the heart of the ruined Reich.

The Schloss Cecilienhof can also be conveniently reached by public transport: take tram #92 from Platz der Einheit north to Alleestrasse and then change to bus #692.

Centre of attraction within is the **Konferenzsaal** or conference chamber, where the Allied delegates worked out the details of the division of Europe, and which resembles the assembly hall of a British minor public school. Everything has been left pretty much as it was in 1945, with the huge round table specially made in Moscow for the conference still in place, despite the fact that in July 1990 there was an arson attack on the hall. The fire brigade arrived within a few minutes and extinguished the fire, but not before considerable damage had been done. A remarkably quick restoration job has left few traces of what happened. It's still not known who was responsible for the attack but local *Faschos* – neofascists – are thought to be the most likely culprits.

It's also possible to visit the delegates' workrooms, furnished in varying degrees of chintziness. The study of the Soviet delegation is about the most tasteless, but the British room (with a bronze stag at bay in the fireplace and furniture that looks like it was bought as a job lot from a defunct presbytery) comes a close second. Cecilienhof has been used as a hotel since 1960 and there's an expensive restaurant which is also only for the deep of pocket (for information, see "Accommodation" on p.202).

A walk along the lake shore to the north of the Schloss is interesting simply because before the *Wende* it was impossible. Until 1990 the view north of the Schloss was cut off by a strip of impassable white concrete and signs warned that this was a border area.

The Berliner Vorstadt and Glienicker Brücke

On the opposite shore of the Heiliger See to the Neuer Garten is the **Berliner Vorstadt**, formerly an elegant Potsdam suburb, whose crumbling villas were given over to various party and social institutions under the SED regime. Here, too, were numerous Imperial army barracks, housing elite units like the Garde du Corps and Hussars, which until the summer of 1994 were in Russian hands. At the end of Berliner Strasse, leading back to Berlin, is the **Glienicker Brücke**, the famous spy-swap bridge which inspired many a Cold War film scene. Here, in 1962, U-2 pilot Gary Powers was traded for a Soviet agent, while more recently, in 1986, Jewish dissident Anatoly Scharansky was freed into the West by the Soviet authorities in an early manifestation of Gorbachev's *glasnost*. The bridge was reopened to normal traffic at the beginning of 1990, and today there are few reminders of the era when people living in the immediate vicinity needed special permits simply to come and go from their own homes. From the Potsdam side of the bridge, tram #93 leads back to Platz der Einheit, while bus #116 crosses over and ends in Wannsee.

Babelsberg

On the eastern bank of the Havel is the town of **BABELSBERG**, now officially part of the Potsdam administrative district. Crossing the Lange Brücke from Potsdam, it's hard not to notice a square tower rising up out of the trees atop the **Brauhausberg** hill on the Babelsberg side. This is the former local SED headquarters or "Kreml" (Kremlin), to give it its local nickname. Originally built as a military college at the turn of the twentieth century, it later served as a state archive building – a dark oval patch on the side of the tower marks where the SED symbol used to be.

The Telegrafenberg and the Einsteinturm

Like Potsdam, Babelsberg has a few secrets ripe for rediscovery. Above the Lange Brücke, Albert-Einstein-Strasse leads up onto the **Telegrafenberg**. This was the site chosen in 1832 for a telegraph station, one of a whole network positioned between Berlin and Koblenz to relay messages by means of mechanical signal arms. Just over forty years later, when the mechanical system had been rendered obsolete, it was decided to build an astronomical observatory here. The complex still stands, finished in the orange- and yellow-striped brickwork typical of the late nineteenth century.

Beyond the observatory, a path leads to the nearby **Einsteinturm**, a twenty-metre-high observatory tower designed by Erich Mendelsohn in 1920. An unrepentently phallic piece of Expressionist architecture, it looks like an element from a Dalí dreamscape and is the most remarkable modern building in the Potsdam area. Experiments testing the Theory of Relativity were carried out here in the presence of Einstein, and scientific work continues here today with research into the sun's magnetic field.

On the eastern side of the Telegrafenberg are a couple of musts for cemetery fans: the **Neuer Friedhof**, laid out in 1866 according to plans drawn up by the architect Lenné, and, below it on the other side of Heinrich-Mann-Allee, the eighteenth-century **Alte Friedhof** with its Classical mausoleum and numerous overgrown monuments, including one to Eleonore Prochaska, who joined the Prussian army in 1813 disguised as a man, successfully fooling her comrades, and later fell in the war against Napoleon.

Nowawes and Park Babelsberg

From the junction of Heinrich-Mann-Allee and Friedrich-Engels-Strasse, bus #698 follows the latter to the centre of Babelsberg. Alighting just north of Lutherplatz, it's a short walk south across this square to **Neuendorfer Anger**, once the heart of the old town, with now only the shell of the **Neuendorfer Dorfkirche** as a reminder. Follow Karl-Liebknecht-Strasse northwards; on either side of the road is an area known as **Nowawes**, where single-storey cottages survive from a settlement of Protestant Czech weavers founded by Friedrich Wilhelm II. The name Nowawes came from *Nowa Ves*, Czech for Neuendorf – "new village" – and the streets either side of Karl-Liebknecht-Strasse today have names like Spindelallee and Jutestrasse, bearing witness to the trades once plied here. A right turn onto Weberplatz brings you to the pretty eighteenth-century **Friedrichskirche**, one of the most appealing buildings in Nowawes.

Between Alt Nowawes and the Tiefer See is the **Park Babelsberg**, Potsdam's third great park complex, designed by Lenné, and neglected by most visitors in favour of Sanssouci. The main entrance is at the end of **Allee nach Glienicke**, the northern extension of Alt Nowawes, although until 1989 this was closed because of the proximity of the border fortifications. A roadway leads through the hilly, roughly wooded park to **Schloss Babelsberg** (April–Oct Tues–Sun 10am–5pm; Nov–March Sat & Sun 10am–4pm; *www.spsg.de*; DM4/€2.05, concessions DM2/€1), a Neo-Gothic architectural extravaganza built by Schinkel at the behest of Prince Wilhelm, brother of Friedrich Wilhelm IV, and inspired by England's Windsor Castle. A couple of nineteenth-century architectural oddities lurk in the park: the **Flatowturm** (April to mid-Oct Sat & Sun 10am–5pm; *www.spsg.de*; DM3/€1.50, concessions DM2/€1), an improbable-looking Neo-Gothic guest house and lookout tower, and the **Matrosenhaus**, a bizarrely styled gabled house built for the men who crewed the royal boats and barges of the Hohenzollerns. The park is also home to the thirteenth-century **Gerichtslaube**, Berlin's Gothic courthouse building, brought here in 1872 after the Rotes Rathaus had displaced it.

The Filmpark Babelsberg and Jagdschloss Stern

Babelsberg has a couple of other curiosities. At the eastern end of town, served by buses #690 and #692 from the centre, is the **Filmpark Babelsberg**, August-Bebel-Strasse 26–53 (entrance on Grossbeeren Strasse; mid-March to Oct daily 10am–6pm; ☎01805/34 56 72; *www.filmpark.de*; DM29/€14.85, concessions DM26/€13.30), a huge complex, originally founded in 1917. As the UFA film studios, during the 1920s this was the heart of the German film industry and rivalled Hollywood as a centre of cinematic innovation. Films produced during the heyday of UFA included Robert Wiene's Expressionist masterpiece *Das Kabinett des Dr Caligari*

("The Cabinet of Dr Caligari"), Fritz Lang's *Metropolis* and *Der Blaue Engel* ("The Blue Angel") starring the young Marlene Dietrich. Under the Nazis the anti-Semitic *Jud Süss* was filmed here in 1940, followed a few years later by the special effects-laden colour epic *Münchhausen*. Later, as the DEFA studios, it was the heavily subsidized centre of the East German film industry, which didn't last much longer than the GDR itself after the *Wende*. These days Babelsberg has reinvented itself as the "Film Experience Park", and visitors can wander through the costume and props departments and watch technicians going through the motions of shooting film scenes for their benefit. It's also possible to visit the hangar-like studio where Fritz Lang may have filmed *Metropolis* (no one is quite sure of the exact location) and admire a reproduction of his futuristic set. Aside from the film-related attractions, there are fairground rides, several featuring German cartoon characters, and animal shows, which usually take place around 11am, though it's best to ring in advance for exact times.

If you have the time or the inclination for yet another royal left-over, take the bus as far as the stop just before Steinstrasse on the eastern edge of town, then follow Jagdhaus Strasse on foot to the **Jagdschloss Stern** (by appointment only – call the Stiftung Preussischer Schlösser und Gärten ☎0331/9 69 42 00), a former royal hunting lodge in gabled Dutch style, built in 1732 by Friedrich Wilhelm I. The Schloss is quite plain, a reflection of the soldier king's preferences, and comes as a surprise after the splendour of Potsdam's other royal palaces. East of the Schloss, well-signposted trails lead through the wooded **Parforceheide**, a one-time hunting ground of the king.

Berlin: Listings

Chapter 11

Accommodation

Finding a room isn't as hard as it used to be in Berlin, and the number and quality of **hotels** in the city has increased considerably in the last few years. However, for anything other than **private rooms**, it's essential to book at least one month in advance normally, and at least two months in advance during important trade fairs and festivals – such as the Love Parade (early July), the Berlin Marathon (first Sun in Oct) and the Berlin Film Festival (Feb) – and at Easter and Christmas. At the bottom end of the market, most of the city's **hostels** are fully booked weeks in advance, and there's no **campsite** anywhere near the city.

On the plus side, **Berlin Tourismus Marketing** and **bed and breakfast agencies** can provide private rooms at moderate prices, and the accommodation agencies known as **Mitwohnzentralen** can almost always find somewhere at reasonably short notice – especially if you're after a long-term stay.

Hostels

Berlin's **hostels** are used extensively by school and sporting parties, and rooms tend to be booked well in advance: it's essential to phone through first.

HI hostels

To stay in any of these hostels, you will need an **HI card**, which can be bought from your own national association (see box overleaf) or the organization's Berlin offices at Tempelhofer Ufer 32, Kreuzberg (☎2 64 92 50; *www.hostel.de*; nearest U-Bahn Möckernbrücke). All hostels include bedding and a spartan breakfast in the price.

Jugendherberge Ernst Reuter, Hermsdorfer Damm 48–50, Reinickendorf ☎4 04 16 10; fax 4 04 59 72. U-Bahn line #6 to Alt-Tegel, then bus #125 towards Frohnau. Situated so far from town that it's the least popular of the hostels and therefore least likely to fill up in summer: worth bearing in mind as an emergency option. Under-27s DM28 (€14.30), others DM35 (€17.90); key deposit DM10 (€5.10).

Jugendherberge Berlin, Kluckstr. 3, Tiergarten ☎2 61 10 98; fax 2 65 03 83. Bus #129 to Gendenkstätte Deutscher Widerstand stop. Central city location close to Potsdamer Platz and the Kulturforum museum complex. Under-27s DM34 (€17.45), others DM42 (€21.45); key deposit DM15 (€7.70). Lockout 9am–noon.

Jugendherberge Wannsee, Badeweg 1, Zehlendorf ☎8 03 20 35; fax 8 03 59 08. S-Bahn Nikolassee. Very pleasantly located, with plenty of woodland walks on hand near the beaches of the Wannsee lakes, but far from the city centre. Under-27s DM34 (€17.45), others DM42 (€21.45); key deposit DM20 (€10.25).

The tourist office leaflets Jugendherbergen und Gästehäuser *and* Berlin Hotels und Pensionen (also available from German National Tourist Offices, see p.17) *have useful lists of hotels and pensions.*

See Hotels and pensions for details of Berlin Tourismus Marketing's advance booking service.

Accommodation

Other hostels

Circus Hostel, Rosa-Luxemburg-Str. 39–41, Mitte ☎ 28 39 14 33; fax 28 39 14 84; *www.circus-berlin.de*. U-Bahn Rosa-Luxemburg-Str. Plain but light-filled rooms with high ceilings and big windows. Located near the attractions of the east. Singles DM50 (€25.50), doubles DM40 (€20.45), DM25 (€12.80) per bed in a five-bed room (breakfast not included). No curfew.

Die Fabrik, Schlesische Str. 18, Kreuzberg ☎ 6 11 71 16; fax 6 18 29 74; *www.diefabrik.com*. U-Bahn Schlesisches Tor. A hip and inexpensive hostel in a converted factory building that appeals to backpackers and other young travellers. Singles DM66 (€33.75), doubles DM94 (€48.05), DM30 (€15.35) per bed in dormitory (four or more beds) rooms.

Globetrotter Hostel Odyssee, Grünberger Str. 23, Friedrichshain ☎ 29 00 00 81; fax 29 00 33 11; *www.hostel-berlin.de*. U-Bahn Frankfurter Tor. Imaginatively decorated rooms, a young staff, and

hard by the emerging scene in Friedrichshain. Doubles DM36 (€18.40), DM24 (€12.30) per bed in eight-bed rooms.

Jugendgästehaus am Zoo, Hardenbergerstr. 9a, Charlottenburg ☎ 3 12 94 10; fax 31 25 50 30. U- and S-Bahn Zoologischer Garten. An excellent western location and extremely popular. Singles DM47 (€24), doubles DM85 (€43.50), DM35 (€17.90) per person in four-bed room. No curfew.

Jugendgästehaus Central, Nikolsburger Str. 2–4, Wilmersdorf ☎ 8 73 01 88; fax 8 61 34 85; *www.jugendgaestehaus-central.de*. U-Bahn Güntzelstr. Institutional and plain, but clean and very well located on a quiet street south of Zoo Station. DM39 (€19.95) per bed with breakfast in 2–6 bed rooms, half-board DM43 (€22), full board DM45 (€23).

Jugendgästehause Deutsche Schreberjugend, Franz-Künstler-Str. 4–10, Kreuzberg ☎ 6 15 10 07; fax 6 14 63 39. U-Bahn Hallesches Tor. Easy access to hot spots in the centre of town. Doubles or triples DM38.50 (€19.70), including breakfast. No curfew.

Lette'm Sleep 7, Lettestr. 7, Prenzlauer Berg ☎44 73 36 23; fax 44 73 36 25; *www.backpackers.de*. U-Bahn Eberswalder Str. Spare but comfortable rooms just steps away from the action in Prenzlauer Berg. DM30 (€15.35) per person in 3–6 bed rooms, or DM45 (€23) per person in double room; breakfast not included.

Hotels and pensions

The following listings indicate some of Berlin's best-value **hotels and pensions**. Broadly, a pension is smaller than a hotel, and usually cheaper, although the categories are not strictly applied. Also there are "Hotel–Pensions", which may be either or both, so it's not worth taking too much notice of the labels (they have been omitted here).

Although a clutch of new places have opened on the eastern side of the city in the past couple of years, moderate and budget hotels and pensions continue to be found in much greater numbers in the west.

Prices are given according to the codes detailed in the box below, though bear in mind that prices can change (usually upwards) and standards can drop; at most places breakfast is included in the price. It's also worth noting that many of the more up-market hotels slash their tariffs at the weekend when the business people have gone home, and that many of the cheaper places will also have more expensive rooms. If you're in a group or arrive out of season, it's often possible to get a price lower than we've quoted.

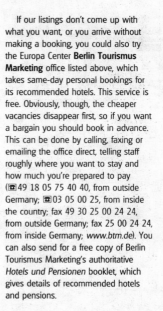

Berlin Tourismus Marketing offices

Main office: Europa Center (entrance on Budapester Str.), Tiergarten ☎25 00 25; fax 25 00 24 24. Mon–Sat 8.30am–8.30pm, Sun 10am–6.30pm.

Brandenburg Gate Daily 9.30am–6pm.

Info-Point KaDeWe, Wittenbergplatz, Charlottenburg. Mon–Fri 9.30am–8pm, Sat 9am–4pm.

Info-Point Tegel airport (main hall, left luggage office) ☎41 01 34 26. Daily 5am–10.30pm.

If our listings don't come up with what you want, or you arrive without making a booking, you could also try the Europa Center **Berlin Tourismus Marketing** office listed above, which takes same-day personal bookings for its recommended hotels. This service is free. Obviously, though, the cheaper vacancies disappear first, so if you want a bargain you should book in advance. This can be done by calling, faxing or emailing the office direct, telling staff roughly where you want to stay and how much you're prepared to pay (☎49 18 05 75 40 40, from outside Germany; ☎03 05 00 25, from inside the country; fax 49 30 25 00 24 24, from outside Germany; fax 25 00 24 24, from inside Germany; *www.btm.de*). You can also send for a free copy of Berlin Tourismus Marketing's authoritative *Hotels und Pensionen* booklet, which gives details of recommended hotels and pensions.

Accommodation

Most of the accommodation options listed are marked on the map on pp.230–231.

ACCOMMODATION PRICE CODES

The codes below indicate prices for the cheapest available double room in high season.

  ① Up to DM100 (€51.10)
  ② DM100–120 (€51.10–61.35)
  ③ DM120–140 (€61.35–71.60)
  ④ DM140–170 (€71.60–86.90)

  ⑤ DM170–260 (€86.90–132.95)
  ⑥ DM260–340 (€132.95–173.85)
  ⑦ DM340–450 (€173.85–230.10)
    and above

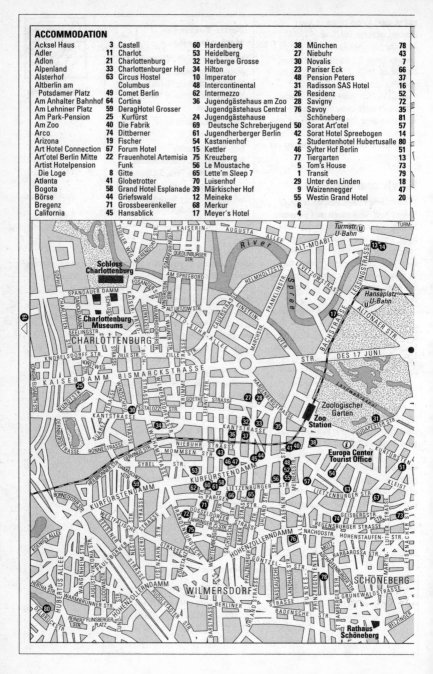

ACCOMMODATION

Acksel Haus	3	Castell	60	Hardenberg	38	München	78
Adler	11	Charlot	53	Heidelberg	27	Niebuhr	43
Adlon	21	Charlottenburg	32	Herberge Grosse	30	Novalis	7
Alpenland	33	Charlottenburger Hof	34	Hilton	23	Pariser Eck	66
Alsterhof	63	Circus Hostel	10	Imperator	48	Pension Peters	37
Altberlin am		Columbus	48	Intercontinental	31	Radisson SAS Hotel	16
Potsdamer Platz	49	Comet Berlin	62	Intermezzo	26	Residenz	52
Am Anhalter Bahnhof	64	Cortina	36	Jugendgästehaus am Zoo	28	Savigny	72
Am Lehniner Platz	59	DeragHotel Grosser		Jugendgästehaus Central	76	Savoy	35
Am Park-Pension	25	Kurfürst	24	Jugendgästehause		Schöneberg	81
Am Zoo	40	Die Fabrik	69	Deutsche Schreberjugend	50	Sorat Art'otel	57
Arco	74	Dittberner	61	Jugendherberger Berlin	42	Sorat Hotel Spreebogen	14
Arizona	19	Fischer	54	Kastanienhof	2	Studentenhotel Hubertusalle	80
Art Hotel Connection	67	Forum Hotel	15	Kettler	46	Sylter Hof Berlin	51
Art'otel Berlin Mitte	22	Frauenhotel Artemisia	75	Kreuzberg	77	Tiergarten	13
Artist Hotelpension		Funk	56	Le Moustache	5	Tom's House	73
Die Loge	8	Gitte	65	Lette'm Sleep 7	1	Transit	79
Atlanta	41	Globetrotter	70	Luisenhof	29	Unter den Linden	18
Bogota	58	Grand Hotel Esplanade	39	Märkischer Hof	9	Waizennegger	47
Börse	44	Griefswald	12	Meineke	55	Westin Grand Hotel	20
Bregenz	71	Grossbeerenkeller	68	Merkur	6		
California	45	Hansablick	17	Meyer's Hotel	4		

CENTRAL BERLIN: ACCOMMODATION

0   500m

N

Former course
of the Wall

WEDDING

Hamburger
Bahnhof

ALT-MOABIT

Neue
Synagoge

Reichstag

Bahnhof
Friedrichstrasse

Bode-
museum

Alte
National-
galerie

Soviet War
Memorial

Neue
Wache

Palast der
Republik

Berliner Dom

Rotes
Rathaus

Fernsehturm

Alexanderplatz
S-Bahn

Siegessäule   Tiergarten

STR. DES 17 JUNI

Brandenburg
Gate

UNTER DEN LINDEN

Staatsoper

Site of Hitler's
Bunker

Französischer Dom &
Hugenottenmuseum

Musikinstrumenten
Museum &
Philharmonie

Schauspielhaus

Deutscher
Dom

Kunstgewerbemuseum

Gemäldegalerie   Kupferstichkabinett

Luftfahrtministerium

Site of
Checkpoint
Charlie

Resistance
Exhibition

Staatsbibliothek

Bauhaus
Archiv

Neue
Nationalgalerie

Gropius-Bau

Anhalter
Bahnhof

KREUZBERG

Kleist
Park

Viktoriapark

Volkspark

Accommodation

Mitte

Adler, Friedrichstr. 124 ☎ 2 82 93 52; fax 2 80 80 57; *www.berliner-zimmerreservierung.de.* About as central as you're likely to get at this price. The pension rooms are spartan but bearable. ①.

Adlon, Unter den Linden 77 ☎ 2 26 10; fax 22 61 22 22; *www.hotel-adlon.de.* The jewel of Berlin's prewar luxury hotels has been re-created in all its excessive splendour. Prices fit for a Kaiser. ⑦.

Artist Hotelpension Die Loge, Friedrichstr. 115 ☎ & fax 2 80 75 13; *die-loge@t-online.de.* Small pension in a prewar building with cosy appointments and a familiar atmosphere. Just steps away from the Scheunenviertel. ①.

Art'otel Berlin Mitte, Wallstr. 70–73 ☎ 24 06 20; fax 24 06 22 22; *www.artotel.de.* Smart, lively hotel with quirky decor and lots of modern art. ⑤.

DeragHotel Grosser Kurfürst, Neue Ross-Str. 11 ☎ 24 60 00; fax 24 60 03 00; *www.deraghotels.de.* Luxury hotel in a renovated turn-of-the-twentieth-century building. ⑤.

Forum Hotel Berlin, Alexanderplatz ☎ 2 38 90; fax 23 89 43 05; *forumberlin@interconti.com.* This big, ugly block dominates Alexanderplatz, but its 900 en-suite rooms are pleasant enough in a bland way, with unbeatable views over the city. ⑥.

Hilton, Mohrenstr. 30 ☎ 2 02 30; fax 20 23 42 69. Luxurious, expensive and not much different to any other *Hilton* hotel in the world; the place to head if you enjoy being completely insulated from the outside world when you visit a city. Features sauna, swimming pool and squash court. ⑦.

Intermezzo, An der Kolonnade 14 ☎ 22 48 90 96; fax 22 48 90 97; *www.hotelintermezzo.de.* Very simply furnished and inexpensive pension for women only, within walking distance of Potsdamer Platz and Unter den Linden. Breakfast not included. ①.

Kastanienhof, Kastanienallee 65–66 ☎ 44 30 50; fax 44 30 51 11. Well-appointed rooms at reasonable prices. Handy for the nightlife of nearby Prenzlauer Berg. ④.

Le Moustache, Gartenstr. 4 ☎ & fax 2 81 72 77. Gay hotel next door to the leather bar of the same name (see p.275). Price includes entry to adjacent swimming pool, Stadtbad Mitte. ①.

Luisenhof, Köpenicker Str. 92 ☎ 2 41 59 06; fax 2 79 29 83. This nineteenth-century coaching company building has been well restored inside and out and is one of the best options in this price range. ⑤.

Märkischer Hof, Linienstr. 133 ☎ 2 82 71 55; fax 2 82 43 31; *hotelmh@t-online.de.* Centrally located, a stone's throw from Oranienburger Strasse and within easy strolling distance of Unter den Linden. Comfortable rooms with TV, minibar etc. Most rooms have showers. ④.

Merkur, Torstr. 156 ☎ 2 82 82 97; fax 2 82 77 65. Fairly comfortable rooms within easy walking distance of city-centre attractions and local nightlife. Most rooms have showers. ③.

Novalis, Novalisstr. 5 ☎ 2 82 40 08; fax 2 83 37 81. Quiet, small hotel not far from Oranienburger Tor S-Bahn station. Rooms have WC, with a separate shower. ④.

Radisson SAS Hotel, Karl-Liebknecht-Str. 5 ☎ 2 38 28; fax 23 82 75 91; *mm@berzh.rdsas.com.* A grand luxury hotel, across from Museum Island and near Alexanderplatz, with every conceivable facility and extra. ⑦.

Unter den Linden, Unter den Linden 14 ☎ 23 81 10; fax 23 81 11 00. A survivor of the GDR; simply furnished but comfortable mid-range place at the junction of Friedrichstrasse and Unter den Linden. ⑤.

Westin Grand Hotel, Friedrichstr. 158–164 ☎ 2 02 70; fax 20 27 33 62. Fully living up to its name, a traditional-style hotel with a little more atmosphere than some of its rivals. ⑦.

Tiergarten

Altberlin am Potsdamer Platz, Potsdamer Str. 67 ☎ 2 61 29 99; fax 2

61 46 37. Large pension just a few minutes' walk from the Tiergarten museums, recently refurbished with turn-of-the-twentieth-century trappings. ④.

Grand Hotel Esplanade, Lützowufer 15 ☎25 47 80; fax 2 65 11 71; www.esplanade.de. Top-class hotel with full facilities and New York-style cocktail bar, *Harry's*, on the ground floor. Great choice if you're not paying. ⑦.

Hansablick, Flotowstr. 6 ☎3 90 48 00; fax 3 92 69 37; reserv@hotel-hansablick.de. A short hop from the Tiergarten, this is one of the few "alternative" hotels in town, being run by a collective. ⑤.

Intercontinental, Budapester Str. 2 ☎2 60 20; fax 26 02 26 00; berlin@interconti.com. Plush modern stopover for high-powered businesspeople and visiting rock stars. Among its legion attractions are a fully equipped health studio, sauna and pool. Absolute luxury. ⑦.

Sorat Hotel Spreebogen, Alt-Moabit 99 ☎39 92 00; fax 39 92 09 99; www.sorat-hotels.com. A spirited hotel housed in a former dairy, though its position across the Spree River means it's isolated from most of the action. ⑥.

Sylter Hof Berlin, Kurfürstenstr. 116, Schöneberg ☎2 12 00; fax 2 14 28 26; info@sylterhof-berlin.de. Well-appointed large hotel just behind Wittenbergplatz and the Ku'damm. ⑤.

Tiergarten, Alt-Moabit 89 ☎39 98 96 00; fax 3 93 86 92; hotel.tiergarten @t-online.de. Intimate hotel in an elegant nineteenth-century building. ⑤.

Charlottenburg

Alpenland, Carmerstr. 8 ☎3 12 39 70; fax 3 13 84 44. Unpretentious and well situated. The broad price range (the more expensive rooms are en suite) means an equally wide range of clientele. ②–⑤.

Am Lehniner Platz, Damaschkestr. 4 ☎3 23 51 00; fax 3 23 93 59. Tiny and economical pension in the middle of an area that's lively at night. ③.

Am Park-Pension, Sophie-Charlotten-Str. 57 ☎3 21 34 85; fax 3 21 34 85. Small, cosy pension, located next to Lietzensee, one of the city's more romantic lakes – peaceful and quiet and surrounded by weeping willows. ②.

Am Zoo, Kurfürstendamm 25 ☎88 43 70; fax 88 43 77 14. A gleaming gold foyer ushers you into a swish hotel, with self-conscious design but excellent facilities. ⑥.

Arizona, Königin-Elisabeth-Str. 47a ☎30 30 90; fax 3 03 09 45; HotelArizona @t-online.de. Reasonably priced 25-room hotel with cable TV. ④.

Art Hotel Connection, Fuggerstr. 33 ☎2 17 70 28; fax 2 17 70 30; arthotel-connection.de. Inexpensive gay hotel located above the famous hardcore *Connection* club. ①.

Atlanta, Fasanenstr. 74 ☎8 81 80 49; fax 8 81 98 72. A simple but comfort-

Accommodation

Lesbian and gay accommodation

There are no hotels or pensions in Berlin specifically for **lesbians**; however, there are two women-only hotels, the *Artemisia* (see "Wilmersdorf", p.235) and *Intermezzo* (see "Mitte", opposite).

    Enjoy Bed & Breakfast (☎2 15 16 66) will arrange gay-friendly private rooms or apartments starting at DM35 (€17.90). For other options, you might check out the classified adverts in the monthly magazine *Siegessäule* (see p.34).

Listed below are some **hotels** popular with gay men.

Arco (see "Western suburbs, p.235)
Art Hotel Connection (see "Charlottenburg", above)
Charlottenburger Hof (see "Charlottenburg", p.234)
Niebuhr (see "Charlottenburg", p.234)
Le Moustache (see "Mitte", opposite)
Tom's House (see "Western suburbs", p.236)

Accommodation

able small hotel housed in a beautiful prewar building on a plush street in the centre of the western side of town. ⑤.

Bogota, Schlüterstr. 45 ☎8 81 50 01; fax 8 83 58 87; *hotelbogota@t-online .de*. Pleasant place offering a touch of luxury in a historic nineteenth-century buiding at affordable prices. ③.

Börse, Kurfürstendamm 34 ☎8 81 30 21; fax 8 83 20 34. Fairly spartan hotel, located on the city's busiest shopping street and near west Berlin's nightlife. ④.

California, Kurfürstendamm 35 ☎88 01 20; fax 88 01 21 11; *info@hotel-california.de*. Well-appointed hotel located in the centre of Ku'damm's shops. En-suite rooms with TV. ⑤.

Castell, Wielandstr. 24 ☎8 82 71 81; fax 8 81 55 48; *messe.castell@t-online .de*. Charming old building, attractively priced and well placed near Ku'damm's shops. The pricier rooms are en suite. ②–④.

Charlot, Giesebrechtstr. 17 ☎3 23 40 51; fax 32 79 66 66. Neatly restored *Jugendstil* building that's efficiently run by friendly staff. Near Adenauerplatz and good value for this area. ③.

Charlottenburg, Grolmannstr. 32–33 ☎88 03 29 60; fax 8 80 32 96 31. Small pension off the Savignyplatz. Cheap and functional. ②.

Charlottenburger Hof, Stuttgarter Platz 14 ☎32 90 70; fax 3 23 37 23; *www .charlottenburger-hof.de*. Stylish, comfortable gay hotel with a 24-hour café. ③.

Columbus, Meinekestr. 5 ☎ & fax 8 81 50 61. Close by the Ku'damm but quiet and comfortable. Child friendly. ②.

Cortina, Kantstr. 140 ☎3 13 90 59; fax 3 12 73 96. Reasonable rooms in a good area, with breakfast included. Ideal for exploring the West End and Savignyplatz. ①.

Dittberner, Wielandstr. 26 ☎8 84 69 50; fax 8 85 40 46. Old-fashioned finery in comfortable surroundings. ④.

Fischer, Nürnberger Str. 24a ☎2 18 68 08; fax 2 13 42 25. Small and very basic pension; breakfast not included. A 15-minute walk from Zoo Station. ①.

Funk, Fasanenstr. 69 ☎8 82 71 93; fax 8 83 33 29. Interesting re-creation of a prewar flat, with furniture and objects from the 1920s and 30s, when it was the home of Danish silent-movie star Asta Nielsen. Given this and its location and price, it's a great bargain. ③.

Hardenberg, Joachimstaler Str. 39–40 ☎8 82 30 71; fax 8 81 51 70. Smack in the action on the west side, on a busy main street filled with tourists – not for those who value peace and quiet. ⑤.

Heidelberg, Knesebeckstr. 15 ☎3 13 01 03; fax 3 13 58 70; *www.bfb.de /hotelheidelberg*. No-frills hotel popular with young travellers; located in an area good for bars and on a street noted for its bookshops. ④.

Herberge Grosse, Kantstr. 71 ☎3 24 81 38; fax 32 76 46 17; *berlin@herbergegrosse.de*. A tiny pension perched high on the fourth floor above busy Kantstrasse. ①.

Imperator, Meinekestr. 5 ☎8 81 41 81; fax 8 85 19 19. Great value, intimate hotel, situated on one of the most exclusive yet friendly streets in the city. Rooms are spacious and stylishly decorated. ③.

Kettler, Bleibtreustr. 19 ☎8 83 49 49; fax 8 82 42 28. A tiny and charming pension on a lively, café-lined street. ③.

Meineke, Meinekestr. 10 ☎88 67 81 90; fax 88 67 92 92. Old-fashioned hotel with an amiable atmosphere; a minute's walk from the Ku'damm. ⑤.

Niebuhr, Niebuhrstr. 74 ☎3 24 95 95; fax 8 81 47 07. Clean and fresh pension in a quiet backstreet location that's within spitting distance of the Ku'damm and Kantstrasse. Breakfast is served in your room at whatever time you desire. Popular with gay guests. ④.

Pension Peters, Kantstr. 146 ☎3 12 22 78; fax 3 12 35 19; *penspeters@aol.com*. Sparse and inexpensive pension right by lively Savignyplatz. ③.

Residenz, Meinekestr. 9 ☎88 44 30; fax 8 82 47 26; *info@hotel-residenz.com*. Situated in a quiet street off the

Ku'damm, with an ambience often lacking in the larger hotel chains. ⑥.

Savoy Hotel, Fasanenstr. 9–10 ☎31 10 30; fax 31 10 33 33; *info@hotel-savoy .com*. Luxury hotel with a traditional, old-world atmosphere. ⑥.

Sorat Art'otel, Joachimstalerstr. 29 ☎88 44 70; fax 88 44 77 00; *www.sorat-hotels-com*. Light, airy and minimalist; popular with passing celebrities. ⑤.

Waizennegger, Mommsenstr. 6 ☎8 83 17 09; fax 8 81 45 28. Cosy little place (eight rooms) with a likeable intimacy and friendly management. ③.

Wilmersdorf

Alsterhof, Augsburgerstr. 5 ☎21 24 20; fax 2 18 39 49; *www.alsterhof.com*. A pleasant modern hotel with warm interior decor. Central, but far enough away from the bustle of the Ku'damm. Pool and sauna. ⑥.

Bregenz, Bregenzer Str. 5 ☎8 81 43 07; fax 8 82 40 09. Small, family-run set-up, a ten-minute walk from Kurfürstendamm. Kids welcome. ①.

Comet Berlin, Kurfürstendamm 175 ☎8 80 41 70; fax 8 82 57 07. Centrally located along Berlin's main shopping street and, considering its position, good value for money. ④.

Frauenhotel Artemisia, Brandenburgische Str. 18 ☎8 73 89 05; fax 8 61 86 53; *Frauenhotel-Berlin @t-online.de*. A popular women-only hotel, with a roof garden and art exhibitions. Fills up quickly, so book well in advance. ⑤.

Gitte, Pfalzburger Str. 87 ☎8 81 84 27; fax 8 83 98 28. Quiet, yet centrally located pension, only 10min from the hustle and bustle of Kurfürstendamm. ④.

München, Güntzelstr. 62 ☎8 57 91 20; fax 85 79 12 22. A straightforward, unpretentious pension with light, bright modern decor, friendly management and prices that make it a highly recommendable bargain. ①.

Pariser Eck, Pariser Str. 19 ☎8 81 21 45; fax 8 83 63 35. Adequate pension in

a pleasant, leafy backstreet. A ten-minute walk from the Ku'damm and with some classy cafés nearby. ①.

Savigny, Brandenburgische Str. 21 ☎8 81 30 01; fax 8 82 55 19; *Hotel.Savigny@t-online.de*. Just 10min south of Adenauerplatz, with decent facilities, including a laundry room, bar and parking space. ③.

Studentenhotel Hubertusalle, Delbrückstr. 24 ☎8 91 97 18; fax 8 92 86 98; *studentenhotel.hubertus-berlin @t-online.de*. Closed Nov–Feb. While the building resembles an ugly college hall of residence, the *Studentenhotel* is right by the Hubertus lake, which makes it pleasant in summer. Its popularity with student groups means you need to book way in advance. ①.

Western suburbs

Am Anhalter Bahnhof, Stresemannstr. 36, Kreuzberg ☎2 51 03 42; fax 2 51 48 97; *www.hotel-anhalter-bahnhof.de*. Not a pretty hotel, but a pleasant one, located just south of Potsdamer Platz and the Kulturforum. ②.

Arco, Geisbergstr. 30, Schöneberg ☎2 35 14 80; fax 2 11 33 87; *www.arco-hotel .de*. Situated in the middle of Berlin's four-star hotel district; a quiet hotel, simple but tasteful, and popular with an international gay/straight crowd. ②.

Brauhaus in Spandau, Neuendorfer Str. 1, Spandau ☎3 53 90 70; fax 35 39 07 11. A charming, if slightly kitsch, small hotel on the far western edge of the city. A brew pub with beer garden rounds out the Bavarian ambience. ⑤.

Estrel Residence and Congress Hotel, Sonnenallee 225, Neukölln ☎6 83 10; fax 68 31 23 45; *m.trottier@estrel.com*. Claims to be the largest hotel in the country, with 1125 rooms. Located quite a way out of the centre, this complex is intended for business travellers and conventioneers and is unlikely to appeal to anyone else. ④.

Grossbeerenkeller, Grossbeerenstr. 90, Kreuzberg ☎7 42 49 84; fax 7 42 39 30. Pleasant, family-run pension that's

Accommodation

Accommodation

better known for its ancient bar of the same name in the cellar. ②.

Humboldt Mühle Sorat, An der Mühle 5–9, Reinickendorf ☎43 90 40; fax 43 90 44 44; *www.sorat-hotels.com*. Modern yet pleasant hotel, housed in a former windmill north of the city. ⑤.

Igel, Friederikestr. 33–34, Reinickendorf ☎4 36 00 10; fax 4 26 24 70. Quiet leafy location, almost on the shores of Lake Havel and far from the centre in Reinickendorf. For those with their own transport. ⑤.

Kreuzberg, Grossbeerenstr. 64, Kreuzberg ☎2 51 13 62; fax 2 51 06 38. Close to Kreuzberg hill at the smarter end of that neighbourhood. This pension offers only basic amenities: communal bathrooms, no lift, no phones. But at the price, who's complaining? ①.

Schöneberg, Hauptstr. 135, Schöneberg ☎7 80 96 60; fax 78 09 66 20; *www.hotel-schoeneberg.de*. Highly recommended pension that borders the leafy surburbs of Friedenau to the south of the city centre. Has some no-smoking rooms. ⑤.

Tom's House, Eisenacher Str. 10, Schöneberg ☎2 18 55 44; fax 2 13 44 64. Clean and friendly gay hotel, popular with those into leather. ④.

Transit, Hagelbergerstr. 53–54, Kreuzberg ☎7 89 04 70; fax 78 90 47 77; *welcome @hotel-transit.de*. Located in a converted factory building in a quiet courtyard, *Transit* attracts a young clientele. ②.

Eastern Suburbs

Acksel Haus, Belforter Str. 21, Prenzlauer Berg ☎44 33 76 33; fax 4 41 61 16. Small off-beat hotel in the midst of the lively Prenzlauer Berg scene. Breakfast not included. ①.

Am Weissen See, Parkstr. 78, Weissensee ☎9 78 90 10; fax 97 89 01 99. Tiny pension out in leafy Weissensee, but with reasonable public transport access to the centre (bus #158, #155 & #255, tram #2, #3, #4 & #13). ③.

Comfort Hotel Lichtenberg, Rhinstr. 159, Lichtenberg ☎54 93 50; fax 54 93 55 11; *lichtenberg@comfort-hotel-berlin.de*. A medium-sized hotel located in a rather dreary neighbourhood, but not far from east Berlin's Tierpark zoo. ⑤.

Greifswald, Greifswalder Str. 211, Prenzlauer Berg ☎4 42 78 88; fax 4 42 78 89; *www.hotel-greifswald.de*. A casual, familiar atmosphere reigns in this pension, tucked away in a quiet rear courtyard not far from Alexanderplatz and the nightlife in Prenzlauer Berg. ③.

Meyer's Hotel, Metzer Str. 26, Prenzlauer Berg ☎44 01 40; fax 44 01 41 04. A new hotel, simply but tastefully furnished, in the quiet courtyard of a renovated turn-of-the-twentieth-century building. ④.

Touristenhaus Grünau, Dahmestr. 6, Lichtenberg ☎6 76 98 08; fax 6 74 44 21. A bit hostel-like (only a handful of rooms have en-suite WCs and bathrooms), but pleasantly situated on the banks of the Langer See out in Grünau. ①.

Private rooms

Private rooms represent one of the best and, at around DM40–60 (€20.45–30.70) per person per night, most cost-effective solutions to finding somewhere to stay in the city. There is also quite a lot of privacy – often you'll barely see your host. Obviously, though, it can be a hit-or-miss undertaking, and service and amenities are usually strictly limited.

Rooms, though, are usually of a good standard: clean and simple, often self-contained. You may be politely requested to return to your room by a reasonable hour – and you should certainly inform the owner if you intend to stay out until the early morning.

Berlin Tourismus Marketing (see p.229 for details) can arrange accommodation free of charge, though their listings are somewhat limited. Flyers from individuals offering rooms are also available at their offices in Europa Center and the Brandenburg Gate. Best bet are the **agencies** that specialize in private rooms, since they pre-screen their offerings.

Bed and breakfast agencies

Bed & Breakfast

Bed & Breakfast Privatzimmervermittlung, Mehringdamm 66, Kreuzberg ☎78 91 39 71; *www.bed-and-breakfast.de* (Mon–Fri 10am–6pm). Part of a national chain, offering rooms ranging from the simple to the luxurious.

Bed & Breakfast in Berlin, Belforter Str. 21, Prenzlauer Berg ☎44 05 05 82; *www.bed-and-breakfast-berlin.de* (Mon–Fri 9am–6.30pm). Single and double rooms starting at about DM65 (€33.25) a night.

Zimmervermittlung Dentler, ☎5 66 78 40; *www.zimmer-berlin.de* (Mon–Fri 8am–6pm). Rooms all over the city, starting from about DM65 (€33.25).

Mitwohnzentralen

Mitwohnzentralen are agencies that can find just about any type of room, and for any length of time – from a week in a bedroom in a shared flat to six months in a luxury apartment. In the summer plenty of places become available for short-term rent while people are away on holiday, and your chances of finding something immediately are high. But where the *Mitwohnzentralen* come into their own is in arranging **longer-term stays**. Monthly charges for a self-contained apartment start at DM650 (€332.30), about half to two-thirds of that if you're prepared to share kitchen and bathroom facilities; agency fees are usually 20–25 percent of the monthly rent. **Shorter stays** will work out a little more expensive than the pro rata rate, and the shortest period of time a *Mitwohnzentrale* will book a room for is usually one week. But, considering this works out to roughly DM40–50 (€20.45–25.50) per person per night, it clearly represents the best cost-cutting option outside the cheapest hostel beds or private rooms. Almost all *Mitwohnzentralen* will take advance bookings by phone, and vary only in the number of places they have on their files – and in some cases, their degree of efficiency.

Agentur Wohnwitz, Holsteinische Str. 55, Wilmersdorf ☎8 61 82 22 (Mon–Fri 10am–7pm, Sat 11am–2pm). Friendly and fairly central, specializing in city-centre rooms. Also has women-only apartments.

Fine & Mine, Neue Schönhauser Str. 20, Mitte ☎2 35 51 20; *www.fineandmine.de* (Mon–Fri 10am–6pm). International agent offering long- and short-term rooms and apartments.

Wohnagentur am Mehringdamm, Mehringdamm 66, Kreuzberg ☎7 86 20 03; *www.wohnung-berlin.de* (Mon–Fri 10am–6pm). A particularly good selection of rooms and apartments in Kreuzberg and Schöneberg.

Home Company, Joachimstaler Str. 17, Charlottenburg ☎1 94 45; *www.homecompany.de* (Mon–Fri 9am–6pm, Sat 11am–2pm). A long-established agency, offering lots of listings.

Mitwohnagentur Streicher, Immanuelkirchstr. 8, Prenzlauer Berg ☎4 41 66 22 (Mon–Fri 11am–2pm & 3–6pm). Helpful agency with rooms and apartments all over the eastern part of the city.

Accommodation

Camping

None of Berlin's **campsites** is close to the centre; each requires time and effort to reach. All the campsites are inexpensive – prices are a uniform DM7.40 (€3.75) per tent plus DM9.90 (€5) per person per night – and well run. During the summer season, from April until the end of September, the campsites are open 6am–1pm and 3–10pm; during the winter season they open one hour later and close one hour earlier, apart from the Dreilinden and Kohlhasenbrück campsites, which close altogether during winter. If you're intending to camp with a group it's recommended that you contact the **Deutscher Camping Club e.V.**, Geisberger Str. 11, 10777 Berlin (☎2 18 60 71), to make a prior reservation.

An exception to the above is the *Internationales Jugendcamp*, which is run

Accommodation

by the Berliner Jugendclub and is located next to their hostel at Ziekowstr. Here, no reservations are necessary, so it's a great option if you haven't pre-booked and arrive at a busy time. It's also quite inexpensive, DM10 (€5.10) a night, but it's open only during the summer months.

If you are looking to cut costs, and intend to stay for a while, bear in mind that a *Mitwohnzentrale* flat may work out to be almost as cheap once you've added the cost of travel to a campsite. Further afield, the Brandenburg region that surrounds Berlin has innumerable sites; the various tourist offices should be able to give you a complete list.

Campingplatz Dreilinden, Albrechts-Teerofen, Wannsee ☎8 05 12 01. Closed Oct–May. U-Bahn to Oskar-Helene-Heim then bus #118 in the direction of Kohlhasenbrück, and get off at the Katchenweg stop. The site is 2.5km from the bus stop, so it's not advisable to stay there unless you have your own transport. Free showers and a small restaurant.

Campingplatz Kladow, Krampnitzer Weg 111–117, Spandau ☎3 65 27 97. U-Bahn to Rathaus Spandau, then bus #134 to Kladow; at the southern end of Kladower Damm (Alt-Kladow stop), change to the #234, get off when the bus swings off Krampnitzer Weg and walk west to the end of the road. Friendly campsite on the western side of the Havel Lake, with the best facilities of all the sites, including a free crèche, bar,

restaurant, shop and showers (DM0.50/€0.25). Six-week maximum stay.

Campingplatz Gatow, Kladower Damm 207–213, Spandau ☎36 80 84 92. U-Bahn to Rathaus Spandau, then bus #134 or #X34 directly to Flugplatz Gatow stop. New facilities not far from the Kladow campsite, with showers, laundry and a restaurant.

Campingplatz Kohlhasenbrück, Neue Kreis Str. 36, Zehlendorf ☎8 05 17 37. Closed Oct–May. A ten-minute walk from S-Bahnhof Griebnitzsee. Has all the basic facilities (showers, laundry etc), a children's playground and a restaurant.

Campingplatz Am Krossinsee, Wernsdorfer Str. 38, Köpenick ☎6 75 86 87. From S-Bahn Grünar take tram #68 to Schmöckwitz, and from there catch bus #463 to the grounds. Pleasantly located in the woods just outside the southeastern suburb of Schmöckwitz, *Am Krossinsee* offers easy access to local lakes. It's also possible to rent a bungalow here.

International Jugendcamp, Ziekowstrasse 161, Reinickendorf ☎4 33 86 40. Closed Sept–June 25. Take U-Bahn #6, direction Alt-Tegel, to the end of the line; it's then a short hop on bus #222, direction Alt-Lübars, to the Titusweg stop. Only those aged between 14 and 26 (which you will be asked to prove) are admitted. You'll be provided with a sleeping mat and blanket. Basic facilities. DM10 (€5.10) per night, breakfast DM3 (€1.50).

Chapter 12

Restaurants

Berlin has all the possibilities you'd expect from a major European capital city, with virtually every imaginable type of cuisine represented: indeed, the national cuisine takes a back seat to Greek, Turkish, Balkan, Indian and Italian food. The more established restaurants are in the west, but in the last few years the eastern districts of the city have experienced a restaurant boom. Generally speaking, these eastern establishments cater to a young and savvy crowd and emphasize modern and foreign cuisine. Particularly in Mitte and Prenzlauer Berg, there is now a wide range of excellent food on offer.

Restaurant eating in Berlin need not be expensive: a sit-down meal starts at around DM12 (€6.15) for a single main course, and drinks aren't hiked up much more than they are in bars. When it comes to **tipping**, add just a few marks to the bill, since a 15 percent service charge is already added. A tip should be given directly to your server when paying, and never left on the table. All restaurants display their menu and prices by the door, where they also indicate which is their *Ruhetag/e* (closing day/s).

Where to eat

Not surprisingly, the places around the Ku'damm and Unter den Linden tend to be overpriced, and for the best-value food, you need to head a little way off the well-beaten tourist routes. It's worth noting that Italian, Yugoslav and – espe-

cially – Greek eateries often provide the best bargains, while if you're on a very tight budget, try the city's *Imbiss* and student *Mensa* restaurants, which offer rock-bottom prices.

German restaurants, on the other hand, are generally expensive. The *Gaststätte*, or traditional German eating places, with their dark wood-panelled walls, waitresses in *dirndls* and huge beer mugs, almost always have a kitsch atmosphere, and the food served is heavy and old-fashioned – dumplings, roast pork, sauerkraut, and the like. However, they are good places to meet the natives, and at the best restaurants the food can be very decent.

What to eat

To enjoy traditional **German cuisine**, it does help if you share the national penchant for solid, fatty food accompanied by compensatingly healthy fresh vegetables and salad.

The **pig** is the staple of the German menu – it's prepared in umpteen different ways, and just about every part of it

Berlin's cafés are covered in Chapter 13.

Eating

Most restaurants are usually able to rustle up something for vegetarians, though a small number of specifically vegetarian restaurants provide a welcome relief from salads. For more information, see p.250.

is eaten. Sausages are the country's most popular snack, while *Kassler Rippen* (smoked and pickled pork chops) and *Eisbein* (pig's trotters) are Berlin favourites – although the fatty *Eisbein* tends to be more of a winter speciality, as does *Boulette*, a sort of German hamburger. *Königsberger Klopse* (meat dumplings in a caper- and lemon-flavoured sauce) can also be found on many menus.

Unusual things are done with **potatoes**, too: try *Kartoffelpuffer* (flour and potatoes mixed into a pancake) or *Pellkartoffeln mit Quark und Leinöl*, a stomach-churning combination of baked potatoes, low-fat cheese and linseed oil that's best digested with lashings of beer or schnapps.

Surprisingly for a country known for its cakes, **desserts** in Berlin's German restaurants are something of an anticlimax. *Rote Grütze* (mixed soft berries eaten hot or cold with vanilla sauce) is one of the few distinctive dishes. Otherwise it's the usual selection of fresh and stewed fruits, cheeses and ice creams; if you have a sweet tooth, you're best off heading for a café that serves one of the delicious cakes or gateaux of which Germans are so fond (see Chapter 13).

Modern German cuisine, known as **Neue Deutsche Küche**, the German equivalent of *nouvelle cuisine*, is a reaction against heavy traditional cooking. While not as minimalistic as the French or Californian versions, like any food trend it tends to be expensive – particularly so for the quantity you get. The places we recommend are, of course, exceptions.

Snacks and budget eating

For cheap, on-the-hoof snacks, head for one of the ubiquitous **Imbiss stands** found on street corners, where for a few marks you can fill up on *Currywurst* – curry-sprinkled sausages that originated in Berlin – and French fries; Turkish stands selling doner or chicken kebabs – in pitta bread with salad – can be found

in equal numbers. Greek stands are also popular, selling Greek doner kebabs, known as *Gyros*, in a puffy pitta-style bread, generally with a tzatziki-type sauce; these are great value at around DM3–6 (€1.50–3.10).

There are also plenty of **fast-food places** and **burger bars**, especially around Friedrichstrasse train station and Zoo Station. Takeaway pizzas are a major boon if you're on a tight budget, with prices as low as DM2 (€1) for a square of cheese, tomato and salami pizza.

For something more substantial but not that much more expensive, **Imbiss restaurants** – a step up from the *Imbiss* street stall – charge between DM7 (€3.60) and DM12 (€6.15) for a meal, handy if you want to refuel cheaply. They come in several guises – some serving German sausages, others Turkish, Greek or Chinese food. Alternatively, at lunchtime, head for any of the city's **Mensas**, officially for university students only but usually open to anyone who broadly fits that description. In either case, make sure you head for the *Bargeld* (cash) queue to avoid being asked for university-issued lunch vouchers.

Some of the *Imbiss* places listed below offer limited seating, but most are standing only.

Al Rai, Grosse Hamburger Str. 20–21, Mitte (see map, pp.252–253). A spacious, informal place, offering delicious Arabian specialities such as couscous and shish kebab.

Ashoka-Imbiss, Alt-Moabit 49, Tiergarten (see map, p.246). Above-average Indian vegetarian dishes, some, such as banana curry, quite unusual.

Baharat Falafel, Winterfeldtstr. 37, Schöneberg (see map, p.246). The best falafels this side of Baghdad. A late-opener, serving till 2am.

Bistro-Tor, Torstr. 195, Mitte (see map, pp.252–253). Family-run, better-than-average place selling chicken doner, salads, pan-fried vegetables and delicious roasted potatoes.

Brooklyn, Oranienstr. 176, Kreuzberg (see map, pp.252–253). Great American-style sandwiches, wonderful cheesecake and brownies.

Café Marché, Kurfürstendamm 14–16, Charlottenburg (see map, p.246). Part of a chain run by Mövenpick, a well-established Swiss catering company. Rather like a glorified canteen, it features a help-yourself buffet, with daily specials. There are always lots of salads, vegetarian dishes, exotic fruit juices and great cakes.

Café Rimon, Krausnick Str. 24, Mitte (see map, pp.252–253). This is the takeaway annexe of the restaurant located at Orienburger Str. 26. Delicious fresh bagels made on the premises, as well as falafel and other Middle Eastern specialities.

Croissant Imbiss, Wittenbergplatz U-Bahn, Schöneberg (see map, p.246). The aroma hits you almost as soon as you get off the train, and makes the wide range of pure butter croissants irresistible. Mon–Fri 6am–6pm.

Die Tofuerei, Krefelderstr. 2, Tiergarten (see map, p.246). As the name suggests, a vegetarian *Imbiss* (though the premises once contained a butcher's shop) with tasty and imaginative daily specials. Closes at 6pm and all day Sun.

Duy Thai Snack, Prenzlauer Allee 226, Prenzlauer Berg (see map, pp.252–253). Inexpensive and tasty Thai cuisine including crispy duck with fruit as well as many vegetarian and noodle dishes.

Einhorn, Mommsenstr. 2, Charlottenburg (see map, p.246). Vegetarian wholefood at its best, in a friendly and relaxed atmosphere. Closes at 6.30pm (4pm on Sat).

Fressco, Oranienburger Str. 48–49, Mitte, and Stresemannstr. 34, Kreuzberg (see map, pp.252–253). Clean, well-lighted places serving excellent quiches, sandwiches, pasta and Italian nibbles. Tables at the Kreuzberg location, stand-up counters only in Mitte, and a no-smoking policy at both. Daily noon–1am.

Habibi, Goltzstr. 24, Schöneberg (see map, p.246). Amiable late-night falafel shop with seating. Open through to 3am.

Humboldt-Mensa, Humboldt-Universität, Unter den Linden, Mitte (see map, pp.252–253). Offers basic *Mensa* food without surprises; just about the cheapest lunch in the area. No ID needed.

Imbiss Konnopke, Schönhauser Allee/Kastanienallee, Prenzlauer Berg (see map, pp.252–253). Beneath the S-Bahn arches, a Prenzlauer Berg legend that serves what's claimed to be the best *Currywurst* in the city.

Letscho, Kastanienallee 15, Prenzlauer Berg (see map, pp.252–253). Small snack shop serving delicious home-made quiche, vegetable rolls, croissant, strudel and salads.

Lotus, Pestalozzistr. 29, Charlottenburg (see map, p.246). Health-food shop with good and inventive vegetarian meals and salads to eat in or take out.

Mai Thai, Zossener Str. 13, Kreuzberg (see map, pp.252–253). Inexpensive, simple Thai fast-food restaurant.

Monsieur Vuong, Gipsstr. 3, Mitte (see map, pp.252–253). Delicious Indochinese soups and noodle dishes. Pleasant atmosphere. Open Mon–Sat noon–midnight.

Nachtigall Imbiss, Ohlauerstr. 10, Kreuzberg (see map, pp.252–253). Arab specialities, including the delicious *Schwarma* kebab – lamb and hummus in pitta bread. Good salads for vegetarians.

Naturkost am Mehringdamm, Mehringdamm 47, Kreuzberg (see map, pp.252–253). Tasty vegetarian sit-down *Imbiss* featuring daily specials: salads, soups, quiches, lasagne, etc. Open during normal office hours.

NK Insel, Friedrichstr. 67 (in the Friedrichstadt Passagen), Mitte (see map, pp.252–253). The best of several affordable snack places in the food court of the upscale Friedrichstadt Passagen shopping mall, featuring casserole dishes and salads that are surprisingly good and fresh.

Eating

Eating

FOOD GLOSSARY

Basics

Frühstück	breakfast
Mittagessen	lunch
Abendessen	supper, dinner
Messer	knife
Gabel	fork
Löffel	spoon
Speisekarte	menu
Teller	plate
Tasse	cup
Glas	glass
Vorspeise	starter
Hauptgericht	main course
Nachspeise	dessert
Brot	bread
Brötchen	bread roll
Butter	butter
Butterbrot	sandwich
Belegtes Brot	open sandwich
Marmelade	jam
Honig	honey
Käse	cheese
Fleisch	meat
Fisch	fish
Ei	egg
Gemüse	vegetables
Obst	fruit
Joghurt	yoghurt
Sahne	cream
Zucker	sugar
Pfeffer	pepper
Salz	salt
Öl	oil
Essig	vinegar
Senf	mustard
Sosse	sauce
Reis	rice
Spätzle	shredded pasta
Maultaschen	form of ravioli
Rechnung	bill
Trinkgeld	tip

Soups and starters

Suppe	soup
Bohnensuppe	bean soup
Erbsensuppe	pea soup
Flädlesuppe, Pfannkuchen- suppe	clear soup with pancake strips
Fleischsuppe	clear soup with meat dumplings
Gulaschsuppe	thick soup in imitation of goulash
Hühnersuppe	chicken soup
Leberknödelsuppe	clear soup with liver dumplings
Linsensuppe	lentil soup
Ochsenschwanzsuppe	oxtail soup
Zwiebelsuppe	onion soup
Leberpastete	liver pâté
Lachsbrot	smoked salmon on bread
Melone mit Schinken	melon and ham
Grüner Salat	mixed green salad
Gurkensalat	cucumber salad
Fleischsalat	sausage and onion salad
Schnittlauchbrot	chives on bread
Sülze	jellied meat loaf

Meat and Poultry

Aufschnitt	slices of cold sausage
Bockwurst	chunky boiled sausage
Bratwurst	grilled sausage
Broiler	chicken
Currywurst	sausage served with piquant sauce
Eisbein	pigs' trotters
Ente	duck
Fasan	pheasant
Frikadelle	meatballs
Froschschenkel	frogs' legs
Gans	goose
Geschnetzeltes	shredded meat, usually served with rice
Gyros	kebab
Hackbraten	mincemeat roast
Hackfleisch	mincemeat
Hammelfleisch	mutton
Hase	hare
Herz	heart
Hirn	brains
Hirsch, Reh	venison

Huhn, Hähnchen	chicken	Kaviar	caviar
Innereien	innards	Krabben	crab
Jägerschnitzel	cutlet in wine and	Lachs	salmon
	mushroom sauce	Makrele	mackerel
Kaninchen	rabbit	Muscheln	mussels
Kassler Rippen	smoked and pickled	Rotbarsch	rosefish
	pork chops	Sardinen	sardines
Kotelett	cutlet (cheapest	Schellfisch	haddock
	cut)	Scholle	plaice
Krautwickerl	cabbage leaves	Schwertfisch	swordfish
	filled with mince-	Seezunge	sole
	meat	Scampi	scampi
Lamm	lamb	Thunfisch	tuna
Leber	liver	Tintenfisch	squid
Leberkäse	baked meatloaf	Zander	pike-perch
Lunge	lungs		

Eating

Fish

Nieren	kidneys	**Vegetables**	
Ochsenschwanz	oxtail	Blumenkohl	cauliflower
Rahmschnitzel	cutlet in cream	Bohnen	beans
	sauce	Bratkartoffeln	fried potatoes
Rindfleisch	beef	Champignons	button mushrooms
Sauerbraten	braised pickled	Erbsen	peas
	beef	Grüne Bohnen	green beans
Saure Lunge	pickled lungs	Gurke	cucumber
Schaschlik	diced meat with	Karotten, Möhren	carrots
	piquant sauce	Kartoffelbrei	mashed potatoes
Schinken	ham	Kartoffelpuree	creamed potatoes
Schnecke	snail	Kartoffelsalat	potato salad
Schnitzel Natur	uncoated cutlet	Knoblauch	garlic
Schweinebraten	roast pork	Knödel, Kloss	potato dumpling
Schweinefleisch	pork	Kopfsalat	lettuce
Speck	bacon	Lauch	leeks
Truthahn	turkey	Maiskolben	corn on the cob
Wiener Schnitzel	thin cutlet in	Paprika	green or red
	breadcumbs		peppers
Wienerwurst	boiled pork sausage	Pellkartoffeln	jacket potatoes
Wild	wild game	Pilze	mushrooms
Wildschwein	wild boar	Pommes frites	chips/French fries
Wurst	sausage	Salzkartoffeln	boiled potatoes
Zigeunerschnitzel	cutlet in paprika	Reibekuchen	potato cake
	sauce	Rosenkohl	Brussels sprouts
Zunge	tongue	Rote Rübe	beetroot
		Rotkohl	red cabbage
Fish		Rübe	turnip
Aal	eel	Salat	salad
Forelle	trout	Sauerkraut	pickled cabbage
Hecht	pike	Spargel	asparagus
Hering, Matjes	herring	Tomaten	tomatoes
Hummer	lobster	Weisskohl	white cabbage
Kabeljau	cod	Zwiebeln	onions
Karpfen	carp		

continued overleaf

Eating

Fruit

Ananas	pineapple
Apfel	apple
Aprikose	apricot
Banane	banana
Birne	pear
Brombeeren	blackberries
Datteln	dates
Erdbeeren	strawberries
Feigen	figs
Himbeeren	raspberries
Johannisbeeren	redcurrants
Kirschen	cherries
Kompott	stewed fruit or fruit mousse
Mandarine	tangerine
Melone	melon
Obstsalat	fruit salad
Orange	orange
Pampelmuse	grapefruit
Pfirsich	peach
Pflaumen	plums
Rosinen	raisins
Schwarze Johannisbeeren	blackcurrants
Trauben	grapes
Zitrone	lemon

Cheeses and desserts

Emmentaler	Swiss Emmental
Käseplatte	cheese board
Schafskäse	sheep's cheese
Weichkäse	cream cheese
Ziegenkäse	goat's cheese
Apfelstrudel	apple strudel
mit Sahne	with fresh cream
Berliner	jam doughnut
Dampfnudeln	large yeast dumplings served hot with vanilla sauce
Eis	ice cream
Gebäck	pastries
Kaiserschmarrn	shredded pancake served with powdered sugar, jam & raisins
Käsekuchen	cheesecake
Keks	biscuit
Pfannkuchen	doughnut
Nüsse	nuts
Nusskuchen	nut cake
Obstkuchen	fruitcake
Schokolade	chocolate
Schwarzwälder Kirschtorte	Black Forest gateau
Torte	gateau, tart

Common terms

art	in the style of
blau	rare
eingelegte	pickled
frisch	fresh
gebacken	baked
gebraten	fried, roasted
gedämpft	steamed
gefüllt	stuffed
gegrillt	grilled
gekocht	cooked
geräuchert	smoked
gut bürgerliche	traditional German
hausgemacht	home-made
heiss	hot
kalt	cold
Küche	cooking
spiess	skewered
Topf, Eintopf	stew, casserole
vom heissen Stein	raw meats you cook yourself on a red-hot stone

Nordsee, Karl-Liebknecht Str. 6, Mitte (see map, pp.252–253). This seafood shop has a takeaway counter offering inexpensive fish sandwiches and seafood salads. A great respite from hamburgers and doner kebabs.

Orientalischer Imbiss, Mehringdamm 63, Kreuzberg (see map, pp.252–253). Arab *Schwarma* specialities: spiced lamb, chickpea puree and salad in pitta bread that are a cut above the rest. Other delicacies include marinated sheeps' tongues with tabbouleh.

Pagode, Bergmannstr. 88, Kreuzberg (see map, pp.252–253). Dishes up Thai meals that enjoy a high reputation among Berlin's *Imbiss* aficionados.

Safran-Falafel, Knaackstr. 14, Prenzlauer Berg (see map, pp.252–253). Where trendy bars appear, falafel takeways are sure to follow – Prenzlauer Berg's first, offering an extensive vegetarian menu.

Solomon Bagels, Joachimsthaler Str. 13, Charlottenburg (see map, p.246). A small, smart stand-up place, featuring hand-baked bagels and fresh tasty toppings. Almost like New York.

Soup Kultur, Kurfurstendamm 224, Charlottenburg (see map, p.246). Soup kitchen with changing daily specials and takeaway; delicious, full-bodied soups. Open noon–8pm; Sat until 4pm.

Situna, Kollwitzstr. 47, Prenzlauer Berg (see map, pp.252–253). A small and friendly African restaurant, featuring Tunisian and Sudanese cooking – good salads and couscous dishes.

Tex-Mex, Georgenstr. 198, Mitte (see map, pp.252–253). A kitsch little place with chilli, tacos and the like.

Tori Katsu, Winterfeldtstr. 7, Schöneberg (see map, pp.252–253). Slightly chaotic Japanese *Imbiss*, here long before sushi became popular, and specializing in dishes with breaded chicken.

TU Mensa, Hardenbergstr. 34, Charlottenburg (see map, p.246). Serves basic casseroles and pasta dishes; buy your meal ticket before getting your food. Mon–Fri 11.15am–2.30pm.

Restaurants

Most of the restaurants listed below are walk-in establishments; where you may need to book, we've included the phone number. Don't forget that many of the cafés and bars listed in the following chapter can be excellent (and inexpensive) choices for food, especially breakfast (see p.259).

Charlottenburg

Akropolis, Wielandstr. 38 (see map, p.246). Taped Greek communist songs accompany the moussaka in a tranquil locale; good, traditional cooking. Moderate.

Eating

> ## Price categories
> **Budget:** Under DM8 (€4.10)
> **Inexpensive:** DM8–14 (€4.10–7.15)
> **Moderate:** DM14–25 (€7.15–12.80)
> **Expensive:** Over DM25 (€12.80)
> *Prices are the average cost per person for a main course without drinks.*

Ana e Bruno, Sophie-Charlotte-Str. 101 ☎3 25 71 10 (see map, p.246). One of the city's finest Italian restaurants with superb regional food made from the freshest ingredients. Interestingly, no dishes are on the menu more than once a year. Open Tues–Sat; booking essential. Expensive.

Angkor Wat, Seelingstr. 34–36 (see map, p.246). Wonderful, subtle Cambodian food that is often surprising and always pleasing. There's another branch in Tiergarten (see p.256). Moderate.

Arche Noah, Fasanenstr. 79 (see map, p.246). Wonderful kosher delights in a good atmosphere. Moderate.

Astir's, Grolmanstr. 56 ☎3 13 63 20 (see map, p.246). Brightly decorated French bistro, kitted out Parisian style with checked cloths, chrome bar and tiled floors. Good portions of classic staples, as well as three-course *prix fixe* menu for under DM30 (€15.35). Moderate.

Athener Grill, Kurfürstendamm 156 (see map, p.246). Ordinary Greek fast-food place that's heavy on grease but handy for late nights. Closes 6am. Inexpensive.

Carpe Diem, Savigny Passage 577 (see map, p.246). Trendy tapas bar underneath the arches near S-Bahn Savignyplatz in an up-market shopping area. Open Tues–Sat. Moderate.

Casa Portuguesa, Helmholtzstr. 15 (see map, p.246). Small, rustic family-run Portuguese, with well-above-average food, musicians some evenings and the freshest of fish. It's in the middle of nowhere, so hop on bus #101, direction Waldstrasse, Alt-Moabit. Moderate.

RESTAURANTS

Akropolis	31	Cour Carrée	20	India-Haus	62	St. Germain	42
Ambrosius	40	Croissant Imbiss	41	India-Palace	21	Storch	60
Ana e Bruno	6	Der Ägypter	23	Kalkutta	33	Tabuna	3
Angkor Wat	10	Die Tofuerei	2	Kashmir Palace	39	Taverna Labrys	50
Arche Noah	29	Diekmanns	48	Khan Mongolian Barbecue	24	Terzo Mondo	30
Ashoka-Imbiss	1	Don Camillo	9	Kyoto	47	Theodors	12
Astir's	16	Einhorn	34	Le Canard	18	Tim's Canadian Deli	56
Athener Grill	52	Florian	19	Litfass	46	Trio	8
Baharat Falafel	58	Foyer	43	Lotus	15	TU Mensa	13
Café Marché	28	Good Friends	22	Luisada	55	Ty Breizh	17
Café Nola	4	Habibi	57	Maharadscha	53	Vietnam	14
Candela	59	Hakuin	51	Never Never Land	61	Wang Hoo	35
Carib	54	Hard Rock Café	49	Paris Bar	27	Wasserwelt	7
Carpe Diem	26	Hitit	11	Sapporo-Kan	32	XII Apostoli	25
Casa Portuguesa	5	Ho Lin Wah	38	Solomon Bagels	45	Zlata Praha	44
Ciao-Ciao	52	Il Calice Enoiteca	36	Soup Kultur	37		

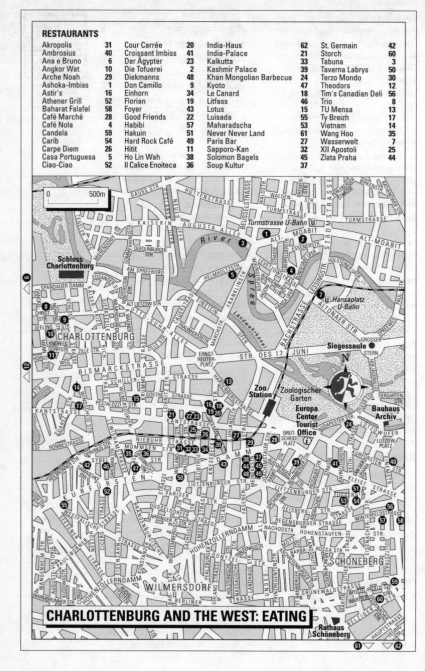

CHARLOTTENBURG AND THE WEST: EATING

Ciao-Ciao, Kurfürstendamm 156, (see map, p.246). Chi-chi Ku'damm trattoria offering excellent, authentic Italian cooking, with patio eating in summer. Moderate–Expensive.

Cour Carrée, Savignyplatz 5 (see map, p.246). Deservedly popular French restaurant with *fin-de-siècle* decor and garden seating. Moderate.

Der Ägypter, Kantstr. 26 (see map, p.246). Egyptian falafel-type meals. Spicy, filling and an adventurous alternative to the safe bets around Savignyplatz, with good vegetarian selections. The Egyptian jewellery shop next door, run by the same owners, is also worth a look. Moderate

Diekmanns, Meinekestr. 7 (see map, p.246). Serves modern German food in a charming ex-grocery store, with much of the original decor. Good large portions. Moderate–Expensive.

Don Camillo, Schlossstr. 7 (see map, p.246). Particularly renowned for its fish, this is one of the best Italians in the city, with a delightful garden terrace. Prices, though, are steep; go if someone else is footing the bill. Expensive.

Florian, Grolmanstr. 52 (see map, p.246). Leading light of the new German cuisine movement in Berlin, this is as much a place to be seen as to eat in. The food, similar to French *nouvelle cuisine*, is light and flavourful. Moderate–Expensive.

Foyer, Uhlandstr. 28 ☎8 81 42 68 (see map, p.246). Tiny Turkish restaurant, tucked away in a Hinterhof off the Kurfürstendamm. A small menu ensures that the food is fresh; closed Sun. Moderate.

Good Friends, Kantstr./Schlüterstr. ☎3 13 26 59 (see map, p.246). One of the city's few Chinese restaurants to offer Peking Duck (24hrs' notice required). Always busy; evening bookings recommended. Moderate.

Hard Rock Café, Meinekestr. 21 (see map, p.246). Loud, cold – the air conditioning is always on full – and totally packaged, the only thing that distinguishes it from other HRCs across Europe is its unusually high prices. Moderate–Expensive.

Hitit, Knobelsdorffstr. 35 (see map, p.246). The proof that Turkish cuisine offers much more than doner kebabs, with an equal mix of meat and vegetarian choices. Moderate.

Ho Lin Wah, Kurfürstendamm 218 (see map, p.246). Something of an oddity, this former Chinese embassy has been transformed into a Chinese restaurant, serving generally excellent dishes. Moderate.

Il Calice Enoiteca, Giesebrechtstr. 19 (see map, p.246). An up-market wine bar serving superb wines and an unusual array of antipasti to Berlin's more bourgeois middle classes. Expensive.

India-Palace, Leibnizstr. 35 (see map, p.246). Serves up a huge variety of Indian dishes at low prices. One of the few places in Berlin to do a halfway decent chicken tikka. Inexpensive.

Kalkutta, Bleibtreustr. 17 (see map, p.246). Arguably the finest Indian restaurant in Berlin. Moderate–Expensive.

Kashmir Palace, Marburger Str. 14 (see map, p.246). Up-market Indian with authentic northern Indian cuisine. Moderate–Expensive

Khan Mongolian Barbecue, Budapester Str. 11–13 (see map, p.246). The Mongolian barbecue hits Berlin: choose your food and grill away. Moderate.

Kyoto, Wilmersdorfer Str. 94 (see map, p.246). Excellent Japanese local, where you can eat sushi to your heart's content. Snooty service at times. Moderate.

Le Canard, Knesebeckstr. 88 ☎3 12 26 45 (see map, p.246). Old, sleepy, much-favoured French restaurant, smack in the centre of town. Often fully booked for business lunches, so call ahead. Expensive.

Litfass, Sybelstr. 49 (see map, p.246). Great portions of Portuguese food and particularly tasty seafood – don't be put off by the bunker-like exterior. Moderate.

Luisada, Kurfürstendamm 132a, ☎8 91 58 69 (see map, p.246). Boisterous Portuguese place renowned for its fish dishes. Moderate.

Eating

Eating

Paris Bar, Kantstr. 152 ☎3 13 80 52 (see map, p.246). This was once the city's most famous meeting place for artists, writers and intellectuals. Now high prices mean that it's wholly the pre-serve of the moneyed middle classes. The food is French/Viennese in style and the service immaculate, but it's probably not worth the outlay. Expensive.

Sapporo-Kan, Schlüterstr. 52 (see map, p.246). Japanese restaurant that's a pop-ular lunchtime spot. Admire the wax culi-nary creations in the window, then eat the real thing inside. Moderate.

St Germain, Damaschkestr. 20 (see map, p.246). Trendy French bistro, heavy on sauces, but with hard-to-find dishes – in Berlin, anyway – like *cassoulet* and con-fit de canard, and a weekly couscous special. Closed Sun. Expensive.

Taverna Labrys, Wielandstr. 26 (see map, p.246). Run-of-the mill Greek fare made exemplary by the use of top-quali-ty ingredients, and on offer at very rea-sonable prices. Inexpensive–Moderate.

Terzo Mondo, Grolmanstr. 28 (see map, p.246). Raucous Greek bar and restau-rant with live music, owned by the Greek star of *Lindenstrasse*, one of German TV's most popular soap operas. Open till 4am daily. Moderate.

Theodors, Theodor-Heuss-Platz 10 ☎3 02 57 70 (see map, p.246). Elegant mosaic interior along the lines of a Parisian brasserie. The usual French fare, though the veg are cooked and present-ed *à l'allemande*. One of the best choic-es for this part of town. Expensive.

Trio, Klausener Platz 14 ☎3 21 77 82 (see map, p.246). A well-kept secret in the middle of town. The house cocktail depends on the time of year: in July, for example, it's *Himbeerbowle* – raspberries and Sekt. Booking essential; closed Wed. Expensive.

Ty Breizh, Kantstr. 75 ☎3 23 99 32 (see map, p.246). Chaotic place serving up mounds of traditional northern French cuisine, including crepes. The colourful owner adds to the fun. Moderate.

Vietnam, Suarezstr. 61 (see map, p.246). One of the city's most popular Vietnamese restaurants, quietly situated in a street of junk shops. Moderate.

Wang Hoo, Wilmersdorfer Str. 75 (see map, p.246). Soothing surroundings draw a thirty-something crowd. Delicious DM35 (€17.90) set menu. Moderate.

XII Apostoli, Bleibtreustr. 49, opposite S-Bahn Savignyplatz ☎3 12 14 33 (see map, p.246). This de luxe pizzeria has been packing them in for years, with out-of-the-ordinary toppings like smoked salmon and cream cheese and five types of calzone. Has a sister restaurant in Mitte (see p.254). Moderate–Expensive.

Zlata Praha, Meinekestr. 4. ☎8 81 97 50 (see map, p.246). Classy Czech restaurant with a nouveau-riche clientele. Moderate–Expensive.

Kreuzberg

Abendmahl, Muskauerstr. 9 ☎6 12 51 70 (see map, pp.252–253). Vegetarian restaurant, magnificent in every respect: excellent food (especially the soups – try the *Kürbis* or pumpkin) and a busy but congenial atmosphere. Moderate–Expensive.

Altes Zollhaus, Carl-Herz-Ufer 30 ☎6 92 33 00 (see map, pp.252–253). Very classy place in an old half-timbered building overlooking a canal, serving modern German food. Several set menus, starting at about DM75 (€38.50). Expensive.

Amun, Möckenstr. 73a (see map, pp.252–253). Egyptian specialities in a relaxing atmosphere that, save for a pic-ture or two of Nefertiti, avoids the usual Egyptian kitsch. Occasional bellydancing. Moderate.

Austria, Bergmannstr. 30 (see map, pp.252–253). Serves excellent Austrian food in generous portions on solid wood tables in dark, rustic surrounds. Moderate–Expensive.

Bar Centrale, Yorckstr. 82 (see map, pp.252–253). Chic Italian locale, popular with the affluent young, and exiled Italians. Moderate.

Café Jolesch, Muskauerstr. 1 (see map, pp.252–253). Noisy, smoky and very popular Austrian restaurant with great food and divine desserts. No credit cards. Expensive.

Cat Food, Körterstr. 8 (see map, pp.252–253). Small and stylish sushi bar that's become a neighbourhood favourite. Moderate.

Chamisso, Willibald-Alexis-Str. 25 ☎6 91 56 42 (see map, pp.252–253). Long-established *Szene* eating spot, with Italian (and French) food on the menu, including good pasta. Booking advisable. Moderate.

Gorgonzola Club, Dresdener Str. 121 ☎6 15 64 73 (see map, pp.252–253). Classy pizzas and freshly made pasta – choose any sauce with any pasta – in a rustic, fun atmosphere that's also, unfortunately, often very smoky. Moderate.

Henne, Leuschnerdamm 25 ☎6 14 77 30 (see map, pp.252–253). Pub-style restaurant serving the best chicken in Berlin. The interior here is original – it hasn't been changed, the owners claim, since 1905. Reservations essential. Inexpensive.

Kleine Markthalle, Legiendamm 32 (see map, pp.252–253). Wonderful crispy chicken in a basic, old-fashioned bar and restaurant. Similar to its better-known neighbour *Henne*, but easier to get into. Inexpensive.

Kulisse, Friesenstr. 14 (see map, pp.252–253). South German specialities. Reasonably priced, but imagination sometime exceeds skill here. Moderate.

Lone Star Taqueria, Bergmannstr. 11 (see map, pp.252–253). A variety of tacos, as the name implies, but lots more, including powerful Margaritas. One of the better of the city's Tex-Mex joints. Inexpensive.

Medici, Lausitzer Str. 25 ☎6 18 68 26 (see map, pp.252–253). New German cuisine in stylish surroundings. Trendy, so book ahead. Daily except Thurs 7pm–1am. Moderate.

Merhaba, Hasenheide 39 (see map, pp.252–253). Highly rated Turkish restaurant that's usually packed with locals. A selection of the starters here can be more interesting than a main course. Moderate.

Osteria No. 1, Kreuzbergstr. 71 ☎7 86 91 62 (see map, pp.252–253). Classy and popular Italian run by a collective. Booking essential. Moderate.

Parlamento, Bergmannstr. 3 ☎6 94 77 45 (see map, pp.252–253). Back-to-basics Italian restaurant, with generous portions of hearty country cuisine and Italian football on the bar's TV set. Moderate.

Publique, Yorckstr. 62 ☎7 86 94 69 (see map, pp.252–253). Friendly French café-cum-restaurant serving tasty and inexpensive food till 2am. Plenty of fish dishes and a set menu. Moderate.

Riehmers, Hagelberger Str. 9 (see map, pp.252–253). Excellent husband-and-wife-run traditional German restaurant with a comfortable ambience and outstanding food and service. Outdoor seating in summer in the historic Riehmer's Hofgarten. Moderate–Expensive.

Sarod's, Friesenstr. 22 ☎6 94 21 84 (see map, pp.252–253). A Thai-run restaurant offering some spectacular and imaginative dishes. Try the *Ente VIP* – duck cooked in coconut milk and green curry paste. Interesting vegetarian options. Moderate.

Slobo's, Heimstr. 8 ☎6 93 09 00 (see map, pp.252–253). One of Berlin's smallest restaurants, creating imaginative dishes with a French/German slant. Booking advised. Closed Wed. Moderate–Expensive.

Tartuffel, Körtestr. 15 ☎6 93 74 80 (see map, pp.252–253). Large sprawling Italian restaurant serving an intriguing selection of dishes featuring the humble potato. Moderate.

Thymian, Gneisenaustr. 57 (see map, pp.252–253). Somewhat austere and self-conscious vegetarian place, but with an inventive menu. Moderate.

Eating

Eating

Berlin ohne Speck – a guide for vegetarians

In the 1930s, Berlin had over thirty vegetarian restaurants, and while the city can't field anything like that amount today, it's still the best place for a vegetarian to be in a country that seems to sustain itself exclusively on dead pig. There is a list of exclusively vegetarian places below: otherwise you should generally steer clear of German restaurants, whether traditional or Neue Deutsche Küche – lard and beef stock are used ubiquitously, and there's an unwritten convention that no meal is really complete until sprinkled with small pieces of *Speck* (bacon). Refuse your plain omelette because it's been so garnished and you'll be treated with incredulity.

Thankfully, the city's cosmopolitan spread of cuisines means that choosing an Italian, Indian or Thai option will usually yield something without meat on the menu, and most upmarket cafés have a flesh-free option. If you're on a budget, head for one of our vegetarian *Imbiss* listings rather than an *Eckkneipe*, where you stand as much chance of getting something meat-free as you do of being thrown out for swearing.

Useful phrases

Remember to be forceful and insistent: to many Germans, small bits of bacon, ham or lard just don't count as meat.

Ich bin Vegetarier. I am a vegetarian.

Ich esse keinen Fleisch oder Fisch. I don't eat meat or fish.

Ich möchte keinen Speck oder keine Fleischbrühe essen. I cannot eat bacon or meat stock.

Gibt's Fleisch drin? Has it got any meat in it?

Gibt's was ohne Fleisch? Do you have anything without meat in it?

Vegetarian restaurants

Abendmahl (see p.248)
Beth Café (see below)
Café Oren (see below)
Hakuin (see p.256)
Little Shop of Food (see p.255)
Thymian (see p.249)
Zenit (see p.257)

Van Loon, Carl-Herz-Ufer 5 ☎6 92 62 93 (see map, pp.252–253). A converted pleasure cruiser moored on the Landwehrkanal. Modern German cooking, with great fish dishes and on-deck eating (weather permitting). Moderate.

Weltrestaurant Markthalle, Pücklerstr. 34 (see map, pp.252–253). Spacious restaurant with long communal tables offering German food in hearty portions. Popular with a young crowd. Moderate.

Zagato, Bergmannstr. 27 (see map, pp.252–253). Tiny local Italian joint, with basic but delicious recipes. Moderate.

Zorbas, Zossener Str. 25 ☎6 91 94 34 (see map, pp.252–253). The most likeable of several Greek places in the neighbourhood (off Gneisenaustrasse in west Kreuzberg), and popular with the Greek locals – always a good sign. Open till late. Inexpensive–Moderate.

Mitte

Astor, Oranienburger Str. 84 (see map, pp.252–253). A heaped plate of excellent fish and chips served American style with tartare sauce or English style with vinegar. Good cakes and desserts and a special pancake brunch served at weekends. Inexpensive.

Beth Café, Tucholskystr. 40 (see map, pp.252–253). Small and spartan vegetarian kosher café featuring Israeli and traditional Eastern European specialities. Moderate.

Borchardt, Französischer Str. 47 ☎20 38 71 17 (see map, pp.252–253). A re-creation of an elegant prewar French restaurant of the same name, and widely considered one of the top restaurants in the city. Expensive.

Café Oren, Oranienburger Str. 28 ☎2 82 82 28 (see map, pp.252–253). Next door to the Oranienburger Strasse synagogue, offering light vegetarian dishes in a stylish interior. Inexpensive–Moderate.

Café Zsolnay, Karl-Leibknecht Str. 9 (see map, pp.252–253). A hold-over from the GDR days, the Eastern European food served here is nothing to write home about, but it's one of the last places you can experience the old pre-unification ambience. Inexpensive.

Canta Maggio, Alte Schönhauser Str. 4 (see map, pp.252–253). Wonderful classic Italian food has made this new Scheunenviertel place deservedly popular. The service can be idiosyncratic, however. Moderate.

Ermeler Haus, Märkisches Ufer 10 (see map, pp.252–253). A Spree-side building containing two different restaurants run by the same people. The main one is a rather pricey German wine restaurant. A better bet is the *Raabediele*, downstairs in the basement, where you can get well-priced traditional dishes in slightly folksy surroundings. Moderate.

Fournier, Gipsstr. 3 ☎ 28 38 66 22 (see map, pp.252–253). Excellent pan-Pacific fare in this upscale art-crowd hangout on fashionable Gipsstrasse. Wine-tasting club in the basement. Moderate.

Französischer Hof, am Gendarmenmarkt, Jägerstr. 36 ☎ 2 04 35 70 (see map, pp.252–253). The decor is typical of the last days of the GDR – expensive-looking but bland. Still, you can enjoy a superb view of the Schauspielhaus and the Französischer Dom, the French specialities are better than average and there's a good wine list. Open until midnight. Moderate–Expensive.

Fridericus, Opernpalais, Unter den Linden 5 ☎ 20 26 83 (see map, pp.252–253). Regional German specialities, with the accent on fish. It's all competently prepared and served and attracts a steady flow of tourists and businesspeople. Moderate–Expensive.

Fuku Sushi, Rosenthaler Str. 61 (see map, pp.252–253). Bright and cheerful restaurant for sushi, sashimi, maki, tamaki and sake, also offering home delivery.

There's a second branch in Prenzlauer Berg (see p.254). Moderate.

Gorki Park,Weinbergsweg 25 (see map, pp.252–253). Authentic Russian café and restaurant featuring a lavish Saturday brunch from 10am to 3pm. The brunch is popular but well worth the wait. Moderate.

Historische Weinstuben, Poststr. 23 (see map, pp.252–253). A reasonable little German wine restaurant in the basement of the Knoblauch-Haus in the Nikolaiviertel. Moderate.

Honigmond, Borsigstr. 28 ☎ 28 54 45 50 (see map, pp.252–253). Understated and tastefully appointed rooms featuring well-prepared, seasonal modern German cuisine. Moderate.

Kamala, Oranienburger Str. 69 (see map, pp.252–253). Thai restaurant in a cramped basement that's deservedly popular: fresh and crisp ingredients enhanced rather than subsumed by chillis. Inexpensive.

Kellerrestaurant im Brechthaus, Chausseestr. 125 ☎ 2 82 38 48 (see map, pp.252–253). Atmospheric restaurant in the basement of Brecht's old house, decorated with Brecht memorabilia, including models of his stage sets. Viennese specialities from recipes said to be dreamed up by Brecht's wife Helene Weigel. Moderate.

Königin Luise, Opernpalais, Unter den Linden 5 ☎ 20 26 84 50 (see map, pp.252–253). High-class German cuisine catering mainly for visitors and the business-expenses crowd. Expensive.

La Riva, Spreeufer 2 ☎ 2 42 51 83 (see map, pp.252–253). Pricey Tuscan cuisine in the Nikolaiviertel. Open until midnight. Moderate–Expensive.

La Rustica, Kleine Presidentenstr. 4 ☎ 2 18 91 79 (see map, pp.252–253). Wonderful gourmet pizzas and excellent pasta and antipasti. Moderate–Expensive.

Los Cucarachas, Oranienburger Str. 38 (see map, pp.252–253). Very popular and spirited Tex-Mex place that fills up just about every night. Burritos and tacos

Eating

MITTE, KREUZBERG AND THE EAST: EATING

WEDDING

Hamburger
Bahnhof

Former course
of the Wall

Neue
Synagoge

Bode-
museum

Alte
Nationalgalerie

Reichstag

Bahnhof
Friedrichstrasse

Neue
Wache

Berliner
Dom

Soviet War
Memorial

Staatsoper

Palast der
Republik

Brandenburg
Gate

UNTER DEN LINDEN

Siegessäule

Tiergarten

Site of Hitler's
Bunker

Musikinstrumenten
Museum &
Philharmonie

Kunstgewerbe-
museum

Site of
Checkpoint
Charlie

Gemäldegalerie

Bauhaus
Archiv

Resistance
Exhibition

Kupferstichkabinett

Luftfahrt-
ministerium

KREUZBERG

Neue
Nationalgalerie

Staatsbibliothek

Gropius-Bau

Anhalter
Bahnhof

SCHÖNEBERG

Kleist
Park

Viktoriapark

Rathaus
Schöneberg

COLUMBIA DAMM

RESTAURANTS

Abendmahl	70	La Riva	60
Al Dente	31	La Rustica	49
Al Rai	45	Letscho	4
Altes Zollhaus	76	Little Shop of Food	7
Amun	91	Lone Star Taqueria	97
Angkor Wat	52	Los Cucarachas	41
Aroma	90	Maa-Rani	28
Asia Inn	17	Mai Thai	82
Astor	47	Mao Thai	15
Austria	102	Medici	78
Bangkok	16	Merhaba	100
Bar Centrale	81	Monsieur Vuong	39
Beth Café	38	Naan	8
Bistro-Tor	34	Nachtigall Imbiss	77
Boikos	86	Naturkost	
Borchardt	61	am Mehringdamm	84
Brooklyn	74	NK Insel	63
Café Arada	3	Nordsee	53
Café Jolesch	73	November	9
Café Oren	42	Offenbach-Stuben	2
Café Rimon	43	Orientalischer Imbiss	89
Café Zsolnay	50	Osteria No. 1	98
Canta Maggio	36	Ostwind	11
Cat Food	85	Pagode	96
Cenone	18	Paris-Moskau	48
Chamisso	105	Parlamento	99
Chez Maurice	29	Pasternak	19
Club	26	Petite Europa	95
Die Krahe	10	Publique	88
Dionysos	66	Restauration 1900	13
Duy Thai Snack	24	Riehmers	83
Edd's Thailändisches	68	Safran-Falafel	21
Ermeler Haus	64	Sarod's	103
Fournier	39	Sawaddi	75
Französischer Hof	62	Situna	22
Fressco (Kreuzberg)	71	Skales	37
Fressco (Mitte)	40	Slobo's	104
Fridericus	58	Suriya Kanthi	27
Fuku Sushi (Mitte)	35	Tadschikische	
Fuku Sushi		Teestuben	56
(Prenzlauer Berg)	12	Tandoor	14
Gorgonzola Club	72	Tartuffel	94
Gorki Park	30	Tex-Mex	55
Gugelhof	23	Thymian	93
Henne	65	Tori Katsu	79
Historische		Trattoria Lappeggi	20
Weinstuben	59	Trattoria Paparazzi	6
Honigmond	33	Tuk-Tuk	87
Humboldt-Mensa	57	Van Loon	80
Imbiss Konnopke	5	Viva Mexico	25
Kamala	44	Weltrestaurant	
Kellerrestaurant		Markthalle	69
im Brechthaus	32	XII Apostoli	51
Kleine Markthalle	67	Yosoy	46
Königin Luise	58	Zagato	101
Kulisse	106	Zorbas	92
La Bodeguita		Zur Nolle	54
del Medio	1		

Eating

from the Mexican side of the border; hamburgers and fried chicken from the Texas side. Inexpensive.

Skales, Rosenthaler Str. 13 ☎2 83 30 06 (see map, pp.252–253). Trendy Greek place in the Scheunenviertel. The food is fairly pedestrian but it's more a place to be seen than anything else. Moderate.

Tadschikische Teestuben, Palais am Festungsgraben ☎2 01 06 95 (see map, pp.252–253). More famous for its tea specialities, but also serving up tasty Russian and Tajik dishes, the latter mainly involving lamb. The intricately decorated interior is a protected monument. Moderate.

Viva Mexico, Chausseestr. 36 ☎2 80 78 65 (see map, pp.252–253). The most authentic Mexican restaurant in Berlin. Fresh ingredients and salsa to die for at this family-owned restaurant. Moderate.

Yosoy, Rosenthaler Str. 37 (see map, pp.252–253). Inexpensive tapas bar perfectly placed for before-drinking or after-clubbing dinners. Inexpensive.

Zur Nolle, Georgenstrasse, In den S-Bahnbogen 203 (see map, pp.252–253). Pleasant restaurant in the railway arches beneath Bahnhof Friedrichstrasse. The reliable menu, featuring the likes of spaghetti bolognese and fillet of salmon, makes it popular with business lunchers. Moderate.

XII Apostoli, Georgenstr. 2 ☎2 01 02 22 (see map, pp.252–253). Located under the train lines by Friedrichstrasse station, this de luxe pizzeria is just as popular as its elder sister in Charlottenburg (see p.248), and offers a piano bar to boot. Moderate–Expensive.

Prenzlauer Berg

Al Dente, Greifswalder Str. 24 (see map, pp.252–253). Traditional Italian food in simple, light surroundings. Great for a hearty meal on cold winter nights. Moderate.

Asia Inn, Knaackstr. 45 at Kollwitzplatz ☎44 04 21 40 (see map, pp.252–253). Regional Chinese including above-average Mongolian, Cantonese and

Szechuan cuisine. Open daily noon–midnight. Moderate.

Bangkok, Prenzlauer Alle 46 (see map, pp.252–253). Authentic and very good Thai food. First choice in Prenzlauer Berg for mid-priced dining. Open daily noon–11pm. Inexpensive.

Café Arada, Lychener Str. 4 (see map, pp.252–253). Deliciously authentic Ethiopian cuisine, eaten with the hands. Closed Mon. Inexpensive.

Cenone, Marienburger Str. 48 (see map, pp.252–253). Northern Italian kitchen with a huge wine list. Fresh breads and Italian delicacies can be bought from their gourmet shop (open until 8pm), and they also do fabulous sandwiches to go. Mon–Fri 11am–8pm, Sat 11am–4pm. Moderate.

Chez Maurice, Botzowstr. 39 ☎4 25 05 06 (see map, pp.252–253). A little out of the way but worth it for the totally authentic food and theatrics of the manic French chef Maurice. Service can be slow when the place is packed so count on enjoying a bottle of wine while spending the better part of the evening here. Reservations recommended. Daily 7pm–2am. Expensive.

Club, Immanuelkirchstr. 31 (see map, pp.252–253). Inexpensive breakfasts and simple home cooking including feta salad, spinach *au gratin*, and trout if you're lucky. Live entertainment. 10am till late into the night. Inexpensive.

Die Krahe, Kollwitzstrasse 86 ☎4 42 82 91 (see map, pp.252–253). Inventive, fresh and seasonal, with a mixed German and French kitchen. Moderate–Expensive.

Fuku Sushi, Husemannstr. 14 (see map, pp.252–253). Bright and cheerful Japanese, which also offers a home delivery service. There's another branch in Mitte (see p.251). Moderate.

Gugelhof, Knaackstr. 37 (see map, pp.252–253). Inventive German, French and Alsatian food, beautifully presented. Moderate.

La Bodeguita Del Medio, Lychener Str. 6 (see map, pp.252–253). Good Cuban food and cocktails in an interesting environment which features a religious shrine in the corner, a large flag of Cuba, and framed photos and icons on the graffiti-decorated walls. Great Cuban coffee. Daily 6pm till after midnight. Moderate.

Little Shop of Food, Kollwitzstr. 90 (see map, pp.252–253). Never disappointing, the vegetarian kitchen here turns out a wonderful and ever-changing selection of soups, entrées and fresh baked goods. Daily noon–10pm; closed Sat. Inexpensive.

Maa-Rani, Immanuelkirchstr. 29 ☎4 42 57 53 (see map, pp.252–253). Pastel frescos of Indian deities contribute to the relaxing atmosphere. Good tandoori and curry. Inexpensive.

Mao Thai, Wörther Str. 30 ☎4 41 92 61 (see map, pp.252–253). A bit overpriced but the food is excellent and the service unfailingly polite. Moderate–Expensive.

Naan, Oderbergerstr. 49 ☎44 05 84 14 (see map, pp.252–253). South of Kastanienallee, an authentic Indian restaurant that's a favourite of the art and student crowd in Prenzlauer Berg. Cheap.

November, Husemannstr. 15 ☎4 42 84 25 (see map, pp.252–253). Imaginative daily modern German specials and the best weekend brunch in Prenzlauer Berg. Moderate.

Offenbach-Stuben, Stubbenkammerstr. 8 ☎4 45 85 02 (see map, pp.252–253). A near legend even in the GDR days, serving fine traditional German dishes. Theatrical decor and intimate seating niches great for late-night conversation. Booking essential. Moderate–Expensive.

Ostwind, Husemannstr. 13 ☎4 41 59 51 (see map, pp.252–253). Serene setting for superb modern and traditional Chinese dining. Inexpensive.

Pasternak, Knaackstr. 24 ☎14 41 33 99 (see map, pp.252–253). Authentic up-scale Russian place. A nice spot for caviar and champagne or a *milch café*. Moderate.

Restauration 1900, Husemannstr. 1 ☎4 42 24 94 (see map, pp.252–253).

Another Prenzlauer Berg culinary highlight, serving traditional German dishes that spring a few surprises. Moderate–Expensive.

Suriya Kanthi, Knaackstr. 4 ☎4 42 53 01 (see map, pp.252–253). Serves tasty Sri Lankan food. Inexpensive.

Tandoor, Rykestr. 42. Sister restaurant to *Naan*, with the same low prices. Closer to the trendy Kollwitzplatz strip. Cheap.

Trattoria Lappeggi, Kollwitzstr. 56 ☎4 42 63 47 (see map, pp.252–253). Embarrassingly trendy restaurant where west Berliners dine when they want to be hip and go to the east. Good food but inattentive service. Moderate–Expensive.

Trattoria Paparazzi, Husemannstr. 35 ☎4 40 73 33 (see map, pp.252–253). Top-rated place with outstanding Italian food and a large wine list. Moderate–Expensive.

Schöneberg

Aroma, Hochkirchstr. 8 ☎7 82 58 21 (see map, pp.252–253). Well-above-average Italian with photo gallery and Italian films on Tues nights. One of the best options in this part of town, it's advisable to book ahead. Inexpensive.

Boikos, Grossgörschenstr. 6 (see map, pp.252–253). Modern Greek cuisine that lightens up the often heavy traditional repertoire. Moderate.

Candela, Grunewaldstr. 81 (see map, p.246). Solid Italian food at reasonable prices, with service that's top of the range. Moderate.

Carib, Motzstr. 31 (see map, p.246). Classic Caribbean cuisine and friendly service from the Jamaican owner. Moderate.

Edd's Thailändisches, Lutzowstr. 81 ☎2 15 52 94 (see map, pp.252–253). A new and sumptuous location for a local favourite. Huge portions of superbly cooked fresh Thai food make this a popular place any day of the week. Booking essential; closed Mon. Moderate.

Eating

Eating

Hakuin, Martin-Luther-Str. 1 ☎2 18 20 27 (see map, p.246). Excellent Japanese vegetarian-macrobiotic, run by a Buddhist order, featuring tofu and tempura dishes, often complemented by a seaweed salad. It's best to book. Quiet and no smoking. Expensive.

India-Haus, Feurigstr. 38 (see map, p.246). Decent quality Indian, with first-rate veggie options. Inexpensive–Moderate.

Maharadscha, Fuggerstr. 21 (see map, p.246). Though the ambience is that of a German farmhouse, the food is pure Indian. Inexpensive.

Never Never Land, Cranachstr. 55 (see map, p.246). Offering ostrich burgers, kangaroo steak, and other delights from Down Under. Moderate.

Petite Europe, Langenscheidtstr. 1 ☎7 81 29 64 (see map, pp.252–253). Unpretentious neighbourhood place with an informal, lively atmosphere. A good selection for vegetarians. Usually full, so booking is advised. Inexpensive.

Sawaddi, Bülowstr. 9 ☎2 16 57 52 (see map, pp.252–253). Thai through and through, but rather pricey. If you feel like a change, opt for the table without seats, and eat traditional Thai-style. Moderate–Expensive.

Storch, Wartburgstr. 54 ☎7 84 20 59 (see map, p.246). Rustic eatery serving cuisine from the Alsace region in what was once – they claim – a brothel. The excellent food, a mix of French and German, is served at long communal tables, so don't come for an intimate chat. Bookings advisable, though none taken after 8pm. Moderate.

Tim's Canadian Deli, Maasenstr. 14 (see map, p.246). One of the best North American restaurants in Berlin, featuring burgers, ribs, club sandwiches and fresh baked cakes and pastries. Inexpensive.

Tuk-Tuk, Grossgörschenstr. 2 ☎7 81 15 88 (see map, pp.252–253). Amiable Indonesian near Kleistpark U-Bahn. Enquire about the heat of your dish before ordering. Booking advisable at weekends. Moderate.

Tiergarten

Ambrosius, Einemstr. 14 ☎2 64 05 26 (see map, p.246). Large portions of cheap German grub at Berlin's answer to the working men's caff. Popular for its *Eisbein* (boiled pork knuckle) – a dish that's guaranteed to spoil the day of any vegetarian. Inexpensive.

Angkor Wat, Paulstr. 22 (see map, pp.252–253). Excellent place, serving subtle variations on traditional Cambodian food. There's another branch in Charlottenburg (see p.245). Moderate.

Café Nola, Dortmunderstr. 9 ☎3 99 69 69 (see map, p.246). An unusual location for an exceptional restaurant that specializes in Californian-style chargrilled dishes and pungent reduced-fruit sauces. Moderate.

Dionysos, Schöneberger Ufer 47 (see map, pp.252–253). Slightly pricey for a Greek place, but much better value than any of the cafés in the surrounding Tiergarten museums. Moderate.

Paris-Moskau, Alt-Moabit 141 ☎3 94 20 81 (see map, pp.252–253). Housed in the former train station stopoff on the Paris to Moscow line, this popular French restaurant manages to be elegant without being too snooty. Expensive.

Tabuna, Alt-Moabit 59 ☎3 90 70 40 (see map, p.246). Israeli restaurant with, the owner claims, the only Tabuna oven in Europe. Unique or not, it delivers up warm and delicate pitta bread, the like of which you've never had before. Moderate–Expensive.

Wasserwelt, Altonaer Str. 20 ☎39 90 69 33 (see map, p.246). Chef Gordon W. does his pan-Pacific magic at this high-style 1960s-inspired spot, with tandoori and fresh fruit drinks a speciality. Moderate.

Out of the centre

Blumenladen, Bahnhofstr. 4a, part of S-Bahn Friedenau, Steglitz ☎8 52 09 09. Crisp, clean Italian located in a former flower shop – hence the name – away from the bustle of the city, with an interesting choice of food and a good wine list. Booking advisable. Moderate.

Britzer Mühle, Buckower Damm 130, Neukölln ☎6 04 10 05; bus #144. Freshly prepared, meaty German fare in one of Berlin's few remaining traditional eating houses, out in the middle of nowhere. The building forms part of a nonworking windmill complex, and has scenic outdoor eating in summer. Booking essential. Moderate.

Frühsammers Restaurant an der Rehweise, Matterhornstr. 101, Zehlendorf ☎8 03 27 20; S-Bahn Schlachtensee. Part of a trend among the city's more elite restaurants: traditional German cooking revamped and refined. Expect some interesting sausage creations from one of Berlin's leading chefs. Expensive.

Kartoffelhaus Alt Rixdorfer, Richardplatz 20, Neukölln ☎6 85 90 41; U-Bahn Karl-Marx-Str. Variations on that German staple, the potato. Soups, dumplings, baked potatoes and pancakes. Portions are large. Moderate.

Ratskeller Köpenick, Alt Köpenick 21, Köpenick; S-Bahn Köpenick. Authentic *Ratskeller* full of locals and serving decent, value-for-money German food. Occasional live music. Moderate.

Wirtshaus Schildhorn, Strasse am Schildhorn 4a, Grunewald ☎3 05 31 11; bus #A18. Housed in an attractive old *Wirtshaus* (a traditional inn) on the edge of Lake Havel, this is a lovely spot to eat. Expensive.

Zenit, Liebenwalder Str. 2, Wedding; U-Bahn Nauner Platz. Vegetarian German food, dumplings, *Käsespätzle* and the like, in a far-flung neighbourhood. Inexpensive–Moderate.

Eating

Chapter 13

Cafés and bars

Nowhere in Berlin is more than a stone's throw from a **bar**. The basic, no-frills drinking hole known as a *Kneipe* is found on street corners throughout the city and is identifiable by its general gloom and all-male clientele. *Kneipen* are the cheapest places to drink – a small beer costs around DM4 (€2.05) and can be fun if the regulars decide to befriend you. Unaccompanied women should bear in mind that such befriending may have unwanted overtones; as a rule, local women do not frequent these places, choosing instead to head for more mixed and more up-market bars – often referred to as *Szene* ("Scene") hangouts, where pose (or self-conscious lack of it) is all – and cafés that make up the bulk of our listings. While the trendier-looking bars are more expensive, few are outrageously so; and, given their tendency to cluster, it's easy to bar-hop until you find a favourite. Almost all the better bars serve food, too, and this can be a bargain – though beware the most chic places, where that interesting-looking item on the menu turns out to be a plate of asparagus tips for DM30 (€15.35).

You'll find that most bars stay open later than elsewhere in Germany: it's quite feasible to drink **around the clock** here, the result of an Allied-era law that requires bars to close for just an hour a day for cleaning. In reality, most bars open at lunchtime and close sometime between 1 and 5am.

However, if you feel you just can't take the pace of nonstop drinking, help is at hand. Berlin also has an established **café scene**, with hundreds of coffee houses acting as additional social hangouts. And if you can't decide whether to drink or not, many places operate as dual-functioning café-bars, so you can change your mind as the evening wears on.

Afternoon is traditionally time for *Kaffee und Kuchen* (coffee and cakes) in one of the self-consciously elegant (and, therefore, ultra-expensive) cafés in the city centre. Although indelibly associated with Austria, these places are just as popular an institution in Germany. Serving various types of coffee with cream cakes, pastries or handmade chocolates, they're the ideal place to head should your mid-afternoon blood sugar level need pepping up.

Finally, if **breakfast** (*Frühstück*) isn't provided with your accommodation, it can be bought at certain cafés (listed below), many of which continue to serve breakfast throughout the afternoon and into the evening. Prices start at around DM5 (€2.50) for a basic bread, eggs and jam affair, rising to DM25 (€12.80) or more for exotic, champagne-swigging delights. Several cafés also have eat-as-much-as-you-like buffets for a reasonable set price. Typically, you'll be offered a small platter of **cold meats** (usually sausage-based) and **cheeses**, along with a selection of marmalades, jams and honey, and,

Cafés and bars

If finances are tight, your best bet for a stand-up morning snack is in one of the bakeries (Bäckerei), where you can get cheap coffee and cake.

BREAKFAST CAFÉS

SCHEUNENVIERTEL
Barcomi's Deli, Sophienstr. 21.
Hackbarth's, Auguststr. 49a.
Strandbad Mitte, Kleine Hamburger
Str. 16.

PRENZLAUER BERG
Café Anita Wronski, Knaackstr. 26–28.
Eckstein, Pappelallee 73.
Kapelle, Zionskirchplatz 22–24.

KREUZBERG
Barcomi's, Bergmannstr. 21.
Café am Ufer, Paul-Lincke-Ufer 43.
Café Übersee, Paul-Lincke-Ufer 44.
Milagro, Bergmannstr. 12.
Morena, Wiener Str. 60.
Rampenlicht, Körtestr. 33.

SCHÖNEBERG
Café Leising, Hauptstr. 85.
Café Savarin, Kulmerstr. 17.
Mediencafé Strada, Potsdamer Str. 131.
S-Bahn Café, S-Bahn Friedenau,
Bahnhofstr. 4c, Friedrichshain.
Tomasa, Motzstr. 60.

**AROUND NOLLENDORFPLATZ AND
WINTERFELDPLATZ**
Café Berio, Maassenstr. 7.
Café Einstein, Kurfürstenstr. 58.
Café M, Goltzstr. 34.
Café Savo, Goltzstr. 3.
Café Sidney, corner of Maasenstr. and
Winterfeldtstr.
Tim's Canadian Deli, Maassenstr. 14.

SAVIGNYPLATZ AND AROUND
Café Bleibtreu, Bleibtreustr. 45.
Café Hardenberg, Hardenbergstr. 1.
Café Savigny, Grolmanstr. 53.
Filmbühne am Steinplatz, corner of
Hardenbergstr. and Steinplatz.
Schwarzes Café, Kantstr. 148.
Zillemarkt, Bleibtreustr. 48.

CHARLOTTENBURG AND THE WEST
Café au Lait, Kantstr. 110.
Wintergarten, inside the
Literaturhaus, Fasanenstr. 23,
Charlottenburg.

occasionally, muesli or another cereal. You're generally given a variety of **breads**, one of the most distinctive features of German cuisine. Both brown and white rolls are popular, often baked with caraway, coriander, poppy or sesame seeds. The rich-tasting black rye bread, known as *Pumpernickel*, is a particular favourite, as is the salted *Bretzel*, which tastes nothing like any foreign imitation.

Coffee (usually freshly brewed) is the normal accompaniment, though **tea** – whether plain or herbal – and **hot chocolate** are common alternatives. A glass of **fruit juice** – almost invariably orange – is sometimes included as well.

Beer

For serious beer drinkers, Germany is the ultimate paradise. Wherever you go, you can be sure of getting a product made locally, often brewed in a distinctive

style. The country boasts around forty percent of the world's breweries, with some 800 (about half the total) in Bavaria alone. It was in this province in 1516 that the **Reinheitsgebot** ("Purity Law") was formulated, laying down stringent standards of production, including a ban on chemical substitutes. This has been rigorously adhered to ever since (even in products made for export), and was also taken up by the rest of the country, but only for beers made for the domestic market. It was not so scrupulously adhered to by the communists, but has since been reintroduced in those East German breweries that survived closure. Unfortunately, the law fell foul of the EU bureaucrats, who deemed it a restriction on trade, since very few foreign beers met the criteria laid down (and so could not be imported). Though the law is now unenforceable, thankfully

Cafés and bars

it hasn't forced the Germans into lowering their own standards, the entire brewing industry having reaffirmed its commitment to the *Reinheitsgebot*. All in all, the current outlook is very rosy: although the odd brewery bites the dust each year, there has been a revival of long-forgotten techniques, often put into practice in new small **Hausbrauereien**.

More generally, there's an encouraging continuation of old-fashioned **top-fermented** brewing styles. Until last century, all beers were made this way, but the interaction of the yeasts with a hot atmosphere meant that brewing had to be suspended during the summer. It was the Germans who discovered that the yeast sank to the foot of the container when stored under icy conditions; thereafter, brewing took on a more scientific nature, and yeast strains were bred so that beer could be bottom-fermented, thus allowing its production all year round. While the *Reinheitsgebot* has ensured that bottom-fermented German brews are of a high standard, the tech-

nique has been a major factor in the insipidity of so much beer in other countries, including Britain. The top-fermentation process, on the other hand, allows for a far greater individuality in the taste (often characterized by a distinct fruitiness), and can, of course, now be used throughout the year, thanks to modern temperature controls. All wheat beers use this process.

Berlin beer specialities include *Berliner Weisse*, a top-fermented "young beer" that's only just fermented and still quite watery and sour, and must be drunk with a shot of fruity syrup or *Schuss*. Ask for it *mit grün* and you get a dash of woodruff, creating a greeny brew that tastes faintly like cough syrup; *mit rot* is a raspberry-flavoured drink that works wonders at breakfast time.

Wine

Many people's knowledge of German **wine** starts and ends with *Liebfraumilch*, the medium-sweet easy-drinking wine. Sadly, its success has obscured the quality of other German wines, especially

---

Wine categories

TAFELWEIN

Tafelwein can be a blend of wines from any EU country; *Deutscher Tafelwein* must be 100 percent German. *Landwein* is a superior *Tafelwein*, equivalent to the French *Vin de Pays*, and medium dry. Like all German wines, *Tafelwein* can be *trocken* (dry), *halb-trocken* (medium dry) or *lieblich* (sweet).

QUALITÄTSWEIN

There are two basic subdivisions of *Qualitätswein*: **Qba** (*Qualitätswein eines bestimmten Anbaugebietes*) and **Qmp** (*Qualitätswein mit Prädikat*). "Qba" wines come from eleven delimited regions and must pass an official tasting and analysis. "Qmp" wines are further divided into six grades:

Kabinett The first and lightest style.

Spätlese Must come from late-picked grapes, which results in riper flavours.

Auslese Made from a selected bunch of grapes, making a concentrated medium-sweet wine. If labelled as a *Trocken*, the wine will have lots of body and weight.

Beerenauslese Wine made from late-harvested, individually picked grapes. A rare wine, made only in the very best years, and extremely sweet.

Trockenbeerenauslese Trocken here means dry in the sense that the grapes have been left on the vine until some of the water content has evaporated. As with *Beerenauslese*, each grape will have been individually picked. This is a very rare wine which is intensely sweet and concentrated.

Eiswein Literally "ice wine", this is made from *Beerenauslese* grapes – a hard frost freezes the water content of the grape, concentrating the juice. *Eiswein* is remarkably fresh, due to its high acidity.

Cafés and bars

those made from the *Riesling* grape, and it's worth noting that the *Liebfraumilch* drunk in Germany tastes nothing like the bilge swilled abroad.

The vast majority of German wine is white since the northern climate doesn't ripen red grapes regularly. If after a week or so you're pining for a glass of red, try a *Spätburgunder* (Germany's answer to the *pinot noir* of Burgundy).

First step in any exploration of German wine should be to understand what's on the label: the predilection for Gothic script and gloomy martial crests makes this an uninviting prospect, but the division of categories is intelligent and helpful − if at first a little complex.

Like most EU wine, German wine is divided into two broad categories: *Tafelwein* ("table wine", for which read "cheap plonk") and *Qualitätswein* ("quality wine"), equivalent to the French *Apellation Controllée*. For a detailed rundown on wine categories, see the box opposite.

Cafés and bars

Berlin's café and bar scene is focused on a number of distinct areas. Both drinking and eating are generally best done away from the obvious tourist strips like Unter den Linden and Kurfürstendamm, where standards tend to be lower and prices higher. The **Scheunenviertel**, just north of the city centre, and the inner-city district of **Prenzlauer Berg** − former East Berlin's hidden heart, and now synonymous with alternative-tinged good times − today boast the city's most eclectic possibilities, hip tourist strips with new bars and cafés springing up all the time. **Friedrichshain**, a district characterized by working-class neighbourhoods and former squats, also seems poised to take off, already playing host to a number of dance clubs and hip bars right on the cutting edge of Berlin's nightlife. To some extent their appeal is based on the novelty value of their being in the east − they are not intrinsically better than their counterparts in the west − but they have a subtle edge that makes traditional Kreuzberg and Schöneberg haunts seem a little tired.

Scheunenviertel apart, the rest of **Mitte**, Berlin's centre and for many years the showpiece core of the GDR capital, has a lively scene, with a number of repro old-Berlin bars worth seeking out.

Cafés and bars

Meanwhile, the institutionalized anarchy of **Kreuzberg** – for so long the area to be after hours – is starting to feel slightly shopworn. Despite all this, it remains a good place to go out, and it would be quite easy to spend a few weeks bar-crawling here before you even began to exhaust the possibilities. Local drinkers include political activist types waxing nostalgic for the days of regular street showdowns with the *Polizei*, punks so lost in time they still think the UK Subs are a great band, and members of the various post-punk tribes wearing their baseball caps and skate-gear with pride. Adjacent **Schöneberg** tends to be a little smarter and a little more sedate; you'll find a smattering of slick cafés alongside corner *Kneipen*, but none of the extremities of its neighbour.

The area around **Nollendorfplatz** and **Winterfeldplatz** attracts an older, less image-conscious crowd. If you haven't visited the city before and are looking for a gentle introduction to Berlin nightlife, this makes a good place to start. It's also an area with plenty of gay bars, which are listed on pp.274–276. By contrast, the newly erected city centre at nearby **Potsdamer Platz** may be an architectural wonder, but its culinary merits are still limited.

One part of town that hasn't been too badly affected by the loss of business to the east is **Savignyplatz**, the haunt of Berlin's conspicuous good-timers – gilded youth in designer casualwear, and their older siblings, well-dressed drivers of flash cars. It is possible to have a good time around here but there is a distinct element of "see and be seen" to it all which can be trying.

For a change of pace, it's worth heading out to some of the **suburban places**, particularly the *Gartenlokalen*, beer-restaurants with outdoor seating, along the shores of the city's lakes.

Scheunenviertel

Aufsturz, Oranienburger Str. 67. Not as hip as some of the local hangouts but comes into its own on those occasional broiling summer days, thanks to outdoor seating on the shady side of the street. An additional attraction is the extensive range of bottled beers, taking in everything from erstwhile GDR premium beer *Radeberger* to cherry-flavoured Belgian *arcana*.

Barcomi's Deli, Sophienstr. 21. Situated in a pleasant courtyard, Barcomi's is a nice place to rest while gallery-hopping.

Cafés and bars – a warning

The ever-changing face of Berlin makes it impossible to guarantee the accuracy of the listings that follow. Yesterday's rough-and-ready squatter hangout can be transformed into a smooth café-bistro in a matter of months, and once-hip places can slide into obscurity, or even disappear altogether just as speedily. Equally, new cafés and bars open all the time. Our listings, therefore, should only form a base to your own wanderings and discoveries: let us know of any you make.

Interesting soups and American-style baked goods.

Beth Café, Tucholskystr. 40. Run by a small Orthodox Jewish congregation, a slightly snooty place for would-be intellectuals to size each other up over the tops of their wire-framed specs.

Café CC, Rosenthaler Str. 39. This cinema-themed café – East German film posters and cinematic lights as decor – attracts a slightly serious, studenty crowd. It's cheapish and pleasant, but perhaps not the place for a raucous night out.

Café Ici, Auguststr. 61. By day pipe-smoking aesthetes sit composing poetry amid the venerable furnishings of this pleasantly soporific café-gallery, and though things tend to liven up a bit in the evening it's still a good place to escape the Scheunenviertel crowds. Open until 3am.

Café Orange, Oranienburger Str. 32. Everything about this arty café, from the opera filtering out of the speakers to the soft wooden furnishings, radiates contrived good taste and a certain preciousness. Catching the barman's attention is a job in itself.

Café Oren, Oranienburger Str. 28. This place, more than any other, is a symbol of the staggering transformation that's occurred around Oranienburger Strasse over the past few years. Watching the earnest diners discuss *Kultur* over vegetarian kosher-style dishes, it's hard to believe that until a few years ago the only possibilities in this neck of the woods were workers' beer joints. Open until 1am.

Café Silberstein, Oranienburger Str. 27. Great place, usually packed to the gills with party people, and celebrated for its weird welded chairs (for sale). Arriving late when everybody's well oiled and starting to let their hair down a bit makes it easier to get to know people. Mutates into a club from 11pm at weekends.

Café Zapata, Oranienburger Str. 54–56. Part of the *Tacheles* multimedia extravaganza. The addition of plate-glass windows and permanent fixtures and fittings have toned this once wild place down a little, but it's still fairly shambolic, attracting a lot of *Szene* tourists from all over Europe. Regular live music.

Edwin Café and Patisserie, Grosse Hamburger Str. 15. Not really part of the Scheunenviertel scene, but a handy place for a coffee-and-cake break if you're exploring the area around the Sophienkirche.

Eimer, Rosenthaler Str. 68. Determinedly alternative café that was one of the first to open post-*Wende*. Worth investigating for gigs and events, though you won't feel too welcome if your face and clothes don't fit.

Gorki Park, Weinbergsweg 25. Artsy street café with tasty and affordable Russian dishes such as *blini* and *pelmeni*. Large *Milchcafé* comes with a delicious molasses cookie, and the weekend brunch buffet is a treat.

Hackbarths, Auguststr. 49a. Dominated by a huge triangular bar that seems to fill the whole place, Hackbarths attracts a very mixed crowd: intellectual but still up for a good time. Good food, including excellent quiche. Open until 3am.

Mendelssohn, Oranienburger Str. 39. Self-consciously trendy, with decent enough food and a cheery crowd of mostly tourists.

Meilenstein, Oranienburger Str. 7. This place can't quite decide whether it's part of the local *Szene* or just a normal café. Nevertheless, it's not a bad place and the food is cheap. The lentil soup (*Linsensuppe*) is a meal in itself – try it with vinegar, like the locals do. Open 9am–5am.

Mitte Bar, Oranienburger Str. 46. Open late and a favourite for bartenders after hours. Small dance floor with music ranging from 1980s to experimental electronica.

Obst und Gemüse, Oranienburger Str. 48. Always crowded, always chaotic, in many ways this is the quintessential Oranienburger Strasse bar, although it's not as hip as it used to be. You can wait

Cafés and bars

Most of the bars in Scheunenviertel centre around Oranienburger Strasse.

Cafés and bars

a while to get served but, as the place attracts quite a lot of tourists, at least you'll be waiting in company.

The Pips, Auguststr. 84. Sophisticated cocktail bar and dance club. Fills up fast and stays that way through the night.

Reingold, Novalisstr. 11. Art Deco, sophisticated cocktail lounge with a clientele in their 20s and 30s.

Roter Salon, Linienstr. 227. Part of the Volksbühne theatre, with lurid red decor and chintzy furniture giving it the feel of a 1950s brothel. Readings, concerts and

club nights are held here. Exhibitionists may enjoy the fact that you can sit on the stage.

Schokoladen, Ackerstr. 169–170. The spartan, bare-brick interior of this former chocolate factory is a hangover from its time as a squatted building in the early post-*Wende* days. Now a venue for theatrical and art events, and with live music on Saturdays. Beer is cheap and there's free chocolate on the bar. Breakfast served Sat & Sun from 8am.

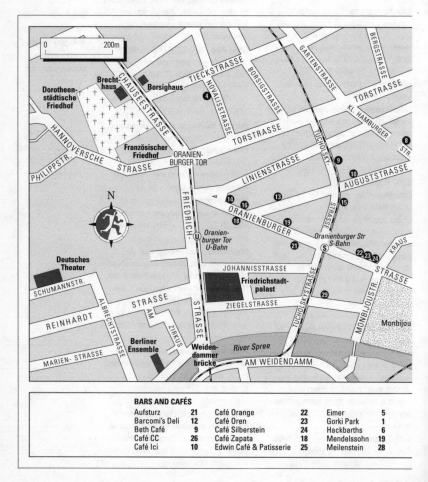

BARS AND CAFÉS

Aufsturz	21	Café Orange	22	Eimer	5
Barcomi's Deli	12	Café Oren	23	Gorki Park	1
Beth Café	9	Café Silberstein	24	Hackbarths	6
Café CC	26	Café Zapata	18	Mendelssohn	19
Café Ici	10	Edwin Café & Patisserie	25	Meilenstein	28

Sophie, Grosse Hamburger Str. 37. A distinctly untrendy old-style pub serving wine, beer and food amid the nineteenth-century facades of Sophienstrasse. Low-key but OK for a quick drink and a bite to eat. Open until 1am.

Strandbad Mitte, Kleine Hamburger Str. 16. At the end of a small street off the beaten tourist track, this inviting café and bar makes a good retreat when it all becomes too much. Excellent breakfasts served 9am–4pm.

Village Voice, Ackerstr. 1a. Read while sipping espresso in an environment inspired by the bookshop/cafés of the US.

Zosch, Tucholskystr. 30. Run by a Turk and an east Berliner, this alternative place started as a squat and is now a good tip for gigs and club nights in the cellar. Usually open until 5am.

Mitte

Café Clara 90, Dorotheenstr. 90 (second courtyard). Office workers and tourists

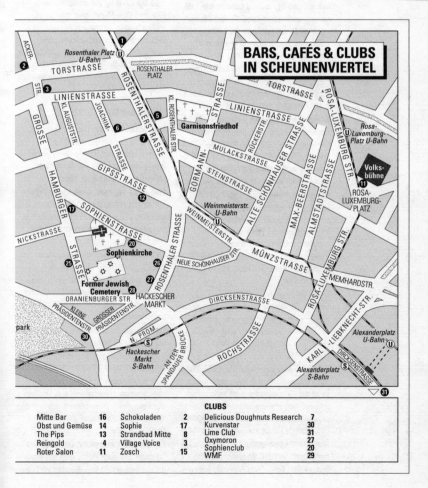

Cafés and bars

Mitte Bar	16	Schokoladen	2	**CLUBS**
Obst und Gemüse	14	Sophie	17	Delicious Doughnuts Research 7
The Pips	13	Strandbad Mitte	8	Kurvenstar 30
Reingold	4	Village Voice	3	Lime Club 31
Roter Salon	11	Zosch	15	Oxymoron 27
				Sophienclub 20
				WMF 29

Cafés and bars

pop in for drinks and snacks by day, while a more arty crowd is drawn by readings and the like at night.

Café Einstein, Unter den Linden 42. A new branch of Kurfürstenstrasse's popular Viennese-style café, but this small outlet can match neither the pomp nor flair of the original.

Café Möhring, Jägerstr./Charlottenstr. Handy for *Kaffee und Kuchen* near the Gendarmenmarkt.

Chagall, Georgenstr., S-Bahn Friedrichstr. in S-Bahn arches. A little piece of Russia in the heart of Berlin: a comfortable café serving up Russian specialities such as *pelmeni* and *soljanka* to the sounds of balalaikas. And a healthy selection of vodkas, of course.

Kaffeestube, Poststr. 19. A Nikolaiviertel café that tries to evoke the atmosphere of a *fin-de-siècle* coffee house. Breakfast is DM7 (€3.60).

Kilkenny Irish Pub, Im S-Bahnhof Hackescher Markt. Three pubs in one in the S-Bahnhof. Guinness, Kilkenny, Irish whiskey. The menu includes Irish stew and that well-known Irish dish tzatziki. Popular with expat construction workers.

Operncafé, Opernpalais, Unter den Linden 5. In a former royal palace, this elegant café evokes the atmosphere of Imperial Berlin for Unter den Linden wanderers. Coffee and amazing cakes make it a recommended stopping-off point after seeing the local sights. Daily 9am–midnight.

Oscar Wilde Irish Pub, Friedrichstr. 112a. Generic Irish bar with all the usual attractions – Guinness, Kilkenny etc. Expats get all dewy-eyed talking about the stews and French fries, but they're not cheap (DM8–20/€4.10–10.25).

Tele-café, Alexanderplatz. This café, 207 metres above Berlin in the upper reaches of the TV tower, turns on its own axis and you can enjoy a wonderful panoramic view of the city while tucking into a pricey ice cream. An essential Berlin tourist experience.

Zur letzten Instanz, Waisenstr. 14–16. One of the city's oldest *Kneipen*, with a wonderful old-fashioned interior, including a classic tiled oven, and a great beer garden. Reasonably priced traditional dishes, all with legal-themed names like *Zeugen-Aussage* ("Eyewitness account"), a reminder of the days when people used to drop in on the way to the nearby courthouse. Open until 1am Mon–Sat.

Zum Nussbaum, Probststr./Am Nussbaum. In the heart of the Nikolaiviertel, a convincing copy of a prewar bar destroyed in an air raid. The original stood on the Fischerinsel and was favoured by the artists Heinrich Zille and Otto Nagel, and though the replica verges on the expensive and flirts dangerously with olde worlde kitsch, it's a good place to soak up a bit of ersatz old-Berlin ambience. *Kneipe* specialities like *Eisbein* and *Kassler Rippchen*.

Prenzlauer Berg

Café ACUD, Veteranenstr. 21. Live rock, blues and, occasionally, acid-jazz sounds, along with cheap beer, are what draws the punters to this scruffy bar spread over a couple of floors.

Café Anita Wronski, Knaackstr. 26–28. This smart Wasserturm café-bar is an excellent place to start local wanderings, though it can get very crowded. Great breakfasts 10am–3pm.

Café Kiryl, Lychener Str. 73. Arty bar that's a good place for whisky fans – it sports a fine selection of single malts. Connected with the alternative publishing house and record label housed in the same building.

Café Manatees, Lychener Str. 64. A new bar catering to a somewhat younger crowd. The distinguishing feature here is a Sunday breakfast that starts at 5am.

Café Schliemann, Schliemannstr. 21. A fairly alternative hangout – if at first you don't get in, it's probably not worth persisting. Holds occasional exhibitions. Open until 6am.

Eckstein, Pappelallee 73. The long frontage and glass doors give this place an airy feel and in fine weather you can sit outdoors. Attracts a trendily bespectacled public who don't seem unduly bothered by the slow service.

Heart of Stone, Käthe-Niederkirchner Str. 34. Dedicated to the music and trappings of the Rolling Stones, and the crowd here is just what you'd expect.

Kaltes Herz, Prenzlauer Allee 32. Despite the name – cold heart – this is a warm and snug café of dark wood, candlelight and cheap and filling food. A nice place to linger over coffee and a book.

Kapelle, Zionskirchplatz 22–24. High ceilings and apricot walls in the shadow of the hulking Zionskirche. A little off the beaten track but worth the detour. Snacks available.

Metzer Eck, Metzer Str. 33. Founded in 1913, this *Kneipe* was a well-known *Szene* haunt during GDR times, as the signed celebrity photos that adorn the walls attest. Its old-fashioned feel makes a change from the slicker, newer places in the neighbourhood.

Cafés and bars

Cafés and bars

Pasternak, Knaackstr. 22–24. An understated establishment that recalls the cafés and restaurants founded by Berlin's large Russian emigré community during the 1920s. There's a good selection of Russian dishes, including *borscht, pelmeni* and *blini,* and an extensive range of vodkas. Popular with discreetly affluent west Berliners. Open noon–2am.

Prater, Kastanienallee 7–9. A traditional beer garden, built in the nineteenth century and recently renovated. In summer you can swig beer, feast on *Bratwurst,* pig's feet or other native food, and listen to German rock from the 1970s. A true Berlin experience.

Santiago Bar, Wörther Str. 36. Light, colourful bar with tasty Latin American snacks and meals. Across the street from Kollwitzplatz.

Schwarz Sauer, Kastanienallee 13–14. A trendy little café with pavement seating. Food (pasta, salads, breakfasts etc) costs up to DM15 (€7.70).

Sevilla Bar, Rykestr. 54. A little north of the action around the Wasserturm, this narrow little cocktail bar gets missed by most tourists, meaning you can enjoy the cocktails and tapas in relative peace.

Times, Husemannstr. 10. The kitchen here is open until 6am – handy if you're out late in the neighbourhood.

Torpedokäfer, Dunckerstr. 69. A vast cockroach mosaic is the first thing to catch your eye in this arty bar. You can buy the works on display, though you'd need to secure a bank loan first. Simple pasta and salad dishes up to DM8 (€4.10).

Uebereck, Prenzlauer Allee/Christburger Str. A long narrow bar with a big silver heating duct running through it. It's all a bit subdued and the emphasis seems to be on events and exhibitions rather than having a good time and meeting people.

Zum Oderkahn, Oderberger Str. 11. A genuine old Berlin *Kneipe* with the kind of atmosphere that encourages impromptu marathon drinking sessions. Early, secret meetings of the opposition group Neues Forum were held here.

Simple dishes like soup and *Bockwurst* from DM3 (€1.50).

Friedrichshain

Astro Bar, Simon-Dach-Str. 40. With its 1970s sci-fi trappings and DJs most nights a week, *Astro Bar* is spearheading Friedrichshain's campaign to be the next boho borough.

Café 100wasser, Simon-Dach-Str. 39. the decoration in here pays homage to the namesake late Austrian artist. Brunch buffet on Sundays.

Supamolly, Jessnerstr. 41. A holdover from Friedrichshain's turbulent squatter days shortly after the fall of the Wall, this cheap bar is still popular with the alternative set.

Tagung, Wühlischstr. 29. Friendly bar with GDR kitsch and memorabilia. Cellar hosts *Cube Club* disco Tues–Sat from 10pm.

Kreuzberg

Ankerklause, Kottbusser Brücke/Maybachufer. A sleepy, nautically themed pub overlooking a bucolic canal has been transformed into a hip bar playing a mixture of techno and easy listening. Usually packed by 11pm.

Atlantic, Bergmannstr. 100. Upmarket and chic, this is Kreuzberg's attempt at a New York bar.

Bar, Skalitzerstr. 64, corner with Wrangelstr. Normally packed, chiefly because the bar staff are apt to forget to measure the drinks.

Barcomi's, Bergmannstr. 21. American-style coffee house with exotic blends accompanied by bagels, brownies and other American baked goods. Scattered copies of the *New Yorker* as well. Branch at Sophienstr. 21 in Scheunenviertel.

Bar Centrale, Yorckstr. 82. Chic Italian locale, popular with alternative types and exiled Italians.

Bierhimmel, Oranienstr. 183. Candlelit bar with a cosy 1950s cocktail lounge out back. Great atmosphere, and a second home to many locals. Cocktail bar open Wed–Sun from 10pm.

Café Adler, Friedrichstr. 206. Small café whose popularity comes from its position by the site of Checkpoint Charlie. Serves breakfast and other meals.

Café Alibi, Oranienstr. 166. Largish murky café-bar that forms part of the Oranienstrasse *Szene*.

Café am Ufer, Paul-Lincke-Ufer 43. Good views of the Landwehrkanal if you sit outside and of the frequent fights if you stay inside. Nevertheless a fun place, with all-you-can-eat breakfasts for DM10 (€5.10) at weekends from 10am.

Café Anfall, Gneisenaustr. 64. Sharp, punk-filled bar that looks as if it were thrown together from local junkshops. Music at maximum distortion level.

Café LebensArt, Mehringdamm 40. A very traditional kind of café, with a long glass counter of wonderful cakes and cookies in front, and several smoky rooms for breakfast and lunch in back. Branch at Unter den Linden/Wilhelmstr.

Café Übersee, Paul-Lincke-Ufer 44. Great location by the canal and a slightly up-market atmosphere for the area – if drinking outside on balmy summer nights, be aware of a 10pm curfew after which you have to move indoors. Breakfast served 10am–2pm.

Die Rote Harfe, Oranienstr. 13. Extreme left-wing ideologists knock back some of the cheapest beer around, while the upstairs eating area looks bizarrely like an old English tearoom.

Enzian, Yorckstr. 77. Wonderfully tacky and lively bar said to be the hangout for one of the country's most popular punk bands, Die Toten Hosen.

espede, Stresemannstr. 28. Sleek, austere café located in the Berlin headquarters of the Social Democratic Party. Good international menu, a little pricey.

Ex, Mehringhof, Gneisenaustr. 2a. Low prices and occasional live music in the bar of the famous alternative Mehringhof collective, with outside drinking on the cobbled Hinterhof (court-yard) in summer.

Futura Café Bar, Adalbertstr./Waldemarstr. Cosy corner

café-bar, deep in Kreuzberg 36, popular with a lesbian crowd.

Golgotha, Viktoriapark. Enormous open-air café and disco (summer only), perched near the top of Kreuzberg's hill. Hugely popular. Breakfast served 11am–3pm.

Kloster, Skalitzerstr. 76. Loud and rau-cous night bar with a religious icon theme, located close to the former bor-der by the Oberbaumbrücke.

Konrad Tönz, Falckensteinstr. 30. Cheesy bar with 1970s trappings; sip moderately priced cocktails while grooving to beat and easy listening.

Locus, Marheinekeplatz 4. Somewhat sober decor, with a small plaza open in summer. Mexican food.

Madonna, Wiener Str. 22. Grimy paint job, a sparse interior, and waning popu-larity, but this still remains one of west-ern Berlin's "in" places. Loud music.

Malheur, Gneisenaustr. 17. Packed (though not uncomfortably so) at most times with the broadest mix possible. Gets going after midnight.

Milagro, Bergmannstr. 12. A bar that's become popular for its imaginative food and huge breakfasts (9am–4pm). *Kloster* beer on tap.

Morena, Wiener Str. 60. Convivial place that serves a generous Spanish or American breakfast and stays open until the wee hours of the morning.

Myslivska, Schlesische Str. 35. Small, under-decorated place that doesn't really get going until the small hours, when it pumps out techno and trip-hop. Serves Thai and Russian foods on some nights.

Rampenlicht, Körtestr. 33. Centrally placed bar-café, a little way north from the Südstern. Good breakfasts (9am–4pm); can get packed at weekends.

Sale e Tabacci, Kochstr. 18. Authentic and beautiful Italian café where alterna-tive journalists and architects linger over espresso and cigarettes.

Wiener Blut, Wiener Str. 14. A sort of compact version of *Madonna*, up the road (see above). Buoyant, spirited atmosphere. Cocktail night Thurs.

Cafés and bars

Cafés and bars

Wirtschaftswunder, Yorckstr. 81. Popular Fifties rock'n'roll theme bar with authentic furniture and a long cocktail list.

Würgeengel, Dresdener Str. 122. Named after the Buñuel film *El angel exterminator* and next to the Babylon cinema, this is a popular hangout for cineastes.

Wunderbar, Körtestr. 38. Large and animated bar with pool room and youthful, varied punters. Perfect for the first drink of the evening when arriving at Südstern U-Bahn, just across the street.

Yorckschlösschen, Yorckstr. 15. Firmly entrenched hippy and alternative crowd; rather like an English pub. Live music Sun.

Zyankali Bar, Grossbeerenstr. 64. Weird cellar bar furnished on the "living-room-as-acid-nightmare" theme. Dimly lit and not that cheap, but good fun.

Schöneberg

Bilderbuch, Akazienstr. 28. Classy yet cosy Viennese-style *Kaffeehaus* with delicious spiked coffee drinks. Live music several nights a week in the back room.

Café Leising, Hauptstr. 85. Minimalist bar decorated with abstract art. Imaginative food; good breakfasts served Sat & Sun 10am–3pm.

Café Savarin, Kulmerstr. 17. Chiefly popular for its breakfast (noon–4pm), homemade quiches and pastries. The back room is preferable, decked out like your great aunt's parlour.

Caracas, Kurfürstenstr. 9. Wild and wacky bar run by Brazilians. The ceiling is full of pink plastic flowers, the bar full of lethal cocktails, the dance floor full of writhing bodies. Good fun.

E&M Leydicke, Mansteinstr. 4. Claims to be the oldest *Kneipe* in western Berlin, and quite aged in feel, though some of the decorations look suspiciously recent. Geared towards tourists.

Felsenkeller, Akazienstr. 2. An unpretentious old bar recently discovered by a young hip crowd. Unchanged by the experience, it continues to pour beer and dish up cheap bar food.

Kleisther, Hauptstr. 5. Large and always crowded with Schöneberg's more style-conscious alternative types. Open till 3am-ish.

Kumpelnest 3000, Lützowstr. 23. Carpeted walls and a mock-Baroque effect attract a rough-and-ready crew of thirtysomethings to this erstwhile brothel. Gets going around 2am. Good fun, and the best place in the area. Normally standing room only.

Mediencafé Strada, Potsdamer Str. 131. Self-styled café for media types (the offices of *Tip* magazine and *Tagesspiegel* daily paper are nearby). Imaginative food, including breakfasts (10am–3pm).

Monte Video, Viktoria-Luise-Platz 6. Hopping place that's been popular for years, though neither the food nor ambience is particularly distinctive. In summer you can make use of a little porch which opens onto picturesque Viktoria-Luise-Platz.

N N Train, Hauptstr. 162. Two subway cars converted into a long, thin cocktail bar. Inside it's buoyant and not as kitsch as you'd think.

Pinguin Club, Wartburgstr. 54. Tiny and cheerful bar with 1950s and 1960s America supplying its theme and background music.

Rössli Bar, Eisenacher Str. 80. Late-night bar with weird fibreglass decor. Try the *Bolk Stoff* beer, if only for the amusing cartoon label. Open till 8am.

S-Bahn Café, S-Bahn Friedenau, Bahnhofstr. 4c. One of the city's smallest bars, collectively run, with a likeable cobbled patio. Breakfasts 10am–4pm.

Tomasa, Motzstr. 60. Rather tacky 1970s-style interior design, but excellent food including breakfast (10am–4pm).

Toronto, Crellestr. 17. Classy wood-panelled café spilling onto a large leafy plaza. Perfect on a fine summer day.

Zoulou Bar, Hauptstr. 5. Compact bar packed after 11pm with Schönebergers. Rather wonderful, in a low-key sort of way.

Around Nollendorfplatz and Winterfeldtplatz

Bar am Lützowplatz, Lützowplatz 7. Distinguished in having the longest bar in the city, this place also has Berlin's best selection of whiskies (63) and a superb range of moderately priced cocktails. A dangerously great bar.

Café Belmundo, Winterfeldtstr. 36. Relative peace – despite the shrieking colour scheme – in one of the busiest night-time areas. Great coffee and snacks.

Café Berio, Maassenstr. 7. Quiet (except during the Wed & Sat market) and civilized bar for those who prefer conversation to music. Breakfast served 8am–midnight.

Café Einstein, Kurfürstenstr. 58. Housed in a seemingly ancient German villa, this is about as close as you'll get to the ambience of the prewar Berlin *Kaffeehaus*; with international newspapers and breakfast served 10am–2pm. Occasional live music, and a good garden. Expensive, though, and a little snooty.

Café Lux, Goltzstr. 35. A desirable alternative to the shrill atmosphere of *Café M* a few doors away. Open (and usually packed) till late.

Café M, Goltzstr. 34. Though littered with tatty plastic chairs and precious little else, *M* is Berlin's most favoured rendezvous for self-styled creative types and the conventionally unconventional. The cool thing to drink is *Flensburger Pils*, from the bottle. Usually packed, even for its famous breakfasts (9am–3pm).

Café Savo, Goltzstr. 3. Low-key bar and café, with a warm, muted red interior, mosaic floor and a mock-1950s bar. Good-value snacks.

Café Sidney, Maassenstr./Winterfeldtstr. Big and brash modern meeting place, especially for breakfast on Sat (9am–2pm). Always crowded.

Green Door, Winterfeldtstr. 50. Somewhat snooty cocktail bar, attracting a well-dressed crowd of young professionals and party-goers. Once you're past the pretension, though, the place can be fun, and they mix a really good cocktail.

Mister Hu, Goltzstr. 39. Cool blue cocktail bar with a great offering of drinks and some of the city's best bartenders.

Mutter, Hohenstaufenstr. 4. Large café and bar of indirect lighting and loud music. Quite popular and usually crowded. Sushi available.

Screwy Club, Frankenstr. 2. The speciality here is frozen drinks, and the place tends to draw a younger set that enjoys such novelties.

Slumberland, Goltzstr. 24. Laid-back, likeable place, with sand on the floor and a tropical theme; one of the better bars in this area.

Tim's Canadian Deli, Maassenstr. 14. It's worth waiting for a table here after visiting Saturday Winterfeldtplatz market; generous breakfasts, scrumptious sweets and hearty meals, including buffalo steak.

Potsdamer Platz

Andy's Diner, Potsdamer Str. 1. Tacky decoration and awful milkshakes (made with powder) aside, this American diner is worth a try for its tasty appetizer combos and lunch specials.

MaxX Bar, Potsdamer Str. 5, Tiergarten. This bar adjunct to the CinemaxX multiplex offers surprisingly good food at humane prices. Try the tapas.

Salomon Bagels, Potsdamer Platz Arkaden, 1st floor. Good selection of bagels, sandwiches and sweets, interesting furniture design, but as with all cafés situated in the Potsdamer Platz mall, the noise and bustle don't exactly create a relaxing atmosphere.

Savignyplatz and around

Café Aedes, Savignypassage. Austere café-bar attached to an art gallery, beneath the arches of Savignyplatz S-Bahn; can get very smoky. Has a branch, *Aedes East*, in Hackesche Höfe, Rosenthaler Str. 40/41, Mitte.

Café Bleibtreu, Bleibtreustr. 45. One of Savignyplatz's more disreputable cafés. Pleasantly down-at-heel, and cheap. Breakfast 9.30am–3.30pm.

Café Hardenberg, Hardenbergstr. 10. Large, old-fashioned café with excellent, cheap food that draws in local students. Breakfast served 9am–midnight.

Cafés and bars

Cafés and bars

Café Savigny, Grolmanstr. 53. Bright, sharp café, with superb coffee, on the edge of Savignyplatz, catering to an arty/media, mixed gay and straight crowd. Breakfast 10am–4pm.

CUT, Knesebeckstr. 16. Over three hundred cocktails in a black cocoon, and certainly a cut above the rest pricewise.

Dicke Wirtin, Carmerstr. 9. Noisy, boozy and popular place, more for the Seventies rock crew than anyone else. Excellent bowls of filling stew for under DM8 (€4.10).

Dralles, Schlüterstr. 69. Notably pricier than other bars in the area, this is the place to see and be seen: the 1950s decor is chic and understated, the clientele aspires likewise. Go beautiful and loaded, or not at all.

Filmbühne am Steinplatz, Hardenbergstr./Steinplatz. One of the least pretentious and more original cafés in Berlin, most of it contained within a cleverly designed conservatory. Breakfast served from 10am.

Florian, Grolmanstr. 52. Watering hole of Western beautiful people, with irregular *Stammtisch* for Russian expats.

Gainsbourg, Savignyplatz 5. The name may pay homage to the master of risqué *chansons*, but the cocktails and food are more like "An American in Paris".

Hegel, Savignyplatz 2. Tiny Russian-themed café on the southeastern side of Savignyplatz that attracts an older crowd. Gregarious fun when someone starts up on the piano.

Lubitsch, Bleibtreustr. 47. Slick bistro-style café, a bit on the expensive side, and very popular with the business classes.

Paris Bar, Kantstr. 152. More famous for its restaurant (see p.247), this was once the local of the city's actors and film crowd, though today it seems to live on a long-dead reputation. Middle-aged, sedate and very expensive. Go if you're not paying.

Rosalinde, Knesebeckstr. 16. Up-market café with an unusual variety of breakfasts, served 9.30am–noon: the *Fitness Frühstück* (muesli, fresh fruit and nuts) does the trick after a rough night out, and there's hot food until 2am.

Rost, Knesebeckstr. 29. Cosy and stylish bar. Great snacks, popular with the theatre crowd.

Schwarzes Café, Kantstr. 148. Kantstrasse's best young, chic hangout, with a relaxed atmosphere, good music and food (like all-day breakfast and a "Black special" of black coffee, a *Sobranie Black* Russian cigarette and black bread). Dated perhaps, but still a classic. Open 24hr (closed Tues 8am–8pm).

Schell, Knesebeckstr. 22. The archetypal Berlin posing parlour, full of people sipping Perrier and rustling through their Filofaxes. Vegetarian food and good breakfasts (9am–2pm).

Wirtshaus Wuppke, Schlüterstr. 21. Old-fashioned *Kneipe* without the sleaze.

Zillemarkt, Bleibtreustr. 48a. Wonderful if shabby bar that attempts a *fin-de-siècle* feel. Unpretentious and fun, and a good place to start Savignyplatz explorations – it's by the S-Bahn. Breakfast 10am–4pm.

Zwiebelfisch, Savignyplatz 7. Corner bar for would-be arty/intellectual types. Jazz, earnest debate and good cheap grub.

Charlottenburg and western Berlin

Bar Bar, Krummestr. 41, Charlottenburg. Located near the Deutsche Oper, this quirky café would be more at home in Schöneberg than Charlottenburg. Tasty snacks and breakfasts.

Berlin Bar, Uhlandstr. 145, Wilmersdorf. Narrow enough to be cosy, expensive enough to make a treat, but cute nevertheless and valued for its intimacy.

Blisse 14, Blissestr. 14, Wilmersdorf. Café-bar designed especially, but not exclusively, for disabled people. A good meeting place.

Café Arc, Fasanenstr. 81a, Charlottenburg. Intimate café in an arch under the elevated train tracks. Predominantly but not exclusively gay.

Café au Lait, Kantstr. 110, Charlottenburg. Small, quirky bar-restaurant with a relaxed atmosphere and Latin American music. Breakfast from 10am.

Café Melanie, Rheinstr. 43, Steglitz. One of the few decent places in the area. Good coffee and late opening (till around 4am) are two attractions.

Café am Neuen See, Lichtensteinallee 1. Smack in the middle of the Tiergarten park, this up-market venue has slick Italian food in a beautiful lakeside setting. Summer outdoor eating is especially pleasant.

Café Rix, Karl-Marx-Str. 141, Neukölln. Part of a cultural complex that's housed in an old dance hall in Neukölln. Pleasant summer seating in a cobbled courtyard, and reasonably priced food, including breakfast (noon–4pm).

Café Slavia, Wiesbadener Str. 79, Wilmersdorf. Art Nouveau café with ample portions of Bohemian food.

Champussy, Uhlandstr. 171, Charlottenburg. Champagne-only bar, where the booze flows freely and everyone pretends they don't care about the bill.

Coxx Café, Nürnberger Str. 17, Charlottenburg. A great find in an area awash with bland tourist drinking holes. Mixed gay/straight crowd, snack lunches and home-made cakes.

Dicker Wirt, Danckelmannstr. 43. Typical neighbourhood pub, full of smoke and besotted regulars. Serves up a particularly good chilli con carne.

Galerie Bremer, Fasanenstr. 37, Wilmersdorf. Gallery with a cocktail bar that's a meeting point for actors and artists of every age and bent. Closed Mon.

Harry's New York Bar, Lützowufer 15 in the *Hotel Esplanade*, Tiergarten. Ritzy piano bar shoehorned into a narrow space in a luxury hotel. Frequented by businesspeople and conventioneers.

Jimmy's Diner, Pariser Str./Sächsische Str., Charlottenburg. An American diner with a replica 1950s interior. Serves American food through to 4am, 6am at weekends.

Kastanie, Schlossstr. 22, Charlottenburg. Amiable bar near Schloss Charlottenburg

that's best on summer evenings for its small beer garden.

Khan, Pariser Str. 20, Charlottenburg. The decor – with one or two minor adjustments – has remained faithful to the bar's origins in the 1960s students' movement.

Kleine Orangerie, Spandauer Damm 20. Bustling café and beer garden across the street from Schloss Charlottenberg. A perfect place to rest up before or after tackling the palace.

Kleine Weltlaterne, Nestorstr. 22, Wilmersdorf. Local artists' hangout, with hardcore regulars – so you might feel left out – but almost the only option in an area quite empty of bars.

Klo, Leibnizstr. 57, Charlottenburg. This one you'll love or hate. A theme bar based on or around things lavatorial (drinks are served in urine sample bottles). If you share the German fascination for anything related to peeing you'll wet yourself laughing; otherwise it's pricey and a bit tacky. Entry DM0.25 (€0.13).

Kronenbourg Café, Pfalzburgerstr. 11, Charlottenburg. Friendly, classy café serving interesting German dishes at affordable prices. Breakfast noon–4pm.

Lentz, Stuttgarter Platz 20, Charlottenburg. Furrow-browed intellectuals and artists on the pick-up. Outdoor seating in summer.

L'Escargot, Brüsseler Str. 39, Wedding. Often described as the only reason to travel to the suburb of Wedding, *L'Escargot* has fabulous and cheap food, imaginatively presented. Many vegetarian options.

Loretta am Wannsee, Kronprinzessinweg 260, Zehlendorf. Popular bar near Wannsee S-Bahn station, with an inviting tree-lined beer garden.

Loretta im Garten, Lietzenburger Str. 89, Charlottenburg. Though angled mainly at the tourist market, this large beer garden can be fun if you're in the right mood.

Luise, Königin-Luise-Str. 40, Zehlendorf. A smaller and more convivial beer garden, just a stone's throw from the Dahlem museums. Usually packed with students from the nearby Free University.

Cafés and bars

Cafés and bars

Nussbaum, Bundesplatz 6, Wilmersdorf. Traditionally minded Berlin pub and beer garden with over a dozen beers on tap and home-made northern German specialities.

Sabine II, Siemenswerder Weg 4, Spandau. This permanently moored yacht on Lake Havel provides the setting for a fun-packed night, since its sequestered location allows revellers to make as much noise as they like. Access by boat also possible. Closed Tues.

Saftladen 2, Wegenerstr. 1, Wilmersdorf. When the booze gets too much, come here, where alcohol-free drinks – some of them quite inventive – are the speciality.

UFA-Café, Viktoriastr. 13, Tempelhof. Amazingly cheap café-bar in the middle of the huge UFA cultural complex.

Wintergarten, Fasanenstr. 23, Charlottenburg. Part of the *Literaturhaus*, an institution given over to poetry readings and other bookish events, the *Wintergarten* has a beautifully renovated interior and a peaceful garden. Moderate prices. Breakfasts from 10am.

Wirtshaus Moorlake, Moorlakenweg 1, Zehlendorf. An easy-going café by the side of the Havel, whose genial beer garden allows you to escape the hordes.

Zur Weissen Maus, Ludwigkirchplatz 12, Charlottenburg. Chic 1920s-style bar with reproductions of Otto Dix and Max Beckmann reflected in the mass of mirrors. Popular with older artists, it has good, if expensive, cocktails. Opens around 10pm.

The eastern suburbs

Café Liebig, Regattastr. 158, Köpenick. Not far from Grünau S-Bahn station, this *Jugendstil* café makes a good starting point for a stroll along the banks of the Langer See.

Eierschale-Zenner, Alt-Treptow 14–17, Treptow. Opel Manta owners limbering up for serious drink-drive sessions do a lot to spoil the ambience of this Spreeside *Gaststätte* after dark. However, it's worth dropping in during the daytime.

Geierwally's, Prenzlauer Promenade 3, Weissensee. Relax on plush sofas and admire the supermarket trolleys welded into the bar in this alternative hangout adjoining the Brotfabrik cinema and theatre.

Marienlust, Am Langen See, Köpenick. A big old *Gartenlokal* overlooking the Langer See, with outdoor seating and decent fish dishes.

Müggelseeklause, Müggelseedamm/Bruno-Wille-Str., Köpenick. A stone's throw from the Müggelsee in Friedrichshagen, and with a bit of old Berlin panache. Art exhibitions are put on here too. Closed Mon.

Müggelseeperle, Am grossen Müggelsee, Köpenick. A good place to interrupt wanderings along the Müggelsee. Outdoor seating.

Müggelturm, In den Müggelbergen, Köpenick. The restaurant in the viewing tower on top of the Müggelberge won't win any prizes for its basic pork and spuds cuisine, but it makes a good target if you're indulging in some city-edge wandering.

Rübezahl, Am grossen Müggelsee, Köpenick. Unreliable food and hideous Alexanderplatz-style architecture, but a good place for a beer looking out over the Müggelsee. Closes at 6pm.

Schmetterlingshorst, Am langen See, Köpenick. Lakeside pork and potatoes with lashings of beer.

Zur Fähre, Müggelseedamm 162, Köpenick. Old-style *Gaststätte* with outdoor seating. Closed Sun.

Gay cafés and bars

The most concentrated area of **gay bars** is between Wittenbergplatz and Nollendorfplatz, south of Kleiststrasse, with Prenzlauer Berg along Schönhauser Allee becoming an eastern gay centre. For more detailed listings, pick up a copy of the guidebook *Berlin von Hinten* (DM22.80/€11.65) or the monthly magazine *Siegessäule* (free), available from most bars, and see also "Gay and lesbian Berlin" in Basics.

Ackerkeller, Ackerstrasse 12 (courtyard), Mitte. Grungy courtyard disco with regular club nights for women and bi's.

Altberliner Bierstuben, Saarbrücker Str. 17, Prenzlauer Berg. A bar with a dual identity: dishing up meat and two veg Berlin specialities to locals during the day, and mutating into a discreet gay bar at night.

Anderes Ufer, Hauptstrasse 157, Schöneberg. Opened at the tail end of the first gay movement heyday in the late 1970s, this classic is still going strong, attracting a mixed gay and lesbian crowd. Regular art and photography exhibitions.

Andreas' Kneipe, Ansbacher Str. 29, Schöneberg. A favourite among Berliners for the last thirty years, and a good place to begin wanderings in the Wittenbergplatz area, especially for the forty-plus set.

Berlin Connection, Martin-Luther-Str. 19, Schöneberg. Modern café-bistro, strewn with palms and mirrors, which attracts a young to late-30s crowd. Second corner bar, and terrace in summer.

Blue Boy Bar, Eisenacher Str. 3, Schöneberg. Tiny, convivial and relaxed bar, far less raucous than many that surround it. Open till 6am.

Burgfrieden, Wichertstr. 69, Prenzlauer Berg. A well-known haunt that's been going since the 1960s, with a 35-plus crowd that takes in everyone from leathermen to transvestites and all points in between. Two bars, one serving beer, the other cocktails.

Café Anal, Muskauer Str. 15, Kreuzberg. Long-established alternative bar in east Kreuzberg and a second home for gay punks. Gets lively after 11pm.

Café am Senefelderplatz, Schönhauser Allee 173, Prenzlauer Berg. Relaxed, long-established East Berlin gay and lesbian hangout with discos every Fri. Various snack dishes, including excellent chips.

Café Amsterdam, Gleimstrasse 24, Prenzlauer Berg. Popular café and bar in emerging Prenzlauer Berg scene. Disco at weekends.

Café Sundström, Mehringdamm 61, Kreuzberg. Small and pleasant café that's low-key and comfortable. The backroom is the current home of the legendary *SchwuZ* club and cultural centre.

Café PositHiv, Alvenslebensstr. 26, Schöneberg. Quiet self-help café run by and for PWAs and men and women who are HIV-positive. Tues–Sun 3pm onwards.

Die Busche, Mühlenstr. 11–12, Friedrichshain. Holdover from the East Berlin gay scene still attracts a fun-loving gay and lesbian crowd with music ranging from ABBA to German *schlager*.

Flipflop, Kulmerstr. 20a. Imaginatively decorated bar/cocktail lounge that attracts a diverse clientele. Popular for its Sunday brunch, served from noon till 4pm.

Hafen, Motzstr. 19, Schöneberg; adjacent to *Tom's Bar* (see below). Longtime popular cruising bar for 20- to 30-year-olds. Always packed, open till late.

Image, Jägerstrasse 67, Mitte. Café off up-market shopping avenue Friedrichstrasse offering cheap breakfast and lunch menus.

Knast, Fuggerstr. 34, Schöneberg. If you're in Berlin for the S&M leather action, look no further. Wicked leather bar in prison-like surroundings: service is from behind a grill and handcuffs line the walls.

Lenz, Eisenacher Str. 3, Schöneberg. Straightforward, likeable *Szene* bar that attracts a good-looking crowd. Specializes in cocktails (125 on its list) and whiskies (80-plus).

Le Moustache, Gartenstr. 4, Mitte. Popular leather bar in the tiled surroundings of an old butcher's shop. Average, but there are few other gay haunts in this part of town. Open from 8pm, though it doesn't usually get going until around 11pm. Closed Mon. Has a pension attached (see p.232).

Pick ab!, Greifenhagener Str. 16, Prenzlauer Berg. As the name suggests, this place is anything but restrained. "Porn videos will be shown", they claim,

Cafés and bars

Cafés and bars

and there's a dark room at the back. Fri & Sat 11pm until dawn or thereabouts.

Schall und Rauch, Gleimstr. 23, Prenzlauer Berg. Tasteful designer elegance in this hip young bar. A place to see and be seen – and eat, thanks to an imaginative and ever-changing menu.

Schoppenstube, Schönhauser Allee 44, Prenzlauer Berg. The best-known gay place in the east. In reality this is two very different bars: a pleasant wine bar upstairs, and a steamy, cruiser's haven downstairs. Knock for entry and if the doorman likes the look of you you're in.

Scheune, Motzstr. 25, Schöneberg. Very popular leather club with regular theme parties for devotees of rubber, uniforms or sheer nakedness. Darkroom, baths and other accoutrements.

Sonderbar, Käthe-Niederkirchner-Str. 34, Prenzlauer Berg. Weekend pre-club rendezvous and chill-out bar, with 55 different cocktails on offer.

Stiller Don, Erich-Weinert-Str. 67, Prenzlauer Berg. An inexpensive gay place that makes an accessible intro to the scene in the former east. More like a slightly intellectual neighbourhood bar with a clientele that runs right across the age spectrum.

Tom's Bar, Motzstr. 19, Schöneberg. Dark, sweaty and wicked cruising bar with a large back room. Possibly Berlin's most popular gay bar, and a great place to finish off an evening.

Twilight Zone, Welserstr. 24, corner with Fuggerstr., Schöneberg. Candlelit basement bar underneath *Connection* disco. On Wed, Thurs and Sun it's leather, rubber or uniforms only. Fairly macho/heavy. Closed Mon & Tues.

Women's cafés and bars

Many of Berlin's **women-only** bars have a strong lesbian following, though straight women are welcome at all of them.

Begine, Potsdamer Str. 139, Schöneberg (women only). Stylishly decorated bar-bistro/gallery with inexpensive food. Hosts films, readings and concerts. See also "Women's Berlin" in Basics.

Café Seidenfaden, Dircksenstr. 47, Mitte. Alcohol-free café, open only until 9pm.

Die Zwei, Am Wasserturm, Spandauer Damm 168, Charlottenburg. An exuberantly tacky and determinedly (nonexclusive) lesbian bar, popular particularly among older women, with music from Marlene via Iron Butterfly to Madonna.

Frauen und Kindercafé, in the EWA e.V Frauenzentrum, Prenzlauer Allee 6, Prenzlauer Berg. An airy café-gallery with a children's play area. Offers advice, discussion and events.

Offenbar, Schreinerstr. 5, Friedrichshain. Lesbian hangout in alternative Friedrichshain.

Pour Elle, Kalckreuthstr. 10, Schöneberg. Intimate disco-bar frequented by the more conservative sort of (generally older) lesbian. Pricey. Closed Mon; women only except Wed.

Roses, Oranienstr. 187, Kreuzberg. Gay bar but with a strong lesbian presence. Currently one of the locales of choice.

Schoko-Café, Mariannenstr. 6, on Heinrichplatz, Kreuzberg. Alternative place in a converted warehouse housing a health-conscious café and offering information on the many activities organized by the Schokofabrik collective. Cliquey atmosphere that's a little intimidating if you're new to the place. The women-only Turkish baths next door are open from September to the end of May (see "Women's Berlin" in Basics). Closed Sat.

SO 36, Oranienstr. 190, Kreuzberg. Outrageous gay disco with a rotating programme of parties and events, often for lesbians. Every third Friday in the month sees the Jane Bond Party for "women, lesbians, drag queens and other feminimities".

Zufall, Pfalzburger Str. 10, Wilmersdorf. Nonexclusive bar-cum-disco, a focal point for Berlin's showier characters.

Hausbrauereien

In the last decade or so Germany has seen a revival of **Hausbrauereien** – small-scale breweries and restaurants brewing and serving their own beer.

These house beers are generally top quality, and often there's a bit of a show too: huge polished copper pots on display filled with suds, lots of serpentine piping, and finally, at the end of the mysterious, magical process, a tap flowing with beer.

Alter Fritz, Brauhaus Johann Albrecht, Karolinenstr. 12, Reinickendorf. One of the oldest pubs in the city, set in a huge and leafy beer garden: a perfect destination for a summer's day journey out of the city.

Aschinger, Kurfürstendamm 26. Old-fashioned underground *Bierkeller*. Catering for tourists, but nonetheless pleasant enough to fill up on unusual beers and traditional German food.

Brauhaus Georgbräu, Spreeufer 4, Mitte. A touristy locale, but popular among locals for its excellent beer and traditional German food.

Brau Haus in Spandau, Neuendorfer Str. 1, Spandau, ☎353 9070. See *"Accommodation"*, p.227.

Lemke, Dircksenstr., S-Bahn arch 143 by Hackescher Markt, Mitte. Always three varieties of the house beer on tap, *Export*, *Bock* and *Festbier*, and, thankfully, a complete lack of kitsch Deutsch decor. Serves, incongruously, Japanese food.

Leopold's Brauhaus, Karl-Liebknecht-Str. 13, Mitte. All the trappings of a Bavarian beer hall, including the excellent beers, re-created in the heart of Berlin.

Luisenbräu, Luisenplatz 1, Charlottenburg. Large bar that brews its own beer (you can see it happening), within sight of Schloss Charlottenburg. Popular with locals and almost a German cliché for its muscular bar staff carrying large numbers of frothing mugs. Beer is served in 0.2 litre glasses "so that it's always fresh".

Rixdörfer Bräuhaus, Glasower Str. 27, Neukölln. Actually part of a brewery, this bar is crammed full of knick-knacks and beer-related paraphernalia, and is Berlin's closest relative to the British pub.

Cafés and bars

Chapter 14

Clubs and live venues

Nothing brought you so much face to face with the pathological distortion of Germany's post-war mentality as the weird nightlife of Berlin. Its grotesqueness destroyed for many of us younger men all the illusions about sex that some people retain throughout their whole lives. One year in Berlin revealed more of the perversions in which man's lower nature can indulge than a normal life-time spent elsewhere.

R. Landauer, describing Weimar Berlin in *Seven.*

Many of the venues listed below are marked on the maps on pp.264–265 and p.267.

Since the time of the Weimar Republic, and even through the lean postwar years, Berlin has had a reputation for having some of the best – and steami-est – nightlife in Europe, an image fuelled by the cartoon-like drawings of George Grosz and films like *Cabaret.* Today the big draw is the **clubs** that have grown up out of the city's techno scene. In a remarkably short space of time these places, many housed in abandoned buildings on or around the former no-go area of the East–West border strip, have spawned a scene that ranks among the most exciting in Europe.

As well as this manic dance music scene, Berlin has a wide range of more traditional clubs and discos, ranging from slick hangouts for the trendy to raucous punky dives.

As far as **live music** goes, there's much of appeal here: venues cover a breadth of tastes and are rarely expen-sive. As ever, it's the tension the city seems to generate that gives the nightlife its colour.

There are two particularly notable and unusual live music venues in the

city: the *Waldbühne* is a large outdoor amphitheatre on the Hollywood Bowl model, just west of the Olympic Stadium. It presents everything from opera to movies to rock – unbeatable in summer. The *Tempodrom,* a tent in Friedrichshain at the Ostbahnhof, set to move to a permanent building near Potsdamer Platz in 2001, hosts concerts and is the venue for the *Heimatklänge* world music festival in summer.

Clubs and discos

Berlin's clubs and discos are smaller, cheaper and less exclusive than their counterparts in London or New York – and fewer in number. You don't need much nous to work out that the places along the Ku'damm are tourist rip-offs: the real all-night sweats take place in the newer **dance-music clubs** that have opened up, mainly in the former East Berlin, where glitz is out and raving is in. For the slightly older crowd, Schöneberg and Kreuzberg tend to be where it's happening. Don't bother turn-ing up until midnight at the earliest, since few places get going much before

278

LISTINGS: CHAPTER 14

then. Admission is often free – when you do pay, it shouldn't be much more than DM15 (€7.70). Some of the ravey places have strict door policies, but if you look the part you'll probably get in. Like most cities, Berlin's turnover in nightspots is rapid: expect the following listings to have changed at least slightly by the time you arrive – this applies particularly to the newer places on the east side of town. Some of the longer established venues (many of these are former Socialist Youth organization clubhouses) in the east also put on **live gigs**.

For the latest information on Berlin nightlife happenings, check the listings magazines *Tip* (*www.tip-berlin.de*) and *Zitty* (*www.zitty.de*), available at any newsstand, and look out for posters and flyers. Two free leaflets, *Flyer* (*www.flyer.de*) and *guide*, list parties and clubs. Both can be picked up in record shops, clubs and *Szene* bars and cafés.

Abraxas, Kantstr. 134, Charlottenburg ☎3 12 94 93. Hot and sweaty dance floor, specializing in salsa and Latin American sounds. Not pretentious, just lots of fun. Tues–Sun 10pm–5am. Free during the week, DM10 (€5.10) Fri & Sat.

Akba Lounge, Sredzkistr. 64, Prenzlauer Berg ☎4 41 14 63. Anything from soul to German pop gets played in this tight but friendly club. Thurs–Sat from 11pm; DM10 (€5.10).

Ankerklause, Kottbusser Damm/Maybachufer, Kreuzberg ☎6 93 56 49. A little café, perched by the Landwehr canal, turns into a funk and soul club by night. Very trendy and very crowded. From 11pm; DM5 (€2.50).

Bastard, Kastanienallee 7–9, Prenzlauer Berg ☎44 04 96 69. Small club and live-music venue nestled in the *Prater* beer garden and theatre complex. Caters to the intelligent electronica and post-rock crowd.

Big Eden, Kurfürstendamm 202, Charlottenburg ☎8 82 61 20. Enormous tourist-trap disco, also popular with teenagers – check out the dance floor first on the video monitors outside. It's

free for women, but drinks are expensive. Sat 7pm–7am, Sun–Fri 7pm–4am.

Blue Note, Courbièrestr. 13, Schöneberg ☎2 18 72 48. Eclectic mix of rock, Latin and (chiefly) jazz sounds. Small dance floor, best after midnight. Tues–Sun 10pm–5am; DM6 (€3.10) on Fri & Sat, otherwise free.

bronx, Wiener Str. 34, Kreuzberg ☎6 11 84 45. All the 1970s rock'n'roll standards in a long-running venue for fans of the era. Nightly from 10pm; DM5 (€2.50).

Casino, Saarbrücker Str./Prenzlauer Allee, Prenzlauer Berg. Housed on grounds of a former baked-goods factory, *Casino* is the rave joint *du jour*, with star DJs like Paul Van Dyk packing them in.

Connection, Fuggerstr. 83, Schöneberg ☎2 18 14 32. Very popular gay disco, attracting a largely leather-clad crowd. Fri & Sat from 10pm.

Delicious Doughnuts Research, Rosenthaler Str. 9, Mitte ☎2 83 30 21. Beautiful party people grooving to acid jazz, trip-hop and funk beats. Excellent cocktails.

Die Insel, Alt-Treptow 6, Treptow ☎5 34 88 51; *www.blinx.de/insel*. Reliable venue for thrash/punk gigs and club nights, with occasional outdoor raves on the large terrace in summer. On a Spree island that's part of Treptower Park. Fri & Sat from 10pm.

Dolmen Club, Schönhauser Allee 6–7, Mitte ☎4 40 60 26. Despite the strange Druid-inspired interior, this club in the basement of *Quinn's Irish Pub* is a popular rendezvous for hip-hop fans. Fri & Sat from 11pm.

Duncker, Dunckerstr. 64, Prenzlauer Berg ☎4 45 95 09. Indie, industrial and unashamedly Goth sounds. Open most nights after 10pm.

El Barrio, Potsdamer Str. 84, Tiergarten ☎2 62 18 53. An irresistible salsa/lambada disco precedes weekend bands; see also p.282.

Far Out, Kurfürstendamm 156, Wilmersdorf (near Lehniner Platz) ☎32 00 07 23. Formerly a Bhagwan disco, now a friendly nightspot for a mix of off-

Clubs and
live venues

Clubs and live venues

beat conservatives and tourists. Gets crowded. Tues–Thurs 10pm–3am, Fri & Sat 10pm–6am; DM6 (€3.10).

Fou-Na-Na, Bachstr. S-Bahn arch 475, Tiergarten ☎3 91 24 42. Caribbean and African sounds underneath the arches of the S-Bahn lines. Tues–Sun from 11pm; DM10 (€5.10).

Golgotha, in the Viktoriapark, Kreuzberg ☎7 85 24 53. Kreuzberg's popular hillside café (see p.269) hosts a daily alfresco disco from 10pm April–Sept; good fun on warm evenings.

Icon, Cantianstr. 15, Prenzlauer Berg. Big and trendy techno and house club.

Knaack-Club, Greifswalder Str. 224, Prenzlauer Berg ☎4 42 70 60; *www.knaack-berlin.de*. Rock in the cellar and dance on the first floor of a big old club building in a Prenzlauer Berg courtyard, drawing a young crowd. Nightly from 10pm; DM3–10 (€1.50–5.10).

Kurvenstar, Kleine Präsidentenstr. 3, Mitte ☎28 59 97 10; *www.kurvenstar.de*. Beautifully decorated retro Seventies club with a bar up front and dance floor in the back. Caters now to a young, not very gregarious hip-hop crowd on Wed & Sat, although other nights feature drum 'n' bass or trip-hop.

Lime Club, Dircksenstr. 105, Mitte ☎2 81 45 85. In an archway under the elevated U-Bahn tracks, Goths come out at night and shake their teased manes to Depeche Mode, the Cure and the like. Fri–Sun from 11pm; DM10–20 (€5.10–10.25).

Madow, Pariser Str. 23, Charlottenburg ☎8 83 92 60. Big unpretentious disco, for a no-nonsense boogie in a friendly atmosphere. Wed–Sun from 10pm; DM10 (€5.10).

Maria am Ostbahnhof, Str. der Pariser Kommune 8–10, Friedrichshain ☎29 00 61 98; *www.klubradio.de*. Club in new *Szene* district Friedrichshain with sounds at the avant garde end of the electronica and rock spectrum. Also a venue for live music. Thurs–Sat from 11pm.

Metropol, Nollendorfplatz 5, Schöneberg ☎2 16 41 22. Berlin's largest disco,

housed in a marvellous Art Deco building but otherwise rather ordinary. Houses fetish *Kit Kat Club* (*www.kitkatclub.de*) on Thurs & Sun.

Ostgut, Mühlenstr. 26–30 (entrance Rummelsburger Platz), Friedrichshain ☎29 00 05 97; *www.klubradio.de*. Generous space for raves, often featuring big name DJs such as Westbam. Also home of *Lab.oratory* gay fetish evenings.

Oxymoron, 40–41 Rosenthaler Str. (in the Hackesche Höfe), Mitte ☎28 39 18 85. House, trip-hop and disco in a big space in the Art Deco Hackesche Höfe retail complex. An Italian restaurant by day. Fri–Sun 10pm–4am.

Privatclub, Pücklerstr. 34 (in the basement of Weltrestaurant Markthalle), Kreuzberg ☎6 11 30 02. Notable for weekend theme parties ranging from 1970s disco trash and new wave to blaxploitation funk, often guest-DJed by local celebrities such as splatter-flick director Jörg Buttgereit.

Salsa, Wielandstr. 13, Charlottenburg ☎3 24 16 42. Exuberant Latin American disco with floor shows and dance lessons thrown in. DM6–12 (€3.10–6.15).

Schleusenkrug, Müller-Breslau Strasse/Landwehrkanal, Tiergarten ☎3 13 99 09. An old-fashioned pub recently transformed into a hip bar and café with techno, house and lounge music played Fri & Sat from 10pm. DM5–15 (€2.50–7.70).

Schwuz, Mehrindamm 61, Kreuzberg ☎69 50 78 89. Dance club well loved by all stripes of the gay community. Always crowded and convivial. Fri & Sat from 11pm.

Soda, Knaackstr. 97, Prenzlauer Berg ☎44 05 87 07. Recently opened club in the newly renovated *Kulturbrauerei* cultural centre located on the grounds of a former brewery. Check out the GDR rock disco Fridays at the neighbouring *Alte Kantine*.

Sophienclub, Sophienstr. 6, Mitte ☎2 82 45 52. This crowded central club puts on different nights for different tastes: taking in soul, funk, house and indie. Nightly from 9pm; DM5 (€2.55), weekends DM10 (€5.10).

S036, Oranienstr. 190, Kreuzberg ☎6 15 26 01. Offers everything from gay-oriented house nights, Turkish and oriental pop to the odd punk concert.

Sternradio, Alexanderplatz 5, Mitte; *www.sternradio-berlin.de*. All-in-one club-bistro-lounge package newly opened on the inhospitable strip between the TV Tower and the Rotes Rathaus. Music runs the full spectrum of electronic dance music, house, techno, and drum 'n' bass, often with big name guest DJs and local heroes such as Clé and Mitja in residency.

Tresor/Globus, Leipziger Str. 126a, Mitte ☎2 29 06 11; *www.tresorberlin.de*; *www.klubradio.de*. A key player in the burgeoning of Berlin's dance music scene since 1990, though the regulars claim that it's not as good as it used to be. Nevertheless trouser-shaking techno in the steamy basement and slightly mellower house and hip-hop beats upstairs still attract clubbers from all over Europe. Wed & weekends 11pm until dawn.

WMF, Ziegelstr. 22, Mitte; *www.wmf-club.de*; *www.klubradio.de*. Legendary club now at its fifth location, still worth checking out if you're into any flavour of house.

90° ("Neunzig Grad"), Dennewitzstr. 37, Kreuzberg ☎2 62 89 84. At the far eastern end of Kurfürstenstrasse, once one of the former West's better clubs. Now it caters to Berlin's self-styled jet set and rich kids jumping the club culture train.

Live music

The way to find out exactly **what's on** and where is by checking the listings magazines *Tip*, *Zitty*, *Prinz* and *Berlin Programm*, or the innumerable fly posters about town.

At the **major venues** you can expect to find international supergroups playing, and you will need to book well in advance for anything even vaguely pop-

ular. Invariably you can't buy tickets from the places themselves, so you'll need to go to one of the ticket offices listed on p.285.

It's also worth remembering that, in addition to the places below, many bars and cafés put on live music.

Major venues

Arena, Eichenstr. 4, Treptow ☎5 33 73 33; *www.arena-berlin.de*. Located almost in the middle of nowhere, this medium-sized hall usually offers rappers, teenie groups and other popular bands for a young audience. Adjacent *Glashaus* hosts regular Sunday morning house breakfasts and hip-hop jams.

ICC Berlin, Messedamm 26, Charlottenburg ☎3 03 81. Vast, soulless hall for trade fairs that often hosts gigs.

Parkbühne Wuhlheide, Wuhlheide Park, Eichgestell, Köpenick. Smaller than the *Waldbühne* (see below), this open-air stage tucked away in the forest has hosted REM and Iggy Pop and is a favourite for summertime festivals.

Velodrom, Paul-Heyse-Str. 29, Prenzlauer Berg ☎44 30 44 30. Home of mega sports events such as the six-day bicycle race, this is also the place to see the likes of Britney Spears or Janet Jackson.

Waldbühne, Glockenturmstr./Passenheimer Str., Charlottenburg ☎3 04 06 76. Open-air spot in a natural amphitheatre near the Olympic Stadium that features movies, bands, classical concerts, and other entertainments. Great fun on summer evenings, but arrive early as it often gets crowded.

Smaller venues

Acud, Veteranenstr. 21, Mitte ☎44 35 94 97; *www.acud.de*. Rock and blues are the mainstay of this no-frills venue, with hip-hop and drum 'n' bass thrown in for good measure. There's also a gallery and movie theatre tucked inside.

A-Trane, Bleibtreustr./Pestalozzistr., Charlottenburg ☎3 13 25 50. Up-and-

Clubs and live venues

Clubs and live venues

coming and well-known jazz artists in a comfortable, intimate setting. Weekends from 10pm; DM15 (€7.70).

Badenscher Hof, Badensche Str. 29, Wilmersdorf ☎8 61 00 80. Lively café-restaurant that draws in the Schöneberg crowd for its frequent jazz concerts, the best of which are at weekends.

b-flat, Rosenthaler Str. 13, Mitte ☎2 80 63 49. Small jazz club with live groups at weekends and a serious audience – don't talk during sets. From 10pm. Entry varies.

ColumbiaFritz, Columbiadamm 9–11, Tempelhof ☎69 81 28 28. Refuge of the owners of the *Loft* when they had to flee the *Metropol*, *ColumbiaFritz* still is heavily alternarock oriented, with the *Fritz* youth radio station throwing in hip-hop and drum 'n' bass club nights.

Columbiahalle, Columbiadamm 13–21, Tempelhof ☎6 98 09 80. Right across the street from the Tempelhof airport, this venue hosts crowd-pleasing international acts.

Eierschale Dahlem, Podbielskiallee 50, Zehlendorf ☎8 32 70 97. Lively venue with large beer garden in summer. Always packed towards the end of the week. Music most nights, often appalling but with free disco before and after the bands. Free.

Eierschale Zenner, Alt-Treptow 14–17, Alt-Treptow ☎5 33 73 70. A large and popular beer garden by the shore of the Spree river, with oldies and other summery music.

El Barrio, Potsdamer Str. 84, Tiergarten ☎2 62 18 53. Berlin's best venue for salsa and South American sounds. Also has a great disco. DM10 (€5.10) upwards.

Flöz, Nassauische Str. 37, Wilmersdorf ☎8 61 10 00. Basement club that's the meeting point for Berlin's jazz musicians and a testing ground for the city's new bands. Also offers occasional salsa and cabaret. Can be wild.

Haus der Kulturen der Welt, John-Foster-Dulles-Allee 10, Tiergarten ☎39 78 71 75; www.hkw.de. The city's number one

venue for world music. Always worth checking out.

Hochschule der Künste, Hardenbergstr. 33, Charlottenburg ☎3 13 70 07. Part of Berlin's art school, and a venue for bands, media performances and dance troupes.

Knaack, Greifswalderstr. 224, Prenzlauer Berg ☎4 42 70 60; www.knaack-berlin .de. Mostly local rock bands, plus the odd visiting post-punk legend.

Kesselhaus@Kulturbrauerei, Knaackstr. 97, Prenzlauer Berg ☎4 41 92 69. Sharing space in a nineteenth-century brewery with an arts and cultural centre, this club offers local and mid-level bands.

Podewil, Klosterstr. 68–70, Mitte ☎24 74 96; www.podewil.bkv.org. Avant jazz, world music and occasional classical concerts. Less lively than some other venues but dedicated to the music.

Pfefferberg, Schönhauser Allee 176, Prenzlauer Berg ☎44 38 31 10. Another converted East Berlin industrial space offering world-music-themed concerts and club nights. Grooving to non-European sounds in the summer beer garden whisks you away from hectic Berlin, at least mentally.

Quasimodo, Kantstr. 12a, Charlottenburg ☎3 12 80 86. Berlin's best jazz spot, with nightly programmes starting at 10pm. A high-quality mix of international, usually American, stars and up-and-coming names. Small, with a good atmosphere. Often free on weekdays.

Saalbau Neukölln, Karl-Marx-Str. 141, Neukölln ☎68 09 37 79. Part of Neukölln's attempt to up its cultural offerings. Live music – both classical and contemporary – literary and poetry recitals, and dance. Interesting location in a 1930s ballroom, with a good café, *Rix*, attached.

Tacheles, Oranienburger Str. 53–56, Mitte ☎2 81 61 19; www.tacheles.de. Concerts from around 10pm. The performers are likely to be pretty eclectic, ranging from guitar bands to industrial noise merchants.

Tempodrom, Str. der Pariser Kommune 8, Friedrichshain; *www.tempodrom-berlin.de*. Tent venue hosting mid-level rock and world music acts. Hosts a free music festival each summer.

Tränenpalast, Reichstagsufer 17, Mitte ☎ 2 38 62 11. A former waiting room at the border between East and West is now a medium-sized hall featuring rock, soul and jazz.

Clubs and live venues

Chapter 15

The arts

When Berlin was a divided city, the West German government poured in subsidies for all kinds of **art**: the annual sum given to the western half of the city by the government (DM550 million) was over half the federal budget for culture for the entire United States. Now, in the mood of glum post-unification realism, things are very different: the plugs have been pulled on almost all subsidies, and orchestras and theatres are being forced to look elsewhere for funding; don't be surprised if some of the companies in these listings are no more by the time you reach the city.

Which is not to say that all is black in Berlin: there are high-quality dance groups performing everything from classical ballet to contemporary experimental works, and scores of mainstream and art-house cinemas. The art gallery scene is thriving, and the city still has one of the world's finest **symphony orchestras**. Unification has left it with a "doubling" of facilities, three magnificent opera houses and one of the liveliest arts scenes of any European city. Berlin's reputation as a leader of the avant-garde is reflected in the number of small, often experimental theatre groups working here. The scene is active, though it's worth remembering that many **theatre companies** take a break in July and August.

Ticket agencies and offices

Ticket offices or **Theaterkassen** are usually the easiest (and occasionally

the only) way of buying tickets for all major music, theatre and dance events in both western and eastern Berlin. Open during working hours (or longer), they charge a hefty commission (up to 17 percent) on the ticket price. The first place to try, especially for fringe-type theatre, less popular classical concerts and dance, is *Hekticket* (see box below for details), which sells half-price tickets, and charges only DM2 (€1) commission on tickets for the same day's performance.

Classical music

For years classical music in Berlin meant one man and one orchestra: Herbert von Karajan and the Berlin Philharmonic. Since his death in 1989, the **Philharmonie**, under conductor Claudio Abbado, has had its former supremacy questioned by the rise of the excellent **Deutsches Sinfonie Orchester** under Vladimir Ashkenazy. And, as elsewhere in the arts, cutbacks in state and senate funding have brought about a more cautious and conservative atmosphere in the classical music world.

The Philharmonie and Deutsche Sinfonie Orchester are by no means the only options. Many smaller orchestras play at sites in and around the city, and museums and historic buildings often host chamber concerts and recitals. It's possible to pick up inexpensive tickets for many performances from *Hekticket* (see above). As ever, see *Zitty* and *Tip* for full and up-to-date listings.

The arts

TICKET OFFICES

Most places listed below take only EC Cards or cash. We've indicated with an asterisk those that also accept MC, Visa and Amex. Note that the box offices themselves all take plastic.

Ars Scribendi
Alte Potsdamer Str. 8, Tiergarten
☎ 25 29 69 87.

Berlin Ticket*
Potsdamer Str. 96, Schöneberg
☎ 23 08 82 30.

Box office
Nollendorfplatz 7, Schöneberg
☎ 2 15 54 63.

Hektiket
Rathausstr. 1, Mitte ☎ 24 31 24 31.

KaDeWe
Tauentzienstr. 21, Schöneberg
☎ 2 17 77 54.

Kant-Kasse
Krumme Str. 55, Charlottenburg
☎ 3 13 45 54.

Ko Ka 36
Oranienstr. 29, Kreuzberg ☎ 6 15 88 18;
and Kollwitzstr. 66, Prenzlauer Berg

☎ 44 05 26 66. Also Internet booking at
www.icf.de/koka36

Karstadt
Hermannplatz, Neukölln ☎ 6 87 40 00.

Telecard*
Birchbuschstr. 14, Steglitz ☎ 8 34 40 73.

Theaterkasse Centrum
Meinekestr. 25, Charlottenburg
☎ 8 82 76 11.
Credit cards accepted only if bookng
from out of town

Ticket Hotline*
☎ 8 09 90 90.
Credit card bookings only.

Wertheim
Kurfürstendamm 231, Charlottenburg
☎ 8 82 25 00.

Wildbad-Kiosk
Rankestr. 1, Charlottenburg
☎ 8 81 45 07.

Orchestras and venues

Berlin Sinfonie Orchester. Founded in 1952 and based in the *Konzerthaus* (see below), this used to be East Berlin's main symphony orchestra, and it maintains its fine reputation today, though it does not compare to the Philharmonic. Currently under the directorship of Michael Schønvandt, who was due to be replaced in 2001 by Eliahu Inbal.

Deutsche Oper Berlin, Bismarckstr. 35, Charlottenburg; box office ☎ 3 43 84 01 (Mon–Sat 11am–6pm); *www.deutsche-oper.berlin.de*. Formerly West Berlin's premier opera house, built in 1961 after the Wall cut access to the Staatsoper. Once the city's most prestigious venue in terms of visiting performers, it now shares that honour with its eastern cousin. This is the place to hear Wagner and Strauss. Tickets DM20–200 (€10.25–102.50).

Deutsche Sinfonie Orchester. Shares the *Konzerthaus* (see below) with the Berlin Sinfonie Orchester. Under conductor Vladimir Ashkenazy, has stolen much of the Berlin Philharmonie's limelight over the last few years. As of 2001 the baton passes to Kent Nagano.

Staatsoper, Unter den Linden 5–7, Mitte; box office ☎ 20 35 45 55 (Mon–Sat 10am–8pm, Sun 2–8pm); *www.staatsoper/berlin.org*. The city's oldest and grandest music venue, built for Frederick the Great in 1742 to a design by Knobelsdorff. While little remains from that time (the building was bombed out in 1941, rebuilt, destroyed again in 1945 and rebuilt to the current specifications in 1955), the interior is all you'd expect a grand opera house to be.

During the GDR years, political isolation meant that performers didn't match the glamour of the venue. The appoint-

The arts

ment of Daniel Barenboim in 1992 as musical director was an attempt to bring the Staatsoper to the forefront of the international opera scene and it certainly seems to be working. Chamber music performances take place in the Apollo Saal and tickets for most operas are around DM13–120 (€6.65–61.40). Be warned that the cheapest seats have only a partial view.

Komische Oper, Behrenstr. 55–57, Mitte; box office at Unter den Linden 41, Mitte ☎ 20 26 03 60 (Mon–Sat 11am–7pm, Sun 1pm to 1hr 30min before performance); *www.komischeoper.line.de*. Less traditional than the *Staatsoper*, but a reliable venue for well-staged operatic productions, under the direction of Harry Kupfer. Expert cutting-edge interpretation of modern works alongside the usual fare – and tickets at half the price of the Deutsche Oper.

Konzerthaus Berlin (Schauspielhaus), Gendarmenmarkt, Mitte; box office ☎ 2 03 09 21 01 (Mon–Sat noon–8pm, Sun and hols noon–4pm); *www.konzerthaus .de*. A super venue, not only for performances by resident Deutsche Sinfonie and Berlin Sinfonie orchestras, but also the Rundfunk Sinfonieorchester Berlin and other visiting musicians, orchestras and ensembles. Two concert spaces occupy the Schinkel-designed building: the Grosser Konzertsaal for orchestras and the Kammermusiksaal (not to be confused with that of the same name in the Philharmonie) for smaller groups and chamber orchestras. Look out for performances on the Konzerthaus's famed organ.

Meistersaal, Köthener Str. 38, Kreuzberg ☎ 2 64 95 30. A worthwhile alternative for those who can't afford the nearby Philharmonie's Kammermusiksaal. The chamber groups and soloists appearing here are often first rate, as are acoustics. Tickets DM10–35 (€5.10–17.90).

Philharmonie, Matthäikirchstr. 1, Tiergarten; box office ☎ 2 61 43 83 (Mon–Fri 3.30–6pm, Sat & Sun 11am–2pm); *www.berlin.philharmonic.com*. Home to

the world-famous Berlin Philharmonic, Hans Scharoun's indescribably ugly building is acoustically near-perfect, and while you'll have to be near-loaded to enjoy it, it's definitely worth it. Though crowds are thinning under Claudio Abbado, expect a surge when Simon Rattle takes over in 2002.

The Philharmonie also contains the smaller **Kammermusiksaal** for more intimate performances, and your best chance of getting a ticket is when guest orchestras are playing. Prices range from DM25 to DM120 (€12.80–61.40); some half-price tickets for students available 30min before performances.

Rundfunk Sinfonieorchester Berlin. After the Philharmonic, the second oldest orchestra in Berlin and a little more daring than its older sister. The orchestra appears at both the Philharmonie and the Konzerthaus and director Fafael Frübeck de Burgos often lends his baton to guest conductor Michael Jurowski.

Theatre

Sad to say, the mainstream **civic and private theatres** in Berlin are, on the whole, dull, unadventurous, and expensive – though it's often possible to cut costs by buying student standby tickets – and in recent years, many professional people have left the birthplace of experimental theatre and returned to Munich and the lure of the film business.

However, Berlin's reputation as Germany's **Theaterstadt** still holds firm for the thousands of eager young Germans who flock to the city every year, rent a space, and stage their work. The city is still a major venue for **experimental work**, and if your German is up to it, a number of groups are worth the ticket price; check under "Off-Theater" in *Tip* or *Zitty* for up-to-the-minute listings. Groups that have the word *Freie* in their name are not dependent on city or state subsidies, which often impose creative constraints on a group's output.

Tickets can be bought for almost all theatre performances other than *Freie* theatre at the ticket offices listed in the box on p.285; costs are between DM15 and DM80 (€7.70–41).

You'll find little in English at the mainstream theatres, but you may have more luck with the small, roving theatre groups.

Civic and private theatres

Berliner Ensemble, Bertold Brecht Platz 1, Mitte ☎2 82 31 60; *www.berliner-ensemble.de*. Recently privatized, Brecht's old theatre now seems a little adrift, performing pieces without a strong sense of artistic direction. Brecht still forms the staple fare here, though thankfully the productions are a little livelier than in GDR days. There are also occasional experimental productions on the *Probebühne* (rehearsal stage).

Deutsches Theater, Schumannstr. 13a, Mitte ☎28 44 12 21; *www.deutsches-theater.berlin.net*. Good, solid productions taking in everything from Schiller to Mamet make this one of Berlin's best theatres. Invariably sold out. Also includes a second theatre, the Kammerspiele des Deutschen Theaters, and Die Baracke, an experimental stage.

Hebbel Theater, Stresemannstr. 29, Kreuzberg ☎25 90 04 27; *www.hebbel-theatre.de*. Hosts short runs of European and American theatre and dance. Often interesting.

Maxim-Gorki-Theater, Am Festungsgraben 2, Mitte ☎20 22 11 15. Consistently good productions of modern works like Tabori's *Mein Kampf* and Schaffer's *Amadeus*. More experimental works are staged on the *Studiobühne* (studio stage).

Prater der Volksbuehne, Kastanienallee 7–9, Prenzlauer Berg ☎4 48 58 89. Second stage of the Volksbuehne (see below). Performance, experimental works and modern adaptations of classics.

Renaissance Theater, Knesebeckstr. 100, Charlottenburg ☎3 12 42 02. Contemporary pieces of theatre from Ayckbourn to Reza, readings and musical revues.

Schaubühne am Lehniner Platz, Kurfürstendamm 153, Wilmersdorf ☎89

00 23; *www.schaubuehne.de*. State-of-the-art theatre that hosts performances of the classics and some experimental pieces. The new directorship that came in in 2000 promises to bring an infusion of young energy – expect more of an accent on dance. Its high reputation means booking ahead is advisable.

Schlosspark Theater, Schlossstr. 48, Charlottenburg ☎7 93 15 15; *www.schlosspark.de*. Interesting, if mainstream, theatre with large local following.

Theater des Westens, Kantstr. 12, Charlottenburg ☎8 82 28 88; *www.theater-des-westens.de*. Musicals and light opera, the occasional Broadway-style show, sometimes in English. Housed in a beautiful *fin-de-siècle* building. Often sold out.

Volksbühne, Rosa-Luxemburg-Platz, Mitte ☎2 47 67 72. Under director Frank Castorf, this has become one of Berlin's most adventurous and interesting theatres. Castorf has gone all out to bring in young audiences with the result that performances are often highly provocative – nudity and throwing things at the audience crop up fairly regularly and there's a statistically high chance of witnessing a partial audience walkout.

Experimental and free theatre

Ballhaus Naunynstrasse, Naunynstr. 27, Kreuzberg ☎25 88 66 44. Renovated former ballroom in the heart of Kreuzberg. Repertoire of events includes mixed-media performances, dance and fringe theatre.

BAT (Studiotheater der Hochschule für Schauspielkunst), Belforter Str. 15, Prenzlauer Berg ☎4 42 79 96. Originally a "workers' and students' theatre", founded in 1975, this one can usually be relied on to come up with challenging experimental offerings, including drama student graduation projects. A meeting point for everyone interested in theatre.

Freunde der Italienischen Oper, Fidicinstr. 40, Kreuzberg ☎6 91 12 11. Tiny courtyard theatre specializing in fringe productions performed in English.

The arts

The arts

Neuköllner Oper, Karl-Marx-Str. 131, Neukölln ☎68 89 07 77. Alternative take on chamber opera and musical theatre.

Out to Lunch Theatre Group ☎8 91 37 25. Fringe theatre group formed by American and English actors, who perform a mixed bag of plays. Phone for venues.

Schaubude, Greifswalder Str. 81–84, Prenzlauer Berg ☎4 23 43 14. Former GDR puppet theatre now presenting shows for adults and children – from *Hansel and Gretel* to *Faust* and performances on atomic physics.

Schiller-Theater-Werkstatt, Bismarckstr. 110, Charlottenburg ☎3 12 65 05. The Schiller Theatre no longer exists as a serious theatre venue, but their experimental group lives on.

Stükke, Palisadenstr. 48, Friedrichshain ☎71 58 11 43. International selection of contemporary theatre and performance works.

Theater 89, Torstr. 216, Mitte ☎2 82 46 56. A small venue putting on modern works in a simple and unaffected style.

Theater Am Halleschen Ufer, Hallesches Ufer 32, Kreuzberg ☎2 51 06 55. Venue for a variety of theatre, performance and dance productions, sometimes in English. Puts up the large-scale shows of Freunde der Italienischen Oper and Tanzfabrik (see below).

Dance and cabaret

Though there are few **dance groups** in the city, those that exist are of a high quality: you can expect to see plenty of original, oddball and unusual performances. Apart from those regular venues listed below, expect dance performances to pop up at *Podewil* (see "*Clubs and live venues*", p.282), as well as at various theatres such as Balhaus Nauenystrasse, UFA-Fabrik, Volksbühne and especially the Schaubühne (see previous page).

In the 1920s and 1930s, Berlin had a rich and intense **cabaret scene**: hundreds of small clubs presented acts that were often deeply satirical and political. When the Nazis came to power these quickly disappeared, to be replaced by anodyne entertainments in line with Party views. Sadly, the cabaret scene has never recovered: most of what's on show today is either semi-clad titillation for tourists or that most German of predilections, the drag show. However, a few places are worth trying, notably the **Chamäleon Variete**, which plays host to some very eclectic acts. Check out the *Mitternachtshow* ("Midnight Show") on Friday and Saturday. Be warned that most cabaret venues make their money by charging very high prices at the bar; entrance is usually around DM30 (€15.35).

Dance

Deutsche Oper Berlin, see "Orchestras and venues". Classical ballet and opera and, to a lesser extent, contemporary work. Mainstream programme lacking in innovation.

Die Etage, Hasenheide 54, Kreuzberg ☎6 91 20 95. Contemporary dance and mime; also runs dance classes.

Hebbel Theater, see "Civic and private theatres". Featuring *Tanz in Winter* and *Tanz in August*, two three-week festivals of contemporary dance.

Komische Oper, see "Orchestras and venues". Modern ballet and experimental works, arguably the most interesting of the established heavyweights.

Staatsoper, see "Orchestras and venues". Ballet and dance under the direction of Michael Denar, formerly of the Paris opera. Note that because of cutbacks in civic financing, at the time of writing plans were afoot to merge the companies of the three opera houses into one "Berlin Ballet" in 2001.

Tanzfabrik Berlin, Möckernstr. 68, Kreuzberg ☎7 86 58 61. Experimental and contemporary works, usually fresh and exciting. This is also Berlin's biggest contemporary dance school.

Theater Am Halleschen Ufer see "Experimental and free theatre". While not primarily a dance venue, it is host to Berlin's contemporary dance scene. Home of the *Tanzzeit* Festivals in June and November and the *Solo Duo* in March.

Cabaret venues

Bar Jeder Vernunft, Scharperstr. 24, Wilmersdorf ☎8 83 15 82. Currently the city's best, younger and hipper than most.

BKA (Berliner Kabarett Anstalt), Mehringdamm 32, Kreuzberg ☎2 51 01 12. Cabaret and one-person shows, often dealing with political themes and current events.

Chamäleon Variete, Rosenthaler Str. 40–41, Mitte ☎2 82 71 18. Very lively, with jugglers, acrobats and the like.

Chez Nous, Marburgerstr. 14, Tiergarten ☎2 13 18 10. Classic feathery drag revue.

Friedrichstadt Palast, Friedrichstr. 107, Mitte ☎23 26 24 74. Big flashy variety shows with leggy chorus girls, but the real stuff is to be found in their small café theatre.

Hackesches Hof Theater, Rosenthaler Str. 40–41, Mitte ☎2 83 25 87. Musical theatre, often with Jewish themes, and klezmer music every week.

Kalkscheune, Johannisstr. 2, Mitte ☎28 39 00 65. Creative shows – authentic but without the nostalgia.

Kleine Nachtrevue, Kurfürstenstr. 116, Schöneberg ☎2 18 89 50. Intimate and torchy, going for that 1920s feel.

La Vie en Rose, Flughafen Tempelhof, Kreuzberg ☎69 51 30 00. A drag variety revue with lots of glitter and lots of skin. There's also piano bar.

Meringhof Theater, Gneisenaustr. 2a, Kreuzberg ☎6 91 50 99. Mixed bag of alternative cabaret.

Roter/Grüner Salon, in the Volksbühne, Rosa-Luxemburg-Platz, Mitte ☎24 06 58 07. Lots of interesting and varied goings on with occasional performances in English.

Scheinbar Variete, Monumentenstr. 9, Schöneberg ☎7 84 55 39. Hip, experi-

mental and fun; open stage on Wed nights.

Wintergarden, Potsdamer Str. 96, Tiergarten ☎23 08 82 30. A glitzy attempt to re-create the Berlin of the 1920s, with live acts from all over the world – cabaret, musicians, dance, mime, etc. Very expensive.

Film

When the all-night drinking starts to get too much, it's always possible to wind down in front of the silver screen. Art-house cinemas, unfortunately, are facing very hard times, but for those who like the mainstream, the corresponding rise of the multiplex theatres means there is more English-language fare available. The two surest bets for English-language films are Cinemaxx at Potsdamer Platz and the UFA Arthouse Kurbel, though old standbys such as Odeon and Babylon, and the newly renovated Neues Off, soldier on with somewhat more interesting choices.

There are still some **smaller cinemas** showing art-house and independently made movies, and some of the more interesting places are listed below. *Tip* and *Zitty* have listings of all the films showing each week: their daily listings are of "off-Ku'damm-Kinos"; the big city cinemas are listed separately under "Ku'damm-Kinos". *(030)* lists everything.

Listings will tell you which language the film is in. If a film is listed as **OF** or **OV** (*Originalfassung*) it's in its original language; **OmU** (*Originalfassung mit Untertiteln*) indicates German subtitles. Otherwise, the film will have been dubbed into German. You may occasionally see films listed as **OmE** – original with English subtitles.

Ticket prices range from DM11 to DM18 (€5.60–9.20); two days a week, usually Tuesday and Wednesday, are designated Kinotag, when prices are reduced to around DM8 (€4.10).

In February, the **Berlin International Film Festival** dominates the city's cultural life. Second only to Cannes among European festivals, it was once the

The arts

The arts

Video rental

The average Berlin video store has the usual schlock-horror selection along with Hollywood hits, all clumsily dubbed into German. For English-language video, you'll need to visit one of the following shops. All will require ID, and it's best to go with a friend registered at a Berlin address to show some proof of residency. Expect to pay around DM7 (€3.60) per night per video.

British Council, Hackescher Markt 1, Mitte ☎31 10 99 10. Classic British films, plus the "Best of the BBC" on tape.

Incredibly Strange, Eisenacher Str. 115, Schöneberg ☎2 15 17 70. Two and a half thousand titles, with lots of weird and wonderful stuff.

Videodrom, Mittenwalder Str. 11, Kreuzberg ☎6 92 88 04. Berlin's largest selection of English-language movies, with over 3500 titles.

Negativeland, Dunkerstr. 9, Prenzlauer Berg ☎44 77 44 77. English videos in the east, finally. Not the biggest or the weirdest, but working on it.

showcase for East German and East European films, and still offers a staggering number of films from all around the world. A limited number of season tickets (DM250/€128; two passport photos required, nontransferable) go on sale a week before opening at the Galerie of the Berliner Volksbank, Linkstr. 10, located at Potsdamer Platz. Otherwise, advance tickets can be purchased at the ticket booths centrally located in the Potsdamer Platz Arcaden shopping mall, the second floor of the Europa Center or at the International (see below). Tickets for the day of the show must be purchased at the cinema box office. For general information, the best bet is to visit the festival's Web site at *www.berlinale.de*. During the festival, programming information is available in the regular listings magazines or the festival's own daily magazine, *Berlinale*, available at all participating theatres.

Cinemas

The following are the usual venues for English-language films, but it pays to look through the listings in *Tip* and *Zitty* as there are always surprises.

Arsenal, Potsdamer Str. 2 in the Sony Filmhaus at Potsdamer Platz ☎26 95 51 00. Specializes in retrospectives, series and experimental work. Sometimes in English, and foreign films, particularly Asian, may have English subtitles.

Babylon, Dresdener Str. 126, Kreuzberg ☎61 60 96 93. New films in English, with and without subtitles.

Babylon Mitte, Rosa-Luxemburg-Str. 30, Mitte ☎2 42 50 76. Central Berlin's best repertory cinema in a landmark theatre. Occasional films with English subtitles.

Camera In Tacheles Oranienburgerstr. 54–56, Mitte ☎2 83 14 98. Mostly foreign and indie films, sometimes in English.

Central, Rosenthalerstr. 39, Mitte ☎2 85 99 93. Main programme is almost all German but bizarre midnight events often occur and are often in English.

Cinemaxx Potsdamer Platz, Potsdamer Platz 5, Tiergarten ☎44 31 63 16. Monster 19-screen multiplex with at least two screens in English.

Eiszeit-Kino, Zeughofstr. 20, Kreuzberg ☎6 11 60 16. Tiny cinema tucked away in a *Hinterhof*, specializing in retrospectives and alternative films. Less English than before but still *the* home of innovative programming.

Hackesche Höfe, Rosenthalerstr. 40–41, Mitte ☎2 83 46 03. Five-screen multiplex on the top floor of the busy Hackesche Höfe. Upscale independent foreign films and documentaries, sometimes in English. Often sold out at weekends, but they take phone reservations.

International, Karl-Marx-Allee 33/Schillingstr., Mitte ☎24 75 60 11. A big, comfortable GDR landmark cinema showing new releases. The Monday night gay programme often shows films in their original language.

Kino in der Brotfabrik, Prenzlauer Promenade 3, Weissensee ☎4 71 40 02. Art-house cinema that's worth checking out. Occasional films in English.

Moviemento I, Kottbusser Damm 22, Kreuzberg ☎6 92 47 85. Less innovative than before but still worth a look.

Odeon, Hauptstr. 116, Schöneberg ☎78 70 40 19. If you're after the more intelligent English-language releases, the Odeon will have them first.

Neues Off, Hermannstr. 20, Neukölln ☎62 70 95 50. Usually picks up films after their run at the Odeon.

UFA Arthouse Kurbel I, II & III, Giesebrechtstr. 4, Charlottenburg ☎8 83 53 25. The latest commercial releases (don't let the "Arthouse" claim fool you), all in English with sneak previews on Mondays at 11pm.

Xenon, Kolonnenstr. 5, Schöneberg ☎7 82 88 50. Often screens English-language independent films with an accent on Queer Cinema.

Zeughaus-Kino, Unter den Linden 2, Mitte. Cinema in the Zeughaus which often unearths fascinating films from the pre- and postwar years. Due to reopen after renovation in 2001.

Art

Like most Berlin phenomena, the Berlin art scene divides sharply into east and west, the latter containing the expensive, more established galleries in **Charlottenburg** and **Tiergarten** and the former reflecting the current energy and attention. The area around **Auguststrasse** in Mitte, which became the breeding ground of wild and crazy art in the first years after the Wall, is now known as the "Art Mile" – after the many galleries that have sprung up along its streets. It seems to be settling down though as it becomes more commercialized. A useful and comprehensive source of information about **what's on**

in the city's galleries is the English/German monthly magazine *artery berlin* (DM3.50/€1.80) found in most galleries. You can pick up the free *Galerien Berlin* listings brochure put out by the Berlin Art Dealers Association in galleries as well, or visit their Web site at *www.berliner-galerien.de*. The quarterly *Berliner Kunstblatt* has selective listings. *Zitty* and *Tip* (under "Galerien" in "Ausstellungen") are also worth checking for up-to-the-minute details. Most galleries are open from about 2 to 7pm and close on Monday; some western galleries open from 11am.

Galleries

Aktions Galerie, Grosse Präsidentenstr. 10, Mitte ☎28 59 96 54; *www.aktions-galerie.de*. Experimental and conceptual art and happenings, generally outrageous. Also organizer of the always interesting *Und ab die Post* show at the Postfuhramt, Oranienburgerstr. 19–21, every May & June.

Arndt & Partner, Auguststr. 35, Mitte ☎2 80 81 23; *www.arndt-partner.de*. International contemporary art and young local artists. Tues–Sat noon–6pm.

Asian Fine Arts Berlin, Sophienstr. 18 (1st Hof), Mitte ☎28 39 13 88; *www.asianfinearts.de*. Focus on new Asian art with a strong international profile. Tues–Sat noon–7pm.

DAAD Galerie, Kurfürstenstr. 58, Tiergarten ☎2 02 20 80 26. Exhibitions

The arts

Municipal art galleries

Several public galleries also exhibit **contemporary/twentieth-century art** – for more details, see the following:

The arts

and occasional readings by big-name artists working in the city on fellowships awarded by the Berlin Artist Exchange of the Deutsche Akademischer Austausch Dienst (German Academic Exchange Service). Daily 12.30–7pm.

EIGEN+ART, Auguststr. 26, Mitte ☎ 2 80 66 05; *www.eigen-art.com*. Run by Gerd Harry Lybke, who opened the first private gallery in the GDR back in the 1980s, this is one of the most important Auguststrasse galleries. Though originally a showcase for East German talent, the programme now covers painting, installations and photography by (predominantly young) international artists. Tues–Fri 2–7pm, Sat 11am–5pm.

Fine Art Rafael Vostell, Knesebeckstr. 30, Charlottenburg ☎ 8 85 22 80; *www.vostell.de*. International artists of the 1960s with a mix of young Berlin painters. Mon–Fri 11am–7pm, Sat 11am–4pm.

Galerie am Chamissoplatz, Chamissoplatz 6, Kreuzberg ☎ 69 40 12 45; *www.tammen-busch.de*. Politically oriented art, on the site of a former bakery in the heart of Kreuzberg. Tues–Fri 1–6pm, Sat & Sun 3–6pm. Also check out their second location, Galerie Tammen & Busch, at nearby Fidicinstr. 40, for larger and more sculptural work. Tues–Fri 1–6pm, Sat 3–6pm.

Galerie Anselm Dreher, Pfalzburgerstr. 80, Wilmersdorf ☎ 8 83 52 49; *www.galerie-anselm-dreher.com*. One of the city's top galleries, showing international avant-garde artists. Tues–Fri 2–6.30pm, Sat 11am–2pm.

Galerie Argus Fotokunst, Marienstr. 25, Mitte ☎ 2 83 30 49. Interesting, often provocative fine art and documentary photographs. Wed–Sun 2–6pm.

Galerie Barbara Thumm, Dirksenstr. 41, Mitte ☎ 28 39 03 47; *www.bthumm.de*. British and Berlin-based artists working in all mediums. Tues–Fri 1–7pm, Sat 1–6pm.

Galerie Berlin, Oranienburgerstr. 27 (in the Kunsthof), Mitte ☎ 2 51 56 15; *www.galerie-berlin.de*. Focus on former East German artists as well as twentieth-

century German Impressionism and Expressionism. Once the official GDR art marketer. Tues–Fri 1–7pm, Sat 1–6pm.

Galerie Bodo Niemann, Auguststr. 19, Mitte ☎ 28 39 19 28. Berlin city life in the 1920s is the theme of this gallery. Tues–Fri 1–7pm, Sat noon–6pm.

Galerie Bremer, Fasanenstr. 37, Wilmersdorf ☎ 8 81 49 08. One of the first places to show work banned by the Nazi regime. Also has a good cocktail bar. Tues–Fri noon–6pm.

Galerie Eva Poll, Lützowplatz 7, Tiergarten ☎ 2 61 70 91; *www.germangalleries.com*. Contemporary art, with an emphasis on international figurative work. Mon 10am–1pm, Tues–Fri 11am–6.30pm, Sat 11am–3pm.

Galerie Franck + Schulte, Mommsenstr. 56, Charlottenburg ☎ 3 24 00 44; *www.fal-fs.de*. Well-presented photographic exhibitions and installations, frequently featuring established artists from America. Mon–Fri 11am–6pm, Sat 11am–3pm.

Galerie Georg Nothelfer, Uhlandstr. 184, Charlottenburg ☎ 8 81 44 05; *www.berliner-galerien.de*. Renowned contemporary art gallery. Tues–Fri 2–6.30pm, Sat 10am–2pm.

Galerie Nierendorf, Hardenbergstr. 19, Charlottenburg ☎ 8 32 50 13. Mainly German Expressionism. Karl Nierendorf's gallery was one of the first to exhibit Die Brücke group, Dix, Kirchner and Kandinsky. Tues–Fri 11am–6pm.

Galerie Paula Böttcher, Klein Hamburgerstr. 15, Mitte ☎ 2 81 12 36. Young energetic presentation of young energetic artists – local and international. Wed–Fri 2–6pm, Sat 1–6pm.

Galerie Springer, Fasanenstr. 13, Charlottenburg ☎ 3 12 70 63. Top-class contemporary painting. One of the galleries foremost in establishing the Berlin art scene after World War II. Mon–Fri 2–7pm, Sat 11am–2pm.

Galerie Wohnmaschine, Tucholskystr. 36, Mitte ☎ 30 87 20 15. Young gallery-owner Friedrich Loock opened his first gallery in his flat (he's one of the few people involved in the Scheunenviertel art scene who actually comes from the area) and now specializes in promoting the works of young, predominantly local artists. Tues–Fri 2–7pm, Sat noon–5pm.

ifa Gallerie, Neustädtische Kirche 15, Mitte ☎ 2 08 07 64; *www.ifa.de*. Promotes international cultural awareness with exhibitions by foreign artists, often from developing countries. Daily except Mon 2–7pm.

Haus Schwarzenberg, Rosenthalerstr. 39, Mitte ☎ 30 87 25 73. Potpourri of local and international artists and installations. Also interesting selection of alternative art books and CDs for sale. Wed–Thurs 4–10pm, Fri 4pm–midnight, Sat 2pm–midnight, Sun 2–10pm.

Kunst-Werke Berlin, Auguststr. 69, Mitte ☎ 2 43 45 90; *www.kw-berlin.de*. Large gallery overrunning a former factory building, heavily subsidized by the city. Varies from has-been American artists carpetbagging their way into the city arts scene to astute reflections on contemporary Berlin. Principal organizer of the *Berlin Biennale* (*www.berlinbiennale.de*). Daily except Mon 2–6pm.

Monster Cabinet, Rosenthalerstr. 39 in the basement of the Central Cinema, Mitte. Not an actual gallery but a permanent installation by the former GDR performance group, The Dead Chickens. Metal-constructed grotesqueries: press the buttons and stand back. Fri 8pm–midnight, Sat & Sun 4pm–midnight.

museumsakademie berlin, Rosenthaler Str. 39, Mitte ☎ 30 87 25 80. In a back courtyard, second floor; shows mainly young Berlin artists. Tues–Sat 2–7pm.

Petersen Galerie, Herderstr. 5, Charlottenburg ☎ 3 13 45 08. Indefinable mix of action art and "happenings". Mon–Fri 2–7pm, Sat 11am–2pm.

Raab Galerie, Potsdamer Str. 58, Tiergarten ☎ 2 61 92 17; *www.germangalleries.com/raab*. Avant-garde and contemporary art; popular meeting place for the art "in" crowd. Mon–Fri 10am–7pm, Sat 10am–4pm.

Radio Berlin, Veteranenstr. 22, Mitte ☎ 01734 077 666. Alternative art for the alternative masses – pop, fun and cheap enough to actually buy. Thurs–Sat 4–10pm.

Zwinger Gallerie, Gipsstr. 3, Mitte ☎ 28 59 89 07. One of the city's most important galleries, presenting a mixture of the avant-garde and conventional. Tues–Fri 2–7pm, Sat 11am–2pm.

The arts

Chapter 16

Children's Berlin

Attitudes to young children in Berlin strike the outsider as oddly ambivalent. While the city has a large number of single-parent families and excellent social service provisions for them, Berliners aren't too tolerant of kids in "adult" places, such as restaurants or bars; and though the city consists of a higher proportion of lakes, parks and woodland than any other European capital, there's little in them directly geared to entertaining children. If you're bringing kids, be prepared to do Berlin versions of the obvious things – zoos, museums and shops – rather than anything unique to the city. On a day-to-day basis, check the listings in *Tip* (under "Kindertheater"), *Zitty* (under "Kinder") and *Berliner Programm* (under "Kinder & Jugend") for details of what's on.

Baby-sitting services

The John F. Kennedy School, an English-language high school, has a list of students willing to **baby-sit**; call the library at ☎80 91 26 63. Other possibilities include Heinzelmännchen der Freien Universität Berlin (☎8 31 60 71; reservations for sitters taken Mon, Tues & Thurs 7am–6pm, Wed & Fri 7am–5pm); and TUSMA der Technischen Universität Berlin (☎3 15 93 40; reservations taken Mon–Fri 7am–7pm, Sat 8am–1pm). Rates are approximately DM20 (€10.25) per hour. Several private baby-sitting firms are listed in the Yellow Pages under "Babysitting".

Parks and activities

With over a third of Berlin being forest or parkland, often with playgrounds dotted around, there's no shortage of spaces for children to go and let off steam. The most central and obvious choice is the **Tiergarten**, northeast of Zoo Station, though this is rather tame compared to the rambling expanses of the **Grunewald** (S-Bahn Grunewald). In both parks paddle and rowing boats can be rented. The Grunewald borders the **Wannsee** lake, and it's fun to take the ferry over to the **Pfaueninsel** (Peacock Island), where there's a castle and plenty of strutting peacocks; see p.167 for details. Alternatively, **Freizeitpark Tegel** (U-Bahn Alt-Tegel, walk to the lake, then turn right) has playgrounds, trampolines, table tennis and paddle boats, while the **Teufelsberg** (Devil's Mountain; bus #149 to Preussenallee stop, then walk for 20min south down Teufelsseechaussee), a large hill to the west of the city, is the place to go kite-flying at weekends. On the southeastern edge of the city, the woods around the **Grosser Müggelsee** (S-Bahn to Friedrichshagen) offer lakeside walking trails, and there's also a good nature trail around the **Teufelssee** (S-Bahn to Köpenick, then bus #169 for five stops), just south of the Müggelsee.

Playgrounds and pools

Of the city's sports facilities, probably of most interest to kids is the **blub Badeparadies**, a slick indoor and outdoor pool complex at Buschkrugalle 64, Neukölln (☎6 06 60 60; www .blub-berlin.de; Mon–Sat 10am–11pm, Sun & hols 9am–11pm; weekdays: DM18/€9.20, children up to 12 DM14/€7.15; weekends: DM21/€10.75, children up to 12 DM16/€8.20; U-Bahn Grenz Allee). It's a bit of a trek out, and expensive to boot, but is worth it for the waterfalls, whirlpools, 12-metre chute and wave machine, to name but a few facilities. There's a similar complex in the eastern suburb of Friedrichshain: the **SEZ-Sport und Erholungszentrum**, Landsberger Allee 77, Friedrichshain (☎42 18 20; tram #5 or #15 from Hackescher Markt). It's not quite as upscale as the blub Badeparadies, but it also offers several pools with slides, chutes and diving boards.

Excursions and trips

For views of Berlin from on high (in ascending order of terror), try the **Siegessäule** (not for little legs; see p.126), the **Fernsehturm** (p.93), the **Funkturm** (p.159) and the **Reichstag** dome (p.57). Also, the **Müggelturm** (p.198) offers mildly hair-raising views of the woods and lakes at the southeastern edge of the city. Older children might appreciate a visit to the **Planetarium am Insulaner**, Munsterdamm 90, Steglitz (guided tours Tues–Fri 8pm, Sat 4pm, 6pm & 8pm, Sun 2.30pm, 4pm & 7pm; adults DM8/€4.10, children DM5/€2.50; S-Bahn Priesterweg), or the **Zeiss Planetarium**, Prenzlauer Allee 80, Prenzlauer Berg (Wed–Fri 10am–noon & 1.30–8pm, Sat & Sun 1.30–8pm; DM8/€4.10; S-Bahn Prenzlauer Allee, tram #1, bus #156).

Circuses and funfairs

The **UFA-Kindercircus** at the UFA-Fabrik, Viktoriastr. 10, Tempelhof (☎75 50 30; www.ufafabrik.de), is a residential circus offering an inventive alternative to the usual lions-and-clowns stuff. Another resident circus, in which youngsters perform, is **Cabuwazi Zirkus**, Weiner Str. 59h, Kreuzberg (☎6 11 92; www

.members.xoom.com/cabuwazi/index.htm), and Bouchéstr. 74, Alt-Treptow (☎5 33 70 16). In addition, professional circus troupes visit the city regularly during the summer months. Check with the tourist office to find out where and when.

Small **funfairs** can be found throughout the summer in Berlin on the small patches of park that dot the city. Again, check with the tourist office for locations.

Children's Berlin

The Zoo and children's farms

The **Zoo**, Hardenbergplatz 8, Charlottenburg (☎25 40 10; www.zoo-berlin.de; daily 9am to sunset; DM14/€7.15, children 3–15 DM7/€3.60; near the train station of the same name, has an array of exotic animals in surroundings that attempt to mimic their natural habitat. Of most interest to kids will be the monkeys, orang-utans and gorillas, the hippo house, the nocturnal rooms (a darkened area where varieties of gerbil-type creatures do their thing), pony and horse-and-trap rides around the zoo, and a playground. The **Aquarium** nearby, at Budapester Str. 32, Tiergarten (☎25 40 10; daily 9am–6pm, last Sat in month & public hols until 10pm; DM14/€7.15, children 3–15 DM7/€3.60; combined tickets with zoo DM22.50/€11.50, children 3–15 DM12/€6.15), is also well worth the money, though probably best seen on a separate trip from the zoo. The huge **Tierpark**, Am Tierpark 125, Lichtenberg (☎51 53 10; www.tierpark-berlin.de; daily 9am to dusk; DM14/€7.15, children 3–15 DM7/€3.60; U-Bahn Tierpark, trams #26, #27 & #28, buses #194 & #296), in the eastern suburb of Friedrichsfelde, is also worth a day out in itself – this sprawling zoo will be enough to exhaust even the most demanding child.

Educationally oriented **Kinder-bauern-höfen**, or children's farms, can be fun without knowing the language: they're to be found at Domäne Dahlem (see "Museums" below for details); in Görlitzer Park at Wiener Str. 59, Kreuzberg (summer Mon, Tues, Thurs & Fri 10am–7pm, Sat & Sun noon–7pm; closes at 5pm

Children's Berlin

during winter months; U-Bahn Görlitzer Bahnhof or bus #129 then follow footpath); and in the UFA-Fabrik, Viktoriastr. 13–18, Tempelhof (open daily from 10am; U-Bahn Ullsteinstrasse).

At the eastern end of town is **the FEZ Wuhlheide**, An der Wuhlheide, Köpenick (☎53 07 11 46; summer: Tues–Thurs 10am–9pm, Fri 10am–10pm, Sat 1–6pm, Sun 10am–6pm; during the school year: Tues–Fri 10am–6pm, Sat 1–6pm, Sun 10am–6pm; S-Bahn to Wühlheide, trams #26, #61 & #67), a large recreation park, packed with play- and activity-areas for kids of all ages and including a popular narrow-gauge railway.

Museums

Almost all museums give a discount for children; the following are the most interesting in terms of special areas for kids, interactive exhibits, and fun things to do.

Deutsches Technikmuseum Berlin, Trebbiner Str. 9, Kreuzberg ☎25 48 40; *www.dtmb.de* (U-Bahn Möckernbrücke, buses #129 & #248). Lots of gadgets to experiment with, plus a great collection of old steam trains and carriages. Highly diverting; the perfect thing for a wet afternoon. See also p.136. Tues–Fri 9am–5.30pm, Sat & Sun 10am–6pm; DM5 (€2.50), children DM2 (€1).

Domäne Dahlem, Königin-Luise-Str. 49, Zehlendorf ☎8 32 50 00; *www.snafu.de/~domaene-dahlem* (U-Bahn Dahlem-Dorf). This working farm and craft museum has plenty to entertain kids besides farmyard animals, especially at weekends when craft fairs are held here, and there are games and shows especially for children. Phone ahead to see what's on. Daily except Tues 10am–6pm; DM3 (€1.50), children DM1.50 (€0.80).

Düppel Museum Village, Clauertstr. 11, Zehlendorf ☎8 02 66 71; *www.dueppel .de* (bus #115). Reconstruction of a medieval country village, with demonstrations of the handicrafts and farming methods of those times. Better for older children. Easter to mid-Oct Thurs 3–7pm, Sun & hols 10am–5pm; DM3 (€1.50).

Juniormuseum im EthnologischenMuseum, Arnimallee 23, Dahlem ☎18 30 12 55; *www.smb .spk-berlin.de* (U-Bahn Dahlem Dorf). A section of the Ethnological Museum in Dahlem, this museum teaches children about different cultures through playful activities and interactive exhibits. Tues–Fri 10am–6pm, Sat & Sun 11am–6pm; free.

Labyrinth Kindermuseum Berlin, Osloer Str. 12, Wedding ☎49 30 89 01; *www.b.shuttle.de/b/labyrinth* (U-Bahn Pankstr., S-Bahn Bornholme Str., trams #23 & #24, bus #227). A converted factory building that offers temporary exhibits, usually very inventive and thoughtful, geared towards hands-on learning and fun. Tues–Fri 2–6pm, Sat 1–6pm, Sun 11am–6pm; DM6 (€3.10), children 3–16 DM5 (€2.50).

Museum for Communication, Leipziger Str. 16, Mitte ☎20 29 40; *www.museumsstiftung.de* (U-Bahn Mohrenstr. or Stadtmitte, buses #142 & #348). For older kids there are lots of computers and devices to play with and three robots careering around the main lobby. Tues–Fri 9am–5pm, Sat & Sun 11am–7pm; free.

Museum for Natural History, Invalidenstr. 43, Mitte ☎20 93 85 91 (U-Bahn Zinnowitzer Str., trams #6, #8 & #50, buses #157 & #245). The main attraction here is the gigantic Brachiosaurus skeleton, and once that's been admired the rest of the display is a bit of an anticlimax. However, it should keep animal-crazy kids happy for an hour or so. Tues–Sun 9.30am–5pm; DM5 (€2.50), children DM2.50 (€1.30).

Theatres and cinemas

Most cinemas show **children's films** during the school holidays but these are likely to be German-language only. The one time you're likely to catch English-language kids' films is during the Berlin Film Festival in February (see p.289), which always offers a children's programme (*Kinderprogramm*). Berlin supports an astonishing number of **puppet** theatres, most of which put on worth-while performances which kids don't need a knowledge of German to enjoy. For details of children's films and theatre performances, check the listings magazines or call the venues.

Berliner Figuren Theater, Yorckstr. 59, Kreuzberg ☎7 86 98 15. Innovative puppet theatre with superbly crafted dolls.

Berliner Kino Museum, Grossbeerenstr. 57, Kreuzberg (no phone). Tiny place with old cinema furniture. Often shows silent comedies featuring Laurel and Hardy and the like.

Charlottchen, Droysenstr. 1, Charlottenburg ☎3 24 47 17. A child-friendly café with a theatre offering funny fairy tales and original pieces in the back.

Figurentheater Grashüpfer, Puschkinallee 16a, Treptow ☎53 69 51 50. Audience participation plays and puppetry for younger children.

Fliegendes Theater Berlin, Urbanstr. 100, Kreuzberg ☎6 92 21 00. Puppet theatre for kids of 4 and over.

Grips, Altonaer Str. 22, Tiergarten ☎39 74 74 77. Top-class children's/young people's theatre; usually all improvised.

Homunkulus Figurentheater, Florastr. 16, Pankow ☎48 09 72 12. Innovative puppet theatre.

Narrenspiegel, Otto-Suhr-Allee 94, Charlottenburg ☎7 81 45 49. Children's theatre presenting fairy tales and original productions.

Schaubude, Greifswalderstr. 81–84, Prenzlauer Berg ☎4 23 43 14. Beautiful, often elaborate puppets and settings in original productions.

Zaubertheater Igor Jedlin, Roscherstr. 7, Charlottenburg ☎3 23 37 77. Jedlin's one-man magic shows have been a hit for years.

Shops

There's a fair but not overwhelming selection of **children's shops** in Berlin, with an emphasis on wooden toys, ecological themes and multicultural education. Plastic pistols and toy soldiers are definitely out of favour and hard to find. For a full list of shops, see Chapter 18.

Anagramm, Mehringdamm 50, Kreuzberg ☎7 85 95 10. Neighbourhood bookstore with an excellent children's section and a reading corner.

Baby-Korb, Bundesallee 17, Wilmersdorf ☎8 83 30 07. Accessories and European designer clothes; middle price range.

British Bookshop, Mauer Str. 83–84, Mitte ☎2 38 46 80. Great selection of books for toddlers and preschool children through to teenagers, all in English.

Elephant's Knot, Meinekestr. 3, Charlottenburg ☎8 83 38 97. Designer kids' clothing including the latest Italian children's fashions.

Fliegender Hamburger, Torstr. 98, Mitte ☎2 82 22 67. Model trains and accessories.

Grober Unfug, Zossener Str. 32, Kreuzberg ☎69 40 14 90. Large display of international comics.

H&M, Kurfürstendamm 234, Charlottenburg ☎8 82 38 44. Now young fans of grown-ups' clothing store H&M (see p.307) have a branch all to themselves. This former *fin-de-siècle* café stocks a wide range of designs.

Jonglerie, Körtestr. 26, Kreuzberg ☎6 91 87 69. Magic tricks, balloons and toys.

Kinderboutique Cinderella, Kurfürstendamm 46, Charlottenburg ☎8 81 28 63. Ralph Lauren for kids, and other top-notch designers.

Pre-Natal, Tauentzienstr. 1, Schöneberg ☎2 11 73 40. Smart kiddies' clothing up to five years. Not cheap, but not a rip-off either considering the prominent location.

Speilbrett, Körtestr. 27, Kreuzberg ☎6 92 42 50. Picture books, games and puzzles.

Stiefelchen, Kurfürstendamm 51, Charlottenberg ☎8 81 29 43. Pricey but classy children's shoes.

Tabularium, Grosser Hamburger Str. 28, Mitte ☎2 80 82 03. One half of this store is dedicated to Judaica, the other half to wooden toys, sophisticated puzzles and children's books.

Children's Berlin

Children's Berlin

Übermuth, Mommsenstr. 64, Charlottenburg ☎8 81 39 50. Charming children's wear, cute without being cutesy. Not cheap.

Vogel Spielwaren, Uhlandstr. 137, Wilmersdorf ☎8 73 23 77. Toys, games and model-making equipment.

Vom Winde Verweht, Eisenacher Str. 81, Schöneberg ☎78 70 36 36. Kites – the place to come before heading off for the Teufelsberg hill.

Werken, Speilen, Schenken, Florastr./Schlossstr., Charlottenburg ☎7 90 80 90. Large store of games and hobby wares, with a kids' book section.

Wundertüte, Reichenhaller Str. 2–3, Neukölln ☎89 51 00 33. New and secondhand kids' clothes and accessories.

Zauberkönig, Hermannstr. 84, Neukölln ☎6 21 40 82. Illusions and tricks for magicians and their apprentices.

Zinnsoldaten, Skalitzerstr. 81, Kreuzberg ☎6 18 38 15. Enormous selection of tin soldiers and figures.

Chapter 17

Sport

While Berliners go in for healthy eating in a big way, they're not famous for being fitness fanatics – they need all their energy for the frenetic nightlife. Nonetheless there is a surprising variety of **participatory sports** available in the city, such as swimming, skating, tennis, cycling etc. As for spectator sports, there's little on offer: the city has only one major **soccer team**, BSC Hertha, who play in the Bundesliga at the Olympic Stadium, and sporting events are rarely at an international level. The only exception is the annual **International Women's Tennis Tournament**, in May, a highly popular event. For details, contact the Rot–Weiss Tennisclub, Gottfried-Von-Cramm-Weg 47–55, Wilmersdorf (☎8 95 75 50; *www.german-open-berlin.de*).

For a complete rundown of all annual sporting events, visit the **Landessportbund Berlin e.V**, Jesse-Owens-Allee 2, Charlottenburg (☎30 00 20), where you can pick up a copy of the yearly *Freizeitsports Kalender*, which has full details of both spectator and participatory sports.

Boat rental

Paddle and rowing boats are a pleasant, if rather strenuous, way of enjoying Berlin's lakes during the summer. Try Strandbad Wannsee, the Neuer See in Tiergarten, or the quieter Schlachtensee. For other waterborne trips, see *Introducing the city*.

Fishing

There are plenty of fishing spots in Berlin: for detailed information and the necessary visitor's fishing licence (*Fischereischein*), contact the **Fischereiamt beim Senator für Stadtentwicklung und Umweltschutz**, Havelchaussee 149, Charlottenburg (☎3 00 69 90), which can also advise on the best places to rent the necessary equipment.

Ice-skating

There are **ice-skating rinks** at **Eissporthalle Berlin**, Jafféstr., Charlottenburg (☎3 03 80; DM8/€4.10; U-Bahn Theodr-Heuss-Platz), an indoor rink with a disco on Monday evenings during the winter from 7.30 to 9.45pm, and **Eisstadion Berlin-Wilmersdorf**, Fritz-Wilding-Str. 9, Wilmersdorf (☎8 24 10 12; DM6/€3.10, children DM3/€1.50; S-Bahn Hohenzollerndamm), an outdoor rink with a limited skating time of up to two hours.

Jogging

The most convenient but crowded spot to **jog** is around the Tiergarten, just behind Zoo Station. Alternatively, there's Volkspark Friedrichshain on the east side and Hasenheide in the south. The lakes around the city are also popular with joggers: try the Schlachtensee, Krumme Lanke or Grunewaldsee.

If you're into long-distance running, a trip around Grunewald lake should

Sport

be more of a challenge, or there's always the **Berlin Marathon** on the last weekend in September. This starts on Strasse des 17 Juni and ends back at the Kaiser-Wilhelm Memorial Church, after passing through Dahlem and along the Kurfürstendamm. To enter, write to **SCM Berlin**, Alt-Moabit 29, 10559 Berlin (☎3 02 53 70; *www.berlin-marathon.com*): closing date for entries is one month before the marathon. The SCM can also supply details on numerous other meetings, including the 10km race along the Kurfürstendamm in August.

Roller-skating and skateboarding

Choices are limited for skateboarding and hot-dogging: there's a large ramp in Kreuzberg's Böckler Park (U-Bahn Prinzenstr), otherwise the locals can be found in Breitscheidplatz or the pavement outside the Neue Nationalgalerie. However, on the first and third Wednesday of each month, **Blade Night** (☎0179 695 1661; *www.bladenight.com*), a huge mobile gathering of thousands of inline skating enthusiasts, said to be the largest in Europe, sets out at 9pm from S-Bahn Station Tiergarten for a skate through the streets of Tiergarten.

Skiing and tobogganing

Believe it or not, there are five **ski slopes** in Berlin and, if there has been sufficient snowfall, skiing lessons on the Teufelsberg take place both day and night. Contact the **Skiverband Berlin**, Bismarckallee 2, Wilmersdorf (☎8 91 97 98), for more information. You can rent skis from *Ski-sport-stadl*, Lützowstr. 104, Tiergarten (☎2 61 58 05).

Tobogganing is a favourite winter pastime in Berlin – and not just for children. The **Teufelsberg**, and to the north of the city, the **Freizeitpark Lübars**, have the most hair-raising slopes, or for more nervous souls there's the **Rodelbahn Goethepark**, Transvaalstrasse, Wedding, and the **Rodelbahn Humboldthain**, Gustav-Meyer-Allee, Wedding.

Swimming pools

Most districts throughout the city have both indoor and outdoor **swimming pools** (not necessarily in the same place). Details of all opening times, prices, special offers and activities can be found in a biannual pamphlet issued by the Berlin Senate called *Öffnungszeiten der Städtischen Bäder Berlins*, available from the tourist office and at all swimming pools, or from the Web site *www.bbb.berlin.de*. Many pools have special women- or families-only days or evenings. Watch out too for **Warmbädetag**, when the water is warmer than usual – and admission usually more expensive.

Bad am Spreewaldplatz, Wiener Str. 59h, Kreuzberg ☎6 12 70 57. Popular indoor pool complete with sauna and wave machine. Tues–Fri 8am–9pm, Sat & Sun 1–9pm; Tues & Thurs women only, Wed men only.

blub Baderparadis, Buschkrugallee 64, Neukölln ☎6 06 60 60; *www.blub-berlin.de* (U-Bahn Grenz Allee). Magnificent indoor and outdoor pool with wave machine, 120-metre chute, whirlpools, waterfalls, sauna and fitness centre. Daily 10am–11pm; weekdays: DM18 (€9.20), children up to 12 DM14 (€7.15); weekends: DM21 (€10.75), children up to 12 DM16 (€8.20).

Freibad Halensee, Königsallee 5a, Wilmersdorf ☎8 91 17 03. Lakeside pool.

Freibad Friedrichshagen, Müggelseedamm 216, Köpenick ☎6 45 57 56. Outdoor swimming in the Müggelsee lakes, including a nudist section.

Olympia-Schwimmstadion, Olympischer Platz (Osttor), Charlottenburg ☎30 06 34 40. Outdoor pool, part of the Olympic Stadium complex.

Schwimhalle Fischerinsel, Fischerinsel 11, Mitte ☎2 01 39 85. GDR-era modern pool that's a convenient place for a dip if you're staying in the city centre.

SEZ (Sport- und Erholungszentrum), Landsberger Allee 77, Friedrichshain

☎ 42 18 20. Sports centre that has a superb pool complex with wave machine, fountains, high diving, saunas and an ice-cold "polar bear pool". Also has an ice rink, a bowling alley and many other facilities. Entry varies for different facilities; swimming pool DM10 (€5.10), DM8 (€4.10) 7–10pm.

Sommerbad Neukölln, Columbiadamm 169–190, Neukölln ☎ 6 27 88 30. Outdoor pool, open from April to mid-Sept.

Stadtbad Charlottenburg (Alte Halle), Krumme Str. 10, Charlottenburg ☎ 34 38 38 60. A delightful, old-fashioned tiled pool with sauna, which is relatively unknown and as a result seldom crowded. Women only Mon & Thurs. Mon–Sat from 7am, Wed from noon, irregular closing time.

Stadtbad Mitte, Gartenstr. 5, Mitte ☎ 30 88 09 10. Centrally located old-fashioned pool.

Stadtbad Neukölln, Ganghoferstr. 3, Neukölln ☎ 68 09 26 53. Swim and relax in a setting resembling a Hungarian spa. Two pools (one heated, one cool) decorated with fountains and mosaic tiles, encased in a maze of archways and colonnades. Sauna and steamroom available. Mon 2–6pm, Tues–Fri 7–8am & 2–9pm, Sat 8am–5pm.

Stadtbad Wilmersdorf, Mecklenburgische Str. 80, Wilmersdorf ☎ 8 21 02 60. Indoor pool with solarium, easily accessible from the city centre. Mon & Sat 7am–7pm, Tues–Fri 7am–9.40pm.

Strandbad Wannsee, Wannseebadweg 25, Zehlendorf ☎ 8 03 56 12. Outdoor pool with beach nearby, lots of activities in the summer and usually packed. May–Sept daily 7am–8pm.

Tennis

Several parks have **tennis courts**, notably the **Freizeitpark Tegel**, Reinickendorf (next to Tegeler See; ☎ 4 34 66 66). This is open from mid-April to mid-October (Mon–Fri 8am–4pm). Courts cost DM20 (€10.25) per hour from 4 to 9pm, bookable up to six days in advance.

Sport

Chapter 18

Shopping

Berlin isn't exactly a shopper's paradise, but it does have an interesting selection of quirky specialist shops and earthy markets, and it's an excellent place to buy secondhand clothes. Glitz and dazzle are the prerogatives of **Wittenbergplatz** and the **Kurfürstendamm**, with its two miles of luxury galleries, antique shops and designer clothes shops, while the recently rebuilt **Friedrichstrasse** in the east, though more modest in size, is no less opulent in wares. The areas around **U-Bahns Wilmersdorfer Strasse**, **Walter-Schreiber-Platz** and **Hermannplatz** are good for chain-store clothes and all-purpose shopping, and **Mitte** and **Prenzlauer Berg** contain a strange mix of funky speciality shops and expensive boutiques. Ethnic foods and the "alternative" businesses are mostly in **East Kreuzberg**, with a more up-market alternative scene in **Charlottenburg**.

Normal **shop opening hours** are Monday to Friday 9am to 8pm & Saturday 9am to 4pm. Smaller shops outside of the major shopping districts tend to close earlier: 6pm on weekdays and 2pm on Saturdays. Except for chains and the larger places, **credit cards** are not widely accepted.

Books, magazines and prints

Berlin boasts a great variety of new and secondhand bookstores, and it's an

ideal city for leisurely, unharassed browsing. There are quite a few places to find **English-language books**, most of them situated in or around Knesebeckstrasse, the street with Berlin's highest concentration of bookstores.

English-language/general

All English Books, Elberfelder Str. 9, Tiergarten ☎39 90 42 76. English-language books on a great variety of subjects, including children's books.

Books in Berlin, Goethestr. 69, Charlottenberg ☎3 13 12 33; www.firstweb.de/books_in_berlin. Small bookstore with a good selection of English-language history and popular fiction.

British Bookshop, Mauerstr. 83–84, Mitte ☎2 38 46 80. Berlin's best and biggest English-language bookstore, with a good selection of books about the city, as well as daily and Sunday papers, magazines, and literature on cassette. Often organizes readings and other happenings.

Buchexpress, Unter den Eichen 97, Lichterfelde ☎8 31 40 04; www.buchexpress.com. Specializes in English and American literature.

Dussmann, Friedrichstr. 90, Mitte ☎20 25 11 11; www.kulturkaufhaus.de. A huge emporium of books, CDs, videos and software. Open Mon–Sat until 10pm.

Fair Exchange, Dieffenbachstr. 58, Kreuzberg ☎6 94 46 75. Secondhand

302 LISTINGS: CHAPTER 18

bookshop that specializes in English literature. Part-exchange possible.

Hugendubel, Tauentzienstr. 213, Charlottenburg ☎21 40 60. Huge general bookstore with a section devoted to English-language paperback fiction. Branches at Friedrichstr. 83, Mitte ☎20 63 51 00, and in the Potsdamer Platz shopping mall, Tiergarten ☎2 53 91 70.

Kiepert, Hardenbergstr. 4–5, Charlottenburg ☎31 18 80. Sprawling over the corner into Knesebeckstrasse, Kiepert has an excellent selection of books under every major subject heading, with a particularly good travel department and a limited but well-chosen assortment of English-language books. Branches at Friedrichstr. 63, Mitte ☎2 08 25 11, and Georgenstr. 2, Mitte ☎2 03 99 60.

Marga Schoeller, Knesebeckstr. 33–34, Charlottenburg ☎8 81 11 12. Rather eccentric shop assistants will point you to a good array of English fiction and nonfiction (this is the best place for esoteric topics in English) and then wrap up your purchases prettily on request.

Discount/secondhand

Another Country, Riemannstr. 7, Kreuzberg ☎69 40 11 60. A living-room atmosphere pervades this intimate English-language used bookshop, run by a British expat. The cellar is full of science fiction.

Buch- und Kunstantiquariat Tode, Dudenstr. 36, Kreuzberg ☎7 86 51 86. In the cellar is a good selection of old Penguins and literature, some in English.

Kauf's im Kilo, Dircksenstr. S-Bahnbogen 136, Mitte ☎0172 3912 317. Good-sized book- and antique shop under the S-Bahn tracks near Hackescher Markt. The name is literal: DM6 (€3.10) per kilo of books.

Knesebeck 11, Knesebeckstr. 11, Charlottenburg ☎3 12 28 36. General bookstore with a section of secondhand books, but also a good venue to scout for more unusual titles. Provides a quick and efficient mail-order service.

Art and architecture

Artificium, Rosenthaler Str. 40–41, in the Hackeschen Höfen, Mitte ☎30 87 22 80; www.artificium.com. Nineteenth- and twentieth-century art, architecture, photography, and the like. Open until 11pm on Fri and midnight on Sat.

Bücherbogen am Savignyplatz, Stadtbahnbogen 593–594, Charlottenburg ☎31 86 95 11. Situated under the S-Bahn arches, a nevertheless airy and spacious setting for specialist books on art, architecture, film and photography.

Kiepert, Hardenbergstr. 4–5, Charlottenburg ☎31 18 80. Art books at knock-down prices, usually on display on the street outside.

Comics and science fiction

Grober Unfug, Zossener Str. 32, Kreuzberg ☎69 10 14 90; www.groberunfug.de. Large display of international comics, plus T-shirts, cards, and the like on sale. Prides itself on being the number-one place for cartoon enquiries. Often has exhibitions of cartoonists' work in the small gallery upstairs.

Modern Graphics, Oranienstr. 22, Kreuzberg ☎6 15 88 10. Small, serious shop stuffed with sci-fi comics, cards, and posters.

Videodrom Basement, Fürbringer Str. 24, Kreuzberg ☎6 92 88 04; www.videodrom.com. Science fiction and subculture books, comics and videos.

Gay, feminist and radical

Chronika, Bergmannstr. 26, Kreuzberg ☎6 93 42 69. General bookstore but with a large department of lesbian literature.

Prinz Eisenherz Buchladen GmbH, Bleibtreustr. 52, Charlottenburg ☎3 13 99 36. The city's best-known gay bookstore, with a large selection of fiction and nonfiction, much in English.

Schwarze Risse, Gneisenaustr. 2a (in back courtyard), Kreuzberg ☎6 92 87 79. Radical bookstore located in the

Shopping

Shopping

Mehringhof complex, home to several left and alternative shops and organizations.

Spiritual

Adhara, Pestalozzistr. 35, Charlottenburg ☎3 12 24 62. Cosy and friendly mind, body and spirit bookshop.

Daulat, Wrangelstr. 11, Steglitz ☎7 91 18 68. Books, body oils, crystals and other esoterica.

Dharma, Akazienstr. 17, Schöneberg ☎7 84 50 80. Books with a slant towards occultism and Oriental philosophies, with a few in English.

Kristall Buchhandlung, Weimarer Str. 16, Charlottenburg ☎3 13 87 93. Large, well-stocked shop with a good variety of titles, several in English.

Theatre and film

Bücherbogen am Savignyplatz, Stadtbahnbogen 593–594, Charlottenburg ☎31 86 95 11. See "Art and architecture".

Kiepert, Hardenbergstr. 4–5, Charlottenburg ☎31 18 80. See "English-language/general".

Kommedia Medienbuchladen, Potsdamer Str. 131, Tiergarten ☎2 16 13 69. Every aspect of media and communications.

Travel

British Bookshop, Mauerstr. 83–84, Mitte ☎2 38 46 80. See *Children's Berlin*, p.294, and "English-language/general", p.302.

Buchhandlung Schropp, Potsdamer Str. 129, Schöneberg ☎23 55 73 20. Specialist travel-book and map store, with a large well-chosen selection. Also stocks detailed cycling maps of Berlin and Germany.

Chatwins, Goltzstr. 40, Schöneberg ☎21 75 69 04. Comfortable shop specializing in travel and guide books.

Newspapers and magazines

Almost any decent-size magazine shop in the central districts of Berlin will stock a few English-language newspapers, usually at least *The Guardian*, *Financial Times* and the *New York Herald-Tribune*. There are several places selling international newspapers and magazines clustered around the Zoo Station area, the best stocked being **Internationale Presse**, Joachimstalerstr. 1, Charlottenburg, open daily until midnight, which has every London-printed morning newspaper by 1pm; a branch just inside the main entrance to Zoo Station also has a wide selection of newspapers and magazines. Alternatively, try the store on the first floor of the **Europa Center**, open daily until 10pm. See also "Information and maps" in Basics.

Posters, prints and cards

Ararat, Bergmannstr. 99a, Kreuzberg ☎6 93 50 80. Huge selection of greetings cards and postcards; posters and prints are across the street at Bermannstr. 9 ☎6 94 95 32.

Scenario, Savigny Passage (next to S-Bahn Savignyplatz), Charlottenburg ☎3 12 91 99. Everything from run-of-the-mill postcards to hand-painted greetings cards. Also part gift shop, Scenario is great for browsing, and not expensive.

CDs, records and tapes

Berlin doesn't have a large number of general record stores but there are plenty of smaller shops dedicated to just one style.

Canzone Importschallplatten, Savigny Passage S-Bahnbogen 583, Charlottenburg ☎3 12 40 27. For lovers of Latin American and Oriental sounds. Expect some unusual finds, and a superb CD selection.

Club Sound Records, Eberswalderstr. 32, Prenzlauer Berg ☎4 49 27 03. Vinyl and CDs of electronic dance music including house, trance, techno, acid, hip-hop and drum 'n' bass. They also sell systems, record bags, etc.

DaCapo, Kastanienallee 96, Prenzlauer Berg ☎4 48 17 71. Vinyl-only new and used record shop with wide selection of jazz, 1960s–80s rock and releases on East German label Amiga.

DNS Records, Alte Schonhauser Str. 39, Mitte ☎ 2 47 98 35. Listening stations and a large selection of the newest of club dance music on CD and vinyl.

Dussmann, Friedrichstr. 90, Mitte ☎ 2 02 50. Good selection of rock, jazz, dance, world, international vocalists. Basement devoted entirely to classical. You can spend a whole afternoon listening to CDs without salesperson interference if you like.

Down-Beat, Dresdener Str. 19, Kreuzberg ☎ 61 60 93 26. Reggae, soul, R&B and jazz, with some rare items.

Flash Point, Schivelbeiner Str. 47, Prenzlauer Berg ☎ 44 65 09 59. Vinyl club and equipment specialists with a PC for music production software testing.

Gelbe Musik, Schaperstr. 11, Charlottenburg ☎ 2 11 39 62. Avant-garde place that's not so much a record shop as a music gallery.

Groove Records, Pücklerstr. 36, Kreuzberg ☎ 6 18 86 39. Small and noisy shop with lots of hardcore but also good dance and jazz sections. New and used CDs and LPs.

Hard Wax, Paul-Lincke-Ufer 44a, Kreuzberg ☎ 61 13 01 11. Premier dance music specialist. Techno, trance: you name it, they should have it. And if they haven't, they'll get it for you.

Jazzcock, Fürbringer Str. 17, Kreuzberg ☎ 6 93 61 33. Over 5000 jazz titles; specialists in European avant-garde.

L&P Classics, Knesebeckstr. 33–34, Charlottenburg ☎ 88 04 30 43. Store devoted entirely to classical music.

Mr Dead & Mrs Free, Bülowstr. 5, Schöneberg ☎ 2 15 14 49. Primarily rock records on independent labels. And a great name.

Musicland, Klosterstr. 12, Spandau ☎ 3 32 20 72. Fine selection of hits ancient and modern, with many discounted items.

New Noise, Schonleinstr. 31, Kreuzberg ☎ 69 04 01 37. Rare imports and under-

ground labels on CDs and vinyl. Will do special orders. Second location at Potsdamer Str. 106, Tiergarten ☎ 2 62 24 33.

Rave Age, Mainzer Str. 5, Friedrichshain ☎ 6 12 30 95. Techno and various forms of club dance music. Vinyl and CDs.

Rockers, Wienerstr. 20, Kreuzberg ☎ 6 18 27 12. Punk, metal and hip-hop, with a good selection of collectibles.

Scratch Records, Zossener Str. 31, Kreuzberg ☎ 69 81 75 91. A large selection of club, world and alternative music. If you can't find what you're looking for, they will order it for you.

Soul Trade, Sanderstr. 29, Kreuzberg ☎ 6 94 52 57. Specialists in black music including soul, hip-hop, funk, house and jazz.

Soundgarden, Hauptstr. 9, Schöneberg ☎ 7 87 58 91. Buys and sells LPs and CDs modern and mainstream.

Soundman-Shop, Urbanstr. 112, Kreuzberg ☎ 6 93 47 58. The latest gadgets and accessories for portable sound, including CD and cassette Walkmans and more.

Tonhalle, Kastanienallee 96, Prenzlauer Berg ☎ 44 04 75 99. Small store with wide selection of techno vinyl.

WOM, Augsburger Str. 35–41 (behind Wertheim on the Ku'damm), Charlottenburg ☎ 8 85 75 40, and at Forum Steglitz, Schlossstr. 1, Steglitz ☎ 7 91 80 83. Huge general shop with all kinds of music, including good selections of folk and world music, blues, and soundtracks.

Clothes

Although they like to think of themselves as such, Berliners aren't exactly trendsetters. Still, it's possible to pick up superb **bargains** at the many **secondhand** clothes stores: you'll find unusual (and trendy) items here at very low prices. Easier access to the discarded wardrobes of the East has brought many odd items of official uniform and clothing since the Wall fell.

Shopping

Shopping

Children's shops are covered in Chapter 16; see pp.297–298.

The main shopping areas at Wilmersdorferstrasse U-Bahn, Wilmersdorf, and Walter-Schreiber-Platz U-Bahn, Steglitz, have plenty of inexpensive name-brand styles. Ku'damm and Friedrichstrasse boast designer clothes shops, but unless you're very rich and very conservative, these aren't worth the time. A couple of exceptions are leather outlets, which have both cheap and good-quality jackets, and the excellent and stylish shoe shops.

Secondhand

More up-market and designer secondhand clothing (Jill Sander, Yves Saint Laurent, etc) can be found by perusing **Mommsenstrasse**, starting at the **Knesebeckstrasse** end, in Charlottenburg.

Checkpoint, Mehringdamm 57, Kreuzberg ☎6 94 43 44. Funky club wear and other brightly coloured youth fashions. Shoes too.

Colours, Bergmanstr. 102 Hinterhof, Kreuzberg ☎6 94 33 48. Kin to Made in Berlin (see below), but with a wider range of clothes.

Garage, Ahornstr. 2, Schöneberg ☎2 11 27 60 (Mon–Sat noon–9pm). Largest secondhand clothes store in Europe; good for jackets, coats and jeans. Prices are according to weight (the clothes', not yours).

Humana, Karl-Liebknecht-Str. 30, Mitte ☎2 42 30 00. Secondhand chain, offering great bargains on items that are (again) in style. Branches at Zoo Station and in Prenzlauer Berg.

La Bottega, Akazienstr. 7, Schöneberg ☎78 70 44 29. Antique outfits and trendy secondhand to rent or buy.

Made in Berlin, Potsdamer Str. 106, Tiergarten ☎2 62 24 31. Popular with the *Szene* crowd and very 1970s at the moment.

Second Coming, Motzstr. 15, Schöneberg. Rather a raggedy selection, but hunt hard enough and you might find a bargain.

Secondo, Mommsenstr. 61, Charlottenburg ☎8 81 22 91. Exclusively designer clothes.

Sgt. Peppers, Kastanienallee 91, Prenzlauer Berg ☎4 48 11 21. Vintage 1960s and 1970s.

Sterling Gold, Oranienburger Str. 32, Mitte ☎28 09 65 00. Vintage prom, evening, cocktail and wedding dresses.

Textil-Basar, Hauptstr. 51, Schöneberg ☎8 59 28 29. Women's designer clothing; some leather goods.

New and designer labels

Clothes shops open, close and change hands almost as fast as bars in Berlin. To find the latest additions, wander down **Bleibtreustrasse** between the Ku'damm and Kantstrasse – this area is also great to browse in during the sales in January (*Winterschluss verkauf*) and July/August (*Sommerschluss verkauf*), when designer and less well-known names are on offer at knockdown prices – the length of **Pestalozzistrasse** (until Wilmersdorfer Strasse), **Oranienstrasse**, **Stuttgarter Platz** and **Ludwigkirschstrasse**, off Uhlandstrasse.

Betty Bund, Oderberger Str. 6, Prenzlauer Berg ☎61 28 44 75. Simple lines and materials, mix and match outfits. Connected to Body Covering store (see below).

Blue Moon, Wilmersdorfer Str. 80, Wilmersdorf ☎3 23 70 88. Ultra-trendy *Szene* shop.

Blutorange, Neu Schonhauser Str. 67, Mitte. Featuring trendy and Italian designs for men and women.

Body Covering, Kopenick Str. 10, Prenzlauer Berg ☎61 28 48 92. High street fashion. Connected to the Betty Bund store (see above).

Boutique Soft, Bleibtreustr. 6, Charlottenburg ☎3 12 14 03. Jean Paul Gaultier, Thierry Mugler, Montana et al.

Claudia Skoda, Linien Str. 156, Mitte ☎2 80 72 11. Berlin's knitmaster and most famous designer.

Dajka, Zossener Str. 37, Kreuzberg ☎6 94 67 53. Updated fashion wear and low-pressure shopping.

Depot 2, Oranienstr. 9, Kreuzberg ☎6 11 46 55. Hip-hop and skating fashion.

DKNY and Donna Karan, Friedrichstr. 71 (in the Friedrichstadt Passagen), Mitte ☎20 94 60 10. The local branch of the wildy popular New York label. The Donna Karan shop is upstairs.

Eisdieler, Kastanienallee 12, Prenzlauer Berg ☎28 38 87 25. Innovative, international collection.

Essence, Nurnberber Str. 50–56, Charlottenburg ☎2 11 20 09. Street, sport, skate and snowboarding clothing.

Evento, Grolmanstr. 53–54, Charlottenburg ☎3 13 32 17. Understated linen and wool designs for women, some belts and bags. Great quality and reasonable prices.

Groopie Deluxe, Goltzstr. 39, Schöneberg ☎2 17 20 38. Trendy German design. Great bags and shoes.

Hallhuber, Kurfürstendamm 13, Charlottenburg ☎8 81 20 78. This store concentrates on affordable high-street fashions using natural fibres, and carries its own label alongside others such as Esprit and Strenesse.

H&M, Kurfürstendamm 20, Charlottenburg ☎8 82 62 99, and Tauentzienstr. 13a, Charlottenburg ☎2 13 90 92. Inexpensive, up-to-the-minute styles. Branches all over town.

Inge Helf, Uhlandstr. 170, Charlottenburg ☎8 83 48 16. International designs and young fashions, in bigger than standard sizes.

Jean Pascale, Europa Center, Tauentzienstr. 9, Charlottenburg ☎2 62 54 90. Similar to H&M, only cheaper.

Jill Sander, Kurfürstendamm 185, Charlottenberg ☎8 86 70 20. Minimal and simple, a favourite designer of the understated.

Levi's, Kurfürstendamm 36, Charlottenburg ☎8 85 78 10, and Schlossstr. 9, Steglitz ☎7 91 70 80. All styles of Levi's jeans stocked, along with Levi's sweatshirts, T-shirts, footwear and bags. Jeans around DM140 (€71.60).

Lisa D., Rosenthaler Str. 40–41 (in the Hackescher Höfe), Mitte ☎2 82 90 61. One of Berlin's very few local designers

to have made a name for herself, Lisa D. favours fitted dresses in muted colours.

Mientus Studio 2002, Wilmersdorfer Str. 73, Charlottenburg ☎3 23 90 77. Casual and formal up-to-the-minute menswear, ranging in price from reasonable to outrageously expensive.

Molotow, Gneisenaustr. 112, Kreuzberg ☎6 93 08 18. The best of west and east Berlin designers; mid-price range.

Morgan, Friedrichstr. 67 (in the Friedrichstadt Passagen), Mitte ☎20 94 58 90. The Paris-based boutique offers its spirited, youthful clothing and accessories in this upscale shopping mall. Second store at Kurfürstendamm 236 (☎88 68 33 00).

Nix, Auguststr. 86, Mitte ☎2 81 80 44. Unusual designs for women from a couple of young east Berliners.

Planet, Schluterstr. 36, Charlottenburg ☎8 85 27 17. Very hip, future styles, club wear, and shoes.

Planet Mini, Kaiser-Wilhelm-Platz 2, Schöneberg ☎7 82 26 91. Outrageous labels and shoes. Smaller sister store to Planet.

Respectmen, Neu Schonhauser Str. 14, Mitte ☎2 83 50 10. Good tailoring and nice design mark this men's store which features suits and casual wear.

Retro Mode, Oranienburger Str. 13, Mitte ☎28 09 77 02. Stylish Italian suits and shoes and, two doors down, a separate shop with leather jackets and coats.

Soma, Alte Schonhauser Str. 27, Mitte ☎2 81 93 80. Young Berlin designers and club wear in the front, secondhand in the rear.

The Black Rose, Danziger Str. 25, Prenzlauer Berg ☎44 05 17 44. Upon entering this shop with the changing room that resembles a coffin, you question if you are back in London or the East Village in 1977. Punk, goth, and heavy metal clothing and accessories.

The World Shop, Oranienstr. 198, Kreuzberg ☎6 18 98 65. T-Shirt mecca – ready-made or special orders.

Shopping

Shopping

For serious cowboy and bike boot shopping, take a stroll along Kantstrasse from Schlüterstrasse to Wilmersdorfstrasse.

To Die For, Neu Shonhauser Str. 10, Mitte ☎28 38 68 34. Featuring innovative Berlin designers.

Uli Knecht, Kurfürstendamm 30, Charlottenberg ☎88 67 78 42. Multibrand shop featuring cool club wear such as Gaultier, Paul Smith and Philosophy.

Unplugged, Gneisenauerstr. 95, Kreuzberg ☎6 94 25 15. Jeans, sweats, sunglasses – at fair prices.

Zeppelin, Oranienburger Str. 87, Mitte. Smart and expensive Italian clothes for men and women.

360, Pariser Str. 23, Wilmersdorf ☎8 83 85 96. Extreme sport clothing and equipment, including blades, windsurfing, surfing and snowboarding outfits. Also organizes adventure activities.

Shoes

Berlin does not have the best selection of great shoes, but there are odd and wonderful things if you look. Small shoe boutiques in the area of Mitte near Hackescher Markt feature innovative styles.

Barfuss oder Lackschuh, Oranienburgerstr. 89, Mitte ☎28 39 19 91. The place to head for everything from designer shoes to workboots.

Budapester Schuhe, Kurfürstendamm 199, Charlottenberg ☎8 81 17 07. World-class, expensive designer shoes such as Prada, Dolce & Gabbana, etc.

Luccico, Goltzstr. 34, Schöneberg; Zossenerstr. 32, Kreuzberg; and Bergmannstr. 97, Kreuzberg. Wild and wacky Italian shoes, plus plainer varieties.

Ludwig Reiter, Fasanenstr. 29, Charlottenberg ☎88 68 17 76. Luxurious formal wear and well-made sports shoes.

Mad Flavor, Krumme Str. 58, Charlottenberg ☎3 12 49 63. Trendy sneakers for the hip-hop and club crowd.

Roots, Kantstr. 57, Charlottenburg ☎3 23 30 21. Specializes in comfortable "earth" styles.

Saloon, Boots and Stuff, Oranienstr. 4, Kreuzberg ☎6 12 54 76. Cowboy boots and other Wild West essentials.

Schuhtick, Savignyplatz 11, Charlottenburg ☎3 15 93 80, and Tauentzienstr. 5, Schöneberg ☎2 14 09 80. Wide range of desirable shoes. Branches at Karl-Liebknecht-Str., Mitte ☎2 42 40 12, and Maassenstr. 5, Schöneberg ☎2 17 08 86.

Trippen, Hackescher Höfe, Rosenthaler Str. 40, Mitte ☎28 39 13 37. Hot Berlin design original specializing in wooden soled shoes with a rounded toe.

Zapato, Maassenstr. 14, Schöneberg ☎2 16 65 67. Full of off-beat styles for men and women.

Underwear

As a rule, any form of underwear not bought in a supermarket – or at H&M (see previous page) – is fiercely expensive in Berlin, and, from a quality point of view, not worth the extra outlay. Tights are individually sized and generally cut small – try a size larger for a good fit.

Falke, Quartier 206, Friedrichstr. 71, Mitte ☎20 94 61 10. The place to go for men's underclothing and socks.

Femme Dessous, Fasanenstr. 31, Charlottenburg ☎8 82 53 39. Luxury lingerie from La Perla.

Fogal, Kurfürstendamm 216, Charlottenburg ☎8 81 15 16. Luxury tights and stockings with amazing colours to match anything.

Körpernah, Maassenstr. 10, Schöneberg ☎2 15 74 71. Well-designed French and Italian underwear; friendly service.

La Perla, Quartier 206, Friedrichstr. 71, Mitte ☎20 94 60 80/81. Lovely lingerie with nice detailing and fit.

Rose, Rosa, Bleibtreustr. 5a, Charlottenburg ☎3 12 21 40. Hanro, Bleyle and other German brands.

Strumpfladen, Kurfürstendamm 66, Charlottenburg ☎8 83 62 54; and in Europa Center, Charlottenburg ☎2 61 20 25. Wide selection of tights, stockings and leggings.

Hair and beauty

There are plenty of places to get made up and smelling good in Berlin, though note that as a rule hairdressers are closed on Monday. As well as the parfumiers listed below, there are also branches of Parfumerie Douglas (several on Kurfürstendamm – notably on the corner of Uhlandstr. and Fasanenstr.) which carry an extensive range of up-to-date and established perfume lines. KaDeWe department store has the largest cosmetic floor in the city, and Quartier 206 on Friedrichstrasse the most exclusive.

Shopping

HAIR

Carlo Piras, Fasanenstr. 42, Charlottenburg ☎ 8 82 11 00. Classy salon in the Italian school of hairdressing.

Dirk I, Goethestr. 15, Charlottenberg ☎ 3 13 71 32. The staff are trained in London to keep up on current trends. Care is given to individual preference, with styles that suit.

Haareszeiten, Danziger Str. 56, Prenzlauer Berg ☎ 44 05 00 02. Expert colourists, understanding of hair disasters, and child-friendly: they also do kids' cuts.

Heinz Schlicht, Uhlandstr./ Kurfürstendamm, Charlottenburg ☎ 8 82 73 05. A favourite among Berliners for twenty years. Service is professional but relaxed, and some of the staff are English.

Jason's Hairpower, Leibnizstr. 102, Charlottenburg ☎ 3 41 90 85. Ultra-hip and ultra-expensive hairstylists that has numbered David Bowie and Brigitte Nielsen among its customers.

Locke & Glatze, Kastanienallee 59, Prenzlauer Berg ☎ 4 48 26 20. If you're undecided and open to suggestions, this trendy salon is the place for you. Another branch at Boxhagener Str., Friedrichshain ☎ 2 94 97 78.

Schnittstelle, Kollwitzstr. 70, Prenzlauer Berg ☎ 44 04 98 70. Good cuts and colour to the sound of techno.

Toni & Guy, Kaiser-Friedrich-Str. 1a, Charlottenburg ☎ 3 41 85 45. Local branch of the London-based hairstylists, and staffed with many English-speakers.

Venus, Goltzstr. 38, Schöneberg ☎ 2 16 47 91. Punk and "normal" hairstyles at reasonable prices.

Vidal Sassoon, Schlüterstr. 38, Charlottenburg ☎ 8 84 50 00. After a successful run in Munich and Hamburg, this outfit has decided at long last to add Berlin to its list. From DM80 (€40.90). Predominantly English and American staff.

Wasser & Welle, Schonhauser Allee 174, Prenzlauer Berg ☎ 4 49 11 62. Friendly relaxing salon for a perfect cut.

PERFUMERIES

Belladonna, Bergmannstr. 101, Kreuzberg ☎ 6 94 37 31. Large choice of natural cosmetics.

Body Shop, Schlossstr. 25, Steglitz ☎ 7 92 25 57; also Zoo Station shopping complex, Charlottenburg, and Friedrichstr. station. Berlin franchise of the familiar British-based concern. Daily until 9pm.

DK Cosmetics, Kurfürstendamm 56, Charlottenberg ☎ 32 79 01 23. Hard-to-find top brands from around the world.

Harry Lehman, Kantstr. 106, Charlottenburg ☎ 3 24 35 82. Mix your smells then take them away, for DM5 (€2.50). Over fifty different brews, including one aptly named "Berlin".

Ligne de Vie, Friedrichstadt Passagen, Friedrichstr. 70, Mitte. Elegant and expensive scents in an upscale shopping complex.

Shopping

Wolford, Meinekestr. 26, Mitte ☎ 8 83 34 00. Lingerie from Austria.

Other accessories

Augenoptik Neumann, Gneisenaustr. 22, Kreuzberg ☎ 6 91 93 34. Large variety of 1950s glasses, currently all the rage here.

Fiona Bennett, Grosse Hamburger Str. 25, Mitte ☎ 28 09 63 30. Unique and avant-garde designer hats for men and women.

Glasses, Nürnberger Str. 50–56, Schöneberg ☎ 2 18 24 74. Optician's set out like a cocktail bar.

Optiker Hübner, Torstr. 119, am Rosenthaler Platz, Mitte ☎ 4 49 61 00. Purveyor of gimmick glasses. Check out the Batman and Robin specs, and the "Windscreenwiper" for those rainy days.

Rio, Bleibtreustr. 52, Charlottenburg ☎ 3 13 31 52. Unusual decorative costume jewellers, specializing in earrings at affordable prices.

Sack & Pack, Kantstr. 48, Charlottenburg ☎ 3 12 15 13. Natural- and black-leather bags in sporty styles.

Scenario, Savigny Passage, Bogen 602, Charlottenburg ☎ 3 12 91 99. Up-market gift shop, with leather goods and jewellery among its wares.

Travel equipment

Bannat, Lietzenburger Str. 65, Charlottenburg ☎ 8 82 76 01. A great selection of travel equipment, particularly for the backpacker and camper.

Camp 4, Karl-Marx-Allee 32, Mitte ☎ 2 42 66 34; *www.camp4.de*. Everything necessary for hiking and mountain climbing.

Farradbüro Berlin, Hauptstr. 146 (next to Kleiststr. U-Bahn), Schöneberg ☎ 78 70 26 00. Every conceivable piece of equipment for bikes.

Department stores

There are no surprises inside Berlin's **department stores** and, with the exception of KaDeWe and Galeries Lafayette, they're only worth popping into to stock up on essentials or to buy **concert and theatre tickets** at the Theaterkassen. Listed below are the most central ones; check the phone book for outlying branches.

Galeries Lafayette, Französische Str. 23, Mitte ☎ 20 94 80. Branch of the upscale Paris-based department store. Surprisingly small, but packed with beautiful and expensive things and including a food department with imports from France.

Hertie, Karl-Marx-Str. 92–98, Neukölln ☎ 68 99 40. Not as wide a range of goods as at Karstadt (see below) and more expensive.

KaDeWe, Tauentzienstr. 21, Schöneberg ☎ 2 12 10. Content rather than flashy interior decor rules the day here. From designer labels to the extraordinarily good displays at the international delicatessen, where you can nibble on some piece of exotica or stock up on double-price El Paso taco mix, everything the consumer's heart desires can be found at this, the largest department store on the Continent.

Karstadt, Wilmersdorfer Str. 118, Charlottenburg ☎ 31 10 50; Schlossstr. 7, Steglitz ☎ 79 00 10; and Hermannplatz, Kreuzberg ☎ 6 95 50. Good basic all-rounder, classier and cheaper than Hertie. The branch at Hermannplatz is the best stocked.

Kaufhof, Alexanderplatz 9, Mitte ☎ 24 74 30. Once the location of the GDR's showcase department store, this is now a quite typical emporium.

Wertheim, Kurfürstendamm 231, Charlottenburg ☎ 88 00 30. A smaller and cheaper version of KaDeWe. Everything is beautifully laid out, with a particularly good menswear department.

Woolworth, Wilmersdorfer Str. 113, Charlottenburg ☎ 3 18 67 30; and Johannisthaler Chaussee 319, Neukölln ☎ 6 66 91 60. Good for cheap basic toiletries and essentials.

Food and drink

Of the city's **supermarket chains**, Pennymarkt, a kind of budget grocery store, is by far the cheapest for food and drink, although it offers less choice than the rest. Ullrich, on Hardenbergstrasse, underneath the railway bridge by Zoo Station, has an excellent selection of foods, wines and spirits and is very cheap despite its central location. The city's **speciality food shops** are spread throughout the town, though the majority of Turkish shops are in Kreuzberg. Health food is very popular, particularly organically grown fruit and vegetables, and almost every neighbourhood has its own health-food shop (*Naturkostladen*), with vegetarian goodies, chemical-free beers and wines. The night shops listed in the box below all close before midnight, and prices are about a third higher than usual.

Bread and cakes

Freshly baked **bread** is one of the delights of Berlin, where small neighbourhood bakeries provide wholemeal loaves fresh from their ovens. For cakes, it's hard to beat the quality and selection on offer at KaDeWe – you may end up paying slightly more here than elsewhere, but you won't regret it.

Brendel, Grossbeerenstr. 16, Kreuzberg ☎2 16 91 55. Speciality breads, rolls, baguettes, etc.

Café Kranzler, Kurfürstendamm/Joachimstalerstr., Charlottenburg ☎8 85 77 20. Pricey café and cake shop, with delicious, rich creations.

Café Möhring, am Gendarmenmarkt, Charlottenstr. 55, Mitte ☎2 03 90 22 40. A long-lived and well-known concern in Berlin, once again located at its original nineteenth-century address on Gendarmenmarkt.

Einhorn, Wittenbergplatz 5, Schöneberg ☎21 47 51 80. Wholegrain breads and cakes.

KaDeWe, Tauentzienstr. 21, Schöneberg ☎2 12 10. The sixth-floor food hall has over 400 different breads.

Leysieffers, Kurfürstendamm 218, Charlottenburg ☎8 85 74 80. Best selection of cakes, chocolates and biscuits in town.

Operncafé, Unter den Linden 5, Mitte ☎20 26 83. An amazing array of baroque extravaganzas in cakes and gateaux. Select one from the display, collect a ticket and give it to the waiter.

Weichardt, Mehlitzstr. 7, Wilmersdorf ☎8 73 80 99; *www.weichardt.de*. Probably the best *Vollkorn* bakery in town: delicious cakes and breads.

Wiener Conditorei Kaffeehaus am Roseneck, Hohenzollerndamm 92, Zehlendorf ☎89 59 69 20. Cakes made by the *Operncafé*, on sale in Zehlendorf.

Coffee and tea

Eduscho, Frankfurter Allee 111, Friedrichshain ☎42 78 03 87 (and branches around town). Good-quality ground coffee, and the cheapest stand-up coffee in the city.

Shopping

Night shops

The following shops open beyond normal hours, but charge considerably for the convenience. Many **Turkish shops** are open Saturday afternoons and Sundays 1–5pm, and **petrol stations** often have shops with basics that are open seven days a week until late.

Lidl, in Ostbahnhof, Friedrichshain (Mon–Fri 8am–9pm, Sat & Sun 9am–9pm).

Metro, in U-Bahn Kurfürstendamm, Charlottenburg (daily 11am–11pm, Sat till midnight).

Nimm's Mit, Zoo Station, Charlottenburg (Mon–Sat 6am–10pm, Sun 8am–10pm).

Reise Point Markt, Friedrichstrasse S- & U-Bahn, Mitte (Mon–Sat 6am–10pm, Sun 8am–10pm). Everything from videos to shaving cream, but at hugely inflated prices.

Shopping

Jade Libelle, Chauseestr. 4, Mitte ☎2 82 91 27. Offering Asian teas and Chinese art objects.

King's Teegarden, Kurfürstendamm 217, Charlottenburg ☎8 83 70 59. Buy your tea downstairs or drink a range of brews upstairs to a background of classical music. Open all day Saturday.

Tchibo, Kurfürstendamm 11, Charlottenburg ☎8 81 11 94 (other branches around the city). The second most popular coffee shop after *Eduscho*, with the advantage that you can mix your own blend of beans from a small choice at the counter.

TeeHaus, Krumme Str. 35, Charlottenburg ☎31 50 98 82. A tea-lover's paradise: teas sold loose and to suit every taste. Also English jams and natural honeys.

Delicatessens and ethnic foods

Alimentari e Vini, Skalitzer Str. 23, Kreuzberg ☎6 11 49 81. A slick shop in scruffy Kreuzberg offering wines, pastas and other Italian deli items.

Aqui Espana, Kantstr. 34, Charlottenburg ☎3 12 33 15. Spanish and South American foods, though rather pricey.

Fuchs & Rabe, Schlossstr. 119, Steglitz ☎7 92 81 68. Row upon row of exotic and unusual cheeses and dishes containing cheese. Made-to-order rolls at lunchtime. Also at Ludwigskirchstr. 2, Wilmersdorf ☎8 82 39 84, for fresh home-made pasta and a good stand-up *Imbiss*.

Galeries Lafayette, Französische Str. 23, Mitte ☎20 94 80. Like the larger KaDeWe, this swank department store offers a gourmet food section with delectables from around the world.

Holland Shop, Mehringdamm 73, Kreuzberg ☎6 92 69 67. Far Eastern specialities, lots of cheap herbs and spices, flavourings and sauces.

KaDeWe, Tauentzienstr. 21, Schöneberg ☎2 12 10. The sixth-floor food hall (*Feinschmecker Etage*) of the giant department store is a gourmet's delight: 400 types of bread, 1200 cheeses and 1400 meats, plus cafés where you can sample lots of the goodies on sale. The dough for their French bakery, Le Notre, is flown in from Paris daily.

Kolbo, Auguststr. 78, Mitte ☎2 81 31 35. Kosher food and wine, and Jewish specialities.

Ku Long, Nollendorfstr. 8, Schöneberg ☎2 16 66 98. Southeast Asian ingredients.

La Cantina, Kreuzbergstr. 76, Kreuzberg ☎7 85 87 93. Top-class Italian deli, with olive oils, fresh pasta and exotic vinegars.

Salumeria da Pino & Enzo, Windscheidstr. 20, Charlottenburg ☎3 24 33 18. Wines and yummy Italian delicacies. Mouthwatering nibbles available for lunch.

Südwind, Akazienstr. 7, Charlottenburg ☎7 82 04 39. Wines and products from Tuscany. Very good value.

Fish and meats

Alternative Fleischerei, Körtestr. 20, Kreuzberg ☎6 91 64 86. Cows and chickens that weren't stuffed with chemicals and hormones before they were killed.

Klaus Gerlach, Greifswalder Str. 205, Prenzlauer Berg ☎4 42 61 83. One of the few butchers located in the eastern part of the city to offer organically raised meat.

Rogacki, Wilmersdorfer Str. 145–146, Charlottenburg ☎3 43 82 50; *www.rogacki.de*. Great selection of fresh and smoked fish, with an eat-in *Imbiss*.

Schlemmermeyer, Schlossstr. 6, Steglitz ☎7 93 31 38. Bavarian sausage, cooked and smoked meat heaven.

Health food

Kräuter Kuhne, Prenzlauer Allee 175, Prenzlauer Berg ☎4 45 69 30. Herbal specialist, with a good selection of sweet and savoury snacks.

Lotus, Pestalozzistr. 29, Charlottenburg ☎31 80 97 40. Health-food shop with vegetarian meals and salads to eat in or take out.

Manne & Tiaré, Weinmeisterstr. 9a, Mitte ☎2 81 73 34. Natural foods and organic cosmetics.

Mutter Erde, Behaimstr. 18, Charlottenburg ☎3 41 79 55. Large stock of organic vegetables and wines and "green" household products.

Naturkost Mitte, Linienstr. 150, Mitte ☎28 87 92 45. Small shop with vegetables and other organically grown products.

Sesammühle, Knesebeckstr. 89, Charlottenburg ☎3 12 51 99. Health foods.

UFA-Fabrik-Laden, Viktoriastr. 13, Tempelhof ☎75 50 31 51. Wholefoods and goods from developing and politically emergent countries.

Wines and spirits

Hardy in Huth, Alte Potsdamer Str. 5, Tiergarten ☎25 29 72 80. Well-stocked store and wine bar in the old Weinhaus Huth, the only prewar building remaining in Potsdamer Platz.

Metzdorf, Saarbrückerstr. 20–21, Prenzlauer Berg ☎44 05 06 55. Features top-quality German wines.

Der Rebgarten, Bergmannstr. 112, Kreuzberg ☎6 94 55 02. Organically grown wines and juices. Open weekday afternoons and Saturday mornings only.

Vendemmia, Akazienstr. 20, Schöneberg ☎7 84 27 28. Bulk-bought Italian wines, so good for bargains. Also sells inexpensive olive oil.

Wein & Glas Compagny, Prinzregentenstr. 2, Schöneberg ☎2 35 15 20. German and French wines (and some glasses).

Weinkeller, Gneisenaustr. 15, Kreuzberg ☎6 93 46 61. Spanish, French, Italian and German wines, and sherries and whiskies from the cask.

Markets

There are several food markets within each quarter of the town, too numerous to mention here; listed below is a selection of the best **flea markets** and **out-**

door food markets. For **junk shops**, Suarezstrasse in Charlottenburg, Gotzstrasse in Schöneberg and Bergmannstrasse in Kreuzberg are the places to head.

Flea markets

Antiquitäten- und Flohmarkt, Bahnhof Friedrichstrasse (under the railway arches 190–203), Mitte. Tending more towards the antique end of things with numerous little shops selling everything from books to jewellery. Not particularly cheap. Daily except Tues 11am–6pm.

Humboldt Universität, Unter den Linden, Mitte. Secondhand books, mostly in German. Daily from 2pm.

John-F-Kennedy-Platz, in front of the Schöneberg City Hall, Schöneberg. Some professionals here selling books and collectibles, but also a good number of amateur vendors who have cleared out the garage or attic and are selling the motley results. Sat & Sun 8am–4pm.

Kunst und Nostalgie Markt, by the Bode and Pergamon Museums, Mitte. A good mix of real antiques, schlock souvenirs, used books and bootleg CDs. Sat & Sun 11am–5pm.

Marheinekeplatz Markthalle, Marheinekeplatz, Kreuzberg. Indoor market with a little of everything and some bargains. Good for fresh fruit and veg and especially fish. Mon–Sat 8am–6pm.

Strasse des 17 Juni, north side of road near Ernst-Reuter-Platz, Charlottenburg. Pleasant enough for a Sunday morning stroll, but the most expensive of the flea markets, and with horribly tourist-oriented wares. Good for embroidery and lace though. Sat & Sun 10am–5pm.

Türken-Markt, Kottbusser Damm/Maybachufer, Neukölln. Definitely worth a visit, especially on Friday when there's a real Oriental flavour. Handy for all things Turkish, especially cheese, bread, olives and dried fruits, all at rock-bottom prices. Tues & Fri noon–6pm.

Winterfeldtmarkt, am Winterfeldtplatz, Schöneberg. Arguably the most popular market in Berlin, with brightly printed

Shopping

Shopping

clothes, exotic smells floating in the breeze, and plenty of cafés nearby for a drink afterwards. Wed & Sat 8am–1pm.

Zille-Hof, Fasanenstr. 14, Charlottenburg. Not so much a flea market as an overgrown junkshop with reproduction curios, old street signs and a miscellany of interesting junk. Not especially cheap, but good fun. Mon–Fri 8.30am–5.30pm.

Flowers and plants

Flowers are frequently given as gifts, and are almost a prerequisite for birthdays and other special occasions. When looking for flowers, avoid the Ku'damm, where prices are steep and quality is poor, and take a look instead along some of the side streets. It's more fun choosing your own bouquet. Simply explain roughly what colours you'd like and the price you'd prefer to pay – try around DM20 (€10.25). The city's many open-air markets also sell interesting arrangements at affordable prices.

Art Floral, Grolmanstr. 29, Charlottenburg ☎8 83 45 84. Beautiful flowers, plants and ceramic pots from DM10 (€5.10).

Blumenladen, Südstern U-Bahn, Kreuzberg ☎6 91 89 24. Flowers on Sunday.

Blumen Röwer, S-Bahnhof Friedrichstr., Mitte ☎20 45 43 49. Conveniently located in the Friedrichstrasse train station.

Exotic Green, Schönebergweg 2–4, Schöneberg ☎6 64 43 01. Bamboo and other indoor plants and trees.

Petit Fleur, Knesebeckstr. 88, Charlottenburg ☎3 12 93 77. Floral arrangements and plants for all occasions; also sells greetings cards and wrapping paper.

Crafts and antiques

Bale-Bale, Savignyplatz 6, Charlottenburg ☎3 12 90 66. Arts and crafts from India, Pakistan and Indonesia.

El Condor, Kantstr. 36, Charlottenburg ☎3 13 98 28. Latin American crafts.

Dritte-Welt-Laden, inside the Gedächtniskirche, Charlottenburg ☎8 31

54 32. Nonprofit organization selling handicrafts from the Third World.

Jukeland, Crelle Str. 14, Schöneberg ☎7 82 33 35. For lovers of 1950s paraphernalia American-style, including a selection of hugely expensive jukeboxes.

Lampen aus 100 Jahren, Mittenwalder Str. 30, Kreuzberg ☎6 92 11 15. Antique and Art Deco lamps, both sophisticated and outrageous.

Miscellaneous

As Germany's largest and most cosmopolitan city, Berlin offers a cross section of unusual and quirky stores – from the trendy to the merely odd.

Atzert-Radio, Kleiststr. 33, Schöneberg ☎2 12 98 41. Do-it-yourself radio and electronics paradise.

Bären–Luftballons, Kurfürstenstr. 31–32, Tiergarten ☎26 97 50. Balloons in all colours, shapes and sizes.

Foto Meyer, Viktoria-Luise-Platz 6, Schöneberg ☎2 35 09 90; www.fotomeyer.de. Reasonably priced cameras and darkroom equipment, plus good-quality film processing.

George Behrendt, Hauptstr. 18, Schöneberg ☎7 81 49 06. Everything for parties, from napkins to costumes to exploding cigars.

Kaufhaus Schrill, Bleibtreustr. 46. Charlottenburg ☎8 82 40 48. An Aladdin's Cave of delights, from fish-shaped ties to fluorescent tutus.

Küchenladen, Knesebeckstr. 26, Charlottenburg ☎8 81 39 08. Everything for the foodie, from tortoiseshell teaspoons to Italian cookbooks.

Münzfachgeschäft Moneta, Friedrichstr. 114, Mitte ☎2 82 67 20. An old-fashioned little shop of coins and medals.

Pfeifenmacher, Bismarckstr. 60, Charlottenburg ☎3 41 63 03. Huge selection of tobaccos and own-brand pipes made on the premises.

Souvenir Shop Boenicke, in Europa Center, Charlottenburg, ☎2 61 46 82. *The* place to get kitsch mementos such as cuckoo clocks and beer steins.

Vom Winde Verweht, Eisenacher Str. 81, Schöneberg ☎78 70 36 36. Small shop that sells all kinds of kites, from the simple to the grandiose.

Zauberkönig, Hermannstr. 84, Neukölln ☎6 21 40 82. Illusions, tricks, and other magicians' equipment.

Zinnfiguren Kabinet, Knesebeckstr 88, Charlottenburg ☎3 15 70 00. Beautifully made model soldiers – not cheap, and certainly not toys.

Zinnsoldaten, Skalitzerstr. 81, Kreuzberg ☎6 18 38 15. Enormous selection of tin figures.

Shopping

Chapter 19

Directory

ADDRESSES The street name is always written before the number and all Berlin addresses are suffixed by a five-figure post code. Street numbers don't always run odd–even on opposite sides of the street – often they go up one side and down the other. *Strasse* (street) is commonly abbreviated to *Str.*, and often joined on to the end of the previous word. Other terms include *Weg* (path), *Ufer* (river bank), *Platz* (square) and *Allee* (avenue). Berlin apartment blocks are often built around courtyards with several entrances and staircases: the *Vorderhaus*, abbreviated as *VH* in addresses, is as the name suggests, the front building; the *Gartenhaus* (garden house) and the *Hinterhof* (*HH*; back house) are at the rear of the building. *EG* means the ground floor, *1 OG* means the first floor, etc. *Dachwohnung* means the "flat under the roof" – ie the top floor.

AIRLINES Aeroflot, Unter den Linden 51, Mitte ☎ 2 26 98 10; Air Canada, Kurfürstendamm 207, Charlottenburg ☎ 8 82 58 79; Air France, Tegel Airport ☎ 0180/5 83 08 30; British Airways, central info number ☎ 0180/5 26 65 22; Deutsche BA, Poststrasse 4–5, Mitte ☎ 2 47 36 80; KLM, Tegel Airport ☎ 0180/5 21 42 01; LTU, Schönefeld Airport ☎ 63 30 62 03; Lufthansa, Kurfürstendamm 220, Charlottenburg ☎ 88 75 88; Sabena, Tempelhof Airport, Tempelhof ☎ 69 51 38 50; Swissair, Kurfürstendamm 206, Charlottenburg ☎ 0181 525 8575.

AIRPORT TAX Tax varies from DM10 (€5.10) to DM120 (€61.50) depending upon destination and time of travel.

BEACHES Berlin has one of the largest inland beaches in Europe, Strandbad Wannsee, on the Havel River at Wannsee to the west of the city centre (see p.167). To the east, the best beaches are on the northern shore of the Müggelsee near the small town of Rahnsdorf (see p.198). Both these beaches include an *FKK* (nudist) stretch. There are also possibilities in Grünau and, just outside Berlin, on the lakes south of Potsdam.

BIKE RENTAL Fahrradstation branches at Bergmannstr. 9, Kreuzberg ☎ 2 15 15 66; Augustr. 29a, Mitte ☎ 28 59 56 61; Bahnhof Friedrichstrasse ☎ 20 45 45 00; and Hackesche Höfe ☎ 28 38 48 48. Their office hours are Mon–Fri 10am–6pm, Sat 10am–2pm, but it's best to phone a reservation through first.

CAR RENTAL Some inexpensive firms, each charging around DM60 (€30.70) a day, are: ACS Rent a Car, Albrechtstr. 117, Schöneberg ☎ 7 92 00 15; City Trans, Wönnichstr. 100, Lichtenberg ☎ 5 12 71 14; C. Nagel, Bundesallee 176, Wilmersdorf ☎ 8 54 30 00. Among the major international firms, you could try Avis, Budapester Str. 43, Charlottenburg ☎ 2 30 93 70; Hertz, Spandauer Str. 5, Mitte ☎ 2 42 44 40; National, Witzlebenstrasse 26, Charlottenburg ☎ 8 85 72 70. The international firms also have offices at Tegel airport and are listed in the phone book under "Autovermietungen".

CONTRACEPTION A glowing spectrum of condoms is available from supermarkets, anywhere selling toiletries, and vending machines in bar toilets. To get a prescription for the pill you'll need to see a doctor, so it's worth stocking up before leaving.

ELECTRICITY The supply is 220 volts, though anything requiring 240 volts (all UK appliances) will work. American visitors, however, will need a voltage converter to run appliances. Sockets are of the two-pin variety, so a travel plug is useful.

EMBASSIES AND CONSULATES Australia, Uhlandstr. 181–183 ☎030/8 80 08 80, *www.australian-embassy.de*; Britain, Wilhelmstr. 70–71 ☎030/20 18 40, *www.britischebotschaft.de*; Canada, Friedrichstr. 95 ☎030/20 31 20, *www.kanada-info.de*; Ireland, Friedrichstr. 200 ☎030/22 07 20; New Zealand, Friedrichstr. 60 ☎030/20 62 10; US, Neustadtische Kirchstr. 4–5 ☎030/2 38 51 74, visa section, Clayallee 170 ☎030/8 32 92 33, *www.usembassy.de*.

HOSPITALS For immediate medical attention, head for one of the major hospitals: Charité, Schumann Str. 20–21, Mitte ☎2 80 20; Krankenhaus Am Urban, Dieffenbachstr. 1, Kreuzberg ☎69 70; Krankenhaus Moabit, Turmstr. 21, Tiergarten ☎3 97 60; Krankenhaus Neukölln, Rudower Str. 48, Neukölln ☎6 00 41; Martin-Luther-Krankenhaus, Caspar-Theyss-Str. 27–31, Grunewald ☎8 95 50; St Hedwig Krankenhaus, Grosse Hamburger Str. 5 ☎2 31 10; St Joseph Krankenhaus, Bäumerplan 24, Tempelhof ☎7 88 20.

ID Bits of official-looking paper go down well in Berlin. For anything requiring proof of age or identity (banking, student discounts and the like) it's a good idea to have your passport on hand. It's essential that you carry all your documentation when driving – failure to do so may result in an on-the-spot fine.

INTERNET ACCESS *Alpha*, Dunckerstr. 72, Prenzlauer Berg ☎4 47 90 67, *www.alpha-icafe.de*; *Cyberb@r Zoo*, in Karstadt Sporthaus, Joachimstaler Str. 5–6, Charlottenburg ☎88 02 40, *www.cyberbarzoo.de*; *Cafe@Home*, Wollankstr. 119, Pankow ☎48 63 76 00, *www.cafe-at-home.de*; *Hai Täck*, Brünhilderstr. 8, Friedenau ☎85 96 14 13, *www.haitaeck.de*; *Website*, Joachimstaler Str. 41, Charlottenburg ☎88 67 96 30, *www.website-cafes.com*; *Webtimes*, Chausseestr. 8, Mitte ☎28 04 98 90, *www.webtimes.de*.

JAYWALKING This is illegal and you can be fined if caught. Even in the irreverent atmosphere of Berlin, locals stand rigidly to attention until the green signal comes on – even when there isn't a vehicle in sight. Cars are not required to stop at crossings; although walking on one should give you right of way, use your judgement and be careful.

LAUNDRIES Rosenthaler Str. 71 (7.30am–10pm); Hermannstr. 74–75 (7.30am–10pm). Other addresses are listed under "Wäschereien" in the Yellow Pages.

LEFT LUGGAGE There are lockers at Zoo Station (DM2/€1, DM3/€1.50 or DM4/€2.05 depending on size), but they don't accept rucksacks. The lockers, on the ground and first floor, are often full, so you may need to use the left-luggage office (DM4/€2.05 per item per day). There are also 24-hour luggage lockers at Friedrichstrasse and Alexanderplatz stations.

LOST PROPERTY Police lost and found, Platz der Luftbrücke 6, Tempelhof ☎69 95. For items lost on public transport, contact the BVG Fundbüro, Fraunhoferstr. 33–36, Charlottenburg ☎25 62 30 40, and for items lost on the S-Bahn system try the Fundbüro at S-Bahn station Schönefeld ☎29 72 96 12.

PETROL STATIONS Aral, Potsdamer Chaussee 6, Zehlendorf; BP, Kurfürstendamm 128, Charlottenburg; Esso, cnr Leibnizstr. and Mommsenstr., Charlottenburg, and Tempelhofer Damm

Directory

Directory

20, Tempelhof; Minol, Prenzlauer Allee 1–4, Prenzlauer Berg, and Holzmarktstr. 36–42, Friedrichshain; Shell, Uhlandstr. 187, Charlottenburg, and Hohenzollerndamm 41, Wilmersdorf

TAXIS Werfelfunk Taxi ☎ 21 01 01 (24hr service); Taxi von Berlin ☎ 6 90 22; Funktaxi Berlin ☎ 26 10 26; Taxifunk ☎ 44 33 22; Saba Taxi ☎ 2 61 70 80.

TIPPING Service is, as a rule, included in the bill. Rounding off the total to the next Mark or five Marks is acceptable in most cases, though when you run up a particularly large tab you will probably want to add some more. If the service was appalling, however, there's absolutely no need to tip. In taxis, add a couple of marks or euros to the total.

TRAVEL AGENTS Autopia Reiseladen, Kurfürstenstr. 153, Schöneberg (☎ 2 61 18 21; *www.autopia-reise.de*), offers lots of cheap flights at youth fares. Express Travel, Giesebrechtstr. 18, Charlottenburg (☎ 3 24 94 20), is a British travel agent. United Planets, Greifswalderstrasse 29, Prenzlauer Berg (☎ 42 80 78 54; *www.united-planets.de*), offers good deals and great service in English. Flugbörse, Schönhauser Allee 185, Prenzlauer Berg (☎ 4 48 54 37), is a chain with over half a dozen shops in the city offering last-minute tickets. Team Reisen, Hauptstr. 9, Schöneberg (☎ 7 80 00 00; *www.teamreisen.de*) offers the benefit of instant ticketing for most flights (apart from same-day departures).

The Contexts

The historical framework

Few cities have a history as tangible as that of Berlin. It's impossible not to be aware of the forces that have shaped the city as you walk through its streets – they have left physical reminders in the shape of shrapnel scars on buildings and, most telling of all, a huge dead swathe right through the middle of the city, now rapidly being transformed by commercial development.

If any city embodies the twentieth century it is Berlin. Even after the darkest days of the Cold War, when agreements between the great powers put an end to the city's role as the prime focus for international tension, Berlin still somehow symbolized the postwar order. And this whole process continues. Though the space where the Wall once ran is gradually being filled, the legacy of forty years of communist government cannot be erased overnight. The unification of Germany has raised startling problems for its capital city: today Berlin is once again the setting for world history's next instalment.

Beginnings

Archeologists reckon that people have lived around the area of modern-day Berlin for about 60,000 years. Traces of hunter-gatherer activity dating from about 8000 BC and more substantial remains of Stone Age farming settlements from 4000 BC onwards have been discovered. The Romans regarded this as barbarian territory and

left no mark on the region. Although **Germanic tribes** first appeared on the scene during the fifth and sixth centuries AD, many of them left during the great migrations of later centuries, and the vacated territories were occupied by **Slavs**. Germanic ascendancy only began in the twelfth and thirteenth centuries, when Saxon feudal barons of the Mark of Brandenburg expelled the Slavs. The **Saxons** also granted municipal charters to two humble riverside towns – where the Berlin story really begins.

The twin towns

Sited on marshlands around an island (today the Museumsinsel and Fischerinsel) at the narrowest point on the River Spree, **Berlin** and **Cölln** were on a major trade route to the east, and began to prosper as municipalities. Despite many links (including a joint town hall built in 1307), they retained their separate identities throughout the fourteenth century, when both received the right to mint their own coinage and pronounce death sentences in local courts. Their admission to the powerful **Hanseatic League** of city-states in 1369 confirmed their economic and political importance. By 1391, Berlin and Cölln were virtually autonomous from the Mark of Brandenburg, which grew ever more chaotic in the early years of the fifteenth century.

Order was eventually restored by **Friedrich Hohenzollern**, burgrave of Nürnberg, whose subjugation of the province was initially welcomed by the burghers of Berlin and Cölln. However, when his son Johann attempted to treat them likewise, they forced him to withdraw to Spandau. It was only divisions within their ranks that enabled **Friedrich II**, Johann's brother, to take over the two cities. Some of the guilds offered him the keys of the gates in return for taking their part against the Berlin-Cölln magistrates. Friedrich obliged, then built a palace and instituted his own harsh rule, forbidding any further union between Berlin and Cölln.

After swiftly crushing a **rebellion** in 1448, Friedrich imposed new restrictions. To symbolize the **consolidation of Hohenzollern power**, a chain was placed around the neck of Berlin's heraldic symbol, the bear, which remained on the city's coat of arms until 1875. After the Hohenzollerns moved their residence and court here, Berlin-Cölln assumed the character of a *Residenzstadt* (royal residence) and rapidly expanded, its old wattle and daub dwellings replaced with more substantial stone buildings – culminating in a Renaissance Schloss finished in 1540. Yet life remained hard, for despite being involved in the Reformation, Berlin-Cölln lagged behind the great cities of western and southern Germany, and in 1576 it was ravaged by plague. The **Thirty Years' War** (1618–1648) marked a low point. After repeated plundering by Swedish troops, the twin towns had lost half their population and one third of their buildings by the end of the war.

The Great Elector

The monumental task of postwar reconstruction fell to the Mark's new ruler, Elector Friedrich **Wilhelm of Brandenburg** (1620–1688), who was barely out of his teens. Massive fortifications were constructed, besides the residences and public buildings necessary to make Berlin-Cölln a worthy capital for an Elector. (Seven Electors – three archbishops, a margrave, duke, count and king – were entitled to elect the Holy Roman Emperor.) In recognition of his achievements, Friedrich Wilhelm came to be known as the **Great Elector**. After defeating the Swedes at the Battle of Fehrbellin in 1675, the Mark of Brandenburg was acknowledged as a force to be reckoned with, and its capital grew accordingly. Recognizing the value of a cosmopolitan population, the Elector permitted Jews and South German Catholics to move here and enjoy protection as citizens.

A later wave of immigrants affected Berlin-Cölln even more profoundly. Persecuted in France, thousands of **Protestant Huguenots** sought new homes in England and Germany. The arrival of five thousand immigrants – mostly skilled craft-workers or traders – revitalized Berlin-Cölln, whose own population was only twenty thousand. French became an almost obligatory second language, indispensable for anyone looking for social and career success. Another fillip to the city's development was the completion of the **Friedrich Wilhelm Canal**, linking the Spree and the Oder, which boosted its status as an east–west trade centre.

Carrying on from where his father had left off, Friedrich III succeeded in becoming king of Prussia to boot (and thus gained the title of Friedrich I), while Berlin continued to expand. The **Friedrichstadt and Charlottenburg quarters** and the **Zeughaus** (now the Deutsches Historisches Museum) were created during this period, and Andreas Schlüter revamped the Elector's palace. In 1709, Berlin-Cölln finally became a single city named **Berlin**. None of this came cheap, however. Both Berlin and the Mark Brandenburg were heavily in debt by the end of Friedrich's reign, to the point where he even resorted to alchemists in the hope of refilling his treasury.

Berlin under the Soldier King

The next chapter in the city's history belongs to Friedrich I's son, **Friedrich Wilhelm I** (1688–1740). Known as the **Soldier King** and generally reckoned to be the father of the Prussian state, he dealt with the financial chaos by enforcing spartan conditions on his subjects and firing most of the servants at court. State revenues were henceforth directed to building up his army, and culture took a back seat to parades (eventually he even banned the theatre). While the army marched and drilled, the populace had a draconian work ethic drubbed into them – Friedrich took to walking about Berlin and personally beating anyone he caught loafing.

Friedrich tried to introduce conscription but had to make an exception of Berlin when the city's able-bodied young men fled en masse to escape the army. Despite this, Berlin became a **garrison town** geared to maintaining the army: the Lustgarten park of the royal palace was transformed into a parade ground, and every house was expected to have space available for billeting troops. Much of modern Berlin's shape and character can be traced back to Friedrich – squares like **Pariser Platz** (the area in front of the Brandenburg Gate) began as parade grounds, and **Friedrichstrasse** was built to link the centre with Tempelhof parade ground. When Friedrich died after watching rehearsals for his own funeral (and thrashing a groom who made a mistake), few Berliners mourned.

Frederick the Great and the rise of Prussia

His son, Friedrich II – known to historians as **Frederick the Great** (1712–1786) and to his subjects as "Der alte Fritz" – enjoyed a brief honey-moon as a liberalizer, before reverting to his father's ways. Soon Prussia was drawn into a series of wars that sent Berlin taxes through the roof, while the king withdrew to Sanssouci Palace in Potsdam, where only French was spoken, leaving the Berliners to pay for his military adventurism. Friedrich's saving grace was that he liked to think of himself as a philosopher king, and Berlin's **cultural life** consequently flourished during his reign. This was thanks in part to the work of the leading figures of the German Enlightenment, like the playwright Gotthold Ephraim Lessing and the philosopher Moses Mendelssohn, both of whom enjoyed royal patronage.

It was the **rise of Prussia** that alarmed Austria, Saxony, France and Russia into starting the **Seven Years' War** in 1756. Four years later they occupied Berlin and demanded a tribute of four million thalers, causing City President Kirchstein to faint on the spot. This was later reduced to 1.5 million when it was discovered that the city coffers were empty. Berlin was eventually relieved by Frederick, who went on to win the war (if only by default) after Russia and France fell out. Victory confirmed Prussia's power in Central Europe, but keeping the peace meant maintaining a huge standing army.

Besides direct taxation, Frederick raised money by establishing **state monopolies** in the trade of coffee, salt and tobacco. Citizens were actually required to buy set quantities of these commodities whether they wanted them or not. This was the origin of some of Berlin's most celebrated culinary delicacies: sauerkraut, *Kassler Rippchen* (salted pork ribs) and pickled gherkins were all invented by people desperate to use up their accumulated salt. Popular discontent was muffled by Frederick's **secret police** and **press censorship** – two innovations that have stuck around in one form or another ever since.

Unter den Linden came into its own during Frederick's reign, as grandiose new edifices like the **Alte Bibliothek** sprang up. Just off the great boulevard, the **Französischer Dom** was built to serve the needs of the Huguenot population, while the construction of Schloss Bellevue in the Tiergarten sparked off a new building boom, as the wealthy flocked into this newly fashionable area.

Decline and occupation

After Frederick's death Prussia went into a **decline**, culminating in the defeat of its once-invincible army by French revolutionaries at the Battle of Valmy in 1792. The decline went unchecked under Friedrich Wilhelm II (1744–1797), continuing into the Napoleonic era. As Bonaparte's empire spread across Europe, the Prussian court dithered, appeasing the French and trying to delay the inevitable invasion. Life in Berlin continued more or less as normal, but by August 1806 citizens were watching Prussian soldiers set off on the march westwards to engage the Napoleonic forces. On September 19, the king and queen left the city, followed a month later by Count von der Schulenburg, the city governor, who had assured Berliners that all was going well right up until he learned of Prussia's defeat at Jena and Auerstadt.

Five days later French troops marched through the **Brandenburg Gate** and Berlin was occupied. On October 27, 1806, Napoleon himself arrived to head a parade down Unter den Linden – greeted as a liberator by the Berliners, according to some accounts. **French occupation** was uneventful, interrupted only by a minor and unsuccessful military rebellion, and ending with the collapse of Napoleon's empire after his defeats in Russia and at the Battle of Leipzig in 1813.

The rebirth of Prussia

With the end of French rule, the Quadriga (the Goddess of Victory in her chariot) was restored to the Brandenburg Gate (see p.56), but the people of Berlin only gained the promise of a constitution for Prussia, which never materialized – a portent of later conflict. The real victor was the **Prussian state**, which acquired tracts of land along the Rhine, including the Ruhr, which contained the iron and coal deposits on which its military might was to be rebuilt.

The war was followed by an era of reaction and oppression, which did so much to stifle intellectual and cultural life in Berlin that the philosopher Wilhelm von Humboldt resigned from the university in protest at the new authoritarianism. Gradually this mellowed out into the **Biedermeier years**, in which Prussia's industrial fortunes began to rise, laying the foundation of its Great Power status. Berlin continued to grow: factories and railways and the first of the city's *Mietskaserne* or **tenement buildings** were constructed – foreshadowing what was to come with full industrialization.

Revolution and reaction

Berlin enjoyed more than thirty years of peace and stability after 1815, but it shared the revolutionary mood that swept Europe in **1848**. Influenced by events in France and the writings of Karl Marx (who lived here from 1837 to 1841), Berliners demanded a say in the running of their own affairs. King Friedrich Wilhelm IV (1795–1861) refused to agree. On March 18, citizens gathered outside his palace to present their demands. The soldiers who dispersed them accidentally fired two shots and the demonstration became a **revolution**. Barricades went up and a fourteen-hour battle raged between insurgents and loyalist troops. According to eyewitness accounts, rich and poor alike joined in the rebellion. During the fighting 183 Berliners and eighteen soldiers died.

Aghast at his subjects' anger, Friedrich Wilhelm IV ordered his troops to withdraw to Spandau, leaving the city in the hands of the revolutionaries, who failed to take advantage of the situation. A revolutionary parliament and citizens' militia were established, but rather than assaulting Spandau or taking other measures to consolidate the revolution, the new assembly concerned itself with protecting the royal palace from vandalism. No attempt was made to declare a republic or seize public buildings in what was turning out to be an unusually orderly – and ultimately doomed – revolution.

On March 21, the king appeared in public wearing the black, red and gold tricolour emblem of the revolution. Having failed to suppress it, he now proposed to join it, along with most of his ministers and princes. The king spoke at the university, promising nothing much but paying lip service to the idea of German unity, which impressed the assembled liberals. Order was fully restored; then in October, a Prussian army under General Wrangel entered Berlin and forced the **dissolution of parliament**. The Berliners either gave up the fight or followed millions of their fellow Germans into exile.

Suppression followed. Friedrich gave up the tricolour and turned to persecuting liberals, before going insane shortly afterwards. His brother Prince Wilhelm – who had led the troops against the barricades – became regent, and then king himself. **Otto von Bismarck** was appointed to the chancellorship (1862), despite the almost universal loathing he inspired among Berliners.

Meanwhile, Berlin itself continued to grow apace, turning into a cosmopolitan, modern industrial city. Its free press and revolutionary past exerted a liberal influence on Prussia's emasculated parliament, the **Reichstag**, to the irritation of Bismarck and the king (who was soon to proclaim himself emperor, or kaiser). However, Bismarck became a national hero after the Prussian victory at the **Battle of Königgrätz** (1866) had smashed Austrian military power, clearing the way for Prussia to unite – and dominate – Germany. Although militaristic nationalism caused liberalism to wither elsewhere, Berlin continued to elect liberal deputies to the Reichstag, which became the parliament of the whole nation after **German unification** in 1871.

Yet Berlin remained a maverick city. It was here that three attempts were made to kill Emperor Wilhelm I; the final one on Unter den Linden (1878) left him with thirty pieces of shrapnel in his body. While the kaiser recovered, Bismarck used the event to justify a **crackdown on socialists**, closing newspapers and persecuting trade unionists. The growth of unionism was a direct result of relentless urbanization. Between 1890 and 1900, Berlin's population doubled to two million and thousands of tenement buildings sprang up in working-class quarters like **Wedding**. These were solidly behind the Social Democratic Party (**SPD**), whose deputies were the chief dissenters within the Reichstag.

By 1890 Wilhelm II had become kaiser and "dropped the pilot" (Bismarck), but the country continued to be predominantly militaristic and authoritarian. While Berlin remained defiantly liberal, it steadily acquired the attributes of a modern capital. Now an established centre for commerce and diplomacy, it boasted electric trams, an underground railway, and all the other technical innovations of the age.

World War I and its aftermath

The arms race and dual alliances that gradually polarized Europe during the 1890s and the first decade of the twentieth century led inexorably towards **World War I**. Its outbreak in 1914 was greeted with enthusiasm by civilians everywhere – only confirmed pacifists or communists resisted the heady intoxication of patriotism. In Berlin, Kaiser Wilhelm II spoke "to all Germans" from the balcony of his palace, and shop windows across the city were festooned with national colours.

Military bands played *Heil dir im Siegerkranz* ("Hail to you in the Victor's Laurel") and *Die Wacht am Rhein* ("The Watch on the Rhine') in cafés, while Berliners threw flowers to the Imperial German army or Reichswehr as it marched off to war. The political parties agreed to a truce, and even the Social Democrats voted in favour of war credits.

The General Staff's calculation that France could be knocked out before Russia fully mobilized soon proved hopelessly optimistic, and Germany found itself facing a war on two fronts – the very thing Bismarck had dreaded. As casualties mounted on the stalemated western front, and rationing and food shortages began to hit poorer civilians, **disillusionment** set in. By the summer of 1915 housewives were demonstrating in front of the Reichstag, a portent of more serious popular unrest to come. Ordinary people were beginning to see the war as an exercise staged for the benefit of the rich at the expense of the poor, who bore the brunt of the suffering. In December 1917, nineteen members of the SPD announced that they could no longer support their party's backing of the war and formed an independent socialist party known as the USPD. This party joined the "International Group" of **Karl Liebknecht** and **Rosa Luxemburg** – later known as the Spartacists – which had opposed SPD support for the war since 1915. It was this grouping that was to form the nucleus of the postwar Kommunistische Partei Deutschlands, or **KPD**. Meanwhile, fuel, food, and even beer shortages added to growing hardships on the home front.

Defeat and revolution

With their last great offensive spent, and America joining the Allied war effort, even Germany's supreme warlord, Erich von Ludendorff, recognized that **defeat** was inevitable by the autumn of 1918. Knowing the Allies would refuse to negotiate with the old absolutist system, he declared (on September 9) a democratic, **constitutional monarchy**, whose chancellor would be responsible to the Reichstag and not the kaiser. A government was formed under Prince Max von Baden, which agreed to extensive reforms. But it was too little, too late, for the bitter sailors and soldiers on the home front, where the contrast between privilege and poverty was most obvious. At the beginning of November the Kiel

Garrison led a **naval mutiny** and revolutionary **Workers' and Soldiers' Soviets** mushroomed across Germany.

Caught up in this wave of unrest, Berliners took to the streets on November 8–9, where they were joined by soldiers stationed in the capital. Realizing that the game was up, **Kaiser Wilhelm II abdicated**. What Lenin described as a situation of "dual power" now existed. Almost at the same time as Philipp Scheidemann of the SPD declared a **"German Republic"** from the Reichstag's balcony, Karl Liebknecht was proclaiming a "Free Socialist Republic" from a balcony of the royal palace, less than a mile away. In the face of increasing confusion, SPD leader Friedrich Ebert took over as head of the government. A deal was struck with the army, which promised to protect the republic if Ebert would forestall the full-blooded socialist revolution demanded by the Spartacists. Ebert now became chairman of a Council of People's Delegates that ruled Berlin for nearly three months.

Between December 16 and 21, a **Congress of Workers' and Soldiers' Soviets** was held, which voted to accept a system of parliamentary democracy. However, many of the revolutionary soldiers, sailors and workers who controlled the streets favoured the establishment of Soviet-style government and refused to obey Ebert's orders. They were eventually suppressed by staunchly anti-revolutionary units of the old Imperial army, further indebting Ebert to the Prussian establishment. This itself relied heavily on the **Freikorps**: armed bands of right-wing officers and NCOs, dedicated to protecting Germany from "Bolshevism".

Things came to a head with the **Spartacist uprising** in Berlin during the first half of January 1919. This inspired lasting dread among the bourgeoisie, who applauded when the Spartacists were crushed by the militarily superior Freikorps. The torture and **murder of Liebknecht and Luxemburg** by Freikorps officers (who threw their bodies in the Landwehrkanal) was never punished once the fighting was over. This hardly augured well for the future of the **new republic**, whose National Assembly elections were held on January 19.

The Weimar Republic

The elections confirmed the SPD as the new political leaders of the country, with 38 percent of the vote; as a result, Ebert was made president, with Scheidemann as chancellor. **Weimar**, the small country town that had seen the most glorious flowering of the German Enlightenment, was chosen as the seat of government in preference to Berlin, which was tinged by its monarchic and military associations.

A **new constitution** was drawn up, hailed as the most liberal and progressive in the world. It aimed at a comprehensive system of checks and balances to ensure that power could not become too concentrated. Authority was formally vested in the people, and the state was given a quasi-federal structure to limit excessive Prussian domination. Executive authority was shared between the president (who could rule by emergency decree if necessary) and the Reich government in a highly complex arrangement. Reichstag deputies were elected by proportional representation from party lists.

While on the surface an admirable document, this constitution was hopelessly idealistic for a people so unfamiliar with democratic practice and responsibilities. No attempt was made to outlaw parties hostile to the system; this opened the way for savage attacks on the republic by extremists at both ends of the political spectrum. The use of proportional representation, without any qualifying minimum percentage of the total vote, favoured a plethora of parties promoting sectional interests. This meant that the Weimar governments were all unwieldy coalitions, whose average life was about eight months and which often pursued contradictory policies in different ministries.

Dada

World War I smashed prevailing cultural assumptions and disrupted social hierarchies. With politics in ferment, culture became another battleground. The leading exponent of the challenge to bourgeois values was the **Dada movement**, which shifted its headquarters from Zurich to Berlin in 1919. A Dada manifesto was proclaimed, followed by the First International Dada Fair (July and August), whose content aligned the movement with the forces of revolution. The right was particularly enraged by exhibits like a stuffed effigy of an army officer with a pig's head, labelled "Hanged by the Revolution", which dangled from the ceiling. All in all, it was an appropriate prelude to the new decade.

Berlin in the 1920s – the Weimar Years

The history of Berlin in the 1920s is bound up with Germany's – much of which was being dictated by the Allies. Resentment at the harsh terms imposed by the **Treaty of Versailles** led to turmoil and a wave of political violence: Matthias Erzberger, leader of the German delegation to Versailles, was among those assassinated. On March 13, 1920, Freikorps units loyal to the right-wing politician Wolfgang Kapp marched on Berlin, unopposed by the army. The government left Berlin but returned a week later, when the **Kapp putsch** collapsed. The army had withdrawn its support after protesters called for a general strike.

The early 1920s was a bad time for Berlin. War reparations to the Allies placed a crippling burden on the German economy. As the mark began to plunge in value, the government was shocked by the **assassination of Walter Rathenau**. As foreign minister, he had just signed the Treaty of Rapallo, aimed at promoting closer economic ties with the Soviet Union, since the Western powers remained intransigent. Rathenau was killed at his own house in the Grunewald by Freikorps officers. When France and Belgium occupied the Ruhr in response to alleged defaults in the reparations payments, a general strike was called across Germany in January 1923.

The combination of reparations and strikes sent the mark plummeting, causing the worst **inflation** ever known. As their savings were wiped out and literally barrowloads of paper money wasn't enough to support a family, Berliners experienced the terrors of hyperinflation. In working-class districts, street fighting between right and left flared up. Foreigners flocked in to pay bargain prices for carpets and furs that even rich Germans could no longer afford, and fortunes were made and lost by speculators. In the midst of all this, on November 8, Berliners' attention was briefly diverted to Munich, where a motley crew of right-wing ex-army officers including General Ludendorff attempted to mount a putsch. It failed, but Berliners were to hear of one of the ringleaders again – **Adolf Hitler**.

Finally, the mark was stabilized under a new chancellor, **Gustav Stresemann**, who proved to be a supremely able politician. Having come to realize that only an economically sound Germany would have any hope of meeting reparations payments, the Allies moderated their stance. Under the Dawes Plan of 1924, loans poured into Germany, particularly from America, leading to an upsurge in the economy.

Nightlife and the arts

Economic recovery affected the social life of Berlin. For many people the centre of the city had shifted from the old Regiurungsviertel (government quarter) around Friedrichsstrasse and Unter den Linden, to the cafés and bars of the Kurfürstendamm. Jazz hit the **nightclubs** in a big way, like drug abuse (mainly cocaine) and all kinds of sex. There were clubs for transvestites, clubs where you could watch nude dancing, or dance naked yourself – and usually the police didn't give a damn. This was the legendary era later to be celebrated by Isherwood and others, when Berlin was briefly the most open, tolerant city in Europe, a Mecca for all those who rejected conventions and traditions.

The 1920s was also a boom time for the arts, as the Dada shockwave rippled through the decade. **George Grosz** satirized the times in savage caricatures, while **John Heartfield** used photomontage techniques to produce biting political statements. Equally striking, if less didactic, was the work of artists like **Otto Dix** and **Christian Schad**.

Producer **Max Reinhardt** continued to dominate Berlin's theatrical life, as he'd done since taking over at the Deutsches Theater in 1905. **Erwin Piscator** moved from propaganda into mainstream theatre at the Theater am Nollendorfplatz, without losing his innovative edge, and in 1928 **Bertolt Brecht's** *Dreigroschen Oper* ("Threepenny Opera") was staged for the first time. Appropriately, Berlin also became a centre for the very newest of the arts. Between the wars the **UFA film studios** (see p.222) at Babelsberg was the biggest in Europe, producing legendary films like **Fritz Lang's** *Metropolis*, *The Cabinet of Doctor Caligari* and *The Blue Angel* (starring Berlin-born **Marlene Dietrich**).

Middle- and lowbrow tastes were catered for by endless all-singing, all-dancing **musicals**, featuring platoons of women in various states of undress. This was also the heyday of the Berlin cabaret scene, when some of its most acidic exponents were at work.

The rise of Nazism

With inflation back under control, Germany experienced a return to relative **political stability**. The 1924 elections demonstrated increased support for centre-right and republican parties. When President Ebert died (February 28, 1925) and was succeeded by the former commander of the Imperial army, **General Field Marshal von Hindenburg**, monarchists and conservatives rejoiced. Nevertheless, it was now that the extreme right began gradually gaining ground, starting in Bavaria.

The **National Socialist German Workers' Party** (NSDAP) began as a ragbag group of misfits and fanatics, whose views were an odd mixture of extreme right and left, as the party's name suggests. It was Hitler who synthesized an ideology from existing reactionary theories, modelled the Nazis on Mussolini's *Fascisti*, and took a leaf from the Communists when it came to red flags, excessive propaganda and street fighting. For this they had the thuggish, brown-shirted **SA** (Sturmabteilung) Stormtroopers. As long as "reds" were the victims, the authorities did little or nothing to curb SA violence. The fear of street violence – foreshadowing a return to the anarchy of the postwar years – was calculated to drive the bourgeoisie towards Nazism, which promised drastic "solutions" to Germany's ills.

The Nazis made no headway in staunchly "red" Berlin until the end of 1926, when Hitler appointed **Joseph Goebbels** as *Gauleiter* (regional head) of the city's party organization. Goebbels reorganized the SA with the intention of confronting the Communists and conquering the streets of Berlin. On February 11 the following year, he rented the Pharus hall as a site for a Nazi demonstration in the predominantly Communist suburb of Wedding. A bloody brawl ensued and an **era of violence** began. Marches by the SA and the Communist Rote Frontkämpferbund (Red Fighters' Front) – often culminating in pitched battles – became a regular feature of street life in Berlin's working-class suburbs. The Nazis were here to stay.

Elections and unrest

In the **1928 elections** the NSDAP won 800,000 votes and gained twelve seats in the Reichstag. In May 1929 there was serious unrest in Berlin when Communist workers clashed with armed police in Wedding. Running street battles occurred and 33 civilians, many of them innocent bystanders, were killed. Fearful for their lives and property should the Communists gain ascendancy, wealthy bourgeois and the captains of finance and industry donated heavily to the Nazis.

In October 1929 Gustav Stresemann, one of Germany's few capable politicians, died. A few weeks later came the **Wall Street Crash**. All American credit ended, and international recession wiped out what was left of Germany's economic stability. By the year's end **unemployment** had reached three million, and the poverty of the

immediate postwar period had returned with a vengeance. A centrist politician, Heinrich Brüning, was appointed chancellor by Hindenburg, but failed to get any legislation passed in the Reichstag and advised Hindenburg to dissolve it, pending elections. Poverty – worsened by a state-imposed austerity programme – polarized society: gangs fought in the streets, while swastika banners and red flags hung from neighbouring tenements.

The **1930 elections** resulted in gains for the Communists, and 107 seats in the Reichstag for the Nazis. There were anti-Semitic attacks throughout Berlin as the newly elected Nazi deputies took their seats in the Reichstag on October 13. By now the parliamentary system had effectively ceased to function and Germany was being ruled by presidential decree. Financial misery and disorder showed no signs of abating, and SA uniforms became a common sight on the streets of central Berlin, where Nazi thugs attacked Jewish shops and businesses, flaunting pornographic hate-sheets like *Der Stürmer*. Their rising influence was confirmed when General Schleicher of the Reichswehr General Staff began to court Hitler, envisaging the Nazis as a bulwark against the left. In Berlin – with its predominantly anti-Nazi population – despair began to mount.

At the **presidential elections** of April 10, 1932, Hindenburg gained an absolute majority, but Hitler won 13.5 million votes. A month later Hindenburg dismissed Brüning for failing to control the economy and disagreeing with his speeches, replacing him with Franz von Papen. Flanked by a cabinet that the left-wing press pilloried as the "Cabinet of Barons", von Papen announced plans for "reform", amounting to a thinly disguised attempt to revive the prewar

■ THE RISE OF NAZISM

BERLIN IN 1932

order. The July **parliamentary elections** saw street violence on an unprecedented scale and made the Nazis the largest party in the Reichstag. Despite a setback at the polls in November 1932, their strength on the streets increased – intimidating Berlin's cabarets and left-wing theatres into muted criticism or silence.

Hitler's last steps to power were assisted by conservatives who sought to use the Nazis for their own ends. First, General Schleicher (by now defence minister, and less enamoured of the Nazis) engineered the removal of von Papen, and personally replaced him as chancellor. Von Papen retaliated by instigating a series of **political intrigues**. To Hindenburg he argued that Schleicher was incompetent to govern Germany, whose political mess could best be resolved by making Hitler chancellor. Von Papen reckoned that the Nazis would crush the left but reveal themselves unequal to the task of government; after a few months Hitler could be nudged aside and power would pass back into the hands of conservatives like himself.

Having come to an agreement with Hitler, he persuaded the virtually senile Hindenburg to appoint Hitler as chancellor and himself as vice chancellor (January 4, 1933). Knowing nothing of this, people were demanding the departure of Schleicher on the streets of Berlin. Two days after his resignation, they were horrified to see **Hitler sworn in as chancellor** on January 30. Life in Berlin would never be the same again, despite the fact that three-quarters of the city's electors had voted against the Nazis at the last elections.

The Nazi takeover

Hitler went immediately to the Reich's Chancellery to make his first public appearance as chancellor. Berlin thronged with Nazi supporters bearing torches, and the SA marched in strength through the *Regierungsviertel* to celebrate their victory. For anti-Nazis in Berlin, it was a nightmare come true.

The Nazi takeover of the state and the suppression of political opposition was spearheaded by **Hermann Göring**. As Prussian minister of the interior, he ordered the police "to make free use of their weapons wherever necessary" and built up a secret political department, soon to become notorious as the **Gestapo** (Geheime Staatspolizei – "Secret State Police"). "It's not my business to do justice; it's my business to annihilate and

exterminate," boasted Göring. The pretext for an all-out assault on the Nazis' opponents was provided by the **Reichstag fire** (February 28, 1933). Whether this was really caused by the Nazis themselves, or by Marius van der Lubbe, the simple-minded Dutch Communist whom they accused, is still a subject for debate. But there's no doubt that the Nazis used the Reichstag fire to their advantage.

An **emergency decree** to "protect the people and the state" was signed by Hindenburg the following day. It effectively abolished habeas corpus and provided the legal basis for a permanent state of emergency. The Nazi propaganda machine played up the Red Menace. Communist offices were raided, and the head of the Communist International, Georgi Dimitrov, was accused of instigating the Reichstag fire. In this atmosphere, the **elections of March 5** took place. The Communist vote dropped by one million, but the Nazis failed to achieve an outright majority, with 43.9 percent of the vote. Nevertheless, Hitler was poised to consolidate his grip on power.

The new Reichstag was opened in the Garrison Church in Potsdam and later transferred to a Berlin opera house. Delegates were asked to approve an **Enabling Act** that would place dictatorial powers in the hands of the predominantly Nazi cabinet. By the arrest of Communist deputies and some of the SPD, and with the support of the traditional right, Hitler was only just short of the two-thirds majority he needed to abolish the Weimar Republic quite legally. The SPD salvaged some self-respect by refusing to accede to this, but the Catholic Centrists failed to repeat their act of defiance against Bismarck, meekly supporting the Bill in return for minor concessions. It was passed by 441 votes to 84, hammering the final nails into the coffin of German parliamentary democracy.

On May 2, the Nazis clamped down on the unions, arresting leaders and sending them to **concentration camps**. In a series of subsequent moves opposition parties were effectively banned, and persecution of Nazi opponents was extended to embrace "active church members, freemasons, politically dissatisfied people . . . abortionists and homosexuals". An **exodus from Berlin** of known anti-Nazis and others with reason to fear the Nazis began. Bertolt Brecht, Kurt Weill, Lotte Lenya and Wassily Kandinsky all left the city, joining the likes of Albert Einstein and

George Grosz in exile. The atmosphere of the city was changing irrevocably. The unemployed were drafted into labour battalions, set to work on the land or building autobahns.

On April 1, the SA launched an enforced **boycott of Jewish shops**, businesses and medical and legal practices in Berlin. Meanwhile, the Nazis put their own men into vital posts throughout local governments – in Berlin and the rest of Germany. This was the first stage of Gleichschaltung ("co-ordination"), whereby the machinery of state, and then society itself, would be Nazified. On May 11, they shocked the world by burning thousands of books that conflicted with Nazi ideology on the Opernplatz in central Berlin. After the concentration camps, the **bookburnings** (Büchverbrennung) remain one of the most potent symbols of Nazi brutality.

The Night of the Long Knives

In 1934 Nazi savagery was briefly turned inwards. Under **Ernst Röhm**, the SA had grown to 500,000 men and boasted of swallowing up the smaller Reichswehr. The SA felt cheated of the spoils of victory and muttered about a "Second Revolution". "Adolf is rotten. He's betraying all of us. He only goes around with reactionaries. . . Are we revolutionaries or aren't we?" Röhm complained. Big business, the regular army and rival Nazis like Himmler and Göring were united in their hostility towards the SA. Hitler was persuaded that Röhm and his allies were conspiring against him, and ordered a wholesale purge later known as the "**Night of the Long Knives**". On the night of June 30, the SA leaders were dragged from their boyfriends' beds in the resort of Bad Wiessee, taken to Stadelheim prison and shot in the courtyard by SS troopers; some believed this was an army coup, and died shouting "Heil Hitler!" In Berlin alone, 150 SA leaders were executed. Röhm's final words before being shot in Stadelheim prison were more appropriate: "All revolutions devour their own children."

Other victims included General Schleicher, von Papen's assistants, and the leader of the radical Nazis, Gregor Strasser. Local police and Gestapo chiefs added personal enemies to the death lists. Some of the victims had no connection with politics, like the Bavarian music critic whom the hit-squad mistook for an SA general of the same name. Aside from Hitler, Göring, and the army, the main beneficiaries of the purge were two

Nazi organizations under the control of a failed chicken-farmer, **Heinrich Himmler**. His black-uniformed **SS** (Schutzstaffel – "Defence Staff"), originally Hitler's personal bodyguard, grew into the nucleus for a Nazi army. Meanwhile, the party's private intelligence service, the **SD** (Sicherheitsdienst or "Security Service"), established itself as a rival to the Gestapo and the army's Abwehr – military intelligence organization.

Following Hindenburg's death later that summer, Hitler merged the offices of president and chancellor and declared himself **Führer** of the German Reich. Defence Minister von Blomberg acceded to Hitler's request that all soldiers of the Reichswehr swear an oath of allegiance to him personally. Having assured Blomberg that the army would remain the "only bearer of arms in the nation", Hitler took the salute from the Leibstandarte Adolf Hitler regiment of the SS and the Hermann Göring Police Battalion – an indication of how he applied the policy of divide and rule even within the Führer state.

The Nazi impact on Berlin

In Berlin as in the rest of the Reich, **Nazi control** extended to all areas of life: the press and radio were orchestrated by Goebbels; children joined Nazi youth organizations; and every tenement building had Nazi-appointed wardens who doubled as Gestapo spies. It was even decreed that women should eschew make-up as an "un-German" artifice – one of the few edicts that wasn't taken seriously. Anti-Nazi criticism – even of the mildest kind – invited a visit from the Gestapo. Although Germans might avoid joining the NSDAP itself, it was difficult to escape the plethora of related organizations covering every aspect of life, from riding clubs and dog breeders to the "Reich Church" or "German League of Maidens". This was the second stage of Gleichschaltung – drawing the entire population into the Nazi net.

As the capital of the Reich, Berlin became a showcase city of banners, uniforms and parades. An image of order and dynamism, of a "new Germany" on the march, was what the Nazis tried to convey. This reached its apotheosis during the **1936 Olympics**, held at a vast purpose-built stadium in the Pichelsdorf suburb of Berlin. Hitler's expectation that the games would demonstrate Aryan racial supremacy was humili-

atingly dashed when black American athlete
Jesse Owens gave the greatest performance of
the Olympics.

Like many previous rulers of Germany, Hitler felt
uncomfortable in Berlin, probably aware that
most Berliners suffered rather than supported
him. He also felt the city was insufficiently
grandiose for the capital of the "Thousand Year
Reich", and from 1936 onwards spent much time
with his favourite architect, **Albert Speer**, drawing
up extensive plans for a remodelled postwar
Berlin, to be called "Germania". Its main purpose
would be to serve as a monument to the expected Nazi victory in the forthcoming war and as the
capital of a vast empire thereafter. Hitler's millen-
nial megalomania inspired hours of brooding on
how future generations might be awed by
Germania's monumental ruins – hence the need
to build with the finest materials on a gigantic
scale. In the meantime, he preferred to spend his
time in the Berghof in Berchtesgaden.

Kristallnacht and the road to war

If the Berlin Olympics had partly glossed over the
realities of Nazi brutality, Kristallnacht exposed
them to the world. On the night of November
9–10, 1938, organized **attacks on Jewish shops
and institutions** took place across Germany, an
escalation in the Nazis' violent anti-Semitism. At
least 36 Jews were murdered, and thousands
injured; in Berlin Jews were beaten on the streets
while passers-by looked on, and 23 of the city's
29 synagogues were destroyed. Many of the
attacks were carried out by SA men in civilian
clothes, to give the impression that these were
spontaneous outbursts by German citizens. In
the wake of Kristallnacht ("Crystal Night" – after
the broken glass), new **anti-Semitic laws** were
brought in, making life difficult and dangerous for
German Jews, and paving the way for the greater
horrors to come.

Throughout the 1930s the Nazis made **prepa-
rations for war**, expanding the army and gearing
the economy for war readiness by 1940. Göring
bragged of putting "guns before butter", but the
real architect of the four-year plan was Hjalmar
Schacht, a respected banker. It dovetailed with
Hitler's foreign policy of obtaining Lebensraum
("living space") from neighbouring countries by
intimidation. In 1936 the German army occupied
the Rhineland (demilitarized under the terms of
the Treaty of Versailles) to token protests from the

League of Nations. The Anschluss ("annexation")
of Austria in 1938 was likewise carried off with
impunity, and a few months later Britain and
France agreed to the dismemberment of
Czechoslovakia at Munich.

Encouraged by their pusillanimity, Hitler made
new demands on Polish territory in 1939. It's
probable that he believed there would be a similar collapse of will by the Western powers, the
more so since he had pulled off the spectacular
coup of signing a nonaggression pact with his
ultimate enemy, the Soviet Union, thus ensuring
that Germany could avoid a war on two fronts.
But two days after the German invasion of
Poland began on September 1, Britain and
France declared war in defence of their treaty
obligations.

World War II

The outbreak of **World War II** was greeted without enthusiasm by Berliners, despite German victories in Poland. According to American journalist
and eyewitness William Shirer (see "Books"),
there were few signs of patriotic fervour as the
troops marched off to war through the streets of
Berlin, and Hitler cancelled further parades out of
pique. On October 11, there was rejoicing when
a radio broadcast on the Berlin radio wavelength
stated that the British government had fallen, and
an immediate armistice was to be declared.
Shirer noted that the Berliners showed more
enthusiasm at the military parade to mark the fall
of France (July 18, 1940), when German troops
marched through the Brandenburg Gate for the
first time since 1871. Still, he reckoned that it was
the spectacle rather than martial sentiments that
attracted crowds of Berliners.

Initially, Berlin suffered little from the war.
Although citizens were already complaining of
meagre rations, delicacies and luxury goods from
occupied Europe gravitated towards the Reich's
capital. What remained of the diplomatic and foreign press community, and the chic lifestyles of
Nazi bigwigs, passed for high life. Open dissent
seemed impossible, with Gestapo informers
believed to lurk everywhere. The impact of
wartime austerity was also softened by Nazi welfare organizations and a blanket of propaganda.

Air raids

Göring had publicly boasted that Germans could
call him "Meyer" (a Jewish surname) if a single

bomb fell on Berlin – notwithstanding which the British RAF dropped some for the first time on August 23, 1940. A further raid on the night of August 28–29 killed ten people – the first German civilian casualties. These raids had a marked demoralizing effect on Berliners, who had counted on a swift end to the war, and Hitler had to reassure the populace in a speech at the Sportpalast. Holding up a Baedeker guide to Britain, he thundered that the Luftwaffe would raze Britain's cities to the ground one by one.

However, these early **bombing raids** caused scant real damage and it wasn't until March 1, 1943 – when defeat in the Western Desert and difficulties on the eastern front had already brought home the fact that Germany was not invincible – that Berlin suffered its first heavy raid. While the RAF bombed by night the Americans bombed by day, establishing a pattern that would reduce Berlin to ruins in relentless stages. "We can wreck Berlin from end to end if the USAAF will come in on it. It will cost us between 400 and 500 aircraft. It will cost Germany the war," the head of Bomber Command, Sir Arthur "Bomber" Harris, had written to Churchill in 1943. The first buildings to go were the Staatsoper and Alte Bibliothek on Unter den Linden. On December 22 the Kaiser-Wilhelm-Gedächtniskirche was reduced to a shell. By the year's end, daily and nightly bombardments were a feature of everyday life.

During the 363 air raids until the end of the war, 75,000 tons of high-explosive or incendiary bombs had killed between 35,000 and 50,000 people and rendered 1,500,000 Berliners homeless. Yet despite the colossal destruction that filled the streets with 100 million tons of rubble, seventy percent of the city's industrial capacity was still functioning at the war's end.

Resistance against the Nazis

Anti-Nazi resistance within Germany was less overt than in occupied Europe, but it existed throughout the war, particularly in Berlin. A group of **Communist cells** run by members of the old KPD operated a clandestine information network and organized isolated acts of resistance and sabotage. But the odds against them were overwhelming, and most groups perished. More successful was the Rote Kapelle (Red Orchestra) headed by Harold Schulze-Boysen, a prewar Bohemian aristocrat who worked in the Air Ministry on Wilhelmstrasse, with agents in most of the military offices, supplying information to the Soviet Union. Eventually it, too, was identified and broken up by the SD and the Gestapo.

The **Kreisau Circle**, a resistance group led by Count Helmut von Moltke, and the groups around Carl Goerdeler (former mayor of Leipzig) and General Beck (ex-chief of staff) talked about overthrowing the Nazis and opening negotiations with the Western Allies, but the most effective resistance came from **within the military**. There had been attempts on Hitler's life since 1942, but it wasn't until late 1943 and early 1944 that enough high-ranking officers had become convinced that defeat was inevitable, and a wide network of conspirators was established. The one-armed Colonel von Stauffenberg was responsible for placing the bomb in Hitler's headquarters at Rastenberg in East Prussia, while Bendlerstrasse officers planned to use Fromm's Replacement Army to seize crucial points in Berlin.

On July 20, 1944, six weeks after the Allied invasion of Normandy, the coup was launched. Stauffenberg heard the bomb explode as he was leaving Rastenberg and signalled for the coup to go ahead. In fact, the **attempt to kill Hitler failed** through bad luck (see pp.144–145), and the conspirators botched their takeover. First they failed to cut communications between Rastenberg and Berlin, and took their time seizing buildings and arresting Nazis. Goebbels succeeded in telephoning Hitler, who spoke directly to the arrest team, ordering them to obey his propaganda minister. Then Goebbels set to work contacting SS and Gestapo units, and reminding army garrisons of their oath of loyalty to the Führer. The final blow came at 9pm, when Hitler broadcast on national radio, threatening to "settle accounts the way we National Socialists are accustomed to settle them".

The ringleaders were either summarily shot, or tortured into implicating others in the basement of Gestapo headquarters on Prinz-Albrecht-Strasse. Several thousand suspects were arrested and hundreds executed. Fieldmarshal Rommel was allowed to commit suicide and receive an honourable burial, but other high-ranking conspirators went before the so-called People's Court in Berlin for a public show trial (August 7–8). All were sentenced to death by the Nazi judge Ronald Freisler and hanged on meat-hooks at Plötzensee Prison, their death agonies being filmed for Hitler's private delectation. Almost all of those who would have been best qualified to lead postwar Germany had thus been killed. Freisler himself was killed by an American bomb following a later show trial.

The fate of Berlin's Jews

For Berlin's Jews (and those living elsewhere in Germany) the terror began long before the war, as a noose tightened around their right to exist. Of the 160,564 Jews in Berlin at the beginning of 1933, many left in the first year of Hitler's chancellorship, when a series of laws banned them from public office, the civil service, journalism, farming, teaching, broadcasting and acting. Still more left when the so-called **Nürnburg Laws** (September 1936) effectively deprived them of German citizenship and defined apartheid-like classifications of "racial purity". Jews who could see the writing on the wall, and had money, escaped while they could (other European countries, the US and Palestine all restricted Jewish immigration); but the majority stayed put, hoping that things would improve, or simply because they couldn't afford to emigrate. After Kristallnacht, their already beleaguered position became intolerable.

Once the war began, the Nazis embarked on outright **genocide**, corralling the Jews of Europe in ghettos, branded by their yellow stars, destined for the concentration camps and eventual extermination. Emigration and murder had reduced the Jewish population of Berlin to about 6500 by 1945. Roughly 1400 of the **survivors** were "U-Boats" who lived perpetually in hiding, usually with the help of Gentile friends; the other 5100 somehow survived in precariously legal conditions, usually by being married to non-Jews, or working as grave diggers in the Weissensee Jewish Cemetery.

The fall of Berlin

Enjoy the war while you can! The peace is going to be terrible . . .

Berlin joke shortly before the fall of the city.

By autumn 1944 it was obvious to all but the most fanatical Nazis that the end was approaching fast. Even so, Hitler would brook no talk of surrender or negotiation. Teenage boys and men in their fifties were conscripted to replace the fallen millions, as Hitler placed his faith in "miracle

weapons" like the V-1 and V-2, and new offensives. A wintertime counterattack in the Ardennes temporarily checked the Allies to the west, but their advance had resumed by January 1945. Meanwhile, the Red Army had launched the largest offensive ever seen on the eastern front, 180 divisions seizing East Prussia within two weeks. The distance between the Allied forces was narrowing inexorably.

On January 27, Soviet forces crossed the Oder a hundred miles from Berlin. Only Hitler now really believed there was any hope for Germany. The Nazis threw all they could at the eastern front and mobilized the Volkssturm, an ill-equipped home guard of old men, boys and cripples. Thirteen- and fourteen-year-old members of the **Hitler Youth** were briefly trained in the art of using the Panzerfaust bazooka, then sent to fight against T-34 tanks and battle-hardened infantrymen. As thousands died at the front to buy a little time for the doomed Nazi regime, life in Berlin became a nightmare. The city was choked with refugees and terrified of the approaching Russians; it was bombed day and night, and the flash of Soviet artillery could be seen on the horizon.

Behind the lines, **flying court martials** picked up soldiers and executed anyone suspected of "desertion" or "cowardice in the face of the enemy". On February 1, 1945, Berlin was declared Verteidigungsbereich (a "zone of defence") – to be defended to the last man and the last bullet. The civilian population – women, children, cripples and forced labourers – were set to work building tank traps and barricades; stretches of the U- and S-Bahn formed part of the fortifications. Goebbels trumpeted a **"fortress Berlin"**, while Hitler planned the deployment of **phantom armies**, which existed on order-of-battle charts, but hardly at all in reality.

As Berlin frantically prepared to defend itself, the Russians consolidated their strength. On April 16, at 5am Moscow time, the **Soviet offensive** began with a massive bombardment lasting 25 minutes. When the artillery fell silent, 143 searchlights spaced 200m apart along the entire front were switched on to dazzle the enemy as the Russians began their advance. Three army groups totalling over 1,500,000 men moved forward under marshals Zhukov, Konev and Rokossovsky – and there was little the vastly outnumbered Germans could do to halt them. By April 20 – Hitler's 56th birthday (celebrated with tea and cakes in the *Führerbunker*) – the Red Army was on the edge of Berlin. Next day the city centre came within range of their guns, and several people queueing outside the Karstadt department store on Hermannplatz were killed by shells. On April 23, Soviet troops were in the Weissensee district, just a few miles east of the centre. The Germans were offered a chance to surrender, but declined.

Hitler's birthday party was the last time the Nazi hierarchy assembled before going – or staying – to meet their respective fates. The dictator and his mistress Eva Braun chose to remain in Berlin, and Goebbels elected to join them in the **Führerbunker** with his family. It was a dank, stuffy complex of reinforced concrete cells beneath the garden of the Reich Chancellery. Here Hitler brooded over Speer's architectural models of unbuilt victory memorials, subsisting on salads, herbal tisanes and regular injections of dubious substances by one Dr Morell. To hapless generals and faithful acolytes, he ranted about traitors and the unworthiness of the German *Volk*, declaring that the war was lost and that he would stay in the bunker to the end, after learning that General Steiner's army group had failed to stop Zhukov's advance.

The Final Days

By April 25, Berlin was completely **encircled by Soviet troops**, which met up with US forces advancing from the west. Over the next two days, the suburbs of Dahlem, Spandau, Neukölln and Gatow fell to the Russians, and the city's telephone system failed. On April 27 the Third Panzer Army was completely smashed; survivors fled west, leaving Berlin's northern flank virtually undefended. The obvious hopelessness of the situation didn't sway the top Nazis' fanatical **refusal to surrender**. Never mind that many of Berlin's defences existed only on paper, or that units were undermanned and poorly armed, with crippling shortages of fuel and ammunition. As the Red Army closed in, Goebbels called hysterically for "rücksichtslose Bekämpfung" – a fight without quarter – and SS execution squads worked around the clock, killing soldiers, Volkssturm guards or Hitler Youth who tried to stop fighting.

In the city the horrors mounted. The **civilian population** lived underground in cellars and air-raid shelters, scavenging for food wherever and

whenever there was a momentary lull in the fighting. Engineers blasted canal locks, flooding the U-Bahn to prevent the Russians from advancing along it. Hundreds of civilians sheltering in the tunnels were drowned as a result (see p.135). On April 27, the Ninth Army was destroyed attempting to break out of the Russian encirclement to the south, and unoccupied Berlin had been reduced to a strip nine and a half miles long from east to west, and three miles wide from north to south, constantly under bombardment. Next the Russians captured the Tiergarten, reducing the **last pocket of resistance** to the Regierungsviertel, where fighting focused on the Reichstag and Hitler's Chancellery, and on Potsdamer Platz, only a few hundred metres from the *Führerbunker*, by now under constant shellfire.

Hitler still hoped that one of his phantom armies would relieve Berlin, but on April 28 his optimism evaporated when he heard that Himmler had been suing for unconditional surrender to the Western Allies. In the early hours of the following day, he married Eva Braun, held a small champagne wedding reception, and dictated his will. As the day wore on, savage fighting continued around the Nazi-held enclave. At a final conference the commandant of Berlin, General Weidling, announced that the Russians were in the nearby Adlon Hotel, and that there was no hope of relief.

A breakout attempt was proposed, but Hitler declared that he was staying put. On the afternoon of April 30, after testing the cyanide on his pet German shepherd dog, **Hitler and Eva Braun committed suicide**: he with a revolver, she by poison. The bodies were taken to the Chancellery courtyard and doused with 200 litres of petrol; Hitler's followers gave the Nazi salute as the corpses burned to ashes. Meanwhile, Soviet troops were battling to gain control of the Reichstag, and at 11pm two Russian sergeants raised the red flag from its rooftop.

According to Hitler's will, Admiral Dönitz was appointed chancellor *in absentia*. In the early hours of May 1, Chief of Staff Krebs was sent out to parley with the Russians. After hasty consultation with Stalin, General Chuikov replied that only unconditional surrender was acceptable. When Krebs returned to the bunker, Goebbels rejected this and ordered the fighting to continue. That night he and his wife killed themselves, having first poisoned their children. The rest of the bunker occupants, with the exception of Krebs and General Burgdorf – Hitler's ADC, who committed suicide – now decided to try and break out. Weidling agreed not to surrender until the following dawn in order to give the fugitives time to **escape from the bunker** and through the railway tunnels towards northern Berlin. Of the 800 or so who tried, about 100 made it – the rest were either killed or captured. No one is sure about the fate of Hitler's deputy, Martin Bormann.

Capitulation and surrender

At 5am, Weidling offered the **capitulation of Berlin** to General Chuikov, who broadcast his surrender proclamation from loudspeaker vans around the city. At 3pm, firing in the city centre stopped, although sporadic, sometimes fierce fighting continued on the outskirts, where German troops tried to break out to the west to surrender to the British or Americans rather than the Russians. Their fears were justified, for the Soviets unleashed an **orgy of rape and looting** on the capital, lasting three days. This was Stalin's reward to his troops for having fought so long and so hard.

The **official surrender of German forces** occurred at a Wehrmacht engineers' school in the Berlin suburb of Karlshorst on May 8, 1945. Wehrmacht forces in the west had already surrendered the day before, and British, French and American delegates flew in with General Keitel, High Commander of the Armed Forces, to repeat the performance for the benefit of the Russians. Berliners had already emerged from their shelters and started to clear the dead and the rubble from the streets. Now the Red Army established field kitchens.

With the final act of surrender complete, it was time to count the cost of the Battle of Berlin. It had taken the lives of 125,000 Berliners (including 6400 suicides and 22,000 heart attacks), and innumerable German soldiers from the 93 divisions destroyed by the Red Army. The Soviets themselves had suffered some 305,000 casualties in the battle, while the city itself had been left in ruins, without even basic services.

Occupation

During the immediate postwar months, civilian rations of food, fuel and medicine were cut to the bone to support the two-million-strong **Soviet occupation forces**. Survival rations were mea-

sured in ounces per day, if forthcoming at all, and civilians had to use all their wits to stay alive. The Soviet Union had taken steps towards establishing a civilian, communist-dominated administration even before the war was over. On April 30, a group of exiled German communists arrived at Küstrin airfield and were taken to Berlin, where they established a temporary headquarters in Lichtenberg. Directed by **Walter Ulbricht**, the future leader of the GDR's communist party, they set about tracking down old Berlin party members and setting up a new **municipal administration**. In each city district, they were careful to ensure that control of education and the police went to communists. This apparatus remained in place even after the arrival of the British and Americans in July.

The **western occupation sectors** had been demarcated by the Allies as far back as 1943, but the troops didn't move in until July 1–4, when fifty thousand British, American and French soldiers replaced the Red Army in the western part of the city. Here, the food situation improved marginally once American supplies began to find their way through, but public health remained a huge problem. Dysentery and TB were endemic, and there were outbreaks of typhoid and paratyphoid, all exacerbated by an acute shortage of hospital beds. British and American soldiers had endless opportunities to profit from the burgeoning **black market**: trading cigarettes, alcohol, gas, NAAFI and PX supplies for antiques, jewellery, or sexual favours. With less to offer, the Russians simply demanded "Davai chas", and took watches at gunpoint. Huge black market centres sprang up around the Brandenburg Gate and Alexanderplatz.

From July 17 to August 3 the **Potsdam conference** took place at the Cecilienhof Palace. It was to be the last great meeting of the leaders of the Big Three wartime alliance. Churchill took the opportunity to visit the ruins of the Reich's Chancellery, followed by a mob of fascinated Germans and Russians. Mid-conference he returned to Britain to hear the results of the first postwar election – and was replaced by the newly elected Labour prime minister, Clement Attlee, who could do little but watch as Truman and Stalin settled the fate of postwar Europe and Berlin.

For Germans, the worst was yet to come. Agriculture and industry had virtually collapsed, threatening acute **shortages of food and fuel** just as winter approached. In Berlin they dug mass graves and stockpiled coffins for the expected wave of deaths, and thousands of children were evacuated to the British occupation zone in the west of the country, where conditions were less severe. To everyone's surprise the winter turned out to be uncommonly mild. Christmas 1945 was celebrated after a fashion, and mothers took their children to the first postwar Weihnachtsmarkt (Christmas fair) in the Lustgarten.

Starvation and unrest

Unfortunately the respite was only temporary, for despite the good weather, food supplies remained overstretched. In March rations were reduced drastically, and the weakened civilian population fell prey to typhus, TB and other **hunger-related diseases**; the lucky ones merely suffered enteric or skin diseases. The Allies did what they could, sending government and private relief, but even by the spring of 1947 rations remained at malnutrition levels. **Crime and prostitution** soared. In Berlin alone, two thousand people were arrested every month, many of them from juvenile gangs that roamed the ruins murdering, robbing and raping. Trains were attacked at the Berlin stations, and in the countryside bandits ambushed supply convoys heading for the city. The winter of 1946–47 was one of the coldest since records began. Wolves appeared in Berlin and people froze to death aboard trains. There were rumours of cannibalism and Berlin hospitals had to treat 55,000 people for frostbite.

Meanwhile, **political developments** that were to have a lasting impact on Berlin were occurring. In March 1946, the social democratic SPD was forced into a shotgun merger with the KPD, to form the **SED** (Sozialistische Einheitspartei Deutschlands – "Socialist Unity Party of Germany"), or future **communist party** of East Germany. In the western half of the city, 71 percent of members voted against union; in East Berlin no voting was permitted, and attempts to hold ballots in the Prenzlauer Berg and Friedrichshain party offices were broken up by Russian soldiers. In October 1946, the first citywide **free elections** since 1933 were held. The SED fared badly and the SPD triumphed, much to the annoyance of the Soviet zone authorities, who abandoned free elections after this setback.

The Berlin airlift

Already the city was becoming **divided along political lines** as the wartime alliance between the western powers (France had also been allotted an occupation zone) and the Soviet Union fell apart, ushering in a new era of conflict that would all too often focus on Berlin. The Allied Control Council met for the last time on March 20, when Marshal Sokolovsky, the Soviet military governor, protested about British and American attempts to introduce economic reform in their occupation zones.

Tension mounted over the next few months as the Allies went ahead with economic reform, while the Russians demanded the right to board Berlin-bound Allied trains, and on June 16 walked out of the four-power Kommandantura that had ultimate control over Berlin. Things came to a head with the **introduction of the D-Mark** in the western zone (June 23, 1948). On that day, the Soviets presented Berlin's mayor with an ultimatum, demanding that he accept their own Ostmark as currency for the whole city. But the city's parliament voted overwhelmingly against the Soviet-backed currency.

Everyone knew that this was asking for trouble, and trouble wasn't long in coming. On the night of June 23–24, power stations in the Soviet zone cut off electricity supplies to the western half of Berlin, and road and rail links between the western part of Germany and Berlin were severed. This was the beginning of the **Berlin blockade**, the USSR's first attempt to force the Western Allies out of Berlin. SPD politician Ernst Reuter, soon to be mayor of West Berlin, addressed a crowd at the Gesundbrunnen soccer field, promising that Berlin would "fight with everything we have".

There was now only one month's food and ten days' coal supply left in the city. The British and Americans realized that they had to support West Berlin, but were unwilling to use military force to push their way in overland. After some consideration it was decided to try to supply Berlin by air, as it was felt that the Soviets wouldn't dare risk intercepting Allied planes. However, there were serious doubts as to whether it was possible to sustain two million people by an airlift. The only previous attempt on a comparable scale – maintaining the German Sixth Army at Stalingrad – had been an utter failure. Berlin's needs were calculated at 4000 tons of supplies per day, yet the available aircraft could carry fewer than 500 tons.

Nevertheless, the **Berlin airlift** that began on June 26, 1948, soon gathered momentum. The Soviets maintained their blockade and made it plain that they regarded Germany as divided and Berlin as the capital of their half. America brought in huge C54 Skymaster transport planes to supplement the smaller C47s and Dakotas that the airlift began with. It soon became an around-the-clock, precision operation. By October, planes were landing every three minutes, bringing in 4760 tons of food and fuel every day. Winter was exceptionally tough. Power cuts and severe food rationing reduced living standards to the level of the immediate postwar period. The Russians made supplies available in the eastern half of the city, but relatively few West Berliners chose to take advantage of them. At municipal elections on December 7, the SPD's **Ernst Reuter** was voted in as mayor of West Berlin, becoming a kind of human symbol of its resistance.

By the spring of 1949, planes were landing or taking off every thirty seconds and shifting 8000 tons a day. At Easter, the Allies mounted a special operation to boost morale and cock a snook at the Soviets. In just 24 hours they flew 13,000 tons of supplies into Berlin. Shortly afterwards the Soviets gave up, lifting the blockade on May 12. The first trucks and trains to reach West Berlin received a tumultuous welcome. The airlift was continued for another four months to ensure that Berlin would be supplied should the blockade be resumed at short notice. Though it cost the lives of 48 airmen and millions of dollars, the airlift thwarted Stalin's attempt to expel the Allies from West Berlin, and dealt the Soviets a resounding propaganda defeat. It also changed most Berliners' perception of the Western powers from occupiers to allies.

The birth of the two Germanys

Within six months, the political division of Germany was formalized by the creation of two rival states. First, the British, French and American zones of occupation were amalgamated to form the **Federal Republic of Germany** (May 1949); the Soviets followed suit by launching the **German Democratic Republic** on October 7. As Berlin lay deep within GDR territory, its eastern sector naturally became the official GDR capital. However, much to the disappointment of many Berliners, the Federal Republic chose Bonn as their capital. West Berlin remained under the overall control of the Allied military commandants, although it was eventually to assume the status of a Land (state) of the Federal Republic.

Although West Berlin's **economic recovery** was by no means as dramatic as that of West Germany, the city did prosper, particularly in comparison to East Berlin. The Soviets had gone in for ruthless **asset-stripping** – removing factories, rolling stock and generators to replace losses in the war-ravaged USSR – and when they eventually turned to reconstructing the GDR, the emphasis was put on heavy industrial production. West Berlin soon became an attractive destination for East Berliners, who were able to cross the **zonal border** more or less freely at this time. Many came to stay, while others worked in the city, benefiting from the purchasing power of the D-Mark. And those who did neither used the city to enjoy the entertainment and culture lacking in the more spartan East.

Political tension remained a fact of life in a city that had become an arena for superpower confrontations. The Soviets and GDR communists had not abandoned the idea of driving the Allies out of Berlin, and mounted diverse operations against them; just as the Allies ran spying and sabotage operations against East Berlin. In this cradle of **Cold War espionage**, the recruitment of former Gestapo, SD or Abwehr operatives seemed quite justifiable to all the agencies concerned. On one side were Britain's SIS (based at the Olympic Stadium) and the American CIA, which fostered the Federal Republic's own intelligence service, the Gehlen Bureau, run by a former Abwehr colonel. Opposing them were the Soviet KGB and GRU (based at Karlshorst), and the GDR's own foreign espionage service and internal security police. The public side of this rumbling underground war was a number of **incidents** in 1952. An Air France plane approaching West Berlin through the air corridor was fired upon by a Russian MiG; the East German authorities blocked streets leading from West to East Berlin and expropriated property owned by West Berliners on the outskirts of the eastern sector.

The Workers' Uprising

The **death of Stalin** on March 5, 1953, raised hopes that the situation in Berlin could be eased, but these were soon dashed. In the eastern sector, the communists unwittingly fuelled smouldering resentment by announcing a ten percent rise in work norms on June 16. For workers already hard-pressed to support their families, this demand to produce more or earn less was intolerable. The first to protest were building workers on block 40 of the prestigious Stalinallee construction project, who downed tools and marched on the city centre, joined by other workers and passers-by. At Strausberger Platz they swept aside Volkspolizei units who tried to stop them and headed, via Alexanderplatz, for Unter den Linden. From here, by now roughly eight thousand-strong, the **demonstration** marched to the House of Ministries, occupying Göring's former Air Ministry on Leipziger Strasse, where they demanded to speak with SED chief Walter Ulbricht and Prime Minister Otto Grotewohl, both of whom declined to appear.

Eventually three lesser ministers were sent out to speak to the demonstrators. Clearly alarmed at the scale of the demonstration, they promised to try and get the work norms lowered. But by now the crowd wanted more, and began calling for political freedom. After declaring a **general strike** for the next day, the protesters returned to Stalinallee, tearing down SED placards on the way. Grotewohl's announcement rescinding the new work norms later that day failed to halt the strike, news of which had been broadcast across the GDR by western radio stations. About 300,000 workers in 250 towns joined in, and by 7am a crowd of 100,000 people was marching through East Berlin towards the House of Ministries.

Ulbricht and Grotewohl feared for their lives and called for Russian help. When **Soviet tanks** appeared in Leipziger Strasse before noon, they found their route blocked by a vast crowd that refused to budge. The Soviet commandant, General Pavel Dibrova, warned by loudspeaker that martial law had been declared, and all violators would face summary punishment – but with little effect. Dibrova ordered his troops to move forward with the tanks following in close support, and it was at this point that the shooting started.

The crowd scattered as the first shots rang out, leaving youths to confront the T-34s with bricks and bottles. **Street fighting** raged throughout East Berlin for the rest of the day, and it wasn't until nightfall that the Soviets reasserted communist control. At least 267 demonstrators, 116 policemen and 18 Soviet soldiers were killed during the fighting, and it's estimated that 92 civil-

ians (including a West Berliner just passing through) were summarily shot after the **suppression of the uprising**. The Western Allies did nothing to prevent this, nor the subsequent trials of "counter-revolutionaries" at which fourteen death sentences and innumerable prison terms were meted out – final confirmation that Berlin was divided.

Bertolt Brecht, who had returned to Berlin in 1949 and elected to live in the East, wrote an epitaph to this episode in a poem called "The Solution":

> *After the rising of 17 June*
> *The secretary of the Writers' Union*
> *Had leaflets distributed in Stalinallee*
> *In which you could read that the people*
> *Had lost the government's confidence*
> *Which it could only regain with*
> *Redoubled efforts. Would it in that case*
> *Not be simpler if the Government*
> *Dissolved the people*
> *And elected another?*

Berlin was relatively quiet for the remainder of the 1950s, but important events were taking place in **West Germany** under Chancellor Konrad Adenauer. Foremost among these was the so-called **"economic miracle"**, which saw West Germany recover from the ravages of war astonishingly quickly and go on to become Europe's largest economy, which couldn't help but give a shot in the arm to the fortunes of West Berlin. On the political front, the **Hallstein doctrine** of non-recognition for the GDR reigned supreme. This was even stretched to the point of not maintaining diplomatic relations with other countries who chose to recognize the GDR. A pragmatic exception was made of the Soviet Union.

The building of the Wall

The economic disparity between East and West Germany (and their respective halves of Berlin) worsened throughout the 1950s. **Marshall Plan aid** and West German capital were transforming West Berlin into a glittering showcase for capitalism, whereas the GDR and East Berlin seemed to languish. Prospects for development in the GDR were undermined by a steady **population drain**, as mostly young and often highly skilled workers headed west for higher living standards and greater political freedom. Roughly 2,500,000 people quit the GDR during the 1950s, mostly via the open border with West Berlin, where an average of 19,000 East Germans crossed over every month. Both the GDR and Soviet governments saw this as a threat to East Germany's existence.

On November 10, 1958, Soviet leader Nikita Khrushchev demanded that the Western Allies relinquish their role in the "occupation regime in Berlin, thus facilitating the normalization of the situation in the capital of the GDR". Two weeks later, Khrushchev suggested that the Allies should withdraw and Berlin should become a free city – coupled with a broad hint that if no agreement was reached within six months, a blockade would be reimposed. The Allies rejected the ultimatum, and the Kremlin allowed the deadline to pass without incident. Tripartite **negotiations** at Geneva (May–Sept 1959) failed to produce a settlement. Meanwhile, tens of thousands of East Germans continued to cross the border into West Berlin.

By 1961 Ulbricht's regime was getting desperate, and rumours that the border might be sealed began to circulate. In mid-June Ulbricht felt compelled to assure the world that no one had "the intention of building a wall". Simultaneously, however, border controls were tightened. Yet the flood of people voting with their feet continued to rise, in what West Berlin's Springer press dubbed "mass escapes . . . of avalanche proportions". It was obvious that something was about to happen.

Shortly after midnight on August 13, 1961, East German soldiers, policemen and Workers' Militia received orders to close the border with the West. At 2am, forty thousand men went into action, stringing barbed wire across streets leading into West Berlin and closing U- and S-Bahn lines to create what their commanders called "an antifascist protection barrier". Many Berliners were rudely evicted from their homes, while others, marginally less unfortunate, had their doors and windows blocked by bales of barbed wire and armed guards. Although the Allies reinforced patrols, they did nothing to prevent the **sealing of the border**.

Despite earlier rumours, most people in West and East Berlin were taken by surprise. Those who lived far from the border area only learned of its closure when they found all routes to West Berlin blocked. Crowds gathered and the border guards were reinforced to prevent trouble. There was little most people could do other than accept this latest development as a *fait accompli*. Others – including a few border guards – managed to take advantage of loopholes in the new barrier, and flee west. But within a few days, building workers were reinforcing the barbed wire and makeshift barricades with bricks and mortar, creating a **provisional version of the Wall**. As an additional measure, West Berliners were no longer allowed to cross the border into East Berlin.

Reaction in the West

Despite public outrage throughout West Germany and formal **diplomatic protests** from the Allies, everyone knew that to take a firmer line risked starting nuclear war. The West had to fall back on symbolic gestures: the Americans sent over General Lucius Clay, organizer of the Berlin airlift, and Vice-President Lyndon Johnson, on August 18. The **separation of families** plunged morale in East Berlin to new depths and **economic problems** hit West Berlin, which was suddenly deprived of sixty thousand skilled workers who formerly commuted in from the GDR. They could only be replaced by creating special tax advantages to attract workers and businesses from the Federal Republic into West Berlin. American support for West Berlin was reaffirmed in August 1963, by President **John F. Kennedy**'s "Ich bin ein Berliner..." speech, but for all its rhetoric and rapturous reception, the West essentially had to accept the new status quo.

From 1961 onwards the GDR strengthened its **border fortifications**, completely sealing off West Berlin from East Berlin and the East German hinterland. The Wall became an almost impenetrable barrier – in effect two walls separated by a Sperrgebiet (forbidden zone) dotted with watchtowers and patrolled by soldiers and dogs. Border troops had orders to shoot to kill and often did so. Yet hundreds of successful **escapes** took place before the GDR was able to refine its techniques, and thousands of people passed over, under or through the Wall by various methods, usually involving extreme danger.

Berlin in the 1960s

The **gradual reduction of political tension** that occurred after the Wall had been standing a couple of years was partly due to improved relations between the superpowers, and mostly to local efforts. Under SPD Mayor **Willy Brandt**, talks were opened between the West Berlin Senate and the GDR government, resulting in the "**Pass**

Agreement" of December 1963, whereby 730,000 West Berliners were able to pay brief visits to the East at the end of the year. Three more agreements were concluded over the next couple of years until the GDR decided to use border controls as a lever for winning **diplomatic recognition** (which the Federal Republic and its Western allies refused to give under the Hallstein doctrine). Access to West Berlin via routes through GDR territory was subject to official hindrance; on one occasion, deputies were prevented from attending a plenary session of the Bundestag, held in West Berlin in April 1965. New and more stringent **passport and visa controls** were levied on all travellers from June 1968 onwards.

As the direct threat to its existence receded, West Berlin society began to fragment along generational lines. Partly because Berlin residents could evade West German conscription, young people formed an unusually high proportion of the population. The immediate catalyst was the wave of **student unrest** in 1967–68, when initial grievances over unreformed, badly run universities soon spread to embrace wider disaffection with West Germany's materialistic culture. As in West Germany, the APO or **extra-parliamentary opposition** emerged as a strong and vocal force in West Berlin, criticizing what many people saw as a failed attempt to build a true democracy on the ruins of Nazi Germany. Another powerful strand was anti-Americanism, fuelled by US policy in Southeast Asia, Latin America and the Middle East. Both these viewpoints tended to bewilder and enrage older Germans.

The police reacted to street demonstrations in Berlin with a ferocity that shocked even conservatives. On June 2, 1967, a student was shot by police during a protest against a state visit by the Shah of Iran. The right-wing **Springer press** (deliberately sited just near the Wall) absolved the police, pinning all the blame on "long-haired communists". When someone tried to kill student leader **Rudi Dutschke** (April 11, 1968), there were huge and violent demonstrations against the Springer press. Although the mass-protest movement fizzled out towards the end of the 1960s, a new and deadlier opposition would emerge in the 1970s – partly born from the West German establishment's violent response to what was initially a peaceful protest movement.

Ostpolitik and détente

The international scene and Berlin's place in it changed considerably around the turn of the decade. Both superpowers now hoped to thaw the Cold War and reach a *modus vivendi*, while elections in the Federal Republic brought to power a chancellor committed to rapprochement with the GDR. On February 27, 1969, US President Richard Nixon called for an easing of international tension during his visit to Berlin. Soon afterwards, **Four Power Talks** were held in the former Allied Control Council building in the American sector. Against a background of negotiations between West Germany and the Soviet Union, and proposals for a European security conference, the participants decided to set aside broader issues in an effort to fashion a workable agreement on the status of the divided city.

This resulted in the **Quadripartite Agreement** (September 3, 1971), followed in December by inter-German agreements regarding transit routes to West Berlin and travel and traffic regulations for West Berliners. These were largely due to the efforts of Chancellor Willy Brandt, whose **Ostpolitik** aimed at normalizing relations between the two Germanys. Treaties were signed with the Soviet Union and Poland in 1970, recognizing the validity of the Oder–Neisse line marking the Polish–German border. Finally, in 1972, the Federal Republic and the GDR signed a **Basic Treaty**. While stopping short of full recognition, it bound both states to respect each other's frontiers and *de facto* sovereignty.

In return for abandoning the Hallstein doctrine, West Germans were given access to friends and family across the border, which had been effectively denied to them (barring limited visits in the mid-1960s). However, the freedom to move from East to West was restricted to disabled people and senior citizens. This marked a concession by the new East German leader, **Erich Honecker**, who was regarded as a "liberal" when he succeeded Ulbricht in 1971. Aside from desiring access to West German know-how, markets and capital, Honecker had a personal reason for wanting closer ties: his own family lived in the Saarland.

The 1970s

During the 1970s Berlin assumed a new identity, breaking with the images and myths of the past. Thanks to the easing of Cold War tensions West

Berlin was no longer a frontline city, and East Berlin lost much of its intimidating atmosphere. Throughout the decade, **West Berlin** had similar problems to those of West Germany: economic upsets triggered by the quadrupling of oil prices in 1974, and a wave of terrorism directed against the establishment. In addition, West Berlin suffered from a deteriorating stock of housing and rising unemployment – both alleviated to some extent by financial help from West Germany.

East Berlin remained relatively quiet. Under Honecker, living standards improved and there was some relaxation of the tight controls of the Ulbricht days. However, most people regarded the changes as essentially trivial, and escapes continued to be attempted, although by now the Wall was formidably deadly. In 1977 a rock concert in Alexanderplatz turned into a brief explosion of street unrest, which the authorities suppressed with deliberate brutality.

The 1980s

Throughout the 1970s and early 1980s, the Quadripartite Agreement and the inter-German treaties formed the backdrop to relations between West and East Berlin. The main irritant was the **compulsory exchange** of D-Marks for Ostmarks, which the GDR raised in value from DM6.50 to DM25 in 1980, deterring significant numbers of visitors. But on the whole, a degree of stability and normality had been achieved, enabling both cities to run smoothly on a day-to-day basis, without being the focus of international tension. Even after the partial resumption of the Cold War, following the Soviet invasion of Afghanistan in 1979, Berlin remained relatively calm. The only notable event was the shooting of an American officer on an alleged spying mission in Potsdam in the spring of 1985.

As elsewhere in West Germany, Berlin witnessed a crystallization of issues and attitudes and the flowering of new radical movements. Concern about the arms race and the environment was widespread; feminism and gay rights commanded increasing support. Left-wing and Green groups formed an **Alternative Liste** to fight elections, and a left-liberal newspaper, *Tageszeitung*, was founded. Organized squatting was the radical solution to Berlin's **housing crisis**. In 1981, the new Christian Democrat administration (elected after a financial scandal forced the SPD to step down) tried to evict the squatters from

about 170 apartment buildings, and police violence sparked rioting in Schöneberg. The administration compromised by allowing some of the squatters to become legitimate tenants, which had a big effect on life in West Berlin. For the first time since the late 1960s, the social divisions that had opened up showed signs of narrowing. Alternative Liste delegates were elected to the Berlin Senate for the first time in May 1981, and the same year witnessed a boom in **cultural life**, as the arts exploded into new vitality.

The **early 1980s** saw a resumption of frostiness in US–Soviet relations, which heightened concern about **nuclear weapons**. Anti-nuclear activists protested during the Berlin visit of President Ronald Reagan in June 1981. But the tension and sabre-rattling that had characterized the Cold War of the 1950s and 1960s didn't return to Berlin. In 1985 the USSR broke with its tradition of geriatric rulers when the dynamic and comparatively young **Mikhail Gorbachev** became general secretary of the Soviet Communist Party. The West was slow to appreciate the full significance of his campaigns for *glasnost* and *perestroika*, and their initial impact on Berlin was slight. The city's status – and the division of Germany into separate states – seemed assured by the Quadripartite Agreement and the Basic Treaty.

Unfortunately, ideological hostility prevented the two halves of the city from jointly celebrating Berlin's 750th anniversary in 1987. Instead, **separate anniversary celebrations** were arranged. In East Berlin, these were preceded by a massive **urban renewal project**, in both the city centre and the inner suburbs. The SED boasted that the GDR was a mature socialist state, advancing to the front rank of European nations. It saw no need for *glasnost* or *perestroika* – indeed, it regarded them with deep suspicion.

In West Berlin, the elections of spring 1989 swept the CDU administration from power, and an **SPD/Alternative Liste coalition** took over, with Walter Momper as mayor. In Kreuzberg, demonstrations against what many regarded as an Alternative Liste sell-out were put down with unwarranted force, sparking running street battles. Further violence occurred on May 1, during the now-traditional annual wrecking spree by anarchists and far-leftists espousing anti-imperialist, anticapitalist motives. For once, however, the police refrained from breaking heads, having been told to go easy by their chief.

The GDR resists perestroika

In the East there were few visible signs of change as the decade wore on, but things were happening behind the scenes. The **Protestant Church** provided a haven for several **environmental and peace organizations**, which formed a nascent opposition. But the regime seemed as intractable as ever, dismissing Gorbachev-style reforms as inappropriate to the GDR. The most memorable rebuff was delivered by SED chief ideologist Kurt Hager, who said in April 1987, "You don't need to change the wallpaper in your apartment just because your neighbour is doing his place up." Open dissent was stamped on: in January 1988, a group of protesters who unfurled banners calling for greater freedom at the official demonstration in memory of Karl Liebknecht and Rosa Luxemburg were immediately arrested and imprisoned, later being expelled from the GDR.

Fearful of the changes sweeping the Soviet Union, Hungary and Poland, the authorities banned the Soviet magazine *Sputnik* and several Russian films from the 1960s, only now released from censorship. As a further insult to their subjects, the GDR's rulers heaped honours on the odious Romanian dictator Nicolae Ceaușescu. Although Poland and Hungary had both embarked on the road to democracy, the GDR was unmoving. SED leader Erich Honecker declared that the Wall would stand for another fifty or one hundred years if necessary, to protect "our republic from robbers". East Germans could only despair.

Few believed any more the endless lies and clichés that spanned the gap between official pronouncements and reality. The SED leadership seemed totally isolated from the mood of the people. There seemed no way out except individual attempts to escape. When Chris Gueffroy was shot dead while trying to cross the border at Neukölln on February 6, 1989, no one realized that he was to be the last person killed in such an attempt.

Something had to give, and give it did in a manner so dramatic and unpredictable that it surprised the whole world.

Die Wende to the present

1989 ranks as the most significant year in German history since 1945. In the space of twelve months a complete and unforseeable transformation (what Germans call Die Wende) occurred. German unification suddenly went from being a remote possibility to reality, forcing everyone to reassess the European order.

Once again Berlin was at the forefront of historical change, manifested in human terms by emotional scenes that caught the imagination of the world. When the Berlin Wall parted on November 9, 1989, it symbolized the end of an era: the Cold War was finally over, and a lifetime's dream had come true for most Germans – above all, those living in the East.

The beginning: exodus through Hungary

It was reform in another Eastern European country that made the incredible events of 1989 possible. On May 2, the Hungarian authorities began taking down the barbed wire along their border with Austria, creating a **hole in the Iron Curtain**. The event was televised worldwide, and thousands of East Germans saw it as a chance to get out. Aware that new visa laws making travel to Hungary more difficult would come into force in the autumn, they seized their chance during summer, when "holidays" provided a pretext.

It wasn't an easy option. Much of the barbed wire was still intact, and Hungarian troops patrolled the border. The lucky ones made it through the woods and swamps, evading soldiers who sometimes, but by no means always, turned a blind eye. In the early months, those who were caught were deported back to the GDR where jail awaited them. Later the Hungarians merely stamped the passports of those whom they intercepted, leaving it to the East German police to deal with them – if they returned home.

Wise to what was going on, the GDR authorities began trying to halt the increasing numbers of would-be escapees. Hungary-bound travellers were stopped and thoroughly searched. Anyone travelling light was deemed to be making a one-way trip and sent back. The same went for people carrying birth certificates and other important documents. Smart **escapers** began booking return tickets to destinations like Bulgaria, and travelling with baggage as if on a family holiday – only to make an unscheduled stop in Budapest.

The whole process was made slightly easier by the **illness of SED leader Erich Honecker**, which put him out of action from July 8 onwards. No one else seemed able to fill the ensuing power vacuum and enforce measures that would have enabled the state to check the draining away of its population. By August, some two hundred East Germans were crossing into Austria every night. Those who were caught could console themselves with the fact that the Hungarians no longer stamped their passports, leaving them free to try again. Many, unable to get through the border and rapidly running out of money, sought **refuge** in the West German embassy in Budapest. The situation was gradually reaching crisis point.

Mass escape

The first **mass exodus** happened on August 19, when seven hundred East Germans surged across the border into Austria, unhindered by Hungarian border guards. They got there under the pretext of holding a frontier peace picnic near Sopron; in fact, the whole escape was pre-arranged by the conservative Paneuropa-Union, with the support of the reformist Magyar politician Imre Pozsgay. On August 24, others were allowed to leave after the Red Cross stamped their documents with a "Permit de Voyage". By now some six thousand people had made it across the border and their success encouraged others to make the journey from the GDR to Hungary. By the beginning of September there were over **20,000 refugees** housed in Hungarian holiday camps and the West German embassy – which was by now overflowing.

Having considered the reactions of East and West Germany, the Hungarian government opted to please the latter, and announced on September 7 that "humanitarian measures" would take place in the next few days. This was diplomatic smooth talk for **opening the border** and allowing all the East Germans to leave. When the instruction was implemented on September 10, East German refugees heard the news at 7pm. Gyula Horn, the Hungarian foreign minister, announced: "The GDR citizens staying in this country can leave with their own, in other words GDR passports, to a country that is willing to receive them." The border opened at midnight, and 300 cars crossed over within fifteen minutes. A couple of hours later the first East German car crossed the Austro-German border at Passau. For those without transport, special buses and trains were laid on. The GDR government could only condemn what it called "an organized trade in human beings", while the West German government – from whom the Magyars hoped for investment – promised it would "not forget this independent decision by Hungary".

Other East Germans had meanwhile made their way to **Prague and Warsaw**, where they took refuge in West German embassy buildings. By the last week of September there were 3500 people in the Prague embassy, while Czech police and Stasi agents tried to hold back the thousands more who hoped to gain admission. Despite strongarm tactics, increasing numbers scaled the fence and swelled the crowd of refugees inside the embassy, where living conditions were daily growing more intolerable. Relief finally came on September 30, when **Hans-Dietrich Genscher**, West Germany's foreign minister, who had himself fled East Germany during the 1950s, appeared on the embassy balcony and announced that the refugees were to be allowed to leave. Special **trains** laid on by the GDR government were to ferry seventeen thousand refugees to West Germany via East German

territory. As the trains passed through towns like Dresden, Karl-Marx-Stadt and Plauen, stations were stormed by people hoping to jump on board, and there were dozens of injuries as the police sealed off the tracks.

The October revolution

Within the GDR, morale plummeted. While people who had applied to leave and were still waiting for exit permits now despaired, thousands of others who had previously been content to make the best of things suddenly began thinking of emigration. Meanwhile, fledgling **opposition groups** like **Neues Forum** emerged, as East Germans took courage from the regime's evident disarray. People risked printing and circulating *samizdat* manifestos calling for reform and dialogue. SED leader Erich Honecker, whom West Germany's *Bild Zeitung* had already assigned to the obituary column, reappeared on the scene in time to join official celebrations marking the GDR's fortieth anniversary. Among the honoured guests were Mikhail Gorbachev, whom most East Germans had eagerly awaited; a delegation from Beijing bearing thanks for the SED's public approval of the Tiananmen Square massacre; and Romanian dictator Nicolae Ceauşescu.

There was tension on all sides at the **anniversary celebrations** on October 7. Gorbachev stressed the need for dialogue, receptivity to new ideas and the West German viewpoint. Honecker took a contrary stance, praising the status quo in stock clichés, seemingly oblivious to growing public discontent. The vainglorious parade of weaponry and floats passed off calmly (only party loyalists were admitted to the televised zone), but side-street protests and scuffles took place along the cavalcade route. As the day wore on, these escalated into a huge demonstration, which the police and Stasi brutally suppressed. Thousands of arrests were made, and prisoners were subjected to degrading treatment and beatings. Simultaneous **demonstrations** in Dresden and Leipzig were dealt with even more harshly. But the people were growing bolder, as the regime's self-confidence diminished.

A week later, most of those arrested on October 7 were released, and sections of the press voiced oblique criticism of the party leadership's handling of the crisis. The Politbüro offered to talk with the opposition, but refused to legalize it. Monday, October 9, saw **nationwide**

demonstrations, which came close to bloodshed in **Leipzig**, where 70,000 people marched through the city. Honecker ordered the local security forces to suppress the protest by any means necessary, including force of arms. City hospitals were alerted, and extra plasma was rushed in to cope with the expected casualties. But the march went ahead and Honecker's orders were never executed. Whether someone in the Politbüro countermanded them, or the local party secretary or security boss simply ignored them, remains unclear. The main point was that elements of the regime drew the line at wholesale slaughter.

Indeed, the whole Politbüro of the SED had become disenchanted with Honecker's rigidity. He was an obvious target for public hatred, and protests were gathering momentum daily. In Leipzig, now the focal point of opposition, the latest protest brought 150,000 people onto the streets. For the leadership, the strain proved too great: after eighteen years as party secretary, **Erich Honecker was suddenly replaced by Egon Krenz** on October 18. It seems that Honecker threatened to resign unless the Politbüro supported his hard line; instead, they accepted his resignation in silence, and he left the room "an old and broken man". Krenz, whom SED-watchers dubbed the "crown prince", was a 52-year-old Politbüro member with a hardline reputation of his own: it was he who had congratulated the Beijing government after it had crushed the Chinese democracy movement. Confounding expectations, however, Krenz immediately announced that the regime was ready for dialogue, although his reputation was to remain a stumbling block when it came to gaining popular trust.

The continuing exodus

Over the next week, as newspaper reports criticizing the government increased in frequency, the opposition gained ground and the exodus of GDR citizens continued. On October 27, the government declared an **amnesty** for those convicted of Republikflucht (fleeing the country) or jailed for demonstrating, but the pressure on the streets kept rising. On November 4, East Berlin witnessed the largest **street protest** since the workers' uprising of 1953, as over one million citizens demonstrated. The vast crowd walked from the headquarters of the ADN state news agency

to Alexanderplatz, where they were addressed by reformists, writers and priests. Banners calling for the demolition of the Wall were unfurled. The author Stefan Heym, a long-time critic of the regime, told the crowd: "It's as if someone's thrown open a window after years of dullness and fug, platitudes, bureaucratic arbitrariness and blindness." Author Heiner Müller added: "If the government should resign during the next week, it will be permitted to dance at demonstrations."

The authorities made hasty **concessions**. The same day, Krenz agreed to allow five thousand East Germans who were packed into the West German embassy in Prague to leave for the West. It was also announced that GDR citizens no longer required visas to visit Czechoslovakia – in effect, permitting emigration via Czechoslovakia. People swarmed across the border to exploit this loophole, and fifteen thousand of them had reached Bavaria by November 6. The same day, 500,000 citizens demonstrated in Leipzig, winning fresh concessions – the promise of thirty days' foreign travel a year – that satisfied no one.

Next, the SED tried placating people with **resignations**. The government of Prime Minister Willi Stoph quit on November 7, with the Politbüro following suit the next day. On the new executive that replaced it, Krenz and Berlin party boss Günter Schabowski were the only relics from the old order; the new prime minister, **Hans Modrow**, had acquired something of a liberal reputation during his previous job as Dresden party chief. Simultaneously, the Ministry of the Interior accepted an application from Neues Forum to be considered a legal group. Across the GDR, hardline officials were resigning in the face of ever-increasing demands from the street, and the exodus of citizens was continuing. By now, 200,000 East Germans had left the country since the beginning of 1989.

The Wall opens

The **opening of the Berlin Wall** was announced almost casually. On the evening of Thursday, November 9, Schabowski told a press conference that East German citizens were free to leave the GDR with valid exit visas, which were henceforth to be issued without delay. Journalists were puzzled: did this really mean that the Wall was effectively open? As news filtered through to the East German population, they sought confirmation by calling the TV stations, which broadcast

Schabowski's announcement several times in the course of the evening. Hardly daring to believe it, citizens started heading for the nearest border crossings, with or without visas. A couple who passed through the Bornholmer Strasse crossing at 9.15pm may well have been the first to leave under the new law.

In both East and West Berlin, people flocked to the Wall. Huge crowds converged on the **Brandenburg Gate**, where an impromptu **street party** broke out. As West Berliners popped champagne corks and Germans from both sides of the Wall embraced, the Volkspolizei gave up checking documents and simply let thousands of East Germans walk through into West Berlin, from which they had been barred for 28 years. The scenes of joy and disbelief were flashed around a world taken by surprise. West German Chancellor **Helmut Kohl** had to interrupt a state visit to Warsaw and rush to West Berlin, where the international press was arriving in droves. Inside the GDR, disbelief turned to joy as people realized that the unimaginable had happened.

The opening of the Wall was a hard act to follow, but events acquired even greater momentum. On November 10, the Jannowitzbrücke U-Bahn station reopened after 28 years, making it possible for East Berliners to go to West Berlin by U-Bahn. On Saturday, November 11, **500,000 East Berliners visited West Berlin**. There were reports of mile-long queues at checkpoints, where 2.7 million exit visas were issued during the first weekend after the opening of the Wall. West Germans – and TV-viewers around the world – gaped at the streams of Trabant cars pouring into West Berlin, where shops enjoyed a bonanza as East Germans spent their DM100 "welcome money", given to all GDR visitors by the Federal Republic. On November 12, the mayors of the two Berlins, Walter Momper and Erhard Krack, met and shook hands at the newly opened Potsdamer Platz border crossing. Just over two years earlier, Krack had spurned an invitation to the West Berlin celebrations marking the city's 750th anniversary, saying that West Berlin "does not exist for us".

Protest and further reform

Inside the GDR the pace of protest didn't slacken, although the opposition was as surprised as anyone by the rapid changes. Demonstrations continued across the country; in places like Leipzig

(now known as the "hero city of the revolution") they had practically become institutionalized. Feelings were still running high against Krenz and other government figures seen as tainted by their association with the old system. Not least of the problems facing Prime Minister Modrow was the **declining value of the Ostmark**. The black market rate fell from ten to twenty Ostmarks per Deutschmark, and enforcing the official rate of 1:1 became virtually impossible. A fiscal crisis loomed on the horizon.

On the second weekend after the opening of the Wall, the GDR authorities announced that **ten million visas** had been issued since November 9 – an incredible statistic considering the whole population of the GDR was sixteen million. By now all eyes were on the Brandenburg Gate, where the Western media was massing in expectation of a grand reopening. Their hopes were dashed on November 19, when Krenz announced that the opening of the Gate was a symbolic affair in which he had no interest at the moment. Attention shifted back to events in the GDR, whose parliament, the Volkskammer, was asserting itself – particularly the hitherto "tame" parties allied to the SED.

The Volkskammer motion **ending the leading role of the SED** was passed (December 1) just as pent-up feeling against the Stasi erupted in a series of demos and sporadic attacks on its premises and members. These calmed down with a promise from the government that the dismantling of the formidable Stasi security service would begin straight away. In the first week of December, **round-table talks** between government and opposition began in an attempt to thrash out the future. After some haggling, the government agreed to one of the opposition's prime demands, pledging **free elections on May 6, 1990** – these were later brought forward to March 18.

At a special **SED conference** (December 15–17), the party decided to emulate the Hungarian Communists and repackage itself as the new, supposedly voter-friendly **PDS** – Partei des Demokratischen Sozialismus or "Democratic Socialist Party". As one of the last representatives of the old guard, Egon Krenz was consigned to political oblivion. His successor, **Gregor Gysi**, was a previously unknown lawyer who had defended a number of dissidents under the old regime. Almost immediately, Gysi and Modrow had to respond to a new initiative from **Chancellor Kohl**, who visited Dresden on December 19. Addressing a huge, enthusiastic crowd as "dear countrymen", Kohl promised that he wouldn't leave them in the lurch, and declared his ultimate goal of a **united Germany**.

Hans Modrow took Kohl's visit as an opportunity to announce the **reopening of the Brandenburg Gate**. Initially it was opened to pedestrians only, with one channel in each direction. Almost simultaneously it was announced that the **removal of visa controls and compulsory currency exchange** for West German visitors to the GDR would be implemented ahead of schedule. By the year's end there were further signs of the two Berlins drawing closer together. Numerous joint economic, industrial and cultural projects were under consideration, and East Berlin city maps began to feature S- and U-Bahn stations in West Berlin (which had previously been represented by blank spaces).

Into the 1990s

On the face of it, Berlin's future had never looked so rosy, but for many Germans in the East, the new decade began under a palpable shadow of disappointment and fear. There was a general anxiety that the change from a planned to a market economy would push up rents, close factories and wipe out the value of pensions and savings, and already the first legal claims by former owners of apartment buildings in East Berlin were being lodged. Politically, reform seemed too slow in coming, and people suspected that the apparatus of SED control had merely gone underground, biding its time. Hence the outrage in January 1990, when the government proposed establishing a new security service based on the old Stasi.

Revelations of **corruption** among the former communist leadership, and the discovery that West Germany's standard of living eclipsed anything offered by the GDR, produced massive disillusionment with the East German state. The notion of **German unification** became increasingly popular, dismaying some of the original opposition activists, who cherished hopes of a separate state, pursuing a "third way" between socialism and capitalism. Groups like Neues Forum began losing ground to parties modelled on Kohl's CDU, the social democratic SPD, and the far-right Republicans, all of which supported unification in one form or another.

When the GDR's first free elections were finally held on March 18, 1990, the result was a victory for a right-wing alliance dominated by the CDU under Lothar de Maizière. In reality this was a victory for Chancellor Helmut Kohl, the self-proclaimed champion of German unification. It was his promises of financial help and investment that had led people back to the CDU in the GDR, and it was to him that people were looking to ease the worsening economic plight.

During the two months following the election it began to seem possible that these hopes would be realized as, after a shaky start, the new government hammered out an agreement with the Federal Republic in mid-April about the introduction of the Deutschmark into the GDR, scheduled for July 1. The agreement on **economic union** was clearly a prelude to one on political union, for which a provisional date of autumn 1991 had been set. This was to be effected according to **article 23** of the Federal Republic's constitution, which made provision for any part of the GDR to request accession to West Germany. On June 17 a Volkskammer delegate called for immediate union by means of article 23: his motion was overturned but the issue of **reunification** was now firmly in the spotlight, and Kohl upped the ante by declaring 1990 the year of German unity.

However, at this stage it was the chancellor himself who was proving the biggest stumbling block en route to a united Germany. His ambiguous public stance (prompted by fear of alienating Republican support) on the inviolability of the Oder–Neisse line and other post-World War II borders was causing alarm in Poland and eliciting testy reactions from the EC countries. The advice of Foreign Minister **Hans Dietrich Genscher** finally forced Kohl to realize that he risked sacrificing German unity to party political expediency, and to affirm German commitment to existing borders.

As planned, **currency union** was rapidly effected on **July 1**, the most enduring image being that of East Berliners thronging into city centre banks to claim their allotment of Deutschmarks. With monetary union the GDR began to fade away rapidly: overnight, eastern produce vanished from the nation's shops, replaced by western consumer goods, and, superficially at least, it seemed as though a second "economic miracle" was about to begin. Yet for many people in the GDR, the expectation that economic reform and West German know-how would substantially improve their standards of living within a few years was tempered by fear of rent increases and factory closures during the transformation to a market economy.

The political background

For the time being, however, fears like these were overshadowed by **political developments**. It was time to address head-on the issue of reunification, and the "two plus four" talks between the two Germanys and the wartime Allies had established that the West would not stand in the way of the Germans – though the final approval of the Soviet Union had yet to be secured.

On July 15 Kohl met with **Mikhail Gorbachev** in the Caucasus, where they worked out a mutually acceptable series of conditions for the union of the two Germanys. It was agreed that Soviet troops would withdraw from Germany over a period of three to four years and that a united Germany would be free to decide for itself to which military alliance it would belong. An important proviso was that no foreign troops or nuclear weapons would be stationed on the territory of the former GDR.

The last obstacle in the way of unification had been removed and it was now possible to set a firm date for the event. On August 23 an all-night Volkskammer session announced that the GDR would become part of the Federal Republic on October 3, 1990, and just over a week later East and West Germany signed an 1100-page **treaty of union**. On September 12, the Allied military commanders of Berlin and the German foreign minister signed an agreement restoring full sovereignty to Germany, and a day later the Federal Republic and the Soviet Union signed a treaty of co-operation, including a nonaggression clause.

Street level changes

The two Berlins, meanwhile, were already drawing together as the border withered away during the course of the year. Passport and customs controls for German citizens had ceased early in 1990 and, by the time of currency union, nationals of other countries, although nominally still subject to control, could cross the border unhindered. During the course of the year most of the central sections of **the Wall** had been demolished and numerous cross-border streets linked up once again.

As border controls in Berlin and elsewhere throughout the former Soviet bloc eased, Berlin became a magnet for the restless peoples of Eastern Europe. First arrivals had been the **Poles**, who set up a gigantic impromptu street market on a patch of wasteland near the Wall, much to the chagrin of Berliners, who felt the order of their city threatened by the influx of thousands of weekend street traders selling junk out of suitcases. They were followed by **Romanians**, mainly gypsies, fleeing alleged persecution at home and hoping, by taking advantage of visa-free access to what was still the GDR, to secure a place for themselves in the new Germany. Post-unification visa regulations were to put a stop to the commuting activities of the Poles, but as asylum-seekers the Romanians had the right to remain, and the sight of gypsy families begging on the streets of Berlin became commonplace.

The Stasi legacy

In East Berlin it was becoming apparent that a united German government was going to be plagued by questions arising from the immediate past of the GDR. In the run-up to reunification, activists from the GDR citizens' opposition groups occupied the former Stasi HQ in Magdalenenstrasse, demanding an end to the removal of **Stasi files** to West Germany. The protesters demanded that the files remain in the former GDR after reunification, mainly so that victims of the Stasi would have evidence of what had happened to them, enabling them to claim compensation and possibly bring their persecutors to justice. The BND (Bundesnachrichtendienst – West Germany's secret service) had other ideas, however, and was keen to get its hands on the files, presumably to dispose of potentially embarrassing revelations about the extent to which the Stasi had penetrated West German political life.

After a promise from the West German government that the files would remain in the GDR for the time being, the protest action fizzled out, and following reunification the German government discreetly removed the remaining files to Bonn.

Unification and beyond

On **October 3, 1990**, the day of **reunification**, Chancellor Kohl spoke to assembled dignitaries and massive crowds in front of the Reichstag. A conscious effort was made to rekindle the spontaneous joy and fervour that had gripped the city on the night the Wall was opened and during Berlin's first post-*Wende* new year, but for many ordinary people already experiencing the economic side-effects of the collapse of the GDR the celebrations left a bitter taste. On the sidelines anti-unification demonstrators marched through the streets, precipitating minor **clashes with the police**.

Just over a month later, on the night of November 13, the reunited Berlin experienced its first **major upheaval** when SPD mayor Walter Momper ordered the police to evict **West Berlin squatters** who had occupied a number of tenement blocks in the eastern Berlin district of Friedrichshain. The violent tactics of the police, coupled with the uncompromising stance of the radical Autonome squatters, who responded with petrol bombs and a hail of missiles from the rooftops, resulted in the fiercest **rioting** seen in the city since 1981, with dozens of police injured and over three hundred squatters arrested. Politically, the unrest resulted in the **collapse** of the fragile Red-Green SPD/Alternative Liste coalition that had governed West Berlin for the previous twenty months.

Elections and New Year problems

These events did much to ensure a **CDU victory** in the **city elections** held on **December 2** to coincide with Germany's first nationwide elections since 1933. Nationally the CDU, in coalition with the FDP (Free Democrats), triumphed easily, though in Berlin the victory was by a narrower margin. One surprise in the Berlin elections (which were marked by irritatingly facile poster campaigns from all parties) was the fact that the PDS secured 25 percent of the vote in eastern Berlin on an anti-unemployment and anti-social inequality ticket.

The immediate result of the city elections in Berlin was the replacement of SPD Mayor Momper by the **CDU's Eberhard Diepgen**, who faced the unenviable task of dealing with the united city's **mounting difficulties**: to the obvious problem of unemployment could be added a worsening housing crisis, increasing right-wing extremism, and rising crime in the eastern part of the city with its demoralized and under-equipped police force. At the start of 1991, with celebrations of the first united Christmas and New Year over, it was time for the accounting to begin in earnest. The new year brought vastly unpopular

tax increases in the western part of Germany to pay for the spiralling **cost of unification**, which an embarrassed government was now forced to admit it had underestimated. As the year wore on and **unemployment** continued to rise, Kohl's honeymoon with the east soon came to an end. The man who had been mobbed in the former GDR only a year previously was now conspicuously reluctant to show himself there, and when he finally did, in April, he was greeted by catcalls and egg-hurlers.

Meanwhile, **ill-feeling** between easterners and westerners, which had first become apparent the previous year, continued. Western Berliners resented the tax increases and rising rents and mourned the passing of their subsidized island existence, while easterners, grappling with economic hardship, resented the fact that their poverty had reduced them to the status of second-class citizens. However, occasional strikes and dark mutterings about a long hot summer to come aside, the early part of the year passed relatively peacefully. The only major unrest in Berlin came with the outbreak of the **Gulf War** in January, which provoked large and sporadically violent **antiwar demonstrations**, recalling the early 1980s when the German peace movement had been a force to be reckoned with.

Post-unification problems

By mid-1991 the reserves of optimism topped up by currency union and unification had evaporated, particularly in the eastern part of the city, where the full force of social dislocation was felt. The loss of subsidies and tax breaks quickly had a **severe economic effect** on the previously immune west. On July 1, over 300,000 workers in subsidized, part-time work were made unemployed; at the same time, the huge **federal subsidies** that had propped up West Berlin's economy throughout the postwar years started to be scaled down to zero, removing DM8.5 million a year – around half the city's budget – from the municipal coffers. Unemployment, spiralling rents, and the wholesale flight of businesses hit the city.

Meanwhile, events at a national level were hardly encouraging. The Red Army Faction's assassination, on April 1, of **Detlev Rohwedder**, head of the Treuhandgesellschaft responsible for privatizing the ex-GDR's industry, did little to bolster hopes of imminent economic improvement.

Neither was general confidence in the government's ability to deal with the situation boosted by the CDU's defeat in local elections in Kohl's local powerbase of Rheinland-Pfalz, a result seen by many as a symptom of growing disenchantment with Kohl's handling of the first months of unification.

On June 20 an unexpected Bundestag decision to **relocate the seat of government to Berlin** (all key functions are to be transferred by 2003 at the latest) provided brief distraction, but by September attention was once more focused on the darker side of reunification. **Attacks on foreigners**, commonplace in the GDR even before the *Wende*, had been increasing steadily since the fall of the Wall. In September they mounted in intensity with one of the worst outbreaks taking place in the small Saxon town of **Hoyerswerda**, where a mob stormed a hostel housing asylum-seekers, necessitating the removal of the residents under police escort.

Hoyerswerda became a symbol for a wave of anti-foreigner violence that extended into western Germany, and which the government seemed unable to deal with. Rather than condemning the attacks in a forthright manner, the political establishment concentrated on calling for the reform of Germany's liberal asylum laws. Electorally this made sense – the far right was gaining ground, as shown by the Republicans gaining 10.5 percent of the vote in Baden-Württemberg's local elections in April 1992 – but many observers felt that such moral haziness only served to offer encouragement to the extremists.

But the main social pressure, one felt particularly strongly in Berlin, was the **growing distance** between west and east Germans. After forty years of separation no one expected the social gulf between them to be bridged overnight, but western anger at higher taxes to subsidize the east, and eastern resentment at what were seen as patronizing and neocolonialist western attitudes to the people of the former GDR, brought about an antipathy bordering on open hatred between the two peoples. Furthermore, it became apparent that the ever-increasing cost of reunification had pushed the German economy into recession.

By the end of 1992 the **civil war in Yugoslavia** had had its effect on the city, as Germany absorbed more Yugoslavs fleeing persecution and violence than any other European nation –

again, much to the distaste of the far right, whose followers were in action elsewhere: in August a Jewish memorial was attacked in the city, and in September, neo-Nazis were convicted of beating an Angolan student to death in the town of Eberswalde-Finow, 35km northeast of Berlin. The November murders of a Berlin left-winger, three Turks (two of whom had been born in Germany), and a man mistakenly thought to be a Jew were all claimed by neo-Nazi groups.

In October 1992 the ex-mayor of the city, founder of *Ostpolitik* and international statesman **Willy Brandt** died at the age of 78: fittingly, he was given the first state funeral reunified Berlin had seen, and was buried in a small forest cemetery at the edge of the city. Meanwhile the hunt for Erich Honecker on charges of having been responsible for the deaths of would-be escapees from East Germany had been abandoned on the grounds of his ill-health. Honecker was allowed to join his daughter in Chile at the start of 1993 and died there the following year.

Nevertheless there were other well-observed trials of GDR officials during the Nineties that brought Politbüro members, border guards, and even sports officials, accused of doping players without their knowledge, before the courts. The general feeling – that the big fish had slipped through – remained however. The trials did manage to foment debates about "victors' justice", and the legality of trying people for actions not illegal under GDR law, again highlighting the continuing role of the GDR past in the political, historical, and even social life of reunified Germany.

The mid-1990s to the present

The summer of 1994 brought the **departure of the troops** of the World War II Allies, which had maintained a presence in the city since 1945. Their exit was a symbolic end to nearly fifty years of occupation and a signal that Berlin was once again in control of its own destiny.

An even more important and dramatic signal of that control, however, came with the national **government's relocation** to Berlin during the latter half of the 1990s: a tremendous task, and one carried out with usual German thoroughness. The Reichstag, seat of the parliament, was completely gutted and redesigned by British architect Sir Norman Foster, who added a glass cupola as a symbol of openness and observability into the government goings-on below, while ambitious buildings were erected to shelter ministries and embassies, new roads laid and U-Bahn lines constructed. In addition, the administration called for surviving Third Reich buildings to be brought into use: the Finance Ministry has moved into Göring's old Luftwaffe headquarters, and the Foreign Ministry now occupies the Central Bank building. The relocation and building are scheduled to continue until 2003, but the key elements are already in place. On April 19, 1999, the Bundestag, the German parliament, met for the first time since 1933 in regular session in the Reichstag.

The **tenth anniversary** of the fall of the Wall in November of the same year brought Mikhail Gorbachev, George Bush and Helmut Kohl to the city to reminisce and congratulate each other. As they spoke inside the Adlon Hotel, a festival attracting close to 100,000 people was held at the Brandenburg Gate to mark the date. A jovial occasion, featuring music, speeches, and, of course, beer and sausages, it was altogether a rather less euphoric gathering than that which took place a decade earlier; time has delivered a realization of the social and economic difficulties – as well as the high cost – of reunification.

More sobering was a gathering held in the same square in front of the Gate earlier in the year, when the extreme right-wing National Partie Deutschland (National Party of Germany) held a demonstration in March 1999. Though the whole affair was dwarfed by a counter-demonstration, it was a shock for many to see **neo-Nazis** march, in an echo of the Sturmabteilung parades of the Third Reich, in the heart of the German capital. Berlin proper is relatively untroubled by the racist violence that occurs fairly regularly in the small towns of Brandenburg, but there's no doubt that neo-Nazi parties have become better organized and brasher of late. Persistent extremism, fuelled in part by youth unemployment, continues to be a problem throughout the former East Germany, and that includes districts in eastern Berlin.

Although the **economy** has picked up somewhat in the last two years, the government, under the neoliberal Chancellor Gerhard Schroeder, is in a cost-cutting mood. One dramatic savings measure due to be implemented is the fusion of the city's districts. By January 2001, the 23 *Bezirke*, many with roots as separate villages, will become twelve districts; some fear that the loss of local power resulting from these larger units will be a significant erosion of democracy. Other changes afoot are the transformation of Schönefeld airport into Berlin-Brandenburg International, and the rebuilding of Lehrter Stadtbahnhof to make it the city's central train junction – changes designed purely to better outfit the capital for its new role: after a decade of integrating and rebuilding, Berlin at the start of the 21st century is poised to take its place as a leading metropolis of Europe.

Books

Publishers are detailed below with the British publisher first, followed by the American publisher, where both exist. Where books are published in one of these countries only, "UK" or "US" follows the publisher's name; where the publisher is the same in the UK and US, only the publisher's name is given, and where the publisher is located elsewhere, we state the city. Books that are out of print (o/p) should be easy to track down in secondhand bookshops. "UP" means University Press.

History

Early and pre-World War II

Michael Farr, *Berlin! Berlin!* (Kyle Cathie, US, o/p). This compressed (200-page) history of the city from its earliest origins has all the main facts and plenty of colour and character. An ideal introductory text, though by no means the deepest or fullest account.

Otto Friedrich, *Before the Deluge: A Portrait of Berlin in the 1920s* (HarperPerrenial, US). An engaging social history, full of tales and anecdotes, of the city when Dada and decadence reigned. An excellent history of Berlin's most engaging period.

Mary Fulbrook, *A Concise History of Germany* (Cambridge UP). "Concise" is the key word for this post-unification history, whose brevity is simultaneously its strength and its weakness. Nevertheless, a useful basic history, and a clear introduction to a difficult subject.

Alex de Jong, *The Weimar Chronicle* (Paddington Press, o/p; New American Library, o/p). While not

the most comprehensive of accounts of the Weimar Republic, this is far and away the most lively. A couple of chapters focus on Berlin, and the book is spiced with eyewitness memoirs and a mass of engaging detail, particularly on the arts in Berlin. Worth hunting the libraries for.

Ebehard Kolb, *The Weimar Republic* (Routledge, UK). The most recent study of the endlessly fascinating but fundamentally flawed state – the only previous attempt at a united and democratic German nation – that survived for just fourteen years. A bad omen?

Giles MacDonogh, *Berlin* (St Martin's Press). A solid history of the city, emphasizing its early years. It's organized geographically rather than chronologically, which makes it at times confusing and repetitive. A good history, but perhaps not the best introduction to the city.

Questions on German History (Bundestag Press, Berlin). English translation of the guide to the Deutsche Dom exhibition of the same name. Handy if you're visiting, and, for the price, a good bargain read on the political history of Germany and Berlin from 1800 to the present.

Alexandra Ritchie, *Fausts's Metropolis* (HarperCollins). A thick and thorough general history of the city, beginning with the very first settlers and ending in the Nineties. Ritchie debunks a number of myths about the city – such as its supposed anti-Nazism – but her conservatism too often intrudes on the narrative.

Ronald Taylor, *Berlin and Its Culture* (Yale UP). A profusely illustrated survey of the cultural movements and personalities that constituted the artistic life of the city, especially good on Weimar writing and cinematography.

Nazism and the war years

Allied Intelligence Map of Key Buildings (After The Battle, UK). This large detailed map is an excellent utility for anyone searching for Nazi and prewar remains in the city.

Christabel Bielenberg, *The Past is Myself* (Corgi, UK). Bielenberg, the niece of Lord Northcliffe, married German lawyer Peter Bielenberg in 1934 and was living with her family in Berlin at the outbreak of the war. Her autobiography (serialized for TV as *Christabel*) details her struggle to survive the Nazi period and Allied raids on the city, and to save her husband, imprisoned in Ravensbrück as a result of his friendship with members of the Kreisau resistance group.

Alan Bullock, *Hitler: A Study in Tyranny* (Penguin; Konecky & Konecky). Ever since it was published, this scholarly yet highly readable tome has ranked as one of the best biographies of the failed Austrian artist and discharged army corporal whose evil genius fooled a nation and caused the deaths of millions.

George Clare, *Berlin Days 1946–1947* (Papermac). "The most harrowing and yet most fascinating place on earth" is how Clare begins this account of his time spent as a British army translator. This is Berlin seen at what the Germans called the *Nullpunkt* – the zero point – when the city, its economy, buildings and society, began to rebuild almost from scratch. Packed with characters and observation, it's a captivating – if at times depressing – read.

Joachim C. Fest, *The Face of the Third Reich* (Penguin; De Capo). Mainly of interest for its biographies of the men surrounding the Führer – Göring, Goebbels, Hess, Himmler, et al.

D. Fisher and A. Read, *The Fall of Berlin* (Pimlico; De Capo). Superb account of the city's Götterdämmerung, carefully researched with a mass of anecdotal material you won't find elsewhere. An essential book for those interested in the period.

Bella Fromm, *Blood and Banquets* (Carol Publishing, US, o/p). Fromm, a Jewish aristocrat living in Berlin, kept a diary from 1930 until 1938. Her job as society reporter for the *Vossische Zeitung* gave her inside knowledge on the top figures of Berlin society, and the diaries are a chilling account of the rise of the Nazis and their persecution of Berlin's Jews.

Anton Gill, *A Dance Between Flames* (Abacus; Carroll & Graf, o/p). Gill's dense but readable account of 1920s-to-30s Berlin has lots of colour, quotation and detail but leans so heavily on a single source – *The Diary of Henry Kessler* – that you feel he should be sharing the royalties. Even so, one of the best books on the period.

Adolf Hitler, *Table Talk* (Phoenix; Enigma). Hitler in his own words: Martin Bormann, one of his inner circle, recorded the dictator's pronouncements at meetings between 1941 and 1944.

Ian Kershaw, *Hitler: 1889–1936 Hubris* and *Hitler: 1937–1945 Nemesis* (W.W. Norton). The definitive biography. Using newly available documents from Soviet archives, and casting a critical eye on others (such as *Table Talk* above), Kershaw extends our understanding of the German demagogue and dictator.

Claudia Koonz, *Mothers in the Fatherland* (St Martin's Press). Recent and brilliantly perceptive study of the role of women in Nazi Germany. Includes a rare and revealing interview with the chief of Hitler's Women's Bureau, Gertrud Scholtz-Klink.

Brian Ladd, *The Ghosts of Berlin: Confronting German History in the Urban Landscape* (University of Chicago Press). Much dense talk of policy issues and urban planning, but within that discussion is an excellent history of the city.

Tony Le Tissier, *The Battle of Berlin* (Jonathan Cape, UK, o/p). Soldierly (the author is a retired lieutenant-colonel) shot-by-shot account of Berlin's final days. Authoritative, if a little dry. His *Berlin Then and Now* (After the Battle, UK) is a collection of photographs of sites in the city during the war years, contrasted with the same places today. This extraordinary book is the best way to find what's left of Nazi Berlin's buildings – a startling number are barely changed – and to correct myths (such as the position of the Führerbunker) that have long gone unchallenged. Beg, steal or borrow a copy if you have any interest in the city's past.

Martin Middlebrook, *The Berlin Raids* (Cassell). Superbly researched account of the RAF's campaign to destroy the capital of the Third Reich by mass bombing. Based on interviews with bomber crews, Luftwaffe fighter pilots and civilians who survived the raids, it's a moving, compassionate and highly exciting read.

Cornelius Ryan, *The Last Battle* (Wordsworth; Touchstone). The Battle of Berlin turned into a sort of historic filmscript, with factual descriptions alongside speculated conversation. While reasonably accurate in its account of what happened, the style can be cloying.

William Shirer, *The Rise and Fall of the Third Reich* (Arrow; Fawcett). The perfect complement to Bullock's book: Shirer was an American journalist stationed in Berlin during the Nazi period, and his history of the German state before and during the war has long been recognized as a classic. Notwithstanding its length and occasionally outdated perceptions, this book is full of insights and is ideal for dipping into, with the help of its exhaustive index.

Hugh Trevor-Roper, *The Last Days of Hitler* (Papermac; University of Chicago Press). A brilliant reconstruction of the closing chapter of the Third Reich, set in the Bunker of the Reich's Chancellery on Potsdamer Platz. Trevor-Roper subsequently marred his reputation as the doyen of British historians by authenticating the forged Hitler Diaries, which have themselves been the subject of several books.

Marie Vassiltchikov, *The Berlin Diaries* (Pimlico; Vintage). Daughter of a Russian emigré family and friend of the Bielenbergs (see above), Vassiltchikov's diaries provide a vivid portrait of wartime Berlin and the July 1944 bomb plot conspirators – whose members also numbered among her friends.

Peter Wyden, *Stella* (Doubleday, US). Stella Goldschlag was a young, very "Aryan"-looking Jewish woman who avoided deportation and death by working for the SS as a "catcher", hunting down Jews in hiding in wartime Berlin – including her former friends and even relatives. The author, who knew the young Stella, traces her life story and tries to untangle the morality and find some explanation for the motives behind what seem incalculably evil actions. A gripping, terrifying story.

Recent history and social studies

John Ardagh, *Germany and the Germans* (Penguin). The most up-to-date characterization of the country and its people, taking into account its history, politics and psyche, and covering almost every aspect of national life. The section on Berlin, while brief, is packed with astute observations and illuminating facts.

Bill Buford (ed), *Granta 30: New Europe!* (Granta, US). Granta's round-up of writing on and from Central Europe published in spring 1990 contains pieces by Jurek Becker on German unification, and Werner Krätschell on the opening of the Wall.

Timothy Garton-Ash, *We the People* (Penguin). An in-depth account of the revolutions in Eastern Europe. There's a brief chapter on the GDR but, as ever, Garton-Ash is best when dealing with the political and intellectual background to the events in Poland and Czechoslovakia.

Norman Gelb, *The Berlin Wall* (Michael Joseph, o/p; Times Books). The definitive account of the building of the Wall and its social and political aftermath – as far as 1986. Includes a wealth of information and anecdotes not to be found elsewhere.

Mark Girouard, *Cities and People* (Yale UP). A well-illustrated social and architectural history of European urban development that contains knowledgeable entries on Berlin, particularly the eighteenth- and nineteenth-century periods.

Jurgen Habermas, *A Berlin Republic: Writings on Germany* (University of Nebraska Press, US). A trenchant collection of essays on Germany's past and the challenges of the future by one of the country's most prominent intellectuals.

Warren Hinckle (ed), *The Fourth Reich* (Argonaut Press, US). This excellent Californian review dedicated most of an issue to the rise of neofascism and other problems confronting the new Germany. The title is a good indication of its slight tendency to alarmism, but there's so much unignorable factual material that the book is essential reading for those interested in contemporary Germany.

David E. Murphy, Serfei A. Kondrashev and George Bailey, *Battleground Berlin: CIA vs KGB in the Cold War* (Yale UP). A detailed account by participants of the tense, crafty skirmishing in Berlin between the spies of the two superpowers.

Michael Simmons, *The Unloved Country* (Abacus, UK, o/p). Pre-*Wende* account of the GDR by the Guardian's man in Eastern Europe. A bit dry and dull at times, but then so was the GDR.

Hermann Waldenburg, *The Berlin Wall Book* (Thames & Hudson; Abbeville). A collection of photographs of the art and graffiti the Wall inspired, with a rather self-important introduction by the photographer.

Art and architecture

Peter Adam, *The Art of the Third Reich* (Harry N. Abrams Inc). Engrossing and well-written account of the officially approved state art of Nazi Germany – a subject that for many years has been ignored or deliberately made inaccessible. Includes over three hundred illustrations, many reproduced for the first time since the war.

Alan Balfour, *Berlin, the Politics of Order: 1737–1989* (Rizzoli, o/p). A highly cerebral historical/architectural deconstruction of the area around Leipziger Platz. Through quotations, structuralist commentary, allusions and reference, a huge picture of a relatively tiny strip of the city is drawn, creating a paradigm of the richness and complexity of Berlin history.

Alan Balfour (ed), *Berlin: World Cities* (Academy Editions; John Wiley). The pictorial version of the above title, this photographic essay chronicles the architectural development of the city, examining current and past projects by world-renowned figures.

Wolf-Dieter Dube, *The Expressionists* (Thames & Hudson). A good general introduction to Germany's most distinctive contribution to twentieth-century art.

Peter Güttler (et al), *Berlin-Brandenburg: An Architectural Guide* (G: Ernst & Sohn). Brick-by-brick guide to the buildings of the city, in German and English. The definitive guide if you're interested in studying the city's architecture.

Post-War Berlin (Architecture Design Profile). A collection of scholarly essays on how the wartime legacy of destruction has been handled by the architects of the former East and West Berlin.

John Willet, *The Weimar Years* (Thames & Hudson; Abbeville). Heavily visual account of art, design and culture in pre-Nazi Germany. The seemingly Dada-influenced layout is a bit of a distraction.

Michael Z. Wise, *Capital Dilemma: Germany's Search for a New Architecture* (Princeton Architectural Press). An engaging discussion of the historical, political, and architectural considerations in the rebuilding of Germany's old and new capital city.

Frank Witford, *Bauhaus* (Thames & Hudson). Comprehensive and well-illustrated guide to the architectural movement that flourished in Dessau and included the Berlin architect Walter Gropius (see p.143).

Guides and travel writing

Stephen Barber, *Fragments of the European City* (Reaktion Books). Written as a series of interlocking poetic fragments, this book explores the visual transformation of the contemporary European city, focusing on Berlin. An exhilarating evocation of the intricacies and ever-changing identity of the city.

Karl Baedeker, *Berlin and its Environs* (Baedeker o/p, but widely available at secondhand book-shops). First published in 1903, the learned old Baedeker is an utterly absorbing read, describing a grand imperial city now long vanished. There's advice on medicinal brine-baths, where to buy "mourning clothes", the location of the Estonian embassy, and beautiful fold-out maps that enable you to trace the former course of long-gone streets (see also our map on pp.328–329). An armchair treat.

Hans Peter Heinicke, *The Secret Sights of Berlin* (G: Wort & Bild Specials). Not quite as intriguing as the title suggests, but with the occasional tit-bit of offbeat information.

Gordon McLachlan, *Germany: the Rough Guide* (Rough Guides). Companion volume to the book you're holding, a highly readable, erudite and comprehensive guide that's packed with practical information. Essential if your travels take you further than Berlin.

John Miller and Tim Smith, *Chronicles Abroad: Berlin* (Chronicle Books). A suitcase-sized anthology of fiction, reportage and impressions of the city, including pieces by Brecht, Kafka, Isherwood, E.T.A. Hoffmann and Josephine Baker.

Uwe Seidel, *Berlin & Potsdam* (G: Peter Rump). Illustrated guide to the city that has much detail on what you can't see any more. Useful if you need more knowledge of the what-stood-where kind.

Fiction

Len Deighton, *Winter: A Berlin Family 1899–1945* (HarperCollins; Ballantine). This fictional saga traces the fortunes of a Berlin family through World War I, the rise of Nazism and the collapse of the Third Reich: a convincing account of the way in which a typical upper-middle-class family weathered the wars. Better known is Deighton's *Funeral in Berlin* (HarperCollins; Acacia), a spy-thriller set in the middle of Cold War Berlin and based around the defection of an Eastern chemist, aided by hard-bitten agent Harry Palmer (as the character came to be known in the film starring Michael Caine). *Berlin Game* (HarperCollins; Ballantine) pits British SIS agent Bernard Samson (whose father appears in *Winter*) against an arch manipulator of the East Berlin secret service, and leaves you hanging for the sequels *Mexico Set* and *London Match*.

Alfred Döblin, *Berlin-Alexanderplatz* (Continuum). A prominent socialist intellectual during the

Weimar period, Döblin went into exile shortly after the banning (and burning) of his books in 1933. This is his weightiest and most durable achievement, an unrelenting epic of the city's proletariat.

Hugo Hamilton, *Surrogate City* and *The Love Test* (Faber, UK, o/p). Hamilton has set two of his recent novels in Berlin. *Surrogate City* is a love story between an Irish woman and a Berliner and is strongly evocative of pre-*Wende* Berlin. *The Love Test* is the tale of a journalist researching the history of a woman's involvement with the Stasi and gives a realistic account of contemporary Berlin.

Robert Harris, *Fatherland* (Arrow; HarperCollins). A Cold War novel with a difference: Germany has conquered Europe and the Soviet Union, and the Cold War is being fought between the Third Reich and the USA. Against this background, Berlin detective Xavier March is drawn into an intrigue involving murder and Nazi officials. All this owes much to Philip Kerr (see below) but Harris's picture of Nazi Berlin in 1964 is chillingly believable.

Lillian Hellman, *Pentimento* (Little, Brown). The first volume of Hellman's memoirs contains "Julia", supposedly (it was later charged to be heavily fictionalized) the story of one of her friends caught up in the Berlin resistance. This was later made into an finely acted, if rather thinly emotional, film of the same name.

Christopher Isherwood, *Goodbye to Berlin* (Minerva; W.W. Norton). Set in the decadent atmosphere of the Weimar Republic as the Nazis steadily gain power, this collection of stories brilliantly evokes the period and brings to life some classic Berlin characters. It subsequently formed the basis of the films *I Am a Camera* and the later remake *Cabaret*. See also Isherwood's *Mr Norris Changes Trains* (Minerva; New Directions), the adventures of the overweight eponymous hero in pre-Hitler Berlin and Germany.

Philip Kerr, *Berlin Noir: March Violets*, *The Pale Criminal* and *A German Requiem* (Penguin). Three great novels on Berlin in one omnibus edition. The first is a well-received detective thriller set in the early years of Nazi Berlin. Keen on period detail – nightclubs, the Olympic Stadium, building sites for the new autobahn – and with a terrific sense of atmosphere, the book rips along to a gripping denouement. Bernie Gunther, its detec-

tive hero, also features in the second title – a wartime Berlin crime novel. But his best work so far, *A German Requiem*, has Gunther travelling from ravaged postwar Berlin to run into ex-Nazis in Vienna.

Ian McEwan, *The Innocent* (Vintage; Bantam). McEwan's novel brilliantly evokes 1950s Berlin as seen through the eyes of a post office worker caught up in early Cold War espionage – and his first sexual encounters. Flounders in its obligatory McEwan nasty final twist, but laden with a superbly researched atmosphere.

J.S. Marcus, *The Captain's Fire* (Knopf, US, o/p). The complaints and reflections of a young American Jew living in the former east of Berlin. Written in an artful and self-conscious style, and spotted with references to Kafka and Walter Benjamin, the book, though full of atmosphere, leaves the reader unfulfilled.

William Palmer, *The Pardon of St Anne* (Vintage; Trafalger Square). The story of a morally shallow Berlin photographer whose professional involvement with the Nazis forces him – and the reader – to reassess his values.

Ulrich Plenzdorf, *The New Sufferings of Young W.* (Continuum, US). A satirical reworking of Goethe's *Die Leiden des jungen Werthers* set in 1970s East Berlin. It tells the story of Edgar Wibeau, a young rebel without a cause adrift in the antiseptic GDR, and when first published it pushed against the borders of literary acceptability under the old regime with its portrayal of alienated, disaffected youth.

Holly-Jane Rahlens, *Becky Bernstein Goes Berlin* (Arcade Books, US). A young Jewish girl from Queens falls in love with a German, emigrates to Berlin and discovers a new love for the city. A bouncy and funny novel full of New York wit.

Peter Schneider, *The Wall Jumper* (Allison & Busby o/p; University of Chicago Press). A series of fascinating cameos that describe life under the Wall, and the intrigue, characters and tragedy it caused.

Ian Walker, *Zoo Station* (Abacus, o/p; Grove Atlantic o/p). Not strictly fiction but a personal recollection of time spent in Berlin in the mid-1980s. Perceptive, engaging and well informed, it is the most enjoyable account of pre-*Wende* life in the city available.

Language

German is not a language you can hope to master in a short time. As English was a compulsory subject in West Berlin's school curriculum, most Germans who have grown up in the west since the war have some familiarity with it, which eases communication a great deal. In the east, Russian was the language most often taught, and you won't find so many English speakers among former inhabitants of the GDR.

But wherever you are, a smattering of German will help. Also, given that the city still has left-overs of the American and British forces, who make little effort to integrate into local communities or learn German, people are particularly sensitive to presumptuous English speakers. On the other hand, most will be delighted to practise their English on you once you've stumbled through your German introduction. Of the many teach-yourself courses available, best is the BBC course, Deutsch Direkt. For the most useful travelling companion, look no further than the *Rough Guide to German*, a practical and easy-to-use **dictionary/phrasebook** that allows you to speak the way you would in your own language.

Pronunciation

English speakers find the complexities of German grammar hard to handle, but pronunciation isn't as daunting as it might first appear. Individual syllables are generally pronounced as they're printed – the trick is learning how to place the stresses in the notoriously lengthy German words.

Vowels and umlauts

a as in father, but can also be used as in hut
e as in day
i as in leek
o as in bottom
u as in boot
ä is a combination of a and e, sometimes pronounced like **e** in bet (eg Länder) and sometimes like **ai** in paid (eg spät)
ö is a combination of o and e, like the French *eu*
ü is a combination of u and e, like true

Vowel combinations

ai as in lie
au as in house
ie as in free
ei as in trial
eu as in oil

Consonants

Consonants are pronounced as they are written, with no silent letters. The differences from English are:

j is pronounced similar to an English y
r is given a dry throaty sound, similar to French
s is pronounced similar to, but slightly softer than an English z
v is somewhere between f and v
w is pronounced same way as English v
z is pronounced ts
The German letter ß, the *Scharfes S*, occasionally replaces ss in a word: pronunciation is identical.

Gender

German words can be one of three genders: masculine, feminine or neuter. Each has its own ending and corresponding ending for attached adjectives. If you don't know any German grammar, it's safest to use either neuter or male forms.

GERMAN WORDS AND PHRASES

Basics

Ja, Nein	Yes, No	*Jenes*	That one
Bitte	Please/ You're welcome	*Gross, Klein*	Large, Small
Bitte Schön	A more polite form of *Bitte*	*Mehr, Weniger*	More, Less
		Wenig	A little
Danke, Danke Schön	Thank you, Thank you very much	*Viel*	A lot
		Billig, Teuer	Cheap, Expensive
Wo, Wann, Warum?	Where, When, Why?	*Gut, Schlecht*	Good, Bad
Wieviel?	How much?	*Heiss, Kalt*	Hot, Cold
Hier, Da	Here, There	*Mit, Ohne*	With, Without
Jetzt, Später	Now, Later	*Wo ist . . . ?*	Where is . . . ?
Geöffnet, offen, auf	All mean "open"	*Wie komme ich nach . . . ?*	How do I get to (a town)?
Geschlossen, zu	Both mean "closed"		
Früher	Earlier	*Wie komme ich zur/zum . . . ?*	How do I get to (a building, place)?
Da drüben	Over there		
Dieses	This one		

Greetings and times

Auf Wiedersehen	Goodbye	*Morgen*	Tomorrow
Auf Wiederhören	Goodbye (telephone only)	*Vorgestern*	The day before yesterday
		Übermorgen	The day after tomorrow
Tschüs	Goodbye (informal)	*Tag*	Day
Guten Morgen	Good morning	*Nacht*	Night
Guten Abend	Good evening	*Woche*	Week
Guten Tag	Good day	*Monat*	Month
Wie geht es Ihnen?	How are you? (polite)	*Jahr*	Year
Wie geht es Dir?	How are you? (informal)	*Wochenende*	Weekend
Lass mich in Ruhe	Leave me alone	*Am Vormittag/ vormittags*	In the morning
Hau ab	Get lost		
Geh weg	Go away	*Am Nachmittag/ nachmittags*	In the afternoon
Heute	Today		
Gestern	Yesterday	*Am Abend*	In the evening

Days, months and dates

Montag	Monday	*September*	September
Dienstag	Tuesday	*Oktober*	October
Mittwoch	Wednesday	*November*	November
Donnerstag	Thursday	*Dezember*	December
Freitag	Friday	*Frühling*	Spring
Samstag	Saturday	*Sommer*	Summer
Sonnabend	Saturday	*Herbst*	Autumn
Sonntag	Sunday	*Winter*	Winter
Januar	January	*Ferien*	Holidays
Februar	February	*Feiertag*	Bank holiday
März	March	*Montag, der erste Mai*	Monday, the first of May
April	April		
Mai	May	*Der zweite April*	the second of April
Juni	June	*Der dritte April*	the third of April
Juli	July		
August	August	*continued overleaf*	

GERMAN WORDS AND PHRASES CONTINUED

Some signs

Damen/Frauen	Women's toilets	*Umleitung*	Diversion
Herren/Männer	Men's toilets	*Vorsicht!*	Attention*!*
Eingang	Entrance	*Geschwindig-*	Speed limit
Ausgang	Exit	*keitsbegrenzung*	
Notausgang	Emergency exit	*Krankenhaus*	Hospital
Ankunft	Arrival	*Polizei*	Police
Abfahrt	Departure	*Nicht rauchen*	No smoking
Ausstellung	Exhibition	*Kein Eingang*	No entrance
Autobahn	Motorway	*Verboten*	Prohibited
Auffahrt	Motorway entrance	*Baustelle*	Building works
Ausfahrt	Motorway exit	*Ampel*	Traffic light

Numbers

1	*eins*	10	*zehn*	19	*neunzehn*	60	*sechzig*
2	*zwei*	11	*elf*	20	*zwanzig*	70	*siebzig*
3	*drei*	12	*zwölf*	21	*ein-und-*	80	*achtzig*
4	*vier*	13	*dreizehn*		*zwanzig*	90	*neunzig*
5	*fünf*	14	*vierzehn*	22	*zwei-und-*	100	*hundert*
6	*sechs*	15	*fünfzehn*		*zwanzig*	1996	*neunzehn-*
7	*sieben*	16	*sechzehn*	30	*dreissig*		*hundert-*
8	*acht*	17	*siebzehn*	40	*vierzig*		*sechs-und-*
9	*neun*	18	*achtzehn*	50	*fünfzig*		*neunzig*

Questions and requests

All enquiries should be prefaced with the phrase *Entschuldigen Sie bitte* (excuse me, please). Note that *Sie* is the polite form of address to be used with everyone except close friends, though young people and students often don't bother with it. The older generation will certainly be offended if you address them with the familiar *Du*, as will all officials.

Sprechen Sie Englisch?	Do you speak English?	*Getrennt oder Zusammen?*	Separately or together?
Ich spreche kein Deutsch	I don't speak German	*Die Speisekarte, bitte*	The menu, please
Könnten Sie bitte langsamer sprechen	Please speak more slowly	*Hallo!*	Hello! (to get attention of waiter/waitress)
Ich verstehe nicht	I don't understand		
Ich verstehe	I understand	*Haben Sie etwas billigeres?*	Have you got something cheaper?
Wie sagt mann das auf Deutsch?	How do you say that in German?	*Haben Sie noch ein Zimmer frei?*	Is there a room available?
Können Sie mir bitte sagen wo . . . ist?	Can you tell me where . . . is?	*Wo sind die Toiletten, bitte?*	Where are the toilets?
Wieviel kostet das?	How much does that cost?	*Ich hätte gern dieses*	I'd like that one
Wann fährt der nächste Zug?	When does the next train leave?	*Ich hätte gern ein Zimmer für zwei*	I'd like a room for two
Um wieviel Uhr?	At what time?	*Ich hätte gern ein Einzelzimmer*	I'd like a single room
Wieviel Uhr ist es?	What time is it?		
Sind die Plätze noch frei?	Are these seats taken?	*Hat das Zimmer eine Dusche, ein Bad, eine Toilette . . . ?*	Does it have a shower, bath, toilet . . . ?
Die Rechnung, bitte	The bill, please		

For a detailed glossary of food terms see pp.242–244.

Glossaries

Art and architecture

ART DECO geometrical style of art and architecture prevalent in the 1930s.

ART NOUVEAU sinuous, highly stylized form of architecture and interior design; in Germany, mostly dates from the period 1900–15, and is known as Jugendstil.

BAROQUE expansive, exuberant architectural style of the seventeenth and early eighteenth centuries, characterized by ornate decoration, complex spatial arrangements and grand vistas. The term is also applied to the sumptuous style of painting from the same period.

BAUHAUS plain, functional style of architecture and design, originating in early twentieth-century Germany.

EXPRESSIONISM emotional style of painting, concentrating on line and colour, extensively practised in early twentieth-century Germany; the term is also used for related architecture of the same period.

GOTHIC architectural style with an emphasis on verticality, characterized by the pointed arch, ribbed vault and flying buttress; introduced to Germany around 1235, surviving in an increasingly decorative form until well into the sixteenth century. The term is also used for paintings of this period.

NEOCLASSICAL late eighteenth- and early nineteenth-century style of art and architecture, returning to classical models as a reaction against Baroque and Rococo excesses.

RENAISSANCE Italian-originated movement in art and architecture, inspired by the rediscovery of classical ideals.

ROCOCO highly florid, light and graceful eighteenth-century style of architecture, painting and interior design, forming the last phase of Baroque.

ROMANESQUE solid architectural style of the late tenth to mid-thirteenth centuries, characterized by round-headed arches and a penchant for horizontality and geometrical precision. The term is also used for paintings of this period.

ROMANTICISM late eighteenth- and nineteenth-century movement, particularly strong in Germany, rooted in adulation of the natural world and rediscovery of the achievements of the Middle Ages.

German terms

ALTSTADT old part of a city.

AUSKUNFT information.

AUSLÄNDER literally "foreigner", the word has come to be a pejorative term for any non-White non-German.

AUSSTELLUNG exhibition.

BÄCKEREI bakery.

BAHNHOF station.

BAU building.

BERG mountain or hill.

BERLINER SCHNAUZE sharp and coarse Berlin wit.

BEZIRK city district.

BRÜCKE bridge.

BURG mountain or hill.

BUSHALTESTELLE bus stop.

DENKMAL memorial.

DOM cathedral.

DORF village.

EINBAHNSTRASSE one-way street.

ELECTOR (KURFÜRST) sacred or secular prince with a vote in the elections to choose the Holy Roman Emperor. There were seven for most of the medieval period, with three more added later.

FEIERTAG holiday.

FLUGHAFEN airport.

FLUSS river.

FREMDENZIMMER room for short-term let.

GASSE alley.

GASTARBEITER "guest worker": anyone who comes to Germany to do menial work.

GASTHAUS, GASTHOF guesthouse, inn.

GASTSTÄTTE traditional bar that also serves food.

GEMÄLDE painting.

GRÜNEN, DIE "The Greens": political party formed from environmental and antinuclear groups.

HABSBURG the most powerful family in medieval Germany, operating from a power base in Austria.

They held the office of Holy Roman Emperor 1452–1806, and by marriage, war and diplomacy acquired territories all over Europe.

HAUPTBAHNHOF main train station.

HAUPTEINGANG main entrance.

HOF court, courtyard, mansion.

INSEL island.

JAGDSCHLOSS hunting lodge.

JUGENDHERBERGE youth hostel.

JUGENDSTIL German version of Art Nouveau.

JUNKER Prussian landowning class.

KAISER Emperor.

KAMMER room, chamber.

KAPELLE chapel.

KAUFHAUS department store.

KINO cinema.

KIRCHE church.

KNEIPE bar.

KONDITOREI cake shop.

KRANKENHAUS hospital.

KUNST art.

MARKT market, market square.

MOTORRAD motorbike.

NEUES FORUM umbrella group for political opposition organizations within the former GDR.

NOT emergency.

OSTPOLITIK West German policy of détente towards the GDR.

PLATZ square.

PRUSSIA originally an Eastern Baltic territory (now divided between Poland and the Soviet Union). It was acquired in 1525 by the Hohenzollerns, who merged it with their own possessions to form Brandenburg-Prussia (later shortened to Prussia); this took the lead in forging the unity of Germany, and was thereafter its overwhelmingly dominant province. The name was abolished after World War II because of its monarchic and military connotations.

QUITTUNG official receipt.

RASTPLATZ picnic area.

RATHAUS town hall.

RATSKELLER cellars below the Rathaus, invariably used as a restaurant serving *burgerlich* cuisine.

REICH empire.

REISEBÜRO travel agency.

RUNDGANG way round.

SAMMLUNG collection.

S-BAHN commuter train network operating in and around conurbations.

SCHICKIE abbreviation of "Schicki-Micki": yuppie.

SCHLOSS castle, palace (equivalent of French chateau).

SEE lake.

STAATSSICHERHEITSDIENST (STASI) the former "State Security Service" or secret police of the GDR.

STADT town, city.

STAMMTISCH table in a pub or restaurant reserved for regular customers.

STIFTUNG foundation.

STRAND beach.

STRASSENBAHN tram.

TANKSTELLE filling station.

TOR gate, gateway.

TRABI conversational shorthand for the now famous Trabant, East Germany's two-cylinder, two-stroke people's car.

TURM tower.

U-BAHN network of underground trains.

VERKEHRSAMT, VERKEHRSVEREIN tourist office.

VIERTEL quarter, district.

VOLK people, folk; given mystical associations by Hitler.

WALD forest.

WECHSEL currency exchange office.

WEIMAR REPUBLIC parliamentary democracy established in 1918 that collapsed with Hitler's assumption of power in 1933.

WENDE literally, "turning point" – the term used to describe the events of November 1989 and after.

ZEITSCHRIFT magazine.

ZEITUNG newspaper.

ZEUGHAUS arsenal.

ZIMMER room.

Acronyms

BRD (Bundesrepublik Deutschlands) official name of former West Germany.

CDU (Christlich Demokratische Union) Christian Democratic (Conservative) Party.

DB (Deutsche Bahn) national train company.

DDR (Deutsche Demokratische Republik) official name of former East Germany.

FDJ (Freie Deutsche Jugend) East German party youth organization.

GDR ("German Democratic Republic") English equivalent of DDR.

NSDAP (National Sozialistiche Deutsche Abrbeiterparte) "National Socialist German Workers' Party", the official name for the Nazis.

SED (Sozialistische Einheitspartei Deutschlands) "Socialist Unity Party of Germany", the official name of the East German communist party before December 1989.

SPD (Sozialdemokratische Partei Deutschlands) Social Democratic (Labour) Party.

STASI slang term for the Staatssicherheitsdienst, the former East German secret police.

VOPO slang for Volkspolizei, a member of the East German police force.

Index

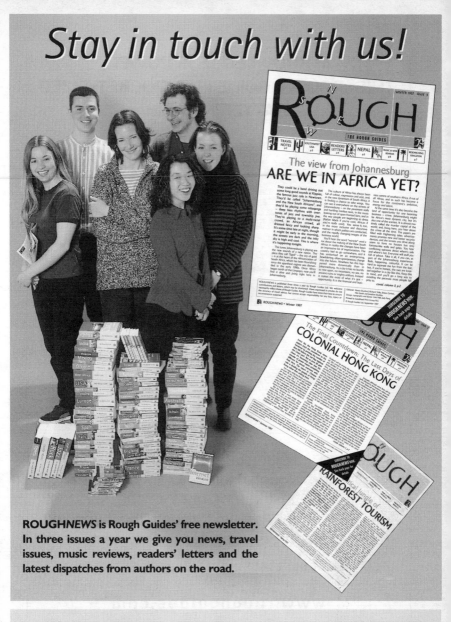

Stay in touch with us!

ROUGHNEWS is Rough Guides' free newsletter. In three issues a year we give you news, travel issues, music reviews, readers' letters and the latest dispatches from authors on the road.

ROUGH GUIDES: Travel

AVAILABLE AT ALL GOOD BOOKSHOPS

ROUGH GUIDES: Mini Guides, Travel Specials and Phrasebooks

MINI GUIDES

Antigua
Bangkok
Barbados
Beijing
Big Island of Hawaii
Boston
Brussels
Budapest
Cape Town
Copenhagen
Dublin
Edinburgh

Florence
Honolulu
Ibiza & Formentera
Jerusalem
Las Vegas
Lisbon
London Restaurants
Madeira
Madrid
Malta & Gozo
Maui
Melbourne
Menorca

Montreal
New Orleans

Paris
Rome
Seattle
St Lucia
Sydney
Tenerife
Tokyo
Toronto
Vancouver

TRAVEL SPECIALS

First-Time Asia
First-Time Europe
Women Travel

PHRASEBOOKS

Czech
Dutch
Egyptian Arabic
European
French
German
Greek

Hindi & Urdu
Hungarian
Indonesian
Italian
Japanese
Mandarin Chinese
Mexican Spanish
Polish
Portuguese
Russian
Spanish
Swahili
Thai
Turkish
Vietnamese